The Cambridge Handbook of Acculturation Psychology

In recent years the topic of acculturation has evolved from a relatively minor research area to one of the most researched subjects in the field of cross-cultural psychology. This edited *Handbook* compiles and systemizes the current state of the art by exploring the broad international scope of acculturation. A collection of the world's leading experts in the field review the various contexts for acculturation, the central theories, the groups and individuals undergoing acculturation (immigrants, refugees, indigenous people, expatriates, students and tourists) and discuss how current knowledge can be applied to make both the process and its outcome more manageable and profitable. Building on the theoretical and methodological framework of cross-cultural psychology, the authors focus specifically on the issues that arise when people from one culture move to another culture, and the reciprocal adjustments, tensions and benefits involved.

David L. Sam is Professor of Cross-Cultural Psychology in the Schools of Psychology and Medicine at the University of Bergen, Norway. He has published extensively on young immigrants' adaptation and received the 2004 Early Career Award from the International Academy for Intercultural Research (IAIR) for his contributions to the field.

John W. Berry is Professor Emeritus at the Department of Psychology, Queen's University, Kingston, Ontario. He is the co-author of *Cross-cultural psychology: research and applications* (2002) and *Human behaviour in global perspective* (1999), and the recipient of the Lifetime Contribution Award from the International Academy for Intercultural Research (IAIR) in 2005.

The Cambridge Handbook of
Acculturation Psychology

Edited by

DAVID L. SAM
University of Bergen, Bergen, Norway

JOHN W. BERRY
Queen's University, Kingston, Ontario, Canada

CAMBRIDGE
UNIVERSITY PRESS

CAMBRIDGE UNIVERSITY PRESS
Cambridge, New York, Melbourne, Madrid, Cape Town, Singapore, São Paulo

Cambridge University Press
The Edinburgh Building, Cambridge CB2 2RU, UK

Published in the United States of America by Cambridge University Press, New York

www.cambridge.org
Information on this title: www.cambridge.org/9780521614061

First published 2006

Printed in the United Kingdom at the University Press, Cambridge

A catalogue record for this publication is available from the British Library

ISBN-13   978-0-521-84924-1 hardback
ISBN-10   0-521-84924-1 hardback

ISBN-13   978-0-521-61406-1 paperback
ISBN-10   0-521-61406-6 paperback

Contents

Figures

Tables

Boxes

Notes on the contributors

LISANNE ACKERMANN obtained her Ph.D. from the University of Oxford. Ackermann's research interests are located on the border area between sociology and social anthropology. She is interested in a number of forced migration and development issues, particularly refugee reintegration, gender, participation in community development, social change, and identity transformation. Her ethnographic interest lies in Mexico and Central America, particularly with the Mayan population in Guatemala where she conducted her doctoral fieldwork. Lisanne worked as College Lecturer at the University of Oxford, and is at present a part-time lecturer at the Free University of Berlin.

JAMES ALLEN is Professor of Psychology at the University of Alaska Fairbanks. His contribution to this volume was written while he was Fulbright Lecturer/Researcher at the Psychosocial Centre for Refugees, University of Oslo. Allen's interests are in cultural and community psychology, and human rights issues relevant to indigenous people, refugees and other groups undergoing involuntary migration, and the seriously mentally ill. Recent research includes publication in the areas of the adjustment of refugees during resettlement, multi-cultural psychological assessment, cross-cultural and participatory research methodologies, alcohol use and sobriety among Alaska Natives, and culturally grounded services for Alaska Native children.

JUDIT ARENDS-TÓTH is currently a post-doctoral research fellow at the Faculty of Social and Behavioural Sciences at Tilburg University in the Netherlands. Her Ph.D. thesis aimed to examine and integrate conceptual and methodological issues associated with the measurement of acculturation of Turkish immigrants in the Netherlands. Her current post-doctoral research project focuses on assessment of acculturation and on markers of ethnic identity of immigrants in the Netherlands. Her main research interests include cultural differences in behavior, psychological assessment of acculturation, and ethnic identity. She has published several articles on acculturation.

UZI BEN-SHALOM completed his Ph.D. on the acculturation and adaptation of immigrant soldiers in Israel at the School of Education, The Hebrew University of Jerusalem, in 2002. He is the head of Behavioural Sciences Research in the Field Command of the Israeli Defence Forces, and a Post Doctoral Fellow at the Department of Psychology, Bar Ilan University. His research interests include cultural transition and military psychology.

JOHN W. BERRY is Professor Emeritus of Psychology at Queen's University, Kingston. He obtained his Ph.D. at the University of Edinburgh (Scotland). He has received Honorary Doctorates from the University of Athens, and Université de Genève, and a Lifetime Achievement Award from the International Academy for Intercultural Research. He has published over thirty books in the areas of cross-cultural, social and cognitive psychology, including co-authoring the textbook *Cross-cultural psychology: research and applications* (Cambridge, 2002), and co-editing the three-volume *Handbook of cross-cultural psychology* (1997). His main research interests are in the areas of acculturation and intercultural relations, with an emphasis on applications to immigration, educational and health policy.

DHARM P. S. BHAWUK is a professor of management, and culture and community psychology, University of Hawaii at Manoa. His research interests include cross-cultural training, intercultural sensitivity, and political behavior in the workplace. He has published several papers in the *Journal of Cross-Cultural Psychology*, *International Journal of Intercultural Relations*, *Applied Psychology: An International Review* and *Journal of Management*. He has also published a number of book chapters and is a co-editor of the book *Asian contributions to cross-cultural psychology* (1996). He has received many awards and honors including Distinguished Scholar Award, Management Department, College of Business Administration (2000), the Distinguished Service Award from the East–West Center (1989), and the Lum Yip Kee Outstanding MBA Student Award from the College of Business Administration, University of Hawaii (1990). He is a founding fellow of the International Academy of Intercultural Research.

STEPHEN BOCHNER is currently a visiting professor in the School of Psychology at the University of New South Wales (UNSW) in Sydney (Australia). From 1987 to 1997, he was the Director of the graduate Applied Psychology program at UNSW. He is currently dividing his time between teaching and research at the University and working as a psychological practitioner in applied organizational settings. His major research interest is the psychology of culture contact. Bochner has an international reputation as an applied cross-cultural psychologist, with a special interest in managing interpersonal relations in culturally diverse workplaces including international education, and has published widely in these areas. His most recent book is *The psychology of culture shock* (2001), co-authored with Ward and Adrian Furnham. Extended sojourns abroad have included visiting fellowships at Oxford and Cambridge universities and the East–West Center at the University of Hawaii.

VIRGINIE BOUTRY is currently finishing her Ph.D. at Université Victor Segalen Bordeaux 2, France. Her research focuses on family dynamics and acculturation processes and their impact on the adaptation of preadolescents living in Moroccan and Comoran communities in France, where she has already published a paper on friendships and attitudes of these two Muslim groups.

GIORGIA DONÀ is Senior Lecturer and member of the Refugee Research Centre at the University of East London. She received her MA and Ph.D. in Psychology at Queen's University (Canada) and obtained her M.Phil. in social anthropology at Cambridge University. She has conducted research and professional work with refugees in Central America and Africa. Her main research interests are in the areas of adaptation and wellbeing, psycho-social issues in forced migration, humanitarian assistance, and children in need of protection. She has co-authored *Rebuilding society's social fabric: a critical look at humanitarian assistance* (1999, in Spanish), *Psychology in humanitarian assistance* (1998), *Overview of the conditions of children outside parental care in institutions and communities* (2003) and *The Rwandan experience of fostering separated children* (2001).

ESTHER EHRENSAFT is Adjunct Professor in the Department of Psychology of Alliant International University, San Francisco, California. She specializes in child development, trauma, and resilience in cross-cultural contexts. Ehrensaft is also in private practice as a child and adolescent clinical psychologist.

EDVARD HAUFF undertook his medical studies at the Royal College of Surgeons in Ireland, his specialist certification in psychiatry in Norway, and obtained his Ph.D. from the University of Oslo. He is presently Professor of Trans-cultural Psychiatry at the University of Oslo and is the Director of Psychiatric Education, Ulleval University Hospital. He has also a part-time private practice in psychotherapy. He is an advisor to the Cambodian National Mental Health Programme and Temporary Advisor to the WHO in Indonesia and in other countries. He is also the Vice-President of the World Association for Psychosocial Rehabilitation (WAPR) with responsibility for the European region. His professional and research interests include: trans-cultural psychiatry, especially mental health in low-income countries; traumatic stress, including refugee mental health and the treatment of survivors of torture and other forms of organized violence; community-based rehabilitation (CBR); medical education; and narrative medicine.

JOHN E. HAYFRON holds a doctorate in economics from the University of Bergen, Norway, and is currently Assistant Professor in Economics at Western Washington University, Bellingham. He also taught labor economics at Coquitlam and Douglas Colleges in Vancouver, Canada. He is affiliated to the Vancouver Centre of Excellence on Immigration at Simon Fraser University where he is a senior researcher. His fields of interest are applied labor economics and economics of immigration. He has published a number of articles in international journals.

GABRIEL HORENCZYK is a senior lecturer at the School of Education and the Melton Centre for Jewish Education, The Hebrew University of Jerusalem. His teaching and research areas include: the psychological study of cultural and ethnic identity; education and immigration; cultural identity processes during inter-group contact; acculturation and identity processes among immigrants. He has recently co-edited two books: *Language, identity, and immigration* (with E. Olshtain), and *National variations in Jewish identity* (with S. Cohen).

ANKICA KOSIC has a doctorate in social psychology from the University of Rome "La Sapienza" where she also worked as a research fellow from 1999 to 2001. Since 2001 she has been working as a research fellow at the European University Institute, Florence, Italy, where she has been involved in a number of large-scale research projects. Her research interests are the issues of immigrants' integration, inter-group relationships, prejudice, and social representation. She has published articles in Italian and international journals. Some of her recent articles appeared in the *Journal of Personality and Social Psychology*, *Journal of Social Psychology*, *International Journal of Psychology* and *International Migration Review.*

SIV KVERNMO is Associate Professor at The Institute of Clinical Medicine, Faculty of Medicine, at the University of Tromsø in Norway. She is also the Head Consultant and Leader of the Child and Adolescent Psychiatric Outpatient Clinic at The University Hospital in North Norway in Tromsø. She has performed epidemiological research in multiethnic areas in North Norway, and is the manager of several adolescent health surveys in this area. Kvernmo is also the head of a clinical multicenter study of young psychiatric patients in North Norway. She is interested in cross-cultural and ethnocultural psychiatry with a special focus on indigenous and Sami mental health issues. Her medical specialty is child and adolescent psychiatry.

DAN LANDIS is Affiliate Professor of Psychology at the University of Hawaii; Professor Emeritus of Psychology and Director Emeritus, Center for Applied Research and Evaluation, University of Mississippi; and President, D. K. Research and Consultation Group. He is a past Dean of the College of Liberal Arts at the University of Mississippi, Chair of Psychology at Indiana University–Purdue University at Indianapolis; and Founder of the Center for Social Development at the University City Science Centre in Philadelphia. Dr. Landis is the author/co-author of over 100 books, articles, technical reports and presentations in areas such as: the measurement of the equal-opportunity climate in military and other organizations, racial discrimination, perception, statistics, sexual behavior and attitudes, and cross-cultural psychology and training. He is the founding and continuing editor of the *International Journal of Intercultural Relations*, the co-editor/author of *Ethnic conflict* (1985) and the co-editor of *Handbook of intercultural training,* now in its third edition (2004).

CHAN-HOONG LEONG recently completed his Ph.D. at Victoria University of Wellington in New Zealand under the supervision of Professor Colleen Ward. Chan-Hoong obtained his Master of Arts degree from the University of Queensland. His Ph.D. thesis involves a multi-level analysis of hosts' attitudes towards Chinese immigrants in New Zealand. His research interests include the assessment of intercultural competence and communication, host nationals' perceptions of immigrants and immigration policies, and Singaporeans' perceptions of citizenships and intention to emigrate. Chan-Hoong is currently employed as a Teaching Fellow at the Nanyang Technological University in Singapore, and he has just embarked on a new line of research to study the perception of corruption as a form of cultural script.

KARMELA LIEBKIND is Professor of Social Psychology at the University of Helsinki, Finland. Her research interests are in inter-group relations, ethnic identity, racism and acculturation processes. She has studied various immigrants, refugees and other minority members in Finland and Sweden, and the attitudes of majority members towards these. She edited and contributed substantially to *New identities in Europe: immigrant ancestry and the ethnic identity of youth* (1989), authored the chapter on "Acculturation" in the *Blackwell handbook of social psychology,* Vol. IV (2001), and has published extensively on ethnic identity, acculturation and inter-group relations in various scientific journals.

KEVIN LO is a doctoral student in international management at the University of Hawaii at Manoa. His research interests include international organizational behavior, cross-cultural training, and China–US comparative management. Prior to entering his doctoral program, he taught Chinese at Iolani School in Honolulu, Hawaii, as well as several different business and communication courses at Chaminade University. He has lived and worked in both Beijing and Taiwan.

ANNE-MARIE MASGORET worked for her doctorate at the University of Western Ontario, Canada, and is currently a Lecturer at Victoria University of Wellington and a Research Fellow of the Centre for Applied Cross-Cultural Research, New Zealand. Her research interests include acculturation, with a focus on the social psychological processes of second/foreign language learning, intergroup relations, prejudice and discrimination. Her research has been recognized by the International Academy for Intercultural Research and the American Council for the Teaching of Foreign Languages. She is currently the Executive Officer representing Australasia for the International Association of Language and Social Psychology.

HUONG H. NGUYEN is an assistant professor at Brandeis University (USA) in the Institute for Children, Youth, and Family Policy at the Heller School of Social Policy and Management. She received her Ph.D. in clinical psychology from Michigan State University, with a specialization in children and families.

Her research centers on the processes of how immigrants become both American and "ethnics" over time, and of their social, psychological and academic adjustment as a result of these processes. She studies the cultural and structural mechanisms that affect children of immigrants, particularly mechanisms that relate to their acculturation, identity and oppression (such as racism, and poverty).

KIMBERLY A. NOELS is an associate professor in the social and cultural psychology area of the Department of Psychology at the University of Alberta, Canada. Her research concerns the social psychology of language and communication processes, with a focus on intercultural communication. Her publications include articles on motivation for language learning, the role of communication in the process of cross-cultural adaptation, the association between language and ethnic identity, and intergenerational communication from a cross-cultural perspective. Her research has been recognized through awards from the Modern Language Association, the International Association of Language and Social Psychology, and the Society for the Psychological Study of Social Issues.

BRIT OPPEDAL has a doctorate in psychology from the University of Oslo. She is currently Project Manager at the Norwegian Institute of Public Health, where she is doing research on the mental health of children and adolescents. Her research focus is on children in immigrant families, and she is particularly interested in how migration and acculturation experiences affect family interaction and the development of children and adolescents. She also has extensive cross-cultural clinical experience, both as a school psychologist in Norway and as a family therapist among Latin-American immigrants in the USA.

KAREN PHALET is a professor of cross-cultural studies and a permanent staff member of the European Research Centre on Migration and Ethnic Relations (ERCOMER) at Utrecht University, the Netherlands. She has been doing cross-cultural research on immigrant families, cultural values, acculturation, ethnic relations and school achievement in various immigrant communities and host countries. She is also an associate editor of the *Journal of Cross-Cultural Psychology* and has published extensively in international journals and in edited volumes. Some of her recent publications include K. Phalet, I. Andriesen and W. Lens (2004). How future goals enhance motivation and learning in multicultural classrooms. *Educational Psychology Review, 16(1)*, 59–89, and K. Phalet and A. Orkeny (eds.), *Ethnic minorities and interethnic relations in context* (2001).

LENA ROBINSON is Professor in Psychology and Social Work at the University of Paisley, Glasgow. She is the author of *Psychology for social workers: black perspectives* (1995); *Race, communication and the caring professions* (1998) *and Cross-cultural child development for social workers* (in press). She has researched on issues related to acculturation and immigrants in Britain.

AMANDA ROGERS is in the write-up stage of her Ph.D. in the area of gambling, with the University of Western Australia, Perth. Since moving from Australia to Norway two years ago she has developed research interests in cross-cultural psychology and has been working as a part-time researcher at the University of Bergen, Norway.

COLETTE SABATIER is Professor of Psychology at Université Victor Segalen Bordeaux 2, France. She received her Ph.D. in Psychology from the University of Quebec in Montreal with a thesis on mother–infant relationships in an immigration context. Her post-doctoral research at Queen's University (Kingston, Ontario) was on the acculturation of immigrant adolescents. Before coming to Bordeaux, she was a faculty member at Université de Haute-Bretagne (Rennes) and Université de Paris X. Her special interest is adolescent and child development within different cultural contexts, and in particular within immigrant families. Her research focuses on socialization, enculturation and acculturation from the points of view of both the child and the parents. She has edited several books on cross-cultural psychology in French and published several chapters in French and in English on this topic.

DAVID L. SAM is Professor of Cross-cultural Psychology at the University of Bergen (Norway), where he divides this position between the Schools of Psychology and Medicine. He teaches courses in developmental psychology, cross-cultural psychology and medical anthropology. His research interests include psychology of acculturation, and the role of culture in health and human development. He has published extensively on young immigrants' adaptation, and in recent years this interest has adopted a more comparative point of view. He was the recipient of the 2004 Early Career Award from the International Academy for Intercultural Research for his contributions to the field of intercultural research.

DAVID SANG, a Vietnamese Australian, has been teaching and researching in cross-cultural and health psychology for the last ten years at the University of Western Australia. As a registered psychologist, he has been involved in the Australian Government's Better Outcomes in Mental Health Care and Counselling Initiative.

MICHEL TOUSIGNANT worked for his doctorate in human development at the University of Chicago. He has taught community psychology at the University of Quebec at Montreal since 1975. He is currently doing research on suicide and culture among Aboriginal peoples of Canada and on the community response to the contagion of suicide. His other interest is the process of resilience after a serious suicide attempt. He has published more than seventy-five articles, and authored or edited six books in France, Canada and the USA. In line with these interests is his book *Ethnicity, immigration and psychopathology* (co-edited with I. Al-Ihsa, 1997).

AINA BASILIER VAAGE was trained as a nurse and worked in the Paediatric Department, Ullevål University Hospital (Norway). Later, as a physician, she obtained specialist certification in psychiatry and in child and adolescent psychiatry. Working with refugee children and families has been a substantial part of her role as a Senior Consultant in Stavanger (Norway). Her main research interests are in trans-cultural psychiatry, particularly in trans-generational transmission of trauma, traumatized refugee children and the mental health services to these groups of children and families. She is currently a research fellow at the Regional Centre for Child and Adolescent Mental Health, the University of Bergen, in cooperation with the University of Oslo.

FONS R. VAN DE VIJVER teaches cross-cultural psychology at Tilburg University in the Netherlands. His research interests are methodological aspects of inter-group comparisons, acculturation, and cognitive differences and similarities of cultures. He is editor of the *Journal of Cross-Cultural Psychology*. With Kwok Leung, he has published a chapter in the second edition of the *Handbook of cross-cultural psychology* (1997) and a book on methodological aspects of cross-cultural studies, *Methods and data analysis for cross-cultural research* (1997).

JAN PIETER VAN OUDENHOVEN is Professor of Cross-cultural Psychology at the University of Groningen (the Netherlands). After working in two psychiatric hospitals (the UNESCO in Latin America, and an Institute for Welfare Training), he joined the University of Groningen. His dissertation dealt with linguistic achievement of disadvantaged students. He has published widely in the areas of educational psychology, inter-group relations and cultural diversity. He has written several books, on group dynamics, management development, cross-cultural psychology and ethnic minorities. His current interests are international attitudes, cultural diversity and immigration issues.

PAUL VEDDER received his doctorate in developmental psychology from Groningen University in the Netherlands in 1985. His thesis was entitled "Cooperative learning: a study on processes and effects of cooperation between primary schoolchildren." Currently he is a professor in the Department of Learning and Instruction at Leiden University, the Netherlands, with a special focus on learning and development in a multi-cultural society. His research focuses on cooperative learning, social competence, multilingualism and inter-ethnic relationships.

COLLEEN WARD is Professor of Psychology, and received her doctorate in social psychology from the University of Durham, England. She has held teaching and research positions in Trinidad, Malaysia, Singapore and New Zealand. She is currently the Director of the Centre for Applied Cross-cultural Research at Victoria University of Wellington, New Zealand. She is past Secretary-General of the International Association for Cross-cultural

Psychology and is currently the President of the Asian Association of Social Psychology. Her research interests are broadly in cross-cultural psychology with particular interests in acculturation. She is co-author, with Bochner and Adrian Furnham, of *The psychology of culture shock* (2001).

CHARLES WESTIN is Professor of Migration and Ethnicity Studies and Director of the Centre for Research in International Migration and Ethnic Relations at Stockholm University, Sweden. He trained as a psychologist. In his research he has dealt with issues relating to acculturation, integration, identity, ethnicity, discrimination, racism and citizenship.

Foreword

Jean S. Phinney

If you ask the average person the meaning of the term *acculturation*, the most likely response will be with reference to immigrants from developing countries arriving in an industrialized country and faced with the need to learn a new language, develop an understanding of new customs, and interact with people whose values and beliefs differ from their own. This image is perhaps the prototypical view of acculturation.

However, as readers of this book will discover, this image is just the tip of the iceberg. Acculturation processes, which encompass the many changes that occur when people from differing cultures come into contact with each other, can be observed among a wide range of people in addition to immigrants, such as refugees forced to leave their home countries, people living abroad as foreign students or as employees of international companies, and aboriginal peoples dealing with the encroachment of other cultures. All such people face challenges, stresses and opportunities that lead to changes in their lives and wellbeing, sometimes for the better and sometimes for the worse. The ways in which the processes of change unfold vary widely depending on one's culture of origin and current cultural context, as well as on personal characteristics such as age, gender, place of birth, and education, and the characteristics of one's group, such as size, structure, status, values and beliefs.

The varied experiences resulting from cultures in contact have been evident throughout human history and have been written about by observers from ancient times to the present. Scholars from a variety of fields of study have taken differing approaches to understanding acculturation. Sociologists, anthropologists, historians and political scientists, among others, have addressed the topic. Psychologists, with their focus on individuals, have only recently become interested in the subject, in part because acculturation is generally thought of in terms of groups of people. However, since the mid-1980s, psychological interest in acculturation has burgeoned from a few studies and reviews to an extensive literature on the subject. There is increasing recognition that acculturation is a worldwide phenomenon that affects the individual lives of millions of people. This expanding field has in fact become a broad area of study in psychology. Many different theoretical and empirical approaches are being used across a wide range of geographic areas to address the psychological issues raised by cultures in contact. Therefore, an overview of psychological acculturation, as provided in this *Handbook*, is most timely.

How is it possible to make sense out of such a broad topic in today's increasingly complex and culturally intermingled world? The editors of this *Handbook* have taken the approach of assembling an outstanding group of scholars to review their particular areas of expertise. The result is a rich smorgasbord of fascinating information that will be eye-opening to anyone who thinks of acculturation in terms of one particular setting or type of culture contact. In addition to the presentation of a number of broad theoretical frameworks for studying acculturation, there are detailed descriptions of particular types of acculturating individuals, including immigrants, sojourners, refugees and indigenous people. Information is provided as well on methods for designing studies and measuring acculturation. The focus is on acculturation in European and European-origin industrialized countries, but the book includes chapters dealing with variability among these countries; these chapters provide absorbing insights into the very different experiences of acculturating people depending on a particular country's history, ethnic and racial makeup, and policies for dealing with cultural diversity. The reader who peruses the *Handbook* will be rewarded with a sense of the immensity and variety of the topic of acculturation and of the highlights of current thinking on the subject.

Furthermore, the appetites of researchers interested in studying acculturation will be whetted by the many issues and questions raised by the authors. In addition to specific questions posed, gaps in our understanding are revealed by the absence of information on particular aspects of the topic; for example, relatively little is known about acculturation in parts of the world not included in this overview or about changes in existing societies as a result of contact with newcomers. Because population shifts throughout the world will continue to bring new groups of people into contact, the study of acculturation will be important for psychologists for the foreseeable future. This *Handbook* is an excellent starting point in providing an overview of our current understanding of psychological acculturation and suggesting future directions for our efforts to better understand our diverse and changing world.

Jean S. Phinney
Los Angeles, California

Acknowledgments

This book represents the growing effort on the part of a number of international scholars who see the need to understand human behavior from a more global perspective. These scholars also consider that theories and research findings are culturally situated and that no one theoretical viewpoint will fully capture the understanding that we desire to gain about human behavior. The opportunity to work with such people has been very inspiring and stimulating for both of the volume editors.

Producing a book like this would not be possible without the help of several people. As editors we are very grateful for the contributions made by all the chapter authors. We would like to thank each of the chapter authors for agreeing to contribute to this volume. We know that producing these kinds of chapters requires much time and effort, and we are very grateful for all the sacrifice they have had to make within all the constraints we imposed. We appreciate the richness of the reviews. The different chapters generally reflect the theoretical and empirical position of the authors and do not necessarily reflect the position of the editors.

We are particularly grateful to Amanda Rogers (of University of Bergen and University of Western Australia) for her invaluable editorial skills in organizing the chapters and coordinating the work of the chapter authors and the editors. We also gratefully acknowledge financial support from the Department of Psychosocial Science, University of Bergen, to cover Amanda's salary. David wants to thank the Department of Psychology at the University of Hawaii at Manoa, Honolulu, where a lot of writing and editing took place, for hosting him during the last part of his sabbatical (Spring 2005).

We also express our thanks to the different editors at Cambridge University Press who have been both understanding and supportive in guiding us through the maze of producing an edited book: we appreciate the efforts of Sarah Caro (who initially commissioned this *Handbook*), of Chris Harrison (who took over in the interim) and finally of Andrew Peart (for seeing us to the finish line).

Chapters 24 and 27 were prepared during David's visit to the Department of Psychology, University of Hawaii at Honolulu, in the Spring of 2005.

Research for Chapter 28 was conducted at the Université du Québec, Montreal, by the co-authors. Dr. Ehrensaft gratefully acknowledges the financial support of her research by the Conseil québécois de recherche sociale.

Finally, we would like to thank our families for their support and encouragement during the entire period.

David L. Sam and John W. Berry

1 Introduction

David L. Sam & John W. Berry

1.1 The scope of acculturation

Contact between peoples of different cultures is not a new phenomenon. Throughout human history, mankind has traveled around the world for various reasons, either in search of greener pastures, fleeing from persecution and catastrophe, to trade or to conquer and colonize, or in search of adventure or fun. These activities have resulted in the meeting of peoples of diverse backgrounds. This process has led to changes in the original patterns of life and cultures of the peoples concerned, as well as to the formation of new societies. The meeting of cultures and the resulting changes are what collectively has come to be known as *acculturation*.

Although acculturation is as old as recorded history, and the field indeed engaged the minds of ancient philosophers, it was not until the last few decades that we saw a major surge in research interest in the topic in psychology. However, in the field of anthropology, the interest in acculturation developed earlier, with research carried out with indigenous peoples (e.g., Hallowell, 1955), and in sociology with immigrants (e.g., Park, 1928). In psychology, books and articles reviewing and integrating the literature on acculturation began appearing in the 1980s and 1990s (e.g., Berry, 1980, 1990; Padilla, 1980), and have continued up to the present (e.g., Chun, Balls-Organista & Marin, 2003). Rudmin (2003) has tracked this trend in psychology, noting a rapid increase in publications from less than 100 in the 1940s, to over 500 in the 1980s and over 1,500 most recently.

We attribute this increased interest in the field of acculturation to several reasons, but they all boil down to two main issues: (i) the increase in worldwide migration, due to natural and man-made disasters such as war, conflict, poverty and famine, as well as to improved means of traveling over larger distances; and (ii) the increasing importance of understanding the link between culture and human behavior that has been advanced by those working in the field of cross-cultural psychology.

1.2 Worldwide traveling and migration

The increase in the global population and the widening in socio-economic differences between low- and high-income countries have acted as "push" factors in sending people from less economically developed regions of the world to the more developed parts in a search for a better livelihood. Concomitantly, urbanization in many countries has led to internal movement of people from rural areas into urban areas. Several regions of the world have witnessed an increase in political, ethnic and religious conflicts that have culminated in collective violence. In its aftermath, there has been a surge in the numbers of people seeking asylum and becoming refugees in other countries. These activities have all contributed to an increase in worldwide migration (Desjarlais, Eisenberg, Good & Kleinman, 1995).

At the start of this century, it was estimated that there were about 175 million people living in countries different from the one in which they were born – a group that is collectively referred to as "migrants" (United Nations, 2002). This number is a doubling in just a quarter of a century. Most of these 175 million migrants are undergoing changes of some sort in their original ways of living, largely because they originate from societies that are culturally different from the one they currently reside in. What are not included in this statistic showing a large number of migrants are the millions of children of these migrants who were born in the country where their parents currently reside. Indeed immigrant children have been identified as one of the fastest-growing sectors of the population in several Western societies (Aronowitz, 1984). For instance, it was estimated that, while the number of immigrant children in the United States grew by 47 percent in the period between 1990 and 1997, the percentage increase in children of native-born parents was only 7 percent during the same period (Hernandez, 1999).

There is hardly any country that is presently not affected by migration in one way or another, either as a sender or as receiver. There are both positive and negative aspects to these migrations. For sending countries, one of their concerns is brain-drain, but, on the positive side, monetary remittances from abroad serve to support their families and bolster their domestic economies. For the receiving countries, they may be concerned with ethnic conflicts and social problems, on the negative side. However, on the positive side, immigrants contribute to their demographic base during times of population decline, as well as to economic development. In spite of the fact that the one major motivating factor in migration is to improve one's personal, social and economic situation, most migrants face several challenges as they traverse two or more cultures. All in all, it is not surprising that migration is not simply a personal issue, but one that attracts vested political interests with important global implications.

Since 1975, the number of international travelers has been rising steadily from 222 million, reaching 500 million in 1993. Projections made by the World Tourism Organization suggest that this figure will increase by an average of 3.6 percent annually until 2010, to a total of 940 million (see Chapter 12). Much international traveling is short-term and is for a specific purpose, such as tourism. Nevertheless, it leads to a meeting between peoples of different backgrounds and in the process leads to changes in the original cultural patterns of the groups concerned. In addition to tourism, international education has also been on the rise since the end of the Second World War. Open Doors (1996/1997) estimates that there may be up to 1 million people studying in countries other than their own each year. One rationale behind the promotion of international education is the idea of international students serving as cultural carriers (Klineberg, 1970). One consequence of international education is the experience of acculturation, for both the student and the receiving institutions.

Worldwide, there are about 350 million people who are considered to be indigenous; these can be classified into at least 5,000 cultural groups ranging from the Inuit and Sami in the Arctic to Maori in New Zealand and Biaka in Africa. Many indigenous people live in remote areas, and although some have willingly come into contact with other cultures as part of programs of national development, others have been colonized, encroached upon and annexed against their will. In this latter group are people who have been forced to live together with, and dominated by, cultures different from their original one, and subsequently to experience acculturation

1.3 Culture and human behavior

In the 1960s, many psychologists became concerned about the cultural bias that was inherent in their discipline. Most theories, data and researchers were rooted in a small cultural corner of the world, while most of the world's peoples were being ignored. Even worse, when other cultural groups became part of the research enterprise of psychology, they were studied using concepts and instruments that were alien and culturally inappropriate. Missing were points of view that matched the cultural realities of these other populations, including meanings and procedures that could allow psychologists to understand people *in their own terms*.

To deal with these problems, a field of psychology developed which became known as *cross-cultural psychology* (for an overview of these trends, see Berry, Poortinga, Segall & Dasen, 2002; Berry *et al.*, 1997; Segall, 1979; Triandis *et al.*, 1980). For this field, the primary question was *how does culture influence human behavior?* The focus was on how the cultural context in which a person develops might shape (either promote or constrain) behavior. Substantial information is now available to answer this question. The field has clearly demonstrated that cultural experiences do indeed shape the development of behavior and its display in daily life. The field has also developed theories, research methods and domains of application that have radically transformed the way psychology views human diversity.

Some psychologists working in this field came to be interested in a parallel question: "how do people born and raised in one society manage to live in another society that is culturally different from the one they are used to?" This is the basic acculturation question, and is the focus of this *Handbook*. It is rooted in the finding of cross-cultural psychology that people develop behaviors that are adapted to living successfully in their own sociocultural contexts. If this is the case, what happens to people when they take their behavioral repertoire to a different cultural context? We can imagine a number of possible answers to this question. One is that their behavior remains unchanged, and they may risk becoming maladapted to their new setting. Another is that their behavior changes rather easily and rapidly as they learn to live well in their new setting. And a third is that there is a complex pattern of both behavioral continuity and change as people negotiate how to live in their new society. This complexity involves many psychological processes, including social learning, stress and coping, identity, resilience, mental illness, conflict and many others. It is this very complexity that has spurred the development of this field of acculturation psychology, and the production of this *Handbook*.

1.4   Contemporary research in psychology of acculturation

Research in the psychology of acculturation now abounds and there is no lack of studies listed on the PsyINFO web-site and in dissertation abstracts. The references at the end of each chapter in this volume are a testimony to how fast the field is growing. Many of these studies have been reported not only in general psychological journals but also in cross-cultural and multidisciplinary journals. The titles of the journals are unending, and for that reason we will not make any effort to list them.

Another important outlet for psychological acculturation research is at international conferences. Many conference presentations are naturally further developed for journal papers and conference proceedings, and therefore may be included in the list of references in this *Handbook*. However, several important and powerful presentations are not developed further and get lost in the system. A list of conferences where acculturation studies abound may therefore be appropriate, but here again there can be no end; mention can, however, be made of the predominant international psychological associations whose conferences are often dominated by acculturation studies. These are the International Association for Cross-Cultural Psychology (IACCP), and the International Academy of Intercultural Research (IAIR). As an example of how acculturation studies dominate several of these conferences, more than 1 out of 5 papers of the nearly 200 presentations at the joint conference between IACCP and ARIC (Association pour la Recherche Interculturelle – a Francophone organization similar to IACCP) in 1994 was on acculturation (see Bouvy, van de Vijver, Boski & Schmitz, 1994).

Furthermore, there have been a number of specialized conferences on acculturation over the last couple of decades, two of which might be mentioned here. The first (Padilla, 1980) drew together psychologists who had made early contributions to conceptualizing acculturation, and who had made empirical contributions to the field. The second (Chun, Balls-Organista & Marin, 2003) was an explicit attempt to replicate and update the earlier conference. Both of these conferences have resulted in very well cited books on acculturation. Unfortunately both books were mainly focused on acculturation research done in only one country (the United States), and are sometimes of less relevance to acculturation taking place in the wider world. This is the same issue of limited cultural coverage that the field of cross-cultural psychology has attempted to deal with.

Although the list of book chapters on acculturation studies is unlimited, with few exceptions (e.g., Ward, Bochner & Furnham, 2001) textbooks entirely devoted to the psychology of acculturation are rare. This general lack of books on the psychology of acculturation in its entirety, coupled with the overwhelming dominance of US acculturation studies, has been one of the motivating factors behind the development of this *Handbook*. Our intention was to organize a book that covers a very broad range of topics within acculturation, as well as to draw on scholars from different parts of the world.

However, we do acknowledge that most of the topics addressed in this *Handbook* are of concern to the more economically developed societies. It is obvious that most acculturation is taking place in Africa, Asia and South America, but there is limited coverage of these phenomena to be found here. This restriction in coverage is partly due to the limited availability of researchers and research funding for work in these other areas. However, we have attempted to include references to such work where it is available. We also acknowledge that the list of authors is largely dominated by scholars working in Europe; this is partly because acculturation as a research topic has a shorter history in Europe compared with the settler societies in North America and the South Pacific, and we wanted to highlight this emerging literature from Europe.

In spite of the abundance of acculturation research, one area of research that is largely lacking is comparative studies that cover more than a few countries. Many of the studies cited focus on a single society and at best a few ethnic groups, making it very difficult to achieve any generalizations about acculturation phenomena (Berry, Kim, Minde & Mok, 1987). The editing of this *Handbook* coincides with the publication of a large-scale cross-national study on young immigrants' psychological acculturation. This is the International Comparative Study of Ethnocultural Youth (ICSEY) project. Several of the chapters in this *Handbook* refer to some of the findings accruing from the ICSEY project (see Berry, Phinney, Sam & Vedder, 2006).

In order to cover a broad range of issues relevant to psychological acculturation, the book is organized in four parts. The first part provides an overview of the main theories and concepts within the field of acculturation, together with a presentation of issues pertaining to research design, methodology and measurement. The second part includes chapters that present some research findings, both general and specific, on the various kinds of acculturating groups that are found in plural societies. Part III reviews research findings from a variety of societies of settlement, where much of the research work on acculturation has been taking place. The fourth and final part is concerned with applications, drawing upon both theory and empirical findings to address issues of work, school, society and health that may arise in plural societies as a result of acculturation.

The chapters in each part will be previewed in a Part Introduction. There, readers will find sufficient information to allow them to locate the kinds of material that meet their main interests. In addition, at the end of the volume, a Subject Index is provided that gives more detailed access to key concepts and findings.

1.5   References

Aronowitz, M. (1984). The social and emotional adjustment of immigrant children. A review of literature. *International Migration Review*, *18*, 237–257.

Berry, J. W. (1980). Acculturation as varieties of adaptation. In A. Padilla (ed.), *Acculturation: theory, models and findings* (pp. 9–25). Boulder: Westview.

   (1990). Psychology of acculturation. In J. Berman (ed.), *Cross-cultural perspectives: Nebraska symposium on motivation* (pp. 201–234). Lincoln: University of Nebraska Press.

Berry, J. W., Kim, U., Minde, T. & Mok, D. (1987). Comparative studies of acculturative stress. *International Migration Review*, *21*, 491–511.

Berry, J. W., Phinney, J. S., Sam, D. L. & Vedder, P. (eds.) (2006). *Immigrant youth in cultural transition: acculturation, identity and adaptation across national contexts*. Mahwah, NJ: Lawrence Erlbaum Associates.

Berry, J. W., Poortinga, Y. H., Pandey, J., *et al*. (eds.) (1997). *Handbook of cross-cultural psychology*. 2nd edn. 3 vols. Boston: Allyn & Bacon.

Berry, J. W., Poortinga, Y. H., Segall, M. H. & Dasen, P. R. (2002). *Cross-cultural psychology: research and applications*. 2nd edn. New York: Cambridge University Press.

Bouvy, A.-M., van de Vijver, F. J. R., Boski, P. & Schmitz, P. (eds.) (1994). *Journeys into cross-cultural psychology*. Lisse: Swets & Zeitinger.

Chun, K., Balls-Organista, P. & Marin, G. (eds.) (2003). *Acculturation: theory, research and applications*. Washington: APA Press.

Desjarlais, R., Eisenberg, L., Good, B. & Kleinman, A. (1995). *World mental health. Problems and priorities in low-income countries*. New York: Oxford University Press.

Hallowell, A. I. (1955). Sociopsychological aspects of acculturation. In A. I. Hallowell, *Culture and experience* (pp. 310–332). Philadelphia: University of Pennsylvania Press.

Hernandez, D. J. (1999). Children of immigrants: health, adjustment and public assistance. In D. J. Hernandez (ed.), *Children of immigrants: health, adjustment and public assistance* (pp. 1–18). Washington, DC: National Academy Press.

Klineberg, O. (1970). Research in the field of educational exchange. In I. Eide (ed.), *Students as links between cultures* (pp. 49–69). Oslo: Universitetforlaget.

Open Doors (1996/1997). *Report on international education exchange*. New York: Institute of International Education.

Padilla, A. (ed.) (1980). *Acculturation: theory, models and some new findings*. Boulder: Westview.

Park, R. E. (1928). Human migration and the marginal man. *American Journal of Sociology*, *33*, 881–893.

Rudmin, F. W. (2003). Catalogue of acculturation constructs: descriptions of 126 taxonomies, 1918–2003. In W. J. Lonner, D. L. Dinnel, S. A. Hayes & D. N. Sattler (eds.), *Online readings in psychology and culture* (Unit 8, Chapter 8), (www.wwu.edu/~culture), Center for Cross-Cultural Research, Western Washington University, Bellingham, Washington.

Segall, M. H. (1979). *Cross-cultural psychology: human behavior in global perspective*. Monterey: Brooks/Cole.

Triandis, H. C., Lambert, W. W., Berry, J. W., *et al.* (eds.) (1980). *Handbook of cross-cultural psychology*. 6 vols. Boston: Allyn & Bacon.

United Nations (2002). *UN population report 2002*. New York: United Nation Statistics Division.

Ward, C., Bochner, S. & Furnham, A. (2001). *The psychology of culture shock*. Sussex: Routledge.

PART I

Theories, concepts and methods

While acculturation research originated in the field of anthropology, and was further developed by sociology, this *Handbook* mainly examines the newer research tradition developed by psychologists. This first part portrays some of these earlier roots in the social sciences, and then focuses on some perspectives that derive mainly from psychological concepts and research interests. In particular, three general traditions, referred to as the *stress*, *culture learning* and *identity* perspectives, are presented in Chapters 4, 5 and 6 respectively, to set the stage for much of the discussion that follows in the *Handbook*. These three general orientations to the field are followed by two chapters that link acculturation phenomena to two basic psychological concepts: *development* (Chapter 7) and *personality* (Chapter 8). The part closes with two chapters that draw our attention to some methodological features of acculturation research. While the field of acculturation psychology shares most of the problems and solutions that are present in cross-cultural psychology, there are some unique features to acculturation research design, assessment and analyses that are addressed here.

2 Acculturation: conceptual background and core components

David L. Sam

2.1 Introduction

Although *acculturation* is now a term commonly used in discussions around immigrants and refugees, the term, its meaning and operationalization within the social sciences still remain elusive. The elusive nature of the concept has, no doubt, limited the scientific exchange of information and meaningful discussion around research findings and theory development. The goal of this chapter is to clarify the concept's definition, its use in the social sciences and the implications of both for research and theory development. As an introduction to the concept in a comprehensive handbook, the main emphasis of the chapter will be to give a broad overview. A more detailed coverage of the various aspects of the concept can be found in other chapters in this *Handbook*, and in particular elsewhere in Part I.

In its simplest sense, "acculturation" covers all the changes that arise following "contact" between individuals and groups of different cultural backgrounds. A more formal definition was proposed by Redfield, Linton and Herskovits in 1936. They defined acculturation as "those phenomena which result when groups of individuals having different cultures come into continuous first-hand contact, with subsequent changes in the original culture patterns of either or both groups" (Redfield *et al.*, 1936:149). In 2004, the International Organization for Migration (IOM) defined acculturation as "the progressive adoption of elements of a foreign culture (ideas, words, values, norms, behavior, institutions) by persons, groups or classes of a given culture." The two definitions just cited highlight some of the important controversies surrounding the use of the concept. The IOM definition for instance overlooks the fact that acculturation could also entail "rejection of" or "resistance to" cultural elements and not simply the "adoption" of foreign cultural elements (see Chapter 3). These issues have important implications for theory development.

Redfield *et al.*'s definition is now regarded as the classical definition of the concept and is perhaps the one most cited by acculturation researchers. Nevertheless, the term is sometimes wrongly and/or synonymously used instead of *assimilation,* as exemplified by an everyday expression such as "he is very much acculturated to . . . ," implying "he is very much assimilated into . . . ," a given society or culture. In recent years where many countries have come to acknowledge the "un-workable" nature of assimilation as a general settlement policy (Berry, Poortinga, Segall & Dasen, 2002), together with increased growth in global migration, there has been a proliferation of new terms such as "biculturalism," "multiculturalism," "integration," "re-socialization" and "ethnic identity." These terms have either been used as an alternative concept or interchangeably with "acculturation." Furthermore, the rapid expansion and exchange of information, trade and economic harmonization have given rise to the concept of "globalization" and idiomatic expressions such as "western-ization" and "coca-colanization" in the current discourse in acculturation. The need to clarify some of these other terms can therefore not be overemphasized.

To complicate matters, "acculturation" and "assimilation" as terms have also sometimes been used *not* as synonyms of each other, but as sub-sets of each other. Specifically, assimilation has sometimes been seen as one form/phase of acculturation and at other times the situation has been reversed (i.e., accultur-ation is one form/phase of assimilation). Gordon (1964) for instance equated acculturation with one phase of assimilation – *cultural or behavioral assimila-tion* – and defined it as "change of cultural patterns to those of the host society." The concept of *segmented assimilation* was recently introduced as a refinement of the original concept of assimilation (Portes & Rumbaut, 2001). Berry (1990, 1997, 2003) on the other hand regards assimilation to be one of four strategies an individual may use during acculturation. Berry defined "assimilation" to be the situation where either (i) an individual turns his back on his original cultural background and identity and chooses to identify and interact with the members of the host society or (ii) a national society expects foreigners to adopt wholly the culture of the larger national society (see Chapter 3 for an elaboration of these views).

Furthermore, Teske and Nelson (1974) viewed acculturation and assimila-tion to be two separate and distinct processes that may be differentiated on a number of dimensions. Teske and Nelson indicate that acculturation is poten-tially bidirectional and reciprocal in terms of influence (i.e., the two groups in contact influence each other). Assimilation on the other hand is unidirectional in its influence (i.e., a host group unilaterally exerts some influence on another group).

Bearing in mind the ubiquitous, albeit elusive, use of the term "accultura-tion," this chapter will first give a brief historical background to the concept as a means to understanding the (mis-)use of the concept. Subsequently the "building blocks" of the concept will be examined to highlight its scope for research and theory development. In addition, related concepts will be defined.

2.2   Historical background

Powell (1880, 1883) is accredited as the first person to have used the term "acculturation" in the English language, although the topic has its roots in antiquity (see Plato, 1969). As a concept, Powell (1883) suggested that "acculturation" referred to psychological changes induced by cross-cultural imitation. McGee (1898), working from an anthropological perspective, defined acculturation to be the process of exchange and mutual improvement by which societies advanced from savagery, to barbarism, to civilization, and to enlightenment. From a sociological perspective, Simons (1901) regarded acculturation to be a two-way process of "reciprocal accommodation." She nevertheless equated the word to the English term "assimilation" and defined "assimilation" as the process of adjustment or accommodation which occurs between the members of two different races giving rise to the synonymous use of the terms.

"Assimilation" and "acculturation" have from the outset been regarded as synonymous even though from two different social science disciplines. While anthropologists preferred to use the term "acculturation," sociologists preferred to use the term "assimilation." Furthermore, anthropologists' use of the term "acculturation" was primarily concerned with how so-called "primitive" societies changed to become more civilized following cultural contact with an enlightened group of people. On the other hand, sociologists' use of the term "assimilation" or "acculturation" was more directed towards "immigrants" who, through contact with the "host nationals," gradually conformed to the ways of life of the host people.

The first confusion surrounding the use of the term arose when anthropologists directed their research attention from the "primitive societies of the world" to "immigrants on their backyard" (i.e., anthropologists changed their original target group of interest to that of sociologists). Instead of using the term "assimilation" as was used by sociologists, anthropologists kept to the term "acculturation" preparing the ground for confusion. Another possible reason behind the confusion is that "assimilation" assumed that an "inferior" group would want to, and would inevitably, become like the "superior" group, reminiscent of the original meaning of "acculturation" when used by anthropologists.

Does it matter whether the two concepts are used interchangeably, and, if it does, is any one of the two terms a better one to use? I believe the synonymous use of the terms matters, because there are some nuances in these two terms that have important ramifications for theory development and interpretation of research findings. Specifically, I argue in this chapter that "acculturation" should be the preferred term.

In his history of acculturation psychology, Rudmin (2003a & b) credits G. Stanley Hall (1904) as possibly the first psychologist to write about the topic. However, it was over 50 years later that psychologists became fully interested in this field of inquiry. Acculturation was originally introduced as a group-level phenomenon (Linton, 1940; Redfield *et al.*, 1936); however, early discussions around the concept also recognized it as an individual level-level phenomenon (see Broom & Kitsuse, 1955; Devereux & Loeb, 1943; Dohrenwend & Smith, 1962; Eaton, 1952; Spiro, 1955; Thurnwald, 1932).

Naturally, psychology's strong interest in the individual contributed towards the formal use of the term "psychological acculturation" and the distinction between individual-level changes arising from acculturation and those taking place at the group level.

"Psychological acculturation" refers to the changes an individual experiences as a result of being in contact with other cultures, or participating in the acculturation that one's cultural or ethnic group is undergoing (Graves, 1967). In addition to the need to make a distinction between group-level and individual-level changes, Berry (1990) indicated that the kinds of changes that take place at the two levels are often different. At the group level, the changes might be in either the social structure of the group, the economic base or the group's political organization. At the individual level, the kinds of changes taking place might be in identity, values, attitudes and behavior. Moreover, the rate at which changes take place within the individual (i.e., attitudes, behavior, etc.) may differ. Thus a comprehensive coverage of the topic requires studying changes occurring at both levels (i.e., group and individual) as well as the relationship between the levels.

2.3   The building blocks

Taking a point of departure in Redfield *et al.*'s (1936) definition of acculturation, three issues can be identified as the building blocks in the process. These are *contact*, *reciprocal influence* and *change*. Within each of these blocks, a number of sub-blocks can also be identified, and these blocks are briefly elaborated on below.

Contact A major prerequisite for acculturation is *contact* following a "meeting" between at least two cultural groups or individuals who come together in a "continuous" and "firsthand" manner. While there may be many different types of contacts in contemporary societies (e.g., living side by side in the same apartment block, internet communication or mass-media broadcasting), the two distinguishing features of an acculturative contact are "continuous and firsthand." True acculturation might be said to be one where the individuals or groups have "interaction" within the same time and space, and not through secondhand experiences (e.g., the experiences of another person who might have been exposed to another culture) or indirect contact (e.g., through pen-pal mail communication). Furthermore, the interaction should be over a period of time. A challenging question raised by the term "continuous" is *how long* should a contact be for it to qualify as an acculturation? If the contact tourists encounter during their brief visit to a place qualifies as an acculturation, then an acculturation contact should be at least twenty-four hours in duration (see Chapter 12 of this *Handbook*). Perhaps, the issues of "how long" or "continuous" contact in themselves are not as important as the resulting *change* following the contact. Consequently, short-term visitors such as tourists who undergo several changes may be experiencing as much acculturation as indigenous peoples who experience cultural contact over several generations.

The groups or individuals commonly identified as undergoing acculturation include immigrants, refugees, asylum seekers, sojourners, ethnocultural groups and indigenous peoples. Precisely who these peoples are, and the terms used in describing them, vary from country to country depending on a number of socio-political factors (Cohon, 1981). Berry (1990) has, however, suggested that the various acculturating individuals and groups can be distinguished along three dimensions: voluntary – involuntary, sedentary – migrant and permanent – temporary, as part of the acculturation contact (see Chapter 3 of this *Handbook*). In this classification, both refugees and immigrants have a relatively permanent contact with another cultural group, and they are migrants. But they differ on the voluntary – involuntary dimension of the contact. Refugees *involuntarily* come into contact with another cultural group, but this contact is *voluntary* for immigrants. Similarly, while sojourners and asylum seekers are *temporarily* in contact with another cultural group, indigenous people and ethnocultural groups have permanent cultural contact. Furthermore, sojourners and asylum seekers are migrants, but the two differ in terms of the voluntariness of their contact. Sojourners voluntarily came into contact with another cultural group, but it is the opposite for asylum seekers. With respect to ethnocultural groups and indigenous peoples, they are both sedentary, but indigenous peoples' contact is involuntary and that of ethnocultural groups is voluntary, even though contact for some of them (e.g., African Americans) might have started off as involuntary.

Reciprocal influence The expression "changes in the original culture patterns of either or both groups" in Redfield *et al.*'s definition of acculturation entails *mutual or reciprocal influences* where in theory both groups influence each other. However, due to power differences, in terms of either economic power, military might or numerical strength, one group exerts more influence than the other. Since one group often exerts more influence (i.e., the dominant group) than the other (i.e., the non-dominant group), it is often and wrongly assumed that only the non-dominant group is changing. This assumption has probably contributed towards the one-sided view of acculturation: the changes taking place in the non-dominant group. It is important that acculturation studies direct as much attention to changes taking place in the dominant group as to those in the non-dominant group.

Although most acculturation research takes place in a dominant – non-dominant relationship, it is important to indicate that "dominance" is not considered a necessary prerequisite for acculturation to take place. Dominance is nevertheless an important variable in explaining the rate of acculturation and the direction of change during acculturation (Teske & Nelson, 1974). In line with this, Bogardus (1949) suggested that there might be three forms of acculturation when discussing cultural pluralism: blind acculturation (i.e., when people of different cultures live near one another and culture patterns are adopted on a chance basis); imposed acculturation (i.e., where there is the forced imposition of one's culture on another people's culture, such as during colonization); democratic acculturation (i.e., where representatives of cultures view each other's culture with respect). In contemporary plural societies, and with particular reference to immigrants, specific settlement policies (as either imposed or democratic acculturation) are often implemented to ensure that the same form of "change" takes place rather than the change being "left to chance."

Change An inherent aspect of contact is *change* which involves both a *process* that is dynamic, and an *outcome* which may be relatively stable. This means that, in studying acculturation, the interest can equally be on the process itself – e.g., how acculturation change comes about (i.e., the process-question) – as well as on what has changed during acculturation (i.e., the outcome-question). While cross-sectional studies may be suitable for addressing the outcome-question, they may be insufficient when dealing with process-questions. With respect to process-questions, longitudinal studies may be better suited. For a better understanding of acculturation, both outcome and process questions need to be addressed, and both cross-sectional and longitudinal study designs pursued.

The classical definition of "acculturation" points to outward "contact between two cultural groups" as a prerequisite to change. However, with psychological acculturation where changes may include personal characteristics such as values, attitudes and identity, it is not always easy to identify the origin of the change, or whether the change is indeed acculturation. All human beings undergo ontogenetic development and this may entail changes in identity or behavior development. In essence it may not be easy to distinguish psychological acculturation from ontogenetic development. The two forms of changes confound each other (see Sam, in press).

Acculturation changes are often thought of as limited to only "cultural" changes. Berry (1991), however, pointed out that acculturation changes could be either physical (e.g., setting up temporary houses and camps to accommodate refugees and asylum seekers), biological (e.g., changes in people's resistance to diseases), political (e.g., the introduction of immigration policies), economical (i.e., the economic contribution of foreign workers), social (e.g., racial and ethnic discrimination) and cultural or a combination, at the group level. Since this *Handbook* is on psychological acculturation, we will limit our discussion to psychological changes.

Psychological acculturation often involves _a_ffective, _b_ehavioral and _c_ognitive changes, in the individual, in what have been termed the ABCs of acculturation by Ward (2001; see Chapter 5 of this *Handbook*). Berry (Berry 1997; Berry & Sam 1997) summarizes these ABCs as behavioral shifts and acculturative stress. These changes tend to be the focus of attention when the interest is in short-term acculturation outcomes. However, as acculturation changes may also continue for a very long time, long-term outcomes, referred to as "adaptation," become a prime concern. Ward and her colleagues (Searle & Ward, 1990; Ward, 2001; Ward & Kennedy, 1993) have distinguished between two kinds of adaptation: psychological and sociocultural adaptations. Broadly speaking, psychological adaptation refers to psychological or emotional well-being and satisfaction while sociocultural adaptation is concerned with the acquisition of the culturally appropriate skills needed to negotiate or "fit into" a specific social or cultural milieu. For detailed discussion, see Chapters 4 and 5 of this handbook.

2.4   Directionality and dimensionality

Two fundamental issues in all acculturation research and theory are *directionality* (i.e. in which direction does change take place?) and dimensionality (i.e., does change take place along a single dimension or two independent dimensions?). Regarding directionality, some writers have suggested that acculturation is a unidirectional process (Gordon, 1964; Graves, 1967). Others (Taft, 1977; Teske & Nelson, 1974) regard it as a bidirectional one. The differences of opinion lie in the previously noted confusion regarding the synonymous use of the concepts of assimilation and acculturation. The assimilation perspective is that change takes place in one direction, namely one group moving unidirectionally towards another group which is "stationary," so to speak. The notion here is that one group changes to become like the other. At the core of the bidirectional perspective is the issue of mutual or reciprocal influence between two individuals or groups in contact. Here, the assumption is that both individuals and groups in contact *can* change, but do not necessarily change towards a neutral or a mid-point. Most current psychological thinking regards acculturation to be bidirectional rather than unidirectional.

The issue of dimensionality is closely linked with the directionality issue. In the uni-dimensional thinking it is assumed that individuals lose their original cultural identity as they acquire a new cultural identity in line with the second culture. That is, the more individuals acquire of the new culture, the less they have of the original culture (LaFromboise, Coleman & Gerton, 1993). The two cultures in contact are seen as mutually exclusive, and therefore it is considered to be psychologically problematic to maintain both cultures (Johnston, 1976; Sung, 1985). This perspective is in line with assimilation assumptions, where one either remains unchanged (i.e., maintains separation), or becomes assimilated.

From the bidimensional perspective, the assumption is that it is possible to identify with or acquire the new culture independently, without necessarily losing the original culture (Berry, 1980). Change can take place along two independent dimensions, one dimension being the maintenance or loss of the original culture and the other being participation in, or adoption of aspects of, the new culture. It is therefore possible for an individual to have more or less of the two cultures in question. The final outcome is one of the relative degree of involvement in the two cultures in contact.

2.5   Managing the process of acculturation

In order to understand how acculturation changes occur, several theorists have suggested that the process passes through several phases or that it can take different forms. In this section, the two main schools of thought around assimilation/acculturation will briefly be discussed. However, for a more detailed discussion of these, see LaFromboise *et al.* (1993).

Perhaps Gordon's (1964) thesis is the most explicit on the phases involved in assimilation (acculturation). Gordon suggested that assimilation involves passing through seven stages in a progressive fashion. These, he termed *cultural or behavioral assimilation, structural assimilation, marital assimilation, attitudinal reciprocal assimilation, behavioral reciprocal assimilation, civic assimilation* and *identificational assimilation*. The crux of the assimilation theory is that, over time and with increasing contact between the foreigner and the host members, the foreigner will become more and more like the host members. Gordon suggested that a self-image as an unhyphenated American (identificational assimilation) was the end product of the process "that began with cultural assimilation, proceeded through structural assimilation and intermarriage and was accompanied by an absence of prejudice and discrimination in the 'core society'" (Rumbaut, 2001:846). These changes are thought to be linear and uniform, or what has been termed "straight line assimilation" (Gans, 1973; Sandberg, 1973). One form of straight line assimilation is what economists refer to as earnings assimilation (see Chapter 26).

While this "assimilation story" might have worked for early groups of immigrants to the United States, this does not appear to be the case for current waves of migrants – and their children – not only to the USA, but to other parts of the world. Consequently, the straight line assimilation hypothesis has been questioned (Alba & Lee, 1997; Glazer, 1993) and the concept of segmented assimilation has been introduced (Portes & Rumbaut, 2001; Zhou, 1997). Within this concept, it is argued that assimilation is contingent on a number of factors including social class differences (between immigrants themselves and in comparison to their host members), the time of arrival, the context of their reception, which together may contribute to a non-linear, non-unidirectional assimilation outcome. Instead, assimilation may result in a number of other possible outcomes where people and individuals may be assimilated into different segments of the society. Segmented assimilation is a reflection of the different contingencies that may impact on the assimilation process to thwart the relatively smooth and straight-line path.

Within psychological acculturation thinking, the framework of Berry (Berry, 1990, 1997; Berry, Kim, Power, Young & Bujaki, 1989; Berry *et al.*, 2002) has received most attention. Berry suggested that the acculturation process proceeds according to the degree to which the individual simultaneously participates in the cultural life of the new society and maintains his or her original cultural identity. The simultaneous participation and maintenance of the two cultures may lead to four different outcomes which Berry called *assimilation, integration, separation* and *marginalization*. These four outcomes are collectively referred to as "acculturation strategies." Chapter 3 of this *Handbook* gives a more thorough discussion of these concepts. It is important to add that these outcomes are not an end in themselves, they are strategies. Since acculturation is a continuous process, an individual may adopt different strategies at different times, and to deal with different life issues. Again, these different strategies should not be thought of as "additive," leading to where one can think of an individual as being fully "integrated." Alternatively, the strategies could be thought of as phases which an individual may pass through over and over, using several strategies at any given time.

2.6   Related concepts

Interculturation is a concept found in the French literature with a similar meaning to "acculturation." The concept is defined as "the set of processes by which individuals and groups interact when they identify themselves as culturally distinct" (Berry & Sam, 1997; Clanet, 1970). In an elaboration of "la psychologie interculturelle" (intercultural psychology) Denoux (1992) defined it as:

> a psychology studying processes of culture-mediated construction. This refers to the construction of cultural diversity in the context of cultural contacts: the relationship between immigrants and host-country, between minority and majority, between traditional and modern culture ... Intercultural psychology has a specific research field (intercultural encounters), a specific research objective (cultural distinctiveness), and a specific mechanism ("interculturation," i.e., the formation of a new culture on the basis of these encounters).   (Cited in Bouvy, van de Vijver, Boski & Schmitz 1994:2.)

As Berry and Sam (1997) have pointed out, there are similarities between interculturation and acculturation. One distinguishing feature is the interest in the "formation of new cultures" in the case of the interculturation approach, which is of somewhat less importance in the acculturation approach.

Enculturation, socialization and re-socialization Enculturation refers to all the learning that occurs in human life without any deliberate effort on the part of someone to impart that learning. It is something that occurs because of the possibilities and opportunities that are present and available within an individual's context. Much of enculturation occurs through observation, but not all observation entails enculturation. In some forms of observation, an individual is asked to observe closely and "imitate" a behavior. This is *socialization*. Enculturation is closely related to socialization, but for one major difference: *socialization* entails deliberate and systematic "shaping" of an individual through teaching. Enculturation does not. Within social and developmental psychology, the term "socialization," however, is used as an all-embracing concept to include both systematic and accidental shaping and learning of the culture of a given society. A more formal definition of socialization is "the continuous collaboration of 'elders' and 'novices,' of 'old hands' and 'newcomers,' in the acquisition and honing of skills important for meeting the demands of group life" (Bugental & Goodnow, 1988:386). This definition brings to light several issues that require further elaboration, but elaborating on these issues will be going beyond the scope of this chapter.

Closely related to socialization is re-socialization which simply entails "re-shaping" of previously acquired skills necessary for meeting the demands of a particular society (see Berry, 2006). This may occur because an individual has moved from one cultural society to another where new skills may be needed in order to meet the demands of this new society. Enculturation, socialization and re-socialization are all processes that often occur during acculturation, but they are not in themselves acculturation.

Globalization This concept has been variously defined depending on the theoretical perspective taken. Within the context of the present discussion, it refers to the process by which societies and cultures influence one another and become more alike through trade, immigration and the exchange of information and ideas. Unlike acculturation where the emphasis is on the changes taking place between two individuals and cultures, globalization encompasses several societies and cultures and is concerned with how they "become alike" or harmonized.

Multiculturalism This refers to a political ideology about how ethnic groups in a society live together and maintain their ethnic and cultural distinctiveness. While most contemporary societies are plural in nature (i.e., the inhabitants of the society belong to various cultural and ethnic backgrounds), plural societies differ in the types of policies they use to determine how the different ethnic and cultural groups should live together and at the same time maintain their ethnic diversity and distinctiveness. "Multiculturalism" is the term used to describe the situation in a society where the different groups are encouraged to maintain their ethnic distinctiveness, and to participate in the daily life of the larger society. This is opposed to one where ethnic diversity is diminished and distinctiveness is harmonized (as in the "melting pot"), or where ethnic differences are allowed but kept out of participation in the life of the larger society ("segregation"). In line with this thinking, a multicultural society may not have a single culture for all the groups and no one culture may take precedence over the others. Thus, a term such as "multicultural education" means an educational system where the educational goals and school curriculum, amongst other things, are equally relevant for all the ethnic groups concerned.

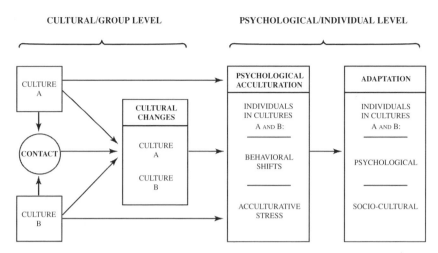

Figure 2.1 *A framework for conceptualizing and studying acculturation*

Ethnic identity This is one form of cultural identity and deals with how individuals and groups define and make sense of themselves, in terms of the ethnic group they originally belonged to and a new cultural group. For many individuals and groups, prior to acculturation, they may not have a very clear sense of their ethnicity as this is taken for granted. However, when the individual or group comes into contact with another group that is culturally different, they may be forced to define a sense of identity in line with their ethnicity. Ethnic identity may therefore be thought of as an aspect of acculturation.

2.7   Implications of the concept for research and theory development

Acculturation involves contact that takes place at both group and individual levels leading to changes which for the individual entail affective, behavioral and cognitive changes (or what may be referred to as behavioral changes and acculturative stress) and subsequent long-term modification of psychological and sociocultural adaptation. Berry (2003) has proposed a framework showing how individual- and group-level factors come together to form acculturation. This is illustrated in Figure 2.1. In the figure, arrows are seen as moving from the group level towards the individual level. What may not be obvious in the figure however, is the mutual influence and change between the two groups in contact. This is, however, implied by including cultures and individuals from both cultures A and B in the headings of all 3 boxes.

From the framework and the discussions, good acculturation research and theory should be able to highlight the contact between two distinct cultures, identify the cultural and psychological changes (both short- and long-term) that are taking place in both groups, and determine how these changes actually come about.

2.8   Limitations of acculturation

At the core of "acculturation" is the concept of "culture" and difficulties in defining and operationalizing culture have important implications for acculturation research and theory formulation. One assumption acculturation researchers make is the existence of some cultural differences in the groups and individuals in contact with each other. Very often, as long as an individual or a group is seen as coming from a different country, some form of difference is assumed. These differences may be linked to such value dimensions as individualism and collectivism without any effort to measure these dimensions in the groups in question. A challenge facing acculturation researchers is how to demonstrate the existence of the cultural difference.

How we define "culture" and its related concepts will undoubtedly affect the results of acculturation studies and the interpretation of these results. This issue is very well demonstrated in the study by Snauwaert and his colleagues (Snauwaert, Soenens, Vanbeselaere & Boen, 2003). In their studies, one dimension of the acculturation orientations was operationalized in three different ways: (i) as contact (i.e., participation in intercultural activities), (ii) as adoption of the culture of the dominant society, or (iii) as identification with the dominant society. These differing phrasings affected individuals' acculturation strategy preferences. This study shows, not surprisingly, that when the bidimensional framework proposed by Berry is operationalized in different ways, different results are obtained.

Closely linked to the definition of culture is the issue of "cultural context." Acculturation does not take place in a "vacuum" but at a specific time and place – cultural context. It is therefore meaningless to speak of acculturation if the context under which the two groups are in contact is not understood. This context may include the socio-political background of the groups in contact as well as the reasons behind the contact. Thus, it is imperative that these cultural contexts are well understood before any meaningful understanding of acculturation can be reached. Part III of this *Handbook* describes some of the major acculturating contexts in the world.

Acculturation studies have primarily focused on changes that have their origins in "physical contact" between individuals and groups. This contact is limited to those taking place within the same time and space. Our IT-world has also changed the way we normally think of time and space. Where do we place *chatting on the internet*? To date, internet chatting has not been defined as a domain of inquiry by acculturation researchers. How do we define the culture context for internet chatting? Obviously people involved in internet chatting are doing so at the same time and in the same space, albeit a special form of space – cyberspace. It is unclear in the definition of "acculturation" where to place internet chatting. The same applies to the several passengers who spend hours in transit at major international airports rubbing shoulders with practically the whole world. Do these contemporary activities fall within the scope of acculturation? These issues are yet to be clarified.

2.9   Conclusions

Efforts have been made in this chapter to clarify the concept of acculturation and how it differs from other concepts such as assimilation. A challenging question which researchers face is whether the interchangeable use of the two terms "assimilation" and "acculturation" really matters in developing research and theory, or whether this is simply an issue of semantics. It is my opinion that acculturation is different from assimilation and that acculturation is a more far-reaching and all-embracing concept in terms of scope and meaning than is assimilation. "Acculturation" is therefore deemed to be a better-suited term to use in formulating clearer research questions and theory development. Progress in acculturation theory development and research is closely tied up with progress in the definition and operationalization of the concept of culture. Likewise, our contemporary world with its technological advances also comes with new challenges yet to be defined as acculturation.

2.10   References

Alba, R. & Nee, V. (1997). Rethinking assimilation theory for a new era of immigration. *International Migration Review, 31*, 826–874.

Berry, J. W. (1980). Acculturation as varieties of adaptation. In A. Padilla (ed.), *Acculturation: theory, models and some new findings* (pp. 9–25). Boulder: Westview.

   (1990). Psychology of acculturation. In J. J. Berman (ed.)., *Nebraska symposium on motivation, 1989: cross-cultural perspectives* (pp. 201–234.) Lincoln: University of Nebraska Press.

   (1991). Managing the process of acculturation for problem prevention. In J. Westermeyer, C. L. Williams & A. N. Nguyen (eds.), *Mental health services for refugees* (pp. 189–204). DHSS Publication no. [ADM] 91–1824. Washington DC: US Government Publishing House.

   (1997). Immigration, acculturation and adaptation. *Applied Psychology: An International Review, 41*, 5–68.

   (2003). Conceptual approaches to acculturation. In K. Chun, P. Balls-Organista & G. Marin (eds.), *Acculturation: advances in theory, measurement and applied research* (pp. 17–37). Washington: APA Books.

   (2006). Acculturation. In J. Grusec & P. Hastings (eds.), *Handbook of socialization research*. New York: Guilford Press.

Berry, J. W., Kim, U., Power, S., Young, M. & Bujaki, M. (1989). Acculturation attitudes in plural societies. *Applied Psychology: An International Review*, *38*, 185–296.

Berry, J. W., Poortinga, Y. H., Segall., M. H. & Dasen, P. R. (2002). *Cross-cultural psychology: research and application*. Cambridge: Cambridge University Press.

Berry, J. W. & Sam, D. L. (1997). Acculturation and adaptation. In J. W. Berry *et al.* (eds.), *Handbook of cross-cultural psychology*, Vol. III: *Social behaviour and applications* (pp. 291–326). Boston: Allyn & Bacon.

Bogardus, E. S. (1949). Cultural pluralism and acculturation. *Sociology and Social Research*, *34*, 125–129.

Bouvy, A.-M., van de Vijver, F. J. R., Boski, P. & Schmitz, P. (1994). Introduction . In A.-M. Bouvy, F. J. R van de Vijver, P. Boski & P. Schmitz (eds.), *Journeys into cross-cultural psychology* (pp. 1–27). Lisse: Swets & Zeitinger.

Broom, L. & Kitsuse, J. I. (1955). The validation of acculturation. A condition to ethnic assimilation. *American Anthropologist*, *57*, 44–48.

Bugental, D. B. & Goodnow, J. J. (1988). Socialization processes. In I. W. Damon & N. Eisenberg (eds.), *Handbook of child psychology*, Vol. III: *Social, emotional and personality development*. 5th edn. (pp. 389–462). New York: John Wiley.

Clanet, C. (1990). *L'interculturel: introduction aux approches interculturelles en éducation et en sciences humaines*. Toulouse: Presses Universitaires du Mirail.

Cohon, J. D. (1981). Psychological adaptation and dysfunction among refugees. *International Migration Review*, *15*, 255–275.

Devereux, G. & Loeb, E. M. (1943). Antagonistic acculturation. *American Sociological Review*, *8*, 133–147.

Dohrenwend, B. P. & Smith, R. J. (1962). Towards a theory of acculturation. *Southwestern Journal of Anthropology*, *18*, 30–39.

Eaton, J. (1952). Controlled acculturation. A survival technique of Hutterites. *American Sociological Review*, *17*, 331–340.

Gans, H. (1973). Introduction. In N. Sandberg (ed.), *Ethnic identity and assimilation. The Polish community*. New York: Praeger.

Glazer, N. (1973). Is assimilation dead? *Annals of the American Academy of Social and Political Sciences*, *530*, 122–136.

Gordon, M. M. (1964). *Assimilation in American life. The role of race, religion and national origins*. New York: Oxford University Press.

Graves, T. D. (1967). Psychological acculturation in a tri-ethnic community. *Southwestern Journal of Anthropology*, *23*, 337–350.

Hall, G. S. (1904). *Adolescence*, Vol. II. New York: Appleton.

Johnston, R. (1976). The concept of the "marginal man": a refinement of the term. *Australian and New Zealand Journal of Science*, *12*, 145–147.

LaFromboise, T., Coleman, H. L. K. & Gerton, J. (1993). Psychological impact of biculturalism: evidence and theory. *Psychological Bulletin*, *114*, 395–412.

Linton, R. (1949). The distinctive aspects of acculturation. In R. Linton (ed.), *Acculturation in seven American Indian tribes* (pp. 501–520). New York: Appleton-Century.

McGee, W. J. (1898). Piratical acculturation. *American Anthropologist, 11*, 243–249.

Plato (1969). Laws XII, trans. A. E. Taylor. In E. Hamilton & H. Cairns (eds.), *The collected dialogues of Plato* (pp. 1488–1513). Princeton, NJ: Princeton University Press.

Portes, A. & Rumbaut, R. G. (2001). *Legacies. The story of the immigrant second generation.* Berkeley: University of California Press.

Powell, J. W. (1880). *Introduction to the study of Indian languages.* 2nd edn. Washington, DC: US Government Printing Office.

(1883). Human evolution: annual address of the President, J. W. Powell, delivered November 6, 1883. *Transactions of the Anthropological Society of Washington, 2*, 176–208.

Redfield, R., Linton, R. & Herskovits, M. J. (1936). Memorandum for the study of acculturation. *American Anthropologist, 38*, 149–152.

Rudmin, F. W. (2003a). Catalogue of acculturation constructs: descriptions of 126 taxonomies, 1918–2003. In W. J. Lonner, D. L. Dinnel, S. A. Hayes & D. N. Sattler (eds.), *Online readings in psychology and culture* (Unit 8, Chapter 8), (www.wwu.edu/~culture), Center for Cross-Cultural Research, Western Washington University, Bellingham, Washington.

(2003b). Critical history of the acculturation psychology of assimilation, separation, integration and marginalization. *Review of General Psychology, 7*, 3–37.

Rumbaut, R. G. (2001). Assimilation of immigrants. In *International Encyclopedia of the Social and Behavioural Sciences* (pp. 845–849). Oxford: Elsevier Science Ltd.

Sam, D. L. (in press). Adaptation of children and adolescents with immigrant background: acculturation or development. In M. H. Bornstein & L. Cote (eds.), *Acculturation and parent–child relationships. Measurement and development.* Mahwah, NJ: Lawrence Erlbaum Associates.

Sandberg, N. (ed.) (1973). *Ethnic identity and assimilation. The Polish community.* New York: Praeger.

Searle, W. & Ward, C. (1990). The prediction of psychological and socio-cultural adjustment during cross-cultural transitions. *International Journal of Intercultural Relations, 14*, 449–464.

Simons, S. E. (1901). Social assimilation. *American Journal of Sociology, 6*, 790–822.

Snauwaert, B., Soenens, B., Vanbeselaere, N. & Boen, F. (2003). When integration does not necessarily imply integration. Different conceptualizations of acculturation orientations lead to different classifications. *Journal of Cross-Cultural Psychology, 3*, 231–239

Spiro, M. E. (1955). The acculturation of American ethnic groups. *American Anthropologist, 57*, 1240–1252.

Sung, B. L. (1985). Bicultural conflicts in Chinese immigrant children. *Journal of Comparative Family Studies, 16*, 255–269.

Taft, R. (1977). Coping with unfamiliar cultures. In N. Warren (ed.), *Studies in cross-cultural psychology* (Vol. I, pp. 143–155). London: Academic Press.

Teske, R. H. C. & Nelson, B. H. (1974). Acculturation and assimilation: a clarification. *American Ethnologist, 1*, 351–367.

Thurnwald, R. (1932). The psychology of acculturation. *American Anthropologist, 34*, 557–569.

Ward, C. (2001). The ABCs of acculturation. In D. Matsumoto (ed.), *The handbook of culture and psychology* (pp. 411–445). Oxford: Oxford University Press.

Ward, C. & Kennedy, A. (1993). Psychological and socio-cultural adjustment during cross-cultural transitions: a comparison of secondary students at home and abroad. *International Journal of Psychology*, *28*, 129–147.

Zhou, M. (1997). Segmented assimilation: issues, controversies and recent research on the new second generation. *International Migration Review*, *31*, 975–1008.

3 Contexts of acculturation

John W. Berry

3.1 Introduction

As we have seen in Chapter 2, acculturation is a process of cultural and psychological change that results from the continuing contact between people of different cultural backgrounds. Following initial contact, most of these contact situations result in the development of societies that have more than one cultural, linguistic or religious entity living in them. As a result, most acculturation research has taken place in societies that are culturally *plural*. In this chapter, we consider the nature of these societies, and some of their salient dimensions. Second, we provide a typology of the kinds of groups that make up plural societies, including such groups as indigenous peoples, immigrants, sojourners and ethnocultural communities. Third, we present one of the core ideas that underlies much contemporary work on acculturation: there are large group and individual differences in how people go about their lives during this process, which we refer to as *acculturation strategies*.

3.2 Plural societies

A culturally plural society is one in which a number of different cultural or ethnic groups reside together within a shared social and political framework (Skelton & Allen, 1999). There are two key aspects to this concept: the continuity (or not) of diverse cultural communities; and the participation (or not) of these communities in the daily life of the plural society.

The first aspect conveys the idea that there could be a unicultural society that has one culture and one people. While it used to be the case that such unicultural societies actually existed, it is now obvious that there is no contemporary society in which one culture, one language, one religion and one single identity characterizes the whole population. Despite this obvious fact, some people continue to think and behave as if their societies were culturally uniform (or if they are not now, they *should* be!). However, others know and accept that there are usually many cultural groups trying to live together in their society, and that there *should not* be attempts to forge a single culture, a single people, out of this diversity.

In a very stark and contrasting way, Figure 3.1 portrays two implicit models of plural societies. In one (the *mainstream–minority*), there is a *melting pot*;

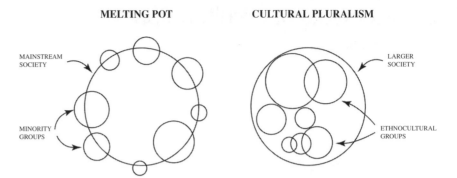

MELTING POT   **CULTURAL PLURALISM**

Figure 3.1 *Two implicit models of culturally plural societies*

here the view is of a single dominant or *mainstream* society, on the margins of which are the various *minority* groups. The common assumption is that such groups should be absorbed into the mainstream in such a way that they essentially disappear. With respect to the two aspects noted above, their cultural continuity is denied, and this absorption is the only acceptable basis for their participation in the society. In this view, there is to be "one people, one culture, one nation" as an overriding goal. It is reminiscent of early conceptions, such as *manifest destiny* in the US American tradition in the last century: "The whole continent of North America appears to be destined by Divine Providence to be peopled by one nation, speaking one language, professing one general system of religious and political principles, and accustomed to one general tenor of social usages and customs" (Quincy Adams, 1811). It is also reminiscent of the colonial policy pursued earlier by the French, and attributed to the philosopher Montaigne: "to gently polish and reclaim for humanity the savages of the world." If such incorporation into a uniform society is not achieved (for whatever reasons), then the groups on the margins literally become marginalized (see below).

A second implicit model, shown on the right of Figure 3.1, is a *multicultural* model, in which there is a mosaic of *ethnocultural groups*. In terms of the two aspects noted above, in the multicultural model individuals and groups retain their cultural continuity and a sense of their cultural identity, and, on that basis, they participate in the social framework of the *larger society*. Such a society is characterized by shared norms about how to live together (such as legal, economic, political), but which permits institutions to evolve in order to accommodate the different cultural interests of all groups. This notion of a larger society is clearly different from that of the mainstream, where the dominant group established the main features of the society.

These two contrasting models are not simply abstract notions, but represent two of the main views in which people conceive of possible ways to arrange themselves when confronting the increasing cultural diversity in their societies.

As a consequence, they serve as important contrasting contexts within which individuals and groups engage the acculturation process.

3.2.1   Groups constituting plural societies

There are many different kinds of groups in plural societies, each one presenting another set of contextual factors (see Figure 3.2). One way to conceive of this variety is by looking at the underlying factors (historical and contemporary) that explain why people of different cultural backgrounds are living together in the same place. While not exhaustive, there are three reasons presented in Figure 3.2. First, groups may find themselves together either because they have sought out such an arrangement *voluntarily*, or alternatively because it has been forced upon them. Second, some groups have remained on home ground, while others have settled far from their ancestral territory (*sedentary* vs. *migrant*). And third, some people are settled into a plural society *permanently*, while others are only *temporary residents*.

Some of the more common terms used to refer to constituent groups in plural societies have been placed in Figure 3.2 in relation to these three dimensions. Starting with the longest-term residents, *indigenous peoples* are those who have "always been there" in the sense that their roots go way back, and there is no evidence of any earlier people whose descendants are still in the population (see Chapter 15). There is considerable controversy in some countries about the term "indigenous" (or "native," or "aboriginal") because of special rights that may be claimed. A similar term, used in some European countries, is *national minority*, such as Basque, Breton, Catalan, Frisian and Sami. The basic characteristic of many indigenous peoples is that their territories have been forcefully incorporated into a larger nation-state, their residual lands are often reduced in size and capacity to sustain life, and they have come to be seen as just another minority group within the larger plural society. They are clearly involuntary, as well as sedentary in Figure 3.2.

Other peoples who have a long history of settlement are the descendants of earlier waves of immigrants who have settled into recognizable groups, often with a sense of their own cultural heritage (common language, identity, etc.). These *ethnocultural groups* can be found the world over, for example in French- and Spanish-origin communities in the New World, in the groups descended from indentured workers (such as Chinese and Indian communities in the Caribbean), from those who were enslaved (such as African Americans), and in Dutch and British immigrant groups in Southern Africa, Australia and New Zealand. Such groups may be large or small, powerful or powerless, depending on the overall history and the national context within which they live. Whatever their histories, most are now voluntary participants in the national life of their contemporary societies.

In contrast to these two sedentary constituents of plural societies, there are others who have developed in other places and been socialized into other

MOBILITY	VOLUNTARINESS OF CONTACT	
	VOLUNTARY	INVOLUNTARY
SEDENTARY	ETHNOCULTURAL GROUPS	INDIGENOUS PEOPLES
MIGRANT permanent temporary	IMMIGRANTS SOJOURNERS	REFUGEES ASYLUM SEEKERS

Figure 3.2 *Varieties of groups in plural societies*

cultures, who migrate to take up residence (either permanently or temporarily) in another society. Among these groups are *immigrants* (see Chapter 11) who usually move in order to achieve a better life elsewhere. For most, the "pull factors" (those that attract them to a new society) are stronger than the "push factors" (those that pressure them to leave). Hence, immigrants are generally thought of as voluntary members of plural societies. The process of settling in will be considered later in the discussion of acculturation and adaptation. For the time being, it is important to note that not everyone becomes a member of the new society in the same way: some jump in with both feet, seeking rapid absorption, while others are more hesitant, seeking to retain a clear sense of their own cultural heritage and identity, thereby revealing different *acculturation strategies* (see below).

While immigrants are relatively permanent participants in their new society, the group known as *sojourners* (see Chapter 12) are there only temporarily in a variety of roles, and for a set purpose (e.g., as international students, diplomats, business executives, aid workers or guest workers). In their case, the process of becoming involved in the plural society is complicated by their knowledge that they will eventually leave, and either return home or be posted to yet another country. Thus there may be a hesitation to become fully involved, to establish close relationships, or to begin to identify with the new society. Despite their uncertain position, in some societies sojourners constitute a substantial element in the resident population (e.g., the Gulf States, Germany, Belgium) and may either hold substantial power, or be relatively powerless.

Among involuntary migrants, *refugees* and *asylum seekers* (now often called collectively "forced migrants"; Ager, 1999) have the greatest hurdles to face: they frequently don't want to leave their homelands, and, if they do, it is not always possible for them to be granted the right to stay and settle into the new society (see Chapters 13 and 14). Those who arrive at the border of a country that has signed the Geneva Convention on Refugees have a right to be admitted and given sanctuary (as asylum seekers) until their claim is adjudicated; if granted permanent admission as refugees, much of the uncertainty that surrounded their life during their flight is reduced. However, most live with the knowledge that "push factors" (rather than "pull factors") led them to flee their homeland and settle in their new society; and, of course, most have experienced traumatic events, and most have lost their material possessions.

There are a number of reasons why the six kinds of groups portrayed in Figure 3.2 were organized according to three factors (voluntary–involuntary; sedentary–migrant; and permanent–temporary), rather than simply listed. The most important reason is that, as groups, they have differential size, power, rights and resources; these factors have an important bearing on how they will engage (as groups or as individuals) in the acculturation process. A second important reason is that the attitudes, motives, values and abilities (all psychological characteristics of individuals in these groups) are also highly variable. These factors, too, impact on how their acculturation is likely to take place.

3.2.2 Cultural dimensions of plural societies

Societies differ from one another in a variety of ways. In those societies that are plural, there are some variations that are particularly salient. These include economic, historical and political contexts that can influence how groups and individuals will relate to each other during acculturation. In this section, however, we focus on those differences that are generally cultural in nature. This is important because evidence shows that the greater the cultural differences between the groups of people in contact during acculturation, then the greater will be the difficulties in experiencing acculturation that is relatively free from stress (see Chapter 4) in achieving successful adaptation and in establishing harmonious relationships (Ward, Bochner & Furnham, 2001). Many dimensions of cultural variation have been proposed by various authors, and have been summarized by Berry (2004): Table 3.1 identifies six of the more important ones.

These six dimensions can be described more fully:

1. *Diversity* Some cultures are fairly homogeneous in terms of what people do, and how they think of themselves. Another aspect of diversity is whether most people share a common regional, or ethnic, identity. For example, in Japan and Iceland, there is minimal variation, whereas in countries such as Australia and Canada, people have rather divergent senses of themselves.

2. *Equality* When differences do occur, they can be treated equally or differentially, in terms of rewards and status. In some societies, there are rigid hierarchies in civic, military and religious spheres (e.g., Pope, cardinals, bishops, priests, monks, believers and heretics). In others there may even be no

Table 3.1 *Dimensions of cultural variation in plural societies that are important in acculturation*

Dimension	Brief description
1. Diversity	How many different positions, roles and institutions are there? Are there other variations within culture (e.g. regional, ethnic)?
2. Equality	Are these differences arranged in horizontal (egalitarian) or vertical (hierarchical) social structures?
3. Conformity	How tightly structured are the various parts; how much are individuals enmeshed in the social order?
4. Wealth	What is the average level of wealth (GDP per person) available to support necessities of life?
5. Space	How do individuals use space during interpersonal relationships? Are eye and body contact frequent?
6. Time	Are people concerned about promptness and schedules; do they engage each other one-on-one, or have multiple interactions at one time?

permanent authority or leadership; coordination of action is by consensus, or by the use of temporary leaders for specific activities. These first two dimensions often interact, with some cultural groups occupying different status levels (eg., indigenous peoples in the Americas, Roma in Eastern Europe, Koreans in Japan).

3. *Conformity* In some societies, people are tightly enmeshed in a system of norms and social obligations to the ingroup, while in others, people are relatively free to "do their own thing." During acculturation, opportunities for independence from one's own group often differ between the members of the larger society and acculturating individuals. Such differences may generate social conflict, both within the cultural community and the family, and psychological conflict within individuals. Such conflict has been observed among Turkish immigrants in Western societies (e.g., Ataca & Berry, 2002).

4. *Wealth* This is perhaps the dimension of cultural variation that is most obvious since it is most concrete: money, possessions, leisure time can be seen by all observers. However, there are other aspects to this dimension that may be less obvious. One of these is the distribution of wealth (is it relatively equally distributed, or are most resources in the hands of a few ethnic or family groups?). Moreover, a number of other features vary with wealth, including education, access to communications and information, health and personal values.

5. *Space* How individuals use space (housing, public places), and how they orient themselves during interpersonal encounters, has one of the largest research literatures, as well as a rich anecdotal base (see Hall, 1959). Close interpersonal distances, and touching, are more common in some cultures than in others, leading to discomfort and misunderstandings.

6. *Time* Similar to the space dimension, cultural variation in the meaning and use of time is not obvious to those having limited intercultural experiences.

However, both empirical studies and personal encounters attest to the importance of these dimensions. Punctuality and personal engagement are sometimes very different on this dimension; it can be one of the main sources of intercultural difficulty.

Emphasis has been placed on these six dimensions of cultural variation because, in addition to variations in language and religion, differences between cultural groups on these dimensions are likely to have an important influence on how individuals interact during acculturation. As noted above, it is now well established that the *cultural distance* between the two groups in contact makes it more difficult for them to adapt to each other. In the area of intercultural relations, one of the most powerful factors affecting mutual attitudes is the degree of *similarity* of the two groups. And in the domain of intercultural communication, both the verbal (language) and nonverbal (e.g., gestures, use of space) aspects are rendered more difficult when there is greater dissimilarity between the cultures.

In addition to economic differences, religious differences also appear to be relevant. Recent analyses (Georgas, van de Vijver & Berry, 2004) show that many psychological characteristics of groups vary according to their placement on two group dimensions: Affluence and Religion. Evidence is that those most different on these two dimensions are most different psychologically, and are most likely to engage in conflictual relations (e.g., Afghanistan and USA; Israel and Palestine). In the field of cross-cultural psychology, it is a basic proposition that individuals develop psychological characteristics that have been nurtured by their cultural backgrounds (Berry, Poortinga, Segall & Dasen, 2002). During intercultural contact, these different cultural and psychological features encounter each other. Hence it is no surprise that greater variations in these cultural and psychological characteristics are predictors of relatively more difficult acculturation, less successful adaptation, and of conflictual, rather than more harmonious, intercultural relationships in plural societies.

3.3   Acculturation strategies

Having set this general stage by looking at variations in contexts of acculturation, we turn now to the concept of *acculturation strategies* (Berry, 1997), which is relevant to all components of the general acculturation framework presented in Chapter 2 (see Figure 2.1). These *strategies* consist of two components: *attitudes* and *behaviors* (that is, the preferences and actual practices) that are exhibited in day-to-day intercultural encounters. Of course, there is rarely a one-to-one match between what an individual prefers and seeks (attitudes) and what one is actually able to do (behaviors). This discrepancy is widely studied in social psychology and is usually explained as being the result of social constraints on behaviors (such as norms, opportunities, etc.). Nevertheless, there is often a significant positive correlation between acculturation attitudes and behaviors, permitting the use of an overall assessment of individual strategies (see Chapter 10, for a review of how to assess these strategies).

The centrality of the concept of acculturation strategies can be illustrated by reference to each component of the general acculturation framework (Figure 2.1). At the cultural level, the two groups in contact (whether dominant or non-dominant) usually have some notion about what they are attempting to do (e.g., colonial policies, or motivations for migration), or what is being done to them, during the contact. Similarly, the goals of the emergent ethnocultural groups will influence their strategies. At the individual level, both the behavioral shifts and acculturative stress phenomena are now known to be a function, at least to some extent, of what people try to do during their acculturation; and the longer term outcomes (both psychological and sociocultural adaptations) often correspond to the strategic goals set by the groups of which they are members.

As we have seen, the original definitions of acculturation foresaw that domination was not the only relationship, and that cultural and psychological homogenization would not be the only possible outcome of intercultural contact. Why not? An answer to this question lies in the observation that people hold different views about how they want to live following contact: not everyone seeks out such contact, and, even among those who do, not everyone seeks to change their culture and behavior to be more like the other (often dominant) group. These two points are those that we identified earlier in this chapter as being characteristics of the distinction between the melting pot and the multicultural societies.

In the 1936 statement on acculturation by Redfield, Linton and Herskovits, it was noted that *assimilation* is not the only form of acculturation; there are other ways of going about it. Taking this assertion as a starting point, Berry (1970; Sommerlad & Berry, 1970) first distinguished between the strategies of *assimilation* and *integration*, and later between *separation* and *marginalization* as various ways in which acculturation (both of groups and of individuals) could take place. As noted, these distinctions involve two dimensions, and are rooted in the distinction between orientations towards one's own group, and those towards other groups (Berry, 1970, 1974, 1980). This distinction is rendered as a relative preference for cultural continuity (Issue 1: maintaining one's heritage culture and identity) or contact (Issue 2: a relative preference for having contact with and participating in the larger society along with other ethnocultural groups). This formulation is presented in Figure 3.3 for both the ethnocultural groups (on the left) and the larger society (on the right). As we shall see, these strategies vary across individuals, groups and societies; they also vary because of the interaction between the strategies of the two groups in contact.

Orientations to the two issues can vary along dimensions, represented by bipolar arrows. Generally positive or negative views about these issues intersect to define four strategies of intercultural relations. These strategies carry

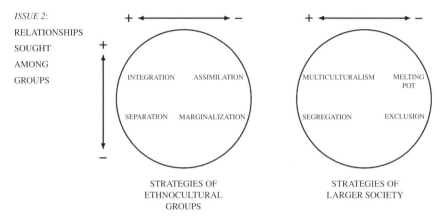

Figure 3.3 *Acculturation strategies in ethnocultural groups and the larger society*

different names, depending on which group (the dominant or non-dominant) is being considered. From the point of view of non-dominant ethnocultural groups, when individuals do not wish to maintain their cultural identity and seek daily interaction with other cultures, the *assimilation* strategy is defined. In contrast, when individuals place a value on holding on to their original culture, and at the same time wish to avoid interaction with others, then the *separation* alternative is defined. When there is an interest in both maintaining one's original culture, and having daily interactions with other groups, *integration* is the option; here, there is some degree of cultural integrity maintained, while at the same time the individual seeks, as a member of an ethnocultural group, to participate as an integral part of the larger social network. Finally, when there is little possibility of, or interest in, cultural maintenance (often for reasons of enforced cultural loss), and little interest in having relations with others (often for reasons of exclusion or discrimination) then *marginalization* is defined.

This presentation was based on the assumption that non-dominant groups and their individual members have the freedom to choose how they want to engage in intercultural relations. This, of course, is not always the case (Berry, 1974). When the dominant group enforces certain kinds of relations, or constrains the choices of non-dominant groups or individuals, then other terms need to be used. This is most clearly so in the case of integration, which can only be freely chosen and successfully pursued by non-dominant groups when the dominant society is open and inclusive in its orientation towards cultural diversity (Berry, 1991). Thus a *mutual accommodation* is required for integration to be attained, involving the acceptance by both dominant and non-dominant groups of the right of all groups to live as culturally different peoples within the same society. This strategy requires non-dominant groups to *adopt* the basic values of the larger society, while at the same time the dominant group must be prepared to *adapt* national institutions (e.g., education, health, labor) to meet better the needs of all groups now living together in the plural society. This latter arrangement was portrayed in Figure 3.3 and was called *multiculturalism*.

Obviously, the integration strategy can only be pursued in societies that are explicitly multicultural, in which certain psychological pre-conditions are established (Berry & Kalin, 1995). These pre-conditions are: the widespread acceptance of the value to a society of cultural diversity (i.e., the presence of a positive *multicultural ideology*); relatively low levels of prejudice (i.e., minimal ethnocentrism, racism and discrimination); positive mutual attitudes among ethnocultural groups (i.e., no specific intergroup hatreds); and a sense of attachment to, or identification with, the larger society by all individuals and groups.

Just as obviously, integration (and separation) can only be pursued when other members of one's ethnocultural group share in the wish to maintain the group's cultural heritage. In this sense, these two strategies are "collectivistic," whereas assimilation is more "individualistic" (Lalonde & Cameron, 1993; Moghaddam, 1988). Other constraints on one's choice of acculturation strategy have also been noted. For example, those whose physical features set them apart from the society of settlement (e.g., Koreans in Canada, or Turks in Germany) may experience prejudice and discrimination, and thus be reluctant to pursue assimilation in order to avoid being rejected (Berry *et al.*, 1989).

These two basic issues were initially approached from the point of view of the non-dominant ethnocultural groups only (as on the left side of Figure 3.3). However, the original definitions clearly established that *both* groups in contact would become acculturated. Hence, in 1974, a third dimension was added: that of the powerful role played by the dominant group in influencing the way in which mutual acculturation would take place (Berry, 1974, 1980). The addition of this third dimension produced a duplicate framework (right side of Figure 3.3). Assimilation, when sought by the dominant group, can be termed the *melting pot* (as depicted earlier, in Figure 3.1); and when strongly enforced, it becomes a Pressure Cooker. When separation is demanded and enforced by the dominant group, it is *segregation*. For marginalization, when imposed by the dominant group it is a form of *exclusion*. Finally, for integration, when cultural diversity is an objective of the society as a whole, it represents the strategy of mutual accommodation now widely called *multiculturalism*.

There are many studies that have examined these acculturation strategies in non-dominant acculturating groups (see Berry & Sam, 1997, for a partial review). Assessment is carried out in a variety of ways (see Chapter 10). Usually, each of the four strategies is assessed with a scale (e.g., Horenczyk, 1996; van de Vijver *et al.*, 1999). Sometimes the two underlying dimensions

(Issues 1 and 2) are measured (e.g., Donà & Berry, 1994; Nguyen, Messe & Stollak, 1999; Ryder, Alden & Paulhus, 2000; Ward & Rana-Deuba, 1999). In a few studies, four vignettes, each portraying one of the four strategies, are used (e.g., Georgas & Papastylianou, 1998; Pruegger, 1993). In most studies, preferences for integration are expressed over the other three strategies, with marginalization being the least preferred. One of the more common exceptions is that of Turks in Germany (Piontkowski *et al.*, 2000), and lower socioeconomic status Turks in Canada (Ataca & Berry, 2002), who prefer separation over integration. A similar result has been obtained for some indigenous peoples in various parts of the world (e.g., Berry, 1999); but in other places, integration is preferred (e.g., Mishra, Sinha & Berry, 1996). In recent work (Berry, Phinney, Sam & Vedder, 2006) with immigrant youth in thirteen countries, these four acculturation attitudes were closely linked with acculturation behaviors, cultural identities and language knowledge and use, yielding four clusters of individuals (termed *acculturation profiles*) that correspond to the four acculturation strategies outlined here.

It is important to note that when all four strategies are assessed, it is possible to have variable degrees of preference for each strategy. For example one could logically have a positive orientation towards both integration and separation, since both strategies involve a preference for the maintenance of one's cultural heritage and identity. Two points arise from this: first, it is not possible to refer to the "degree" or "level" of acculturation (e.g., as in "highly acculturated"), only degree or level of support for each of the four strategies. When "level of acculturation" is used in the literature, it is often intended as "level of assimilation" only (see also the discussion in Chapter 2). Second, however, if one is referring to length or frequency of contact, or to the degree of participation in the larger society, then the notion of "level" is appropriate; this usage has been conceptualized as *contact acculturation* (e.g., Berry *et al.*, 1986; Mishra *et al.*, 1996).

While the original definition of acculturation identified it as a mutual process, fewer studies of acculturation preferences in the larger society have been carried out. One continuing program in Canada (Berry, Kalin & Taylor, 1977; Berry & Kalin, 1995) has employed a scale (termed *multicultural ideology*) in national surveys. This scale represents items supporting integration at its positive pole, and items supporting the other three strategies at its negative pole. These views held by members of the larger society have been termed *acculturation expectations* (Berry, 2003). Since the early 1980s, the preference for multiculturalism (integration) has risen from about 65 percent to about 70 percent, indicating a general and increasing acceptance of the multicultural model of a plural society presented in Figure 3.1.

In another approach to this side of the coin, Horenczyk (1996) asked Russian immigrants to Israel about their perception of the *acculturation ideologies* of Israeli society (in addition to their own views). Integration was the most frequently expected way for immigrants to acculturate, followed by assimilation and separation. This pattern was interpreted as representing a major shift away from the earlier Israeli "absorption" or assimilationist ideology, and as presenting a better match with the immigrants' own acculturation strategies, which were largely integrationist. Bourhis and colleagues (Bourhis *et al.*, 1997) have recently begun a series of studies using an *interactive acculturation model* that examines attitudes of both groups in contact. They find that there are individual differences in these preferences, and, most importantly, differences between the non-dominant and dominant groups studied (see Chapters 17 and 19, for more detail).

A study in Europe (see Chapter 20) of views in the larger society (Piontkowski *et al.*, 2000) employed samples in Germany, Switzerland and Slovakia, using measures of the two basic issues, rather than the four attitudes. Members of non-dominant groups (Hungarians, Turks and former Yugoslavians) living in Germany and Switzerland were also studied. Overall, integration was preferred, although the pattern varied across dominant/ non-dominant pairs. For example, in dominant samples in both Germany and Switzerland, a preference for integration was followed by assimilation; however, there was "remarkable support for separation and marginalization" (p. 11) among the Swiss with respect to Yugoslavians. And in Slovakia, there was roughly similar support (around 30 percent each) for integration, assimilation and marginalization with respect to Hungarians living there. (As already noted, the non-dominant groups in this study preferred integration, with the exception of Turks in Germany, who preferred separation.) There is a very clear mismatch between these two sets of acculturation strategies, especially for Turks in Germany (integration vs. separation), for Yugoslavians in Switzerland (integration vs. marginalization) and for Hungarians in Slovakia (also integration vs. marginalization).

3.3.1   Locus of strategies

As just discussed, these various strategies can be used by individuals and groups in both the ethnocultural groups and the larger society (Figure 3.3); they can also be used by institutions within the larger society. One way to view the locus of intercultural strategies is presented in Figure 3.4. This shows six places in which these various orientations can be found. On the right are the views held by the various ethnocultural (or "minority") groups (who usually are non-dominant in the contact situation); on the left are the views held by the larger (or "mainstream") society. There are three levels, with the most encompassing group level (the national society or ethnocultural groups) at the top; in the middle are the least encompassing (the individuals who are members of these groups); and at the bottom are various social groupings (called "institutions"), which can be governmental agencies, and educational, justice and health systems.

LEVELS	DOMINANT	NON-DOMINANT
	• Mainstream	• Minority group
	• Larger society	• Cultural group
NATIONAL	National policies	Group goals
INDIVIDUAL	Multicultural ideology	Acculturation strategies
INSTITUTIONAL	Uniform or plural	Diversity and equity

Figure 3.4 *Locus of acculturation strategies*

At the first level, we can examine national policies and the stated goals of particular ethnocultural groups within the larger plural society. For example, the Canadian and Australian national policies of multiculturalism correspond to the integration strategy (Berry, 1984) by which both heritage cultural maintenance and full participation in the larger society by all groups are promoted. Many ethnocultural groups also express their preferences in formal statements: some seek integration into the larger society (e.g., Maori in New Zealand), while some others seek separation (e.g., Scottish National Party or Parti Québécois, who seek full independence for their groups). At the individual level, as we have seen, we can measure *acculturation expectations* (Berry, 2003) in the larger society; this concept was discussed earlier as *multicultural ideology*. At the institutional level (which is now introduced as a third place in which to examine these acculturation orientations), competing visions rooted in these alternative strategies confront and even conflict with each other daily. Most frequently, non-dominant ethnocultural groups seek the joint goals of diversity and equity. This involves, first, the recognition of the group's cultural uniqueness and specific needs, and, second, having their groups' needs be met with the same level of understanding, acceptance and support as those of the dominant group. The dominant society, however, may often prefer more uniform programs and standards (based on their own cultural views) in such core institutions as education, health, justice and defence. The goals of diversity and equity correspond closely to the integration and multiculturalism strategies (combining cultural maintenance with inclusive participation), whereas the push for uniformity resembles the assimilation and melting pot approach (see Berry, 1984).

With the use of the framework in Figure 3.4, comparisons of acculturation strategies can be made between individuals and their groups, and between non-dominant peoples and the larger societies within which they are acculturating. The ideologies and policies of the dominant group constitute an important element of acculturation research (see Berry *et al.*, 1977; Bourhis *et al.*,

1997), while preferences of non-dominant peoples are a core feature in understanding the process of acculturation in non-dominant groups (Berry, 2000). Inconsistencies and conflicts between these various acculturation preferences are sometimes sources of difficulty for acculturating individuals. Generally, when acculturation experiences cause problems for acculturating individuals, we observe the phenomenon of *acculturative stress* (see Chapter 4).

3.4   Conclusions

This chapter has identified a number of characteristics of societies in which many different cultural groups have come to live. These plural societies vary in numerous ways, including their general ideological orientation to diversity, the types of constituent groups, their attitudes and strategies for dealing with acculturation, and the locations where all these aspects can be found and studied. These variations all provide differential contexts within which the process of acculturation can take place. Research clearly shows that acculturation is not a uniform process, with a single outcome. Earlier views that non-dominant cultural groups and their individual members would inevitably disappear by being absorbed into a dominant society have proven to be a false assumption. Instead, the research provides support for the alternative view of acculturation as a highly variable process; these variations are rooted in the many contextual differences outlined in this chapter. A similar perspective will be taken in Chapter 4, where an earlier assumption that acculturation is inevitably conflict-ridden for groups and stressful for individuals will be questioned. In its place, we find, once again, large variation in adaptation outcomes, rooted in many of the contextual factors outlined in this chapter.

3.5   References

Ager, A. (ed.) (1999). *Refugees: perspectives on the experience of forced migration.* London: Cassell.

Ataca, B. & Berry, J. W. (2002). Sociocultural, psychological and marital adaptation of Turkish immigrant couples in Canada. *International Journal of Psychology, 37,* 13–26.

Berry, J. W. (1970). Marginality, stress and ethnic identification in an acculturated Aboriginal community. *Journal of Cross-Cultural Psychology, 1,* 239–252.

(1974). Psychological aspects of cultural pluralism: unity and identity reconsidered. *Topics in Culture Learning, 2,* 17–22.

(1980). Acculturation as varieties of adaptation. In A. Padilla (ed.), *Acculturation: theory, models and findings* (pp. 9–25). Boulder: Westview.

(1984). Multicultural policy in Canada: a social psychological analysis. *Canadian Journal of Behavioural Science, 16,* 353–370.

(1991). Understanding and managing multiculturalism. *Journal of Psychology and Developing Societies, 3,* 17–49.

(1997). Immigration, acculturation and adaptation. (Lead article with commentary.) *Applied Psychology: An International Review*, *46*, 5–68.

(1999). Intercultural relations in plural societies. *Canadian Psychology*, *40*, 12–21.

(2000). Sociopsychological costs and benefits of multiculturalism. In J. Dacyl & C. Westin (eds.), *Governance of cultural diversity* (pp. 297–354). Stockholm: UNESCO.

(2003). Conceptual approaches to acculturation. In K. Chun, P. Balls-Organista & G. Marin (eds.), *Acculturation: theory, method and applications* (pp. 17–37). Washington: APA Press.

(2004). Fundamental psychological processes in intercultural relations. In D. Landis and J. Bennett (eds.), *Handbook of Intercultural Research*. 3rd edn. (pp. 166–184). Thousand Oaks: Sage Publications.

Berry, J. W. & Kalin, R. (1995). Multicultural and ethnic attitudes in Canada. *Canadian Journal of Behavioural Science*, *27*, 310–320.

Berry, J. W., Kalin, R. & Taylor, D. (1977). *Multiculturalism and ethnic attitudes in Canada*. Ottawa: Supply & Services.

Berry, J. W., Kim, U., Power, S., Young, M. & Bujaki, M. (1989). Acculturation attitudes in plural societies. *Applied Psychology*, *38*, 185–206.

Berry, J. W., Phinney, J., Sam, D. & Vedder, P. (eds.) (2006). *Immigrant youth in cultural transition: acculturation, identity and adaptation across national contexts*. Mahwah, NJ: Lawrence Erlbaum Associates.

Berry, J. W., Poortinga, Y. H., Segall, M. H. & Dasen, P. R. (2002). *Cross-cultural psychology: research and applications*. 2nd edn. New York: Cambridge University Press.

Berry, J. W. & Sam, D. (1997). Acculturation and adaptation. In J. W. Berry, M. H. Segall & C. Kağitçibaşi (eds.), *Handbook of cross-cultural psychology*, Vol. III: *Social behavior and applications* (pp. 291–326). Boston: Allyn & Bacon.

Berry, J. W., van de Koppel, J., Annis, R. C., *et al.* (1986). *On the edge of the forest: ecology, acculturaltion and psychological adaptation in Central Africa*. Lisse: Swets & Zeitlinger.

Bourhis, R., Moïse, C., Perrault, S. & Sénécal, S. (1997). Towards an interactive acculturation model: a social psychological approach. *International Journal of Psychology*, *32*, 369–386.

Donà, G. & Berry, J. W. (1994). Acculturation attitudes and acculturative stress of Central American refugees in Canada. *International Journal of Psychology*, *29*, 57–70.

Georgas, J. & Papastylianou, D. (1998). Acculturation and ethnic identity: the re-migration of ethnic Greeks to Greece. In H. Grad, A. Blanco & J. Georgas (eds.), *Key issues in cross-cultural psychology* (pp. 114–127). Lisse: Swets & Zeitlinger.

Georgas, J., van de Vijver, F. & Berry, J. W. (2004). The ecocultural framework, eco-social indices and psychological variables in cross-cultural research. *Journal of Cross-Cultural Psychology*, *35*, 74–96.

Hall, E. T. (1959). *The silent language*. New York: Doubleday.

Horenczyk, G. (1996). Migrant identities in conflict: acculturation attitudes and perceived acculturation ideologies. In G. Breakwell & E. Lyons (eds.), *Changing European identities* (pp. 241–250). Oxford: Butterworth-Heinemann.

Lalonde, R. & Cameron, J. (1993). An intergroup perspective on immigrant accultura-
    tion with a focus on collective strategies. *International Journal of Psychology*,
    28, 57–74.

Mishra, R. C., Sinha, D. & Berry, J. W. (1996). *Ecology, acculturation and psycholog-
    ical adaptation among Adivasi in India*. Delhi: Sage Publications.

Moghaddam, F. M. (1988). Individualistic and collective integration strategies among
    immigrants. In J. W. Berry & R.C. Annis (eds.), *Ethnic psychology* (pp. 69–
    79). Amsterdam: Swets & Zeitlinger.

Nguyen, H., Messe, L. & Stollak, G. (1999). Toward a more complex understanding
    of acculturation and adjustment. *Journal of Cross-Cultural Psychology*, *30*,
    5–31.

Piontkowski, U., Florack, A., Hoelker, P. & Obdrzalek, P. (2000). Predicting accultur-
    ation attitudes of dominant and non-dominant groups. *International Journal
    of Intercultural Relations*, *24*, 1–26.

Pruegger, V. (1993). Aboriginal and non-aboriginal work values. Unpublished doctoral
    thesis: Queen's University, Kingston, Ontario.

Redfield, R., Linton, R. & Herskovits, M. (1936). Memorandum on the study of accul-
    turation. *American Anthropologist*, *38*, 149–152.

Ryder, A., Alden, L. & Paulhus, D. (2000). Is acculturation unidimensional or
    bi-dimensional? *Journal of Personality and Social Psychology*, *79*, 49–65.

Skelton, T. & Allen, T. (eds.) (1999). *Culture and global change*. London: Routledge.

Sommerlad, E. & Berry, J. W. (1970). The role of ethnic identification in distinguishing
    between attitudes towards assimilation and integration of a minority racial
    group. *Human Relations*, *23*, 2329.

Van de Vijver, F., Helms-Lorenz, M. & Feltzer, M. (1999). Acculturation and cognitive
    performance of migrant children in the Netherlands. *International Journal of
    Psychology*, *34*, 149–162.

Ward, C., Bochner, S. & Furnham, A. (2001). *The psychology of culture shock*. Hove:
    Routledge.

Ward, C. & Rana-Deuba, A. (1999). Acculturation and adaptation revisited. *Journal
    of Cross-Cultural Psychology*, *30*, 422–442.

4 Stress perspectives on acculturation

John W. Berry

John W. Berry

4.1 Introduction

As noted in Chapter 1, there are two main theoretical perspectives on how groups and individuals manage the process of acculturation. One is the "stress, coping and adaptation" approach, which is the focus of this chapter. The other is the "cultural learning" perspective, which will be the focus of Chapter 5. In the general framework presented in Chapter 2, a distinction was made between two kinds of change: the first are those cultural and psychological changes that take place easily in a relatively straightforward way through a process of culture learning and culture shedding; the second are those changes that generate stress for the group and individual. In the latter case, cultures can clash, especially when the purpose of the contact is hostile; and individuals can conflict, especially when there are scarce resources. Moreover, the process of culture learning and shedding may involve psychological conflict, where, for example, there are incompatible values held by members of the dominant and non-dominant groups.

To deal with this problematic aspect of acculturation, the concept of acculturative *stress* was proposed (Berry, 1970). Acculturative stress is a response by people to life events that are rooted in intercultural contact. Frequently, these reactions include heightened levels of depression (linked to the experience of cultural loss) and of anxiety (linked to uncertainty about how one should live in the new society). This notion is broadly similar to that of *culture shock* (Oberg, 1960; see also Ward, Bochner & Furnham, 2001), but acculturative stress is preferred for two reasons. First, the term *shock* is essentially a negative one, implying that only difficulties will result from culture contact. It is reminiscent of the idea of "shell shock" that was proposed to account for the complete psychological breakdown of soldiers exposed to horrendous war experiences (now also changed to "posttraumatic stress disorder"). However, the term *stress* has a theoretical basis in studies of how people deal with negative experiences (called *stressors*) by engaging in various *coping* strategies, leading eventually to some form of adaptation (see Lazarus & Folkman, 1984). Within this frame of reference, people are seen as potentially able to deal effectively with stressors in their lives and to achieve a variety of outcomes (adaptations) ranging from very negative through to very positive. Thus, from a stress (in contrast to a shock) perspective, acculturation experiences can be advantageous (such as providing opportunities and interesting experiences), as well as undermining life's chances (such as limiting opportunities and diminishing experiences that provide meaning to life). However, an experience of a "shock" may still be present in the very early stages of the acculturation process, particularly when it is accompanied by sudden and negative events (e.g., war, famine or ethnic conflict).

A second reason to prefer the notion of *acculturative stress* is that the source of the stressful experiences lies in the interaction between cultures (hence *acculturative*), rather than in one culture or the other. Thus, by using the term *culture*, it is possible to misidentify the root of the difficulty as being in a single culture. True, it may sometimes lie in the dominant culture (e.g., when there is prejudice and discrimination) or in the non-dominant culture (e.g., when there is a lack of resources, such as education, to adapt to the new situation). However, even in these two examples, a case can be made that prejudice and resource shortage are essentially problems that are located in the interaction between the two cultures, rather than uniquely in one or the other. Thus for these two reasons, the term *acculturative stress* is preferred to *culture shock*.

There is a massive literature on the phenomenon of acculturative stress. A framework to help understand the various findings is presented in Figure 4.1. It elaborates some of the features of Figure 2.1, showing the processes involved, the factors affecting the course of acculturative stress, and the eventual outcomes (adaptation).

On the left are aspects of the groups in contact, and the resultant acculturation. On the right is the central flow of psychological acculturation (at the mid-level) from contact experiences to eventual adaptation. Above are those pre-existing individual characteristics that influence this flow, and below are those that arise during the process of acculturation. To expand on Figure 4.1 we consider in detail the various situational and personal factors that are widely believed to influence psychological acculturation.

4.2   Society of origin

A complete study of acculturation needs to start with a comprehensive examination of the two societal contexts: that of origin and that of settlement. In the society of origin, the cultural characteristics that accompany individuals into the acculturation process need description, in part to understand (literally) where the person is coming from, and in part to establish cultural features for comparison with the society of settlement as a basis for estimating *cultural distance* between the two groups in contact. The combination of political, economic and demographic conditions being faced by individuals in their society of origin also needs to be studied as a basis for understanding the degree of voluntariness in the *migration motivation* of acculturating individuals. Arguments by Richmond (1993) suggest that migrants can be ranged on a continuum

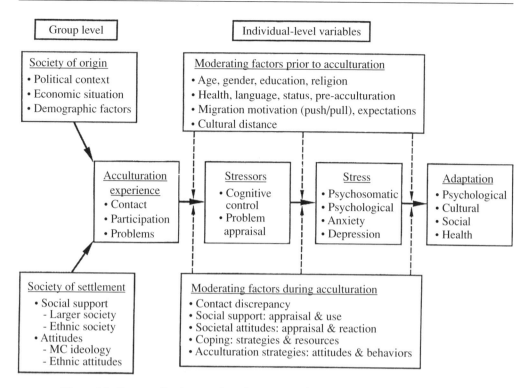

Figure 4.1 *Factors affecting acculturative stress and adaptation*

between *reactive* and *proactive*, with the former being motivated by factors that are constraining or exclusionary, and generally negative in character, while the latter are motivated by factors that are facilitating or enabling, and generally positive in character; these contrasting factors have also been referred to as push/pull factors in the earlier literature on migration motivation.

4.3   Society of settlement

Of importance here are the general orientations of a society and its citizens towards immigration and pluralism. The important issues here are the historical and attitudinal situation faced by migrants. As outlined in Chapter 3, some societies seek to encourage cultural communities to maintain and share their heritage cultures and identities; they are accepting of the resulting cultural pluralism, taking steps to support the continuation of cultural diversity as a shared communal resource. This orientation represents a positive *multicultural ideology* (Berry & Kalin, 1995) and corresponds to the integration strategy outlined earlier. Others seek to reduce immigration and diversity through policies and programs of assimilation, while others attempt to segregate or marginalize diverse populations in their societies. Murphy (1965) has argued that societies that are supportive of cultural pluralism (that is, with a positive multicultural ideology) provide a more positive settlement context for two reasons. First, they are less likely to enforce cultural loss (assimilation) or exclusion (segregation and marginalization) on immigrants. Second, they are more likely to provide social support, both from the institutions of the larger society (such as culturally sensitive health care, multicultural curricula in schools, etc.) and from the continuing and evolving ethnocultural communities that usually make up pluralistic societies. However, even where pluralism is accepted, there are well-known variations in the relative acceptance of specific cultural, racial and religious groups, leading to hierarchies of acceptance and rejection across groups (Berry & Kalin, 1995; Hagendoorn, 1993). Those groups that are less well accepted (i.e., are the objects of negative ethnic attitudes) experience hostility, rejection and discrimination, one factor that is predictive of poor long-term adaptation (Clark, Anderson, Clark & Williams, 1999; Liebkind & Jasinskaja-Lahti, 2000; Noh, Beiser, Kaspar, Hou & Rummens, 1999).

4.4   Process of acculturative stress

The central line in Figure 4.1 represents the main phenomena included in the process of *psychological acculturation*, beginning with *group level of acculturation* and individual *acculturation experience* and ending with some long-term *adaptation*. This process is highly variable for two main reasons. First is the operation of moderating factors that existed prior to major acculturation taking place (and hence which cannot be much changed by public policies in the society of settlement), and second are those moderating factors that may arise during the process of acculturation (and which are controllable, to some extent). These moderating factors are important for both groups and individuals, and can be seen as both risk factors and protective factors, depending on their degree or level. Because they influence the course of events along the central line they will be discussed following the presentation of this course.

The main features of psychological acculturation have received many different names in both the general and acculturation literatures. However, there is broad agreement (see, e.g., Aldwin, 1994; Lazarus, 1990) that the process of dealing with life events begins with some causal agent that places a load or demand on the organism. During acculturation, these demands stem from the experience of having to deal with two cultures in contact, and having to participate to various extents in both of them.

Second, individuals consider the meaning of these experiences, evaluating and appraising them as a source of difficulty (i.e., as *stressors*), or as benign, sometimes even as opportunities. The outcome of this appraisal is variable: when acculturation experiences are judged to pose no problem for the individual, changes are likely to be rather easy and behavioral shifts will follow smoothly. Most often this process has been termed *adjustment* (Ward, 1996; Ward & Kennedy, 1993), because the adaptive changes all take place in the acculturating individual, with few changes occurring among members of the larger society. These adjustments are typically made with minimal difficulty, in keeping with the appraisal of the acculturation experiences as non-problematic. However, some degree of conflict may occur, which is usually resolved by the acculturating person yielding to the behavioral norms of the dominant groups; in this case, *assimilation* is the most likely outcome.

When greater levels of conflict are experienced, and the experiences are judged to be problematic, but controllable and surmountable, then *acculturative stress* results. In this case, individuals understand that they are facing problems resulting from intercultural contact that cannot be dealt with easily or quickly by simply adjusting or assimilating to them. Drawing on the broader stress and adaptation paradigms (e.g. Lazarus & Folkman, 1984), this approach advocates the study of the process of how individuals deal with acculturative problems on first encountering them, and over time. In this sense, acculturative stress is a stress reaction in response to life events that are rooted in the experience of acculturation.

Third, as we have noted, individuals engage in strategies that attempt to deal with the experiences that are appraised as problematic. These basic coping strategies can be understood in relation to the intercultural strategies outlined earlier. Within the general stress and adaptation approach, other strategies have been proposed, and are linked to the notion of coping. Lazarus and Folkman (1984) have identified two major functions: *problem-focused* coping (attempting to change or solve the problem); and *emotion-focused* coping (attempting to regulate the emotions associated with the problem). More recently, Endler and Parker (1990) have identified a third: *avoidance-oriented* coping.

These analyses of coping may or may not be valid cross-culturally; Aldwin (1994) and Lazarus (1990) suggest that cross-cultural variations are likely to be present in these distinctions, and in which ones are preferred. One key distinction, made by Diaz Guerrero (1979), is between *active* and *passive* coping. The former seeks to alter the situation, and hence may be similar to problem-focused coping. It may have only limited success if the problem lies in the dominant society, especially if there is little interest in the dominant group in accommodating the needs of acculturating individuals. Passive coping reflects patience and self-modification, and resembles the assimilation acculturation strategy. These strategies are likely to be successful only if the dominant society has positive attitudes towards, and is willing to accept, members of the acculturating groups. If attitudes are hostile, the passive coping strategies may well lead to unacceptable levels of exclusion or domination.

The fourth aspect of psychological acculturation is a complex set of immediate effects, including physiological and emotional reactions, coming closest to the notion of stress as a "reaction to conditions of living" (Lazarus, 1990:5). When behavioral shifts have taken place without difficulty, stress is likely to be minimal and personal consequences are generally positive. When acculturative problems (stressors) do arise, but have been successfully coped with, stress will be similarly low and the immediate effects positive; but when stressors are not completely surmounted, stress will be higher and the effects more negative. And when acculturative problems have been overwhelming, and have not been successfully dealt with, immediate effects will be substantially negative and stress levels debilitating, including personal crises, and commonly anxiety and depression.

The last of the five main features of psychological acculturation is the long-term *adaptation* that may be achieved. As we saw earlier, "adaptation" refers to the relatively stable changes that take place in an individual or group in response to environmental demands, and has two main facets: *psychological* and *sociocultural* adaptation (see below).

4.5   Factors affecting acculturation stress

We are now in a position to consider the moderating factors that exist prior to and those that arise during the process of acculturation. Although termed "moderating" (i.e., influencing the relationship between the main events in Figure 4.1), they sometimes serve as "mediating" variables (i.e., intervene directly between the main events). Different empirical studies assign different roles to these factors: it is not possible at this point in acculturation research to claim them to be unambiguously one or the other.

4.5.1   Factors existing prior to acculturation

Individuals begin the acculturation process with a number of personal characteristics of a demographic, psychological and social nature. In particular one's age has a known relationship to the way acculturation will proceed. When acculturation starts early (e.g., prior to entry into primary school), the process is generally smooth (Beiser *et al.*, 1988). The reasons for this are not clear; perhaps full enculturation into one's primary culture is not sufficiently advanced to require much culture shedding or to create any serious culture conflict; or perhaps personal flexibility and adaptability are maximal during these early years. However, older youth do often experience substantial problems (Aronowitz, 1992; Sam & Berry, 1995), particularly during adolescence. It is possible that conflict between demands of parents and of peers are greater at this period, or that the problems of life transitions between childhood and adulthood are compounded by cultural transitions. For example, developmental issues of identity come to the fore at this time (Phinney, 1990) and interact with questions of ethnic identity, thus multiplying the questions about who one really is. If acculturation begins in later life (e.g., on retirement, or when older parents migrate to join their adult offspring under family reunification programs) there appears to be increased risk (Beiser *et al.*, 1988). Perhaps the same factors of length of enculturation and adaptability suggested for children are also at work here: a whole life in one cultural setting cannot easily be ignored when one is attempting to live in a new setting.

Gender has variable influence on the acculturation process. There is substantial evidence that females may be more at risk for problems than males (e.g., Beiser *et al.*, 1988; Carballo, 1994). However, this generalization probably itself depends on the relative status and differential treatment of females in the two cultures: where there is a substantial difference, attempts by females to take on new roles available in the society of settlement may bring them into conflict with their heritage culture (e.g. Naidoo, 1992), placing them at risk.

Education appears as a consistent factor associated with possible adaptations: higher education is predictive of lower stress (Beiser *et al.*, 1988; Jayasuriya *et al.*, 1992). A number of reasons have been suggested for this relationship. First, education is a personal resource in itself: problem analysis and problem solving are usually instilled by formal education and likely contribute to better adaptation. Second, education is a correlate of other resources, such as income, occupational status, support networks, etc., all of which are themselves protective factors (see later). Third, for many migrants, education may attune them to features of the society into which they settle; it is a kind of pre-acculturation to the language, history, values and norms of the new culture.

Related to education is one's place in the economic world. Although high status (like education) is a resource, a common experience for migrants is a combination of status loss and limited status mobility (Aycan & Berry, 1996). One's *departure status* is frequently higher than one's *entry status*: credentials (educational and work experience) are frequently devalued on arrival (Cumming, Lee & Oreopoulos, 1989). Sometimes this is due to real differences in qualifications, but it may also be due to ignorance and/or prejudice in the society of settlement, leading to status loss, and the risk of stress. For similar reasons, the usual main goal of migration (upward status mobility) is thwarted, leading again to risk of various disorders, such as depression (Beiser, Johnson & Turner, 1993). In a sense, these problems lie in personal qualities brought to the acculturation process, but they also reside in the interaction between the migrant and the institutions of the society of settlement: hence, problems of status loss and limited mobility can usually be addressed during the course of acculturation.

Reasons for migrating have long been studied using the concepts of *push/pull motivations* and *expectations*. As we noted earlier, Richmond (1993) has proposed that a reactive – proactive continuum of migration motivation be employed, in which push motives (including involuntary or forced migration, and negative expectations) characterize the reactive end of the dimension, while pull motives (including voluntary migration and positive expectations) cluster at the proactive end. Such a single dimension allows for more concise conceptualization and ease of empirical analysis. Viewing previous research in this light permits some generalizations about the relationship between motives and stress and adaptation. For example, Kim (1988) found that, as usual, those with high push motivation had more psychological adaptation problems. However, those with high pull motivation had almost as great a number of problems. It appears that those who are reactive are more at risk, but so too are those who are highly proactive; it is likely that these latter migrants had extremely intense or excessively high (even unrealistic) expectations about their life in the new society, which were not met, leading to greater stress.

Cultural distance (how dissimilar the two cultures are in language, religion, etc.), too, lies not uniquely in the background of the acculturating individual but in the dissimilarity between the two cultures in contact. The general and consistent finding is that the greater the cultural differences, the less positive is the adaptation. This is the case for sojourners, and immigrants (Ward & Kennedy, 1993) and for indigenous people (Berry, 1976). Greater cultural distance implies the need for greater culture shedding and culture conflict leading to poorer adaptation.

Personal factors have also been shown to affect the course of acculturation. In the personality domain, a number of traits have been proposed as both risk and protective factors, including locus of control, introversion/extraversion (Ward & Kennedy, 1992), and self-efficacy (Schwarzer, Hahn, & Schröder, 1994). However, consistent findings have been rare, possibly because, once again, it is not so much the trait by itself but its "fit" with the new cultural setting that matters. Kealey (1989) has advocated such a person-by-situation approach to studying sojourner adaptation.

One finding (Schmitz, 1994), among a group of immigrants to Germany, is that stress reaction styles are related to a person's preferred acculturation strategy. Using the Grossarth-Maticek and Eysenck (1990) Psycho-Social Stress Inventory, the "Approach" style was positively related to a preference for assimilation, the "Avoidance" style to separation, the "Flexible" style to integration, and "Psychopathology" to marginalization.

4.5.2 Factors arising during acculturation

It is now clear that the phase of acculturation needs to be taken into account if stress and adaptation are to be understood. That is, how long a person has been experiencing acculturation strongly affects the kind and extent of problems. The classical description of positive adaptation in relation to time has been in terms of a U-curve: only a few problems are present early, followed by more serious problems later, and finally a more positive long-term adaptation is achieved. However, there is little empirical evidence for such a standard course, nor for fixed time (in terms of months or years) when such variations will occur. Church (1982:452) has concluded that support for the U-curve is "weak, inconclusive and overgeneralized," although there are occasional longitudinal studies suggesting fluctuations in stress over time (e.g., Beiser, 1999; Ward & Kennedy, 1993; Zheng & Berry, 1991).

An alternative to a fixed, stage-like conceptualization of the relationship between length of acculturation and problems experienced is to consider the specific nature of the experiences and problems encountered as they change over time (e.g., initially learning a language, obtaining employment and housing, followed by establishing social relationships and recreational opportunities), and the relationship of such problems to the personal resources of the migrant and to opportunities in the society of settlement (Ho, 1995). This approach emphasizes the high degree of variability to be expected over the time course from initial contact to eventual long-term adaptation.

Acculturation strategies have been shown to have substantial relationships with positive adaptation: integration is usually the most successful; marginalization is the least; and assimilation and separation strategies are intermediate. This pattern has been found in numerous studies, and is present for all types of acculturating groups (Berry, 1990; Berry & Sam, 1997; Berry, Phinney, Sam & Vedder, 2006). Why this should be so, however, is not clear. In one interpretation, the integration strategy incorporates many of the other protective factors, such as a willingness for mutual accommodation (i.e., having two social support systems), and being flexible in personality. In sharp contrast, marginalization involves rejection by the dominant society, combined with own-culture shedding (even though it may be voluntary), and separation involves rejection of the dominant culture (perhaps reciprocated by them). In the simplest version of this explanation, integration involves two positive orientations, marginalization involves two negative ones, while assimilation and separation involve one positive and one negative relationship.

Another possible reason for the finding that integration is the most adaptive strategy is that most studies of the relationship between acculturation strategies and adaptation have been carried out in multicultural societies, in which there is acceptance of cultural diversity. That is, there could be benefits to persons matching their acculturation strategies to that generally advocated and accepted in the larger society. However, in some studies in societies that are more assimilationist in orientation, the integration strategy remained the most adaptive (and marginalization was the least adaptive) strategy. For example, this was the case among Indian immigrants to the USA (Krishnan & Berry, 1992), and Third World immigrant youth in Norway (Sam & Berry, 1995); and Schmitz (1992:368), working with a variety of immigrant groups in Germany, concluded that "The findings suggest that integration seems to be the most effective strategy if we take long term health and well-being as indicators."

Related to acculturation strategies are the coping strategies discussed earlier. Some empirical evidence supports the relationship between coping and acculturation strategies. For example, in the same study Schmitz (1992) found, using the three coping styles identified by Endler and Parker (1990), that integration is positively correlated with task orientation, segregation is positively correlated with emotion and avoidance orientation, and assimilation is positively correlated with both task and emotion orientation. And, as we have just noted, these strategies were related to health outcomes for immigrants to Germany.

In the field of psychological wellbeing generally, the variable of social support has been widely studied (Lin, Dean & Ensel, 1986). Its role in adaptation to acculturation has also been supported (e.g., Furnham & Alighai, 1985; Jayasuriya *et al.*, 1992; Vega & Rumbaut, 1991). For some, links to one's heritage culture (i.e., with co-nationals) are associated with lower stress (e.g., Vega, Kolody, Valle & Weir, 1991; Ward & Kennedy, 1993); for others links to members of the society of settlement are more helpful, particularly if relationships match one's expectations (e.g., Berry & Kostovcik, 1990); but in most studies, supportive relationships with *both* cultures are most predictive of successful adaptation (Berry *et al.*, 1987; Kealey, 1989). This latter finding corresponds to observations made earlier about the advantages of the integration strategy.

It has been widely reported that the experience of prejudice and discrimination has a significant negative effect on a person's wellbeing (e.g., Halpern, 1993; Noh *et al.*, 1999). In groups experiencing acculturation, this can be an added risk factor (Beiser *et al.*, 1988). Murphy (1965) has argued that such prejudice is likely to be less prevalent in culturally plural societies, but it is by no means absent (e.g., Berry & Kalin, 1995). Indeed Fernando (1993) has designated racism as the most serious problem and risk factor facing immigrants and their mental health.

4.6   Adaptation

The last part of Figure 4.1 shows various kinds of *adaptation*. This refers to the long-term ways in which people rearrange their lives and settle down to a more-or-less satisfactory existence. It is "more-or-less" because adaptation can range from being a very positive through to a very negative way of living in the new cultural setting. "Adaptation" refers to the relatively stable changes that take place in an individual or group in response to external demands. Moreover, adaptation may or may not improve the "fit" between individuals and their environments. It is thus not a term that necessarily implies that individuals or groups change to become more like their environment (i.e., adjustment by way of assimilation) but may involve resistance and attempts to change their environments, or move away from them altogether (i.e., by separation). Adaptation can be seen as ranging from achieving *primary control* to achieving *secondary control* as discussed previously. Moreover, adaptation is an outcome that may or may not be positive in valence (i.e., meaning only *well*-adapted). Thus, long-term adaptation to acculturation is highly variable, ranging from well-adapted to poorly adapted; varying from a situation where individuals can manage their new lives very well, to one where they are unable to carry on in the new society.

Adaptation is also multifaceted. The initial distinction between *psychological* and *sociocultural* adaptation was proposed and validated by Ward and colleagues (Ward, 1996; Ward & Rana-Deuba, 1999). Psychological adaptation largely involves one's psychological and physical wellbeing (Schmitz, 1992), while sociocultural adaptation refers to how well an acculturating individual is able to manage daily life in the new cultural context.

While conceptually distinct, they are empirically related to some extent (correlations between the two measures are in the $+.4$ to $+.5$ range). However, they are also empirically distinct in the sense that they usually have different time courses and different experiential predictors. Psychological problems often increase soon after contact, followed by a general (but variable) decrease over time; sociocultural adaptation, however, typically has a linear improvement with time. Analyses of the factors affecting positive adaptation reveal a generally consistent pattern: good psychological adaptation is predicted by personality variables, life-change events and social support, while good sociocultural adaptation is predicted by cultural knowledge, degree of contact, and positive inter-group attitudes; both aspects of adaptation are usually predicted by the successful pursuit of the integration acculturation strategy, and by minimal cultural distance (Ward & Kennedy, 1993b; Ward, 1996). Two specific kinds of sociocultural adaptation have been suggested. For one kind, *economic adaptation*, Aycan and Berry (1996) showed that psychological and sociocultural adaptation were predicted by much the same set of variables as in Ward's studies, while economic adaptation was predicted by some other variables, including migration motivation, perception of relative deprivation and status loss on first entry into the work world. A second kind has been identified by Ataca and Berry (2002) who proposed that *marital adaptation* is a core aspect of adaptation when married couples are studied as a unit that is experiencing acculturation.

Research relating adaptation to acculturation strategies allows for some further generalizations (Berry, 1997; Ward, 1996). In most cases, for all forms of adaptation, those who pursue and accomplish integration appear to be better adapted, while those who are marginalized are least well adapted. And again, the assimilation and separation strategies are associated with intermediate adaptation outcomes. In studies of sojourners, Kealey (1989) found this pattern for international aid workers from Canada. However, Ward and Rana-Deuba (1999) found that integration predicted better psychological adaptation only, while a preference for assimilation predicted better sociocultural adaptation. In a study of Irish immigrants to the UK, Curran (2003) found that integration was the most successful strategy for achieving positive psychological wellbeing. And in their large-scale study of immigrant youth, Berry, Phinney, Sam and Vedder (2006) found that involvement in both of the cultures (ie., integration) positively predicted both forms of adaptation relative to the other three acculturation orientations. Moreover, in this study, it was better sociocultural adaptation that influenced better psychological adaptation, rather than the other way around.

4.7   Conclusions

In this chapter, we have presented an overview of one of the approaches to the study of the relationship between acculturation and adaptation. In some contrast to the culture learning approach (in Chapter 5), the emphasis has been on a theoretical approach that was developed in literature dealing with the psychology of emotions and health. It takes the position that acculturation experiences can challenge individuals and their groups, that resources and strategies can be marshaled to cope with these challenges, and that the variable success of using various forms of coping will lead to variable degrees of adaptation. Beyond the basic literature on *coping strategies* in health psychology, this chapter has borrowed the concept of *acculturation strategies* from Chapter 3, and used them to contribute further to our understanding of the various ways that people attempt to navigate their way through the acculturation process. When combined, these two sets of strategies allow us to identify patterns of relationships between acculturation experiences and adaptation that suggest ways to deal with the challenges of acculturation that will enhance the adaptation outcomes. Once contact has taken place between the two cultures, and individuals have begun to experience the demands of dealing with, and making sense of, both cultures, it appears that involvement in both cultures leads to more positive outcomes than involvement in either one or the other culture, or in neither.

4.8   References

Aldwin, C. (1994). *Stress, coping and development*. New York: Guilford Press.

Aronowitz, M. (1992). Adjustment of immigrant children as a function of parental attitudes to change. *International Migration Review, 26*, 86–110.

Ataca, B. & Berry, J. W. (2002). Sociocultural, psychological and marital adaptation of Turkish immigrant couples in Canada. *International Journal of Psychology, 37*, 13–26.

Aycan, Z. & Berry, J. W. (1996). Impact of employment-related experiences on immigrants' psychological well-being and adaptation to Canada. *Canadian Journal of Behavioural Science, 28*, 240–251.

Beiser, M. (1999). *Strangers at the gate*. Toronto: University of Toronto Press.

Beiser, M., Barwick, C., Berry, J. W. *et al.* (1988). *After the door has been opened: mental health issues affecting immigrants and refugees*. Ottawa: Departments of Multiculturalism and Health and Welfare.

Beiser, M., Johnson, P. & Turner, J. (1993). Unemployment, underemployment and depressive affect among Southeast Asian refugees. *Psychological Medicine, 23*, 731–743.

Berry, J. W. (1970). Marginality, stress and ethnic identification in an acculturated Aboriginal community. *Journal of Cross-Cultural Psychology, 1*, 239–252.

   (1974). Psychological aspects of cultural pluralism: unity and identity reconsidered. *Topics in Culture Learning, 2*, 17–22.

   (1976). *Human ecology and cognitive style: comparative studies in cultural and psychological adaptation*. New York: Sage Publications / Halsted.

   (1990). Psychology of acculturation. In J. Berman (ed.), *Cross-cultural perspectives: Nebraska symposium on motivation* (pp. 201–234). Lincoln: University of Nebraska Press.

   (1997). Immigration, acculturation and adaptation. (Lead article with commentary.) *Applied Psychology: An International Review, 46*, 5–68.

Berry, J. W. & Kalin, R. (1995). Multicultural and ethnic attitudes in Canada. *Canadian Journal of Behavioural Science, 27*, 301–320.

Berry, J. W., Kim, U., Minde, T. & Mok, D. (1987). Comparative studies of acculturative stress. *International Migration Review, 21*, 491–511.

Berry, J. W. & Kostovcik, N. (1990). Psychological adaptation of Malaysian students in Canada. In A. Othman (ed.), *Psychology and socioeconomic development* (pp. 155–162). Bangi: Penerbit Universiti Kebangsaan Malaysia.

Berry, J. W., Phinney, J. S., Sam, D. L. & Vedder, P. (eds.) (2006). *Immigrant youth in cultural transition: acculturation, identity and adaptation across national contexts*. Mahwah, NJ: Lawrence Erlbaum Associates.

Berry, J. W. & Sam, D. (1997). Acculturation and adaptation. In J. W. Berry, M. H. Segall & C. Kağitçibaşi (eds.), *Handbook of cross-cultural psychology*, Vol. III: *Social behavior and applications* (pp. 291–326). Boston: Allyn & Bacon.

Carballo, M. (1994). *Scientific consultation on the social and health impact of migration*. Geneva: International Organization for Migration.

Church, T. (1982). Sojourner adjustment. *Psychological Bulletin, 91*, 540–572.

Clark, R., Anderson, N., Clark, V. & Williams, D. (1999). Racism as a stressor for African Americans: a biopsychosocial model. *American Psychologist, 54*, 805–816.

Cumming, P., Lee, E. & Oreopoulos, D. (1989). *Access to trades and professions*. Toronto: Ontario Ministry of Citizenship.

Curran, Michael J. (2003). *Across the water – the acculturation and health of Irish people in London*. Dublin: Psychology Dept., Trinity College, and Allen Library.

Diaz Guerrero, R. (1979). The development of coping style. *Human Development, 22*, 320–331.

Endler, N. & Parker, J. (1990). Multidimensional assessment of coping. *Journal of Personality and Social Psychology, 58*, 844–854.

Fernando, S. (1993). Racism and xenophobia. *Innovation on Social Science Research, 6*, 9–19.

Furnham, A. & Alighai, N. (1985). The friendship networks of foreign students. *International Journal of Psychology, 20*, 709–722.

Grossarth-Maticek, R. & Eysenck, H. (1990). Personality, stress and disease. *Psychological Reports, 66*, 355–373.

Hagendoorn, L. (1993). Ethnic categorisation and outgroup exclusion. *Ethnic and Racial Studies, 16*, 26–51.

Halpern, D. (1993). Minorities and mental health. *Social Science and Medicine, 36,* 597–607.

Ho, E. (1995). Chinese or New Zealander? Differential paths of adaptation of Chinese adolescent immigrants in New Zealand. *New Zealand Population Review, 21,* 27–49.

Jayasuriya, L., Sang, D. & Fielding, A. (1992). *Ethnicity, immigration and mental illness: a critical review of Australian research.* Canberra: Bureau of Immigration Research.

Kealey, D. (1989). A study of cross-cultural effectiveness: theoretical issues, practical applications. *International Journal of Intercultural Relations, 13,* 387–428.

Kim, U. (1988). Acculturation of Korean immigrants to Canada. Unpublished doctoral thesis: Queen's University, Kingston, Ontario.

Krishnan, A. & Berry, J. W. (1992). Acculturative stress and acculturation attitudes among Indian immigrants in the United States. *Psychology and Developing Societies, 4,* 187–212.

Lazarus, R. (1990). Theory-based stress measurement. *Psychological Inquiry, 1,* 3–13.

Lazarus, R. S. & Folkman, S. (1984). *Stress, appraisal and coping.* New York: Springer.

Liebkind, K. & Jasinskaja-Lahti, I. (2000). The influence of experiences of discrimination on psychological stress: a comparison of seven immigrant groups. *Journal of Community, Applied Social Psychology, 10,* 1–16.

Lin, N., Dean, A. & Ensel, N. (eds.) (1986). *Social support, life events and depression.* New York: Academic Press.

Murphy, H. B. M. (1965). Migration and the major mental disorders. In M. Kantor (ed.), *Mobility and mental health* (pp. 221–249). Springfield: Thomas.

Naidoo, J. (1992). The mental health of visible ethnic minorities in Canada. *Psychology and Developing Societies, 4,* 165–186.

Noh, S., Beiser, M., Kaspar, V., Hou, F. & Rummens, J. (1999). Perceived racial discrimination, depression and coping: a study of Southeast Asian refugees in Canada. *Journal of Health and Social Behaviour, 40,* 193–207.

Oberg, K. (1960). Cultural shock: adjustment to new cultural environments. *Practical Anthropology, 7,* 177–182.

Phinney, J. (1990). Ethnic identity in adolescents and adults. *Psychological Bulletin, 108,* 499–514.

Richmond, A. (1993). Reactive migration: sociological perspectives on refugee movements. *Journal of Refugee Studies, 6,* 7–24.

Sam, D. & Berry, J. W. (1995). Acculturative stress among young immigrants in Norway. *Scandinavian Journal of Psychology, 36,* 10–24.

Schmitz, P. (1992). Acculturation styles and health. In S. Iwawaki, Y. Kashima & K. Leung (eds.), *Innovations in cross-cultural psychology* (pp. 360–370). Lisse: Swets & Zeitlinger.

(1994). Acculturation and adaptation process among immigrants in Germany. In A. Bouvey *et al.* (eds.), *Journeys into cross-cultural psychology* (pp.142–157). Lisse: Swets & Zeitlinger.

Schwarzer, R., Hahn, A. & Schröder, H. (1994). Social integration and social support in a life crisis. *American Journal of Community Psychology, 22,* 685–706.

Vega, W., Kolody, B., Valle, R. & Weir, J. (1991). Social networks, social support, and depression among immigrant Mexican women. *Human Organization, 50,* 154–162.

Vega, W. & Rumbaut, R. (1991). Ethnic minorities and mental health. *Annual Review of Sociology, 17*, 56–89.

Ward, C. (1996). Acculturation. In D. Landis & R. Bhagat (eds.), *Handbook of intercultural training* (pp.124–147). Newbury Park: Sage Publications.

Ward, C., Bochner, S. & Furnham, A. (2001). *The psychology of culture shock.* Hove: Routledge.

Ward, C. & Kennedy, A. (1993). Where is the "culture" in cross-cultural transition? Comparative studies of sojourner adjustment. *Journal of Cross-Cultural Psychology, 24*, 221–249.

Ward, C. & Rana-Deuba, A. (1999). Acculturation and adaptation revisited. *Journal of Cross-Cultural Psychology, 30*, 422–442.

Zheng, X. & Berry, J. W. (1991). Psychological adaptation of Chinese sojourners in Canada. *International Journal of Psychology, 26*, 451–470.

5 Culture learning approach to acculturation

Anne-Marie Masgoret & Colleen Ward

In their 2001 publication *The psychology of culture shock*, Ward, Bochner and Furnham identified three major theoretical approaches to the study of intercultural contact and change. Termed the *ABCs of Acculturation*, (i) the stress and coping framework, (ii) the culture learning approach and (iii) the social identification perspective were taken to highlight the respective importance of Affect, Behavior and Cognition in the acculturation process (Figure 5.1). A developmental dimension has more recently been incorporated into this volume's comprehensive analysis of international theory and research on acculturation and adaptation.

This chapter examines behavioral dimensions of acculturation, elaborating the culture learning approach to acculturation, outlining its history and development, introducing the concepts of communication competence and sociocultural adaptation, and reviewing empirical research on their antecedents, correlates, consequences and temporal variations. The chapter also features contemporary theory and research on a relatively neglected, but important, area in acculturation research – language learning. We conclude with an overall evaluation of the culture learning approach and its contribution to the international literature on acculturation.

5.1 Culture learning theory: history and development

The culture learning approach has its roots in social and experimental psychology and has been strongly influenced by Argyle's (1969) work on social skills and interpersonal behaviors. The approach is based on the assumption that cross-cultural problems arise because cultural novices have difficulties managing everyday social encounters. Adaptation, therefore, comes in the form of learning the culture-specific skills that are required to negotiate a new cultural milieu (Bochner, 1972).

Historically, researchers who have adopted a culture learning approach to intercultural contact and change emphasized the significance of culture-specific variables in the adaptation process. Attention was particularly paid to differences in intercultural communication styles, including their verbal and nonverbal components, as well as rules, conventions and norms, and their influences on intercultural effectiveness. Early work by Stephen Bochner and

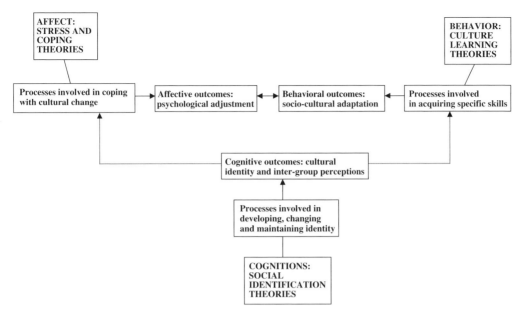

Figure 5.1 *The ABC model of culture contact*
Source: Ward, Bochner & Furnham (2001)

Adrian Furnham in the Oxford tradition (e.g., Bochner, 1972; Furnham & Bochner, 1982), including their research with the Social Situations Questionnaire, exemplified this approach. Culture learning theory similarly occupied a significant position in Brislin's (1981) *Cross-cultural encounters,* and in the 1986 edition of *Culture shock* Furnham and Bochner advocated it as an alternative to the outmoded clinical approaches that were widely used in the field.

More recently, culture learning theory has evolved in two directions. On one hand, aspects of the "social psychology of the intercultural encounter" (Argyle, 1982; Bochner, 1982) have been integrated and subsumed under the overarching framework of communication styles or communication competence. This development is reflected in the work of social psychologists and communication theorists such as Cynthia Gallois, Howard Giles, William Gudykunst and Y. Kim (e.g., Gallois, Franklyn-Stokes, Giles & Coupland, 1988; Gudykunst & Kim, 1984; Kim, 1991). On the other hand, researchers have broadened the traditional line of inquiry about cultural differences in communication styles, norms and values, to concentrate on the definition and prediction of sociocultural adaptation, that is, the ability to "fit in" or negotiate interactive aspects of life in a new cultural milieu. While early research by Hammer, Gudykunst and Wiseman (1978) and Kealey (1989) on intercultural effectiveness underpins this development, more recent work by Ward and colleagues (e.g., Searle & Ward, 1990; Ward & Kennedy, 1999) perhaps best exemplifies this contemporary approach.

The influence of culture learning theory can be seen in early communication studies by Kim (1977), which demonstrated that language competence, acculturation motivation, and interpersonal and mass media accessibility are major determinants of intercultural communication competence. In her more recent discussions, Kim (1991) highlights the significance of cultural differences within the communication process and provides a number of suggestions on how to minimize failed communications across cultures. The influence of culture learning theory is also seen on Gudykunst's (1993) approach to effective communication. Gudykunst's model includes a major skills component, with emphasis on the ability to gather and use appropriate information and the ability to be adaptable in intercultural communication. Although a number of studies have demonstrated that communication competence is associated with cultural learning, the majority of these have tended to focus on the role of overt communication behaviors, such as frequency of intercultural contact and one's level of language fluency, and have focused less attention on the quality of such contact and the social psychological mechanisms underlying communication behaviors.

Culture learning theory also underpins the work by Furnham and Bochner on intercultural encounters, and research by Ward and colleagues, which has expanded the notions of communication competence and effective social interaction to the broader construct of sociocultural adaptation. Situated in the behavioral domain, sociocultural adaptation refers to the ability to "fit in" or negotiate effective interactions in a new cultural milieu. It incorporates knowledge and skills and includes not only proficiency in fundamental communication and social interaction skills, but also adaptation to new ecologies, norms, values and world-views. Ward has distinguished sociocultural and psychological adaptation in her acculturation research, with the latter defined in terms of psychological wellbeing and satisfaction. She has also noted that the two adaptation outcomes are best understood and explained in terms of different theoretical frameworks – culture learning and stress and coping, that they are generally predicted by different types of variables, and that they exhibit different patterns of variation over time (Ward, 2001). An in-depth discussion of the stress and coping framework and psychological adaptation during acculturation is presented in Chapter 4.

In this chapter we bring together the two strands of culture learning research to provide a more comprehensive overview of the theoretical derivatives and their applications. In order to do this, a graphic representation of the relationship between language proficiency and communication competence, effective intercultural interaction and sociocultural adaptation is provided in Figure 5.2. Fundamentally, language proficiency and broader communication competence are at the core of sociocultural adaptation. These complementary components are required for effective social interaction, which, in turn, is part of the broader construct of sociocultural adaptation.

There is no doubt that one of the most important factors in determining effective communication with members of the host community, and arguably

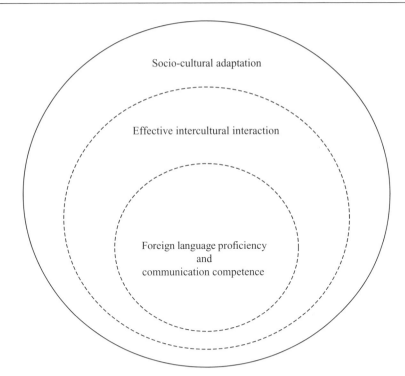

Figure 5.2 *Interactive model of foreign-language proficiency, communication competence, effective intercultural interaction and sociocultural adaptation*

the most central one, is one's facility to speak their language. Indeed, if individuals making cross-cultural transitions are to communicate successfully across cultures, they will be required, at least to some extent, to speak the language of the receiving community. Language skills are relevant to the performance of daily tasks and are important in establishing interpersonal relationships in a foreign country as they affect the quality and quantity of intercultural interactions. Few studies, however, have focused specifically on the relationship between variables relating to second/foreign language acquisition and culture learning, though a number of researchers have suggested that one's level of proficiency or fluency in the language of the host country is associated with general adaptation to the new culture. This relationship has been often attributed to the newcomers' increased ability to use the language in interactions with members of the receiving culture (Gullahorn & Gullahorn, 1966).

Studies have found that language fluency bears a straightforward relationship to sociocultural adjustment; it is associated with increased interaction with members of the host culture and a decrease in sociocultural adjustment problems (Ward & Kennedy, 1993a). For this reason, it seems important to examine the role of language-related variables in facilitating foreign language acquisition and communication competence, which includes both effective and appropriate communicative behaviors (Spitzberg, 1988).

A number of studies have suggested that the relationship between language fluency and social interaction is most likely a reciprocal one, with increased language competence leading to greater participation in the host community which, in turn, leads to improved proficiency in the host language (Clément, Noels & Deneault, 2001). As immigrants become increasingly fluent in the language of the receiving community, their ability to participate in various intercultural experiences is increased. According to this view, the development of language fluency and other communication competencies and the development of interpersonal relationships with members of the receiving community appear to function dynamically in the ongoing process of culture learning. Thus, foreign language skills provide the migrant with the means to establish the interpersonal relationships and social support that have been shown to facilitate culture learning and sociocultural adjustment (Ward, 1996).

Although culture learning theory is relevant to anyone engaged in intercultural contact, the bulk of the research undertaken from this perspective has focused on groups that have undergone a cross-cultural transition. Immigrants and sojourners have received particular attention, and this emphasis will be reflected in the following review. The wider utility of culture learning theory, however, should not be ignored. For example, culture learning theory forms the basis of most intercultural training programs, including those designed for members of "majority" groups in culturally plural societies (Ward, 2004).

The culture learning approach emphasizes the significance of social skills and social interaction. Extending work from the intracultural domain, it begins by identifying the cross-cultural differences in verbal and nonverbal communication, rules, conventions, norms and practices that contribute to intercultural misunderstandings. It then sets about proposing ways in which confusing and dissatisfying encounters can be minimized. As the approach considers intercultural effectiveness as essentially no different from other desirable activities or behavioral goals, it can be achieved through the application of the basic principles of learning.

5.2   Cross-cultural differences and culture learning

Communication is at the heart of intercultural contact, and language proficiency, as well as familiarity with cultural differences, are required for effective intercultural interchanges. Adroit social interaction also demands knowledge about and skill in the rules and conventions of social intercourse in a particular cultural context. Finally, sociocultural adaptation requires understanding of relevant norms and values. This is not to suggest that a sojourner or immigrant must take on board a new set of values to adapt to a new culture, but they should be aware of value differences and have behavioral strategies for effectively dealing with them. This section gives a brief overview of some of the cross-cultural differences that may act as barriers to effective communication, positive social relations and broader sociocultural adaptation. In short, this section considers *what* must be learned.

5.2.1   Differences in language

Linguists have reported the use of as many as 6,000 different spoken languages in the world today. Parallel to the diversity of norms and behaviors among cultures, languages may differ in a number of ways, such as by "language family" as well as by their written and verbal systems. Languages from the different families derive from disparate linguistic ancestors and share few basic similarities. Language scripts can also vary markedly, with alphabetic written scripts differing from ideograms or pictographs. Other differences in written language include types of scripts (e.g., Persian, Roman, Arabic), and the direction in which the language is written/read. Spoken forms of language differ in grammatical constructions, tonality and honorifics. Even within a single language there can be many variations in accents and dialects.

   Knowledge of the language spoken in the receiving community plays a central role within the cultural learning process, since language is viewed as the primary medium through which cultural information is communicated. Because language and cultural learning are intimately linked, miscommunications will likely result if migrants and sojourners do not acquire at least some fundamental verbal skills.

5.2.2   Differences in nonverbal communication

Intercultural competence and cultural learning require more than the learning of a language, and competent communication requires the learner to face a number of challenges. For example, social pragmatic differences can lead to breakdowns in communication. Thus, although language fluency is a significant part of communication, nonverbal forms of communication are also salient in the intercultural communication process.

   There are numerous aspects of nonverbal communication, including activities such as culture-specific gestures, display of gaze, adoption of preferred body postures, the expression of emotions and the performance of ritualized routines such as greetings and leave-takings. Such nonverbal acts often carry implicit messages that define the nature of relationships within a culture, and these messages can vary widely across cultures. In many ways, learning nonverbal forms of communication can present a bigger challenge to cultural travelers than achieving language fluency since it is often difficult to acquire the heuristic knowledge that is embedded within a culture. Because nonverbal behaviors are essential to effective intercultural communication, it is important that they are in accordance with cultural expectations. Indeed, experimental research on intercultural interaction has shown that culturally congruent nonverbal behaviors are a more powerful predictor of interpersonal attraction than ethnicity (Dew & Ward, 1993).

   Nonverbal forms of communication vary markedly across cultures, and these variations frequently contribute to cross-cultural misunderstandings. For example, cultures may differ in how they display physical contact, mutual gaze, and gestures (Argyle, 1975, 1982). Individuals from high-contact cultures, such as those of Southern Europe and Latin America, have small areas of interpersonal space and make frequent physical contact, whereas those from low-contact cultures, such as East Asian societies, appear less intimate. When individuals from high- and low-contact cultures meet, the former may be perceived as intrusive, while the latter are likely to be seen as cold and unfriendly.

Differences in mutual gaze patterns and gestures also vary widely across cultures and affect person perception. Arabs and members of Latin American cultures display a comparatively high frequency of mutual gaze, while Europeans exhibit a lower frequency. When intercultural interactions occur, persons from high-gaze cultures may be seen as disrespectful or threatening, whereas those from low-gaze cultures are likely to be perceived as impolite, bored or dishonest. In terms of cultural differences relating to body gestures, those from Latin-based cultures are known to be very expressive, while the Nordic people make little use of gestures. The meaning and significance of gestures also differ across national and cultural groups. For example, the "thumbs up" gesture used widely in the United States to indicate a sign of approval is seen as an insult in Greece (Collett, 1982). On a more general level, there are cross-cultural differences in the liking of or preference for body postures. The Japanese prefer closed postures, while the Americans tend to respond more positively to those with open body postures (McGinley, Blau & Takai, 1984).

One of the most powerful forms of nonverbal communication is achieved through the use of silence, and this is known to vary in its frequency, duration, intentionality and meaning across cultures. The Japanese, for example, use silence more often than Americans (Lebra, 1987). Polynesians are more comfortable with silence than Caucasian New Zealanders, but do not use it in the same way to imply consent (Metge & Kinloch, 1978).

Facial expression of emotion is subject to cross-cultural variation and related to display rules. Friesen's (1972) classic study demonstrated that Americans expressed negative emotions in reaction to a horrifying film whether alone or with someone else, while Japanese repressed the expression of negative emotions in the presence of another person. How an audience affects the expression of emotion also varies cross-culturally. Matsumoto and Hearn (cited in Matsumoto, 1994), for example, reported that Poles and Hungarians display fewer negative emotions and more positive emotions in ingroups compared to Americans, while the reverse is true for outgroup interactions.

5.2.3 Differences in rules and conventions

In addition to culturally disparate nonverbal behaviors, the rules that govern interpersonal behavior are a major source of difficulty in intercultural interactions. Many of the differences in rules and conventions have been associated more broadly with cross-cultural variations in values, particularly individualism–collectivism and power distance (Hofstede, 1980). Members of

individualistic cultures see the individual as the basic unit of social organization, in contrast to members of collectivist cultures, who emphasize the significance of the larger group. Individualists are idiocentric; they value autonomy,
uniqueness and "standing out." Collectivists, on the other hand, value "fitting
in," finding and maintaining one's proper place among others (Triandis, 1989).
Theory and research have suggested that people from individualist societies,
such as the United States, prefer directness, take longer and more unevenly
distributed turns in conversation, speak louder, and are more willing to express
negative emotions in public. Because collectivists, particularly people from
East Asian societies, value group harmony and face-saving to a greater extent,
they are less willing to engage in activities that might be seen as disruptive to the
larger group. Consequently, they often appear more restrained in social interactions. Asian subtlety and indirectness are often interpreted as inscrutability
by Westerners. This is compounded by the fact that, in many Asian countries,
the word *no* is seldom used in response to a request, so that a response of "yes"
may actually mean "no" or "maybe."

Cross-cultural variations in power distance reflect differences in the prevalence of established hierarchies, the preference for vertical versus horizontal
relationships, and the importance of status. Americans prefer horizontal or
equal relationships and tend to be informal in their interactions, including the
widespread use of first names as a form of address. Societies that are high
in power distance, such as those of Mexico and India, are more likely to
employ forms of address that reflect status differences, including the use of
titles.

Recent work by Ting-Toomey (2004) on face-negotiation provides an excellent example of cross-cultural differences in rules and conventions. She notes
that all cultures engage in interactive processes to maintain and negotiate face
in communication situations, but that the cultural dimensions of variability, particularly individualism–collectivism and power distance, influence the preference for self-versus-other facework. These preferences are manifest in making
requests, gaining compliance, offering apologies and compliments, making
decisions, showing politeness and dealing with conflicts. According to Ting-
Toomey, competent intercultural face-work is achieved through the integration
of knowledge, mindfulness and communication skills. The emphasis on the
knowledge and skills components of face-negotiation is consistent with the
basic principles of culture learning theory.

5.2.4   Differences in norms and values

The rules and conventions of communication practices are not the only learned
behaviors affected by cross-cultural differences in values. Broader aspects
of social activities, including inter-personal and inter-group interactions, are
also influenced by value differences. Hofstede's (1980) distinction of individualism, uncertainty avoidance, power distance and masculinity provides one

framework for organizing and analyzing value differences. Triandis (1989) has discussed individualism–collectivism, cultural looseness–tightness and cultural complexity as overarching cultural characteristics that dictate social behavior, while Schwartz (1994) has identified seven cultural value dimensions – mastery, hierarchy, conservatism, harmony, egalitarian commitment, intellectual autonomy and affective autonomy – as sources of cultural variation. A more recent and innovative approach is found in the work of Leung and Bond on social axioms, which has identified five "operating principles" (social cynicism, reward for application, spirituality, social complexity and fate control) that vary across cultures (Leung et al., 2002).

An important question pertaining to cross-cultural differences in values is the extent to which sojourners or immigrants are required to accept new values to adapt to a novel cultural context. A recent study by Kurman and Ronen-Eilon (2004) addresses this issue. The researchers examined both the individual-level value dimensions identified by Schwartz and colleagues (Schwartz, Melech, Lehmann, Burgess & Harris, 2001) and social axioms distinguished by Leung et al. (2002) in native-born Israelis and immigrants from the former Soviet Union and Ethiopia who were resident in Israel. Immigrants reported on their actual values and axiomatic principles as well as their impressions of Israeli values and axioms. These data permitted the assessment of objective knowledge of Israeli society as well as value and axiomatic discrepancies between the migrants and native-borns. The results revealed two important findings: (i) lack of knowledge about social axioms was a stronger predictor of sociocultural adaptation problems than discrepancies between immigrants and Israelis; and (ii) lack of knowledge about social axioms was a stronger predictor of sociocultural adaptation than lack of knowledge about values. The authors concluded that: "Values may help in understanding a culture, but they have less to do with concrete, mundane behaviors" (p. 203). A similar conclusion was reached by Ward and Searle (1991) who failed to establish a link between value discrepancies and sociocultural adaptation in a sample of international students in New Zealand. Overall, the studies converge to suggest that adopting new axioms or accepting new values is not critical to the sociocultural adaptation process; knowledge and awareness of cross-cultural differences in axioms and values, however, exert a significant influence on adaptation outcomes.

5.2.5   Other factors

Culture learning theory concentrates on the social aspects of intercultural contact impinging on sociocultural adaptation, particularly those arising from differences in language, communication styles and patterns of social interaction. There are, however, other differences that confront cross-cultural travelers that require adaptation, and these are also more effectively managed through context-specific learning. Aspects of the social and physical environment are important. For example, in an innovative observational study Levine and Bartlett (1984) demonstrated significant variations in pace of life and punctuality across Japan, Taiwan, Indonesia, Italy, England and the United States and discussed the implications of these differences for health indicators. Ecological factors, including temperature and climate, vary across cultures and are often a source of discomfort. When asked about the most difficult thing about living in New Zealand, weather was amongst the twelve spontaneously generated replies in a sample of 2,700 international students (Ward & Masgoret, 2004)! Although climate and pace of life may be classified as environmental factors, problems arising from these sources can be circumvented by learning, and such difficulties are often included in the assessment of sociocultural adaptation.

5.3   Factors affecting language and culture learning

There is considerable variation in learning outcomes across individuals and groups. This section considers the major factors that affect language and culture learning, with particular emphasis on their implications for sociocultural adaptation. This includes a discussion of personal factors – such as motivation, expectations, personality and individual differences – and situational factors – such as previous experience, length of residence in a new culture, intercultural contact and cultural distance.

5.3.1 Factors related to the person

5.3.1.1 Motivational factors and expectations

Language-related variables are crucial to the culture learning process and to sociocultural adaptation, since they are considered key elements in language acquisition and effective intercultural communication. Studies have demonstrated that attitudinal and motivational variables influence how successful an individual will be in learning another language (Masgoret & Gardner, 2003). For example, studies by Gardner and his associates have focused attention on a set of related measures known as *integrativeness*, which refers to an individual's attitudes towards the foreign language community, an openness to other cultural groups in general, and a willingness and interest in engaging in social interactions with members of the foreign language community (Gardner & Clément, 1990). Numerous studies have demonstrated that integrativeness is positively associated with second language motivation and subsequent proficiency (Gardner, 1985, 2000; Masgoret & Gardner, 2003). The underlying dynamics have been attributed to the association of such variables with higher levels of intercultural contact, as was demonstrated in Masgoret and Gardner's (1999) study of a sample of Spanish immigrants living in Canada. Here, the role of positive attitudes towards Canadian language and culture was not only relevant to English language proficiency, but also to the frequency and quality of contact with English-speaking Canadians.

Second language confidence refers to the belief in being able to communicate in an adaptive and efficient manner when using the second language (Clément & Bourhis, 1996). Studies have demonstrated that one's confidence in using a second language is an important predictor of foreign language proficiency (Clément, 1980; Clément, Dörnyei & Noels, 1994). Related research has identified the goal of achieving effective intercultural interactions as an important predictor of language motivation and proficiency. For example, studies have demonstrated that an individual's success in learning the language of the host community is influenced by their willingness to communicate with members of that community (MacIntyre, Dörnyei, Clément & Noels, 1998).

Implicitly underpinning many of these individual language-related characteristics are the past communicative experiences and future expectations held by the immigrant or sojourner. Studies by Clément and colleagues have proposed that language confidence, along with subsequent language achievement, is a function of the frequency and quality of contact one has with members of the host language community (Clément & Kruidenier, 1985). However, it should be noted that the frequency and quality of contact require not only the willingness of the newcomer to communicate with members of the host community, but also the willingness of host nationals to interact with newcomers (Smart, Volet & Ang, 2000).

Sociocultural difficulties may arise if the sojourner's expectations regarding effective communication are not met. For example, a study by Takai (1989) found that increases in language fluency in Japanese were associated with decreases in sociocultural adaptation in a sample of foreign students in Japan. This finding was attributed to the students' high expectations of interacting effectively with members of the host community, together with the difficulties they encountered in doing so.

A small number of studies have considered the role of more general cultural expectations within the sociocultural adaptation framework. One approach has been to consider the influence of sojourners' expectations on their adaptation processes by focusing on their expectation–experience discrepancies. For example, Searle and Ward (1990) examined the "what-you-expect-is-what-you-get" phenomenon and found that expectations about cross-cultural difficulties were related to actual difficulties in sojourner adaptation. Similarly, Hawes and Kealey (1980) reported significant relationships between sojourners' expectations of a positive sojourn and competent performance on overseas assignments in a sample of Canadian technical assistants. Both of these studies, however, relied on retrospective ratings of expectations whose accuracy may have been influenced by the actual experiences of sojourners. A longitudinal study by Masgoret (2002) found a strong positive relationship between expected sociocultural adaptation and sojourner's level of adaptation after a 1-month period abroad. Overall, it seems reasonable to conclude that positive attitudes and expectations about a new language and culture can have a favorable influence on sojourners and immigrants.

5.3.2 Personality and individual differences

The "Big Five" model of personality has provided a popular framework for the investigation of the relationship between personality and sociocultural adaptation, including the possible mediating influences of intercultural interactions. As Neuroticism has been broadly associated with skills deficits in the mainstream social psychology and organizational literature, it is not surprising that it is also linked to greater sociocultural adaptation problems (Ward, Leong & Low, 2004). Ones and Viswesvaran's (1997) suggestion that Extraversion underpins effective and satisfying intercultural relations has been borne out in research by Ward and Searle (1991), which additionally demonstrated that Extraversion is a significant predictor of sociocultural adaptation (see also Masgoret, Bernaus & Gardner, 2000). Openness, Agreeableness and Conscientiousness have also been linked to positive sociocultural outcomes (Ward, Berno & Main, 2002; Ward *et al.*, 2004). Other personality factors that have been associated with social adjustment and/or sociocultural adaptation during cross-cultural transitions include cultural empathy, flexibility and emotional stability and resilience (van der Zee & Van Oudenhoven, 2000; Ward *et al.*, 2004).

In contrast to the emphasis on personality, Early and Ang (2003) have provided a new perspective on culture learning and acculturation with the introduction of the concept of cultural intelligence (CQ): "Cultural intelligence refers to a person's capability to adapt effectively to a new cultural context" (p. 59). Its structure consists of cognitive, motivational and behavioral components. The cognitive component is knowledge-based, the motivational component incorporates a sense of self-efficacy, and the behavioral component requires a repertoire of responses appropriate to a given situation. The behavioral dimension of CQ is perhaps the most relevant to culture learning theory, and Early and Ang argue that behavior and CQ are linked in direct and indirect ways. Cultural intelligence entails both aptitudes (capacity) and abilities (actualities), and these vary across individuals. Although CQ is based on relatively stable individual differences and can be assessed by psychometric scales, it can also be improved through training. While CQ has offered a novel perspective on acculturation, it is time to move away from the conceptual development of the construct to an empirical base that can establish its predictive influence on adaptation outcomes.

5.4   Situational factors

5.4.1   Previous experience and length of residence

Studies have suggested that such factors as general knowledge about a new culture (Searle & Ward, 1990) and previous experience abroad (Klineberg & Hull, 1979) play an important role in relation to cross-cultural adjustment.

For example, Masgoret (2002) found that background experiences with the language and culture of the host community were significantly related to the degree of sociocultural adaptation in British sojourners who were employed as teachers of English in Spain. Similarly, previous cross-cultural experience abroad has been shown to facilitate sociocultural adaptation, suggesting that generic skills learned in overseas settings might be applied to new cultural contexts. This was demonstrated in a study by Parker and McEvoy (1993), which found that greater international experience tended to enhance adjustment and the ability to deal with a new cultural environment.

In line with these findings, research has found that sojourner adjustment tends to increase with length of residence (Masgoret *et al.*, 2000; Ward & Kennedy, 1992, 1994). In a study by Ward and Kennedy (1996) that examined Malaysian and Singaporean students in New Zealand, sociocultural adaptation was found to increase markedly between one and six months of residence in the country and then improved only slightly over the next six-month period. Similar results were reported in a study of Japanese students in which sociocultural adaptation improved significantly over a four-month period in New Zealand, but no further significant increments in sociocultural adaptation occurred at six or twelve months (Ward, Okura, Kennedy & Kojima, 1998). Consistent with a skills acquisition model of cross-cultural adaptation, these studies demonstrate a "learning curve" pattern in which sociocultural adaptation increases steadily over the first four to six months, and then tends to level off nearing the end of the first year.

5.4.1.1 Intercultural contact

Beyond previous cultural experiences, one of the most reliable means for sojourners and immigrants to acquire, improve, and eventually master their intercultural expertise in a new cultural milieu is through their interactions with host nationals. Based on the culture learning approach, many studies have focused on the importance of effective communication skills and the ability to establish intercultural relationships as two key components influencing socio-cultural adaptation (Hammer, Gudykunst & Wiseman, 1978; Hannigan, 1990). Moreover, a number of researchers have considered positive interactions with members of the host community to be a necessary condition for sociocultural adaptation (Klineberg & Hull, 1979).

Research findings have converged to indicate that increased contact and satisfaction with that contact are associated with fewer sociocultural difficulties (Ward & Kennedy, 1993b; Ward & Searle, 1991). Even more specifically, close intercultural friendships can enhance social skills. This has been discussed by Bochner and his colleagues (Bochner, McLeod & Lin, 1977; Furnham & Bochner, 1982) who propose that culture learning is a direct function of the number of host culture friends that a sojourner possesses. Based on this view, studies have demonstrated that, on the whole, sojourners who have more extensive contact with host nationals and those who are satisfied with these relationships experience fewer sociocultural adaptation problems (Searle

& Ward, 1990). Despite these findings, studies have consistently shown that although sojourners expect and desire contact with host nationals, the level of contact tends to be relatively low and intercultural friendships infrequent (Bochner *et al.*, 1977; Furnham & Bochner, 1982; Ward & Masgoret, 2004).

Aside from these direct forms of intercultural contact, communication research has examined indirect channels, such as mass media usage and exposure (Kim, 1988). Early studies demonstrated the association of mass media usage and exposure with positive adaptation outcomes in immigrants (Ryu, 1976). Making use of various forms of mass communication, such as television (Graves, 1967), radio (DeFleur & Cho, 1957), newspapers and magazines (Richmond, 1967), and the internet, can assist in the culture learning process not only through providing foreign language exposure and practical day-to-day information, but also by providing knowledge about cultural norms and values for interpreting the cultural environment. Kim has demonstrated that the adaptive function of the media tends to be weaker than that of direct intercultural communication (Kim, 1977), and that it tends to occur during the initial phase of the adaptation process (Ryu, 1976).

5.4.1.2 Cultural distance

Cultural distance has been defined as the perceived similarities and differences between culture of origin and culture of contact. The culture learning approach suggests that cross-cultural transitions are less difficult when the contact cultures are similar. Furnham and Bochner's (1982) work with international students in the United Kingdom clearly demonstrated that social adaptation is a function of cultural distance. More specifically, students from the "far" group (Middle Eastern and Asian countries such as Egypt, Saudi Arabia, Indonesia and Japan) experienced more sociocultural difficulties than those from the "intermediate" group (Southern European and South American countries such as Italy, Spain, Venezuela and Brazil) and the "near" group (Northern European countries such as the Netherlands and Sweden). Data have also indicated that sedentary groups experience fewer sociocultural difficulties than sojourners (Ward & Kennedy, 1999).

This cultural distance effect has been shown repeatedly in research with sojourners, including international students (Searle & Ward, 1990) and business people (Dunbar, 1994). Through a series of studies, Ward and her colleagues have demonstrated that immigrants and sojourners who perceive more similarities between the host culture and their own generally experience higher levels of sociocultural adaptation (Ward, Bochner and Furnham, 2001). For example, a study examining sojourners in Singapore demonstrated that Malaysian and Chinese sojourners adapted more readily to life in Singapore than did Anglo-European ones. Similarly, Malaysian students in Singapore experienced less difficulty than Malaysian and Singaporean students in New Zealand (Ward & Kennedy, 1999). These findings converge with Furnham and Bochner's (1982) original work on cultural distance, suggesting that as cultural distance increases, individuals will tend to have more difficulty learning new culture-specific skills.

5.5   Culture learning and adaptation

This chapter has conceptualized culture learning as the process by which individuals engaged in intercultural contact progress towards sociocultural adaptation. Language learning and the acquisition of broader communication skills are at the heart of intercultural effectiveness. Language proficiency and communication competence underpin effective intercultural relations, and increased contact with members of the host culture reciprocally reinforces and improves communication skills. Language, communication and social interaction skills, along with a wider knowledge of norms and values, all contribute to sociocultural adaptation.

Cross-cultural adjustment, however, is not confined to sociocultural domains. As indicated in Figure 5.1, both psychological and sociocultural dimensions of adaptation are important outcomes of acculturation. Research has clearly demonstrated that the two components of cross-cultural adaptation are related. Across a range of studies involving diverse groups such as foreign students, diplomats, aid workers and business people, Ward and colleagues have consistently found a positive relationship (.20 to .62 with a median correlation of .32) between psychological and sociocultural adaptation (Ward & Kennedy, 1999). More recently, the inter-relationship between psychological and sociocultural outcomes of acculturation has been supported in the International Comparative Study of Ethnocultural Youth, a large and impressive international project involving over thirty ethno-cultural groups in thirteen countries (Berry, Phinney, Sam & Vedder, 2006).

Although the relationship between psychological and sociocultural adaptation has been consistently documented, its strength and magnitude vary. Evidence suggests that the association is stronger under conditions involving a greater level of social and cultural integration. For example, the relationship between psychological and sociocultural adaptation is stronger in acculturating individuals who are culturally similar, rather than dissimilar, to hosts; it is greater in sedentary groups, compared to groups involved in cross-cultural relocation; it increases over time; and it is stronger in those adopting integrationist and assimilationist strategies of acculturation, compared to the separated and the marginalized (Ward *et al.*,1998; Ward & Kennedy, 1996; Ward & Rana-Deuba, 1999).

5.6   Conclusions

This chapter has presented traditional and contemporary perspectives on culture learning theory and acculturation research. It has argued that cultural learning theory can provide a unifying meta-theoretical basis for current work on language learning and communication competence, and empirical work on the prediction of sociocultural adaptation. This permits the broader synthesis of work by linguists, communication theorists and psychologists. In addition, the principles of cultural learning theory form the foundation of intercultural training techniques and programs, which are discussed in detail in Chapter 30 of this *Handbook*.

Culture learning theory offers one of the three major theoretical perspectives on acculturation. Its emphasis on learning and behavioral outcomes provides a complementary approach to the prominence of affective factors in stress and coping approaches and the cognitive dimensions of social identification theories. Although cultural learning theory makes a valuable contribution to the study of acculturation in its own right, in conjunction with stress and coping and social identification theories, a more comprehensive understanding of acculturation can be achieved.

5.7 References

Argyle, M. (1969). *Social interaction*. London: Methuen.

(1975). *Bodily communication*. London: Methuen.

(1982). Intercultural communication. In S. Bochner (ed.), *Cultures in contact: studies in cross-cultural interaction* (pp. 61–79). Oxford: Pergamon.

Berry, J. W., Phinney, J. S., Sam, D. L. & Vedder, P. H. (2006). *Immigrant youth in cultural transition: acculturation, identity and adaptation across national contexts*. Mahwah, NJ: Lawrence Erlbaum Associates.

Bochner, S. (1972). Problems in culture learning. In S. Bochner & P. Wicks (eds.), *Overseas students in Australia* (pp. 65–81). Sydney: University of New South Wales Press.

(1982). The social psychology of cross-cultural relations. In S. Bochner (ed.), *Cultures in contact: studies in cross-cultural interaction* (pp. 5–44). Oxford: Pergamon.

Bochner, S., McLeod, B. M. & Lin, A. (1977). Friendship patterns of overseas students: a functional model. *International Journal of Psychology, 12*, 277–297.

Brein, M. & David, K. H. (1971). Intercultural communication and the adjustment of the sojourner. *Psychological Bulletin, 76*, 215–230.

Brislin, R. (1981). *Cross-cultural encounters*. New York: Pergamon.

Clément, R. (1980). Ethnicity, contact, and communicative competence in a second language. In R. Giles, W. P. Robinson & P. M. Smith (eds.), *Language: social psychological perspectives* (pp. 147–154). Oxford: Pergamon.

Clément, R. & Bourhis, R. (1996). Bilingualism and intergroup communication. *International Journal of Psycholinguistics, 12*, 171–191.

Clément, R., Dörnyei, Z. & Noels, K. (1994). Motivation, self-confidence, and group cohesion in the foreign language classroom. *Language Learning, 44*, 417–448.

Clément, R. & Kruidenier, B. G. (1985). Aptitude, attitude and motivation in second language proficiency: a test of Clement's model. *Journal of Language and Social Psychology, 4*, 21–37.

Clément, R., Noels, K. A. & Deneault, B. (2001). Interethnic contact, identity and psychological adjustment: the mediating and moderating roles of communication. *Journal of Social Issues, 57*, 559–579.

Collett, P. (1982). Meetings and misunderstandings. In S. Bochner (ed.), *Cultures in contact: studies in cross-cultural interactions* (pp. 81–98). Oxford: Pergamon.

DeFleur, M. L. & Cho, C. S. (1957). Assimilation of Japanese born women in an American city. *Social Problems, 4*, 244–257.

Dew, A.-M. & Ward, C. (1993). The effects of ethnicity and culturally congruent and incongruent nonverbal behaviors on interpersonal attraction. *Journal of Applied Social Psychology, 23*, 1376–1389.

Dunbar, E. (1994). The German executive in the U.S. work and social environment: exploring role demands. *International Journal of Intercultural Relations, 18*, 277–291.

Early, P. C. & Ang, S. (2003). *Cultural intelligence: individual interactions across cultures.* Stanford: Stanford University Press.

Friesen, W. V. (1972). Cultural differences in facial expressions in a social situation: an experimental test of the concept of display rules. Unpublished doctoral dissertation: University of California, San Diego.

Furnham, A. & Bochner, S. (1982). Social difficulty in a foreign culture: an empirical analysis of culture shock. In S. Bochner (ed.), *Cultures in contact: studies in cross-cultural interactions* (pp. 161–198). Oxford: Pergamon.

(1986). *Culture shock: psychological reactions to unfamiliar environments.* London: Methuen.

Gallois, C., Franklyn-Stokes, A., Giles, H. & Coupland, N. (1988). Communication accommodation theory and intercultural encounters: intergroup and interpersonal considerations. In Y. Y. Kim & W. B. Gudykunst (eds.), *International and intercultural communication annual*, Vol. XII: *Theories in intercultural communication* (pp. 157–185). Newbury Park, CA: Sage Publications.

Gardner, R. C. (1985). *Social psychology and second language learning: the role of attitudes and motivation.* London: Edward Arnold.

(2000). Correlation, causation, motivation, and second language acquisition. *Canadian Psychology, 41*, 10–24.

Gardner, R. C. & Clément, R. (1990). Social psychological perspectives on second language acquisition. In H. Giles & W. P. Robinson (eds.), *Handbook of language and social psychology* (pp. 495–515). London: John Wiley & Sons Ltd.

Graves, T. D. (1967). Acculturation, access, and alcohol in a tri-ethnic community. *American Anthropologist, 69*, 306–321.

Gudykunst, W. B. (1993). Toward a theory of effective interpersonal and intergroup communication. In R. Wiseman & J. Koester (eds.), *Intercultural communication competence* (pp. 33–71). Newbury Park, CA: Sage Publications.

Gudykunst, W. B. & Kim, Y. Y. (1984). *Communicating with strangers: an approach to intercultural communication.* New York: Random House.

Gullahorn, J. E. & Gullahorn, J. T. (1966). American students abroad: professional vs. personal development. *Annals, 368*, 43–59.

Hammer, M., Gudykunst, W. B. & Wiseman, R. L. (1978). Dimensions of intercultural effectiveness: an exploratory study. *International Journal of Intercultural Relations, 2*, 382–393.

Hannigan, T. (1990). Traits, attitudes, and skills that are related to intercultural effectiveness and their implications for cross-cultural training: a review of the literature. *International Journal of Intercultural Relations, 14*, 89–111.

Hawes, F. & Kealey, D. (1980). *Canadians in development*. Ottawa: Canadian International Development Agency.

Hofstede, G. (1980). *Culture's consequences: international differences in work-related values*. Beverly Hills, CA: Sage Publications.

Kealey, D. J. (1989). A study of cross-cultural effectiveness: theoretical issues and practical applications. *International Journal of Intercultural Relations, 13*, 387–428.

Kim, Y. Y. (1977). Communication patterns of foreign immigrants in the process of acculturation. *Human Communication Research, 4(1)*, 66–77.

(1988). *Communication and cross-cultural adaptation*. Clevedon: Multilingual Matters Ltd.

(1991). Intercultural communication competence: a systems-theoretic view. In S. Ting-Toomey & F. Korzenny (eds.), *Cross-cultural interpersonal communication* (pp. 259–275). Newbury Park, CA: Sage Publications.

Klineberg, O. & Hull, W. F. (1979). *At a foreign university: an international study of adaptation and coping*. New York: Praeger.

Kurman, J. & Ronen-Eilon, C. (2004) Lack of knowledge of a culture's social axioms and adaptation difficulties among immigrants. *Journal of Cross-Cultural Psychology, 35*, 192–208.

Lebra, T. S. (1987). The cultural significance of silence in Japanese communication. *Multilingua, 6*, 343–357.

Leung, K., Bond, M. H., Carrasquel, S. R., *et al.* (2002). Social axioms: the search for universal dimensions of general beliefs about how the world functions. *Journal of Cross-Cultural Psychology, 33(3)*, 286–302.

Levine, R. & Bartlett, K. (1984). Pace of life, punctuality and coronary heart disease in six countries. *Journal of Cross-Cultural Psychology, 15*, 233–255.

MacIntyre, P. D., Dörnyei, Z., Clément, R. & Noels, K. A. (1998). Conceptualizing willingness to communicate in L2: a situational model of L2 confidence and affiliation. *Modern Language Journal, 82(4)*, 545–562.

McGinley, H., Blau, G. L. & Takai, M. (1984). Attraction effects of smiling and body position. *Perceptual and Motor Skills, 58*, 915–922.

Masgoret, A.-M. (2002). Investigating cross-cultural adjustment, and the influence of foreign language instructors on second language achievement. Unpublished doctoral thesis: The University of Western Ontario.

Masgoret, A.-M., Bernaus, M. & Gardner, R. C. (2000). A study of cross-cultural adaptation by English-speaking sojourners in Spain. *Foreign Language Annals, 33*, 548–558.

Masgoret, A.-M. & Gardner, R. C. (1999). A causal model of Spanish immigrant adaptation in Canada. *Journal of Multilingual and Multicultural Development, 1*, 216–236.

(2003). Attitudes, motivation, and second language learning: A meta-analysis of studies conducted by Gardner and associates. *Language Learning, 53(1),* 167–211.

Matsumoto, D. (1994). *People: psychology from a cultural perspective.* Pacific Grove, CA: Brookes/Cole.

Metge, J. & Kinloch, P. (1978). *Talking past each other.* Wellington, New Zealand: Victoria University Press.

Ones, D. S. & Viswesvaran, C. (1997). Personality determinants in the prediction of aspects of expatriate job success. In Z. Aycan (ed.), *New approaches to employee management,* Vol. IV: *Expatriate management: theory and research* (pp. 63–92). Greenwich, CT: JAI Press.

Parker, B. & McEvoy, G. M. (1993). Initial examination of a model of intercultural adjustment. *International Journal of Intercultural Relations, 17,* 355–379.

Richmond, A. H. (1967). *Post-war immigration in Canada.* Toronto: University of Toronto Press.

Ryu, J. S. (1976). Neo-socialisation function of the mass media working among foreign students. Paper presented at the annual meeting of Mass Communication Association, San Francisco, CA.

Schwartz, S. H. (1994). Are there universal aspects in the structure and content of human values? *Journal of Cross-Cultural Psychology, 33,* 286–302.

Schwartz, S. H., Melech, G., Lehmann, A., Burgess, S. & Harris, M. (2001). Extending the cross-cultural validity of the theory of basic human values with a different method of measurement. *Journal of Cross-Cultural Psychology, 32,* 519–542.

Searle, W. & Ward, C. (1990). The prediction of psychological and sociocultural adjustment during cross-cultural transitions. *International Journal of Intercultural Relations, 14,* 449–464.

Smart, D. F., Volet, S. & Ang, G. (2000). *Fostering social cohesion in universities: bridging the cultural divide.* Canberra: Australian Education International Department of Education, Training and Youth Affairs.

Spitzberg, B. H. (1988). Communication competence: measures of perceived effectiveness. In C. H. Tardy (ed.), *A handbook for the study of human communication* (pp. 67–106). Norwood, NJ: Ablex.

Takai, J. (1989). The adjustment of international students at a third culture-like academic community in Japan: a longitudinal study. *Human Communication Studies, 17,* 113–120.

Ting-Toomey, S. (2004). Translating conflict face-negotiation theory into practice. In D. Landis, J. M. Bennett & M. J. Bennett (eds.), *Handbook of intercultural training.* 3rd edn. (pp. 219–248). Thousand Oaks, CA: Sage Publications.

Triandis, H. C. (1989). The self and social behaviour in differing cultural contexts. *Psychological Review, 96,* 506–520.

Ward, C. (1996). Acculturation. In D. Landis & R. Bhagat (eds.), *Handbook of Intercultural Training.* 2nd edn. (pp. 124–147). Thousand Oaks, CA: Sage Publications.

(2001). The ABCs of acculturation. In D. Matsumoto (ed.), *Handbook of culture and psychology* (pp. 411–445). New York: Oxford University Press.

(2004). Psychological theories of culture contact and their implications for intercultural training. In D. Landis, J. Bennett & M. Bennett (eds.), *Handbook of intercultural training*. 3rd edn. (pp. 185–216). Thousand Oaks, CA: Sage Publications.

Ward, C., Berno, T. & Main, A. (2002). Can the Cross-cultural Adaptability Inventory (CCAI) predict sojourner adjustment? In P. Boski, F. J. Main, P. Van de Vijver & A. M. Chodynicka (eds.), *New directions in cross-cultural psychology*. Warsaw: Polish Academy of Sciences Publishers.

Ward, C., Bochner, S. & Furnham, A. (2001). *The psychology of culture shock*. Sussex: Routledge.

Ward, C. & Kennedy, A. (1992). Locus of control, mood disturbance, and social difficulty during cross-cultural transitions. *International Journal of Intercultural Relations, 16*, 175–194.

(1993a). Psychological and socio-cultural adjustment during cross-cultural transitions: a comparison of secondary students at home and abroad. *International Journal of Psychology, 28*, 129–147.

(1993b). Where's the culture in cross-cultural transition? Comparative studies of sojourner adjustment. *Journal of Cross-Cultural Psychology, 24*, 221–249.

(1994). Acculturation strategies, psychological adjustment, and sociocultural competence during cross-cultural transitions. *International Journal of Intercultural Relations, 18*, 329–342.

(1996). Crossing cultures: the relationship between psychological and sociocultural dimensions of cross-cultural adjustment. In J. Pandey, D. Sinha & D. P. S. Bhawuk (eds.), *Asian contributions to cross-cultural psychology* (pp. 289–306). New Delhi: Sage Publications.

(1999). The measurement of sociocultural adaptation. *International Journal of Intercultural Relations, 56*, 1–19.

Ward, C., Leong, C.-H. & Low, M. (2004). Personality and sojourner adjustment: an exploration of the Big Five and the Cultural Fit proposition. *Journal of Cross-Cultural Psychology, 35*, 137–151.

Ward, C. & Masgoret A.-M. (June 2004). *The experiences of international students in New Zealand: report on the results of the National Survey*. New Zealand: International Policy and Development Unit, Ministry of Education.

Ward. C., Okura, Y., Kennedy, A. & Kojima, T. (1998). The U-curve on trial: a longitudinal study of psychological and sociocultural adjustment during cross-cultural transition. *International Journal of Intercultural Relations, 22*, 277–291.

Ward, C. & Rana-Deuba, A. (1999). Acculturation and adaptation revisited. *Journal of Cross-Cultural Psychology, 30*, 372–392.

Ward, C. & Searle, W. (1991). The impact of value discrepancies and cultural identity on psychological and socio-cultural adjustment of sojourners. *International Journal of Intercultural Relations, 15*, 209–225.

6 Ethnic identity and acculturation

Karmela Liebkind

6.1 Introduction

There is no widely agreed definition of ethnic identity: empirical research on this topic is characterized by the absence of a consistent and systematic approach. As the concept of the person varies cross-culturally, even the very concept of identity as we know it may be meaningless in some cultures (Jasinskaja-Lahti & Liebkind, 1998; Liebkind, 1992; Phinney, 1990; Verkuyten, 2000). However, almost all definitions of ethnic identity link ethnicity to origin and culture, although in different ways. The meaning of "ethnicity" stems from its real or imagined common descent and shared culture. History and culture are the two main ingredients of ethnicity. History has relevance for understanding issues of ethnic minority identity and inter-ethnic relations. Collective representations of the past are not only shaped by the present but also influence present conditions, perceptions and behavior (Verkuyten, 2000). Broadly, then, "ethnic identity" refers to an individual's sense of self in terms of membership in a particular ethnic group (Liebkind, 1992, 2001; Phinney, 1990; Phinney, Horenczyk, Liebkind & Vedder, 2001). Although the term is sometimes used to refer simply to one's self-label or group affiliation, ethnic identity is generally seen as embracing various aspects, including self-identification, feelings of belongingness and commitment to a group, a sense of shared values, and attitudes towards one's own ethnic group.

This chapter will first outline the ethnic and cultural dimensions of ethnic identity. Next, changes in ethnic identity during acculturation will be described and related to various theories of acculturation. Questions of the most adaptive forms of ethnic and national identity during acculturation will be raised in the subsequent section, which also deals with the importance of the particular social context where acculturation takes place. Finally, some common pitfalls in the research of ethnic identity in acculturation will be addressed and theoretical improvements suggested.

6.2 The ethnic and cultural dimensions of ethnic identity

As a term, "ethnicity" has its roots primarily in anthropology and ethnology, but the concept of ethnicity is defined in many different ways across disciplines (e.g. Hutchinson & Smith, 1996; Phinney *et al.*, 2001). Ethnicity is primarily a sense of belonging to a particular (assumed) ancestry and origin (e.g. Cornell & Hartmann, 1998; DeVos, 1995; Roosens, 1994). An ethnic group is thought to exist whenever the belief in common descent is used to bind people together to some degree. This sense of origin is often accomplished by defining ethnicity in terms of metaphors of kinship: ethnicity is family writ large (Verkuyten, 2000).

This conceptualization is not without implications. For one thing, we should be careful not to overstate the extent to which ethnic identities should be examined as being transient, flexible and voluntary and thus amenable to change in the acculturation process. Ethnicity can be manipulated, although not situationally created out of nothing. While there is a need to link ethnic identity to context and to avoid problems of reification and essentialism, this must not lead to a neglect of more enduring identities with long-term commitment and connections to, for example, former and future generations. For many ethnic minorities, continuities with, and obligations towards, former and future generations have important self-defining meanings (Verkuyten, 1997, 1999, 2000; Verkuyten, Drabbles & van den Nieuwenhuijzen, 1999). In addition, studies have shown that questions of acceptance by one's own ethnic minority group and ingroup hassles may be even more stressful and problematic for ethnic minority members than negative reactions of the majority group (Lay & Nguyen, 1998; Verkuyten, 2000).

A person's ethnicity is thus ascribed in the sense that one cannot choose the ethnic group into which one is born, but it is achieved to the extent that the meaning it acquires for one's total identity is a matter of choice. The ascribed aspect of ethnicity can be played down to the extent that ethnic identity is made equal to other social identities. However, transmitted as it is in primary socialization, ethnicity can be a most pervasive part of identity. Ideas and beliefs of past ancestry may play a crucial role in the ethnic part of one's identity. Given that gender is deeply implicated in the complex of social processes and institutions devoted to ancestry, sexual coupling, procreation and care of progeny, also one's gender role may be given particularistic meanings by one's ethnicity (Liebkind, 1992).

Studying ethnic identity inevitably raises all kinds of cultural questions, related, for example, to the way culture is implicated in ethnicity, acculturation, group relations and many other psychological processes. It is not possible in this chapter to address all the difficulties in conceptualizing "culture." However, one central problem connected with the concept of "culture" has to be discussed: since social classes, because of social segregation, differ from one another in relation to leisure time, mobility, marriage patterns and way of life, these also develop over time into cultural collectives of a kind. Often ethnic groups and nationalities have laid the foundation for society's other layers, either in that some group has placed itself as conqueror above others, or in that some groups, either as later arrivals or as the vanquished, have been left in society's bottom layers. In later historical development the destinies of different cultural groups differ greatly from each other. Cultural differences are thus tied to historical experiences, some of which are based on socio-economic stratification of a relatively recent nature, while others are rooted in a distant past of which nobody is conscious. This historically older cultural influence is sometimes called "deep culture," as it is embedded in language, ethnicity, religion and/or nationality as such (Liebkind, 1992).

What can be said, therefore, is only that most members of an ethnic group usually identify themselves with a group, they have – or they think they have – a common ancestry, and they display some distinctive cultural patterns. However, on the individual level self-conscious ethnic identity does not in itself imply cultural distinctiveness, as culture may be in continual transformation and ethnic minorities do not live as closed cultural entities. Elements of culture may be transformed or filled with new meaning and take on a new significance in the acculturation process which follows contact with other ethnic/cultural groups (Liebkind, 1992). Sometimes cultural features may explain the finding of strong group identification and positive ingroup evaluation among many ethnic minority groups: groups may differ in the emphasis placed on ethnicity. A sense of enduring group membership may be related to cultural features such as a strong collectivist value orientation in which "ingroup centrism" predominates (Verkuyten, 2000).

6.3   Ethnic identity and acculturation

Changes in self-identification during acculturation involve issues similar to those used to identify acculturation attitudes, such as whether or not to adopt the host country label and whether or not to retain the ethnic label (Berry & Sam, 1997; Phinney, 2003; Phinney et al., 2001). Empirically, ethnic identity has been defined in many different ways. It has been treated as the ethnic component of social identity, as ethnic self-identification, as feelings of belongingness and commitment, as a sense of shared values and attitudes, or as attitudes towards one's own group (Liebkind, 2001). Mere ethnic/cultural self-identification or categorization fails to tell us what attitudes the individual holds towards his or her heritage culture or how much he or she actually identifies with the self-applied category. Yet the strength and nature of actual identification with the ingroup will determine much of the individual's response to acculturation.

For first-generation immigrants, change of self-label is unlikely, but for second and subsequent immigrant generations the use of a compound or bicultural label becomes more common (Phinney, 2003). However, some degree of ethnic identification may be retained in several later generations. One reason for this may lie in other-ascribed labels: members of visible minorities are likely to be ethnically labeled by others, if not by themselves, regardless of their degree of acculturation. Another reason is that, although the strength and positive valence of ethnic identity may decline from the first to the second generation, the decline is much slower in later generations. Generation is not, however, the strongest predictor of ethnic identity. With generation controlled, ethnic identity change is strongly related to retention of ethnic cultural involvement and largely independent of orientation towards the dominant culture (Phinney, 2003). The strength of ingroup identification should not, however, be confused with cultural orientation in terms of endorsement of heritage culture and/or adoption of host culture. In many studies on acculturation, cultural identity is simply equated with the degree of cultural heritage maintenance. However, one may identify strongly with one's cultural ingroup and also have a positive attitude towards maintenance of one's heritage culture, yet fail to endorse that culture oneself (Liebkind, 1996, 2001; Phinney, 1990).

Ethnic identity is a salient part of the acculturation process. There are two main perspectives among the numerous theories of acculturation (for a review, see Liebkind, 2001). One emphasizes a linear process of assimilation, and the other emphasizes cultural plurality (Berry, 1997; Nguyen, Messé & Stollak, 1999; Sayegh & Lasry, 1993). The former posits a unidirectional change towards the mainstream society and implies an eventual disappearance of the original ethnic/cultural identity (Laroche, Kim, Hui & Tomiuk, 1998; Nguyen et al., 1999; Sayegh & Lasry, 1993). In contrast, the latter model is two-dimensional in the sense that it recognizes that ethnic groups and their members preserve, albeit in varying degrees, their heritage cultures while adapting to the mainstream society. Compared to ethnic identity, however, there has been far less attention paid to conceptualizing and studying immigrants' identification with the new society. Some researchers have focused simply on the labels used. However, like ethnic identity, national identity is a more complex construct than is conveyed by a label; it involves feelings of belonging to, and attitudes towards, the larger society (Phinney & Devich-Navarro, 1997; Phinney et al., 2001).

Recent research on acculturation has witnessed a shift from unidimensional conceptualizations of acculturation to bidimensional ones that assume two independent acculturation dimensions (Snauwaert, Soenens, Vanbeselaere & Boen, 2003). Berry (1997) suggests the following two questions as a means of identifying strategies used by immigrants in dealing with acculturation: is it considered to be of value to maintain one's cultural heritage? Is it considered to be of value to have contact with and participate in the larger society? Four acculturation strategies – integration, assimilation, separation and marginalization – can be derived from "yes" or "no" answers to these two questions. Integration is defined by positive answers to both questions, and marginalization by negative answers to both. A positive response to the first and negative to the second defines separation, and the reverse defines assimilation. This model allows for multiculturalism, which asserts that different cultures may coexist in a society (Phinney *et al.*, 2001).

However, it seems that the relationship between the constructs of acculturation and ethnic/cultural identity is both unexplored and ambiguous, and often the two concepts are used almost interchangeably (Liebkind, 2001; Nguyen *et al.*, 1999). A central question is whether ethnic identity is directly related to the degree of acculturation or whether, conversely, it is independent (Phinney *et al.*, 2001). Although Hutnik's (1986, 1991) own studies suggest that ethnic identity and acculturation are independent constructs, Snauwaert and his colleagues (2003) describe the former's bidimensional identification model as an "acculturation model" and compare it both conceptually and empirically with two other bidimensional acculturation models. Hutnik herself found no correlation between ethnic identification patterns (Indian and/or British) on the one hand and cultural attitudes and behavior on the other, among young Asians in Britain. She described four strategies of self-categorization that are determined by the degree to which individuals define themselves within the bounds of the minority and the majority group. The individual who identifies with both the majority and the minority group is acculturative. The assimilative individual concentrates on the majority group aspect of her or his identity, the dissociative individual defines herself or himself entirely within the bounds of the ethnic minority group, and the marginal individual identifies with neither group (Hutnik, 1986, 1991). A similar model, built in analogy with the acculturation model of Berry (1997), has been developed by Phinney and her colleagues (2001). In this model, an integrated or bicultural identity corresponds to Hutnik's acculturative identity, a separated identity to Hutnik's dissociative identity, and the assimilated and marginalized identities have the same labels in both models (Phinney *et al.*, 2001). Research generally supports a bidimensional model of ethnic and national identity among immigrants, but this relationship varies across immigrating groups (Hutnik, 1991; Phinney, Cantu & Kurtz, 1997) and across national settings (Phinney *et al.*, 2001).

Snauwaert and his colleagues (2003) labeled Hutnik's (1986, 1991) original model the *identification conceptualization* of acculturation. In contrast, they labeled the bidimensional acculturation model developed by Berry (1990, 1997) the *contact conceptualization* of acculturation, as it is based on a combination of the attitude towards maintenance of the ingroup culture and the attitude towards contact with the autochthonous group. The third model, proposed by Bourhis and his colleagues (Bourhis, Moïse, Perreault & Sénécal, 1997) was labeled the *adoption conceptualization*, because it replaces the issue of contact and participation by the issue of culture adoption (Snauwaert *et al.*, 2003). Bourhis and his colleagues (1997) substituted the dimension of contact and participation in Berry's (1997) model with a dimension pertaining to host culture adoption: "Is it considered to be of value to adopt the culture of the host community?" (Bourhis *et al.*, 1997:378).

Although Snauwaert and his colleagues (2003) falsely categorize Hutnik's (1986, 1991) model as an acculturation model, they rightly criticize research in this area for overlooking important conceptual differences between these three models. In their study on Moroccans and Turks in Belgium they followed the suggestions of Liebkind (2001) and compared the three models empirically. In accordance with their hypotheses, Snauwaert and his colleagues (2003) found that ethnic minority members were less inclined to identify with the host population than to adopt the culture of the host society or have regular contacts with its members. In addition, their respondents found it more important to have contacts with Belgians than to adopt parts of Belgian culture, and they attached more importance to adopting parts of Belgian culture than they self-categorized as Belgians. The three conceptualizations yielded substantially different distributions of the participants over the acculturation orientations as a function of the contact, adoption and identification conceptualizations. For example, when the contact conceptualization was used, 82% of the participants favored integration and 10% favored separation. With the adoption conceptualization, 37% of the participants were classified as integrationists and 56% as separationists, and with the ethnic identification conceptualization, only 10% of the respondents were classified as acculturative and 80% as dissociative (Snauwaert et al., 2003).

These results have important implications. First, they illustrate that a strong attachment to one's own minority culture is not necessarily incompatible with a contact integration orientation. Of the integrationists according to the contact conceptualization, 80% exhibited a dissociative ethnic identity: lack of identification with the majority does not imply a rejection of intercultural contacts. Even those who were separationists according to the adoption conceptualization of Bourhis and his colleagues (1997) found it important to have contacts with members of the host society. Second, the results emphasize the relative robustness of ethnic identity. An acculturative ethnic identity – and to some extent also an adoption of integration orientation – seem to be psychologically more demanding than the contact integration acculturation orientation (Snauwaert et al., 2003). As a consequence, acculturation should be conceptualized as a broader construct than ethnic identity, encompassing a wide range of behaviors, attitudes and values that change with contact between cultures. In contrast, ethnic identity is that aspect of acculturation that focuses on the subjective sense of belonging to a group or culture (Phinney, 1990; Phinney et al., 2001).

Finally, the findings of Snauwaert and his colleagues (2003) not only have theoretical implications but also are important for the public discourse on multiculturalism. The multiple conceptualizations of acculturation orientations may complicate clear communication on, for example, integration or separation. Jasinskaja-Lahti and her colleagues (Jasinskaja-Lahti, Liebkind, Horenczyk & Schmitz, 2003) found in their comparison between the acculturation attitudes of hosts and repatriates in four countries that both immigrants and hosts expressed the normative orientation towards integration as their first preference. Yet there was a mismatch between the attitudes of immigrants and the hosts when their second choices were acknowledged. The rhetoric of integration may not have the same meaning for these two groups; given that integration involves both the maintenance and the relinquishment of the culture of origin, hosts and migrants may disagree on the preferred degree of weakening of the newcomer's previous identity (Horenczyk, 1996).

In sum, then, ethnic minority members may acculturate to some degree, i.e. acquire a certain level of competence in the ways of the dominant culture, yet they possess the freedom to maintain, explore, rediscover or reject their ethnic identity. Oftentimes, ethnic identity will be the last to change (Liebkind, 2001).

6.4   Ethnic identity, adaptation and the importance of social context

The literature has generally shown that integration is the most adaptive mode of acculturation and the most conducive to the immigrants' wellbeing as compared to other acculturation options (Berry, 1997; Berry & Sam, 1997; Phinney et al., 2001; Ward, 1996). Marginalization is the least beneficial strategy for adaptation, while assimilation and separation are intermediate. This pattern has been found in virtually every study, and is present for all types of acculturating groups (Berry, 1997). The host national group seems to provide the avenue for the acquisition of culturally appropriate skills in that host national contacts are indispensable for culture learning. In contrast, the co-national group forms the important social support network, as it is satisfaction with these relations that underpins psychological adjustment (Ward & Kennedy, 1993).

Similarly, with regard to identity, positive psychological outcomes for immigrants tend to be related to a strong identification with both their ethnic group and the larger society. LaFromboise, Coleman and Gerton (1993) suggest that a bicultural identity is the most adaptive, although the meaning of being bicultural is interpreted differently across studies. However, when the contributions of each type of identity (ethnic and larger society) are included as separate variables in analyses of wellbeing, the results vary (Phinney et al., 2001). Research with Mexican American adolescents in the United States (Phinney & Devich-Navarro, 1997) showed that ethnic identity, but not American identity, was a predictor of self-esteem. Generally, research provides support for the view that a strong, secure ethnic identity makes a positive contribution to psychological wellbeing (Liebkind, 1996; Nesdale, Rooney & Smith, 1997; Phinney et al., 1997, 2001).

However, the interactional model of acculturation proposed by Phinney and her colleagues (2001) suggests that the relationship between ethnic identity and adaptation will be influenced by the particular settings and by the minority members' perceptions of their place in those settings. The relationship between identity and adaptation is likely to be moderated by a number of additional factors. Several researchers (Berry, 1997; Horenczyk, 1997; Jasinskaja-Lahti *et al.*, 2003; Phinney, 1990; Phinney *et al.*, 2001) have emphasized the importance of contextual influences on the relationship between acculturation orientations and adaptation. Although there is evidence that the bicultural option (or integration) may be the most satisfactory and the marginal the least, the other two possibilities (only ethnic identification or only mainstream, i.e. assimilation) may also provide the basis for a good self-concept, if the person is comfortable with these alternatives and is in an environment that supports them (Phinney, 1990).

The assertion that identity is the product of the interaction of the individual with influences in the physical and social world is not new (Liebkind, 1992). For example, Breakwell (1986) describes the social context of identity as structurally comprised of interpersonal networks, group memberships and inter-group relationships. Each individual is located within the matrix of these relationships, and each of them provides roles for the individual to adopt. Also the salience of ethnic or cultural identity varies as a function of situational factors (Liebkind, 2001). LaFromboise and her colleagues (1993) proposed an *alternation model* of second culture acquisition which, like other bidimensional models, assumes that it is possible for an individual to have a sense of belongingness in two cultures without compromising his or her sense of cultural identity. Building on situated identity theory, Clément and Noels (1992) have proposed a similar model, where ethnolinguistic identity is viewed as dynamic and situationally dependent, and the ability to develop and maintain competence in both cultures and to shift between them as required by contextual demands as crucial for psychological wellbeing. It has been found that feelings of ethnic group belonging vary among Francophones and Anglophones in Canada across a variety of relevant situations (Clément & Noels, 1992) and that Chinese students in Canada feel either Chinese or Canadian – but not both simultaneously – in most situations (Noels, Pon & Clément, 1996). Focusing on a performative mode of social identity and emphasizing its dynamic nature in communication, Carbaugh (1996) claims that people enact different social identities depending not only on the intrinsic salience of these identities, but also on where the individual is, with whom he or she is, and what he or she can ably do in that particular situation.

With regards to immigrants, Phinney and her colleagues (2001) have stressed that the ethnic and national identities of immigrants and their role in adaptation can best be understood in terms of an interaction between the attitudes and characteristics of the immigrants and the responses of the receiving society, moderated by the particular circumstances of the immigrant group and the immigrant policies of the new society. For example, Nguyen and her colleagues (1999) found in their study that only the US cultural dimension was related to better outcomes for the different indices of adjustment used. The results obtained by Sánchez and Fernández (1993) point in the same direction. Nguyen and her colleagues (1999) conclude, however, that for their Vietnamese respondents who lived in a predominantly Anglo-American community with only 703 Vietnamese inhabitants, it is not ethnic involvement as such which is maladaptive but the discrepancy between the individual's skills and the demands of his or her context.

However, evidence for links between policies and ethnic identity is generally weak. Some studies show that the decisive factors for identity formation and psychological adaptation are not national policies, but more local circumstances (for example, dispersal versus high local concentration of a particular group), personal relationships (family, peers) and activity settings such as school and neighborhood (Crul, 2000; Gold, 1992; Keaton, 1999; Phinney et al., 2001). These local situations may be independent of the official national immigrant policies (Oriol, 1989). Verkuyten (2000) has found that the notion of "context" is ill defined across many psychological paradigms. For example, "context" may be taken to refer only to the particular task or activity people are engaged in, such as the comparative context in eliciting group evaluations or the public or private expression of these evaluations (e.g. Ellemers, Barreto & Spears, 1999). In other studies, the notion of "context" may be used for historical or cultural circumstances (e.g. Rosenthal & Feldman, 1992), and actual social situations, such as in schools, neighborhoods and workplaces (e.g. Ethier & Deaux, 1994).

These different notions of "context" may account for inconsistent empirical findings. For example, for ethnic minorities actual local conditions may be more important than national policies because of the differential experiences with racism, stereotyping and discrimination, and the opportunities for friendship and social support (Verkuyten, 2000). In most studies, ethnic minority groups are considered to have low status and lack of power. This may be an adequate assessment on the level of society and in many other contexts. However, local situations may differ. Relationships in the wider society do interfere in local situations but cannot be applied self-evidently to, for example, the lives of people in many urban quarters (e.g. Back, 1996; Mac an Ghaill, 1999). In these situations status and power differences are actively defined and challenged, making a simple majority–minority model inadequate for understanding identities and group relations (Verkuyten, 2000).

Ethnic identity is a dynamic construct that evolves and changes in response to contextual factors. The implication is that, although ethnic and national identities may be theoretically independent, the relationship between them varies empirically. Some contexts support the possibility of integration and make it easier to develop a bicultural identity, while others make this resolution difficult. Yet others may foster separation rather than integration. Ethnic identity is likely to be strong when immigrants have a strong desire to retain their identities and when pluralism is encouraged or accepted. When there is pressure towards assimilation and groups feel accepted, the national identity is likely to be strong. In the face of real or perceived hostility towards immigrants or towards particular groups, some immigrants may downplay or reject their own ethnic identity; others may assert their pride in their cultural group and emphasize solidarity as a way of dealing with negative attitudes. The relationship of these identities to adaptation will likewise be influenced by the interaction of characteristics of specific immigrant groups with those of particular settings (Phinney *et al.*, 2001).

One problem with theories of and empirical studies on ethnic identity is that they generally assume ethnic identity to derive from membership in one group only (Liebkind, 2001). The implicit assumption behind many approaches is that ethnic minorities define their identity in relation to the dominant majority group, which is implicitly assumed to be the only really significant other. However, ethnic minority identity is dependent on a diversity of comparisons that are being made and their relation to each other. In multiethnic societies there is a variety of groups in relation to whom people define their ethnic identity (e.g. Hagendoorn, 1995; Verkuyten, 2000). The human environment encompasses, for each individual, quite a large number of social categories, i.e. identity groups. As a consequence, the number of categories generating social identities is enormous. The greater the number of membership groups, the greater the likelihood of the occurrence of conflict, ambiguity or other strains between them, but also the greater the possibility of alternative sources of positive identity (Liebkind, 1992).

As a consequence, a single ethnic label may be inaccurate. Ethnic minority members typically face multiple group allegiances and may define themselves as only partly ethnic and partly mainstream (Jasinskaja-Lahti & Liebkind, 1998; Liebkind, 1992). However, some allegiances are clearly more important to us than others. The individual's identification of the self with some category (for example immigrant or Black) may loom so large in his or her consciousness that all else pales by comparison. Occasionally, some specific social identity may function nearly to the exclusion of all other identity dimensions. The various elements of self are arranged in a hierarchy of salience, some being in the center of the individual's concerns, others being more peripheral. Although the immediate salience of identity elements may vary from one situation to another, the basic hierarchy between them changes more slowly (Liebkind, 1992).

6.5   Ethnic minority identity is more than a negative social identity

In a number of studies, ethnic identity is treated as being similar to any other social identity and defined simply as the ethnic component of social identity (Liebkind, 2001). Social identity theory (SIT: Tajfel, 1974, 1978, 1981, 1982) holds that people's self-image has two components, personal identity and social identity. SIT proposes that the social part of our identity derives from the groups to which we belong, it is simply "that part of an individual's self-concept that derives from his knowledge of his membership of a social group (or groups) together with the value and emotional significance attached to that membership" (Tajfel, 1981:255).

Tajfel (1978) distinguished between numerical and psychological minorities, and defined the latter as a group that feels bound together by common traits that are held in low regard (Verkuyten, 2000). Although this definition makes it possible to see, for example, the Black South Africans as a minority, it strengthens the connection between the concept of minority and psychological states of uncertainty (Liebkind, 1992). Tajfel (1978, 1981) focused on the status and power differential between the majority and the minority group and addressed the question of the psychological effects of minority membership with respect to the threat to social identity that a minority position implies. He described how, depending on the perceived legitimacy and stability of the social system, individuals can accept or reject a negative social identity, and how minority groups may alter the valuation of their group by creativity or social competition (Tajfel & Turner, 1986). One reaction is simply to leave the group (Liebkind, 2001). There are many examples of members of "inferior" groups distancing themselves physically or psychologically from their group (Brown, 2001).

Such an individualistic strategy of social mobility may not always be possible, especially if the group boundaries are relatively fixed and impermeable. In cases like this, SIT suggests that a number of other avenues may be pursued. One is to limit the comparisons made to other similar or subordinate groups, another is to sidestep the main dimensions of comparison and either invent new dimensions or change the value of existing dimensions. These ways are expressions of social creativity (Liebkind, 2001). Yet another route is to confront directly the dominant group's superiority by agitating for social and economic change (Brown, 2001). Which of these tactics will be chosen depends on the prevailing social climate. If it is such that no real alternatives to the status quo may be conceived, subordinate groups are unlikely to challenge the existing order openly and attempt social change. A key factor in generating social unrest among subordinate groups is a sense of relative deprivation, either in relation to their own group in the past or, more often, in relation to the dominant group (Brown, 2001).

Following this conceptualization, many social psychological studies have investigated ethnic minority identity primarily as an example of the more general effect of status differences between groups (Verkuyten, 2000). That is, the "minority" aspect of ethnic minorities is considered central. Being a member of a minority group is supposed to pose a threat to one's self-concept. Ethnic minority group members are thought to counteract the threat by accentuating positive distinctiveness. In the Netherlands, for example, many studies (e.g. Kinket & Verkuyten, 1997, 1999; Verkuyten, 1995, 2000) have shown that ethnic identity is psychologically more salient and important for ethnic minorities than for majority group members. Furthermore, members of ethnic minority groups have been found consistently to feel more committed to their group than majority members. According to SIT, this is a consequence of ethnic group boundaries being perceived in European countries as relatively impermeable and inter-group status as relatively stable (Verkuyten, 2000). As a consequence, ethnic awareness, identification and positive ingroup evaluation among ethnic minority members are often seen as reactions or responses to status differences and the predicaments of negative stereotypes, discrimination and forms of racism (Verkuyten, 2000). Indeed, many studies have found that these conditions are crucial for understanding ethnic minority identity and can have various detrimental psychological effects (Jasinskaja-Lahti & Liebkind, 2001; Jasinskaja-Lahti *et al.*, 2003; Liebkind & Jasinskaja-Lahti, 2000a & b).

However, there are limits to using an exclusively social position perspective. Ethnic identity is not composed simply of minority status and treating it as such greatly limits the ability to examine and understand the richness of the meanings and experiences associated with this identity. In focusing on the "minority" aspect, ethnic minority groups are treated as any low-status or powerless group to which the same social psychological processes are applied. As a result, the "ethnic" aspect is ignored and there is a failure to theorize ethnicity (Verkuyten, 2000). In an attempt to promote theorizing of ethnic identity in acculturation, Liebkind (2001) has emphasized that ethnic minority members may take a variety of positions in the face of devaluation of their group, depending on the nature of the identity threat, the specific component of identity being threatened, and the level of identification with the devalued group. Thus, according to Liebkind (2001), research on acculturation should distinguish between at least the following aspects of ethnic/cultural/social identity.

(i) *Subjective and "objective" (or self-recognized and alter-ascribed) social/ethnic/cultural identity.* Only self-recognized ingroup devaluation can result in an internalized negative ethnic/cultural identity. Even subjective perceptions of the ingroup as devalued do not necessarily threaten global self-esteem, if this devaluation is not attributed internally.

(ii) *Social and cultural/ethnic identity.* Devaluation which derives from specific ethnic or cultural characteristics differs from that which derives from socio-economic disadvantage. Only the former can, under certain conditions, become an incentive to cultural assimilation. The latter can be an incentive to individual or collective social mobility, but is relatively independent of the former kind of devaluation. In accordance with Berry's (1997) notion of integration, acculturating individuals may desire a change in their social status, i.e., express a wish to participate individually or collectively in the larger society, yet may not want to change their cultural identity or orientation

(iii) *Degree of identification with different ethnic/cultural groups*

(a) Degree and nature of the identification with the ethnic/cultural ingroup, including self-categorization, strength of identification with the ingroup, and ethnic/cultural pride, i.e. the degree to which the individual considers the ingroup to be a desirable membership group.

(b) Degree and nature of the identification with the ethnic/cultural outgroup, including self-categorization, strength of identification with the outgroup and the degree to which the individual considers the outgroup to represent a desirable membership group (Liebkind, 2001).

One source of confusion in the literature on social/ethnic identity is that the term "social identification" (point [iii] above) may be used to refer to the content of that social or ethnic identity itself, as well as to indicate the level of identification, i.e., the strength of association with a particular group. These are essentially different components of identity, which, although related, may operate relatively independently of each other (Ellemers, Spears & Doosje, 2002). Some researchers (e.g. Ellemers et al., 2002) try to avoid this confusion by substituting the term "identification" with the term "commitment" and reserving the term "social identity" to refer only to the nature or content of a particular identity. This conceptual distinction may make it easier to understand that people may identify strongly with, i.e. feel strongly committed to, groups that confer a negative identity upon them (Ellemers et al., 2002). Ellemers and her colleagues (2002) argue that it is precisely the level of commitment to the ingroup which will determine how individuals react to various pressures or threats towards their social identities, including their ethnic identity.

From a social psychological perspective, it could be argued that perceptions of the future of the ethnic group create a different kind of threat to ingroup identity from perceptions of its present position. The social context provides feedback about both of these threats (Ellemers et al., 2002). The feedback on the present social position of one's group in relation to other groups can provide a sense of security or engender a source of threat to self. But the social context also includes factors related to the permeability of group boundaries and thus provides feedback on the probability of maintaining the distinctiveness of the group in the future (Ellemers et al., 2002). For non-visible minorities, the question of future vitality is intimately connected with collective survival, i.e. the threat of assimilation or "group death" and the total loss of group distinctiveness (Giles, Leets & Coupland, 1990; Landry, Allard & Henry, 1996). Also the stability of the context plays a role here; if the numerical size of an ethnic group is perceived to be constantly diminishing as a result of the acculturation process, the distinctiveness threat is increased.

In the real world, group size and group status often overlap: minority size is frequently (though not always) associated with disadvantage in status, resources, culture and power within the overall social context (Leonardelli & Brewer, 2001; Liebkind, Nyström, Honkanummi & Lange, 2004; Simon, Aufderheide & Kampmeier, 2001). In most studies, however, group disadvantage is taken for granted and determined a priori on objective grounds. This is perhaps understandable, as the field studies in this area mostly deal with visible minority groups like Blacks, for whom future "group death" through assimilation is not a realistic option (e.g. Schmitt & Branscombe, 2002). However, multilingual contexts, for example, may be less clear-cut in this respect, and the status of language groups may be more ambiguous. In such cases, it becomes necessary to assess the group members' subjective perceptions of disadvantage (Harwood, Giles & Bourhis, 1994).

Outgroups can also be a more direct source of threat to the value of one's group identity: threatening information or behavior can be intentionally directed at the ingroup by the outgroup and take the form of prejudice or discrimination (Branscombe, Ellemers, Spears & Doosje, 1999). Branscombe and her colleagues (Branscombe, Schmitt & Harvey, 1999; Schmitt & Branscombe, 2002) have emphasized the importance of subjective perceptions of prejudice and discrimination for understanding the victims' reactions. There is a complex interaction between ingroup identification and different kinds of threat to identity. One response among group members who expect to encounter prejudice directed at their group may be to try to rid themselves of, or attempt to conceal, that group membership. In contrast to this individual mobility ("passing") approach, such an identity threat may be coped with by adopting a more group-based strategy (Jetten, Branscombe, Schmitt & Spears, 2001). However, the choice of strategy is likely to depend on other simultaneous threats towards one's ethnic identity. Research on strategies adopted regarding ethnic identity in acculturation thus has to acknowledge the extent of discrimination, present group disadvantage and future loss of ethnic distinctiveness as subjectively perceived by the ethnic group members themselves.

6.6   Conclusions

Ethnic identity has been studied within the framework of many different disciplines. This fact is partly responsible for some conceptual and methodological inconsistencies in the use of this concept. However, there is some consensus across researchers as to the role of ethnic identity in the acculturation process. First, ethnic identity seems to be conceptually distinct from other formulations of the acculturation process and fairly resistant to change. Second, ethnic identity should be viewed as distinct from social identity which derives purely from the social position of one's membership group. Ethnic minority members may want to change their social identity but not necessarily at the cost of losing their ethnic identity. Third, the kind of ethnic identity which best fosters adaptation in the acculturation process is largely dependant on contextual factors of the acculturating groups and the larger society. In addition, multiple group membership should be taken into account as a viable option for acculturating ethnic minorities.

Finally, there are different kinds of threat to identity and individual differences in the responses to these. Some threats concern social identity and derive from subjective perception of low status, others involve future prospects of the ingroup and may pose a threat to its distinctiveness. Yet another kind is more direct: deliberate aggression in the form of prejudice, racism and discrimination can be directed towards the self because of one's group membership. The reactions to these threats will vary according to a number of factors, including the level of ingroup identification (Ellemers *et al.*, 2002). The value of these responses for adaptation, in turn, will depend on the social context in which the acculturation process takes place.

6.7   References

Back, L. (1996). *New ethnicities and urban culture: racisms and multiculture in young lives.* London: UCL Press.

Berry, J. W. (1990). Psychology of acculturation. In J. J. Berman (ed.), *Cross-cultural perspectives. Current theory and research in motivation* (pp. 201–234). Nebraska Symposium on Motivation 1989, 37. Lincoln: University of Nebraska.

(1997). Immigration, acculturation and adaptation. *Applied Psychology: An International Review, 46,* 5–34.

Berry, J. W. & Sam, D. L. (1997). Acculturation and adaptation. In J. W. Berry, M. H. Segall & C. Kağitçibaşi (eds.), *Handbook of cross-cultural psychology,* Vol. III: *Social behaviour and applications.* 2nd edn. (pp. 291 – 326). Boston: Allyn & Bacon.

Bourhis, R. Y., Moïse, L. C., Perreault, S. & Sénécal, S. (1997). Towards an interactive acculturation model: a social psychological approach. *International Journal of Psychology, 32,* 369–386.

Branscombe, N. R., Ellemers, N., Spears, R. & Doosje, B. (1999). The context and content of social identity threat. In N. Ellemers, R. Spears & B. Doosje (eds.), *Social identity. Context, commitment, content* (pp. 35–58). Oxford: Blackwell.

Branscombe, N. R., Schmitt, M. T. & Harvey, R. D. (1999). Perceiving pervasive discrimination among African Americans: implications for group identification and well-being. *Journal of Personality and Social Psychology, 77,* 135–149.

Breakwell, G. (1986). *Coping with threatened identities.* New York: Methuen & Co.

Brown, R. (2001). Intergroup relations. In M. Hewstone & W. Stroebe (eds.), *Introduction to social psychology* (pp. 480–515). Oxford: Blackwell.

Carbaugh, D. A. (1996). *Situating selves: the communication of social identities in American scenes.* SUNY Series, Human Communication Processes. Albany, NY: State University of New York Press.

Clément, R. & Noels, K. A. (1992). Towards a situated approach to ethnolinguistic identity: the effects of status on individuals and groups. *Journal of Language & Social Psychology, 11,* 203–232.

Cornell, S. & Hartmann, D. (1998). *Ethnicity and race. Making identities in a changing world.* London: Pine Forge Press.

Crul, M. (2000). *De sleutel tot success* [The key to success]. Amsterdam: Spinhuis.

DeVos, G. A. (1995). Ethnic pluralism, conflict and accommodation. In L. Romanucci-Ross & G. DeVos (eds.), *Ethnic identity: creation, conflict, and accommodation*. Walnut Creek, CA: AltaMira.

Ellemers, N., Barreto, M. & Spears, R. (1999). Commitment and strategic responses to social context. In N. Ellemers, R. Spears & B. Doosje (eds.), *Social identity. Context, commitment, content* (pp. 127–146). Oxford: Blackwell.

Ellemers, N., Spears, R. & Doosje, B. (2002). Self and social identity. *Annual Review of Psychology, 53*, 161–186.

Ethier, K. A. & Deaux, K. (1994). Negotiating social identity when contexts change: maintaining identification and responding to threat. *Journal of Personality & Social Psychology, 67*, 243–251.

Giles, H., Leets, L. & Coupland, N. (1990). Minority language group status: a theoretical conspexus. *Journal of Multilingual and Multicultural Development, 11*, 37–55.

Gold, S. J. (1992). *Refugee communities: a comparative field study*. Newbury Park, CA: Sage Publications.

Hagendoorn, L. (1995). Intergroup biases in multiple group systems: the perception of ethnic hierarchies. In W. Stroebe & M. Hewstone (eds.), *European Review of Social Psychology* (Vol. VI, pp. 199–228). Chichester: Wiley.

Harwood, J., Giles, H. & Bourhis, R. Y. (1994). The genesis of vitality theory: historical patterns and discoursal dimensions. *International Journal of the Sociology of Language, 108*, 167–206.

Horenczyk, G. (1996). Migrant identities in conflict: acculturation attitudes and perceived acculturation ideologies. In G. Breakwell & E. Lyons (eds.), *Changing European identities: social psychological analyses of social change* (pp. 241–250). Oxford: Butterworth-Heinemann.

(1997). Immigrants' perceptions of host attitudes and their reconstruction of cultural groups. *Applied Psychology: An International Review, 46*, 34–38.

Hutchinson, J. & Smith, A. D. (eds.) (1996). *Ethnicity*. Oxford: Oxford University Press.

Hutnik, N. (1986). Patterns of ethnic minority identification and modes of social adaptation. *Ethnic and Racial Studies, 9*, 150–167.

(1991). *Ethnic minority identity. A social psychological perspective*. Oxford: Clarendon Press.

Jasinskaja-Lahti, I. & Liebkind, K. (1998). Content and predictors of the ethnic identity of Russian-speaking immigrant adolescents in Finland. *Scandinavian Journal of Psychology, 39*, 209–219.

(2001). Perceived discrimination and psychological adjustment of Russian-speaking immigrant adolescents in Finland. *International Journal of Psychology, 36*, 174–185.

Jasinskaja-Lahti, I., Liebkind, K., Horenczyk, G. & Schmitz, P. (2003). The interactive nature of acculturation: perceived discrimination, acculturation attitudes and stress among young ethnic repatriates in Finland, Israel and Germany. *International Journal of Intercultural Relations, 27*, 79–97.

Jetten, J., Branscombe, N. R., Schmitt, M. T. & Spears, R. (2001). Rebels with a cause: group identification as a response to perceived discrimination from the mainstream. *Personality and Social Psychology Bulletin, 27*, 1204–1213.

Keaton, T. D. (1999). Muslim girls and the "other France": an examination of identity construction. *Social Identities*, *5*, 47–64.

Kinket, B. & Verkuyten, M. (1997). Levels of ethnic self-identification and social context. *Social Psychology Quarterly*, *60*, 338–354.

(1999). Intergroup evaluations and social context: a multilevel approach. *European Journal of Social Psychology*, *29*, 219–237.

LaFromboise, T., Coleman, H. L. K. & Gerton, J. (1993). Psychological impact of biculturalism. Evidence and theory. *Psychological Bulletin*, *114*, 395–412.

Landry, R., Allard, R. & Henry, J. (1996). French in South Louisiana: towards language loss. *Journal of Multilingual and Multicultural Development*, *17*, 442–468.

Laroche, M., Kim, C., Hui, M. K. & Tomiuk, M. A. (1998). Test of a nonlinear relationship between linguistic acculturation and ethnic identification. *Journal of Cross-Cultural Psychology*, *29*, 418–433.

Lay, C. & Nguyen, T. (1998). The role of acculturation-related and acculturation non-specific daily hassles: Vietnamese-Canadian students and psychological distress. *Canadian Journal of Behavioural Science*, *30*, 172–181.

Leonardelli, G. J. & Brewer, M. B. (2001). Minority and majority discrimination: when and why. *Journal of Experimental Social Psychology*, *37*, 468–485.

Liebkind, K. (1992). Ethnic identity – challenging the boundaries of social psychology. In G. M. Breakwell (ed.), *The social psychology of identity and the self concept* (pp. 147–185). London: Academic Press.

(1996). Acculturation and stress. Vietnamese refugees in Finland. *Journal of Cross-Cultural Psychology*, *27*, 161–180.

(2001). Acculturation. In R. Brown & S. Gaertner (eds.), *Blackwell handbook of social psychology: intergroup processes* (pp. 386–406). Oxford: Blackwell.

Liebkind, K. & Jasinskaja-Lahti, I. (2000a). Acculturation and psychological well-being among immigrant adolescents in Finland. A comparative study of adolescents from different cultural backgrounds. *Journal of Adolescent Research*, *15*, 446–469.

(2000b). The influence of experiences of discrimination on psychological stress among immigrants: a comparison of seven immigrant groups. *Journal of Community and Applied Social Psychology*, *10*, 1–16.

Liebkind, K., Nyström, S., Honkanummi, E. & Lange, A. (2004). Group size, group status and dimensions of contact as predictors of intergroup attitudes. *Group Processes and Intergroup Relations*, *7*, 145–159.

Mac an Ghaill, M. (1999). *Contemporary racisms and ethnicities: social and cultural transformations*. Buckingham: Open University Press.

Nesdale, D., Rooney, R. & Smith, L. (1997). Migrant ethnic identity and psychological distress. *Journal of Cross-Cultural Psychology*, *28*, 569–588.

Nguyen, H. H., Messé, L. A. & Stollak, G. E. (1999). Toward a more complex understanding of acculturation and adjustment: cultural involvements and psychosocial functioning in Vietnamese youth. *Journal of Cross-Cultural Psychology*, *30*, 5–31.

Noels, K. A., Pon, G. & Clément, R. (1996). Language, identity, and adjustment: the role of linguistic self-confidence in the acculturation process. *Journal of Language & Social Psychology*, *15*, 246–264.

Oriol, M. (1989). Modèles idéologiques et modèles culturels dans la réproduction des identités collectives en situation d'émigration [Ideological and cultural models for the reproduction of a sense of collective identity in the emigration situation]. *Revue internationale d'action communautaire / International Review of Community Development, 21*, 117–123.

Phinney, J. S. (1990). Ethnic identity in adolescents and adults: review of research. *Psychological Bulletin, 108*, 499–514.

(2003). Ethnic identity and acculturation. In K. M. Chun, P. Balls-Organista & G. Marin (eds.), *Acculturation: advances in theory, measurement, and applied research* (pp. 63–81). Washington, DC: American Psychosogical Association.

Phinney, J. S., Cantu, C. L. & Kurtz, D. A. (1997). Ethnic and American identity as predictors of self-esteem among African American, Latino, and White adolescents. *Journal of Youth and Adolescence, 26*, 165–185.

Phinney, J. S. & Devich-Navarro, M. (1997). Variations in bicultural identification among African American and Mexican American adolescents. *Journal of Research on Adolescence, 7*, 3–32.

Phinney, J. S., Horenczyk, G., Liebkind, K. & Vedder, P. (2001). Ethnic identity, immigration, and well-being: an interactional perspective. *Journal of Social Issues, 57*, 493–510.

Roosens, E. (1994). The primordial nature of origins in migrant ethnicity. In H. Vermeulen & C. Covers (eds.), *The anthropology of ethnicity: Beyond "ethnic groups and boundaries"* (pp. 81–104). Amsterdam: Spinhuis.

Rosenthal, D. A. & Feldman, S. S. (1992). The nature and stability of ethnic identity in Chinese youth: effects of length of residence in two cultural contexts. *Journal of Cross-Cultural Psychology, 23*, 214–227.

Sánchez, J. I. & Fernández, D. M. (1993). Acculturative stress among Hispanics: a bidimensional model of ethnic identification. *Journal of Applied Social Psychology, 23*, 654–668.

Sayegh, L. & Lasry, J.-C. (1993). Immigrants' adaptation in Canada: assimilation, acculturation, and orthogonal identification. *Canadian Psychology, 34*, 98–109.

Schmitt, M. T. & Branscombe, N. R. (2002). The meaning and consequences of perceived discrimination in disadvantaged and privileged social groups. In W. Stroebe & M. Hewstone (eds.), *European Review of Social Psychology* (Vol. XII, pp. 167–199). Chichester: John Wiley & Sons.

Simon, B., Aufderheide, B. & Kampmeier, C. (2001). The social psychology of minority–majority relations. In R. Brown & S. L. Gaertner (eds.), *Blackwell handbook of social psychology: intergroup processes* (pp. 303–323). Oxford: Blackwell.

Snauwaert, B., Soenens, B., Vanbeselaere, N. & Boen, F. (2003). When integration does not necessarily imply integration. Different conceptualizations of acculturation orientations lead to different classifications. *Journal of Cross-Cultural Psychology, 34*, 231–239.

Tajfel, H. (1974). Social identity and intergroup behaviour. *Social Science Information, 13*, 65–93.

(1978). *The social psychology of minorities*. London: Minority Rights Group.

(1981). *Human groups and social categories*. Cambridge: Cambridge University Press.

(ed.). (1982). *Social identity and intergroup relations*. European Studies in Social Psychology. Cambridge: Cambridge University Press.

Tajfel, H. & Turner, J. C. (1986). The social identity theory of intergroup behaviour. In S. Worchel & W. Austin (eds.), *Psychology of intergroup relations*. 2nd edn. (pp. 7–24). Chicago: Nelson-Hall.

Verkuyten, M. (1995). Self-esteem, self-concept stability and aspects of ethnic identity among minority and majority youth in the Netherlands. *Journal of Youth and Adolescence, 24*, 155–175.

(1997). Discourses of ethnic minority identity. *British Journal of Social Psychology, 36*, 565–685.

(1999). *Etnische identiteit: theoretische en empirische benaderingen*. Amsterdam: Spinhuis.

(2000). The benefits to social psychology of studying ethnic minorities. *European Bulletin of Social Psychology, 12(3)*, 5–21.

Verkuyten, M., Drabbles, M. & van den Nieuwenhuijzen, K. (1999). Self-categorisation and emotional reactions to ethnic minorities. *European Journal of Social Psychology, 29*, 605–619.

Ward, C. (1996). Acculturation. In D. Landis & R. S. Bhagat (eds.), *Handbook of intercultural training* 2nd edn. (pp. 124–147). Thousand Oaks, CA: Sage Publications.

Ward, C. & Kennedy, A. (1993). Where's the "culture" in cross-cultural transition? Comparative studies of sojourner adjustment. *Journal of Cross-Cultural Psychology, 24*, 221–249.

7 Development and acculturation

Brit Oppedal

In this chapter we will present a dynamic model of development intended to fit the particular circumstances of children growing up in multicultural societies. We expand on the concept of culture competence as the basis of acculturation development and present an argument that culture competence originates in the psycho-social dynamics of inter-personal relationships. Embedded in acculturation development is the child's growing consciousness of belonging to various sociocultural groups and ethnic identity formation. Some children encounter problems in making choices about cultural roles and an ethnic identity crisis may arise. Finally we discuss how culture competence may be linked with psychological adaptation and mental health in children of immigrants.

7.1 Introduction

Acculturation development is a process towards gaining competence within two distinct cultural domains in order to have a sense of belonging and be able to participate successfully within both (Sam & Oppedal, 2002). The concept of "acculturation" has cultural idiosyncrasies as its core and cultural values as one of the key elements. The ways people behave and evaluate their experiences are guided by their values, and even if basic values appear to be universal, their individual importance and priority vary between persons and between nations (Schwartz, 1992, 1994). A particular group's "value profiles," or "models of virtue," are central markers of the competence necessary to contribute to and take part in that group's activities. An important task for children of immigrants and other ethnic minority children is to figure out how these models of virtue are expressed in everyday routines, patterns of behaviors, rituals and traditions within their own ethnic group and within the majority society.

The concept of acculturation development has been proposed to accommodate the particular circumstances of children and adolescents with ethnic minority background – both immigrants and ethnocultural groups (Berry & Sam, 1997). It has been argued that, with regards to children of immigrants, acculturation must be considered as part of life-span ontogenetic development rather than as a separate adaptation process (Sam & Oppedal, 2002). *Acculturation development* is distinguished from the traditional notion of acculturation (see Introduction and Chapter 2) in two important ways. Firstly, it is anchored in a holistic approach to development which provides a framework for understanding how various aspects of culture guide developmental processes. This is obtained by fusing the notion of "developmental niche" described by Super and Harkness (1986, 1994) to comprehensive contextual models of life-span development (for other examples of integrated developmental models, see Dasen, 2004).

In the Acculturation development model we describe the developmental niche as situated in the midst of two different sociocultural domains: that of the child's own ethnic group and that of the majority society (Figure 7.1). Each domain consists of various sociocultural settings like, for example, religious community, ethnic group peers, sports clubs, school, etc., that affect the child's development in various direct and indirect ways. Through the child's interaction and participation within each of the two sociocultural domains the child develops domain-specific cultural working models to guide and direct its activities. In contrast, the term *acculturation* presupposes already existing cognitive and behavioral structures that might change as a result of cross-cultural interaction. This way of thinking may seem appropriate with regards to explaining adaptation processes in adult immigrants, but it seems a less useful framework for the study of children and adolescents. Even if many immigrant children grow up in areas characterized as ethnic enclaves, their development is embedded in both their own ethnic reality and their awareness of the surrounding majority society. Thus, rather than changes in existing cognitive structures and behavioral patterns, acculturation development involves an ongoing inculcation of own ethnic and host society culture competence.

Secondly, by conceptualizing acculturation as embedded in life-span development it may be easily observed that both the onset and the progress of the process differ for ethnic minority and host children. Children of ethnic minority background have their primary life experiences within an ethnic group that is a sociocultural minority within a larger cultural context. This is a mixed group that includes labor-force immigrants, asylum seekers, refugees, and sojourners and ethnocultural groups (Chapter 3). Nevertheless, they have in common experiences of racism, which is said to be a marker of ethnic minority status, in addition to their bicultural reality. The various immigrant groups further share the consciousness of a second home country and a history of migration. Even if the acculturation development model may be of value also for examining development of domestic children in multicultural societies, the fact that they experience cultural concordance between the social settings of most importance to them must be taken into consideration. The traditional way of describing acculturation may in principle involve changes in both immigrant minority groups and host majority populations. Research has demonstrated differences in attitudes and behavior in domestic youth as a result of cross-cultural contact. An interesting Norwegian study among tenth-grade students, for example, showed that host youth in multicultural high schools with a large proportion of Muslim students had a lower intake of alcohol than students in predominantly mono-ethnic Norwegian schools (Amundsen *et al.*, 2005). It is, however, commonly accepted that cross-cultural contact does not affect the adaptation of host populations to the same extent as immigrants. It may be argued that, in this situation, "acculturation" refers to the way selected characteristics of the social environment may condition certain behavioral patterns, rather than involving acquisition of culture competence.

7.2   A sociocultural contextual model of development

The Acculturation development model has included perspectives from ecologically based developmental theories and cultural psychology. Life-span developmental contextualism, as presented by Lerner (2002), integrates knowledge from biological and social psychology, and is based on the idea of a continuous and reciprocal dynamic interaction between the organism and the context. Lerner's model shares with other comprehensive environmental and ecological developmental models the idea of culture as an all-encompassing external force. Culture is typically depicted as the outmost circle of the various sociocultural settings or systems that comprise the child's developmental context to illustrate its major importance in the experiences of the growing child. These models seem to suggest a homogeneous culture, in terms of shared beliefs, values, traditions and habits, which is extrinsic to human behavior. Thus it is difficult to fit two or more different cultural domains into them. In addition, they also lack more specific guidelines as to how culture affects various developmental processes.

These challenges have been met by adding to the models the perspective from cultural psychology that both human beings and the context are culturally constituted and interdependent upon each other (Valsiner, 2000; Super & Harkness, 1986). All our activities are imprinted by an individual culture constructed as part of our experiences and activities in the social and cultural environment. To illustrate the dualism of the relationship between individual and context Valsiner argues that human beings exist in a context and contexts exist because they are constructed by humans. In the same line of thought, in Lerner's contextual model one fundamental principle is the reciprocal influence of the various sociocultural settings upon each other throughout the life span. As illustrated by Figure 7.1, the child's developmental context is thus a complex organization of interacting individuals and sociocultural contexts that may affect the child either directly or indirectly. The various sociocultural settings of the developmental context are classified as institutional (e.g. schools, workplaces, health care institutions) or as individual (friends, neighborhood). The activities within the two types of settings may be characterized either by the host majority or by the ethnic minority cultural domains. On the individual level, each person's activity is mostly an expression of his or her personal

Interaction characterized mainly by majority culture

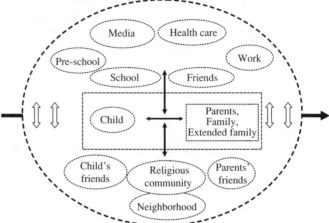

Interaction characterized mainly by minority culture

Figure 7.1 *A dynamic contextual model of acculturation development, adapted from Sam & Oppedal (2003)*

culture and may be dominated by the culture of ethnic group members. On the institutional level, however, the activities are to a larger extent a manifestation of values, beliefs and traditions that are shared on an ethnic, societal or national group level. In a multicultural society, the major institutions typically represent the host national culture. Schools, for example, even with large proportions of immigrant students, are guided by laws, knowledge, values and beliefs that are shared between the majority of the host group members, even if there may be individuals within the system who may hold contrasting personal cultures. This is true also for other institutions like health care, workplaces and mass media: the activities are mainly directed by the superimposed majority culture even if the people within these settings represent several different cultural backgrounds.

As a reminder that change is always occurring throughout the life-span, the time dimension is illustrated in Figure 7.1 by the thick, black arrow that cuts through all levels of the system. The mutuality and interactional principle is illustrated in different ways by permeable membranes and arrows inside the circle that exemplifies the child's developmental context. First of all the developmental niche of the family system is depicted as the social setting of most importance to the child, consisting of the child and his or her parents, family and extended family. The two-headed arrow between the child and the rest of the family implies that childrearing is an interactional process in which the family's efforts to mold the child are affected by the offspring's individual characteristics. The black arrows from each of the cultural domains into the family system denote the impact of the various social settings either directly on the child, or indirectly through the effect on the caregivers. From a more distant location, the parents' work colleagues, for example, may influence the child's development indirectly through the impact they may have on the parents' attitudes and behaviors. Again, the arrows are two-headed to illustrate the mutual influence between the family and the other social systems it is part of. The white arrows represent the interaction between the different social settings, not only within each cultural domain, but also between them. (For a more detailed description of the contextual model, see Lerner 2002:ch. 8.)

7.2.1 Psycho-cultural working models as the basis of culture competence

In a review paper of various approaches to acculturation Ward (2000) summarizes current viewpoints of acculturation in terms of "the ABCs" referring to affective, behavioral and cognitive perspectives, thereby indicating their joint importance. Research within these domains embraces Berry's important thesis that individuals with ethnic minority background have to assess the value both of retaining their own cultural identity and of having contact with the mainstream society (Chapter 3). It is assumed that each person's answer to these two basic questions is predictive of specific patterns of behavior and adaptation. However, there is a missing link in Ward's review in terms of a striking lack of a developmental perspective on the psychological adaptation of ethnic minorities.

From a different viewpoint, Ramirez (1983) defines acculturation as "continued growth and development in the person's original culture as well as in the lifestyles and values of other sociocultural systems in which he or she participates." Within the same line of thought, Cuéllar (2000) refers to acculturation in terms of biculturalism and bi-cognitive adaptation. Contrary to the traditional focus on the potentially stressful characteristics of migration and relocation, these definitions also concentrate on the potentially advantageous gains from biculturalism. The notion that bicultural children develop bi-cognitive capabilities was suggested by Ramirez and Castañeda (1974) who noticed how children could perform effectively and comfortably in both their own and the mainstream cultures, and established friendships with peers from both groups. Research based on Ramirez' bicultural model of culture change and identity development concluded that growing up in a multicultural context provides the individual with advantageous personality-building elements that make him or her more flexible, adaptable, and with more empathy for others (Ramirez, 1983).

The suggestion that there is a cognitive developmental benefit to biculturalism is supported by recent research findings concerning acquisition of language. These have demonstrated that bilingual children learn how to switch back and forth between tasks when the rules change, are better able to focus attention and ignore distraction, and have superior levels of conceptual abstraction and rule switching compared to monolinguals. By means of modern technology (MRI scans), it has been possible to demonstrate that constant rule switching makes the brain recruit extra neural circuits, which is not the case when rule switching is not involved in the task (Bialystok, 2003; Diamond, Kirkham & Amso, 2002; Flynn, Martohardjono & O'Meil, 1998).

Bicultural children learn that different rules can guide their activities within host and own ethnic sociocultural settings, not only with regards to cognitive, but also concerning affective, behavioral and social tasks. D'Andrade (1995) argues that children develop hierchically organized cultural *scripts or working models* based on the meaning and motivation their activities have within their specific cultural system. The working models comprehend culture-specific skills and communicative styles. But more important, they include knowledge about the framework that provides meaning to skills, communication and inter-personal relations. This framework is the culture's ideology, values, traditions, belief systems, ritualized routines, gestures, motives, attitudes and expression of feelings. A corollary of D'Andrade's notion of cultural working models is that children who participate actively within their own cultural domain and that of the hosting society develop cultural working models appropriate for each domain. In the same way as children automatically focus attention, disregard distraction and switch codes as they change between using one language and the other, they also switch codes when it is demanded to accommodate other activities to the appropriate sociocultural context.

These working models are the basis for the development of culture competence. The integration of cultural knowledge, skills and experiences into one's behavioral repertoire is what makes it possible to participate competently and confidently within the relevant sociocultural setting. From this perspective the acquisition of cultural competence is a developmental task, affected by maturation and growth within the affective, cognitive and social domains, and with idiosyncratic challenges to be resolved at different stages in life. The more relevant and elaborated the cultural working models are, the more sophisticated the culture-specific competence. An ease of conceptual abstraction and ability to focus attention and disregard distraction in rule switching are probably helpful resources in coping with the potential stress of having working models with conflicting or incompatible content.

The proposition that immigrants construct culture-specific working models and engage in cultural frame switching in response to situational cues has been presented in the scientific literature on different occasions (see, e.g., Hong, Morris, Chiu & Benet-Martínez, 2002). Interestingly, Benet-Martínez, Leu & Lee (2002) found that responses to cultural cues were dependent upon whether the bicultural individuals perceived their two cultural domains as compatible and complementary or as oppositional and contradictory to each other. In the first situation, bicultural Chinese Americans responded on the basis of a Western meaning system (working model) of attribution when primed with American cues and a Chinese meaning system when exposed to Chinese primes. However, when bicultural Chinese-Americans perceived their cultures as highly contradictory, a contrast effect was observed in their responses. That is; they had a tendency to react on the basis of a Western working model in response to Chinese primes and vice versa. Benet-Martínez *et al.* (2002) suggested that this tendency of reversed priming effects could be explained by a strong cognitive–affective linking of the two meaning systems, and that activation of one system spread to the other.

To the extent that the child's cultural working models facilitate interaction, close relations and achievement of important goals within the relevant socio-cultural settings, they are assumed to be associated with positive developmental processes.

7.3   Developing culture competence

The notion of acculturation development underscores several important considerations about the adaptation of children of immigrants. On the one hand, it is a reminder that acculturation is but one of the developmental tasks ethnic minority children are dealing with. On the other hand it focuses attention on the age-specific attributes of culture competence. The competencies that are adaptive for children differ from those which adolescents and adults need to have available. Further, host and ethnic culture competence may follow dissimilar developmental trajectories and be of unequal value to children's adaptation at different developmental stages. It is implied that ethnic competence should be assessed according to standards of the ethnic culture, and host culture competence be considered according to standards in the majority culture. A final prerequisite of the notion of acculturation development that should be mentioned is that culture competence is postulated as a resource for the individual. Acculturation development thus involves both adaptive and maladaptive opportunities. This is in contrast to the traditional focus on acculturation as a risk factor for maladaptation and poor mental health (Garcia Coll & Magnusson, 1997).

7.3.1 Ethnic culture competence

It is easily seen from Figure 7.1 that the social settings of the ethnic culture domain are key socialization arenas for the child during infancy and childhood. The acquisition of ethnic competence and commitment to traditional family values is instrumental in the formation of ingroup loyalties and connectedness, and provides a sense of psychological security, feelings of continuity and self-esteem (Jasinskaja-Lahti & Liebkind, 2001). Ethnic culture competence is also associated with social support from the family (Oppedal, Røysamb & Sam, 2004). Own ethnic group beliefs, values and behavioral scripts are inculcated through the interactions within the family and ethnic community. As suggested by the lower part of the figure, the extent to which interaction within these communities is directed by traditional culture depends on several socio-economic and demographic factors. The size of the ethnic groups in question and whether they are organized in enclave-like neighborhoods is of importance, as is the number and kind of ethnic institutions and organizations. Presumably also the group's or family's length of stay in the host country is important to intergenerational culture transmission. The upper half of the figure indicates that the family's contact with the host culture is to a large extent mediated through institutions like childcare, school, mass media and workplace, but also through informal social networks. Education level seems to be an indicator of contact with the dominant society, implying that families with better educated adults may have adopted more aspects of the host culture into their daily routines and behaviors. Socio-political characteristics of the receiving countries are most likely of importance to groups' and individuals' preferences for assimilation, segregation or integration as mode of adaptation. However, so far it has proven difficult to single out the most crucial societal dimensions with respect to immigrants' adjustment.

The foundation for ethnic culture competence is established during infancy through the child's interaction with her parents (and/or other caregivers). Parents' "cultural models of virtue" represent the competence they consider appropriate and functional for the child in relation to particular contexts. These are age-specific goals and standards the children have to deal with. Early on, these models are promoted to offspring through feeding routines, sleeping routines and other modes of interaction (Levine & Norman, 2001). Parents' sensitivity to the needs of the child in terms of accessibility, emotional availability and understanding of the child's signs and gestures, their promptness, and timing of responses are best understood against the tapestry of their models of virtue (Crittenden, 2000; Levine & Norman, 2001). Based on these early experiences, the child starts constructing working models of the self in relation to others in terms of attachment, preferred social distance, sensitivity to the feelings of others, and conversational exchange that scaffold their ethnic culture competence. Presumably the early intra-family dynamics are also of importance with regards to the child's later motivation to advance its competence within the ethnic cultural domain.

One interesting question then is in what ways immigrant parents change their models of virtue to accommodate to new social realities. Kağitçibaşi (1996) described three alternative models of family interaction and parenting styles. She reasons that parents have modified their models of virtue regarding relatedness and agency to meet conflicting demands in traditional versus urban industrialized cultures. An authoritarian parenting style in traditional societies promotes control and obedience and a relational self. In the urban industrialized setting an authoritative parenting style promotes control in relation to ingroup members and autonomy regarding materialistic issues. The self is perceived as autonomous–relational in contrast to the separated self prototypical of modern Western societies and the overall relational self of traditional cultures.

From a different perspective, studies of intergenerational transmission of collectivist values are also based on the idea that parents' goals and values are passed on to their offspring through their childrearing practices. Schönpflug (2001) found that parenting style was important in the transmission of values from Turkish fathers to their sons. She also demonstrated that collectivist, but not individualist values, were passed on from one generation to the next both in immigrant Turkish families living in Germany and in families who continued living in Turkey. In another cross-cultural study of immigrants in Germany and the Netherlands, Phalet and Schönpflug (2001) showed that value transmission is dependent upon sociocultural context. Whereas Turkish immigrant parents in Germany transmitted values of achievement and collectivist family values to their offspring, this was only true for the family values in the Netherlands. The differences in the parents' motivation to pass on values of achievement was explained by parents in the Netherlands perceiving a more secure access to extensive social rights and services than the German parents.

7.3.2   Host culture competence

To prepare children to participate efficiently both within their own ethnic networks and within the host society involves several challenges for immigrant parents. First of all they themselves need to have a certain level of competence within the host culture. Secondly, they need to make choices about the specific host values and behavioral patterns they will integrate into their models of virtue. Finally, they must find efficient means to promote this foundation of host culture competence in their children. Considering all these challenges, it may seem a relief to some that parents are not the only educators of children.

Television is probably the earliest source of host culture competence in children of immigrants. But to the extent that they attend pre-schools and schools they also gain basic competence within the host culture, to guide their social interaction with outgroup peers and school behavior. Working models of behavioral patterns grow vertically as they become more abstract with cognitive maturation, and horizontally as the children have new experiences. We suggest that, at a high level of organization, experiences are structured horizontally according to their ethnic group or host society characteristics. Thus immigrant children as they grow older organize their mental representations of values, traditions and social interaction patterns separately according to the cultural context which they are part of. This assumption implies that the child establishes a working model of, for example, eating behavior through family interaction and participation in activities with co-ethnics. This may be paralleled with a different working model for the same behavior by means of the child's interaction with host children and adults. The abstraction of *eating behavior* then includes two models or structures of behavioral patterns categorized in some form as "ethnic" and "host." The amount of information in each model may differ according to the range of the child's experiences in each domain. The "ethnic" model of the abstraction of *classroom behavior* may be rudimentary because it was based on parents' stories of memories from their school days. The "host" model on the other hand has its base in the child's own activities and will therefore grow more complex and sophisticated with maturation and advanced experiences. The more elaborate the cultural working models, the better is the foundation for the child's competent participation within both sociocultural domains that constitute his or her developmental niche.

Ethnic culture competence is based on the infant's interaction with his or her parents when experiencing pleasure, distress or threat (Ainsworth, Blehar, Waters & Wall, 1978; Bowlby, 1969). In contrast, host culture competence probably has its most important origin in playful interaction with peers and achievement-related behavior in the school setting. Cognitive maturation, broadening social contexts, and the intensified peer relations that are characteristic of pre-adolescence and adolescence are accompanied by an expansion in outgroup orientation and growth of host culture competencies.

During middle and high school years it becomes increasingly essential to the young immigrants to be able to participate competently within the host sociocultural setting in order to gain acceptance and be acknowledged as part of the mainstream society. Harter (1990) has demonstrated that feelings of self-worth in young people are based on their idiosyncratic relations not only with parents, but also with classmates and teachers. Research findings concerning immigrant adolescents have shown that host culture competence facilitates support from the two latter networks (Oppedal *et al.*, 2004). Furthermore, host culture competence is a necessary means to succeeding within the educational institutions and job market. During the adolescent years, several decisions are at stake regarding future educational opportunities and hence placement within the labor market. The achievement pressure is high, as grades to a considerable extent determine academic choices. But for immigrant youngsters school success is not only indispensable for the range of future choices they have, it is also an indicator of success within the mainstream society's arena. Consequently, during the adolescent years, host culture competence is a necessary resource for social integration into the host society networks, for future academic and economic success in the mainstream society, and for feelings of being accepted as part of the mainstream society.

7.3.3   Ethnic identity and ethnic identity crisis

Identity formation has an idiosyncratic status during adolescence as the most important developmental task (Erikson, 1968). Phinney has in her work given excellent accounts of how formation of ethnic – or social group – identity is an integrated part of this process (see, e.g., Phinney, 1989; Phinney & Tarver, 1988; and also Chapter 6 of this volume). She has described four possible outcomes of ethnic identity formation. Integration involves high levels of both own ethnic and majority society identity. Separation is portrayed as high ethnic and low majority identity, in contrast to assimilation in which the ethnic identity is low but the majority society identity high. Finally, marginalized ethnic identity is an expression of low levels of identification with both sociocultural groups (Phinney, Horenczyk, Liebkind & Vedder, 2001). This formulation matches the proposition of four acculturation strategies suggested by Berry (Berry & Kim, 1988). Each mode of acculturation strategy and social group identity is supposed to be linked with certain sociocultural conditions and also to be related to specific social and behavioral goals and ways of attaining these. In particular, the two theoretical frameworks have in common the assumption that marginalized acculturation strategy / identity is associated with maladaptation and mental health problems.

In contrast to the concept of a "marginalized ethnic identity" we have proposed a notion of ethnic identity crisis that is more closely linked to Erikson's theory of identity formation and crisis (1968) in which commitment to different roles is central (Oppedal *et al.*, 2004). The concept is building upon the notion of an identity deficit crisis which involves an inability to make decisions about role choices (Baumeister, Shapiro & Tice, 1985). During social group (ethnic) identity exploration, there may be phases of uncertainty and indecision. In this process some young immigrants may encounter difficulties in making role choices and committing to the goals and values of either one or both of the cultural domains. Ethnic identity crisis has been found to be a negative predictor of both internalizing and externalizing problems in young immigrants of several different national origins (Oppedal, Røysamb & Heyerdahl, 2005).

7.4   Culture competence and mental health

The process of migration – in particular the resettlement part of it – is considered a risk factor in relation to mental health of children of immigrants. Beliefs, values and traditions of the hosting society that are perceived as incompatible with those of the immigrant families may create distressing conflicts (Cuéllar, 2000). Experiences of racism and exclusion are also threatening the mental health of immigrants and other ethnic minorities (Clark, Anderson, Clark & Williams, 1999; Fisher, Wallace & Fenton, 2000). However, in spite of these acculturation-specific factors that may increase the risk of mental health problems, several immigrant youngsters report mental health as good as – or even better than – that of their host peers (Oppedal *et al.*, 2005; Roberts, Roberts & Chen, 1997). This piece of evidence draws attention to individual and environmental factors that may protect against the hazards of stressors and promote wellbeing and mentally healthy children in immigrant families.

One interesting question in this scenario is that of the extent to which culture competence plays a part in the migration – mental health link. The question is relevant as an impressive array of studies has demonstrated the association between the construct of competence (in terms of, e.g., self-perception, self-efficacy, mastery, control) and mental health outcomes (Bandura, 1986; Harter, 1985).

From the perspective of the acculturation development model, one way to assess culture competence would be to describe culture-specific normative patterns of behavior and consider the child's activity with reference to these. This perspective is particularly useful with regards to basic psychological developmental processes, and behaviors that are related to these. Another way is to assess culture competence in terms of the child's sense of self-efficacy in relation to central developmental tasks within the two principal cultural domains.

The acculturation development model implies that culture competence is rooted in interpersonal relationships, and interwoven with affective, behavioral and cognitive developmental outcomes. Thus the development of culture competence is not merely a matter of quantity of contact with co-ethnic and majority society members, but is even more affected by the quality of these relations. This has been extensively documented with respect to one of the primary working models the child constructs, which is that of attachment strategies. Constructive parenting practices and caregiver sensitivity are the basis of patterns of attachment that promote psychologically healthy development. Neglectful and otherwise insensitive parenting may undermine the development of culturally sound working models of attachment strategies which may have repercussions for later psychological and social functioning (Crittenden & Claussen, 2000; Van IJzendoorn & Sagi, 1999). In this way early seeds of ethnic competence that develop within a context of caregiver–child interaction are associated with later mental health outcomes.

The acculturation development model is based on the assumption that culture competence is important to children of immigrants, because it improves their chances of being accepted and succeeding within the relevant sociocultural domain. Both theoretical formulations and empirical findings regarding the linkage between competence and mental health suggest that the association is especially significant when performance is assessed in domains that are valued as important by the individual (Bandura, 1986; Harter, 1985). This is true for competence that promotes the sense of belonging and facilitates supportive interpersonal relationships. Accordingly, research among young immigrants has shown that culture competence indeed has an effect on mental health because it increases self-esteem and social support (Oppedal *et al.*, 2004). In line with the theoretical propositions of acculturation development, host culture competence was found to be associated with social support from classmates, whereas ethnic competence was related to support from the family. Even more intriguing were the findings that competence within one cultural domain compensated for lack of supportive resources in the other. When a decrease in family support was associated with a decrease in host culture competence, there was a strong increase in mental health problems. However, when the reduction in family support was accompanied by an *increase* in host culture competence, there were no changes in mental health whatsoever. The availability of multiple cultural models of competent behaviors may contribute to an advantageous personality with flexible and adaptable reservoirs as observed by Ramirez (1983). Under such conditions culture competence scaffolds a healthy development, both mentally and otherwise.

7.5   Summary and future perspectives

In this chapter we have suggested that, when children and adolescents with immigrant parents are concerned, acculturation is best understood as a developmental process whose goal is the acquisition of culture competence. Mental representations of patterns of behavior and their culture-specific meanings are hierarchically structured and organized according to the cultural domain they belong to. Children are able to switch between these "working models" which is the basis for their successful participation both within their own ethnic networks and in the majority society's arena. As part of acculturation development adolescents may experience an ethnic identity crisis involving problems in choosing and committing to roles within one or both sociocultural domains. An ethnic identity crisis may cause distress and behavioral problems.

We have not specifically dealt with the way the political and economic situations in countries that receive immigrants affect their psychological development. The distinction between socio-economic and sociocultural conditions is not clear-cut. It is, however, important to include economic perspectives in the studies of immigrant children's development, as they have proved to impact on family dynamics in important ways (Garcia Coll, Crnic, Lamberty, Wasik, Jenkins & Garcia, 1996).

Further research regarding the development and implications of age appropriate cultural working models may provide us with a better understanding of the behavior and adaptation of children of immigrants. In particular, investigations that elucidate *the processes underlying* both the construction of culture-specific working models and how they affect behavior may inform our knowledge of the dynamics of development in multicultural contexts.

There are several trajectories to adaptation available to children whose parents have migrated from their country of origin to resettle in another nation with the challenges and opportunities of different social and cultural conditions. The acculturation development model focuses our attention on some of the stumbling blocks that may be encountered underway. But, more importantly, our attention is directed to the resources embedded in multicultural contexts with the potential of numerous pathways to a positive development for children and adolescents.

7.6   References

Ainsworth, M. D. S., Blehar, M. C., Waters, E. & Wall, S. (1978). *Patterns of attachment: psychological study of the strange situation.* Hillsdale, NJ: Lawrence Erlbaum Associates.

Amundsen, E. J., Rossow, I. & Skurtveit, S. (2005). Drinking pattern among adolescents with immigrant and Norwegian background: a two-way influence? *Addiction, 100 (10),* 1453–1464.

Bandura, A. (1986). The explanatory and predictive scope of self-efficacy theory. Special issue. Self-efficacy theory in contemporary psychology. *Journal of Social Clinical Psychology, 4,* 359–373.

Baumeister, R. F., Shapiro, J. P. & Tice, D. M. (1985). Two kinds of identity crisis. *Journal of Personality, 53,* 407–424.

Benez-Martínez, V., Leu, J. & Lee, F. (2002). Negotiating biculturalism: cultural frame switching in biculturals with oppositional versus compatible cultural identities. *Journal of Cross-Cultural Psychology, 33,* 492–516.

Berry, J. W. & Kim, U. (1988). Acculturation and mental health. In P. R. Dasen, J. W. Berry *et al.* (eds.), *Health and cross-cultural psychology: towards applications* (pp. 207–236). London: Sage Publications.

Berry, J. W. & Sam, D. L. (1997). Acculturation and adaptation. In J. W. Berry, M. H. Segall *et al.* (eds.), *Handbook of cross-cultural psychology* (pp. 291–326). Boston: Allyn & Bacon.

Bialystok, E. (2003). Developing phonological awareness: is there a bilingual advantage? *Applied Psycholinguistics, 24,* 27–44.

Bowlby, J. (1969). *Attachment and loss,* Vol. I. New York: Basic Books.

Clark, R., Anderson, N. B., Clark, V. R. & Williams, D. (1999). Racism as a stressor for African Americans: a biopsychosocial model. *American Psychologist, 54,* 805–816.

Crittenden, P. M. (2000). A dynamic-maturational exploration of the meaning of security and adaptation: empirical, cultural and theoretical considerations. In P. M. Crittenden & A. H. Claussen (eds.), *The organization of attachment relationships. Maturation, culture, and context* (pp. 358–385). New York: Cambridge University Press.

Crittenden, P. M. & Claussen, A. H. (2000). *The organization of attachment relationships. Maturation, culture, and context.* New York: Cambridge University Press.

Cuéllar, I. (2000). Acculturation and mental health: ecological transactional relations of adjustment. In I. Cuéllar & F. A. Paniagua (eds.), *Handbook of multicultural mental health* (pp. 45–62). San Diego, CA: Academic Press.

D'Andrade, R. (1995). *The development of cognitive anthropology.* Cambridge: Cambridge University Press.

Diamond, A., Kirkham, N. & Amso, D. (2002). Conditions under which young children CAN hold two rules in mind and inhibit a prepotent response. *Developmental Psychology*, *38*, 352–362.

Erikson, E. H. (1968). *Identity: youth and crisis.* New York: W. W. Norton & Company Inc.

Fisher, C. B., Wallace, S. A. & Fenton, R. E. (2000). Discrimination distress during adolescence. *Journal of Youth and Adolescence*, *29*, 679–695.

Flynn, S., Martohardjono, G. & O'Meil, W. (1998). *The generative study of second language acquisition.* Mahwah, NJ: Lawrence Erlbaum Associates.

Garcia Coll, C., Crnic, K., Lamberty, G., Wasik, B. H., Jenkins, R. & Garcia, H. V. (1996). An integrative model for the study of developmental competencies in minority children. *Child Development*, *67*, 1891–1914.

Garcia Coll, C. & Magnusson, K. (1997). The psychological experience of immigration: a developmental perspective. In A. Booth, A. C. Crouter, & N. Landale (eds.), *Immigration and the family. Research and policy on U.S. immigrants.* Mahwah, NJ: Lawrence Erlbaum Associates.

Harter, S. (1985). Competence as a dimension of self-evaluation: toward a comprehensive model of self-worth. In R. L. Leahy (ed.), *The development of the self* (pp. 55–122). New York: Academic Press.

(1990). Self and identity development. In S. S. Feldman & G. R. Elliot (eds.), *At the threshold. The developing adolescent* (pp. 352–387). Cambridge, MA: Harvard University Press.

Hong, Y., Morris, M. W., Chiu, C. & Benet-Martínez, V. (2002). Multicultural minds: a dynamic constructivist approach to culture and cognition. *American Psychologist*, *55*, 709–720.

Jasinskaja-Lahti, I. & Liebkind, K. (2001). Perceived discrimination and psychological adjustment among Russian-speaking immigrant adolescents in Finland. *International Journal of Psychology*, *36*, 174–185.

Kağitçibaşi, C. (1996). *Family and human development across cultures: a view from the other side.* Mahwah, NJ: Lawrence Erlbaum Associates.

Lerner, R. M. (2002). *Concepts and theories of human development.* Mahwah, NJ: Lawrence Erlbaum Associates.

Levine, R. A. & Norman, K. (2001). The infant's acquisition of culture: early attachment re-examined in anthropological perspective. In C. Moore & H. Mathews (eds.), *The psychology of cultural experience* (pp. 83–104). New York: Cambridge University Press.

Oppedal, B., Røysamb, E. & Heyerdahl, S. (2005). Ethnic group, acculturation, and psychiatric problems in young immigrants. *Journal of Child Psychology and Psychiatry*, *46(6)*, 646–660.

Oppedal, B., Røysamb, E. & Sam, D. L. (2004). The effect of acculturation and social support on change in mental health among young immigrants. *International Journal of Behavioral Development*, *28*, 481–494.

Phalet, K. & Schönpflug, U. (2001). Intergenerational transmission of collectivism and achievement values in two acculturation contexts: the case of Turkish families in Germany and Turkish and Moroccan families in the Netherlands. *Journal of Cross-Cultural Psychology*, *32*, 186–201.

Phinney, J. S. (1989). Stages of ethnic identity development in minority group adolescents. *Journal of Early Adolescence*, 9, 34–49.

Phinney, J. S., Horenczyk, G., Liebkind, K. & Vedder, P. (2001). Ethnic identity,
immigration, and well-being: an interactional perspective. *Journal of Social
Issues*, 57, 493–511.

Phinney, J. S. & Tarver, S. (1988). Ethnic identity search and commitment in black and
white eight graders. *Journal of Early Adolescence*, 8, 265–277.

Ramirez, M. (1983). *Psychology of the Americas: multicultural perspectives in personality and mental health*. New York: Pergamon Press.

Ramirez, M. & Castañeda, A. (1974). *Cultural democracy, bicognitive development
and education*. New York: Academic Press.

Roberts, R. E., Roberts, C. R. & Chen, Y. R. (1997). Ethnocultural differences in prevalence of adolescent depression. *American Journal of Community Psychology*,
25, 95–110.

Sam, D. L. & Oppedal, B. (2002). Acculturation as a developmental pathway. In W. J.
Lonner, D. L. Dinnel *et al.* (eds.), *Online readings in psychology and culture*
(www.ac.wwu.edu/~culture), Western Washington University.

Schönpflug, U. (2001). Intergenerational transmission of values: the role of transmission belts. *Journal of Cross-Cultural Psycholog*, 32, 174–185.

Schwartz, S. H. (1992). Universals in the content and structure of values: theoretical
advances and empirical tests in 20 countries. In M. P. Zanna (ed.), *Advances
in experimental social psychology* (pp. 1–65). San Diego, CA: Academic
Press Inc.

(1994). Beyond individualsm/collectivism: New cultural dimensions of values. In
U. Kim, H. C. Triandis, Ç. Kağitçibaşi, S.-C. Choi & G. Yoon (eds.), *Indi-
vidualism and collectivism: theory, method, and applications* (pp. 85–119).
Thousand Oaks, CA: Sage Publications.

Super, C. M. & Harkness, S. (1986). The developmental niche: a conceptualization
of the interface of child and culture. *International Journal of Behavioral
Development*, 9, 545–570.

(1994). The developmental niche. In W. J. Lonner & R. Malpass (eds.), *Psychology
and culture* (pp. 95–99). Needham Heights, MA: Allyn & Bacon.

Valsiner, J. (2000). *Culture and human development*. Thousand Oaks, CA: Sage
Publications.

Van IJzendoorn, N. H. & Sagi, A. (1999). Cross-cultural patterns of attachment: universal and contextual dimensions. In J. Cassidy & P. R. Shaver (eds.), *Handbook
of attachment: theory, research and clinical applications* (pp. 713–734). New
York: Guilford Press.

Ward, C. (2000). The A, B, Cs of acculturation. In D. Matsumoto (ed.), *The handbook
of culture & psychology* (pp. 411–445). New York: Oxford University Press.

8 Personality and individual factors in acculturation

Ankica Kosic

Paralleling the larger societal questions posed by immigration are the considerable challenges newcomers are confronted with as individuals. Whether they arrive as refugees, guest workers or the seekers of a better life, the entrants often find themselves in a veritable "crossfire" of social and psychological forces. These give rise to the immigrants' fundamental dilemma as to whether, and to what degree, they should assimilate into the receiving society (often in the face of considerable hostility and rejection by the local population), and in what part to retain their cultural identity and maintain close ties to the society of origin (whose members may offer an invaluable lifeline of support in the times of hardship which life in the "promised land" often represents). There are very likely to be individual differences in the psychological characteristics that a person brings to the acculturation process, which means that not every person would necessarily participate in the process to the same extent (Berry, 1997). In a microcosm of their individual personalities, the immigrants have their own "acculturation" to grapple with and to optimally manage as they attempt to find their own suitable ways of being in the new setting. It is thus important to examine acculturation in all its complexity, taking into consideration not only the numerous social factors, but also individual factors. This has been suggested by many authors (Berry, 1997, 2003; Berry, Poortinga, Segall & Dasen, 2002; Padilla & Perez, 2003; Schmitz, 2001; Ward, 1996, 2001).

Personality is a very broad concept and in this chapter it is regarded as an amalgam or configuration of personality dimensions, coping strategies and cognitive processes, and as such it could be used interchangeably with the term *self*. When examining the psychological literature on acculturation, one becomes surprised by the paucity of research on acculturation and personality or the *self*, and this raises a number of concerns. The first concern is the degree to which tests and personality measures, developed for the most part within North American and European cultures, might apply to the members of the different cultures immigrants belong to. The conceptual problems in research with immigrants and refugees refer to the appropriate use of instruments and their translations (Pernice, 1994). The second concern is the debate over the universality or specificity of personality across cultures. This debate is destined to replay many of the issues which have framed the debate between different trends: those who believe in behaviors as controlled primarily by traits or endogenous dispositions in the individual, and those who believe that social behavior is produced and regulated by the requirements of situations and environments. There are three positions identified in cross-cultural psychology (Berry *et al.*, 2002): *relativist, absolutist* and *universalist*. The relativist position is advocated by many anthropologists and cultural psychologists (e.g., Markus & Kitayama, 1998) who hold the view that constructs of personality or *self* have different meanings in different cultural contexts. They therefore question the importance of traits in understanding or predicting behavior. In contrast the absolutist position assumes that traits and psychological processes are invariant across cultures and are unaffected by culture (Eysenck & Eysenck, 1983). Within this approach, McCrae and Costa (1997) claim that, even if cultures differ in the extent to which they encourage the expression of personality, all cultures must allow for the expression of basic individual differences. To support their position, they indicate that similar personality dimensions, as expressed in the five factor theory, can be found in many different cultures. The universalists (e.g., Berry *et al.*, 2002) take an intermediate position: that there are some common personality traits across cultures but that cultural factors influence their development and behavioral display.

Research on the role of personality in acculturation shows a number of contradictory findings. It also shows that personality factors typically have low explained variance. All these together ask for a thorough review of what has been done up until now and what could be further examined. This chapter gives an overview of major theories and empirical studies on the relationship between personality and immigrants' acculturation. The effort to be broadly inclusive in the available space does not allow, however, an exhaustive presentation of everything psychologists have said about personality and individual factors in cross-cultural adjustment. In the first section, different individual traits and personality dimensions which play a role in the immigrants' adaptation, both as risk and protective factors, are presented from an analytical perspective. The second section focuses on the interaction between personality characteristics and situational factors in the process of acculturation. The third and final section deals with the impact of acculturation on immigrants' personality. In this chapter, the term "immigrant" is used as a generic one and refers to different acculturating individuals, both "immigrants" and refugees (including asylum seekers) as well as sojourners (such as foreign students).

8.1   Individual and personality dimensions in acculturation: risk and protective factors

Acculturation studies on personality have usually considered a single personality characteristic or ability, and examined its effect on stress reduction in the adaptation process. Examined factors can be distinguished in terms of self- and others-orientation (Leiba-O'Sullivan, 1999). Self-orientation refers to the experience of reflexive consciousness by which an individual is aware of the self, his/her personality and identity. Without this capacity, selfhood would be absent or meaningless: the self could not take the perspective of others, exercise self-control, and produce creative accomplishments, or experience pride, self-esteem, anxiety, and locus of control. Others-orientation includes skills and attributes that assist in the development and maintenance of relationships and effective communication in a foreign country (e.g., extraversion, sociability, and coping strategies). Few attempts have been made to analyze integrative models which take into account different variables together.

8.1.1   Self-orientation

There are certain beliefs about the self and personal characteristics which may either become salient and central, or may remain neglected and overlooked. Favorable views of the self may form a valuable resource for coping with stresses and setbacks, whereas negative views of the self are linked to mal-adjustment, depression and other problems. Self-attention is therefore highly evaluative and motivational. People feel bad when they fall short of their stan-dards and ideals, and so they may be motivated to do one of two things: improve in order to meet the standards, or escape from the aversive state of self-awareness. A study conducted by Csikszentmihalyi and Figurski (1982) revealed that people spend a small amount of time in thinking about themselves and their psychological states. In part this may be because the outer world is more salient (except for the "absent-minded" type of person). However, self-awareness could make emotional states salient and is usually higher in the situations of failure. It seems that the more we want to avoid these unpleas-ant states of self-awareness, the more we think about them. Different studies, especially in clinical psychology, revealed that an excessive self-orientation and cultural self-awareness in immigrants are linked to depression and low self-esteem (Furnham & Bochner, 1986).

8.1.1.1   Self-esteem

Self-esteem is the evaluative aspect of reflexive consciousness and it is a kind of resource that enables people to continue functioning well in the face of failure and other problems. In this view, people who think well of themselves have more of a resource than people who think poorly of them-selves. It is therefore not surprising that self-esteem emerges as a strong predictor of adaptation among immigrants (Valentine, 2001). Sam and Virta (2003) examined this construct in three immigrant groups (Chileans, Turks and Vietnamese) in Norway and Sweden and revealed that having an integrated or bicultural attitude was related to higher self-esteem. Maintaining good self-esteem is a constant effort in a foreign country, and this is important because the more one values oneself, the more likely one is to make an extra effort to adapt. Immigrants face many situations (e.g., prejudice and discrimination

[Sam & Virta, 2003] and downward mobility – see Chapter 26 of this *Handbook*) which might threaten their self-esteem.

A great deal of the research in social psychology relies on the assumption that people are motivated to protect and enhance their self-esteem. It has been hypothesized that immigrants would adopt various strategies in order to achieve a positive self-concept and/or to preserve their self-esteem. This may be achieved either through a positive interpretation of their migration experience in the face of harsh living and working conditions, or through favorable comparisons with the host-nationals and co-nationals. In a study on Albanian and Polish immigrants in Italy (Kosic & Triandafyllidou, 2002), findings show that for young people, migration is understood and experienced both in relation to economic status and in relation to personal achievement. These immigrants initially regarded migration and contact with other cultures as an opportunity to travel and to learn about other societies. However, for many young Albanians and Poles, the "traveling" and "learning" options have remained a dream or an illusion, and they found themselves trapped in menial low-paid jobs. As a strategy to preserve their self-esteem, they used re-interpretation of the situation. The unpleasant, menial and irregular jobs were seen as part of the "price" that had to be paid for future benefits. Thus, despite the difficulties, many immigrants saw the migration experience as positive because it allowed them to improve their own financial situation and that of their family. Moreover, they link migration experiences with positive personal development associated with change and maturity. It therefore seems that immigrants prefer to present themselves not as "victims" but as individuals who have responsibilities, and who can draw upon rich cultural and personal experiences in defining themselves. This probably helps them to make sense of their world and, at the same time, to protect their self-esteem. While self-esteem is clearly implicated in advantageous and positive outcomes in the process of acculturation, the distribution of causes and consequences is not clear. If self-esteem helps one to cope better, what in turn enhances one's self-esteem?

8.1.1.2 Motivation

Beliefs about the self are almost always subject to motivational forces. Motivation has been examined from many perspectives and classified in different ways (see Higgins & Kruglanski, 2000). Perhaps the most applied taxonomy of motivation is the trichotomy developed and operationalized by McClelland (1987). This theory emphasized three needs: need for power, need for affiliation, and need for achievement. Boneva and Hanson Frieze (2001) suggest that individuals who choose to emigrate possess a specific set of motivational needs that differentiates them from those who do not have the intention to emigrate. These authors showed that those who want to emigrate tend to have higher achievement and power motivation, but lower affiliation motivation. High "achievers" may migrate in order to find better opportunities; they look for something more challenging and want to avoid routine. Furthermore, those high in power motivation are more willing to take risks in reaching their goals in order to be recognized and to impress others. Tartakovsky and Schwartz (2001) proposed another conceptualization of the motivation to emigrate: preservation (physical, social and psychological security), self-development (personal growth in abilities, knowledge and skills), and materialism (financial wellbeing, wealth). This conceptualisation could be related to the discourse of self-enhancement mentioned above. These authors not only confirmed the relative importance of motivations in predicting group identifications, subjective wellbeing, and the economic situation of immigrants, but also in determining the first step of the immigration process: the decision to emigrate.

8.1.1.3 Coping strategies

Coping strategies can be conceptualized as cognitive and behavioral efforts that are used by an individual to reduce the effects of stress (Lazarus & Folkman, 1984). Although coping responses may be classified in many ways, most approaches distinguish between problem-oriented strategies and emotion-oriented strategies (Lazarus & Folkman, 1984). Problem-oriented strategies are directed towards the management of the problem (doing something to alter the source of stress, trying to solve the problem), whereas emotion-oriented strategies are directed at reducing the level of emotional distress associated with the stressful situation (focus on the expression of tensions and frustrations, ventilate the feelings, self-controlling, etc.). Endler and Parker (1994) have identified a third strategy: avoidance-oriented coping (describing distraction and passivity).

These strategies have emerged as a key concept affecting adjustment in Lazarus and Folkman's (1984) transaction model of stress. Coping strategies depend on two main classes of cognitive processes. One cognitive process refers to how the situational stressors are perceived and interpreted. This is called "primary appraisal." The second cognitive component is called "secondary appraisal" and refers to the individual's belief about his or her own strategic resources and the effectiveness of these coping strategies in a stressful situation. Empirical findings presented by Schmitz (1992a) point to the relevance of these cognitive appraisal processes as central intervening variables in immigrants' acculturation. Moreover, in another study, Schmitz (1992b) showed that acculturation strategies were significantly correlated to Endler's coping styles of task-, emotion- and avoidance-orientations. Integration was positively related to task-orientation, assimilation was positively related to both task- and emotion-orientations, but negatively related to avoidance-orientation, whereas separation was positively correlated to emotion- and avoidance-coping. Further evidence of the close relationship between acculturation strategies and coping behavior has been reported in other studies (Kosic, 2004). Using a revised version of Endler's scale, this study found that relationships with the host group were also negatively associated with avoidance and emotional coping, and positively related to problem-oriented coping. On the other hand, maintenance of one's original culture was positively related to both emotional and problem-oriented coping.

8.1.1.4 Anxiety

Few studies have examined anxiety as a factor that might influence the acculturation process. Roccas and Brewer (2002) found that anxiety could be detrimental to task performance when attention and deliberate effort are required, as in the case of learning a foreign language. More often than not, studies conceptualize anxiety as an acculturation outcome. There is no doubt that immigrants face a variety of stressors during the process of adaptation to a new society. An immigrant faces problems in finding a job and accommodation, acquiring a new language, dealing with immigration regulations and authorities, adjusting to a different educational system, dealing with a different system of values, beliefs and customs, and so on. Chataway and Berry (1989) compared stress, anxiety, coping, and appraisal measures among three groups of students in Canada – Hong Kong Chinese, French-Canadian, and English-Canadian. They found that Hong Kong Chinese foreign students reported higher trait anxiety associated with communication difficulties and acculturative stress.

8.1.1.5 Need for cognitive closure

Studies have also found close links between "need for cognitive closure" (NCC) and acculturative stress and anxiety. NCC has been defined as the desire for a firm answer to a question, and an aversion towards ambiguity (Kruglanski & Webster, 1996: 264). Webster and Kruglanski (1994) assumed that NCC varies along a continuum from high NCC at one end to high need to avoid closure at the other. Research (Kosic, 2002a) found that immigrants with high NCC suffered greater stress, expressed as emotional disorder and psychosomatic symptoms, although no causal links between the two variables could be established. Need for cognitive closure may be induced by demanding and stressful situational factors, as well as by an organismic state (e.g., tiredness). On the one hand, the different stressful situations immigrants face can give rise to fatigue, which in turn may induce need for cognitive closure. On the other hand, need for cognitive closure – expressed as the dispositional need for order, predictability and mental closure, and intolerance for ambiguity – may give rise to high levels of stress in new and ambiguous situations. Another study investigated how some aspects of immigrants' acculturation may be related to NCC (Kosic, Kruglanski, Pierro & Mannetti, 2004). This study tried to link social reality upon arrival in the host country, social comparison, and acculturation strategies with NCC. The evidence showed that if, upon arrival, immigrants found a welcoming social support network of co-ethnics, individuals with higher NCC clung more tightly to their culture of "origin." This is due to the fact that the co-ethnic company served as a gratifying source of social reality which validated their prior belief systems. Such a situation may impede the migrants' assimilation to the new culture. In contrast, if immigrants were predominantly in contact with members of the society of settlement during their initial post-entry period, their presence would represent a salient new social reality for the immigrants, with the old social reality quickly fading away. Under these circumstances, "lone," or ethnically isolated, migrants with high NCC might assimilate more quickly to the host culture than their counterparts with low NCC.

8.1.1.6 Locus of control

A major aspect of the self is its executive function: the self makes decisions, initiates actions, and exerts control over both self and environment. This aspect has received considerable attention in cross-cultural studies of personality and adjustment (see Ward, 2001). External locus of control is the generalized expectation that outcomes are determined by outside forces such as powerful others, luck or fate (e.g. bad horoscope) and it is the opposite of internal locus of control, which is the generalized expectation that outcomes depend exclusively on one's own actions. Different studies have consistently demonstrated that an internal locus of control facilitates immigrants' cross-cultural adjustment, whereas an external locus is associated with symptoms of psychological distress (Ward, Chang & Lopez-Nerney, 1999; Ward & Kennedy, 1992). We have to mention that some immigrants come from cultures which traditionally "feed" a more fatalistic explanation of events which could moderate their perception of self-confidence and control over events.

8.1.1.7 Psychological differentiation

Berry (1976) predicted that each individual will experience acculturative influence to a different extent, depending on his level of psychological differentiation. Highly differentiated individuals are those who have a field-independent cognitive style, or, better, who are independent of environmental events and manage to keep the self separate from the social context. On the other hand, individuals who are less differentiated have a field-dependent cognitive style, and thus limited analytic and structuring skills in perception and cognition, which may predispose them to be dependent on environmental events. In their study, Witkin and Berry (1975) found that those individuals who were highly differentiated were able to maintain the self in the face of change and thereby suffered less stress, while those who were less differentiated were more embedded in cultural changes and thereby suffered greater stress.

8.1.2 Others-orientation

As mentioned previously, the self is an interpersonal being. People learn who and what they are from other people and they always have identities as members of social groups. An others-orientation also includes competencies which contribute to effective communication in a foreign country and interactions with others. The most obvious and proactive way in which the self participates in social life is through self-presentation. In general, people want to present themselves favorably. However, self-presentation often occurs in the tension of opposing forces. These forces are related to presenting oneself in a manner consistent with one's own values and ideals, or with those of the interaction partner. One line of research in the area of individual characteristics and acculturation explored the role of self-presentation or self-monitoring.

8.1.2.1 Self-monitoring

As a concept, self-monitoring was introduced into the psychological literature by Snyder (1974) to indicate the ability of individuals to "monitor" their own actions and self-presentation in social situations. Studies suggested that immigrants high in self-monitoring displayed greater adjustment (Montagliani & Giacalone, 1998). Lennox & Wolfe (1984) proposed two independent dimensions to the concept of self-monitoring: getting-ahead and getting-along. Different studies suggest that individuals high on getting-ahead (or high self-monitoring) are perspicacious and good at attending to social cues, which together make them good at establishing social relationships with people (Gangestad & Snyder, 2000; Snyder, 1974). These individuals easily learn new ways of reacting and they are also able to modify their responses in relation to the "feedback" they receive from the social context. The tendency of getting-along is guided instead by the desire to avoid social disapproval, a characteristic related to social anxiety, shyness and low self-esteem. Research (Kosic, 2002b) examined the relationships between "getting-ahead" and "getting-along" as self-monitoring styles in the choice of acculturation strategies and immigrants' adaptation. In this study, getting-ahead was found to be positively related to one's relationship with the host group, whereas getting-along was negatively related to relations with the host group. It seems that the positive social relationships which immigrants high on getting-ahead manage to achieve with the host group go a long way in making them feel more accepted in the new society. They therefore are psychologically and socioculturally well adapted. On the other hand, high cultural maintenance was positively correlated with both styles of self-monitoring: getting-ahead and getting-along. These findings confirm that a motivation for self-presentation in socially desirable ways to obtain social acceptance underlies the personality of people high on getting-along. This attitude appears to be directed first and foremost to people with whom immigrants are familiar in terms of values and culture. This induces less social anxiety than when interacting with a non-familiar group and culture. Furthermore, these findings suggest that immigrants high on getting-along may favor the separation strategy.

8.1.2.2 Extraversion

Of the various individual dimensions relevant within others-orientation, great attention in cross-cultural studies has been focused on extraversion.

Extraversion refers to how individuals express themselves, and it is doubt-less that one of the important tasks for an immigrant is to create and cultivate new social contacts. As suggested by McCrae and Costa (1997), the indi-viduals high on this trait tend to enjoy interacting with others. Nevertheless, studies on this dimension have produced inconsistent results (cf. Ward, 2001). Researchers have found positive, negative and non-significant relationships between extraversion and immigrants' adaptation (Ones & Viswesvaran, 1999). According to some researchers, extraversion includes the ability one has to establish interpersonal relationships with others, including host nation-als. Establishing friendships with host nationals consequently facilitates social learning of culture-specific skills, easing cross-cultural adjustment. However, it should be remembered that some dominant cultures favor intraverted qualities.

8.1.2.3   Big Five

Recent studies have tried to examine more integrated personality models, considering together different factors of self- and others-orientations. Here, above all, we can mention those focused on the "Big Five" traits: extraver-sion, emotional stability, agreeableness, conscientiousness and neuroticism. Ward, Leong and Low (2004) demonstrated that four of the Big Five personal-ity factors are significantly related to cross-cultural adjustment. Psychological adaptation is associated with extraversion, agreeableness, conscientiousness and (less) neuroticism. Sociocultural adaptation is linked to greater extraver-sion and less neuroticism, and to greater agreeableness and conscientiousness. Agreeableness generally facilitated effective communication and social rela-tionships. Those high on this trait are more sympathetic towards others and more cooperative. Conscientiousness, on the other hand, refers to the extent to which individuals are careful, diligent and self-disciplined. Ones and Viswes-varan (1999) found that conscientiousness was the strongest of the Big Five traits in its prediction of several dimensions of immigrants' effectiveness. Fur-thermore, Caligiuri (2000) found that extraversion, agreeableness and emo-tional stability were negatively related to the immigrants' desire to return home.

   Schmitz (1994) combined Big Five dimensions with other personality char-acteristics in an attempt to give a more complex picture of risk versus protective factors in the process of acculturation. His studies revealed that differences in personality dimensions may predispose people to respond with different acculturation strategies. Thus, integration seems to be negatively correlated with neuroticism, aggressiveness, impulsivity, anxiety and field-dependence, and positively correlated with extraversion, emotional stability, sociability, agreeableness, sensation seeking and open-mindedness. Assimilation showed positive correlations with agreeableness and sociability, but also with neu-roticism, anxiety, closed-mindedness and field-dependence. Separation was positively correlated with neuroticism, anxiety, impulsivity, sensation seeking and aggressiveness, and negatively correlated with extraversion, sociability, self-assurance and self-esteem. Finally, marginalization was associated with high unsociability, neuroticism, anxiety and closed-mindedness. Persons who preferred integration were found to be more open-minded and flexible. Emotional stability and a low degree of anxiety appeared to facilitate this process. Immigrants favoring assimilation or segregation did not show this degree of flexibility and openness. This is probably because they are not able or willing to construe more complex behavior systems which combine elements of behavior patterns belonging to different cultural backgrounds. Similar results have been obtained by Ryder, Alden and Paulhus (2000). Here the heritage maintenance subscale was associated with higher conscientiousness and lower neuroticism, whereas the mainstream subscale was associated with higher scores on conscientiousness, extraversion and openness, as well as with lower scores on social anxiety, shyness and neuroticism.

Other authors have focused on personality characteristics and skills which predict an effective appraisal of, and response to, stressful intercultural situations: for example cultural empathy, open-mindedness, social initiative, flexibility and emotional stability (Mol, Van Oudenhoven & Van der Zee, 2001; Van der Zee, Van Oudenhoven & De Grijs, 2004). "Cultural empathy" refers to the ability to empathize with the feelings, thoughts and behaviors of members of different cultural groups. Their sensitivity makes individuals high in this trait less likely to experience communication problems in culturally diverse teams. "Open-mindedness" refers to an unprejudiced attitude towards outgroup members and towards different cultural norms and values (Arthur & Bennet, 1995). Openness is regarded as a facilitator of cross-cultural adjustment because individuals higher in this characteristic are thought to have less rigid views, and will make a greater effort to learn about the new culture or to modify their own behavior to make it more congruent with the cultural norms (Mendenhall & Oddou, 1985). In an experimental study among students, a combined factor comprising cultural empathy and open-mindedness was found to be associated with the tendency to appraise intercultural situations as challenging and to respond positively to those situations (Van der Zee, Atsma & Brodbeck, 2004). A third intercultural dimension is social initiative, defined as the ability to establish social contacts. Emotional stability, which refers to a tendency to respond calmly to stressful events, appeared most consistently as a predictor both of the ability to deal effectively with an intercultural situation and of psychological adjustment (Caligiuri, 2000; Ones & Viswesvaran, 1999). Cultural flexibility is the capacity to substitute activities or interests enjoyed in one's home country with existing activities in the host country. Flexible persons generally tend to perceive new and unknown situations rather as a challenge than as a threat. Flexibility was a predictor of job satisfaction among immigrants (Van Oudenhoven, Mol & Van der Zee, 2003), and of positive relationships with host nationals (Black, 1990). A factor comprising emotional stability and flexibility was found to be associated with a tendency to appraise intercultural situations as less threatening (Van der Zee et al., 2004).

After all, it seems that there has been little convergence in studies that have examined the predictive influence of personality on immigrants' adjustment, and in those rare instances where a degree of consistency has been observed, it has been limited to relatively few trait domains. Schmitz (2001) has pointed out that personality characteristics fail to explain the high percentage of variance of immigrants' acculturation.

8.2   Interaction between personality characteristics and situational factors in the process of acculturation

Searle and Ward (1990) proposed the "cultural fit" hypothesis. They highlighted the significance of the person × situation interaction and suggested that the "fit" between the personal characteristics and norms in the new cultural setting could be a better predictor of immigrants' adaptation than personality *per se*. In their study, Ward and Chang (1997) noted that immigrants from Western countries (USA) in Singapore were more extravert than host nationals and consequently experienced frustration or rejection in response to their persistent attempts to initiate and sustain social relations with the locals. In that case, although extraversion *per se* did not relate to psychological wellbeing, those immigrants who perceived the host-society norms as less discrepant with their norms had a lower level of psychological distress and depression.

8.3   Impact of acculturation on personality

Personality variables have also been studied in relation to ethnic or cultural differences. For example, Triandis (2001) and Markus and Kitayama (1991) coined the terms *collectivism/individualism* and *independent-self/ interdependent-self*, respectively. They demonstrated that the way in which people perceive their social environment depends on their cultural background. An individualistic/independent or idiocentric person, typical of Western European and North American cultures, is concerned with the promotion of individual goals and self-reliance. In a collectivist or interdependent society, typical of many Asian, African and Latin American cultures, people are concerned with how they relate to the society. Personal goals are surrendered in favor of group goals.

Thus, despite the common perception of personality as stable and unchanging, there is some evidence to suggest that cultural differences may be a potential source of variation in personality (Heine, Lehman, Markus & Kitayama, 1999). Few longitudinal studies have examined personality changes secondary to cross-cultural living. Kauffmann (1983) compared 126 American undergraduate students who had spent a semester abroad (in different countries) with 19 peers who had not. Using the Omnibus Personality Inventory and in-person interviews, the author found that those who had lived abroad became more intraverted in their thinking than those who had not. This difference persisted a year after the period abroad. The students also became more sensitive and more interested in aesthetics than their peers who had not studied abroad. These findings are particularly striking given the very short period of time the students lived abroad. These changes may partly be due to the students' developmental stage and to maturation changes rather than cross-cultural living. Another study found that recent Chinese immigrants to North America have personality profiles which closely resembled those found in Hong Kong. Later-generation Chinese have profiles that are similar to those of North Americans, suggesting a predominantly cultural rather than a biological origin for basic personality (McCrae, Yik, Trapnell, Bond & Paulhus, 1998). However, such a "linear gradient" has not always been evident.

8.4   Conclusions

The inconsistent findings on the relationship between personality characteristics and the acculturation-adjustment process suggest the need for a meta-analysis of the literature and further studies. In future research on immigrants' adaptation, it is essential to consider a wider range of individual variables in relation to the situational and cultural-level factors. Furthermore, most of the acculturation research has been confined to correlational studies. There are few studies which have tried to draw causal relationships and a more integrated model between different variables. Personality dimensions cannot be abstracted from the context in which they operate. Studies testing the "cultural fit hypothesis" are therefore particularly interesting.

8.5   References

Arthur, W. & Bennett, W. (1995). The international assignee: the relative importance of factors perceived to contribute to success. *Personnel Psychology*, *48*, 99–114.

Berry, J. W. (1976). *Human ecology and cognitive style: comparative studies in cultural and psychological adaptation*. New York: Sage Publications / Halsted.

(1997). Immigration, acculturation and adaptation. *Applied Psychology: An International Review*, *46*, 5–34.

(2003). Conceptual approaches to acculturation. In K. M. Chun, P. B. Organista & G. Marin (eds.), *Acculturation, advances in theory, measurement, and applied research* (pp. 17–37). Washington, DC: American Psychological Association.

Berry, J. W., Poortinga, Y. H., Segall, M. H. & Dasen, P. R. (2002). *Cross-cultural psychology research and applications*. 2nd edn. Cambridge: Cambridge University Press.

Black, J. S. (1990). The relationship of personal characteristics with the adjustment of Japanese expatriate managers. *Management International Review*, *30*, 119–134.

Boneva, B. S. & Hanson Frieze, I. (2001). Toward a concept of a migrant personality. *Journal of Social Issues*, *57*, 477–491.

Caligiuri, P. M. (2000). Selecting expatriates for personality characteristics: a moderating effect of personality on the relationship between host national contact and cross-cultural adjustment. *Management International Review*, *40*, 61–80.

Chataway, C. & Berry, J. W. (1989). Acculturation experiences, appraisal, coping, and adaptation: a comparison of Hong Kong Chinese, French, and English students in Canada. *Canadian Journal of Behavioural Science*, *21*, 295–309.

Csikszentmihalyi, M. & Figurski, T. (1982). Self-awareness and aversive experience in everyday life. *Journal of Personality*, *50*, 15–28.

Endler, S. N. & Parker, D. A. J. (1994). Assessment of multidimensional coping: task, emotion, and avoidance strategies. *Psychological Assessment*, *6*, 50–60.

Eysenck, H. J. & Eysenck, S. B. G. (1983). Recent advances in the cross-cultural study of personality. In J. N. Butcher & C. D. Spielberger (eds.), *Advances in personality assessment* (Vol. II, pp. 41–69). Hillsdale, NJ: Lawrence Erlbaum Associates.

Furnham, A. & Bochner, S. (1986). *Culture shock. Psychological reactions to unfamiliar environments*. London: Methuen.

Gangestad, S. W. & Snyder, M. (2000). Self-monitoring: appraisal and reappraisal. *Psychological Bulletin*, *126*, 530–555.

Heine, S. J., Lehman, D. R., Markus, H. R. & Kitayama, S. (1999). Is there a universal need for positive self-regard? *Psychological Review*, *106*, 766–794.

Higgins, E. T. & Kruglanski, A. W. (2000). Motivational science: the nature and functions of wanting. In E. T. Higgins & A. W. Kruglanski (eds.), *Motivational science: social and personality perspectives* (pp. 1–20). Philadelphia, PA: Psychology Press.

Kauffmann, N. (1983). The impact of study abroad on personality change. Unpublished doctoral dissertation: School of Education, Indiana University.

Kosic, A. (2002a). Acculturation attitudes, Need for Cognitive Closure and adaptation of immigrants. *Journal of Social Psychology*, *2*, 179–201.

(2002b). Le strategie di acculturazione degli immigrati in funzione di Self-monitoring e delle caratteristiche socio-demografiche [Acculturation strategies of immigrants in function of their Self-monitoring and socio-demographic characteristics]. *Giornale Italiano di Psicologia*, *4*, 757–775.

(2004). Acculturation strategies, coping process and immigrants' adaptation. *Scandinavian Journal of Psychology*, *45*, 269–278.

Kosic, A., Kruglanski, A. W., Pierro, A. & Mannetti, L. (2004). The social cognition of immigrants' acculturation: effects of the need for closure and the reference group at entry. *Journal of Personality and Social Psychology*, *86*, 796–813.

Kosic, A. & Triandafyllidou, A. (2002). *Making sense of Italy as a host country. A qualitative analysis of immigrant discourse*, 3rd Project Report, February 2002, European University Institute, Florence, downloadable from www.iue.it/RSC/IAPASIS.

Kruglanski, A. W. (1989). *Lay epistemics and human knowledge: cognitive and motivational bases*. New York: Plenum Press.

Kruglanski, A. & Webster, D. M. (1996). Motivated closing of the mind: "seizing" and "freezing." *Psychological Review*, *103*, 263–283.

Lazarus, R. & Folkman, S. (1984). *Stress, appraisal, and coping.* New York: Springer Publishing.

Leiba-O'Sullivan, S. (1999). The distinction between stable and dynamic cross-cultural competencies: implications for expatriate trainability. *Journal of International Business Studies, 30,* 709–725.

Lennox, R. D. & Wolfe, R. N. (1984). Revision of the Self-Monitoring Scale. *Journal of Personality and Social Psychology, 46,* 349–364.

Markus, H. & Kitayama, S. (1991). Culture and the self: implications for cognition, emotion, and motivation. *Psychological Review, 98,* 224–253.

(1998). The cultural psychology of personality. *Journal of Cross-Cultural Psychology, 29,* 63–87.

McClelland, D. C. (1987). *Human motivation.* Cambridge: Cambridge University Press.

McCrae, R. R. & Costa, P. T., Jr. (1997). Personality trait structure as a human universal. *American Psychologist, 52,* 509–516.

McCrae, R. R., Yik, M. S. M., Trapnell, P. D., Bond, M. H. & Paulhus, D. L. (1998). Interpreting personality profiles across cultures: bilingual, acculturation, and peer rating studies of Chinese undergraduates. *Journal of Personality and Social Psychology, 71,* 1041–1055.

Mendenhall, M. E. & Oddou, G. (1985). The dimensions of expatriate acculturation: a review. *Academy of Management Review, 10,* 39–47.

Mol, S. T., Van Oudenhoven, J. P. & Van Der Zee, K. I. (2001). Validation of the Multicultural Personality Questionnaire among an internationally oriented student population in Taiwan. In F. Salili & R. Hoosain (eds.), *Research in multicultural education and international perspectives,* Vol. I: *Multicultural education: issues, policies and practices* (pp.167–186). Greenwich, CT: Information Age Publishing.

Montagliani, A. & Giacalone, R. (1998). Impression management in cross-cultural adaptation. *Journal of Social Psychology, 138,* 598–608.

Ones, D. S. & Viswesvaran, C. (1999). Relative importance of personality dimensions for expatriate selection: a policy capturing study. *Human Performance, 12,* 275–294.

Padilla, A. M. & Perez, W. (2003). Acculturation, social identity, and social cognition: a new perspective. *Hispanic Journal of Behavioral Sciences, 25,* 35–55.

Pernice, R. (1994). Methodological issues in research with refugees and immigrants. *Professional Psychology. Research and Practice, 25,* 207–213.

Roccas, S. & Brewer, M. B. (2002). Social identity complexity. *Personality and Social Psychology Review, 6,* 88–106.

Ryder, A. G., Alden, L. E. & Paulhus, D. L. (2000). Is acculturation unidimensional or bidimensional? A head-to-head comparison in the prediction of personality, self-identity, and adjustment. *Journal of Personality and Social Psychology, 79,* 49–65.

Sam, D. L. & Virta, E. (2003). Social group identity and its effect on the self-esteem of adolescents with immigrant background. In R. G. Craven, H. W. Marsh & D. M. McInerney (eds.), *International advances in self research* (pp. 347–373) Sydney: Information Age Publishers.

Schmitz, P. G. (1992a). Acculturation styles and health. In S. Iwawaki, Y. Kashima & K. S. Leung (eds.), *Innovations in cross-cultural psychology* (pp. 360–370). Amsterdam: Swets & Zeitlinger.

(1992b). Personality, stress-reactions, and diseases. *Personality and Individual Differences, 13*, 683–691.

(1994). Acculturation and adaptation process among immigrants in Germany. In A. M. Bouvy, F. J. R. van de Vijver & P. G. Schmitz (eds.), *Journeys into cross-cultural psychology* (pp. 142–157). Amsterdam: Swets & Zeitlinger.

(2001). Psychological aspects of immigration. In L. Loeb Adler & U. P. Gielen (eds.), *Cross-cultural topics in psychology* (pp. 229–245). Westport, CT: Praeger Publishers.

Searle, W. & Ward, C. (1990). The prediction of psychological and sociocultural adjustment during cross-cultural transitions. *International Journal of Intercultural Relations, 14*, 449–464.

Snyder, M. (1974). Self monitoring of expressive behavior. *Journal of Personality and Social Psychology, 30*, 526–537.

Tartakovsky, E. & Schwartz, S. H. (2001). Motivation for emigration, values, well-being, and identification among young Russian Jews. *International Journal of Psychology, 36*, 88–99.

Triandis, H. C. (2001). Individualism-collectivism and personality. *Journal of Personality, 69*, 907–924.

Valentine, S. (2001). Self-esteem, cultural identity, and generation status as determinants of Hispanic acculturation. *Hispanic Journal of Behavioral Sciences, 23*, 459–468.

Van der Zee, K., Atsma N. & Brodbeck F. (2004). The influence of social identity and personality on outcomes of cultural diversity in teams. *Journal of Cross-Cultural Psychology, 35*, 283–303.

Van der Zee, K., Van Oudenhoven, J. P. & De Grijs, E. (2004). Personality, threat, and cognitive and emotional reactions to stressful intercultural situations. *Journal of Personality, 72*, 1069–1096.

Van Oudenhoven, J. P., Mol, S. & Van der Zee, K. I. (2003). Study of the adjustment of Western expatriates in Taiwan ROC with the Multicultural Personality Questionnaire. *Asian Journal of Social Psychology, 6*, 159–170.

Ward, C. (1996). Acculturation. In D. Landis & R. Bhagat (eds.), *Handbook of intercultural training.* 2nd edn. (pp. 124–147). Thousand Oaks, CA: Sage Publications.

(2001). The A, B, Cs of acculturation. In D. Matsomuto (ed.), *The handbook of culture and psychology* (pp. 411– 445). Oxford: Oxford University Press.

Ward, C. & Chang, W. C. (1997). "Cultural fit": a new perspective on personality and sojourner adjustment. *International Journal of Intercultural Relations, 21*, 525–533.

Ward, C., Chang, W. & Lopez-Nerney, S. (1999). Psychological and sociocultural adjustment of Filipina domestic workers in Singapore. In J. C. Lasry, J. Adair & K. Dion. (eds.), *Latest contributions to cultural psychology* (pp. 118–134). Lisse: Swets & Zeitlinger.

Ward, C. & Kennedy, A. (1992). Locus of control, mood disturbance, and social difficulty during cross-Cultural transitions. *International Journal of Intercultural Relations, 16*, 175–194.

Ward, C., Leong, C. H. & Low, M. (2004). Personality and sojourner adjustment: an exploration of the "Big Five" and the "Cultural Fit" proposition. *Journal of Cross-Cultural Psychology, 35*, 137–151.

Webster, M. D. & Kruglanski, W. A. (1994). Individual differences in need for cognitive closure. *Journal of Personality and Social Psychology, 67*, 1049–1062.

Witkin, A. A. & Berry, J. W. (1975). Psychological differentiation in cross-cultural perspective. *Journal of Cross-Cultural Psychology, 6*, 4–87.

9 Design of acculturation studies

John W. Berry

9.1 Introduction

This chapter serves as a bridge between the conceptual frameworks for understanding acculturation that were presented in Chapters 2, 3 and 4, and the concrete proposals for the assessment of acculturation phenomena that will be made in Chapter 10. It is an extension and an update of ideas that were published twenty years ago (Berry, Trimble & Olmedo, 1986). First, it identifies the many specific elements that constitute acculturation phenomena at both the cultural group level, and the individual psychological level. The chapter then considers a variety of research issues that go beyond the usual interest in extent of contact and change, acculturation strategies and adaptation. This includes the examination of various designs, including cross-sectional and longitudinal designs. Of particular interest are one-, two- and three-sample designs which involve, respectively, sampling (i) the non-dominant acculturating group only, (ii) this group plus the dominant larger society, and (iii) these two groups plus the society of origin. We also consider single-setting and comparative designs.

The inclusion of acculturation as a phenomenon in research designs has two roots. In the *ecocultural approach* to cross-cultural psychology, it has been considered to be a counterpart to ecological and related cultural factors in searching for the origins of human behavioral diversity (Berry, Poortinga, Segall & Dasen, 2002). Without the inclusion of acculturation as a variable, the explanation of similarities and differences in human behavior across populations would remain incomplete, since acculturation experiences have an obvious impact on most human behaviors. And second, acculturation phenomena have become a core interest in the field in their own right, taking on a life that is independent of the earlier cross-cultural use of the concept as part of the search for the explanation of behavior across cultures. The earlier chapters in this handbook attest to this active area of research.

9.2 Levels of research

As described in Chapter 2, acculturation phenomena take place at two distinct levels: the cultural group level and the individual psychological level. The original concept, proposed by anthropologists to meet their own interests, was that acculturation is *culture change*; at the time, there was little interest in phenomena of individual or psychological change. However, in 1967, Graves proposed the concept of *psychological acculturation* to focus attention on the obvious fact that individuals who are members of cultural communities that are in a culture contact situation will experience personal changes in their behaviors and underlying psychological attributes, such as attitudes, values and motives.

9.2.1 Cultural level prior to contact

In this section, we outline the numerous features of cultures that change following contact, many of which were originally identified by anthropologists. Referring back to Figure 2.1, we begin our exploration with some of the core phenomena that are brought to the contact setting by each of the original cultures.

Culture A This can be considered to be the dominant cultural group in a particular contact setting. For example, these can be colonizing powers that dominate indigenous peoples, or established societies in which immigrants and refugees settle. What are the characteristics of such dominant groups that need research attention? The essential ones are:

1.   *Purpose* Why is the contact taking place; what are its goals? Clearly acculturation phenomena will vary according to whether the purpose is colonization, enslavement, trade, military control, evangelization, education or international aid.
2.   *Length* For how long has the contact been taking place, and does it occur daily, seasonally or annually? Once again, variations in acculturation may be present due to the history, phase and persistence of contact.
3.   *Permanence* Is the dominant group there to stay; have they settled in, or is it a passing venture?
4.   *Population* How many are there; do they form a majority, or are there only a few people who control the situation?
5.   *Policy* What are the policies being exercised towards non-dominant acculturating groups? Are they assimilation, eventual extermination, indirect rule, segregation/ghettoization, dispersion, etc.?
6.   *Cultural qualities* Are there cultural qualities possessed by the dominant group that can meet specific needs, or improve or undermine the quality of life, of the acculturating group? Potentially desirable cultural traits such as medicines, guns and traps (for hunter populations), seeds, plows, and irrigation techniques (for agricultural populations) will likely lead to acceptance and acculturative changes more than will unwanted or nonfunctional culture traits (such as hostility, discrimination, enforced labor).

These six characteristics are not an exhaustive list, but only serve as examples of the kinds of cultural variables that may contribute to the ways in which acculturation takes place. Without some indication of the nature of these variables, no account of acculturation would be complete.

Culture B A parallel account is needed of the characteristics of Culture B (the non-dominant group) that are brought to the contact setting. The first three features are those that were identified in Chapter 3 as contributing to variations in the kinds of groups making up plural societies.

1. *Purpose* Is the group in contact voluntarily (e.g. immigrants) or under duress (e.g. native peoples)? In some cases, the answer is not entirely clear, requiring sensitive research enquiry.
2. *Location* Is the group in its traditional location, with its land and other resources available, or is it displaced to some new, perhaps less desirable, environment (e.g. reservations, refugee camps)?
3. *Length and permanence* These variables are much the same as for the description of Culture A. In particular, the phase of acculturation needs to be specified: has contact only just begun; have acculturative pressures been building up; has a conflict or crisis appeared in relationships between the two groups?
4. *Population* How many are there; are they a majority or minority; is the population vital (sustaining or increasing in number) or declining?
5. *Policy* To what extent does the group have an organized response to the contact and the resulting acculturation? If there is a policy orientation, is it one of resistance (to get rid of acculturative influence), of inclusion (accepting the influence) or of control (selective inclusion according to some scale of acceptability)?
6. *Cultural qualities* Are there certain aspects of the pre-contact culture which affect the acculturative process? For example, hunter–gatherers are susceptible to habitat destruction due to war, forest reduction or mineral exploration, while agricultural peoples may be dispossessed of their land by permanent settlers from Culture A. More structurally complex societies may be able to organize better politically and militarily than less complex societies in order to alter the course of acculturation, while nomads may be in a position to disperse to avoid major acculturative influences.

Contact In addition to the features brought to the contact setting by the two separate cultural groups, we need to consider some joint features of their interaction. We have already noted some of these (e.g., purpose, permanence and duration of the interaction).

One feature that has been examined extensively in the acculturation literature is the concept of "cultural distance," or "difference" (e.g., Ward, Bochner & Furnham, 2001). This refers to how similar or different the two groups are on some cultural dimensions, such as language, religion, values, status and "race" (i.e., the "visibility" of the non-dominant group in the larger society). Many of these dimensions have been identified by anthropologists, and often the placement of the two groups in contact can be found in the extant literature. For example, are differences in the value placed by the two groups on "hierarchy" or "individualism" a factor in how well they adapt to each other? Do differences in religion make it difficult for the groups to accommodate each other, or do great differences in language (e.g., different language families) make mutual understanding a problem? In addition to these being factors at the level of cultural groups, they are also of importance as an individual-level variable. We will consider below how an individual's perception of these cultural similarities and differences may be important in acculturation research.

9.2.2   Individual level prior to contact

We now turn to the individual level of research interest.

Individual B While there are individual differences in any acculturating group (a point that was emphasized in Chapters 3 and 4), it is likely that there are some psychological phenomena that are characteristic of a particular group that will affect the acculturation process. These have not been widely studied, but one example in the literature (Berry, 1976; Hallowell, 1945) is that of the independence of individuals in hunter–gatherer societies; it has been argued that the values of independence and egalitarianism make it difficult for such persons to accept the new authority and hierarchical arrangements that often arrive with acculturation, and as a consequence the process of acculturation tends to be much more difficult and uneven among nomadic than among sedentary groups.

In addition to these specific psychological characteristics which may be discerned in particular groups, it is also important to consider how the set of cultural-level phenomena listed above for Cultures A and B is distributed across individuals in the group: do they vary according to the person's age, sex, family position, personal abilities, etc.? The crucial point is that not every person in the dominant or non-dominant acculturating groups will necessarily enter into the contact setting and the acculturation process in the same way or to the same degree. This point is at the core of the need for the assessment of individual acculturation as an important psychological aspect of acculturation research.

9.2.3   Cultural level changes following contact

We now turn our attention to the changed cultures of both groups, following their contact, as depicted in Figure 2.1. This focus on culture change is of equal importance for both groups in contact; it is now clear that dominant societies are challenged and changed in various ways, just as non-dominant groups are.

We need to understand the changes that have actually taken place as a result of the acculturation process (recognizing, of course, that in many cases the acculturative influences continue to affect the group, and changes are ongoing). These global consequences of acculturation have received considerable attention in the literature (see Berry, 1980, for an early review of some conceptual approaches to "social change"), and include such global descriptors as Westernization, Modernization, Industrialization, Americanization, Russification, Sinofication, Sanskritization, Toyotafication, Cocacolonization, etc. For the purposes of this chapter such broad characterizations are considered to be too general (Kağitçibaşi, 1996). Instead, we will attempt to look more closely at some specific phenomena which can be organized according to a number of headings.

1.   *Political* Have there been changes in political characteristics as a result of acculturation? For example, in the dominant society, has there been political reaction, and policy change (such as a rise in prejudice and discrimination) resulting from increased intercultural interaction? In the non-dominant group, has independence been lost, have previously unrelated (even warring) groups been placed within a common political framework, are there new authority systems (e.g. chiefs, mayors, governors)?

2.   *Economic* Has the economic role of the dominant group been changed, for example by assuming higher-status jobs, or by becoming financial elites (in a newly established hierarchical system)? In the non-dominant group, has the subsistence base been changed, or the distribution of wealth been altered? For example, have hunter–gatherers been converted into herders or farmers, or others into industrial or wage workers? Have previous concentrations of wealth in certain families or regions been eliminated, or, conversely, has a new wealthy class emerged from a previously uniform system? Have new economic activities been introduced, such as mining, forestry, game management, tourism and manufacturing?

3.   *Demographic* Has there been a change in the population size of the two groups? Following initial contact, non-dominant population size often declines due to the introduction of disease, changes in nutrition, war or enslavement. Have there been changes in the population's urban/rural distribution, its age or sex profile, or in regional dispersion?

4.   *Cultural* To what extent are there new languages, religions, modes of dress, schooling, transportation, housing, and forms of social organization and social relations in the two acculturating groups? How do these relate to the previous norms; do they conflict with them, partially displace them, or merge? For example, in language, do people become bilingual or develop a Creole; or in religion do syncretic beliefs appear as in some African Christian churches?

All of these, and possibly many more depending on the location of one's research, are important markers of the extent to which cultural-level acculturation has taken place in the two groups.

9.2.4 Individual level changes following contact

We now consider the psychological characteristics of individuals who are changing, or who have changed, as a result of contact. As noted above, there are very likely to be individual differences in the psychological characteristics that people bring to the acculturation process; moreover, not every person will necessarily participate to the same extent in the acculturation process. These individual differences in contact and participation will inevitably lead to individual differences in the psychological changes that have actually taken place. For example, one of the most substantial relationships found in the acculturation literature is that a person's degree of participation in formal Western-type schooling is associated with changes in their performance on cognitive tasks, attitudes and values. This means that we need to shift our focus away from general characterizations and assessments of acculturation phenomena at the group level, to a concern for individual variation in the sample of persons who are taken to represent the group undergoing acculturation.

What individual-level phenomena need our research attention? An answer to this question would require a review of virtually all research on psychological acculturation. Since this *Handbook* is an attempt to achieve this, only a simple and partial listing of psychological phenomena can be provided here, following Figure 2.1. First, we need to consider some way of characterizing the degree of contact and participation that an individual has undergone. These include such indicators as their experience of formal schooling, wage employment, urbanization, media use, political participation, and exposure to new languages and religions.

Second, numerous phenomena can be included in the category of *behavioral shifts* (in Figure 2.1). Many of these are examined in Chapter 10, where the focus is on their assessment. First, research often considers a person's daily behaviors (such as their diet, language, dress, social relations); many of these are selected as domains in research on their acculturation attitudes (their preferences) and their actual behaviors (together termed *acculturation strategies*). Second, since defining oneself becomes particularly salient in intercultural settings, changes in one's cultural identity are often an important topic of research (Liebkind, 2001; Phinney, 1991; see also Chapter 6). In this research, there is usually substantial interest in the relative changes in identity as a member of one's heritage culture (*ethnic identity*) and as a member of the larger society (*national identity*).

Beyond these behavioral changes, the category of *acculturative stress* was also presented in Figure 2.1. As noted in Chapter 4, these are the changes that arise as a result of challenges to an acculturating person that exceed their ability to cope effectively. Individuals may become nostalgic, "home sick" or even depressed, as a result of loss of culture, society or habitat. They may also become anxious, as a result of uncertainty about how they should be living at the intersection of the two cultures: should they act in one culturally appropriate way or the other; should they alternate depending on context, or blend the two behavioral repertoires? All of these, and many more, are usually included in acculturation research assessment that focuses on individual behavioral change.

On the right-hand side of Figure 2.1 are various individual adaptation phenomena. As noted in Chapter 4, these can be primarily *psychological*, or *socio-cultural*; typically, both aspects are involved in how (and how well) a person carries out their life in the contact setting. In addition to these two concepts, others are involved here, including *appraisal*, *coping*, and some longer-term indicators of successful adaptation in the world of work, and other aspects of participation in one's new society. All of these, and many more, are important aspects in the study of the individual level of acculturation.

Finally, we need to be aware that individual acculturation (as well as group-level phenomena) does not cohere as a nice neat package. Not only will groups and individuals vary in their participation and response to acculturative influences, some domains of culture and behavior may become altered without comparable changes in other domains. For example, attitudes towards the value of traditional technology may change without a parallel change in beliefs and behaviors associated with it. That is, the process of acculturation is an uneven one, and does not affect all cultural and psychological phenomena in a uniform manner.

9.3   Cross-sectional and longitudinal designs

As we have noted, acculturation is a process which takes place over time, and which results in changes both in the culture and in the individual. As for all processes, it is really only possible to observe change when the study design is longitudinal. The measurement of change, between two or more points in time, is a topic which has a considerable literature in developmental and educational psychology, but not much in anthropology or in cross-cultural psychology. This lack has been highlighted for anthropology by a volume devoted to conducting long-term, even continuous, field work (Foster, Scudder, Colson & Kemper, 1978), but no similar treatment exists for cross-cultural psychology.

Culture change, as well as individual change, can only be noted and assessed when two sets of data are compared over time using the same people. While this is ideal, in practice such a two-point comparison is not practicable in most acculturation research settings. Instead, a more usual practice is that many of the cultural features are identified from other sources (e.g., earlier ethnographic accounts) or partially reconstructed from reports of the older and/or the less-influenced members of the community. Similarly, individual change can ideally be assessed by longitudinal research, and this is often plagued with problems of loss through death or out-migration, and by problems of the continuing relevance of research instruments.

A common alternative to longitudinal research is cross-sectional research in which a time-related variable, such as length of residence or generational status, is employed. For example, among immigrants, those who have resided longer in the dominant society may experience more acculturative contact and change than those residing for a shorter period (usually controlling for present age and age of arrival). Similarly, it is common to classify group members by their generation (first generation are themselves immigrants, second generation are their offspring, etc.). An assumption here is that acculturation is a linear process over time, an assumption which we will consider and challenge later.

One longitudinal study (Berry, Wintrob, Sindell & Mawhinney, 1982) which employed both a longitudinal and cross-sectional design, was concerned with how the Cree communities and individuals of James Bay (northern Quebec) would respond to a large-scale hydroelectric project being constructed in their midst. Initial field work with adults and teenagers was carried out before construction was announced or began. Eight years later (after construction was completed, and villages relocated), about half the original sample was studied again, supplemented by an equal number of new individuals who were the same ages as the original sample was eight years earlier. This provided a longitudinal analysis for one group (who were compared at two points in time), and a cross-sectional analysis to maintain an age control. Another longitudinal study with indigenous peoples who were also refugees was carried out by Donà and Berry (2000), as reported in Chapter 14. In that study, Guatemalan Mayan refugees were the focus of research in camps in Mexico, then later in their new villages on return to Guatemala.

A longitudinal study of immigrants was carried out by Ho (1995) in New Zealand, with Chinese adolescents from Hong Kong. She tracked the acculturation attitudes of these young immigrants over time, from their arrival until they had been settled for one year. At first, their preferences were widely distributed across the four attitudes, but over time they gradually shifted towards a stronger preference for integration as opposed to assimilation, separation or marginalization.

A longitudinal study of sojourners was carried out by Zheng and Berry (1991) with a sample of visiting research fellows who relocated from China to Canada. The study was designed to assess their acculturation preferences and adaptation at intervals from before their arrival, during their sojourn, until their return to China. The study took place in 1989, and the sojourn was interrupted by events in Tiananmen Square; a number of the participants became unavailable for follow-up, and many did not return to China. Hence, the longitudinal period was curtailed, and was limited to six months. Nevertheless, a plot of changes in these acculturation phenomena was possible over this shorter time interval. Another study with sojourners was carried out by Kealey (1989) who studied Canadian international development workers on assignment abroad. He interviewed them prior to departure, during their posting in a number of countries, and on their return to Canada. He was able to link their acculturation strategies to their adaptation, including their own satisfaction, and their peer-rated job effectiveness. These studies illustrate the possibilities of doing longitudinal research on acculturation, as well as the kinds of problems that can be encountered in naturalistic settings.

Other designs may be needed in other acculturation arenas. For example, among a settled population where longitudinal work is not done, length of residence and generational status are not appropriate variables. Here a respondent's age may be a suitable surrogate, since younger persons are usually more exposed to acculturative influences (such as schooling, television, popular Western culture) than older members of the community. Moreover, older members have a longer history of enculturation in their original culture and hence may be more resistive to exposure and change. The essential issue, though, is to ensure that both the design and the measures match as well as possible the local acculturation phenomena, rather than emulating more precise but irrelevant or impossible designs which are standard in other domains of research.

9.4   Number of samples

As we have just argued, since acculturation involves change, it should ideally be assessed by using longitudinal designs. However, acculturation can also be examined using quasi-experimental designs. Although most studies in the literature focus only on one acculturating group such as immigrants, this is far from ideal. With such a single group design, it is not possible to note whether they differ from those already living in the society of settlement, or from those who remain out of the acculturative arena by staying in the country of origin. Thus, some researchers have sampled peers from the society of settlement (providing a two group comparison), and some have also sampled peers in the home country (providing a three-group comparison).

An example of the two-group design is the study of immigrant youth (Berry, Phinney, Sam & Vedder, 2006). In this study, samples of young immigrants were taken in 13 societies of settlement, along with parallel samples of their non-immigrant peers. This design allows for the examination of similarities and differences in how well both sets of youth are adapting both psychologically (e.g., wellbeing) and socioculturally (e.g., in school). Other two-group designs focus on distinguishing between stressors that are specific to the acculturation process, and those that are shared by all people in their daily lives (e.g., Lay & Nguyen, 1998).

A few three-group designs have been carried out; these now include samples of those who have remained in their home country. For example, Ataca (1998) studied immigrant Turkish married couples in Canada, non-immigrant couples in Turkey, and non-Turkish couples in Canada. Using this design, she was able to distinguish between acculturation-specific phenomena and those that occur in lives unaffected by the immigration process.

9.5   Number of societies; the comparative advantage

A longstanding problem in acculturation studies has been the very limited sampling of societies in which acculturating groups have been studied. Most acculturation research has been conducted in just a few societies (e.g., Australia, Canada, USA), while most acculturation is taking place in other parts of the world (eg, in China, India, and in African, European and South American societies). Moreover, most studies are carried out in only one society, and often with only one acculturating group in that society. This is the problem faced by most psychological research, and which has led to the emergence of cross-cultural psychology as a field of comparative enquiry. While it is important to know about acculturation phenomena in one group in one society, there is the possibility that such limited research findings will be generalized beyond the setting in which they were obtained. Hence, comparative studies of acculturation have long been advocated (e.g., Berry, Kim, Minde & Mok, 1987), but few have been accomplished until now. There are now well-known problems to be encountered when doing such comparative research. However, there are also many solutions to these problems of comparability and equivalence (e.g. Berry, 1969; Van de Vijver & Leung, 1997). Since these problems and their solutions are closely connected with assessment issues, they will be addressed in Chapter 10.

Some comparative studies of acculturation have been carried out as part of a program of research into the acculturation of indigenous peoples (Berry, 1976) and immigrants (Berry *et al.*, 1987). More recently, in a study of Indian youth in three countries, Ghuman (2003) was able to show patterns of similarities and differences across Australia, Canada and the UK. Another such study is reported by van Oudenhoven in Chapter 11, in which immigrants from Friesland were sampled and compared in three societies.

As mentioned previously in this *Handbook*, the International Comparative Study of Ethnocultural Youth (the ICSEY project) sampled youth from over thirty different immigrant groups in thirteen societies of settlement, and included samples of non-immigrant peers. This study was explicitly designed to examine patterns of similarities and differences in acculturation, identity and adaptation, comparatively across groups and societies. One of the main findings was the large similarity among individuals in these phenomena across groups and societies; most of the variance was due to individual differences, and much less to group and national society differences (Berry *et al.*, 2006). This finding speaks directly to the generalizability of research results obtained in only one society; youth appear to be acculturating in similar ways, with similar adaptation outcomes, and with a similar pattern of relationships between *how* they acculturate and *how well* they acculturate.

9.6   Conclusions

In this chapter, we have attempted to expand the range of acculturation phenomena beyond the conventional examination of a small set of behaviors in one acculturating group in one society. We have emphasized that understanding the cultural level of acculturation phenomena is of equal importance to the psychological-level phenomena. This is one of the basic tenets of the field of cross-cultural psychology which argues that knowing the cultural context is essential in order to interpret any psychological phenomena. A second tenet of the field is that multiple samples in multiple societies are required if we are ever to comprehend human behavior in all its cultural variety. Hence, we have argued that *context* and *comparison* are both core elements in designing complete acculturation research studies.

Beyond these two general principles, numerous components at both the cultural and psychological levels have been identified as part of the vast array of acculturation phenomena available to be examined. This should enable us to increase the range of acculturation phenomena to be included in a particular study. No longer should we be limited to examining such well-established and core concepts as acculturation attitudes, identities and wellbeing.

A "complete" acculturation research design should ideally range over all of these phenomena, in multiple samples in multiple societies, allowing for comprehensive findings that match the complex realities that occur during acculturation. Of course, no single researcher, in any single study, can hope to achieve this ideal. However, by laying out such a full design, we will be in a position to sample elements from it systematically, and be better able to understand both the potential and the limitations of the project that is undertaken.

9.7   References

Ataca, B. (1998). Psychological, sociocultural and marital adaptation of Turkish couples in Canada. Unpublished doctoral thesis: Queen's University, Kingston, Ontario.

Berry, J. W. (1969). On cross-cultural comparability. *International Journal of Psychology*, *4*, 119–128.

(1976). *Human ecology and cognitive style: comparative studies in cultural and psychological adaptation*. New York: Sage Publications / Halsted.

(1980). Social and cultural change. In H. C. Triandis & R. Brislin (eds.), *Handbook of cross-cultural psychology* (Vol. V, pp. 211–279). Boston: Allyn & Bacon.

Berry, J. W., Kim, U., Minde, T. & Mok. D. (1987). Comparative studies of acculturative stress. *International Migration Review, 21*, 491–511.

Berry, J. W., Phinney, J. S., Sam, D. L. & Vedder, P. (eds.) (2006). *Immigrant youth in cultural transition: acculturation, identity and adaptation across national groups*. Mahwah, NJ: Lawrence Erlbaum Associates.

Berry, J. W., Poortinga, Y. H., Segall, M. H. & Dasen, P. R. (2002). *Cross-cultural psychology: research and applications*. 2nd edn. New York: Cambridge University Press.

Berry, J. W., Trimble, J. & Olmedo, E. (1986). The assessment of acculturation. In W. J. Lonner & J. W. Berry (eds.), *Field methods in cross-cultural research* (pp. 291–324). Newbury Park: Sage Publications.

Berry, J. W., Wintrob, R., Sindell, P. & Mawhinney, T. (1982). Psychological effects of acculturation among the James Bay Cree. *Naturaliste Canadien, 109*, 965–975.

Donà, G. & Berry, J. W. (2000). Refugee acculturation and re-acculturation. In A. Ager (ed.), *Refugees: perspectives on the experience of forced migration* (pp. 169–195). New York: Continuum.

Foster, G., Scudder, T., Colson, E. & Kemper, R. (eds.) (1978). *Long-term field research in anthropology*. Orlando: Academic Press

Ghuman, P. A. S. (1991). Best or worst of two worlds? A study of Asian adolescents. *Educational Review, 33*, 121–132.

(2003). *Double loyalties: South Asian adolescents in the West*. Cardiff: University of Wales Press.

Graves, T. (1967). Psychological acculturation in a tri-ethnic community. *South-Western Journal of Anthropology, 23*, 337–350.

Hallowell, A. I. (1945). Sociopsychological aspects of acculturation. In R. Linton (ed.), *The science of man in the world crisis* (pp. 310–332). New York: Columbia University Press.

Ho, E. (1995). Chinese or New Zealander? Differential paths of adaptation of Chinese adolescent immigrants in New Zealand. *New Zealand Population Review, 21*, 27–49.

Kağitçibaşi, C. (1996). *Family and human development across cultures: a view from the other side*. Hillsdale, NJ: Lawrence Erlbaum Associates.

Kealey, D. (1989). A study of cross-cultural effectiveness: theoretical issues, practical applications. *International Journal of Intercultural Relations, 13*, 387–428.

Lay, C. & Nguyen, T. (1998). The role of acculturation-related and acculturation non-related hassles: Vietnamese-Canadian students and psychological distress. *Canadian Journal of Behavioural Science, 30*, 5–14.

Liebkind, K. (2001). Acculturation. In R. Brown & S. Gaertner (eds.), *Blackwell handbook of social psychology: intergroup processes* (pp. 386–406). Oxford: Blackwell.

Phinney, J. (1990). Ethnic identity in adolescents and adults: a review of research. *Psychological Bulletin, 108*, 499–514.

Van de Vijver, F. & Leung, K. (1997). *Methods and data analyses for cross-cultural research*. Newbury Park: Sage Publications.

Ward, C., Bochner, S. & Furnham, A. (2001). *The psychology of culture shock*. Hove: Routledge.

Zheng, X. & Berry, J. W. (1991). Psychological adaptation of Chinese sojourners in Canada. *International Journal of Psychology, 26*, 451–470.

10 Assessment of psychological acculturation

Judit Arends-Tóth & Fons J. R. van de Vijver

10.1 Assessment of psychological acculturation: choices in designing an instrument

Despite the relevance of acculturation for plural societies, major issues in its conceptualization and measurement remain unresolved. The assessment of acculturation[1] has not yet become an integral part of assessment in multicultural groups, possibly because no widely accepted conceptualizations and measurement methods are available (e.g., Suzuki, Ponterotto & Meller, 2001). The main aim of this chapter is to compare and integrate current approaches, models and measurement methods of acculturation in order to optimize its assessment.

The chapter is divided into four parts: the first part describes a framework of acculturation variables. The second part discusses theoretical models and measurement methods in acculturation research. The third part addresses some important choices in designing an acculturation instrument and discusses conceptual and methodological issues. Finally, in the fourth part implications and promising directions in acculturation research are discussed.

10.2 Framework of acculturation variables

The first step which is needed, in our view, in order to clarify acculturation and assess it properly is to make a distinction among different acculturation variables. Acculturation variables can be broadly divided into three groups: conditions, orientations and outcomes (see Figure 10.1). This figure is an extension of Figure 2.1, developed in order to highlight features that are specific to assessment issues.

We introduce the concept of acculturation conditions to refer to the background setting that is relevant in the assessment of acculturation. These conditions define the limits and demands of the acculturation process involving group and individual characteristics. At the group level, variables involve characteristics of the receiving society, of the society of origin, of the immigrant group, and perceived inter-group relations. At the individual level, conditions

---

[1] The terms *acculturation* and *psychological acculturation* are used as synonyms in this chapter.

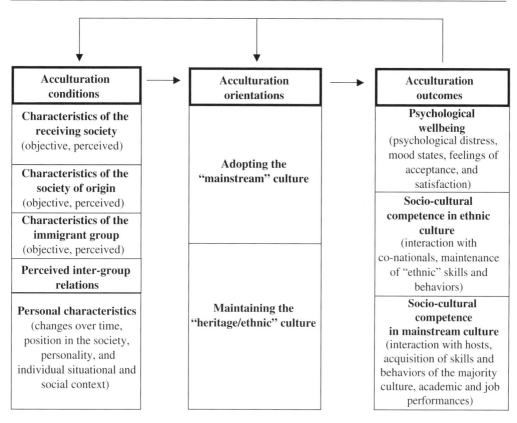

Figure 10.1 *Framework of acculturation variables*

can refer to changes over time, to position in the society, to personality characteristics and abilities, and to individual situational or social context.

Acculturation orientations structure the acculturation process by relating acculturation conditions to outcomes. According to Berry (1997) they refer to two fundamental issues facing immigrants:[2] one involves the decision to maintain one's culture of origin and the other refers to the extent to which the immigrant wishes to have contacts with and participation in the mainstream culture. Bourhis, Moïse, Perreault and Sénécal (1997) proposed a refinement by changing the nature of the second aspect, making it cultural instead of social. These authors state that the two underlying fundamental issues refer then to maintaining key aspects of the ethnic culture and adopting key aspects of the majority group.

Acculturation outcomes refer to the degree of success of the acculturation process (in the broadest sense). Various indices of acculturation outcomes have been examined (e.g., psychological wellbeing and sociocultural competence including the nature and extent of interaction with hosts, the acquisition

[2] The term *immigrants* is used in this chapter to cover various groups involved in an acculturation process, such as immigrants, refugees, asylum seekers and sojourners.

of behaviors and skills of the mainstream culture, academic and job performances). Although sociocultural competence focuses on the level of competence in the mainstream culture, from a theoretical point of view it is also important to address the level of sociocultural competence in the ethnic culture (e.g., interaction with co-nationals, maintenance of "ethnic" skills and behaviors) and changes in this competence as an outcome variable.

10.3   Theoretical models and measurement methods

Many studies of how immigrants cope with intercultural contact focus on acculturation orientations. Although most researchers agree with the definition of acculturation orientations, there are differences in the ways in which they have been operationalized and measured. Current theoretical models of acculturation differ in two aspects: dimensionality and domain specificity.

10.3.1   Dimensionality

The relationship between the two main aspects of acculturation orientations, maintenance of the heritage culture and adoption of the mainstream culture, has been the focus of much acculturation research. Two models of acculturation prevail, which are called the unidimensional and the bidimensional model.

The unidimensional model assumes that change in cultural orientation takes place along a single continuum whereby different aspects of the heritage culture are lost as aspects of the majority culture are adopted (Gordon, 1964). For example, the ability to speak the heritage language is expected to decrease as immigrants become more proficient in the mainstream language.

The bidimensional model sees cultural maintenance and adoption of the mainstream culture as two, presumably independent, dimensions (e.g., Hutnik, 1986; LaFromboise, Coleman & Gerton, 1993; Sánchez & Fernández, 1993; Sayegh & Lasry, 1993; Szapocznik, Kurtines & Fernández, 1980). The ability to speak the heritage language is assumed not to influence the ability to speak the language of the mainstream society. The most widely researched bidimensional acculturation model was developed by Berry (see Chapter 3). Based on the sectors defined by the two dimensions, four acculturation strategies are defined. *Assimilation* involves a preference for relinquishing the heritage culture and participating in the new culture; *integration* refers to a preference for both maintaining one's heritage culture and participating in the new culture; *separation* involves a preference for maintaining one's heritage culture without participating in the new culture; and *marginalization* involves non-adherence to both of the two cultures.

In a third proposed model that could be called a *fusion model*, an acculturating individual mixes both cultures in a new "integrated culture." This integrated culture may either contain a mix of the two cultures (combining "the best of both worlds") or may contain unique aspects that are atypical of either culture (Coleman, 1995; Roosens, 1989). This model implies that acculturation is not only a choice between characteristics of two cultures, but also a mixture of these characteristics. This form of acculturation has also been examined among indigenous peoples in India, where it was termed *coexistence* (Mishra, Sinha & Berry, 1996).

10.3.2 Domain specificity

Domain-specific models start from the assumption that acculturation preferences and practices vary across life domains (e.g., Keefe & Padilla, 1987). For example, one may seek economic or work assimilation and linguistic integration, while maintaining separation in family and marriage.

Another argument in favor of domain-specific models comes from studies in which acculturative changes are studied across time (e.g., comparing first- and second-generation immigrants). These studies show that acculturative change does not take place at the same rate across life domains; attitudes towards specific life domains (e.g., social contacts, language use) may be altered without comparable changes in others (e.g., cultural values, childrearing). The use of a single index of acculturation (one score or a cumulative scale score) may obscure variation of acculturation preferences across domains (e.g., Birman & Trickett, 2001; Mendoza, 1989; Padilla, 1995).

The models of domain specificity that have been proposed in the literature differ in their levels of abstraction (i.e., the breadth of the domain). Three levels of abstraction of domain specificity can be distinguished (see Table 10.1). In our work we find that the first level is constituted by two broad domains: the public (functional, utilitarian) and the private (social-emotional, value-related) domain (Arends-Tóth & Van de Vijver, 2003). Turkish-Dutch reported that they prefer to adopt the Dutch culture more in the public domain than in the private domain, while maintaining the heritage culture is important in both domains. The second level of domain specificity is formed by specific life domains (e.g., education and language, which belong to the public domain, and childrearing and marriage, which belong to the private domain). The third level refers to specific situations; an individual's preference for adopting the mainstream culture or maintaining the heritage culture may vary across specific situations. Researchers have shown that the salience of cultural orientation can vary as a function of specific situations (e.g., Clément & Noels, 1992; Taylor & Lambert, 1996). Sodowsky and Carey (1988) described certain dual characteristics of first-generation Asian Indians in the USA, who preferred Indian food and dress at home and American food and dress elsewhere. Similarly, Phalet, Van Lotringen and Entzinger (2000) found that Dutch immigrant youth preferred cultural maintenance at home and valued Dutch culture outside of the home.

Table 10.1 *A classification of acculturation models: domain specificity and dimensionality (Arends-Tóth & Van de Vijver, 2004)*

| | Dimensionality | | |
Domain specificity	Unidimensional models	Bidimensional models	Fusion models
Trait models (domain-aspecific models)	Immigrant adopts the mainstream culture	Immigrant has two attitudes: maintaining heritage culture and adopting the mainstream culture	A new culture emerges
Level 1: cluster of domains (e.g., public and private domains) Level 2: specific life domains (e.g., childrearing, news) Level 3: specific situations (e.g., childrearing outside home)	Speed of adopting the mainstream culture varies across domains/situations	Same as above, but now applied for life domains/situations	A new culture emerges in a domain/ situation

10.3.2.1   Culture-specific and culture-general domains

Acculturation measures can also be categorized as either culture-specific or culture-general. Culture-specific acculturation scales are more appropriate for individualized clinical services, whereas more general instruments are useful in assessing commonalities among immigrants, particularly when they differ in ethnic background or country of settlement.

10.3.3   Acculturation measurement methods

There tends to be a close link between theoretical models and measurement methods of acculturation orientations. In the unidimensional model, a *one-statement measurement method* has been employed, characterized by a bipolar scale, ranging from maintaining the heritage culture at one pole to adopting the mainstream culture at the other pole. In some studies, a cumulative scale score is used indicating the acculturation status (Celano & Tyler, 1991; Cuéllar, Harris & Jasso, 1980; Suinn, Ahuna & Khoo, 1992), while in other studies domain-specific unidimensional models have been proposed (e.g., Triandis, Kashima, Shimada & Villareal, 1988).

For the bidimensional model, two measurement methods have been proposed: the *two-statement measurement method* and the *four-statement measurement method*. In the two-statement method, acculturation is assessed by using two separate scales: one representing orientations towards the mainstream culture and the other representing orientations towards the heritage culture (e.g., Donà & Berry, 1994; Padilla, 1995; Sánchez & Fernández, 1993; Stephenson, 2000). In the four-statement method, the orientations towards each of the four acculturation strategies distinguished by Berry are assessed in separate items.

As no standardized or widely accepted acculturation measures exist, researchers often design their own acculturation instruments. In order to assess acculturation adequately, some important decisions have to be made. In the following section, we address with examples some important choices in designing an acculturation instrument.

10.4   Important choices in the assessment of acculturation

At least six choices are important in designing an acculturation instrument:

1.   The clear and explicit formulation of research goals (what is the rationale for including acculturation measures?) and a choice of acculturation variables.
2.   The choice of acculturation aspects (e.g., knowledge, values, attitudes or behavior) (what to study?).
3.   The choice of research methodology (how to study?).
4.   The choice of a theoretical model and measurement method (how to assess acculturation?).
5.   The choice of life domains and situations to be dealt with in the items (in which domains and situation to assess?).
6.   The choice of item wording.

The questions are described below in more detail.

10.4.1   Clarity about research aims and acculturation variables

The first essential step in designing an acculturation instrument is a clear and explicit formulation of research aims and expectations. Unfortunately, this is not always the case. Acculturation is often used in research with immigrants without a priori addressing its utility or practical and theoretical relevance. Immigrants are often asked to fill in questionnaires about their acculturation without looking for other relevant related constructs. Using acculturation as an explanation variable without explicitly measuring it is another often-encountered problem in research. Measuring one's occupational, educational or generational status as a proxy may not be effective, as it does not provide the level of detail that is needed for an adequate understanding.

After deciding that acculturation measures are relevant and needed in a study, the next step is to decide which acculturation variables should be addressed. Is acculturation a condition, a moderator/mediator or an outcome in the study?

If the distinction is not clearly made and features are combined in a single score, it can be difficult to interpret acculturation scores and its relationship with other variables.

10.4.2   Choices of acculturation aspects

Acculturation orientations, the most widely used acculturation variables, refer to different aspects, such as knowledge, values, beliefs, identity, attitudes and behaviors. Although there are individual and group differences in acculturation orientations, there are also some common underlying processes. Changes in various aspects of acculturation are likely to occur at different rates: values, ideologies and world-views do not modify as easily as other aspects of acculturation such as knowledge and behaviors. Although the different aspects of acculturation may well yield a different picture (as they do not change in a uniform way), much acculturation research does not make a clear distinction among them and uses a mixture of acculturative aspects in questionnaires.

Ethnic identity and acculturation attitudes have often been used interchangeably in acculturation research. Many authors seem to agree that they have different connotations, although there is disagreement about their relationship (see Chapter 6). Acculturation attitudes refer to preferences given to the cultures involved in the process (e.g., Ward, Bochner & Furnham, 2001), whereas ethnic identity refers to the subjective sense of belonging to an ethnic group or culture (LaFromboise *et al.*, 1993; Phinney, 1990). Changes in attitudes and identity are likely to occur at different rates: acculturation attitudes change easier than ethnic identity.

Studies with Turkish-Dutch adults, which addressed the relations between acculturation attitudes and behaviors (Arends-Tóth & Van de Vijver, 2006) showed that attitudes and behaviours yield partly complementary information. A high overall level of structural equivalence between acculturation attitudes and behaviors was found, implying that both have the same psychological structure and that they can be conceptualized using a single theoretical model; yet, the studies also indicated that attitudinal and behavioral aspects cannot be interchanged as the mean scores for both can be substantially different. Therefore, it is important to consider both attitudinal and behavioral aspects in the assessment of acculturation and the two aspects should be measured with separate subscales.

10.4.3   Research methodologies in acculturation

After the choice of acculturation aspects, the choice of how to study them has to be addressed. Various research methodologies have been used in acculturation, such as observations, case studies, questionnaires, scales, vignette studies, interviews, and information from significant others. The most widely used methodology is a (self-report) questionnaire. Because self-reports have known limitations (e.g., social desirability), researchers could obtain convergent (and divergent) validation by sources of information other than the respondent's report, such as observations, research in experimental settings, and information from friends and relatives. In addition, attaining supplementary information on other aspects of acculturation orientations, including attitudes, cognitions and values, would greatly enhance the scope (and also the accuracy) of acculturation studies.

10.4.4 Measurement methods

The next step in designing an acculturation instrument is how to assess acculturation aspect(s). All measurement methods (the one-, two- and four-statement method) have their own advantages and limitations; examples of the acculturation measurement methods can be found in Box 10.1. The one-statement method has the advantage of yielding an efficient, short instrument, because it allows for a simple interpretation in multicultural assessment by defining acculturation scores as a distance from the mainstream culture. However, the method has an important limitation: if individuals score on the midpoint of the scale, no difference can be made between those who value both cultures equally highly (integration) and those who do not want to relate to either culture (marginalization). Adding an extra response alternative (indicating adherence neither to the mainstream culture, nor the heritage culture) to the answer categories may solve this problem.

A study of the association between the heritage and mainstream dimensions of acculturation (measured with the two-statement method) is theoretically interesting. A strong negative correlation between the two aspects would support the unidimensional model while a low or zero correlation would support the existence of two orthogonal dimensions, as often assumed in the literature on this model. Empirical studies of their association have shown considerable disagreement. Correlations have been found to be negative (e.g., Birman & Trickett, 2001; Elias & Blanton, 1987; Kim, Laroche & Tomiuk, 2001; Laroche, Kim & Hui, 1997; Nguyen, Messé & Stollak, 1999), low and non-significant (e.g., Hutnik, 1986; Sánchez & Fernández, 1993; Sayegh & Lasry, 1993), and positive (e.g., Ward & Kennedy, 1994).

Different procedures have been proposed to transform the two dimension scores into Berry's four acculturation strategies. An overview of the procedures is given in Box 10.2.

The four-statement method is the only one in which the four acculturation strategies are independently assessed and, hence, can show any degree of relationship in empirical data. In spite of this advantage, this method has also some limitations. Because acculturation strategies are defined as arising from two attitudes towards two cultures, the Likert items tend to be "double-barreled." Participants can interpret such items in different ways or may answer to only a part of the item. Also, the use of negations (marginalization items tend to

Box 10.1 Examples of acculturation measurement methods

One-statement measurement method
One item is formulated per domain.

Instruction: Choose one option

I find it important to have...
- ☐ only Turkish friends
- ☐ more Turkish than Dutch friends
- ☐ as many Turkish as Dutch friends
- ☐ more Dutch than Turkish friends
- ☐ only Dutch friends
- ☐ no Turkish and no Dutch friends (this option can be added to measure marginalization)

Two-statement measurement method
Two items are formulated per domain. One refers to adopting the mainstream culture and the other to maintaining the heritage culture. It is important to formulate the two items in such a way that they differ only regarding the dimensions and not in using words or in another way.

Instruction: Indicate agreement on a five-point Likert scale
   I find it important to have Dutch friends (mainstream culture)
   I find it important to have Turkish friends (heritage culture)
Response alternatives: totally disagree – disagree – neutral – agree – totally agree

Four-statement measurement method
Four items that refer to the acculturation strategies (i.e., integration, separation, assimilation, and marginalization) are formulated per domain. Different applications of the four-statement method can be envisaged:
1. Simultaneous measurement via four separate subscales
   Instruction: Indicate agreement on a five-point Likert scale:

Integration: I find it important to have Dutch friends and I also find it important to have Turkish friends.
Separation: I find it important to have Turkish friends but I do not find it important to have Dutch friends.
Assimilation: I find it important to have Dutch friends but I do not find it important to have Turkish friends.
Marginalization: I do not find it important to have Dutch friends and I also do not find it important to have Turkish friends.

Response alternatives: totally disagree – disagree – neutral – agree – totally agree

2. Choosing the most preferred acculturation strategy
See example 1, but in this case respondent has to choose one of the four subscales. Instruction: Select which of the four you prefer.

3. Ranked preferences of the four separate statements See example 1, but in this case respondent has to rank the four subscales.

4. The same as described in examples 1, 2 and 3 but now using vignettes. For each of the four orientations a separate vignette is written and the respondent has either to indicate the level of agreement with each, or to choose the most preferred vignette, or to rank them.

Switching and mixing the cultures
Items are formulated per domain.

Instruction: Indicate agreement on a five-point Likert scale:

General: I mix the Turkish and the Dutch cultures in my life.
Domain language: In a conversation with my Turkish friends, I switch back and forth between Dutch and Turkish.

Response alternatives: totally disagree – disagree – neutral – agree – totally agree

have double negations) makes this method cognitively complex (Rudmin & Ahmadzadeh, 2001).

Although there is a clear need to integrate and compare the three acculturation measurement methods, relatively little attention has been devoted to their systematic comparison. In our study, in which we compared the three measurement methods of acculturation in a group of Turkish-Dutch (Arends-Tóth & Van de Vijver, 2006), we found major convergence in the results obtained with the one-, two- and four-statement methods. A structural equation model in which the three methods loaded on the same underlying acculturation attitude factor showed a good fit. Furthermore, it was found that the one- and two-statement measures had less impact on the measurement outcomes than the four-statement measure. The methodological concerns and the problems participants reported with the latter method (e.g., the occurrence of items with complex formulations) make the four-statement method the least appropriate of the three measurement methods. The one- and two-statement methods are appropriate measures of acculturation in unidimensional and bidimensional models. However, the two-statement method provides a more detailed picture.

The fusion model, which holds that acculturation often amounts to a creative mixture of characteristics of two cultures, has not yet been investigated empirically. Researchers, however, could consider this model by addressing

Box 10.2 Procedures to transform the two dimensions into Berry's four acculturation strategies

One of the main advantages of having scores on two dimensions is the opportunity to use these independently or to combine these in a single score. If there is reason to assume that the two dimensions show their own dynamics (e.g., distinct developmental trajectories over time), the use of the two independently obtained is to be preferred. However, in some cases there may be a need to combine the two dimension scores in a single overall measure. Different computational procedures can be envisaged to combine the scores on the two dimensions.

Subtracting the scores produces a difference score that ranges from completely maintaining the heritage culture to completely adopting the mainstream culture, with sums close to zero representing integration. This method of scoring is meaningful if the aim of the scoring is to produce a scale (like in the one-statement method) with separation at one end, integration and marginalization in the middle, and assimilation at the other end.

Multiplying the independent scores of the two dimensions produces a distribution of scores where higher scores reflect higher involvement on both dimensions and lower scores suggest lack of involvement in either dimension. This method of scoring can be useful if the aim is to juxtapose integration and all other strategies.

In the *median and mean split procedures*, responses are categorized as being lower or higher than a cut-off value (the median or mean of the sample). This procedure is based on the characteristics of the sample of the cultural group under study, and categorizes participants into one of the four strategies independently of where they score on the scale. These procedures may give a distorted image in a homogeneous sample (which is the case when many participants have either a high or low score on either or both dimensions).

In the *midpoint split procedure*, scale scores above the midpoint on the Likert scales are taken to indicate agreement to the scale construct and are classified "high" on the scale while scores below the midpoint refer to disagreement and are classified "low" on the scale. A midpoint split procedure has a firmer theoretical basis than the median and mean split procedures. A problem with this procedure is that the midpoint is often an answer option (e.g., a score of 3 on a scale ranging from 1 to 5) and there is no agreement in the literature as to how to resolve the ambiguity in its interpretation. In some studies midpoint scores have been interpreted as disagreement with the item (e.g., Donà & Berry, 1994), in others as agreement (e.g., Lasry & Sayegh, 1992), and in still others as unclassifiable (e.g., Rudmin & Ahmadzadeh, 2001).

According to the *proximity procedure*, the two dimensions can be seen as defining a two-dimensional space. Each of Berry's four strategies can be represented by a "prototypical point" in the space. For example, on a 7-point Likert scale (ranging from 1 to 7) assimilation is revealed by a score of 1 on the dimension that deals with maintaining the heritage culture and a score of 7 on the dimension that deals with adopting the mainstream culture. The Euclidean distances between the ideal score of each of the four acculturation strategies and the score obtained for an individual can be computed. This procedure has the advantage that it does not classify participants into one of the four categories, but yields a score for all participants on all strategies. A disadvantage of this scoring method is the lack of independence of the scores on the acculturation strategies (i.e., the same problem that holds for the other scoring procedures based on the two-statement measures). Scores for integration and marginalization show a negative correlation and the same is true for assimilation and separation.

the nature and extent of switching and mixing of the two cultures (in general and in a specific domain) in their acculturation instruments.

10.4.5   Acculturation across life domains and situations

Researchers have varied in their sampling of life domains in the assessment of acculturation. The most frequently assessed domain is language use; most of the published acculturation scales have used changes in and preferences for language use. Within this domain, measures differ in their specificity of context; some scales use general items, while others assess use in specific social situations such as with family members at home, at work, or with friends. Other frequently used domains involve social relations and affiliations, habits in daily life (such as food eaten, music, television, and media use), cultural traditions, and beliefs. An overview of domains is given in Box 10.3. It is important to base the choice of life domains on the purpose of the study. For example, if one is interested in a comprehensive measure of acculturation (as is usually the case), a measure based on language use is incomplete.

A related issue involves the number of items used to measure acculturation (single-item indices or a set of items addressing different life domains in different situations). Some researchers state that single-index measures are a valid or at least an adequate proxy measure of acculturation. Although single-item measures such as language use can cover important aspects of the acculturation process, they are almost always suspect because of their limited coverage of the concept of acculturation. Given the multifaceted nature of acculturation, assessment based on a single indicator is often inadequate.

Box 10.3 Examples of life domains relevant in acculturation

> Language ability (understand, read, write and speak), use and preference
> Social contacts, relations, friendships, way of dealing with people, communication style, family life
> Daily living habits: food, music, dance, shopping, clothing, plays, television soaps, artists, films, radio, sport, jokes, going to professionals (e.g., doctors), recreation activities, and cultural activities
> Media, newspapers, radio, news
> Education, lessons, teachers
> Work, employee preference
> Marrying, dating
> Childrearing practices, choosing child's name
> Celebrations and holidays
> Identity
> Values
> General knowledge, knowledge of rules, history, historical figures, symbols
> World-view, political ideology, pace of life, religious beliefs
> Specific cultural habits/customs

10.4.6   Item wording

The last step in designing an acculturation instrument is the choice of appropriate items. Some examples of item wording are given in Box 10.4. Researchers should aim at using simple and single-notion statements. In addition, besides the theoretical and methodological considerations, the designed instrument should also be "user-friendly." In our experience participants prefer to have all items involving a particular life domain immediately after each other (rather than scattered over the whole questionnaire), as it helps to focus the attention on one specific topic at a time.

10.5   Comparative research

Most acculturation studies are designed to examine similarities and differences across ethnic groups or generations within or between societies. There is an increasing interest in comparisons of acculturation orientations across countries (see Chapter 9 for a description of some of the features of comparative research designs). For example, a study of the impact of immigration policies will typically involve a comparison of various ethnic groups across various countries. An important methodological issue in comparison

Box 10.4 Examples of measures of acculturation aspects using the two-statement method: measuring the mainstream dimension

Attitude (domain friends)
    Preference: I like to have English friends.
    Evaluation/importance: I find it important to have English friends.
Response alternatives: totally disagree – disagree – neutral – agree – totally agree

Knowledge (domain language)
    My English is good.
    I have some difficulties in finding the right words and expressions in English.
Response alternatives: totally disagree – disagree – neutral – agree – totally agree

Behavior (cultural activities) as acculturation orientation or outcome
    The items on the behavioral acculturation scale consist of self-reported behaviors. The person is asked to report on a five-point Likert scale the relative frequency with which she or he engages in each behavior.
    I participate in English sport activities.
    I attend English clubs.
Response alternatives: never – sometimes – regularly – often – always

Beliefs/views
    The English way of life is good/peaceful/comfortable.
    English people are polite.
Response alternatives: totally disagree – disagree – neutral – agree – totally agree

Values
    Independence is a main value in my life.
    I should do what is best for me.
Response alternatives: totally disagree – disagree – neutral – agree – totally agree

Ethnic identity
    I feel English.
    I consider myself English.
Response alternatives: totally disagree – disagree – neutral – agree – totally agree

Affections
    I am happy to be English.
    It feels bad to be English.
Response alternatives: totally disagree – disagree – neutral – agree – totally agree

across groups involves the question of the adequacy of an instrument in all cultural groups studied. Before researchers compare scores among groups they have to be sure that the concept they are measuring (i.e., acculturation) has the same psychological meaning for the groups (equivalence). This means that the level of correspondence has to be established by using techniques developed in cross-cultural research. *Structural equivalence* is obtained when the concept has the same psychological meaning for different groups. Such a finding justifies the usage of the concept and its comparison among different groups. If structural equivalence is not found, the concept is no longer adequate as a basis for cultural comparison.

Structural equivalence is often assessed using exploratory or confirmatory factor analysis of two or more data sets with a view to establishing whether similar factors emerge. Similarity of factors is the criterion for structural equivalence. In exploratory factor analysis correspondence between factors is expressed in terms of some factorial agreement index, such as Tucker's phi (see Van de Vijver & Leung, 1997 for an extended discussion of issues and methods involved in making cross-cultural comparisons).

10.6　Implications

The main aim of this chapter was to compare and integrate current approaches, models and measurement methods of acculturation. The chapter clearly shows that acculturation is a complex process, which involves numerous aspects. No single measure or method can reveal the complexity of acculturation in a comprehensive manner. It is a basic problem in acculturation research that, on the one hand, we do not yet have enough insight into the concept, while, on the other hand, there is an urgent need for a reliable and practical acculturation measure. In order to assess acculturation adequately, various important interdependent decisions have to be made. The first one is an explicit formulation of research goals, followed by the choice of acculturation variables, aspects and research methodology. The choice of a theoretical model, measurement method, and life domains and situations to be dealt with in the items received much attention in this chapter.

Acculturation can be seen as a layered concept. At the highest level of the hierarchy, individuals have general (i.e., domain-aspecific) preferences vis-à-vis acculturation. These general preferences are related to more specific preferences regarding domains and situations (e.g., public and private domains), which, in turn, are related to very specific preferences (specific domains and situations). The choice of the level of generality and of domains and situations should be based on theoretical considerations.

Integration, the combination of adopting the mainstream culture and maintaining one's heritage culture, is the acculturation strategy most frequently preferred by immigrants (see, for an overview, Berry & Sam, 1997). There may be, however, large variations in what is meant by integration; it could include a wide variety of different possible combinations of the cultures. Therefore, the term *integration* needs to be more precisely defined, and more knowledge is needed about how integration is managed and negotiated. It could even be argued that most variation among immigrants occurs within the integration option and not between acculturation orientations. "Integration" is an umbrella concept that can have various meanings. First, integration can have a connotation of assimilation rather than a preference for both adoption and cultural maintenance. This may be because in the past the terms "integration" and "assimilation" were often used interchangeably. Second, "integration" can refer to an equal combination of domain-aspecific, independent components (adopting the mainstream culture and maintaining the heritage culture). However, the question is what constitutes an equal combination: does it refer to "completely adopting the mainstream culture and completely maintaining the heritage culture" or to "adopting 50% and maintaining 50%"? Third, immigrants can have access to both cultural systems and shift from the one to the other depending on the context ("dual monocultural" individuals who switch between maintaining the heritage culture at home and adopting the mainstream culture outside). Finally, integration can also refer to merging cultures, creating a "new culture" from the old ones.

"Integration" is a heterogeneous term with high face validity, because almost all immigrants have some aspects of both cultures. In future research, methodology needs to be developed to understand the different ways in which individuals can refer to integration. An example of a methodology for studying what is meant by "integration" can be found in the experimental studies of cultural frame switching (e.g., Benet-Martínez, Leu, Lee & Morris, 2002). In this paradigm bicultural individuals are first primed with cues from either the country of origin or the country of settlement and are then asked to answer questions that are supposedly related to cultural background.

10.7   Conclusions

The need for culturally appropriate assessment and interventions is increasingly apparent as societies become more culturally diverse. Individual differences in acculturation can be measured at different levels of generality and specificity depending upon the purpose of the assessment. At a relatively broad level, the one-statement measure can be applied as a domain-independent, overall rating of acculturation. For a more detailed and comprehensive assessment of an individual's acculturation, the use of the two-statement measurement method with separate scales for a set of domains is useful. At a more specific level, acculturation can be measured in various concrete situations (e.g., at home with children, in shops, with friends) and life domains (e.g., childrearing practices, eating, social contacts). The most effective instruments are likely to be those developed for clearly defined purposes and for use within a specific context.

In order to advance acculturation research it is important to develop standardized, or at least widely accepted, measurement methods. The two-statement measurement method (independent measurement of acculturation dimensions in the mainstream and heritage culture) in a range of different domains and situations is a useful tool in achieving this goal.

10.8 References

Arends-Tóth, J. & Van de Vijver, F. J. R. (2003). Multiculturalism and acculturation: views of Dutch and Turkish-Dutch. *European Journal of Social Psychology*, *33*, 249–266.

(2004). Domains and dimensions in acculturation: implicit theories of Turkish-Dutch. *International Journal of Intercultural Relations*, *28*, 19–35.

(2006). Issues in the conceptualization and assessment of acculturation. In M. H. Bornstein & L. R. Cote (eds.), *Acculturation and parent–child relationships: measurement and development* (pp. 33–62). Mahwah, NJ: Lawrence Erlbaum Associates.

Benet-Martínez, V., Leu, J., Lee, F. & Morris, M. W. (2002). Negotiating biculturalism: cultural frame switching in biculturals with oppositional versus compatible cultural identities. *Journal of Cross-Cultural Psychology*, *33*, 492–516.

Berry, J. W. (1997). Immigration, acculturation, and adaptation. *Applied Psychology: An International Review*, *46*, 5–68.

Berry, J. W. & Sam, D. L. (1997). Acculturation and adaptation. In J. W. Berry, M. H. Segall & C. Kağitçibaşi (eds.), *Handbook of cross-cultural psychology.* 2nd edn. (Vol. III, pp. 291–326). Boston, MA: Allyn & Bacon.

Birman, D. & Trickett, E. J. (2001). Cultural transitions in first-generation immigrants: acculturation of Soviet Jewish refugee adolescents and parents. *Journal of Cross-Cultural Psychology*, *32*, 456–477.

Bourhis, R. Y., Moïse, L. C., Perreault, S. & Sénécal, S. (1997). Towards an interactive acculturation model: a social psychological approach. *International Journal of Psychology*, *32*, 369–386.

Celano, M. P. & Tyler, F. B. (1991). Behavioral acculturation among Vietnamese refugees in the United States. *Journal of Social Psychology*, *131*, 373–385.

Clément, R. & Noels, K. A. (1992). Towards a situated approach to ethnolinguistic identity: the effects of status on individuals and groups. *Journal of Language and Social Psychology*, *11*, 203–232.

Coleman, H. L. K. (1995). Strategies for coping with cultural diversity. *Counseling Psychologist*, *23*, 722–740.

Cuéllar, I., Harris, L. C. & Jasso, R. (1980). An acculturation scale for Mexican American normal and clinical populations. *Hispanic Journal of Behavioral Sciences*, *2*, 199–217.

Donà, G. & Berry, J. W. (1994). Acculturation attitudes and acculturative stress of Central American refugees. *International Journal of Psychology*, *29*, 57–70.

Elias, N. & Blanton, J. (1987). Dimensions of ethnic identity in Israeli Jewish families living in the United States. *Psychological Reports*, *60*, 367–375.

Gordon, M. M. (1964). *Assimilation in American life*. New York: Oxford University Press.

Hutnik, N. (1986). Patterns of ethnic minority identification and models of social adaptation. *Ethnic and Racial Studies*, *9*, 150–167.

Keefe, S. E. & Padilla, A. M. (1987). *Chicano ethnicity*. Albuquerque: University of New Mexico Press.

Kim, C., Laroche, M. & Tomiuk, M. A. (2001). A measure of acculturation for Italian Canadians: scale development and construct validation. *International Journal of Intercultural Relations*, *25*, 607–637.

LaFromboise, T., Coleman, H. L. K. & Gerton, J. (1993). Psychological impact of biculturalism: evidence and theory. *Psychological Bulletin*, *114*, 395–412.

Laroche, M., Kim, C. & Hui, M. K. (1997). A comparative investigation of dimensional structures of acculturation for Italian Canadians and Greek Canadians. *Journal of Social Psychology*, *137*, 317–331.

Lasry, J. & Sayegh, L. (1992). Developing an acculturation scale: a bidimensional model. In N. Grizenko, L. Sayegh & P. Migneault (eds.), *Transcultural issues in child psychiatry* (pp. 67–86). Montreal: Editions Douglas.

Mendoza, R. H. (1989). An empirical scale to measure type and degree of acculturation in Mexican-American adolescents and adults. *Journal of Cross-Cultural Psychology*, *20*, 372–385.

Mishra, R. C., Sinha, D. & Berry, J.W. (1996). *Ecology, acculturation and psychological adaptation: a study of adivasis in Bihar*. Thousand Oaks, CA: Sage Publications.

Nguyen, H. H., Messé, L. A. & Stollak, G. E. (1999). Toward a more complex understanding of acculturation and adjustment: cultural involvements and psychosocial functioning in Vietnamese youth. *Journal of Cross-Cultural Psychology*, *30*, 5–31.

Padilla, A. M. (ed.). (1995). *Hispanic psychology: critical issues in theory and research*. Thousand Oaks, CA: Sage Publications.

Phalet, K., Van Lotringen, C. & Entzinger, H. (2000). *Islam in de multiculturele samenleving* [Islam in the multi-cultural society]. Utrecht: European Research Centre on Migration and Ethnic Relations.

Phinney, J. S. (1990). Ethnic identity in adolescents and adults: review of research. *Psychological Bulletin*, *108I*, 499–514.

Roosens, E. E. (1989). *Creating ethnicity: the process of ethnogenesis*. Newbury Park: Sage Publications.

Rudmin, F. W. & Ahmadzadeh, V. (2001). Psychometric critique of acculturation psychology: the case of Iranian migrants in Norway. *Scandinavian Journal of Psychology*, *42*, 41–56.

Sánchez, J. I. & Fernández, D. M. (1993). Acculturative stress among Hispanics: a bidimensional model of ethnic identification. *Journal of Applied Social Psychology*, *23*, 654–668.

Sayegh, L. & Lasry, J. (1993). Immigrants' adaptation in Canada: assimilation, acculturation, and orthogonal cultural identification. *Canadian Psychology*, *24*, 98–109.

Stephenson, M. (2000). Development and validation of the Stephenson Multigroup Acculturation Scale (SMAS). *Psychological Assessment, 12*, 77–88.

Sodowsky, G. R. & Carey, J. C. (1988). Relationships between acculturation-related demographics and cultural attitudes of an Asian-Indian immigrant group. *Journal of Multicultural Counseling and Development, 16*, 117–136.

Suinn, R. M., Ahuna, C. & Khoo, G. (1992). The Suinn-Lew Asian self-identity acculturation scale: concurrent and factorial validation. *Educational and Psychological Measurement, 52*, 1041–1046.

Suzuki, L. A., Ponterotto, J. G. & Meller, P. J. (eds.). (2001). *Handbook of multicultural assessment: clinical, psychological, and educational applications.* 2nd edn. San Francisco: Jossey-Bass.

Szapocznik, J., Kurtines, W. M. & Fernández, T. (1980). Bicultural involvement and adjustment in Hispanic-American youth. *International Journal of Intercultural Relations, 4*, 353–365.

Taylor, D. M. & Lambert, W. E. (1996). The meaning of multiculturalism in a culturally diverse urban American area. *Journal of Social Psychology, 136*, 727–740.

Triandis, H. C., Kashima, E., Shimada, E. & Villareal, M. (1988). Acculturation indices as a means of confirming cultural differences. *International Journal of Psychology, 21*, 43–70.

Van de Vijver, F. J. R. & Leung, K. (1997). *Methods and data analysis for cross-cultural research.* Newbury Park: Sage Publications.

Ward, C., Bochner, S. & Furnham, A. (2001). *The psychology of culture shock.* London: Routledge.

Ward, C. & Kennedy, A. (1994). Acculturation strategies, psychological adjustment, and socio-cultural competence during cross-cultural transitions. *International Journal of Intercultural Relations, 18*, 329–343.

PART II

Research with specific acculturating groups

Chapters in the first section of this *Handbook* presented acculturation in broad terms. The chapters in this section go a step further by examining some of the key concepts and variables presented earlier in four kinds of acculturating groups: immigrants, sojourners, refugees and indigenous peoples. Chapter 11 reviews immigration trends in the Western world and how countries of settlement affect immigrants. The chapter also uses a comparative approach to examining how a group of immigrants from the Netherlands are acculturating in three major immigrant-receiving countries. The chapter also looks at the role of some personality factors on immigrants' adaptation. The chapter on sojourners (Chapter 12) draws heavily on the cultural learning approach to acculturation to examine some key aspects of this approach in three groups of sojourners: tourists, international students and expatriates. An interesting perspective taken in this chapter is the reciprocal influence the two acculturating groups have on each other.

The next two chapters of this section are devoted to refugees and asylum seekers. While the two chapters have much in common, they differ in their emphasis. Chapter 13 provides a broad overview of refugees, asylum seekers, internally displaced individuals and trafficked individuals and their acculturation experiences. The chapter also uses the experiences of refugees and asylum seekers to make a bridge between acculturation and human rights. In contrast, Chapter 14 is more specific in its approach, focusing primarily on refugees in camps. A unique contribution of this chapter is its focus on the acculturation of returnees. Both chapters devote some sections to trauma and posttraumatic stress disorders (PTSD) but they look at these experiences from two different points of view and complement each other.

The last chapter of this section focuses on indigenous people, a group often neglected in acculturation studies, largely because they tend to be colonized by a larger group or country, where the larger group or country often imposes its rule and way of life on them. As a result of this domination, they are often seen and treated as just a part of the larger group or country. The chapter singles out the unique experiences of different indigenous peoples in their various societies, as well as their common experience of being dominated by a larger group.

11 Immigrants

Jan Pieter van Oudenhoven

11.1 Introduction

Migration is not a new phenomenon. People have always been on the move. China started to build its Great Wall in the seventh century BC with the aim – without much success, however – of preventing northern tribes from invading the empire. The history of the Middle East is another example of a long series of occupations, expansions and invasions of nations. The creation of the Persian, the Roman and the Ottoman empires led to tremendous population drifts. A larger, more global move in history started in the fifteenth and sixteenth centuries with the "discovery" voyages by the Portuguese and Spanish, followed by the colonization of Africa, Asia and the Americas by the Portuguese, Spanish, Dutch, British and French.

Never, however, have there been more migrants in the world than at present times. Some flee their country for fear of oppression or violence, others are sent abroad for a couple of years by their company, and many just like to travel abroad for a short period. These are the refugees, expatriates and tourists, respectively. In contrast to these short-term migrants, immigrants settle down in a new country for long periods or – in most cases – permanently. Another characteristic of immigrants is that they (or their parents) had strong motives to move to their new country. They may have been pulled to the new country by personal, political or religious reasons, but most often they went there to find a better economic position, or to be reunited with family members. Currently, 175 million persons live outside their country of birth (United Nations, 2004). The majority of them are immigrants. Although there are many exceptions, as is illustrated by the *brain drain* phenomenon, immigrants often come from lower socio-economic classes (Stalker, 2001).

Due to the combination of the just mentioned characteristics, the permanence (or long duration) of stay and high motivation, we may assume that immigrants have certain expectations that they wish to fulfil in their new country. These expectations will probably be extra high because individuals who want to emigrate tend to have a stronger achievement motivation than individuals who prefer to stay in their home country (Boneva & Frieze, 2001). Therefore, the question of the form of acculturation they prefer as a way of realizing their expectations is very relevant, as is the question of their success of adaptation. Consequently, I will focus on the adaptation of immigrants throughout this chapter. First, I will discuss the impact of current immigration streams on four main immigration areas. Second, I mention a study illustrating how – vice versa – nations may influence the adaptation of immigrants. Subsequently, an explanation is given of why people, both immigrants and host society, find it less than pleasant to deal with cultural differences. Next, I will underline the importance of the concept of attachment styles to the acculturation research. The chapter ends with the question of whether immigrants are to be pitied, or rather whether they are predisposed to be successful.

11.2 Important immigration areas

Currently the four most important immigration-receiving countries or regions are the United States, Western Europe, Canada and Australia, but many other regions or countries have absorbed immigrants as well. For example, large numbers of Italians, Arabs and Jews found their way to Argentina; Indians to East Africa and the West Indies; and Filipino women to Arabia, Japan, Malaysia and Singapore. When we focus on the four major immigration areas we must conclude that recent immigration streams have brought about fundamental changes in each of these four areas. In all four, this process may be called "de-Westernization," although this de-Westernization process takes a different form in each area. It may mean less European, or less Anglo, or less Christian. Let us take a look at the major changes in each area:

➢   The USA (293 million inhabitants) has for centuries been culturally dominated by European Americans, while African Americans formed the largest minority with roughly 12% of the population. Remarkably, African Americans have recently been surpassed by the Hispanics who – with 40 million – now form 13% of the population. Hispanics keep arriving and have a higher birth rate than Americans of European descent. After Mexico and Spain the USA has the world's largest Spanish-speaking population. Within fifty years, Hispanics will form a quarter of the US population (Nagayama Hall & Barongan, 2001). Moreover, almost twenty Spanish-speaking countries south of the USA back them culturally and linguistically. We may safely predict that the USA is becoming a country with two powerful cultures, the Anglo-Western and the Hispanic, and two important languages: English and Spanish.

➢   In Western Europe (311 million inhabitants) the situation is more diverse, because each country has its own language and its particular immigration history. In the 1960s when economic growth in Western Europe led to a scarcity of labor, many "guest workers" from Turkey, Morocco and some other North African countries moved to Germany, Belgium, France and the Netherlands. Most of them have settled there and have been reunited with their families. The overall majority of them are Muslims. Later, refugees from Muslim countries such as Afghanistan, Iraq and Somalia strengthened the Muslim community. Nowadays, Muslims form 5 to 10% of the population in Western Europe. In some of the bigger cities they form the largest religious community. Their number is still growing whereas the native population is declining. Again, we may predict that Western Europe too is – with respect to religion – becoming more bicultural: on the one hand it has had a long Christian tradition, on the other hand it is experiencing a vital and growing Islamic input. This process will certainly be reinforced when Turkey joins the European Union.

➢ Canada (32.5 million inhabitants) is probably the most multicultural country. Canada used to be a bicultural country, consisting of an Anglo majority group and a strong French minority group. The Anglo part of the population has been decreasing over the last few decades and has ceased to be the majority group. The percentage of Canadians of French European descent is declining as well. In the early years after the Second World War, many other European nationals (Germans, Ukrainians, Italians and Dutch) immigrated to Canada. Subsequently, large numbers of refugees from Soviet-dominated Eastern Europe (Hungarians, Czechoslovaks and Poles) followed. Since the new Immigration Law of 1978, which deleted some discriminatory elements, large groups of immigrants from Asia, Latin America, Africa and the Middle East were allowed to enter the country. Altogether, they have transformed Canada into a truly rainbow nation. This has been formalized by the adoption of the Multiculturalism Act in 1988. Although English will stay the dominant language and even become more important, the dominant Anglo cultural identity will gradually be replaced by a pluralistic cultural identity.

➢ Australia (over 20 million inhabitants) has been the most Anglo-dominated immigration country. According to the 1971 census 83% of the population originated from the British Isles. Other immigrants were primarily Italians, Greeks, Germans and Dutch. The dismantling of the White Australian Policy in the early seventies opened the doors to immigrants from non-European countries. Immigrants from Asia, in particular from China and Vietnam, have benefited from the immigration policy change. At present, more than 7% of the population of Australia originates from Asia. In 1986 Australia officially adopted a policy of multiculturalism. In view of the higher birth rate of Asians within Australia, but – more importantly – of the proximity of densely populated Asian countries, it is to be expected that Australia will have an important Asian cultural input. In the same way that the Hispanics in the USA are culturally backed by a host of Latin American countries, Asians in Australia will feel culturally backed by an overwhelming number of Asians surrounding the country.

In contrast to the opinion of many people that the acculturation of immigrants will primarily be a one-way process of influencing from majority group to immigrants, we see that, in the four major immigration areas immigrants are drastically transforming the dominant culture. This leads in all four regions – in different forms – to a less Western culture. This process will probably be intensified by the fact that it is taking place simultaneously in four important regions.

11.3   The influence of nations on immigrants

Few immigration studies have examined the impact of nations on immigrants' adaptation. A great exception is the ICSEY project (International Comparative Study on Ethnocultural Youth) in which researchers from at least thirteen nations participate. Although the strength of such a project is the possibility to make generalizations, comparative data on immigration are still difficult to interpret (e.g., Phinney, Horenczyk, Liebkind & Vedder, 2001), because nations differ on linguistic, religious, economic, and many other aspects, and immigrants do so too. Some groups of immigrants might do well due to a religious or a linguistic fit between the host society and the country of origin, while other groups might fail because of too great a cultural discrepancy between the two societies. The success of their adaptation may also depend on the economic situation in the country. Periods of economic growth make it easier for any immigrant to succeed. Therefore, in order to be able to draw conclusions, one ought to have comparable groups of immigrants across nations. Moreover, the nations should not differ on too many aspects in order to prevent the confounding influence of many variables. It is a difficult task to find such a combination of countries and immigrants. Luckily, however, we (Van Oudenhoven, Van der Zee & Bakker, 2002) had the opportunity to examine the acculturation of a large, culturally homogeneous, group of immigrants from the Netherlands in three different Anglo-Saxon countries.

11.3.1   A brief description of the study

The sample consisted of 1,562 first-generation immigrants to Canada (N = 861), USA (N = 417) and Australia (N = 284). Of these, 40% were women, 60% men; the average age was 64 (range 18 to 99); the average time spent in the country of immigration was 42 years. All the immigrants came from Friesland, one of the most rural and culturally homogeneous provinces in the Netherlands. Approximately 85% of the immigrants had Frisian (a distinct language) as their native language. As comparison countries we took Australia, Canada and the USA because these are important immigration countries and because they are highly comparable with respect to economic situation, use of

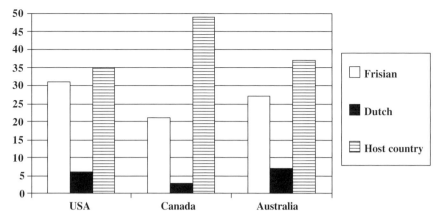

Figure 11.1 *Percentage of self-labels used by Frisian immigrants from three immigration countries*

language (the study did not include immigrants in French-speaking Canada), and culture. According to Hofstede (1991), all three nations score relatively low on power distance and uncertainty avoidance, but high on individualism and – moderately – high on masculinity. The immigrants were remarkably similar across the three countries on the major demographic variables: there were hardly any differences with respect to age, gender, educational level or occupation. Nor did we find any differences on five personality dimensions of intercultural effectiveness (Open-mindedness, Cultural Empathy, Flexibility, Emotional Stability and Social Initiative). Although the Frisian immigrants were almost identical on all personal variables across nations, they did differ, however, on some adjustment variables, which we will discuss briefly.

11.3.2 Results

First, we looked at their ethnic identification. The Frisian immigrants clearly identify more with their Frisian than with their Dutch background, but – in all three countries – they identify even more with their host society. This happens when they have to rate themselves on subjective ethnic identity with respect to their Frisian background, their Dutch background and their host society, respectively. An example of an item is: "I'm proud to be Frisian/Dutch/ American, Australian or Canadian." The results are even clearer when they are asked to label themselves freely (see Figure 11.1). In particular, immigrants in Canada identify themselves with their host society. This is an interesting finding because Canadian policy is very tolerant towards immigrants expressing their own cultural identity.

Second, we looked at their acculturation strategies (Berry, 1997). As we saw in Chapter 3, immigrants are faced with two fundamental questions: "Is it of value to maintain my cultural heritage?" and "Is it of value to maintain relations with other groups?" On the basis of the answers to these questions, four acculturation strategies may be distinguished: (a) integration (it is important both to maintain own cultural identity and to have positive relations with other groups); (b) assimilation (only positive relations with other groups are important); (c) separation (only maintaining own cultural heritage is of importance); and (d) marginalization (neither outcome is important). As was found in many other studies, integration is also the favorite strategy for the Frisian immigrants (45%), followed by assimilation (29%). Only 12% opted for the separation strategy, and another 14% for that of marginalization. This is an important finding, because it indicates that a group of immigrants who are culturally very close to the host society (the Dutch culture only differs on the masculinity dimension from the three Anglo nations, and the Frisian language is more similar to English than Dutch) also have a preference for integration. These results are in line with Berry and colleagues, who equally found evidence for integration being the most favored acculturation response across immigrants (Berry, Kim, Power, Young & Bujaki, 1989) and refugees (Donà & Berry, 1994) in Canada. In most studies, integration is related to a higher level of wellbeing. This was not the case in the present study. When we looked at their Satisfaction With Life, measured by Diener's widely used five-point scale (Diener, Emmons, Larson & Griffin, 1985), differences between the acculturation strategies were found (F [3,1224] $= 7.97$; $p < .001$). Preference for integration was not related to a higher Satisfaction With Life (4.15) than preference for assimilation (4.17), but both "integrators" and "assimilators" did have a higher Satisfaction With Life than "marginalizators" (4.00) and "separators" (3.89). The high Satisfaction With Life for persons with a preference for assimilation may be explained by the relatively small cultural difference between the Frisian immigrants and the post-war Canadian population.

Figure 11.2 shows the relation between subjective ethnic identity and adaptation strategy. It nicely illustrates the description presented in Chapter 3 of the four acculturation strategies distinguished by Berry (1980): integration implies a double identification with the host and the original society, assimilation a strong identification with the host society, whereas separation primarily involves identification with the original society. Marginalization is only weakly related to identification with either society. Remarkable are the differences in acculturation strategies across nations: in the USA and Canada most Frisians opt for integration (53% and 45%, respectively) and then assimilation (20% and 31% respectively), whereas the Frisian Australians are more evenly divided between assimilation (36%), integration (31%) and marginalization (23%).

Third, we examined the reported levels of wellbeing in each country. No substantial differences were found across the nations on Satisfaction With Life or on Psychological Health. However, Frisian Australians reported lower levels of physical health and perceived success of emigration than their fellow immigrants in Canada and the United States. What may we conclude from these

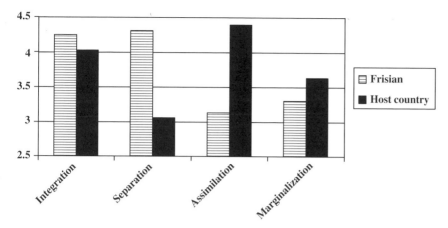

Figure 11.2 *Subjective ethnic identity and acculturation strategies of Frisian immigrants (N = 1562) (1 = low; 5 = high)*

results? The differences we found are small, but they are real. Immigrants in Canada appear to be the most successfully adapted: they identify most strongly with the host society, without necessarily having to give up their original identity; and they include the smallest numbers of marginalisators (10%). Immigrants in Australia seem to be less well adapted: they include a higher percentage of marginalisators (23%), report a slightly less favorable physical health and they perceive their emigration as – slightly – less successful than their fellow Frisians in the USA and Canada. We did not find any demographic or personal characteristics that might explain the differences, except religion. In Canada there were more Calvinistic than Lutheran immigrants, whereas in Australia there were more Lutherans than Calvinists. However, when we controlled for religion, the differences in wellbeing across the nations remained unaffected. Both Calvinists and Lutherans were better off in Canada than in Australia. Therefore, differences in wellbeing may speculatively be explained by the three countries' immigration policies. Canada has the longest tradition of multiculturalism. Australia has the strongest tradition of emphasizing assimilation. Although it has officially adopted a multicultural policy, there is – still – little endorsement of such a policy (Betts, 1991). The USA has held an intermediate position with its *melting pot* ideology: immigrants have been free to a large degree to choose their own strategy in private values, but there has been a strong informal pressure on them to blend into the mainstream culture. By doing so, immigrants add a slightly different flavor to that mainstream culture.

Apparently, Frisian immigrants are doing well in Canada and less well in Australia. This result might be attributed to a lucky combination of type of immigrant and country of immigration. However, in another series of studies, Ghuman (1994, 2000) found that Punjabi Sikhs, a group that is culturally very remote from Frisians, were also much better acculturated in Canada than in

Australia, and – to a lesser degree – than in the United Kingdom. Ghuman attributes the unsatisfactory acculturation in Australia to anti-Asian socio-political attitudes at the time of the study. Altogether the results support the multiculturalism policy. Further evidence comes from the ICSEY project that provides strong evidence that immigrants prefer integration and experience positive consequences of such a choice (see Chapter 29). More evidence is needed, however, to be able to state firmly that multiculturalism is the most favorable policy for achieving a successful adaptation.

11.4   The attractiveness of cultural similarity

Canada is probably the only nation with a clear pluralist policy. Australia officially has a multicultural policy as well, but this is not fully endorsed by the population. Most nations, though, tend to have an assimilation ideology, which implies that immigrants are expected to abandon their cultural and linguistic distinctiveness and adopt the core values of the host society (Bourhis, Moïse, Perreault & Sénécal, 1997). In most cases, majority members also prefer that immigrants assimilate. In Germany, Zick, Wagner, Van Dick and Petzel (2001) reported a preference for assimilation among nationals. Similar results were found in Slowakia (Piontkowski, Florack, Hoelker & Obdrezalek, 2000). In a study in the Netherlands too, a stronger preference was found for immigrants who assimilate rather than immigrants who integrate (Van Oudenhoven, Prins & Buunk, 1998). This tendency has become stronger after "9/11," particularly in Europe. In a survey, which took place a year after "9/11" among a representative sample of the Dutch population, 85% of the respondents declared it to be "important" or "rather important" that immigrants "adopt Dutch norms and values." This constituted an increase of 10% as compared to a survey which took place in 1994. In Israel, Horenczyk (1996) also found that members of the receiving community were more in favor of assimilation than were the immigrants. Admittedly, not all nations prefer assimilation. A lucky exception are the New Zealanders who prefer integration (Ward & Masgoret, 2004).

Why is there such a preference for assimilation? Why are cultural differences not appreciated? The similarity-attraction hypothesis (Byrne, 1971) offers an easy explanation why people do not appreciate cultural differences. According to the similarity-attraction hypothesis, which is more of a robust empirical datum than a theory, similarity leads to attraction. We like other individuals who are seen to be similar to ourselves or our own group with respect to attitudes, values, abilities and many other variables. Similarity may reduce insecurity in inter-personal and inter-group relations. Cultural similarity, in particular, may be rewarding because it confirms that our beliefs and values are correct. As a consequence interactions between individuals and groups occur more smoothly.

Clear support for the similarity-attraction hypothesis was found in a large survey of Dutch-speaking citizens of the Netherlands who were asked to indicate their liking of several social categories (Van Oudenhoven, Judd & Hewstone, 2000). The study included ethnicity, religion and employment. These categorizations were used because they are very relevant ones to issues of discrimination in current Dutch society. Because of the size of our sample, it was possible to employ a between-subjects design in which each respondent made judgments about only a single target individual.

11.4.1 A brief description of the study

A representative sample of the Dutch-speaking population of the Netherlands participated in the study. A total of 2,389 respondents answered questions on personal computers, which were provided to them by a survey organization. This response format necessarily means that illiterate citizens were not included in the sample. Additionally, many recent immigrants were not included because of their lack of fluency in Dutch. Not more than 1% of the respondents were immigrants. Respondents' age ranged from 16 to 85 years; 45% of these were female, 55% male. Respondents were randomly assigned to the cells of a $2\times2\times2$ experimental between-subjects design. These three factors manipulated ingroup/outgroup status on three different category memberships (Nationality, Religion and Employment Status) of a hypothetical target individual whom the respondent judged. As one question in a lengthy survey, respondents were given the following scenario:

"Suppose you got some new neighbors. You have a brief introductory chat with the man and the woman. You don't know whether they are married, but you do know that they are [Dutch/Turkish], that the man has [a job / no job], and that [they do not practice their religion, but that they do celebrate Christmas, Easter and Sinterklaas[1] / they are Muslim]."

The three variables that were manipulated between subjects are given in brackets in the above scenario. Thus each respondent was told either that the couple was Dutch or that they were Turkish, either that the man was employed or that he was unemployed, and so forth. The assumption was that outgroups for the three categorizations are the Turkish, the unemployed and the Muslim. Since the sample consisted of Dutch-speaking citizens, 99% self-identified as Dutch in demographic questions. Unfortunately, no question was asked about religious preference. However, fewer than 1% of Dutch adults are Muslim and most Dutch celebrate Christmas, Easter and "Sinterklaas," and over 60% of the Dutch self-identify as Christian. Finally, only 4% of the respondents said they were unemployed. After reading this scenario, respondents were asked to

---

[1] Sinterklaas, or St Nicholas' Birthday, is a traditional Christian holiday celebrated by most Dutch, like Christmas and Easter.

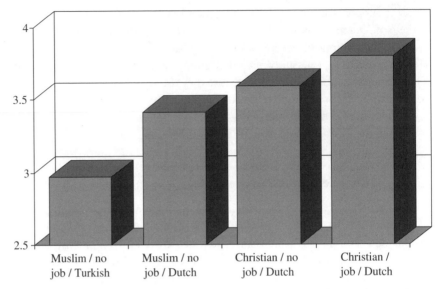

Figure 11.3 *Sympathy scores (1 = low; 5 = high) depending on the target's nationality, religion and employment status (N = 2389)*

answer the question: "Would you like these people as neighbors?" (1 = not at all; 5 = very much so).

11.4.2   Results

The results of this study, using real targets from affect-laden social categories, show that outgroup membership on each social category *adds* to a decreased liking of the target (see Figure 11.3). As long as the target does not share all characteristics of the ingroup, he or she is liked considerably less than the target that shares all characteristics of the ingroup. Respondents indeed felt most attracted to the employed Dutch "Christian" neighbor, who was assumed to be most similar to themselves ($M = 3.80$), and felt least attracted to the unemployed Turkish, Muslim neighbor, who was assumed to be most dissimilar to themselves ($M = 2.97$). This strong additive effect may be explained by the similarity-attraction hypothesis (Byrne, 1971). The data allowed us to further test this hypothesis by giving the targets a similarity score ranging from 1 to 4 according to the number of overlapping categories (1 = no overlapping category; 2 = one overlapping category; 3 = two overlapping categories; 4 = three overlapping categories). Similarity based on number of overlapping categories indeed significantly predicted liking.

The similarity-attraction hypothesis is further supported by a number of survey studies in which acceptance of immigrants appeared to depend on their cultural distance from the host society. In a study by Ho, Niles, Penney and

Thomas (1994), for instance, Australian respondents were more reluctant to recommend the acceptance of immigrants from Asia and the Middle East than from Britain or Southern Europe. Another study in Australia by Nesdale and Mak (2000) reported a related phenomenon, i.e. that the ethnic identification with the culture of origin of immigrants is stronger the more they differ culturally from the host society. In a Dutch study Hagendoorn (1996) found that there was a rank order of immigrants in the eyes of the majority group, with the culturally least distant groups being on the top of the hierarchy. The same pattern was found in Great Britain in a recent poll for *The Economist* (*The Economist*, 2004): whereas 63% of the natives would disapprove if more Iraquis moved into their neighborhoods, less than 5% would mind if the newcomers were Australians. Russians equally show preferences for culturally related groups: whereas more than 50% would not like to work with Roma or Chechens, less than 10% would mind working with West Europeans (*The Economist*, 2005). This phenomenon of "ethnic hierarchy," a sequence of preferences according to the cultural distance from the ingroup, appears to be a general phenomenon (see also Brewer & Campbell, 1976; Osbeck, Moghaddam & Perrault, 1997). Ward and Leong reach similar conclusions in Chapter 29, but they notice that in non-Western countries different patterns are found, that may be attributed to status differentials. In Malawi, for instance, culturally different but high-status Westerners were preferred above Africans from neighboring countries.

11.5   Reactions to "strange" situations

Although national policies and receiving communities may have an impact on the acculturation strategies and eventually on the wellbeing of immigrants, personality factors do have an important effect on immigrants' acculturation and adaptation as well. Most studies on personality and adaptation to new cultures have been done in the domain of the selection of international employees; these studies have focused on a variety of personality factors, and on the "Big Five," in particular (e.g. Caligiuri, 2000; Ones & Viswesvaran, 1999). There are a growing number of studies, though, on personality and immigration as well. In Chapter 8 Ankica Kosic discusses several relevant personality characteristics, such as self-efficacy, self-esteem, assertiveness, likeability, etc., and above I mentioned five dimensions of intercultural effectiveness that are related to the success of acculturation of migrants. However, acculturation has rarely been associated with attachment styles. This is remarkable, because attachment theory refers to the way parents and other caregivers have taught young children to approach others, particularly in new situations. Because acculturation implies interaction with others in new situations we may expect attachment styles to be related to acculturation attitudes and behavior.

Originally formulated by John Bowlby (1969), attachment theory states that over the course of unfolding experiences with their caregivers, children develop different attachment styles. Children internalize their experiences with caregivers into working models, that is mental schemas, of the self as either worthy or unworthy and of others as either dependable or undependable. Once established, these working models are believed to function as a framework for interpreting experiences with other people, thereby affecting subsequent relationships. For this reason, attachment theory has emerged as an important theoretical framework in the study of adult close relationships. Bartholomew and Horowitz (1991) have proposed a classification of attachment styles involving two dimensions that correspond to Bowlby's original working models of the self and others. They distinguish four attachment styles. The *secure* attachment style is characterized by a working model of the self as positive and an expectation that others are trustworthy. The *preoccupied* attachment style indicates a sense of unworthiness of the love of others, combined with a positive evaluation of others. In contrast, individuals with a *dismissive* attachment style have a positive working model of the self and a negative disposition to others. Finally, *anxious* attachment indicates a working model of the self as unworthy combined with an expectation that others are rejecting.

Mikulincer and Shaver (2001) emphasized the relevance of attachment theory for understanding inter-group attitudes. They found that secure attachment was related to less negative reactions towards outgroup targets. Another study that underlined the adaptational importance of attachment styles for individuals in new situations was carried out among college students (Lapsley & Edgerton, 2002). In their study adjustment to college life was positively associated with secure attachment and negatively with insecure attachment. Using a self-report measure of adult attachment which has separate scales for each attachment style in Bartholomew and Horowitz' model (Van Oudenhoven, Hofstra & Bakker, 2003), we related attachment styles to psychological and sociocultural adjustment. The study (Bakker, Van Oudenhoven & Van der Zee, 2004) took place among 847 first generation Dutch immigrants in Canada, the USA, Europe, Australia, New Zealand and some other countries. A first set of predictions concerned psychological adjustment: the secure attachment style would be positively, and the preoccupied and anxious attachment styles would be negatively, related to the psychological adjustment among immigrants. Although dismissive attachment is characterized by a positive self-model, no relationship with the indicators of psychological adjustment was expected given the fact that dismissive individuals tend to use a defensive strategy towards emotion-related self-report measures. Indeed, positive relations were found between secure attachment and psychological adjustment, and the anxious and preoccupied styles were negatively associated with psychological adjustment, whereas the dismissive attachment was not related to psychological adjustment.

The second set of predictions concerned sociocultural adjustment. The indicators of sociocultural adjustment focused on immigrants' orientation towards the host culture, but they also included their orientation towards the *native* culture. The secure attachment style was expected to be positively related to contact with both host and native nationals. Anxious and preoccupied individuals either avoid making close bonds with others because they fear being rejected (anxious attachment) or have difficulties approaching others on account of their low self-worth (preoccupied attachment). We thus predicted a negative association between these styles and contact with host nationals. For contact with the original culture, the opposite was expected. Despite their difficulty in approaching others, preoccupied and anxious individuals do seem to have a wish to affiliate with other people. In an intercultural context, preoccupied and anxious individuals, in order to serve this need, may seek out the company of members of their own cultures because they feel relatively close to, and safe among, them. Accordingly, a positive relationship was expected between these styles and contact with members of the original culture. This dependency on others sets the preoccupied and anxious styles apart from the dismissive attachment style. Dismissive individuals have a generally negative disposition towards others. We therefore expected a negative relationship between this style and contact with both the host and the native culture. Positive relations were indeed found between secure attachment and social relations with both the host and the native culture; the anxious and preoccupied styles were negatively associated with the host culture, but positively with the native culture. Dismissive attachment was mildly negatively related to both the host and the native culture. Interestingly, the attachment styles were able to explain variance in sociocultural adjustment beyond that explained by the Big Five.

In a second study 180 immigrants in the Netherlands (58 Chinese, 56 Surinamese and 66 Turks) participated. The purpose of this study was to test the relationship between immigrants' attachment styles and their acculturation strategies. As said before, Bartholomew and Horowitz (1991) classified the four styles of attachment on the dimensions of self- or other-orientation: secure style (positive about oneself and others), dismissing style (positive about oneself and negative about others), preoccupied style (negative about oneself and positive about others), and anxious style (negative about oneself and others). Interestingly, Berry's classification of acculturation strategies can also be characterized by two analogue basic attitudes (orientation towards own group and towards host society group). Integration is orientated towards own and other group, separation towards own group but not to the other group, assimilation is not oriented towards own group but to the other group, and marginalization is oriented to neither group. The expectation was that a secure style would be related to a preference for integration, whereas the two attachment styles with a lack of trust towards others (dismissing and anxious styles) would be negatively related to integration and positively to separation. Individuals with a preoccupied style were expected to have a preference for assimilation because of their positive image of the other group and their negative self-image, but due to the difficulty preoccupied individuals experience in

Table 11.1 *Correlations between attachment styles and positive and negative feelings towards adaptation strategies*

Strategies	Assimilation		Integration		Marginalization		Separation	
Feeling	Pos.	Neg.	Pos.	Neg.	Pos.	Neg.	Pos.	Neg.
Secure			.31*		.11	.14	−.12	.17
Dismissive	.24	−.19	−.25	.36*	.13	−.14	.40**	−.45**
Preoccupied	.24	−.33*			.25*	−.26*	.22	−.23
Anxious		.14		.33			.24	−.30*

Note: *p < .05; **p < .01; numbers in bold refer to theoretically expected relations

approaching the majority group they might opt for marginalization as well. Attachment styles were measured with the above-mentioned questionnaire. The immigrants' acculturation strategies were determined by their affective reactions towards four different scenarios of immigrants behaving in ways that corresponded to Berry's four acculturation strategies. These scenarios were presented at random, one for each respondent. An advantage of the scenario approach, in which each respondent responds to only one scenario, is that the social desirability bias towards choosing integration as the favorite strategy is reduced. The results confirmed the expectations to a great extent (see Table 11.1). A secure attachment style is indeed related to positive feelings towards integration, whereas individuals with an avoidant style (dismissive or anxious) react with negative feelings to integration and with positive and less negative feelings towards separation. As expected, preoccupied individuals sympathize with the assimilating immigrant in the scenario, but also with the marginalized and the separating person.

Although attachment styles have barely been the focus of interest from an acculturation point of view, they can fruitfully be linked to acculturation variables, because both attachment theory and acculturation theory deal with human beings approaching other persons in new situations. Moreover, the relationship has been empirically established in these two studies. Attachment styles indeed appear to be important factors for the choice of acculturation strategies of immigrants and for their psychological and sociocultural adjustment. Because attachment styles are important for the attitudes of immigrants towards members of the host society, it seems desirable to create conditions for immigrants that stimulate the development of secure attachment styles. It is an interesting question whether we can translate the concept of secure attachment to the society level: are societies able to create conditions in which people have a positive image of their own culture and at the same time approach other cultures with trust? Canada seems to be a positive example of such a society. A subsequent topic of research may be whether attachment styles differ from culture to culture and, if they do, whether the differences can be related to the degree of integration of immigrants.

11.6   Are immigrants pitiable or are they predisposed to success?

Too much emphasis has been placed on the negative side of immigration. Very often however, immigrants are hardworking, ambitious and successful citizens. Quite a few of them seem to benefit from their multicultural background. Indeed, we can easily come up with a long list of extraordinarily successful immigrants, for instance: Arnold Schwarzenegger, Kurt Lewin, George Gershwin, Andy Warhol, Vladimir Nabokov, Peter Ustinov, etc. What factors cause some immigrants to be successful? Is there such a thing as cosmopolitanism, which makes some persons more successful than others? Cosmopolitanism is a belief that several cultures, including one's own culture can possess valuable elements; it is an open and at the same time a detached attitude towards several cultures. In an exploratory study among 141 employed immigrants in the Netherlands we looked at the relation between cosmopolitanism and some other variables. Cosmopolitanism was measured with six items, such as: "I like to adopt ideas from other cultures" and "I like to try foreign food." The concept is associated with intercultural competencies, in particular with open-mindedness ($r = .43$), cultural empathy ($r = .32$) and social initiative ($r = .29$). Moreover, it is related to the immigrants' perceived level of success ($r = .29$), but also to their financial success, as measured by their monthly income ($r = .25$). In a subsequent study among 369 students a 10-item version of the scale was used. Cosmopolitanism, not surprisingly, was associated with a preference for the integration strategy ($r = .42$) (see also Betts, 1996) and with social complexity ($r = .21$), a concept introduced by Leung and Bond. Social complexity refers to "the belief in multiple ways of achieving a given outcome, and agreement that human behaviour is variable across situations" (Leung *et al.*, 2002). According to Leung and Bond it is one of the five social axioms or general beliefs, which "are basic premises that people endorse and use to guide their behaviour in daily living."

This section started with the question of whether immigrants are pitiable or predisposed to success. This important question has not been answered yet. The concept of cosmopolitanism may be valuable in the process of finding an answer. Immigrants may by their acculturation process have become more cosmopolitan and interculturally more effective as compared to non-immigrants. This is an interesting hypothesis that has to be empirically tested.

11.7   Conclusions

Immigration is a hot topic worldwide and will remain so for decades to come. In this short chapter I have tried to formulate some conclusions beyond the ones we usually find in the empirical journals and at conferences. Yet, they are based on or inspired by the research presented in journals and at conferences. In short my conclusions are:

➢   Immigration is not a new phenomenon. Even before history was written large streams of people left their "homes" to settle down in new unknown areas.

➢   Immigrants are not a passive factor in acculturation. They may bring about drastic changes in the receiving societies.

➢   Currently, large groups of newcomers in four main immigration areas are making the Western world culturally more diverse and "de-Westernizing" it to some degree.

➢   Nations' immigration policies and their cultural majorities influence the form and the success of immigrants' acculturation.

➢   In general, cultural differences are not appreciated. The larger the cultural distance between groups the more difficult it is to experience mutual sympathy.

➢   Research on attachment styles suggests that early and later childhood experiences may make some individuals more adaptive immigrants than others. It is a challenging idea to find out whether some cultures can create favorable conditions for the development of secure attachment styles.

➢   Immigrants very often are surprisingly successful. Their intense personal experience with more than one culture may foster an attitude of cosmopolitanism which makes them more effective in current multicultural societies.

11.8   References

Bakker, W., Van Oudenhoven, J. P. & Van der Zee, K. I. (2004). Attachment styles, personality, and Dutch emigrants' intercultural adjustment. *European Journal of Personality, 18*, 387–404.

Bartholomew, K. & Horowitz, L. M. (1991) Attachment styles among young adults: a test of a four-category model. *Journal of Personality and Social Psychology, 61*, 226–244.

Berry, J. W. (1980). Acculturation as varieties of adaptation. In A. Padilla (ed.). *Acculturation: theory, models and some new findings* (pp. 9–25). Boulder: Westview.

    (1997). Immigration, acculturation and adaptation. *Applied Psychology: An International Review, 46*, 5–34.

Berry, J. W., Kim, U., Power, S., Young, M. & Bujaki, M. (1989). Acculturation attitudes in plural societies. *Applied Psychology, 38*, 185–206.

Betts, K. (1991). Australia's distorted immigration policy. In D. Goodman, D. J. O'Hearn and C. Wallace-Crabbe (eds), *Multicultural Australia: the challenges of changes* (pp. 149–177). Newham, Australia: Scribe.

    (1996). Immigration and public opinion in Australia. *People and Place, 4*, 9–20.

Boneva, B. S. & Frieze, I. H. (2001). Toward a concept of migrant personality. *Journal of Social Issues*, *57*, 477–491.

Bourhis, R. Y., Moïse, L. C., Perreault, S. & Sénécal, S. (1997). Towards an interactive acculturation model: a social psychological approach. *International Journal of Psychology*, *5*, 1–18.

Bowlby, J. (1969). *Attachment and loss*, Vol. I: *Attachment*. New York: Basic Books.

Brewer, M. D. & Campbell, D. T. (1976). *Ethnocentrism and intergroup attitudes*. New York: Sage Publications.

Byrne, D. (1971). *The attraction paradigm*. New York: Academic Press.

Caligiuri, P. M. (2000). The Big Five personality characteristics as predictors of expatriates' desire to terminate the assignment and supervisor-rated performance. *Personnel Psychology*, *53*, 67–88.

Diener, E., Emmons, R. A., Larsen, R. J. & Griffin, S. (1985). The Satisfaction with Life scale. *Journal of Personality Assessment*, *49*, 71–75.

Donà, G. & Berry, J. W. (1994). Acculturation attitudes and acculturative stress of Central American refugees. *International Journal of Psychology*, *29*, 57–70.

The Economist (2004). Out with the new. December 11, pp. 33–34.

    (2005). Russian xenophobia. The new Jews. February 19, pp. 26–27.

Ghuman, P. A. S. (1994). Canadian or Indo-Canadian: a study of Asian adolescents. *International Journal of Adolescence and Youth*, *4*, 224–243.

    (2000). Acculturation of South Asian adolescents in Australia. *British Journal of Educational Psychology*, *70*, 305–316.

Hagendoorn, L. (1996). Intergroup biases in multiple group systems: the perception of ethnic hierarchies. *European Review of Social Psychology*, *6*, 199–228.

Ho, R., Niles., S., Penney, R. & Thomas, A. (1994). Migrants and multiculturalism: a survey of attitudes in Darwin. *Australian Psychologist*, *29*, 62–70.

Hofstede, G. (1991). *Cultures and organizations. Software of the mind.* London: McGraw-Hill.

Horenczyk, G. (1996). Migrant identities in conflict: acculturation attitudes and perceived acculturation ideologies. In G. Breakwell and E. Lyons (eds), *Changing European identities: social psychological analyses of social change* (pp. 241–250). Oxford: Butterworth.

Lapsley, D. K. & Edgerton, J. (2002). Separation–individuation, adult attachment style, and college adjustment. *Journal of Counseling and Development*, *80*, 484–492.

Leung, K., Bond, M. H., Reimel de Carrasquel, S., *et al.* (2002). Social axioms: the search for universal dimensions of general beliefs about how the world functions. *Journal of Cross-Cultural Psychology*, *33*, 286–302.

Mikulincer, M. & Shaver, P. R. (2001). Attachment theory and intergroup bias: evidence that priming the secure base schema attenuates negative reactions to outgroups. *Journal of Personality and Social Psychology*, *81*, 97–115.

Nagayama Hall, G. C. & Barongan, C. (2001). *Multicultural psychology.* Upper Saddle River, NJ: Prentice Hall.

Nesdale, D. & Mak, A. S (2000). Immigrant acculturation attitudes and host country identification. *Journal of Community & Social Psychology*, *10*, 483–495.

Ones, D. S. & Viswevaran, C. (1999). Relative importance of personality dimensions for expatriate selection: a policy-capturing study. *Human Performance*, *12*, 275–294.

Osbeck, L. M., Moghaddam, F. M. & Perrault, S. (1997). Similarity and attraction among majority and minority groups in a multicultural context. *International Journal of Intercultural Relations*, *21*, 113–123.

Phinney, J. S., Horenczyk, G., Liebkind, K. & Vedder, P. (2001). Ethnic identity, immigration, and well-being: an interactional perspective. *Journal of Social Issues*, *57*, 493–510.

Piontkowski, U., Florack, A., Hoelker, P. & Obdrezalek, P. (2000). Predicting acculturation attitudes of dominant and non-dominant groups. *International Journal of Intercultural Relations*, *24*, 1–26.

Stalker, P. (2001). *The no-nonsense guide to international migration*. Oxford: New Internationalist Publications.

United Nations (2004). *World economic and social survey 2004. Part II. International migration.* www.un.org.

Van Oudenhoven, J. P., Hofstra, J. & Bakker, W. (2003). Ontwikkeling en evaluatie van de Hechtingstijlvragenlijst [Development and evaluation of the Attachment Styles Questionnaire]. *Nederlands Tijdschrift voor de Psychologie en haar Grensgebieden*, *58*, 95–102.

Van Oudenhoven, J. P., Judd, C. M., & Hewstone, M. (2000) Additive and Interactive Models of Crossed-Categorisation in Correlated Social Categories. *Group Processes and Intergroup Relations, 3,* 285–295.

Van Oudenhoven, J. P., Prins, K. S. & Buunk, B. P. (1998). Attitudes of minority and majority members towards adaptation of immigrants. *European Journal of Social Psychology*, *28*, 995–1013.

Van Oudenhoven, J. P., Van der Zee, K. I. & Bakker, W. (2002). Culture, identity, adaptation strategy, and well-being of Frisians abroad. In D. Gorter & K. I. van der Zee (eds.). *Frisians abroad* (pp. 57–69). Ljouwert: Fryske Akademy.

Ward, C. & Masgoret, A.-M. (2004). New Zealanders' attitudes toward immigrants and immigration. Paper presented at New Directions, New Settlers, New Challenges: Foundation for Science, Research and Technology End-users Seminar on Migration, Wellington, New Zealand.

Zick, A., Wagner, U., Van Dick, R. & Petzel, T. (2001). Acculturation and prejudice in Germany: majority and minority perspectives. *Journal of Social Issues*, *57*, 541–557.

12 Sojourners

Stephen Bochner

12.1 Introduction

The term *sojourner* refers to individuals who travel abroad to attain a particular goal within a specified period of time. The expectation is that these culture travelers will return to their country of origin after completing their assignment. Unlike permanent settlers, such as immigrants or refugees, sojourners have a finite perspective and this influences how they acculturate to their host society.

The idea of *culture contact* is a useful organizing principle for an analysis of sojourner acculturation. Contact between culturally diverse individuals is an inescapable aspect of life in the twenty-first century, and sojourners constitute a major contact category. After a brief discussion of intercultural contact, we will make a distinction between different groups of sojourners in terms of *who* they are and *what* they do while abroad. We will then move on to a discussion of *how* sojourners respond to their intercultural experiences, and also *why* there are differences between various categories of sojourners regarding their ability to navigate through unfamiliar cultural settings. And because culture contact always involves meetings between at least two groups, we will briefly review the role of host-country attitudes and practices in sojourner acculturation.

12.2 Culture contact

Narratives from the past indicate that contact between culturally diverse individuals has a long history. People brought up in one culture have always traveled to other societies in order to trade with, learn from, teach, convert, pillage or exploit them. The journals of Captain Cook, Marco Polo, Xenophon, Columbus, Drake and Burton provide excellent accounts of such intercultural visits. However, until quite recently, the number of cultural travelers was relatively small. Individuals who did venture abroad were members of the elite, or specialized groups such as traders, missionaries and military personnel. In ancient times most ordinary persons seldom ventured further than a few miles from the place where they were born. The intervening centuries have witnessed a steady increase in the incidence of people moving across national and ethnic boundaries.

Three factors account for this development: technological change, changes in the attitudes and legal regulations of both sending and receiving countries, and an increase in natural and human-made disasters. Developments in the technology of human mobility provided the prerequisite condition, culminating with the jumbo jet and the modern era of mass travel. Culture contact is now a universal experience, with most people in the world being exposed to second culture inflluences, either as visitors or as members of receiving societies.

Advances in the technology of travel were accompanied by a corresponding liberalization in the attitudes and what are sometimes called "the border-protection policies" of receiving countries, with respect to both sojourners and settlers. The main categories of sojourners include overseas students; tourists; expatriate workers ranging from executives to laborers, employees of international not-for-profit or non-government agencies (NGOs); and military personnel. Overseas students now constitute a major source of revenue and are regarded as a part of the export market by many receiving countries. The globalized nature of commerce and industry requires the services of expatriate managers and technical personnel. Many countries import so-called "guest laborers" to work in jobs that the locals are unwilling or unqualified to perform. The economies of many nations are boosted by the tourists they attract.

On a global level, the proliferation of not-for-profit and international NGOs has given rise to a new breed of transnational civil servants with defined job descriptions and career paths. One of their major functions is to respond to natural and human-made disasters such as civil war, drought, floods and famine. Finally, large numbers of uniformed personnel are engaged in so-called "peace-keeping" as well as more conventional forms of warfare, and are deployed in countries other than their own. Accurate figures are difficult to come by, but a conservative estimate would indicate that sojourners as the term is used in this chapter would number in the tens of millions.

12.3   The terminology of the sojourn experience

As indicated, *culture contact* provides a useful general theoretical framework for this topic. To guide specific research we have developed the *ABC* model of acculturation (Ward, Bochner & Furnham, 2001), spelling out the consequences of contact on the *A*ffective (emotional), *B*ehavioral and *C*ognitive reactions of sojourners. Our particular interest is in tracing how the sojourners' affective, behavioral and cognitive repertoires *change* when they are exposed to a new culture.

Sojourners go abroad to achieve a particular purpose and then return to their country of origin. The physical and sociocultural characteristics of the *destination* influence how the sojourners adapt, giving rise to the terms *visited group* and *host nation* or *culture*. In the past, research and theorizing concentrated on how the visitors coped with and adapted to their novel environments. It was assumed that host societies, by virtue of their monolithic status, would be largely unaffected by the presence of the sojourners. This assumption has been found to be untenable, and contemporary research takes an *interactionist* approach that includes assessing the sojourners' impact on their host societies. Another research question has been to determine if sojourners perform as agents of change, in particular whether their activities increase or decrease inter-group harmony and mutual understanding (see Chapters 5 and 29).

Contact variables include the *time frame* of the visit, its *purpose*, the *cultural attitudes* of members of the host society to *outsiders*, the sojourners' *emotional involvement* with the host society, and the *culture distance* separating the sojourners from host-society members.

12.4   Sojourners categories

The main sojourner groups include *tourists, international students, expatriate workers, international civil servants* and *military personnel*. The main sojourner characteristics are the *purpose* of the visit and its *time frame*, which can stretch from a few days to several years.

Tourists generally spend a relatively short term abroad, typically two or three weeks at most. Their main *purpose* is to relax, indulge and enjoy themselves. Sub-groups include eco-tourists who express a wish to learn about the societies they visit; and sex tourists, whose purpose is to take part in sexual experiences that are not available or legal in their countries of origin. The overall effect of tourism on the visited societies can range from beneficial to catastrophic.

Overseas (or international) students constitute a prominent group of sojourners. Their *purpose* is to study and gain professional qualifications. Their *time frame* generally ranges from several months in the case of language students, to several years if they attend university. Increasingly, some students also complete the last couple of years of high school abroad, further extending their sojourn.

The term *expatriate* refers to sojourners whose *purpose* is to pursue commercial activities abroad. They include executives employed by multinationals to manage their overseas subsidiaries; skilled professional staff who run overseas-owned technical facilities; and less-skilled workers including manual laborers, maids and service-industry personnel, such as cleaners, cooks and restaurant staff. Their *time frame* can range from a few months, if related to a specific project, to several years.

International civil servants are a growing category of sojourners, and include the employees of the United Nations and its agencies and non-governmental welfare and humanitarian organizations. Their primary *purpose* is to relieve human suffering, and their *time frame* is a function of how long their assistance is required. Many of these sojourners return to the field more than once, and quite a few make a life-long career as international aid workers. *Military personnel* are another category, whose *purpose* is territorial defense and peace-keeping. Their *time frame* can extend from several months to a number of years depending on the nature of the actual or potential conflict.

12.5 Other contact variables

Other variables that have a significant effect on the A, B and C reactions of sojourners are host-country attitudes towards *newcomers, outsiders* and people whose *physical appearance* differs from the local norm. The ability and willingness of sojourners to *participate* in the affairs of the visited society interact with how welcoming it appears. The degree of a sojourner's *emotional investment* in their host societies can be inferred from the nature of their *social networks*, in particular whether they have local friends and associates. International students often develop quite significant relationships with their local peers and teachers, although there is a large minority who lead fairly isolated lives. Likewise, there are considerable variations in the extent to which expatriates engage with their hosts, ranging from those who immerse themselves in the local social and commercial scene, to those who live behind the walls of self-segregated compounds reserved for foreigners (Bochner, 1999; Torbiorn, 1994; Tucker, Bonial & Lahti, 2004). Some sojourners do develop intense interdependent relationships with local persons or institutions, which can be a mixed blessing. When these sojourners return to their home country they can experience *reverse* or *re-entry culture shock*, referring to the difficulties of reintegrating into their culture of origin (Bochner, Lin & McLeod, 1980; Harvey, 1997; Hickson, 1994; Klineberg, 1981; Martin & Harrell, 1996: Tung, 1987). See also Chapter 14 on repatriated refugees.

12.6 Culture contact and culture learning

Social psychologists have been the driving force in studying contact-induced behavioral changes. A pioneer in this field was Michael Argyle (Argyle, 1982; Argyle & Kendon, 1967) who regarded interpersonal encounters as a skilled performance in which the participants respond to each other's cues in a continuing feedback process. Verbal and non-verbal communications serve as key coordinating mechanisms in social interaction. The words that people say to each other, supported by gestures, turn taking, tone of voice, posture, proximity between the communicators and touching, are the main variables (Collett, 1982, 1994). What people say and when and how they speak are governed by a set of socially constructed rules and conventions that differ across cultures and sub-cultures (Brislin, 1993; Burgoon, Buller & Woodall, 1989). Participants who do not share the assumptions, perceptions or interpretations of each other's behavior may end up at cross-purposes, leading to misunderstanding, inter-personal awkwardness, confusion, uncertainty, and possibly to hostility. This in turn can adversely affect the capacity of sojourners to achieve their objectives.

An advantage of the culture learning approach is its implications for remedial action. It follows that the key to a successful sojourn is the person's ability and willingness to attain those culturally relevant social skills which facilitate the achievement of the goals of the assignment.

12.7   Adjustment patterns of the three major sojourner groups

12.7.1   Tourists

International tourists are the largest group of sojourners, and their numbers are steadily growing. International tourism is big business, generating US$ five trillion of economic activity each year. It employs 125 million people directly, accounts for 7 percent of the total of world exports, and 18 percent of the total world trade in services (Baldacchino, 1997). The economies of many regions have become highly dependent on income from visitors.

Most of what is written about tourism has analyzed its demographic, economic and geographic aspects. More recently, there has been a greater emphasis on the psychological aspects of tourism. Of special interest are issues relating to whether contact between tourists and hosts is a pleasant or stressful experience; whether the motives for travel include culture learning; the affect, behaviors and cognitions that such contact evokes in both sojourners and host-society members; and whether tourism contributes to inter-group harmony and world peace.

The time frame for most tourists is quite short, and their involvement with the host society tends to be rather superficial. Many have only minimal contact with members of the host culture, particularly those who travel in groups as part of package tours. The travelers most likely to make contact with ordinary members of the visited societies are backpackers. They are usually (but not exclusively) young and open to new experiences, and often set out actively to learn the cultures of their host societies. They are also more likely to be personally touched by their travels, presumably achieving greater understanding of and tolerance for the cultures they have visited. However, the overwhelming majority of tourists return home with their belief systems unchanged.

In contrast, it is difficult for members of the visited society to ignore the tourists in their midst. The shop-keeper, bus driver, restaurant owner, or just the local person in the street is likely to recognize those who are visibly foreign as tourists, and respond accordingly. The emotions and behavior that these encounters arouse in the locals has been the subject of considerable research. The attitudes of host-society members towards tourists have been found to vary from hostile, through neutral, to mildly positive, depending on self-interest, tourist densities (Faulkner & Tideswell, 1997), and the relative wealth, sophistication and economic development of the respective cultures (Dogan, 1989).

The effect of tourists on the societies they visit is mixed. Tourism injects massive amounts of money into the economies of the visited places, but this does not always translate into genuine improvement in the quality of local life. Often, the natural and built environments suffer. Indigenous cultural practices, artistic and spiritual manifestations are distorted, and family patterns and collective social arrangements may be impaired.

12.7.1.1   Tourism and international understanding

Two contrasting views exist about the effects of international travel. Some prominent optimists are on record as saying that even a brief overseas sojourn promotes tolerance and understanding of other cultures. Mahatma Gandhi, cited in Theobald (1994), called travel the language of peace. John F. Kennedy (1963) believed that travel had become one of the great forces for peace and understanding. Ronald Reagan (1985) wrote that travel for pleasure between countries helps to achieve understanding and cooperation. Many social scientists, on the other hand, have pointed out that there is very little empirical evidence that tourism promotes peace. Several reasons have been offered, including the shallowness of the experience for the majority of tourists; the adverse effects that tourism can have on the host society; and because most tourist–host interactions tend to occur between high-status visitors and low-status locals, such asymmetry not being conducive to inter-group respect and esteem.

12.7.2   Student sojourners

In contrast, culture contact is a central aspect of the sojourn of international students. In order to achieve their purpose, students usually live in the visited country for a significant duration, typically three or four years. This is sufficient time to allow them to learn some of the aspects of their host culture, if they are so inclined and have the opportunity to do so. The function of international educational exchange in promoting mutual understanding across cultures has exercised scholars and politicians over the years. More recently, the economic and sociocultural effects of student sojourners on their host societies have become a major research interest.

12.7.2.1   Historical perspective

International education has a long history, with accounts of traveling scholars dating back to ancient times. Global technical aid is mentioned in the Bible, describing how Solomon asked King Hiram of Tyre for assistance with the construction of the Holy Temple in Jerusalem. In ancient Persia (531-579) the University of Jundishapur became what today would be called an "intellectual center of excellence" for comparative cultural studies, specializing in Greek, Jewish, Christian, Hindu and Persian beliefs. In China, the emperors of the T'ang Dynasty (620–907) fostered international educational relations. In Europe, Alexander the Great set up an early version of a Rhodes scholarship, to bring both domestic and international students to Alexandria. Later, the University of Athens began to attract students from various countries. In the Middle Ages, universities in Seville, Paris, Rome and Bologna encouraged missionary, cultural and commercial studies that went beyond national frontiers. A detailed historical account of international education can be found in Fraser and Brickman (1968).

The history of international education reveals that it was driven by two themes reflecting the motives of the rulers and politicians who initiated and funded the programs. The first objective was geo-political. Right from the beginning cross-cultural education was used as an instrument of foreign policy to expand the political and commercial influence of what today would be called the host states. The second purpose was to spread the values of the dominant culture. In practice this usually meant the dissemination of religion, in particular the Buddhist, Muslim, Confucian and Christian faiths. Later, this shaded into more secular goals such as spreading democratic values and fostering international harmony. Both strands are still evident in contemporary international education.

12.7.2.2   Students, national development, and international understanding

The end of the Second World War saw a growing number of individuals going abroad to seek higher education (Klineberg, 1981). Most of the students were sponsored, usually by the countries in which they were studying. In the United States publicly supported schemes such as the Fulbright Program and the East–West Center at the University of Hawaii were supplemented by funds from the Carnegie, Ford, Rockefeller and Hazen Foundations. The Australian government established the Colombo Plan. In Britain, a variety of programs including the well-known Rhodes scholarships supported a large number of foreign students from British Commonwealth countries. Russia provided university places for students from Africa, and Germany and France also sponsored overseas students.

The programs were driven by modern versions of the two pragmatic reasons mentioned earlier. The first was to accelerate the post-war reconstruction of countries damaged by the war. In practice, this meant that students from countries in some parts of Europe, most of Asia, the Pacific Rim and parts of South America were supported to study abroad in the developed world. The declared intention was to train scientists, technologists and other professionals who would return to their countries of origin and contribute to the economic and social development of their societies. However, these laudable objectives were not altogether altruistic, because the sponsoring countries anticipated that such educational exchange programs would project their socio-political and economic influence into the sojourners' countries of origin.

The second aim was to promote international goodwill in order to prevent future global conflicts. This was based on the assumption that overseas students would develop a positive outlook towards the host countries that had provided them with an education. A second assumption was that after returning home their careers would prosper and they would attain positions of influence. The rather naive expectation was that their policies would favor their erstwhile sponsors. Both questions generated a great deal of research. An example is the work of Otto Klineberg, supported by UNESCO. During a long and productive life Klineberg grappled with the question of whether "foreign students . . . [have] . . . taken their role as culture-carriers seriously? Have they contributed to better mutual understanding? Have they brought the nations concerned closer together?" (Klineberg, 1981:114).

The evidence is mixed, to say the least. Because the assumptions were used to justify soliciting funds from governments and foundations, there was some reluctance to probe too closely into their validity. Most of the contemporary evaluation studies lacked rigor in their design or the conclusions they drew. Reports that were skeptical about the outcomes, such as Tajfel and Dawson's (1965) book called *Disappointed guests*, were largely ignored. So were instances of returned students who rose to prominence in their home countries on a platform of hostility towards the nations where they had received their education.

The theory underlying these assumptions is the "contact hypothesis," usually attributed to Amir (1969). It is based on the belief that inter-ethnic conflict is fueled by ignorance of each other's cultures. It is assumed that once culturally diverse individuals come into contact with each other, through their interactions each will get to know the other's point of view, leading to better mutual understanding, greater tolerance and better cross-cultural acceptance. However, the evidence regarding the contact hypothesis is also mixed. That is because cross-cultural contact promotes better inter-group relations only under quite specific conditions. These include equal status of the participants; no history of inter-group conflict; both parties gaining a benefit from the interaction; and that the meetings are a pleasant experience for everyone taking part. If these conditions are not met, then the contact can intensify existing hostility and increase ethnocentrism. Research has shown that student exchanges are not immune to these adverse effects (Smith & Bond, 1998).

12.7.2.3   The psychological effects of the sojourn on students

The student sojourn experiences can range from being enjoyable and productive to being unpleasant and fruitless. These emotions will play a major role in shaping the sojourners' attitudes towards their host country and its individual members.

Culture learning

Research has shown that the degree and quality of engagement with the host culture is a significant determinant of sojourner adjustment. Students who are more inclusively integrated with the local community do better in their studies; tend to be more satisfied with their sojourn; are less anxious; and report higher self-esteem (Ward & Kennedy, 1993a & b). Engagement with the host culture is mediated by the social networks of the sojourners. Culture learning does not occur in a vacuum. Having a host friend facilitates becoming knowledgeable about local customs and traditions. However, many international students do not acquire a single host-country friend even after several years as sojourners.

Research conducted in various parts of the world has found that overseas students tend to belong to three distinct social networks, each serving a particular psychological function. Their primary network is with conationals, has a strong emotional component, and one of its important functions is to rehearse, express and reinforce the culture of origin. Next in importance are social links with other non-conational international students. The function of this network is largely recreational. It also provides a means of sharing common experiences and mutual support based on a common foreignness. A third network is with host nationals. Its function is largely utilitarian, is related to the academic aspirations of the sojourners, and consists of formal contacts with university administrators and academics, counseling services and government officials. Sometimes, host families also feature in this network, and there the ties tend to be more personal. Students may also form friendships with some host-country students, but in relative terms the number of local peer acquaintances is low. The advent of e-mail has greatly facilitated the maintenance of culture-of-origin bonds, potentially having the unintended consequences of further reducing the sojourners' engagement with their host societies. For a review of Bochner's functional model of friendship networks, see Ward *et al.* (2001:147–150).

Culture shock

Culture shock (Bochner, 1994, 2000; Oberg, 1960) is a term that has been used to describe the reactions of sojourners on arriving in their new society. It refers to the feelings of disorientation, anxiety and confusion that unfamiliar cultural environments arouse. As the sojourn progresses, the students may or may not adjust and adapt to their new circumstances. There is general agreement that acculturation is something that occurs sequentially over time and should therefore be regarded as a developmental process. However, there is disagreement as to the nature of the progression. That is because at least two different patterns of adjustment have been observed. A number of longitudinal studies of emotional adjustment have found that, on arrival in the new society, many students initially express optimism and elation, looking forward to an exciting and productive sojourn. However, these feelings of eagerness are soon replaced by anxiety, stress and disquiet once the person is faced with actually having to overcome the everyday difficulties associated with setting themselves up in an unfamiliar and possibly alien environment. Gradually, as they begin to cope, which in practice means learning the culture of their host country, they regain their sense of security, confidence and wellbeing. This pattern has been called the "U-curve of adjustment."

The U-curve has been contrasted with a linear learning curve of adjustment, reflecting another pattern also found in student sojourners. Many international students do not exhibit any feelings of exhilaration on arrival. Rather, they start their sojourn in a condition of culture shock, and gradually work their way up the scale towards an acceptable level of emotional adjustment. As indicated, both of these developmental curves have been reported in the literature (for a review of this debate, see Ward *et al.*, 2001:80–83, 147–150, 159–165). The inconsistent results are probably due to adjustment interacting with the size of the distance between the culture of the sojourner and the culture of the host society. Research has shown that adjustment difficulties intensify as the distance between the two cultures increases (Dunbar, 1994; Triandis, 2003). This suggests that students sojourning in a "closer" culture should experience less initial acculturation stress than sojourners visiting a more "distant" society, and would therefore also be more likely to follow a U-curve adjustment pattern.

Reverse culture shock is experienced by many sojourners returning home after an extended period abroad (Cox, 2004), because they now have to re-learn their culture of origin. For some returned students this is a daunting task (Bochner *et al.*, 1980; Harvey, 1997; Hickson, 1994; Klineberg, 1981; Martin & Harrell, 1996; Tung, 1987). Sojourners from traditional societies exposed to Western liberal influences in areas such as gender relations, attitudes towards authority and alcohol consumption, may find it hard to revert back to the practices expected of them by their families, religious leaders and employers. In their professional roles, they may be frustrated in their attempts to transfer the technical knowledge they acquired overseas to workplaces that lack the required resources, organizational culture and infrastructure. It is not surprising that many returned students ultimately emigrate, usually to the country where they had been trained. This exodus was given the label of *brain drain* (Rao, 1979), receiving considerable attention because it was inconsistent with one of the key aims of earlier international educational exchange, namely raising the technological capabilities of the countries of origin.

12.7.2.4 The effects of international students on their host societies

To some extent, all this is now history. Most of the nations that used to send students to developed countries for functional reasons are now themselves advanced, at least economically and technically. In contemporary times, over-seas students no longer serve as the agents of economic aid or technical reconstruction. Foreign students now are a "market" (OECD, 2004). Universities in the West sell their courses and degrees to the wealthy elites in the developing world, who have varying motives for sending their children to study abroad, including securing citizenship for their offspring in the host country. Ironically, overseas students have become part of the export industry of the very countries which in earlier times footed their bills. Many higher education institutions have become greatly dependent on the income generated in this way.

The greater visibility of international students has had adverse effects similar to those observed when tourist densities increase. All of the countries that attract large numbers of foreign students have reported an increase in incidents that in the literature are called "hate crimes" (Levin & McDevitt, 1993). These range from serious offences such as physical assaults and verbal racial vilification, to harassment, bullying and discriminatory behavior. Although most of the offenders tend to be members of the general public, fellow students and racist groups on campus are also sometimes involved (Turpin-Petrosino, 2002). The authorities have taken note, and programs are being developed to counter this rising threat to inter-group harmony (Civil Rights Project, 2003).

12.7.3 Expatriates

The next largest group of sojourners comprise expatriate workers who are sent overseas to locations where their organization has a subsidiary or runs a joint venture with a local company. They are usually required to remain abroad for a finite period of time, and expected to achieve a specified set of work-related goals. In order to meet their objectives the expatriates will have to be willing and able to interact successfully with their local counterparts. Expatriates, like other long-term sojourners, experience the dislocation associated with prolonged exposure to unfamiliar cultural settings. Like students, they tend to reside in their host culture long enough to engage socially with local people and institutions, if that is their wish. Unlike students, expatriate sojourners tend to be older; about 80 percent are married and more than 70 percent take their children with them (Ali, Van der Zee & Sanders, 2003). Another issue specific to international workers is that their career path may be affected for better or worse by agreeing to serve their employers abroad.

Individuals from practically all occupations participate in work-related cross-cultural travel, ranging from laborers and domestic staff to highly skilled professionals and managerial personnel. We will restrict our discussion to sojourners at the executive end of the spectrum. This group is of special interest because expatriate professionals serve as the human link in international trade and in the growing integration and globalization of the world's economies. Their behavior has a direct bearing on the profitability and indeed the viability of multinational companies. A major issue is the early repatriation of inadequately performing executives and their families. It is estimated that between 20 percent and, in some cases, up to 50 percent of expatriate executives return prematurely (Adler, 1997; Harris & Moran, 1991), a costly burden on their employers.

12.7.3.1   The psychological effects of the sojourn on expatriates

Culture learning

Two important features of the jobs of expatriate executives are to negotiate with local business partners and to manage subordinates. There are major differences between cultures in negotiating styles and the way in which power is exercised (Hofstede, 1998; Triandis, 1994). Many non-Western cultures tend to be more indirect in their bargaining (Brew & Cairns, 2004), and prefer leaders who are authoritarian rather than participative (Bass & Avolio, 1994; Jung & Avolio, 1999). More generally, management and business practices do not transfer easily across cultural boundaries (Bochner, 1992). What works in New York may not be the appropriate strategy in Jakarta. Effective expatriates have to realize this, discard what they learned in their MBA courses and embark on the acquisition, or at least the expression, of appropriate work-related cognitive styles and responses. However, this is easier said than done. As Hofstede (1998) said "Nobody can think globally . . . Management in general, and personnel management in particular, are culturally constrained" (p. 7).

Emotional adjustment

Many expatriates suffer mild to severe culture shock, and contemplate early termination of their assignment (Adler, 1997). Research has also shown that the spouses of expatriates play a major role in determining not only the person's emotional adjustment but also their job performance (Harvey, 1998; Hechanova, Beehr & Christiansen, 2003). Although there are now increasing numbers of women who take on overseas assignments, most of the expatriates still tend to be men (Caligiuri, Joshi & Lazarova, 1999). If they are accompanied by their families, the good sociocultural adjustment of their wives and children is crucial to the success of the assignment (Copeland & Norrell, 2002; James, Hunsley, Navara & Alles, 2004). There is a large literature devoted to this topic (reviewed in Ward *et al.*, 2001), including the roles of pre-departure training, second-culture preparation, and during-sojourn support for expatriates and their dependents.

The psychological adaptation of expatriate personnel is also affected by the attitudes of the host-society members. In some countries there is specific hostility towards particular expatriate national groups (Stewart & DeLisle, 1994), as well as a more generalized prejudice towards foreign multinationals (Kopp, 1994). The adjustment and coping difficulties of expatriate sojourners increase with the distance between their culture of origin and that of the host society. For instance, the Swedish psychologist Torbiorn (1994) found that Scandinavian expatriate managers in Europe encountered fewer difficulties than those working in Africa.

12.7.3.2   The effects of expatriate sojourners

Expatriate executives comprise one of the major agents of the global diffusion of innovations and the integration of the world's economic systems. Despite its high contemporary profile, the globalization process is not an entirely new phenomenon. In the 1960s R. D. Lambert (1966) coined the term 'cocacolonisation' to refer to this trend, in passing drawing attention to two of its characteristics: that the world was moving towards cultural homogeneity, and that the dominant influence came from the West (Erez & Gati, 2004). More recently, similar comments have been made about American-based multinational companies such as McDonald's restaurants and the Starbucks coffee chain. These and other similar institutions are accused of being responsible for reducing differences between cultures and imposing Western values and life styles on non-Western societies. The violent anti-globalization demonstrations that are a regular occurrence on the political scene are similarly motivated by a desire to maintain the uniqueness of particular cultures, and to preserve diversity and heterogeneity at the global level. A discussion of the desirability or otherwise of global cultural convergence is beyond the scope of this chapter, other than to note that cultures seem to be more resilient to the forces of globalization than its opponents allege.

In part the opposition to globalization is due to the changes that can be observed at the local grass-roots level. Factories that used to function on the basis of labor-intensive and collectivist principles and were often family-owned-and-operated, are being replaced by the modern capital- and technology-intensive subsidiaries of foreign companies. Corner stores face competition from international supermarket chains, and the small farm is fast disappearing under the onslaught of multinational agribusinesses. The resulting changes do not just have economic consequences, but tend to undermine, and in some extreme cases obliterate, longstanding traditions, rituals and social structures. These are some of the more visible consequences of the expatriate presence.

12.8 Conclusions

Intercultural contact has now become a daily fact of life for billions of human beings, either as visitors or as members of the visited societies. The word *sojourner* is the technical term for those travelers who are expected to return to their country of origin after achieving their goals. This feature distinguishes them from permanent settlers such as immigrants and refugees. In this chapter three major categories of sojourners were described: tourists, students and expatriates respectively.

Many sojourners tend to be relatively inexperienced international travelers. For them, the sudden transition to an unfamiliar environment can have adverse effects on their emotional adjustment and their personal and professional well-being and competence. Sojourners have a profound effect on the economies and sociocultural systems of their host countries, with consequences ranging from the positive to the destructive. At the global level, depending on the conditions of the contact, sojourners can contribute to either an increase or a decrease in inter-group harmony and mutual understanding.

Sojourners have been the prime agents of the global integration of industry, commerce, and the arts and sciences. Sojourners play a key role in the trend towards the homogenization of the world's cultures, which in practice means a shift towards Western values and customs in most instances. Where this will lead to in the future is currently a hot topic both in cross-cultural psychology and among political scientists. The pessimists predict a gradual and ultimately total global homogenization, leading to the elimination of most cultural diversity. The more optimistically inclined argue that "modern," that is basically Western, technological innovations are at least in principle capable of being adapted and modified to make them compatible with indigenous sociocultural practices and beliefs.

12.9   References

Adler, N. J. (1997). *International dimensions of organizational behavior*. 3rd edn. Cincinnati, OH: Southwestern College Publishing.

Ali, A., Van der Zee, K. & Sanders, G. (2003). Determinants of intercultural adjustment among expatriate spouses. *International Journal of Intercultural Relations, 27*, 563–580.

Amir, Y. (1969). Contact hypothesis in ethnic relations. *Psychological Bulletin, 71*, 319–343.

Argyle, M. (1982). Inter-cultural communication. In S. Bochner (ed.), *Cultures in contact: studies in cross-cultural interaction* (pp. 61–79). Oxford: Pergamon.

Argyle, M. & Kendon, A. (1967). The experimental analysis of social performance. In L. Berkowitz (ed.), *Advances in experimental social psychology* (Vol. III, pp. 55–98). New York: Academic Press.

Baldacchino, G. (1997). *Global tourism and informal labour relations: the small-scale syndrome at work*. London: Mansell.

Bass, B. M. & Avolio, B. J. (1994). *Improving organizational effectiveness through transformational leadership*. Thousand Oaks, CA: Sage Publications.

Bochner, S. (1992). The diffusion of organizational psychology across cultural boundaries: issues and problems. In J. Misumi, B. Wilpert & H. Motoaki (eds.), *Organizational and work psychology*. Hove: Lawrence Erlbaum Associates.

  (1994). Culture shock. In W. J. Lonner and R. Malpass (eds.), *Psychology and culture*. Needham Heights, MA: Allyn & Bacon.

  (1999). Cultural diversity within and between societies: implications for multicultural social systems. In P. Pedersen (ed.), *Multiculturalism as a fourth force* (pp. 19–36). Philadelphia, PA: Brunner/Mazel.

  (2000). Culture shock. In A. E. Kazdin (ed.), *Encyclopedia of psychology*. (Vol. II, pp. 410–413). New York: Oxford University Press.

Bochner, S., Lin, A. & McLeod, B. M. (1980). Anticipated role conflict of returning overseas students. *Journal of Social Psychology, 110*, 265–272.

Brew, F. P. & Cairns, D. R. (2004). Do culture or situational constraints determine choice of direct or indirect styles in intercultural workplace conflicts? *International Journal of Intercultural Relations, 28*, 331–352.

Brislin, R. (1993). *Understanding culture's influence on behavior*. Orlando, FL: Harcourt Brace Jovanovich.

Burgoon, J. K., Buller, D. B. & Woodall, W. G. (1989). *Nonverbal communication: the unspoken dialogue*. New York: Harper Collins.

Caligiuri, P. M., Joshi, A. & Lazarova, M. (1999). Factors influencing the adjustment of women on global assignments. *International Journal of Human Resource Management, 10*, 163–179.

Civil Rights Project (2003). Know your rights on campus: a guide on racial profiling, and hate crime for international students in the United States. Cambridge, MA: Harvard University.

Collett, P. (1982). Meetings and misunderstandings. In S. Bochner (ed.), *Cultures in contact: studies in cross-cultural interaction* (pp. 81–98). Oxford: Pergamon.

(1994). *Foreign bodies: a guide to European mannerisms*. London: Simon & Schuster.

Copeland, A. P. & Norell, S. K. (2002). Spousal adjustment on international assignments: the role of social support. *International Journal of Intercultural Relations, 26*, 255–272.

Cox, J. B. (2004). The role of communication, technology, and cultural identity in repatriation adjustment. *International Journal of Intercultural Relations, 28*, 201–219.

Dogan, H. (1989). Forms of adjustment: sociocultural impacts of tourism. *Annals of Tourism Research, 16*, 216–236.

Dunbar, E. (1994). The German executive in the U.S. work and social environment: exploring role demands. *International Journal of Intercultural Relations, 18*, 277–291.

Erez, M. & Gati, E. (2004). A dynamic, multi-level model of culture: from the micro level of the individual to the macro level of a global culture. *Applied Psychology: An International Review, 53(4)*, 583–598.

Faulkner, B. & Tideswell, C. (1997). A framework for monitoring community impacts on tourism. *Journal of Sustainable Tourism, 5*, 3–28.

Fraser, S. E. & Brickman, W. W. (1968). *A history of international and comparative education*. Glenview, IL: Scott Foresman.

Harris, P. R. & Moran, R. T. (1991). *Managing cultural differences*. 3rd edn. Houston, TX: Gulf.

Harvey, M. (1997). "Inpatriation" training: the next challenge for international human resource management. *International Journal of Intercultural Relations, 21*, 393–428.

(1998). Dual-career couples during international relocation: the trailing spouse. *International Journal of Human Resource Management, 9*, 309–331.

Hechanova, R., Beehr, T. A. & Christiansen, N. D. (2003). Antecedents and consequences of employees' adjustment to overseas assignment: a meta-analytic review. *Applied Psychology: An International Review, 52(2)*, 213–236.

Hickson, J. (1994). Re-entry shock: coming "home" again. In W. J. Lonner & R. Malpass (eds.), *Psychology and culture* (pp. 253–257). Needham Heights, MA: Allyn & Bacon.

Hofstede, G. (1998). Think locally, act globally: cultural constraints in personnel management. *Management International Review, 38*, 7–26.

James, S., Hunsley, J., Navara, G. S. & Alles, M. (2004). Marital, psychological, and sociocultural aspects of sojourner adjustment: expanding the field of enquiry. *International Journal of Intercultural Relations, 28*, 111–126.

Jung, D. I. & Avolio, B. J. (1999). Effects of leadership style and followers' cultural orientation on performance in group and individual task conditions. *Academy of Management Journal, 42*, 208–218.

Kennedy, J. F. (1963). A free trade in ideas. *Saturday Review*, February 16, 43–44.

Klineberg, O. (1981). The role of international university exchanges. In S. Bochner (ed.), *The mediating person: bridges between cultures* (pp. 113–135). Cambridge, MA: Schenkman.

Kopp, R. (1994). International human resource policies in Japanese, European, and United States multinationals. *Human Resource Management, 33*, 581–599.

Lambert, R. D. (1966). Some minor pathologies in the American presence in India. *Annals of the American Academy of Political and Social Science, 368*, 157–170.

Levin, J. & McDevitt, J. (1993). *Hate crimes: the rising tide of bigotry and bloodshed.* New York: Plenum.

Martin, J. N. & Harrell, T. (1996). Reentry training for intercultural sojourners. In D. Landis & R. S. Bhagat (eds.), *Handbook of intercultural training.* 2nd edn. (pp. 307–326). Thousand Oaks, CA: Sage Publications.

Oberg, K. (1960). Cultural shock: adjustment to new cultural environments. *Practical Anthropology, 7*, 177–182.

OECD (2004). *Education at a glance: OECD indicators.* Paris: Organisation for Economic Cooperation and Development.

Rao, G. L. (1979). *Brain drain and foreign students.* St. Lucia: University of Queensland Press.

Reagan, R. (1985). *Correspondence to the 25th session of the executive council of the World Tourism Organisation. April 18, 1985.* Washington, DC: The White House.

Smith, P. B. & Bond, M. H. (1998). *Social psychology across cultures.* 2nd edn. London: Prentice Hall Europe.

Stewart, S. & DeLisle, P. (1994). Hong Kong expatriates in the People's Republic of China. *International Studies of Management and Organization, 24*, 105–118.

Tajfel, H. & Dawson, J. L. (eds.) (1965). *Disappointed guests.* London: Oxford University Press.

Theobald, W. (ed.) (1994). *Global tourism: the next generation.* Oxford: Butterworth.

Torbiorn, I. (1994). Operative and strategic use of expatriates in new organizations and market structures. *International Studies of Management and Organizations, 24*, 5–17.

Triandis, H. C. (1994). Cross-cultural industrial and organizational psychology. In H. C. Triandis, M. D. Dunnette & L. M. Hough (eds.), *Handbook of industrial and organizational psychology.* 2nd edn. (Vol. IV, pp. 103–172). Palo Alto, CA: Consulting Psychologists Press.

(2003). The future of workforce diversity in international organizations: a commentary. *Applied Psychology: An International Review, 52(3)*, 486–495.

Tucker, M. F., Bonial, R. & Lahti, K. (2004). The definition, measurement and prediction of intercultural adjustment and job performance among corporate executives. *International Journal of Intercultural Relations*, *28*, 221–251.

Tung, R. L. (1987). Expatriate assignments: enhancing success and minimizing failure. *Academy of Management Executive*, *1*, 117–125.

Turpin-Petrosino, C. (2002). Hateful sirens: who hears their song? An examination of student attitudes toward hate groups and affiliation potential. *Journal of Social Issues*, *58(2)*, 281–301.

Ward, C., Bochner, S. & Furnham, A. (2001). *The psychology of culture shock*. 2nd edn. Hove: Routledge.

Ward, C. & Kennedy, A. (1993a). Psychological and sociocultural adjustment during cross-cultural transitions: a comparison of secondary students at home and abroad. *International Journal of Psychology*, *28*, 129–147.

(1993b). Where's the culture in cross-cultural transition? Comparative studies of sojourner adjustment. *Journal of Cross-Cultural Psychology*, *24*, 221–249.

13 Refugees and asylum seekers in societies

James Allen, Aina Basilier Vaage & Edvard Hauff

Refugees leave their homeland to escape significant human rights violations (HRVs). These HRVs include exposure to torture, imprisonment, imminent threat of harm, or otherwise dangerous or significantly adverse environments. In addition to the involuntary nature of refugee acculturation processes, refugees must typically simultaneously cope with the consequences of trauma associated with HRVs while undergoing acculturation.

Recently, longitudinal studies have begun to unravel the long-term outcome of trauma exposure among refugees. In contrast to emerging findings showing a high prevalence of resilience and healthy functioning following trauma exposure in the general population (Bonanno, 2004), the refugee research shows greater variability. Among Vietnamese refugees, who are the most frequently researched refugee group, one ten-year longitudinal study in Canada (Beiser, 1999) showed low unemployment and no heightened risk for mental health problems. However, a somewhat different picture emerges from longitudinal research with Vietnamese refugees in Norway that found high unemployment rates (Hauff & Vaglum, 1993) and a frequent, though not invariable, pattern of chronic psychiatric and health symptom profiles (Lie, 2002).

Acculturation theory can assist understanding of these diverging findings, with implications for receiving-country social policy, and effective prevention and treatment interventions. Despite promise in providing a more complete understanding of refugee experience and resilience processes, acculturation has only recently been explored in refugee research. In addition, limited work addresses how acculturation, and particularly acculturative stress, interacts with HRV-related trauma.

We present here an integrated human rights conceptual framework for understanding refugee acculturation. The framework outlines some of the additional complexities trauma experience and coping bring to refugee acculturation processes, along with mechanisms by which HRV trauma experience interacts with acculturation, heightening risk for trauma symptomatology and acculturative stress.

Because refugee experience typically involves trauma and stress, much of the existing research literature focuses on prevalence of resultant psychiatric disorder and disability, with emphasis on posttraumatic stress disorder (PTSD), as well as specific phobia, generalized anxiety disorder, depression and physical disease. Instead, we will emphasize research on the acculturation process and linkages with resiliency and protective factors influencing refugee adaptation.

In this chapter we define a refugee and describe the current global refugee situation. We next present an integrated human rights conceptual framework for understanding refugee experience, in order to locate the study of acculturation processes in refugee studies within a broader human rights perspective. The framework is proposed as a model to assist in the identification of important variables in refugee acculturation and as a means to evaluate the existing refugee acculturation research. The model may also prove useful as a tool for service providers in helping them to understand the individual acculturation processes of refugees receiving medical and psycho-social services, and as an aid to planners of interventions and social policy. Selected current research is reviewed through this framework to provide recommendations for future refugee acculturation research.

13.1 Defining refugees

Contemporary definitions of *refugee* make frequent reference to the *United Nations convention relating to the status of refugees* established in 1951; refugees were defined by the Convention as people leaving their country of origin because of a "well-founded fear of being persecuted for reasons of race, religion, nationality, membership of a particular social group or political opinion" (UNHCR [United Nations High Commissioner for Refugees], 1996:16). The *UNHCR protocol relating to the status of refugees* in 1967 extended the 1951 definition through establishment of the principle of nonreturn (non-refoulment) to one's home country (UNHCR, 1996). A total of 145 countries have signed the 1951 Convention and/or its 1967 Protocol (UNHCR, 2003).

Asylum seekers are those individuals who travel to a receiving country to escape persecution in their country of origin, but may or may not be allowed to remain in this country as place of final asylum. The *Comprehensive plan of action* (United States Department of State, 1989) established a uniform agreement, signed by over 50 countries, that granted asylum seekers a status determination process to determine if their claim to refugee status was legitimate, based on the criterion of persecution, and, at the same time, asserted that asylum seekers who failed to meet this criterion must return to their country of origin.

The year 1990 represented a turning point in asylum practices in Europe and elsewhere. Beginning in 1990, multiculturalism and immigration increasingly came under attack in many of the resettlement countries of Europe and North America (Prins & Slipper, 2003). Countries became less willing to grant protection to asylum seekers, reflected in a quantitative shift in 1990 to relatively low recognition rates of asylum applications in European Union (EU) countries (Vink & Meijerink, 2003); forced repatriation of asylum seekers and even wholesale closing of borders to refugees became more common, as definitions of a refugee, the criteria for identification and recognition of persecution, and the admission of refugees increasingly became subject to political interests in receiving countries.

Also beginning in 1990, refugee advocates highlighted the increasingly broadening scope of a global refugee humanitarian crisis. Accordingly, the International Roundtable on the Movement of People, convened in San Remo, Italy, in 1990, concluded, "The refugee definition contained in the Refugee Convention of 1951 and the Protocol of 1967 is too narrow to apply to situations where movements of people result from generalized violence, internal armed conflicts or other severely adverse social, economic, and political conditions" (International Organization of Migrants, 1990:1). A UNHCR working group considered these issues and proposed an expanded definition of refugee that we adapt here, to include individuals (i) covered by the 1951 Convention and 1967 Protocol, (ii) covered by the Organization for African Unity 1969 Convention Governing the Specific Aspects of Refugee Problems in Africa,[1] (iii) covered by the Cartagena 1984 Declaration on Refugees[2] which is pertinent to Latin America, (iv) forced to leave or prevented from returning to their country of origin because of HRV or man-made disaster, (v) who are stateless, or (vi) who are *internally displaced persons* (IDPs), in that they are forced to leave home for another location in the same country, because of HRV or man-made disaster (Siem & Appleyard, 1991).

Recent research documents that IDPs share common elements with other refugee groups in the form of high levels of HRV-related trauma exposure (Amowitz *et al.*, 2002) along with the experience of involuntary and forced migration. This displacement, particularly when it occurs in non-Western and developing world settings, often takes place within the context of quite disparate regional and tribal cultural differences within national borders, constituting contact between two cultural groups and an acculturation process. Finally, the HRV dimensions of *human trafficking*, and the plight of *trafficked individuals*, who are abducted or deceptively moved to a new country for the purpose of slave labor, including sexual slavery, has received recent increased attention (Landesman, 2004), and constitutes an emerging area of research (Beyrer, 2001; Chukakov, Ilan, Belmaker & Cwikel, 2002; Dinan, 2002; O'Neill, 2001).

---

[1] Under the Organization for African Unity 1969 Convention, the term *refugee* includes those individuals who fall within the definition of the 1951 Refugee Convention and "every person who, owing to external aggression, occupation, foreign domination or events seriously disturbing public order in either part of the country or the whole country of origin or nationality, is compelled to leave his place of habitual residence in order to seek refuge in another place outside his country of origin or nationality" (OAU, 1969).

[2] Under the Cartagena 1984 Declaration the term "refugee" includes persons forced to move "because their lives, safety or freedom have been threatened by generalized violence, foreign aggression, internal conflicts, massive violations of human rights or circumstances which have seriously disturbed public order" (Colloquium on the International Protection of Refugees in Central America, Mexico and Panama, 1984).

In this chapter, we adopt this broader definition of a refugee encompassing all categories of individuals *forcibly displaced* through HRV, including those granted refugee status, seeking asylum, stateless, internally displaced, or trafficked. While noting important differences in the circumstances and needs of these different categories of refugees, these groups share a common involuntary element within the acculturation experience, along with HRV-related traumatic experience.

13.2 Extent and nature of the refugee experience

Breakdowns in civil order have led to increasingly large-scale population displacements in the past thirty years. In 1976, 2.7 million refugees were reported globally (UNHCR, 1997); this number increased to over 20 million by 2003 (UNHCR, 2003). There is disagreement regarding the actual figure as it probably includes undocumented individuals. For example, Human Rights Watch (2004) estimated 22 million IDPs globally in 2001, and the number of trafficked individuals is unclear. In 2001, 78% of all refugees came from 10 areas: Afghanistan, Angola, Burma, Burundi, Congo-Kinshasa, Eritrea, Iraq, the Palestinian territories, Somalia and Sudan, with Palestinians comprising more than one fourth of all refugees (Human Rights Watch, 2004). Most refugees reside in non-Western regions: in 2003 Asia hosted 46% of all refugees, with Africa 22%, Europe 21%, and the Americas 10% (UNHCR, 2003). Collectively, displaced people suffer documented HRVs in over 150 countries (Amnesty International, 1997); globally, mass violence and warfare comprise the most common cause of death and disability (Desjarlais, Eisenberg, Good & Kleinman, 1995).

13.3 The role of acculturation processes within an integrated human rights conceptual framework for refugees

Silove (1999) has described an integrated conceptual framework for understanding the psycho-social experience of refugees. The framework provides a model for understanding ways in which HRV trauma experience influences refugee functioning, adaptation, and resettlement outcome. This integrated human rights conceptual framework is intended for application on both the individual/psychological and the group/cultural levels. This framework also provides linkages to acculturation theory; acculturation processes and HRV trauma experience affect several of the same domains within the framework.

The destruction of civil order that typically creates the conditions for HRVs blurs distinctions between HRV survivor, war-affected community, and

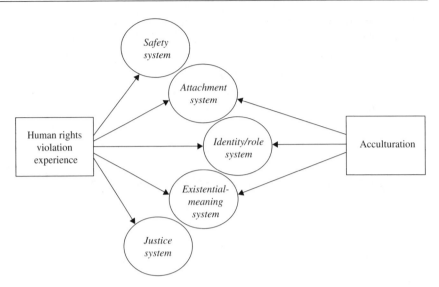

Figure 13.1 *The role of acculturation processes within an integrated human rights conceptual framework for refugee individuals and groups (adapted from Silove, 1999)*

perpetrator, in that these conditions undermine five major adaptive systems supporting the psychological equilibrium of individuals and communities: *personal safety, attachment and bond maintenance, justice, existential-meaning* and *identity/role functioning.* The personal safety system is negatively affected by HRV trauma through the perception of threat engendered. The attachment and bond maintenance system is impacted by multiple experiences of actual and symbolic loss, and its impact on inter-personal bonds. The justice system is affected by the injustice of HRVs, and their often unmitigated or even unacknowledged nature. The existential-meaning system is shaken by a loss of faith in human beneficence resulting from exposure to human cruelty through HRVs. And finally, one of the key aims of torture and other HRVs is to undermine identity, sense of cohesion and agency in individuals and communities, through insult to the identity/role system.

An integrated human rights framework links refugee trauma experience to both its psychosocial meanings and its subsequent impact upon adaptation. It also links refugee acculturation to the process of meaning making and adaptation. The framework specifies how acculturation interacts with response to trauma. This trauma reaction among refugees from diverse cultural backgrounds is more broadly conceived in the framework than the symptom expression associated with the disorder of PTSD. As presented in Figure 13.1, within an integrated human rights framework for refugees, acculturation is an important variable in understanding resilience processes in refugees because it describes a key process in successful adaptation within the identity/role system of a refugee, with additional linkages to the attachment and existential-meaning systems. Acculturative stress can negatively affect these three adaptive systems already impacted by HRV trauma in refugees. An integrated human rights framework specifies testable hypotheses regarding specific variables in refugee outcome and can potentially assist in identification of resilience and protective pathways for prevention and treatment.

13.4   A conceptual framework for understanding refugee acculturation

Individuals exposed to a new cultural context experience a "complex pattern of continuity and change in how [they] go about their lives" (Berry, 1997:6). In refugees, this complexity is intensified by virtue of the premigration (precontact) experience with HRV trauma (Marsella, Bornemann, Ekblad & Orley, 1994); most refugees simultaneously cope with the consequences of traumatic experience as they undergo contact and learn a second culture. Characteristics of the response to trauma can include PTSD, depression, anxiety, or other culturally mediated symptom expression that impacts multiple adaptive systems. These responses can impede exploratory behavior, along with attention, concentration and other cognitive processes (Everly & Lating, 2004) important in both motivation and learning ability during contact and learning of a second culture. From a human rights conceptual framework, the experience of HRV trauma affects survivors at the most profound level of meaning, identity and values; its impact upon adaptive systems induces changes in attitudes, world-view, coping styles and social functioning.

A conceptual framework provided by Berry (2003) is adapted to refugee acculturation and presented in Figure 13.2. It maps additional complexities implicit in acculturation among refugees; elements proposed in the framework constitute important variables in refugee acculturation research. Figure 13.2 describes processes within the area labeled *acculturation* in Figure 13.1. Figure 13.2 emphasizes the *group* and *individual* levels of analysis, the impact of acculturative contact, and the different mechanisms of influence upon members of the *refugee-group culture* and the *receiving-country culture*.

13.5   Cultural/group level

In understanding the acculturation of refugees, the group level of analysis occupies particular importance. Key group elements are presented on the left side of Figure 13.2, converging around *contact*. The *receiving-country culture* and its associated responses to the concerns of refugee resettlement are critical to understanding the nature of the acculturation process as it unfolds for a refugee group in that country. These larger societal factors in turn provide the context within which acculturation processes emerge on the individual level.

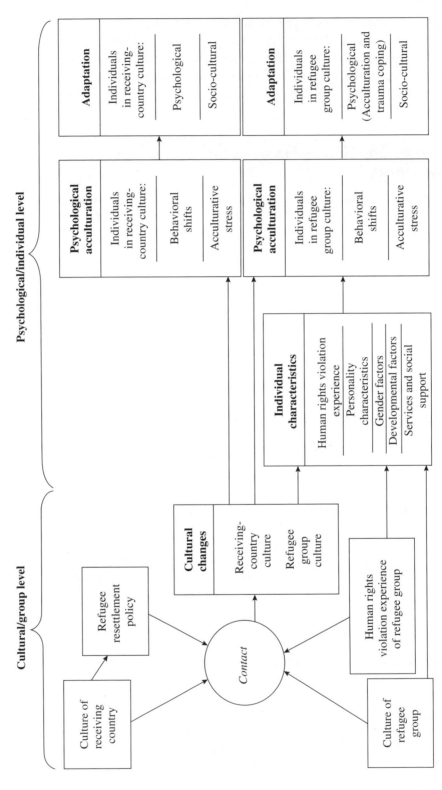

Figure 13.2 *A preliminary framework for understanding refugee acculturation within an integrated human rights conceptual framework: cultural and psychological levels (adapted from Berry, 2003)*

Refugees experience acculturative influences through the receiving-country culture in ways similar to other immigrant and ethnic minority groups; the receiving country's majority-culture views, attitudes, and acceptance of immigrants, minority groups and cultural difference, along with its ideology and social policy regarding the strategy for acculturation, exert powerful influences. For refugees, the response of the receiving-country culture extends beyond the *acculturation strategies* (Berry 2003) of the society to include status determination processes and specific refugee services that are aspects of *refugee resettlement policy*. Resettlement policy of the receiving country includes the services and social supports extended to refugees to assist relocation, resettlement and cultural transition, *and* the amelioration of the HRV trauma. It also includes a country's receiving process for refugees and asylum seekers, which comprises both the legal protections and political rights afforded refugees by the country's legal institutions, and the procedures through which unwanted asylum seekers are excluded from the country. A human rights perspective also emphasizes other important group-level variables in refugee acculturation related to the *HRV experience of the refugee group* that is particular to each refugee group. The premigration historical experience of HRV exposure in a refugee-group society can constitute a collective, group-level psycho-social traumatic process; this *cultural trauma* (Comas-Diaz, Lykes & Alarcón, 1998) is the "concrete crystallization in individuals of aberrant and dehumanizing social relations" (Martín-Baró, as quoted in Aron & Corne, 1994:125) and can strongly influence contact between refugee-group and receiving-country cultures.

Some authors (e.g. Berry, 1986) have argued that precontact HRV trauma experience may be more important to an understanding of refugee behavior than the contact experience itself. While we believe this extremely important, we hypothesize instead that refugee behavior, including acculturation, adaptation and resettlement outcome, is better understood through the interaction of this precontact experience with features of the receiving-country response; for refugees, characteristics of the response of the receiving-country culture exerts powerful influence. This response includes the receiving-country social policy for resettlement, the acculturative strategies adopted by the society towards refugees, as well as potential structural barriers and discrimination in housing and the labor market. Additionally, because asylum seekers often face violence, persecution, prison, torture or death if returned to their country of origin, they occupy an especially precarious position as guests of the receiving country. In these cases, high stakes and enormous pressure drive the acculturation process, with implications for enhanced risk of acculturative stress, since safe return to their home cultural setting is often not an option as is the case with other immigrant groups. The growing trend worldwide of high rates of detention of asylum seekers pending adjudication and of rejection of applications for asylum in most resettlement countries (Keller *et al.*, 2003) contributes to this pressure in the initial phases of the acculturation process. As indicated on the left side of Figure 13.2, these group factors interact during contact, and result in varying degrees of *cultural change* on the group level in both receiving-country and refugee-group cultures, which in turn exerts a major influence on acculturation at the individual level.

13.6 Psychological/individual level

At the individual level, located to the right of group level in Figure 13.2, individuals in both receiving-country and refugee groups undergo a process of *psychological acculturation,* defined as acculturation on the individual level, involving several phenomena. During this process, individuals initiate *behavioral shifts* to varying degrees; these can involve change in dress, food, language, manner of speaking, and other behaviors. Other changes that may prove problematic for the individual constitute an *acculturative stress* response (Berry, 1976), characterized by depression, anxiety, dysphoria and uncertainty. On an internal level, this process also involves varying degrees of individual *adaptation*, which are the outcomes of the psychological acculturation. These outcomes include *psychological* adaptation, affecting such underlying self-perception processes as self-esteem and identity formation, and *sociocultural* adaptation, involving relationship formation and other links among individuals between the cultures, which are facilitated by cross-cultural competencies in various activities of daily living.

A human rights perspective includes additional considerations for refugee acculturation at the individual level of analysis. These special individual-level considerations for refugees appear in the center of Figure 13.2, immediately to the right of group level. Each refugee has a unique *individual refugee precontact experience*. Characteristics of the refugee-group culture, the group precontact experience, and the nature and extent of the individual refugee's precontact experience, including trauma exposure, interact with several *individual characteristics*. These characteristics include *personality characteristics* such as temperament, coping resources and other variables. The model notes the importance of *developmental factors* and *gender factors* in the process of refugee acculturation. For example, as with other immigrant groups, refugee children often acculturate at different rates and use different strategies from their parents, and refugee women may confront challenges related to quite different gender role norms in their new cultural setting, as compared to their home culture. While we feel the analysis of developmental and gender factors is an important and often overlooked factor in much of the current work on acculturation, we believe its consideration is elevated in refugee acculturation, particularly in such cases as unaccompanied refugee minors, and the re-unification situations of many refugee couples and families. Finally, there is a marked variation in the quality of *services and supports* available to individuals within the same receiving country, including legal experiences and detention, resettlement services, and medical and behavioral health services. These individual processes influence the process of psychological acculturation as well as the individual's response to HRV trauma exposure; individual processes influence both the extent and nature of an individual's behavioral shifts and acculturative stress response.

During *psychological adaptation*, other important differences in refugee acculturation emerge. Successful psychological adaptation for refugees involves negotiation of two simultaneous psychological processes: the changes in self-perception processes common to the contact experience occur along with *trauma coping* that is in many ways distinct from the experience of cultural contact. Longitudinal research shows long-term consequences of trauma exposure among refugees; significant and often unchanged psychiatric symptomatology can persist for years following resettlement (Lie, 2002; Mollica, Sarajlic, Chernoff, Lavelle, Vukovic & Massagli, 2001). Successful coping with this trauma is individually defined, and can vary from an extreme of resolution of severe symptoms of PTSD, to a more universal need to find existential meaning in a personal world altered by HRVs. The trauma response when maladaptive can have pervasive negative effects on multiple areas of functioning, including learning, and even in the adaptive resolution of traumatic events, trauma can constitute a psychological crisis that considerably challenges personal resources (Herman 1992). Extended discussion of trauma exposure and symptomatology, and approaches to the prevention and treatment of trauma symptomatology among refugees, can be found elsewhere in the literature (e.g. Hauff & Vaglum, 1995; Gong-Guy, Cravens & Patterson, 1991; Keller *et al.*, 2003; Lustig *et al.*, 2004; Mollica *et al.*, 1993; Mollica, McInnes, Sarajlic, Lavelle, Sarajlic & Massagli, 1999; Williams & Berry, 1991).

13.7 Phases of acculturation

Berry (1991) described six phases of acculturation for refugees: *predeparture, flight, first asylum, claimant period, settlement period* and *adaptation*. During the predeparture period, refugees are exposed to HRV traumatic events. The predeparture period has additional impact upon acculturation attitudes within a context of globalization; individuals develop attitudes about the culture of the receiving country or receiving area prior to departure. This experience previous to direct cultural contact can influence both the decision of where to take flight to and the later acculturation process.

Flight often represents a continuation of trauma experience involving risk of capture, exploitation, piracy, physical and sexual assault, other crimes, injury or death. Privation, including hunger, discomfort, and intense physical challenges, is often involved. Typically, loss of attachment bonds with family, friends and community, along with loss of material possessions and monetary wealth, occurs.

Many refugees arrive at a location of first asylum where they may or may not remain long term. This may involve arrival at a border-area camp where danger continues or detainment resembles imprisonment. Though safety and physical needs are typically most critical, attitudes towards host societies and acculturation can be impacted at this time, as can later health, behavioral health, and social outcomes.

During the claimant phase, a refugee requests asylum in a receiving country. Though signatories to the Convention of 1951 have in theory agreed to clear principles and criteria embodied in it and the 1967 Protocol, in practice, definitions of a refugee and the criteria of persecution have been subject to changing political interests, and many asylum seekers are turned away. This serves to heighten uncertainty and fear in an already traumatized population. Differing experiences with the wide variation in status determination bureaucracies, and health and social services in different receiving countries impact attitudes. In formulations of acculturation theory, the situation of the refugee in the claimant phase is defined as marginalization (Berry, 1987, 1991); this acculturation strategy, when adopted by the receiving country, includes separation of the marginalized group from the mainstream of society within a subordinate position regarding legal rights and access to the benefits of that society. The combination of this acculturative strategy with the involuntary nature of refugee immigration is high-risk for acculturative stress; acculturative stress interacting with HRV trauma can potentiate increased trauma symptom expression. Accordingly, recent research has found exacerbated psychological symptoms in detained asylum seekers in the USA (Keller *et al.*, 2003). On the group level, receiving countries, including those not intending to admit all claimants, can make excellent use of their available health and social resources during the claimant period, as these resources comprise indicated prevention interventions for a high-risk and often symptomatic group. The social policy of the receiving country, and the range of services and experiences offered, can have marked positive impact at the group and individual acculturation levels in refugee adaptation.

If a refugee is granted asylum, he or she enters into the resettlement phase wherein acculturation is impacted by the acculturative strategy of the receiving country interacting with the individual refugee's selection of acculturative strategy. The proposed framework for refugee acculturation is most relevant to this phase, and most existing refugee acculturation research has been conducted during resettlement.

Many engaged in clinical work with refugees have noted that individuals can move on to a point where "they cease to be a refugee." By this is meant some resolution regarding the meaning of refugee life and experience, including HRV, within a person who no longer views himself or herself as a refugee from their home country, but, instead, as a citizen of the country where he or she now lives. This restoration of equilibrium to adaptive systems can be termed the adaptation phase; however, at present, there is scant longitudinal research on this proposed final phase.

It is also important to note not all refugees go through all these phases. Many may never reach adaptation; refugees are often sent back during the claimant phase or captured during flight. In addition, phases may differ across different involuntary groups. For example, some refugees are more fortunate in that they wish to and are allowed to settle in their country of first asylum. In less favorable contrast, IDPs typically do not undergo a claimant process, and instead navigate the existing internal systems of a nation state and the external systems of foreign aid and non-governmental organizations, often in the midst of a conflict-torn region. Trafficked individuals also undergo no claimant process; they are typically not recognized under the Convention of 1951, are in danger of recapture by their captor–enslavers in the resettlement country, are often at first inaccurately viewed as criminals by authorities despite the coerced nature of prostitution or work without a residence visa, and sometimes authorities presume such individuals will return to their country of origin though return may be dangerous or not be possible (Landesman 2004).

13.8   Conclusions and recommendations

Though there has been significant work in the area of refugee mental health since the mid-1970s, direct study of psychological acculturation among refugees is a more recent research area; our review located almost 100 studies. Formulating general conclusions and recommendations from the refugee acculturation literature involves numerous complexities. On the group level, there exists extreme variation in refugee circumstances. On the individual level, important variables interact with acculturation, including premigration experience, acculturative stress experience, and individual characteristics. The range of theoretical and methodological approaches, the diversity of investigative topics, the variation in study sample characteristics, and the differing acculturation measurement approaches utilized in the literature all underscore these points, but have also contributed to inconsistent findings and contradictory conclusions; therefore, it is useful to identify several methodological issues that warrant attention in refugee acculturation research. Some of the issues raised are identified by others in the general acculturation literature (e.g., Chun & Akutsu, 2003), while others are unique to refugees. Methodological concerns include a general pattern of studying trauma and acculturative stress in isolation, problematic conceptual formulations and measurement strategies of refugee acculturation, incomplete description and mapping of the scope of variables impacting refugee acculturation, and limited research on the acculturation process over time. These concerns relate to six central findings of the refugee acculturation research.

13.8.1 Premigration and postmigration experience interact in refugee acculturation processes

Acculturative stress interacts with HRV trauma as an important determinant in refugee resettlement outcome. A human rights framework proposes theoretical linkages for these variables, suggesting dependent variables and downstream causal model variables for research. We argue it is inappropriate to consider, as some authors assert (e.g. Nicholson, 1997), that such factors as extended bereavement over multiple losses constitute a task of acculturation. A human rights framework conceives of adaptation at the individual level as including two separate facets: *acculturation* co-occurs with *trauma coping* as distinct processes involving both overlapping and unique psychological mechanisms. Research exploring both variables in a common causal pathway predicting refugee behavior and resettlement outcome is still in its infancy; typically trauma-related or acculturative stress have been a focus of inquiry as if each functioned somewhat in isolation from the other.

13.8.2 Acculturation in refugees is a multidimensional and dynamic construct

Though this assertion appears repeatedly and is discussed at length in other chapters in this book, the fundamental weakness of unidirectional, unidimensional, noninteractive and static models of acculturation processes has become particularly apparent in the findings of recent refugee acculturation research. Among some refugee populations, as in the case of Soviet Jewish refugees, it may be more appropriate to consider multiple rather than just two cultural identities (Birman & Tyler, 1994); in some cases these processes may be orthogonal while in others they may not (Birman & Trickett, 2001), and to understand acculturative processes more completely, it is important to tap these processes across multiple life domains, where they can have differential effects (Birman, Trickett & Vinokurov, 2002).

13.8.3 Acculturation measurement in refugee research requires a consistent, sufficiently elaborated, and conceptually grounded approach

Flaws in the theoretical elaboration of the construct of acculturation in refugee research have led to flawed measurement strategies. Some measurement strategies in refugee research have confused the acculturation strategy of assimilation with acculturation, inappropriately conceptualizing it as unilevel and unidirectional. Other strategies have confused assimilation with measures of life satisfaction. Acculturation measures must explore the range of refugee acculturative strategies, including separation, marginalization, and integration or biculturalism among potential possibilities. Other approaches tap a restricted set or even single dimension of acculturation, such as a single behavioral indicator (e.g. second-language skill) to quantify acculturation, or employ proxy variables, such as years in resettlement. Strategies using proxy variables provide a poor and inconsistent relation to acculturative processes; for example, among Afghani refugee children, age of arrival in resettlement provided a better outcome predictor than years in resettlement (Mghir, Freed, Raskin & Katon, 1995). The multiple life domains impacted by these processes require investigation, including work, school, home and recreation.

Measures of acculturative stress often evidence similar conceptual confusion in the research. Many inadequately tap multiple life domains, confuse general hassles of life with the more specific category of acculturative stressors, confound stressors with the distress produced by them, and do not assess their frequency or perceived impact (Vinokurov, Trickett & Birman, 2002). Some studies have used broad measures of general psychopathology symptomatology as an indicator of acculturative stress in refugees, ignoring the confound of HRV trauma exposure upon scores on such measures.

As a result, numerous studies in the literature describe only restricted components of the acculturation process, explore only one facet of acculturation, or, at worst, inaccurately map the process. This can lead to contradictory findings as different measurement approaches to acculturation, through their methodological deficiencies, can produce different relationships to dependent variables.

In the limited number of studies that explore the relation of acculturative processes to refugee behavior as a dependent variable, there is often a lack of grounding of measurement strategy with acculturative theory and models that could guide theory-driven inquiry. Silove's (1999) human rights framework and, within it, Berry's (2003) acculturation framework adapted for refugees are examples of possible theoretical frameworks that can guide inquiry.

As the measurement of acculturative processes progresses, it is important to test measures with each new refugee group. As acculturation is a construct, meaning it is inferred and cannot be directly evaluated, construct validation (Cronbach & Meehl, 1955) assumes significant importance in refugee acculturation studies. In addition to tests of measures' internal validity commonly reported in the current refugee acculturation literature, construct validity investigation as a routine component of refugee acculturation research designs can guide efforts to identify and resolve issues relevant to acculturation measurement among specific refugee populations, and can assist in further elaboration and refinement of our understanding of the causal network of variables operative in refugee acculturation, behavior, and resettlement outcome. Adoption of a perspective informed by multiple methodologies also encourages researchers to incorporate qualitative methodologies.

Qualitative research can expand our understanding of the causal network of variables in refugee acculturation. The work of Palinkas and Pickwell (1995), exploring links between acculturation and chronic disease among Cambodian refugees, provides one example from the literature. In this study, qualitative inquiry provided rich, elaborated ethnographic description both of the change in social and psychological processes associated with cultural contact in this refugee group, and of the nature of the interaction of acculturative stress with other key pre- and postmigration refugee variables, including HRV-related trauma, as they influenced refugee outcomes across different domains. Themes derived from coding and analysis of qualitative interview data can inform selection of new variables for quantitative studies of refugee acculturation and outcome.

13.8.4   Macrolevel, cultural/group influences are critically important to an understanding of refugee acculturative processes

An integrated human rights framework proposes pathways by which individual psychological acculturation is influenced by group-level processes such as the historical HRV trauma experience and the cultural characteristics of a refugee group. In involuntary immigration and, in particular, within the context of the often dire survival options during asylum seeking, macrolevel processes in the receiving country can exert stronger influence than is typical with other immigrant groups. Status determination policy, resettlement policy, and acculturative attitudes of the receiving country can exert profound influences on refugee acculturation.

Limited attention has been devoted to macrolevel influences; descriptive research on group-level variables, including comparative studies on asylum determination and resettlement policy in various countries, constitutes an important starting point. Immigration studies, such as the work of Gran and Hein (1997) in France, have begun to explore contextual determinants of receiving-country acculturative attitudes and strategies for immigration; similar work is needed in refugee studies. In addition, comparative studies contrasting such variables as asylum determination and resettlement policy in various countries with their associated refugee acculturation and adaptation outcomes would provide modes of naturalistic inquiry into the effectiveness of various social policies and cultural responses to the refugee situation.

13.8.5   Refugee acculturation is differentially determined through a breadth of divergent refugee experience

The dynamic nature of acculturation requires conceptualization and study of refugee acculturation processes across development, location, cohort, ethnicity and gender. The existing developmental literature highlights several distinguishing attributes in the acculturation experience of children. Similarly, the acculturation stressors for teens can be expected to differ in important ways from those in young adults, and those in young adults will differ from those in mid- and late adulthood. Recent work has highlighted important differences in the experience of refugees in the developing or majority world – where most refugees live – compared with refugee status in the West, where most refugee research is conducted (Thapa, Ommeren, Sharma, de Jong & Hauff, 2003). Refugee experience in the majority world can be quite different; refugees in these countries often face additional stressors including poverty and limited services. There exists an emerging literature on asylum seekers, but research on IDPs is currently at the level of documentation of the HRV exposure this population endures (Amowitz *et al.*, 2002), and even less is known regarding the acculturative experience of trafficked individuals; important differences may exist in the contact experience of each group. Ethnicity is another important variable for research; not all refugee groups are valued in the same way by receiving countries, and not all refugees within a country face the same acculturation attitudes (Williams & Berry, 1991). The experience of European refugees in European resettlement countries may be quite different than that of non-European refugees. Similarly, the experience across gender appears to differ; recent research has identified important gender differences in factors associated with psychological distress among immigrants to Oslo from low- and middle-income countries (Thapa & Hauff, 2005). Yet gender also remains an important under-examined variable in refugee acculturation research. Finally, within ethnic group and gender, important cohort differences may exist between waves of refugees in the same receiving country; Chung, Bemak and Wong (2000) found important within-gender differences in mental health status, acculturative strategies and social support across first- and second-wave Vietnamese refugees in the USA. All these considerations highlight a need for greater specificity in description of the refugee population under study in research reports, and examination of the impact of these contextual variables on acculturation.

13.8.6 Study of refugee acculturation as a process requires longitudinal research designs

Six distinct developmental phases are described in the refugee process. Differing acculturative strategies and stressors are proposed as being likely in different phases, with changes over time predicted in the nature of the acculturative process. Similarly, different acculturative stresses and strategies are expected during lifespan development. Coping with HRV trauma also follows a developmental path, and can interact with acculturative stress in potentially different ways at different times in this pathway. Longitudinal studies of refugees are only now appearing in the literature. Generally these studies have explored such factors as economic adjustment and psychiatric outcome (Beiser, 1999; Hauff & Vaglum, 1993, 1995; Lie, 2002); few studies report on refugee acculturation processes over time or the longitudinal pathways of acculturation interacting with HRV trauma coping.

13.9   Future directions in refugee acculturation for research and practice

Study of refugee acculturation has potential for important contributions to the broader study of acculturation within cultural psychology. Within psychiatry, community and clinical psychology, social work and public health, better understanding of acculturation processes among refugees can inform development of improved models of therapeutic intervention for refugees by facilitating our understanding of effective prevention efforts, psychotherapy process, and social support systems for this group. Advances in measurement of acculturation have direct clinical utility in assessment and in culturally competent service delivery models (e.g., Dana, 2000). In refugee research, acculturative processes constitute an important variable determining outcome; acculturative stress interacts with HRV trauma as a predictor of refugee health, mental health, and adaptation. Finally, the study of acculturative processes in refugees, asylum seekers, IDPs and trafficked individuals holds promise for advancing our understanding of other groups facing involuntary acculturation, such as global indigenous peoples, and, more generally, can advance the understanding of resiliency and protective factors, particularly with regard to response to trauma when accompanied by rapid social transition.

13.10 References

Amnesty International (1997). *Amnesty International report*. London: Amnesty International Publications.

Amowitz, L. L., Reis, C., Lyons, K. H., *et al.* (2002). Prevalence of war-related sexual violence and other human rights abuses among internally displaced persons in Sierra Leone. *Journal of the American Medical Association, 287*, 513–521.

Aron, A. & Corne, S. (eds.) (1994). *Writings for a liberation psychology: Ignacio Martín-Baró*. Cambridge, MA: Harvard University Press.

Beiser, M. (1999). *Strangers at the gate: the "boat people's" first ten years in Canada*. Toronto, Ontario: University of Toronto.

Berry, J. W. (1976). *Human ecology and cognitive style: comparative studies in cultural and psychological adjustment*. New York: Sage Publications / Halsted.

(1986). The acculturation process and refugee behavior. In C. L. Williams & J. Westermeyer (eds.), *Refugee mental health in resettlement countries* (pp. 25–38). Washington, DC: Hemisphere Publishing Corporation.

(1987). Acculturation and psychological adaptation among refugees. In D. Miserez (ed.), *Refugees – the trauma of exile*. Dordrecht, The Netherlands: Martinus Nijhoff Publishers.

(1991). Refugee adaptation in settlement countries: an overview with an emphasis on primary prevention. In F. L. Ahearn, Jr., & J. L. Athey (eds.), *Refugee children: theory, research, and services* (pp. 20–38). Baltimore, MD: Johns Hopkins University Press.

(1997). Immigration, acculturation, and adaptation. *Applied Psychology: An International Review*, *46*, 5–34.

(2003). Conceptual approaches to acculturation. In K. M. Chun, P. B. Organista & G. Marín (eds.), *Acculturation: advances in theory, measurement, and applied research* (pp. 17–37). Washington, DC: American Psychological Association.

Beyrer, C. (2001). Shan women and girls and the sex industry in Southeast Asia: political causes and human rights implications. *Social Science & Medicine*, *53*, 543–550.

Birman, D. & Trickett, E. J. (2001). Cultural transitions in first-generation immigrants: acculturation of Soviet Jewish refugee adolescents and parents. *Journal of Cross-Cultural Psychology*, *32*, 456–477.

Birman, D., Trickett, E. J. & Vinokurov, A. (2002). Acculturation and adaptation of Soviet Jewish refugee adolescents: predictors of adjustment across life domains. *American Journal of Community Psychology*, *30*, 585–607.

Birman, D. & Tyler, F. B. (1994). Acculturation and alienation of Soviet Jewish refugees in the United States. *Genetic, Social, & General Psychological Monographs*, *120*, 101–115.

Bonanno, G. A. (2004). Loss, trauma, and human resilience: have we underestimated the human capacity to thrive after extremely aversive events? *American Psychologist*, *59*, 20–28.

Chukakov, B., Ilan, K., Belmaker, R. H. & Cwikel, J. (2002). The motivation and mental health of sex workers. *Journal of Sex & Marital Therapy*, *28*, 305–316.

Chun, K. M. & Akutsu, P. D. (2003). Acculturation among ethnic minority families. In K. M. Chun, P. B. Organista & G. Marín (eds.), *Acculturation: advances in theory, measurement, and applied research* (pp. 95–119). Washington, DC: American Psychological Association.

Chung. R. C., Bemak, F. & Wong, S. (2000). Vietnamese refugees' levels of distress, social support and acculturation: implications for mental health counseling. *Journal of Mental Health Counseling*, *22*, 150–161.

Colloquium on the International Protection of Refugees in Central America, Mexico and Panama. (1984). *Cartagena declaration on refugees*. Resolution adopted by the Colloquium on the International Protection of Refugees in Central America, Mexico and Panama, Cartagena, Colombia. Retrieved November 16, 2004, from www.unhcr.ch/.

Cronbach, L. J. & Meehl, P. E. (1955). Construct validity in psychological tests. *Psychological Bulletin*, *52*, 281–302.

Dana, R. H. (ed.) (2000). *Handbook of cross-cultural and multicultural personality assessment*. Hillsdale, NJ: Lawrence Erlbaum Associates.

Desjarlais, R., Eisenberg, L., Good, B. & Kleinman, A. (1995). *World mental health*. New York: Oxford University Press.

Dinan, K. A. (2002). Migrant Thai women subjected to slavery-like abuses in Japan. *Violence Against Women*, *8*, 1113–1139.

Everly, G. S., Jr., & Lating, J. M. (2004). Neuropsychological assessment and posttraumatic stress. In G. S. Everly & J. M Lating (eds.), *Personality-guided therapy for posttraumatic stress disorder* (pp. 89–99). Washington, DC: American Psychological Association.

Gong-Guy, E., Cravens, R. B. & Patterson, T. E. (1991). Clinical issues in mental health service delivery to refugees. *American Psychologist, 46*, 642–648.

Gran, B. K. & Hein, J. (1997). International migration, ethnopolitics, and the French nation-state: explaining natives' views of immigrant assimilation. *Social Science Quarterly, 78*, 369–384.

Hauff, E. & Vaglum, P. (1993). Integration of Vietnamese refugees into the Norwegian labour market: the impact of war trauma. *International Migration Review, 27*, 388–405.

(1995). Organised violence and the stress of exile: predictors of mental health in a community cohort of Vietnamese refugees three years after resettlement. *British Journal of Psychiatry, 166*, 360–367.

Herman, J. L. (1992). *Trauma and recovery*. New York: Basic Books.

Human Rights Watch (2004). *Refugees*. Retrieved March 18, 2004, from www.hrw.org.

International Organization of Migrants (1990). *International roundtable on the movement of people: new developments*. Geneva, Switzerland: International Institute of Humanitarian Law.

Keller, A. S., Rosenfeld, B., Trinh-Shevrin, C., *et al.* (2003). Mental health of detained asylum seekers. *Lancet, 362*, 1721–1723.

Landesman, P. (2004). The girls next door. *The New York Times Magazine*, January 24, 30.

Lie B. (2002). A 3-year follow-up study of psychosocial functioning and general symptoms in settled refugees. *Acta Psychiatrica Scandinavica, 106*, 415–425.

Lustig, S. L., Kia-Keating, M., Knight, W. G., *et al.* (2004). Review of child and adolescent refugee mental health. *Journal of the American Academy of Child & Adolescent Psychiatry, 43*, 24–36.

Marsella, A. J., Bornemann, T., Ekblad, S. & Orley, J. (1994). Introduction. In A. J. Marsella, T, Bornemann, S. Ekblad & J. Orley (eds.), *Amidst peril and pain: the mental health and wellbeing of the world's refugees* (pp. 1–16). Washington, DC: American Psychological Association.

Mghir, R., Freed, W., Raskin, A. & Katon, W. (1995). Depression and posttraumatic stress disorder among a community sample of adolescent and young adult Afghan refugees. *Journal of Nervous & Mental Disease, 183*, 24–30.

Mollica, R. F., Donelan, K., Svang, T., *et al.* (1993). The effect of trauma and confinement on functional health and mental health status of Cambodians living in Thailand/Cambodia border camps. *Journal of the American Medical Association, 270*, 581–586.

Mollica, R. F., McInnes, K., Sarajlic, N., Lavelle, J., Sarajlic, I. & Massagli, M. P. (1999). Disability associated with psychiatric co-morbidity and health status in Bosnian refugees living in Croatia. *Journal of the American Medical Association, 282*, 433–439.

Mollica, R. F., Sarajlic, N., Chernoff, M., Lavelle, J., Vukovic, I. S. & Massagli, M. P. (2001). Longitudinal study of psychiatric symptoms, disability, mortality and emigration among Bosnian refugees. *Journal of the American Medical Association, 286*, 546–555.

Nicholson, B. (1997). The influence of pre-emigration and postemigration stressors on mental health: a study of Southeast Asian refugees. *Social Work Research, 21*, 19–31.

OAU (1969). *Convention governing the specific aspects of refugee problems in Africa.* Adopted by the Heads of State and Government assembled in the city of Addis Ababa. Retrieved November 16, 2004, from www.africa-union.org/Official_documents/Treaties_%20Conventions_%20Protocols/Refugee_Convention.pdf.

O'Neill, T. (2001). "Selling girls in Kuwait": domestic labour migration and trafficking discourse in Nepal. *Anthropologica, 43,* 153–164.

Palinkas, L. A. & Pickwell, S. M. (1995). Acculturation as a risk factor for chronic disease among Cambodian refugees in the United States. *Social Science & Medicine, 40,* 1643–1653.

Prins, B. & Slijper, B. (2003). Multicultural society under attack: an introduction. *Journal of International Migration and Integration. Special Double Issue: Multicultural Society Under Attack, 3,* 313–328.

Siem, H. & Appleyard, R. (1991). *Refugee movements and human migration. Some conceptual issues.* Paper presented at the International Conference on Refugee Mental Health and Well-being, Stockholm, Sweden, November.

Silove, D. (1999). The psychosocial effects of torture, mass human rights violations, and refugee trauma: toward an integrated conceptual framework. *Journal of Nervous and Mental Disorder, 197,* 200–207.

Thapa, S. B. & Hauff, H. (2005). Gender differences in factors associated with psychological distress among immigrants from low and middle-income countries: findings from the Oslo Health Study. *Social Psychiatry and Psychiatric Epidemiology, 40,* 78–84.

Thapa, S. B., Ommeren, M. V., Sharma, B., de Jong, T. V. M. J. & Hauff, E. (2003). Psychiatric disability among tortured Bhutanese refugees in Nepal. *American Journal of Psychiatry, 160,* 2032–2037.

UNHCR (1996). *Convention and protocol relating to the status of refugees: text of the 1951 convention relating to the status of refugees – text of the 1967 protocol relating to the status of refugees.* Resolution 2198 (Xxi) adopted by the United Nations General Assembly. Retrieved March 16, 2004, from www.unhcr.ch/cgibin/texis/vtx/home?page =PROTECT&id=3c0762ea4.

  (1997). *The state of the world's refugees.* Oxford: Oxford University Press.

  (2003). *Refugees by numbers 2003 edition.* Retrieved March 19, 2004, from www.unhcr.ch/.

United States Department of State (1989). *Comprehensive plan of action.* Washington, DC: United States Department of State.

Vink, M. & Meijerink, F. (2003). Asylum applications and recognition rates in EU member states 1982–2001: a quantitative analysis. *Journal of Refugee Studies, Special Issue: European Burden-sharing and Forced Migration, 16,* 97–315.

Vinokurov, A., Trickett, E. J. & Birman, D. (2002). Acculturative hassles and immigrant adolescents: a life-domain assessment for Soviet Jewish refugees. *Journal of Social Psychology, 142,* 435–445.

Williams, C. L. & Berry, J. W. (1991). Primary prevention of acculturative stress among refugees: application of psychological theory and practice. *American Psychologist, 46,* 632–641.

14 Refugees in camps

Giorgia Donà & Lisanne Ackermann

14.1 Introduction

This chapter examines the process of acculturation of refugees in camps from a space and time perspective. The study of this phenomenon in camps is important for understanding acculturation in the global context for four main reasons. First, most of the research on this topic describes the experience of refugees in the West, and this chapter documents acculturation in non-Western settings, exploring the role of cultural similarity and distance between country of origin and host country. Second, this chapter examines those refugees who are not expected to settle in the host country and thus is complementary to research on refugees who are settled in the West as discussed in this *Handbook* by Allen, Vaage and Hauff. Third, individuals and groups experience acculturation when living intermingled among host community members; refugees in camps differ by living in collective settings where interactions with conationals while residing in host countries predominate. Fourth, while traditionally acculturation refers to psychological and cultural change and maintenance in host countries, recent research has studied acculturation beyond exit migration to include return, leading to the examination of re-acculturation (Donà & Berry, 1999). This chapter contributes to the *Handbook* by adding a new dimension to acculturation research, the phenomenon of return. It places acculturation and re-acculturation in the continuum of exile and return by examining the impact of the acculturation experience in camps on the re-acculturation process.

The chapter begins with an overview of life in refugee camps, continues with an analysis of psychological acculturation and re-acculturation, and concludes with a brief examination of the relationship between acculturation and wellbeing. The general literature about life in refugee camps has been analyzed for its relevance to the phenomenon under study, and research with Guatemalan refugees in Mexico and with returnees has been used to explain concepts and develop ideas.

14.2 General overview of refugees in camps

According to the United Nations High Commissioner for Refugees (UNHCR) the number of individuals of concern to the agency at the end of 2003 was 17.1 million, excluding 4 million Palestinians under the United Nations Relief and Works Agency (UNRWA). Of these 57 percent, that is 9.7 million, are refugees, and the remaining are asylum seekers, internally displaced, stateless individuals and others of concern. This excludes all refugees who self-settle and are not under the protection and assistance of UNHCR. The number of refugees in camps is 4,477,441 in comparison to 1,907,760 forced migrants in urban areas and 6,954,434 dispersed refugees in other settings. Thus, refugees in camps constitute 34 percent of the population of concern to the agency (UNHCR, 2004).

The term *camp* encompasses a range of settings from short-term transit camps to more permanent settlements. The differences reflect the continuum from first emergency phases to rehabilitation and long-term development, from plastic sheeting shelter to more permanent housing. Camps were originally created as a temporary and short-term solution to refugee movements but an increasing number of refugees spend considerable time there and de facto they have become a semi-permanent solution. Staying in camps for more than five years, which is known as a protracted refugee situation, is recognized as a feature of camp life and as occurring in most parts of the world, but mainly in Africa (Crisp, 2003). For understanding acculturation, such semi-permanency offers an interesting setting in which psychological temporariness and stability coexist.

Another feature of camps that impacts on acculturation is their level of seclusion, which varies from close to open. The former includes barbed-wire-walled camps for South-East Asian refugees in Hong Kong, restrictive exit permits for Palestinians in the Gaza and West Bank, and mobility limited to a few kilometers outside the camp for Burmese in Thailand. A higher degree of openness can be found in the case of Guatemalans in Mexico, allowed to move freely within the region but not to other parts of the country. Permeable borders between refugees and locals exist for Sudanese refugees in Uganda.

Independently of temporal and spatial variations, the experience of refugees in camps is described as being characterized by: traumatization (Bilanakis & Pappas, 1996; Breslau, 2004; Moreno & Gibbons, 2002), dependency (Hitchcox, 1990; Kibreab, 1993, 2004), politicization/ideologization (Malkki, 1995; Kauffer Michel, 2002; Peteet, 1995) and institutionalization (Street, 1985). The concept of camp culture can be introduced to understand the somewhat self-contained way of life that refugees lead where they are confronted with psychological temporariness and limbo that affect their wellbeing, and where they develop coping strategies for survival.

However, most camps are not self-contained entities. Psychological and cultural changes occur, making for an interesting study of the interaction among camp culture, and the cultures of the home country and of host societies. The very definition of refugees proposed by Harrell-Bond and Voutira (1996) assumes a process of psychological acculturation for refugees in general and in camps. For the authors, refugees are individuals who live in a state of limbo, neither here nor there, and who in order to move on with their lives need to be incorporated into the host society or be able to return to their society of origin. Therefore, acculturation can be seen as a central feature of the refugee experience. The next section examines one particular context in which acculturation takes place and the phenomenon unfolds, that of Guatemalan refugees in Mexico.

14.3   Guatemalan refugees in Mexico

In the early 1980s, thousands of Guatemalans from the rural areas fled across the border into Mexico following a scorched-earth policy by the government. At first, refugees were hosted by Mexicans with whom they had had previous contacts through seasonal labor migration. The refugee influx continued until 1984 with 46,000 formally recognized Guatemalan refugees living in 92 small camps, mostly across the southern Mexican border in Chiapas (*Refugees*, 1990). The high number of refugees led the Mexican government to relocate them to the south-eastern part of Mexico, in Campeche and Quintana Roo. In 1987, following a socio-demographic survey, the Mexican government, supported by UNHCR, promoted a policy of self-sufficiency and integration, allocating land to the refugee communities and supporting economic and social exchanges (*Refugees*, 1990).

At the same time, refugees began to strengthen their own internal socio-political structures, including the election of representatives to negotiate the conditions for returning to Guatemala. On October 20, 1992, after ten years in exile, an agreement was signed that stipulated the conditions for a voluntary, collective and organized return, which was different from repatriation, meaning spontaneous and individual return. The collective return was implemented in 1993 and formally came to an end in 1998 with approximately 20,000 returnees (Crosby, 2000). Back in Guatemala, all returnee groups settled in regions they had fled from. However, only a few groups moved to their exact place of origin. For instance Ackermann (2002) examined the impact of refugee life among returnees belonging to a community composed of five different ethnic groups who settled in an area where only one of these returnee groups had close ethnic and kinship links with those who had stayed behind.

14.4   Psychological acculturation in camps

Psychological acculturation often occurs in the context of cultural proximity and/or previous cultural contact. When refugees first cross borders they often find protection in neighboring countries, either among the host population or more often in camps which vary in degrees of closure and openness. These settings influence the acculturation process.

14.4.1   Cultural proximity

Psychological acculturation needs to be seen in the context in which camps are created in relation to space and time. Most refugee camps are located in neighboring countries and often close to the border. The African context is emblematic of how artificial boundaries were superimposed across ethnic groups and forced migration across borders does not entail a different cultural encounter. Previous cultural contact is likely to have existed and ethnic affinities are to be found. However, the existence of nation states means differences in economic standards, cultural norms, national identities and, for refugees, political histories. In relation to time, when refugees cross borders the first groups tend to disperse among host communities with whom there have been pre-existing historic, economic and social cultural links (Freyermuth Enciso & Hernández Castillo, 1992). It is only with an increasing number of individuals and groups crossing the border that camps are set up, and, even when they are an option, there are refugees who decide to settle among the local population in villages and towns (Malkki, 1995).

Similarity in language, history, ethnic belonging, etc., has an impact on acculturation. For instance, in both Guatemala and Southern Mexico, the indigenous population shares a common history and identity as descendants of the Maya who suffered discrimination and marginalization, though to different degrees. In addition, long-term seasonal labor migration across the border has over time promoted social cultural exchanges. For Mexican employers Guatemalans represent cheap and efficient farm labor, and products are bought and sold between the two groups. This economic exchange becomes the first point of contact from which social and cultural interactions develop. The economic contact triggers social relations, with Mexicans and Guatemalans becoming friends and godfathers (Kauffer Michel, 2002). However, standards of life, cultural identities and recent political histories in Southern Mexico and Guatemala mean that sociocultural differences exist.

Given the proximity of countries of origin and settlement, this case also highlights a context in which the shared past history of colonization and Mayan culture converge and diverge in recent history, manifesting themselves as adaptation through forced migration. Thus, the crossing of borders by Guatemalan refugees in the early 1980s, which could be seen as the beginning of the process of acculturation, was in reality the beginning of a *new cycle of acculturation*. Differently from previous cycles, this was characterized by collective migration to a specific physical location, the camp.

14.4.2   Villages and camps

Literature on refugee resettlement to Western countries describes acculturation of individuals interspersed among host communities. In the case of refugees crossing borders into neighboring countries, persons from the same country of origin and residing in the same host country may either live dispersed among local communities or together in camps as a community. These two settings affect the way in which people from the same country of origin position themselves and interact with both the host society and one another. For instance, when the first groups of Guatemalan refugees crossed into Mexico, they were hosted in villages. For fear of being recognized and expelled, they changed their appearance in the way they dressed, an important element of self, collective and political identity. Indeed, for the Guatemalan Mayas, cloth has a psychological and cultural symbolic meaning. It is a form of self-identification with one's ethnic group and during the years of the repression it was used by the military to identify and target specific ethnic groups, even though all indigenous people suffered persecution. Once refugees moved into camps, they regained this symbol of identity.

The setting refugees inhabit affects not only their relations with the host society but also perceptions they have of one another. When comparing Burundian Hutu refugees living in camps and in local villages in Tanzania, Malkki (1995) found that the Burundian Hutus living in camps felt they were the real Hutus because they had maintained their ethnic purity, and perceived those living in the villages as being impure and contaminated. Therefore, not only acculturation differs depending on whether refugees live dispersed or in camps – location also impacts on the relations among conationals fleeing for the same reasons but ending up in different settings. What vary are not only relations with home and host country but also relations *between* the acculturating groups.

14.4.3   Open and closed camps

When focusing on camps, their degree of openness or closure is influential for acculturation, especially as it relates to policy orientations discussed by Berry in Chapter 3. In the context of closed camps, refugees are subjected to host-country policies and practices of *forced separation* or *segregation*, which compare unfavorably with the advantages of multiculturalism (Berry, 2001). The negative impact of segregation on refugees is described, for instance, by Bartolomei, Pittaway and Pittaway (2003) for refugees in northern Kenya. For minorities who feel marginal in home nation states, such as the Iraqi Assyrians (Al-Rasheed, 1994), the Kurds (Griffith, 2000), or the Palestinians (Hart, 2002) in Israel, the juxtaposition of home and host-country policies of segregation means that these refugees in camps are subjected to policies of *marginalization*. In the context of open camps, policies of *integration or multiculturalism*, though varying in degrees and types, are put into practice. The Mexican Government for instance implemented a policy of integration, with the goal of supporting economic and social exchanges.

In conclusion, the setting in which refugee camps are located is important for acculturation. First, cultural proximity between country of origin and host country means that, while acculturation takes place, it is not necessarily a new phenomenon but can be described as a new cycle of an already existing process. Second, acculturation strategies of individuals from the same country residing in the same host country are different depending on whether refugees live in camps or outside them. Third, the degree of closure or openness of the camps is an indicator of host-country policy orientations towards forced migrants. After having examined the setting in which acculturation takes place, the next section describes the phenomenon itself: the acculturation strategies that refugees adopt while living in camps.

14.5   Acculturation strategies

Berry's (1980) model of acculturation describes four strategies, integration, assimilation, separation and marginalization, resulting from the intersection of two underlying dimensions: cultural maintenance and cultural contact. Life in camps shapes both these components.

14.5.1   Cultural maintenance

As culture is dynamic and varies in time and space, cultural maintenance in camps takes on different meanings and representations from those in the home country. The concept of frozen culture, which is used to refer to the idea of the culture left behind at the moment of departure that refugees, migrants and sojourners carry with them after migration, is different from the culture that continues to change back home.

For refugees living communally in camps, in addition to the culture of origin and that of the host country, a *camp culture* also develops and impacts on acculturation. Life in camps differentiates refugees from those who stayed behind and from members of the host country. For example, Guatemalans who had been living in camps for years called themselves "el pueblo refugiado" (the refugee people) or "el pueblo Maya" (Mayan people) rather than "Guatemalans" or "Mexicans." In terms of social identity, they switched from a national or ethnic identity related to their own ethnic group, such as Quiche or Chuj, to a transnational one that relied on historic categorizations or present conditions. Such new self identification was explained in relation to being more modern and developed than those who had stayed behind and at the same time to being able to maintain strong socio-political ties with the place of origin.

These were strengthened by the idea of return, which is implicit in the temporary nature of camps. Imagining the return keeps alive links with the home country and thus some degree of cultural maintenance. In refugees' minds, return does not only mean going back to the homes that were left but to places of historic cultural meanings, such as the Middle East for the Jewish survivors of the concentration camps or pre-colonial state boundaries for the

Kurds living in camps in Mesopotamia. In these situations, returning home after having spent years or having been born in exile, means beginning a new cycle of acculturation to places and peoples who have undergone very different acculturation experiences.

Imagining and preparing for return while in camps give rise to a strong sense of social cohesion and political identity that shape daily social organization and cultural maintenance (Malkki, 1995; Zetter, 1991). The Guatemalans in camps, for instance, developed a strong socio-political awareness linked to the idea of a collective return. Refugees elected representatives who regularly fed the results of ongoing negotiations back to the community. The refugees' sociocultural cohesion reached its peak when they sat at the negotiating table with the Guatemalan government, the Mexican government and international agencies. This is one of the few examples in history of refugee participation in international negotiations, and which resulted in the signing of an agreement for a voluntary and collective return. Therefore, cultural maintenance evolves and transforms itself through camp culture to become not only a distinctive feature of life in camps but also a new kind of underlying dimension of acculturation. The other dimension is cultural contact, which refers to interactions with members of the host society and other ethnic groups.

14.5.2   Culture contact

Interactions between acculturating groups and host-society members develop differently when living interspersed with the host society or in separate refugee camps. By definition refugees living in camps do not live interspersed with host-society members. However, cultural contact occurs when refugees go outside to sell and purchase products, or, in the case of the Palestinians in Lebanon, when host-society members go into and sometimes live in camps in order to engage in economic and sociocultural interactions (Weighill, 1997).

Culture contact happens to different degrees depending on the meaning attributed to the term *host*. Host country, society and communities are not necessarily the same entity. Guatemalan refugees who moved across the border into southern Mexico were surrounded by Mexicans of Mayan descent or poor ladino peasants with whom they shared social cultural features that were different from those of Mexicans living in other parts of the country or rich ladinos. Culture contact and change within the broader society was called "hacerse mexicano" (to make oneself Mexican). This was evident in changes in appearance such as switching the *huipil* (colorful hand-woven top worn by Mayan women) for a blouse, coloring black hair to make it become light brown and shortening braids. It was also manifested by changes in survival strategies, especially the switch from land cultivation to other forms of employment, thus relinquishing a peasant identity of the Mayans as the people of the corn.

While cultural contact generally refers to relations with mainstream society and other ethnic groups, in refugee camps it also means interaction with aid workers. These include foreign, often Western humanitarian or development workers, representatives of international agencies such as the UNHCR or the Red Cross, and aid workers from the host society. Such agencies and employees play a significant role in refugees' acculturation, at times an influence more important than that of the host society. This is due to the fact that refugees depend on external agents for survival and development. Daily interactions with aid workers occur and transferral of values, policies and practices takes place through the allocation of funds and the implementation of projects, and this is even more influential when agencies are based inside the camps.

14.5.3   Acculturation strategies

Both cultural maintenance and cultural contact are therefore *multi-layered* and embrace different elements that impact upon the four acculturation strategies resulting from their interaction. The increased length of time that refugees spend in camps implies a shift from a situation of temporariness to one of alleged permanency. However, psychologically refugees continue to perceive their situation as temporary. This affects their preferred acculturation strategies, with separation and/or integration being their preferred options. This is evident in the case of the Burundian Hutu refugees in Tanzania (Malkki, 1995), Guatemalans in Mexico (Donà, 1993), and Greek Cypriots in Cyprus (Zetter, 1991).

However, the multi-layered composition of the two dimensions means that acculturation strategies are not necessarily homogeneous categories. For instance, Guatemalan refugees in camps generally adopt separation or integration strategies with reference to Guatemalan and Mexican cultures (Donà, 1993) but they show greater variation when attitudes towards aid workers (Mexicans, Guatemalans, foreigners) are discussed, depending on the acculturation issue being considered (Donà & Berry, 1999).

Palestinian refugees in camps in Jordan, where they are in a position of marginality to both the Jordanian nation state and the Palestinian national identity, develop integration but of a new kind (Hart, 2002). Here, children develop creative visions for their own collective future which are not necessarily drawn from the culture of their home or host country but rather from their particular spatial and historical context.

These examples point to the usefulness of Berry's model as an overall framework for understanding acculturation and to the need for further research into the specificities of the underlying dimensions. In particular, acculturation research in camps indicates that while the *process* underlying the development of these strategies is the same in different contexts and across groups, the *content* of the strategy (e.g., what integration means) differs according to specific sociocultural contexts, and research with refugees in camps points to the possibility of moving beyond the cultural maintenance and contact towards new forms of interactions.

14.6   Acculturation in camps and re-acculturation after return

Acculturation refers to the process of culture contact that generally occurs through movement from a place of origin to a different place of settlement. Although camps are becoming a semi-permanent solution to refugee movements, they are not seen as a durable solution. Rather, refugees are encouraged, as soon as conditions in the home country change, to return to the place of origin. While in the past repatriation was seen as the end of the refugee cycle, more recent research has challenged this idea by showing that returnees continue to move to become internally displaced (Black & Koser, 1999) or transnational migrants (Ackermann, 2002). The Palestinian case is paradoxical in that, for them, returning home actually means to camps. Indeed, Palestinians returning from the diasporas to the home country, the Palestinian territories, find themselves in refugee camps (Awwad, 2004).

The acculturation cycle therefore does not end in the camps but continues during and after repatriation, and camp life has a powerful impact on it. Similarly, social cultural changes occur also for those who stayed behind. In this sense the collective return of large groups of refugees to places of origin or to new locations within the country of origin (Eastmond & Öjendal, 1999) generates a new cycle of adjustment, a process of *re-acculturation* (Donà & Berry, 1999). In her study with Guatemalan returnees from five ethnic groups into an area which only one group had links with, Ackermann (2002) showed that their re-acculturation experience challenged the practice of juxtaposing returnee with ethnic identities. Returnees, independently of their ethnic affiliation, felt different from those living in the neighboring village who had stayed behind, and attributed this dissimilarity to their refugee experience. But members of the ethnic group who had close ethnic links to the neighboring community experienced tension in reconciling returnee and ethnic identities.

The acculturation experience in exile has an impact on returnees' life. Rousseau, Morales and Foxen (2001) compared two returnee communities in Guatemala whose paths differed slightly and showed how cultural change (social change) and maintenance (tradition) manifested themselves differently in the returnee communities because of the acculturative experience in exile. Outside support from international organizations and cohesion within the camps enabled young people in one community to disclose their traumatic past from a position of strength and confrontation as key to social change. Differently, avoidance of recent history took place in the other community, while tradition became the bridge between past and future.

Similarly, acculturation influences social identity and reciprocal inter-group perceptions between those who left and those who stayed behind. For instance, Eritrean youth returning from Sudan showed an awareness of social cultural differences between the host and home countries (Farwell, 2001), and children of Malawian refugees who had grown up in exile developed a distinct social identity and patterns of social interactions after return (Cornish, Peltzer & Maclachlan, 1999). While in exile, Guatemalan refugees perceived internally displaced Mayans as brothers, emphasizing similar histories of persecution and discrimination. After return, perceptions shifted and returnees referred to the internally displaced as "less developed." This was due to their experience in the camps, which they saw as positive but which created differences and a degree of separation (Donà & Berry, 1999).

The acculturative experience in camps shapes refugees' lives in exile and also upon return. The assumption that return from a condition of temporariness to one of stability means the end of the refugee cycle has been challenged (Black & Koser, 1999). Similarly, the idea that acculturation is about exit rather than entry can be questioned, and the concept of re-acculturation may explain the new cycle which confronts returnees, internally displaced and those who stayed behind. The experience of exile profoundly shapes identities, perceptions and inter-group relations after return and these components need to be researched further.

Conceptually, it is interesting to note that with the exception of the term "assimilation," which is replaced by "re-integration," the other terms used to describe the acculturation strategies in Berry's model are found in the forced migration literature to explain re-acculturation. The term "re-integration" is the one that is most often found to describe efforts at rebuilding communities in post-conflict situations. "Separation" is used to refer to distinct identities that returnees become aware of; to a lesser extent, "marginalization" is indirectly used to illustrate tension and social disarray found among some returnee communities.

In conclusion, this section has shown that re-acculturation may explain the new cycle which confronts returnees, internally displaced and those who stayed behind, after return. In this way, it complements acculturation research. Both processes influence identities, perceptions and inter-group relations. They also impact differently on wellbeing, both individual and societal. In previous chapters, this has been framed within the stress, sociocultural adaptation, resilience and human rights models. In the next section wellbeing of refugees in camps and repatriates will be discussed through a social cultural approach.

14.7   Acculturation and wellbeing

The relationship between acculturation and wellbeing is supported in the literature and summarized by Berry in this *Handbook*; acculturating individuals adopting an integration strategy manifest lower levels of acculturative stress and overall better mental health than those adopting other strategies. In camps, the relationship between acculturation and wellbeing yielded similar findings. Guatemalan refugees choosing an integration strategy (in an environment that favored integration policies) had better mental health, lower acculturative stress, better quality of life, happiness, and life satisfaction, than those adopting other strategies (Donà, 1993).

The literature on refugees details their wellbeing from a medical perspective, relying especially on concepts such as trauma and Posttraumatic Stress Disorder. Tibetan refugees in India have been described as manifesting symptoms of intrusion-avoidance, anxiety and depression (Terheggen, Stroebe & Kleber, 2001) and refugees living in camps in Serbia (Bilanakis & Pappas, 1996) as exhibiting Posttraumatic Stress Disorder. These findings adopt a universal approach to understanding the experience of refugees in camps that is culturally insensitive.

Refugees rely on their own cultural systems to express and give meaning to their experiences. For instance, Guatemalan refugees described their experience of violence and forced migration to the camps by relying on cultural Mayan cosmo-vision. *El susto*, a fear that is often translated as "soul loss," was used to refer to the fear and helplessness of Guatemalan peasants (Eastmond, 2000). Englund (1998) problematises two central tenets of Western psychological work with refugees: the primacy of the past and the use of verbalization over bodily manifestations. In the context of Mozambican refugees in Malawi, cultural practices such as funerals and spirit exorcism become more important than individual therapeutic practices for the improvement of refugees' wellbeing.

Bracken, Giller and Summerfield (1997) argue that, since conflicts leading to forced migration are by their very nature collective experiences, wellbeing must also be considered a collective social phenomenon. Expressions of sociocultural wellbeing are linked to acculturation. When thinking about cultural changes, increased levels of empowerment and community participation in camps become manifestations both of cultural change and of sociocultural wellbeing. When considering cultural maintenance, communal rituals, which provide a sense of continuity in crisis, become a way of maintaining social wellbeing at community level. Harrell-Bond and Wilson (1990) write of the efforts that refugees in camps make to ensure that rituals are performed according to tradition to ensure social wellbeing there. Mozambican refugees used blankets received from aid agencies to wrap the body of the deceased in order to ensure a smooth passage from this world to another one. Such rituals prevent spirits of the dead from coming back to haunt the community and cause illnesses and disharmony in the camps.

The above shows that the focus on individual wellbeing in camps tends to ignore the role that culture has in the expression of wellbeing, and it also views culture and the acculturation experience as the independent variable impacting on wellbeing as the dependent variable. A shift in level of analysis from individual to collective wellbeing helps to identify a stronger conceptual link between acculturation and wellbeing, in the sense that social manifestations of wellbeing become symbols of both sociocultural health and cultural changes.

14.8 Conclusions

This chapter examined the process of acculturation of refugees in camps from a space and time perspective highlighting some of the distinctive features of camps for an understanding of acculturation globally. The analysis of the spatial context in which psychological acculturation takes place contributes to the *Handbook* by (i) introducing the idea of cycles of acculturation, (ii) linking types of camps to host-country policies and acculturation strategies of larger societies, and (iii) discussing reciprocal perceptions of the same acculturating groups in camps and villages.

The fact that most camps are located in the south and often in neighboring countries or regions facilitated the exploration of the role of cultural proximity in acculturation, leading to the proposition that, in such contexts, acculturation needs to be conceptualized as cycles rather than as a uniform phenomenon with a distinct beginning.

Furthermore, Berry's (2001) support for the benefits of multiculturalism as a policy for the larger society is echoed in this chapter. It could be added that the experience of refugees crossing borders with pre-existing inter- and intra-cultural exchanges could be seen as informal multiculturalism in local practices through exchanges and integration of languages, clothes, markets and crafts. Formal host-country policies determining the establishment of more or less open camps were seen as indicators of attitudes leading to policies and practices of forced separation/segregation and marginalization for closed camps and different degrees of integration or multiculturalism for open camps.

Acculturation of refugees in non-settlement contexts differs from that of other acculturating individuals because the former live predominantly in collective settings where interactions with conationals are widespread while residing in host countries, while the latter experience acculturation when living intermingled among host-community members. The same group of refugees living in the same host country experienced different types of acculturation that varied according to the setting: camps or villages. Differences among conationals in camps and villages emerged not only in relation to attitudes towards home and host country but also in relation to reciprocal perceptions of the two acculturating groups.

The analysis from a time perspective shows that during re-acculturation returnee and ethnic identities may compete, coexist or shift. While acculturation generally refers to cultural change and maintenance in host countries, the chapter examined the impact of life in exile upon return and re-acculturation. The case of the Guatemalan refugees and the literature on refugees in camps supports Bhatia's (2002) argument that identity in exile (and return) is shaped by and linked to cultural and political issues of race, gender, colonization and power present in home and host countries. The chapter placed acculturation and re-acculturation in a continuum between exile and return. Thus, it expanded

Berry's model and opened a discussion on re-acculturation. Having been a refugee and having spent often a considerable amount of time in camps influence social identity and reciprocal inter-community perceptions in regions of return.

Moving into the analysis of the process and content of psychological acculturation in camps, the chapter illustrated the usefulness of Berry's model as an overall framework for understanding acculturation. Further research in this area would be beneficial, and Kibreab's (2004) proposition of the coexistence of different systems that vary depending on the point of reference seems relevant for the acculturation model. By examining the phenomenon of cheating in refugee camps, he discovered that two different moral systems were in place, depending on who the interlocutor was. An act of cheating committed for self-interest disregarding the concern for relatives, neighbors or villagers, was considered disgraceful and inappropriate, while the same act committed against faceless entities such as aid agencies and governments was often considered heroic. This example indicates that relations with culture of origin, in this case relatives and members of the home community, and host culture, meaning aid workers for refugees in camps, rather than intersecting to create the four acculturation strategies of Berry's model, coexist as complementary shifting systems.

Acculturation research in camps also informed the content of psychological acculturation. While the process underlying the development of acculturation strategies was the same in different contexts and across groups, the content of the strategy (e.g. what integration means) differed. Hart's (2002) study described integration of a new kind that was not necessarily drawn from the culture of home or host country but rather on particular spatial and historical context.

While there are many phases of the refugee experience, such as settlement, resettlement, repatriation, transnational movements, and often long periods in camps, all of which can be seen as acculturation trajectories, the chapter focused on a non-settlement environment. The analysis of psychological acculturation in non-Western, temporary and collective settings pointed to the usefulness of testing the acculturation model in different contexts of culture contact and to the value of bringing together context, process and content.

14.9   References

Ackermann, L. (2002). Violence, exile and recovery: reintegration of Guatemalan refugees in the 1990s – a biographical approach. Unpublished doctoral thesis: University of Oxford. http://fmo.qeh.ox.ac.uk/fmo/.

Al-Rasheed, M. (1994). The myth of return: Iraqi Arab and Assyrian refugees in London. *Journal of Refugee Studies, 7(2/3)*, 199–219.

Awwad, E. (2004). Broken lives: loss and trauma in Palestinian–Israeli relations. *International Journal of Politics, Culture and Society, 17(3)*, 405–414.

Bartolomei, L., Pittaway, E. & Pittaway, E. E. (2003). Who am I? Identity and citizenship in Kakuma refugee camp in northern Kenya . *Development*, *46(3)*, 87–93.

Berry, J. W. (1980). Acculturation as varieties of adaptation. In A. Padilla (ed.), *Acculturation: theory, models and some new findings* (pp. 9–25). Boulder, CO: Westview.

   (2001). A psychology of immigration. *Journal of Social Issues*, *57(3)*, 615–631.

Bhatia, S. (2002). Acculturation, dialogical voices and the construction of the diasporic self. *Theory and Psychology*, *12(1)*, 55–73.

Bilanakis, N. & Pappas, E. E. (1996). War refugees in a refugee camp: the impact of war stress on mental health. *European Psychiatry*, *11(1004)*, 372–373.

Black, R. & Koser, K. (eds.) (1999). *The end of the refugee cycle? Refugee repatriation and reconstruction.* Oxford: Berghahn Books.

Bracken, P., Giller, J. E. & Summerfield, D. (1997). Rethinking mental health work with survivors of wartime violence and refugees. *Journal of Refugee Studies*, *10(4)*, 431–442.

Breslau, J. (2004). Cultures of trauma: anthropological views of PTSD in international health. *Culture, Medicine and Psychiatry*, *28(2)*, 113–126.

Cornish, F., Peltzer, K. & Maclachlan, M. (1999). Returning strangers: the children of Malawian refugees come "home"? *Journal of Refugee Studies*, *12(3)*, 264–283.

Crisp, J. (2003). No solutions in sight: the problem of protracted refugee situations in Africa. *UNHCR New Issues in Refugee Research Working Paper No. 75.* www.unhcr.org, accessed October, 2004.

Crosby, A. (2000). Organizational challenges for Guatemalan refugee women. *Refuge*, *19(3)*, 32–37.

Donà, G. (1993). Acculturation, coping and mental health of Guatemalan refugees living in settlements in Mexico. Unpublished doctoral thesis: Queen's University, Kingston, Ontario. (http://fmo.qeh.ox.ac.uk/fmo/)

Donà, G. & Berry, J. (1999). Refugee acculturation and re-acculturation. In A. Ager (ed.), *Refugees: perspectives on the experience of forced migration* (pp. 169–195). New York: Continuum.

Eastmond, M. (2000). Refugees and health: ethnographic approaches. In F. L. Ahearn (ed.), *Psychological wellness of refugees: issues in qualitative and quantitative research* (pp. 67–87). Oxford: Berghahn Books.

Eastmond, M. & Öjendal, J. (1999). Revisiting a "repatriation success": the case of Cambodia. In R. Black and K. Koser (eds.), *The end of the refugee cycle? Refugee repatriation and reconstruction* (pp. 38–55). Oxford: Berghahn Books.

Englund, H. (1998). Death, trauma and ritual: Mozambican refugees in Malawi. *Social Science and Medicine*, *46(9)*, 1165–1174.

Farwell, N. (2001). Onward through strength: coping and psychological support among refugee youth returning to Eritrea from Sudan. *Journal of Refugee Studies*, *14(1)*, 43–69.

Freyermuth Enciso, G. & Hernández Castillo, R. A. (eds.) (1992). *Una década de refugio en México: los refugiados guatemaltecos y los derechos humanos* [Ten years of refuge in Mexico: Guatemalan refugees and human rights].

Mexico: Centro de Investigaciones y Estudios Superiores en Antropología Social; Instituto Chiapaneco de Cultura; Academia Mexicana de Derechos Humanos.

Griffith, D. J. (2000). Fragmentation and consolidation: the contrasting cases of Somali and Kurdish refugees in London. *Journal of Refugee Studies, 13(3)*, 281–302.

Harrell-Bond, B. & Voutira, E. (1996). Refugees. In D. Levinson and M. Ember (eds.), *Encyclopaedia of cultural anthropology* (Vol. III, pp. 1076–1081). New York: Henry Holt and Company.

Harrell-Bond, B. E. & Wilson, K. (1990). Dealing with dying: some anthropological reflections on the need for assistance by refugee relief programmes for bereavement and burial. *Journal of Refugee Studies, 3(3)*, 228–243.

Hart, J. (2002). Children and nationalism in a Palestinian refugee camp in Jordan. *Childhood, 9(1)*, 35–47.

Hitchcox, L. (1990). *Vietnamese refugees in South East Asian camps*. London: MacMillan.

Kauffer Michel, E. F. (2002). Leadership and social organisation: the integration of the Guatemalan refugees in Campeche, Mexico. *Journal of Refugee Studies, 15(4)*, 359–387.

Kibreab, G. (1993). The myth of dependency among camp refugees in Somalia, 1979–1989. *Journal of Refugee Studies, 6(4)*, 321–349.

(2004). Pulling the wool over the eyes of the strangers: refugee deceit and trickery in institutionalised settings. *Journal of Refugee Studies, 17(1)*, 1–26.

Malkki, L. H. (1995). *Purity and exile: violence, memory and national cosmology among Hutu refugees in Tanzania*. Chicago: University of Chicago Press.

Moreno, I. T. & Gibbons, J. L. (2002). Trauma events, residence in refugee camps, and educational attainment as predictors of trauma symptoms of Albanian refugees in Macedonia. *International Journal of Group Tensions, 31(2)*, 155–174.

Peteet, J. M. (1995). Transforming trust: dispossession and empowerment among Palestinian refugees. In E. V. Daniel and J. Knudsen (eds.), *Mistrusting refugees* (pp. 168–186). Berkeley: University of California Press.

Refugees (1990). *Refugees*, December, *81*, 33–35.

Rousseau, C., Morales, M. & Foxen, P. (2001). Going home: giving voice to memory strategies of young Mayan refugees who returned to Guatemala as a community. *Culture, Medicine and Psychiatry, 25(2)*, 135–168.

Street, J. (1985). Vietnamese refugees in the Hong Kong closed camp. Unpublished report.

Terheggen, M. A., Stroebe, M. S. & Kleber, R. J. (2001). Western conceptualizations and eastern experience: a cross-cultural study of traumatic stress reactions among Tibetan refugees in India. *Journal of Traumatic Stress, 14(2)*, 391–403.

UNHCR (2004). *2003 Global refugee trends: overview of refugee populations, new arrivals, durable solutions, asylum seekers and other persons of concern to UNHCR*. www.unhcr.ch/.

Weighill, M. L. (1997). Palestinian refugees in Lebanon: the politics of assistance. *Journal of Refugee Studies, 10(3)*, 294–312.

Zetter, R. (1991). Labelling refugees: forming and transforming a bureaucratic identity. *Journal of Refugee Studies, 4(1)*, 39–63.

15 Indigenous peoples

Siv Kvernmo

The construct of acculturation is for indigenous peoples strongly associated with the process of colonization over centuries, initially characterized by involuntary contact. Forced assimilation, leading to loss or extensive change of traditional practice, norms and beliefs, relocation and loss of lands, acculturative stress and psycho-social disaster are concepts often associated with this process. Although early research on acculturation dealt with the impact of modernization on indigenous people and traditional groups, the focus in recent research has been turned towards immigrants and other ethnic minority groups. While the main part of research on acculturation among indigenous people has been on North American groups, little research has been conducted on European indigenous groups such as the Sami and Greenlanders, or indigenous peoples from Russia, or Asia, Africa and Oceania where the strongest impact of acculturation has taken place (Berry & Sam, 1997). In anthropological and psychological research, concepts such as deculturation, ethnic identification, cultural change, cultural orientation, ethnic identity, biculturalism and modernization are often used interchangeably with acculturation or in describing much of the same process. In this chapter therefore, the term *acculturation* will be treated broadly, including some of these related constructs. This chapter deals with the history of the acculturation process among indigenous peoples worldwide and the outcome of the process, particularly with respect to emotional and physical health.

At least 350 million people worldwide can be considered to be indigenous and can be separated into at least 5,000 peoples ranging from the Sami, Nenets and Inuit in the Arctic to the Maori in New Zealand, and from the forest peoples of the Amazon to the tribal peoples of India. Most of the indigenous people live in remote regions and inhabit areas or land which are rich in natural resources and minerals. Compared to the dominant or majority population, indigenous groups are likely to be much less powerful (militarily, economically, politically and socially) (Berry & Sam, 1997). The indigenous peoples are also characterized by a younger population (Durie, 2000; Gracey, 1998; Kvernmo, 2004; Young *et al.*, 2002). In general, the health status for many indigenous peoples is lower in terms of medical disorder, psychiatric disorders, alcohol- and drug-use-associated disorders, suicide and injury death rates (Blum, 1992; Clarke, 1997; Gracey, 2000; Hunter, 2002; Hunter & Harvey, 2002; Huriwai, 2002; Stevenson, 1998), but there is also evidence of more healthy conditions compared to the majority group such as in some American Indian tribes (Kim, Lujan & Dixon, 1998) and among Arctic indigenous Sami (Hassle, Sjölander, Barnekow-Bergkvist & Kadesjö, 2001).

15.1   Who are indigenous peoples?

In spite of there being no internationally accepted definition of there being "indigenous peoples," the following criteria are often applied under international law, and by United Nation bodies and agencies, to distinguish indigenous peoples (UNDP, 2000):

➢   residence within or attachment to geographically distinct traditional habitats, ancestral territories, and natural resources in these habitats and territories;

➢   maintenance of cultural and social identities, and social, economic, cultural and political institutions separate from mainstream or dominant societies and cultures;

➢   descent from population groups present in a given area, most frequently before modern states or territories were created and current borders defined;

➢   self-identification as being part of a distinct indigenous cultural group, and the display of the desire to preserve that cultural identity.

The United Nations Developmental Programme (UNDP) notes that "despite common characteristics, no single accepted definition of indigenous peoples that captures their diversity exists. Therefore, self-identification as indigenous or tribal is usually regarded as a fundamental criterion for determining indigenous or tribal groups, sometimes in combination with other variables such as language spoken and geographic location or concentration" (UNDP, 2000).

15.2   The history of acculturation among indigenous peoples

15.2.1   The colonization process

Prior to the encounter with immigrants, indigenous peoples to a great extent varied in cultural adaptation, ranging from sedentary, stratified and complex societies (e.g. in much of Africa, Asia and in Meso-America) to nomadic, egalitarian and loosely structured societies (e.g. frequently present in Australia, Scandinavia, North and South America and to some extent in Africa and Asia). Owing to the fact that many colonizing powers were highly structured societies and forced their hierarchical structures on indigenous peoples, it has been assumed that indigenous groups who were more similar to the dominant groups would face fewer problems. On the other hand, those being most dissimilar were supposed to experience relatively more problems, and thereby experience greater acculturative stress (Berry and Sam, 1997). Early research suggests that at the cultural level loosely structured, egalitarian societies have indeed been most vulnerable to problems induced by colonization. At the psychological level, nomadic groups, which are based on hunting, gathering and herding, have faced more acculturative stress than comparable sedentary groups (Sinha, Mishra & Berry, 1992).

A significant precontact factor influencing the acculturation of indigenous peoples has, according to Berry and Sam (1997), been the lack of warning of, or preparation for, their cultural encounter, and the rapid cultural changes which took place, particularly among indigenous groups in the Western hemisphere and Oceania where colonial settlement often happened within a few years. The authors further suggest: "the lack of foreknowledge and the speed of onset remain a plausible explanation of why indigenous peoples had initially (and perhaps why they continue to have) relatively great difficulty with acculturation."

The acculturation process among indigenous peoples has mainly been subject to contradictory policies – which were, first to segregate, then to assimilate (Berry & Sam, 1997). For most indigenous groups, their colonization was initially a genocide, driven by both physical and cultural means, with the aim of moving or eliminating indigenous people for land expansion. Indigenous people were viewed as inferior compared to the European or White culture. Warfare, disease and alcohol were all used to decimate the numbers of indigenous people. As genocide gained less and less acceptance, disputes over land grew in number and intensity. Enforced removal and relocation to reservations or urban areas were thought to be a simple resolution to many land-title disputes, but were also a way to disrupt indigenous cultures through removal from the traditional homelands which were important to customs, beliefs and traditions. In general, indigenous peoples' relationship with the land and nature is of utmost importance, providing not only physical but also transcendental nurturance for their living, culture and traditions. An ever-expanding colonizing population led historically to relocation of most indigenous peoples and tribal groups. This was the case for American Indians, Australian Aboriginals, Inuk, Sami, etc., who historically were systematically stripped of their land and relocated to reserves and often disadvantaged rural areas (Grose, 1995). This break in their previously virtually unlimited access to earth resulted in great cultural change (Choney, Berryhill-Paapke & Robbins, 1995). Relocation from homelands is still an ongoing policy in some areas (e.g. in South America).

While relocation into reservations and areas set aside for the exclusive use of indigenous people, with the restriction to only reside there, can be considered as segregation, the assimilation policy was actuated by other means. As it became evident that neither extermination nor relocation was a viable method of complete cultural destruction and neither would lead to subsequent adoption of European cultural standards by the indigenous groups, ideas related to the power of Christianization and education to change ways of living were introduced. Through the use of missionaries, indigenous people were forced to give up their original religions and adopt Christianity. In some countries like Australia, new communities for relocated Aboriginals were set up as church missions (Shannon, 2002). Elsewhere, Arctic indigenous groups such as Inuk (Eskimo) in Greenland, Alaska and Canada were infantilized by being considered as inferior ("people under tutelage": Honigmann & Honigmann, 1965) by colonial authorities, as their lives were dependent on missionaries, teachers, police, traders from the colonizers for acceptable living conditions (Berry & Hart Hansen, 1985; Freeman, 1988; O'Neil, 1986). The intention was to coerce them to change their original indigenous daily life by altering their beliefs, behavior and culture. A common result of these efforts was the marginalization of large numbers of indigenous peoples. As Berry and Sam (1997) state, "through attempts at assimilation they became deculturated, losing essential features of their heritage (language, identity and survival skills); through segregation, they were kept from full participation in the larger society, not acquiring the values or skills necessary to live successfully there."

15.2.2   Boarding schools

Many indigenous children were forcibly removed from their families, communities and tribal life and brought to boarding schools run by federal governments and various churches or missions. The schools acted strongly as assimilation agencies by often being far away from the indigenous communities and families, by forbidding children to practice their religion and their native language or participate in any aspect of their cultures (Dlugokinski & Kramer, 1974). Government-sponsored boarding schools were, for instance, common until the late 1960s to mid-1970s among Native Americans, Sami in Scandinavia, Aboriginals in Australia and First Nation peoples in Canada. Many indigenous children and adolescents are still educated in boarding schools, often funded by the indigenous culture (Dick, Manson & Beals, 1993).

   The consequences of the residential school policy were disruption of children's attachment to their families, communities and cultures and discontinuity of their group identity. Since access to the dominant culture and community was strongly limited (Stiffarm & Lane, 1992), the original culture was not replaced by the dominant and alienation and marginalization were often the outcome. Family separation in the kinship-dominated American Indian culture was assumed to contribute to high incidences of psychosomatic symptoms and primarily among younger children (Leon, 1969, in Kleinfeld & Bloom, 1977). Boarding schools are shown to be associated with mental and physical health problems in indigenous youngsters, such as Inuk children in the USA (Krush & Bjork, 1965; Krush, Bjork, Sindell & Nelle, 1966; Kleinfeld & Bloom, 1977) but are also shown as a predictor of mental health problems and substance abuse in later adult life (Dinges & Duong-Tran, 1994). Originally a European idea, boarding schools diametrically opposed indigenous ways of parenting and learning (Bull, 1991; Morrissette, 1991) by replacing them with Western methods of upbringing.

15.2.3   Cultural revitalization

Today many indigenous peoples are still excluded from mainstream society and often even deprived of their rights as equal citizens of a state. Nevertheless, they are determined to preserve, develop and transmit to future generations their ancestral territories and their ethnic identity. Self-identification as an indigenous individual and acceptance as such by the group is an essential component of indigenous peoples' sense of identity. Their continued existence as peoples is closely connected to their ability to influence their own fate and to live in accordance with their own cultural patterns, social institutions and legal systems. During the last decades there has been a pervasive revitalization process taking place in many indigenous groups. Often this process has been connected to and led to more extended political, cultural and social rights for the group, resulting in education in the indigenous language, an increase in culture-specific behavior, maintenance and practice of indigenous traditions and religion, and even certain land rights, as in Canada, and political self-government, as in Greenland and among the Sami.

15.3   The acculturative process among indigenous peoples

As acculturation is a process that takes place over time and changes both the culture and the individual (Berry, 1990a), longitudinal research is important to examine the nature of these changes. A common suggestion is that there is resistance to change and a majority of negative consequences in terms of sociocultural disorganization and personal disintegration. According to the literature, this is not inevitable. The character of the adaptations depends upon specific features of the cultures in contact and upon the quality of their relationships (Berry, Wintrob, Sindell & Mawhinney, 1982). In the 1970s Berry and his colleagues (1982) conducted a study among Cree Indian communities concerning their response to a large-scale hydroelectric project constructed on their hunting and trapping territory. The study, which included both adults and teenagers, had both a longitudinal and a cross-sectional design. The fieldwork was initiated before the construction began, and repeated eight years later (after the construction). About half of the original sample was re-examined, supplemented by an equal number of new individuals who were at the same ages as the original sample eight years earlier. In this way, longitudinal analysis was provided for one group who were compared at two time points, but also two cross-sectional analyses were undertaken to maintain age control. The study showed that both continuity and change in cultural and psychological characteristics had taken place among the Cree people. In spite of a large-scale community and regional change and an upheaval in political and economic life, the Crees wanted to remain collectively as a Cree nation. Broad-ranging evidence of psychological continuity in abilities, attitudes and behaviors among the Cree people was found. The study also showed that increasing institutional control among the Cree people themselves, and individual cognitive control, helped to decrease acculturative stress over the eight-year follow-up period. Among Norwegian Sami, a similar process took place in the 1970s and '80s due to a large-scale hydroelectric project planned and placed in a reindeer herding area by the Norwegian government. The government proposal caused considerable resistance among both Norwegians and the Sami themselves, leading to an extensive focus upon the Sami people and later achievement of several Sami rights and revival of the culture replacing the previous assimilation process.

Maintenance of cultural identification with the group of origin was also seen among Inuk people in Alaska in the 1950s who were Westernized into mainstream-culture technology and social institutions. In an early study of the Barter Island Inuk people in Alaska, Chance (1968) found that, in spite of dramatic changes that had occurred in the community, the extent of community integration was not adversely affected. According to Chance, six factors appeared to be significant for a successful adjustment in the acculturation process. First, a predisposition to change was already built into their sociocultural system, with emphasis on adaptability rather than on conformity. Second, the change in a large part of their social and cultural life was voluntarily chosen to fit the new culture. Third, the majority of the goals associated with change were capable of realization. Fourth, the community members participated collectively as a group. Fifth, most of the alterations to previous cultural patterns occurred together in such a manner as to preserve a total cultural balance. Finally, the people were able to control their own internal village affairs without external constraints. The study also showed that personal adjustment to the acculturation processes was not solely related to the group contact or identification index themselves, but to the combination of less contact and weaker identification with their ethnic group (Chance, 1965).

15.4 Effects of the acculturation process

15.4.1 Cognitive skills

Several studies indicate that during the Westernization of indigenous peoples, cognitive skills generally become more like those of the Western peoples: familiarity with Western ways increases; school performance, perceptual characteristics and IQs gradually approach Western norms (Berry, 1971). This has been assumed to be related to education as an agent for acculturation as school performance improves in childhood, due to increased use of the dominant

language. Among northern indigenous groups in Canada an already high level
of spatial perceptual skills is found to increase during acculturation, indicating combined effects of traditional and modern educational influence on these
skills (Berry, 1971). Also, habits of perceptual inference change with acculturation, as shown among Inuk people who approached Western perception styles
in their susceptibility to certain illusions (Berry, 1968). For other cognitive and
intelligence test results, changes occur with increased cultural contact.

Early studies found great diversity in IQ test results, with some indigenous
groups scoring higher than or equal to the White reference group (Havighurst &
Hilkevitch, 1944; Havighurst, Gunther & Pratt, 1946), and others lower than
Whites (MacArthur, 1968, 1969). The early studies also showed interesting
differences between hunting–gathering people and agricultural peoples, with
those belonging to the former group doing better on visuospatial tests, and the
latter weaker on these but better on verbal ones (Berry, 1966; Dawson, 1967).
Intragroup variations have also been revealed among indigenous groups, with,
for instance, Inuk boys living in rural areas scoring higher on visuospatial
tests than same-ethnic-group peers living in more urbanized areas with more
unemployment (Vernon, 1966). Another interesting finding is the lack of gender differences in visuospatial tests in indigenous peoples, which are usually
obtained with Whites and other ethnic groups (Berry, 1966; MacArthur, 1969).
Presumably, hunting and gathering groups, including their female members,
are brought up to be autonomous and adapted to the environments, as good
perceptual skills are needed, particularly in harsh climes such as the Arctic,
while agriculturalists are brought up for conformity and dependence on the
community.

Assessment of cognitive skills in indigenous groups needs not only to reflect
the linguistic conventions and the social context of cultures, but also to be
sensitive to the dynamics that influence social interaction with indigenous
peoples. This is particularly important for individuals who live traditionally
and are separated, those skilled only in the indigenous language, and elders
(Cattarinich, Gibson & Cave, 2001).

15.4.2 Mental health

Owing to the significant cultural, social, economic and political impacts of
colonization, indigenous peoples have existed under conditions of extreme
stress for multiple generations. Although this stress phenomenon has influenced health in general, often it is in reports and research related to social
and psychological pathology and can be seen as a product of forced acculturation. Berry (1970), in an early study of Aboriginals, found that a certain
level of propensity for deviance, psychosomatic stress and negative attitudes
towards the dominant White society was related to psychological marginality.
People who were most traditionally oriented were those who suffered the most
psychological marginality rather than those who wanted to move on but were

not able to. An interesting finding was that the level of personal discomfort seemed to decrease when the conflict was solved not by reacting against or rejecting, but by assuming, an Australian identity. This finding is supported in Sami adolescents where a strong identification with the Norwegian society reduced behavioral problems (Kvernmo & Heyerdahl, 2003).

In an early study by Cawte and his colleagues (Cawte, Bianchi & Kiloh, 1968), three main sub-groups of Australian Aborigines on Mornington Island in the north of Australia were examined with regard to health condition: the Lardil who, due to exposure to missionary influence, had rather high levels of acculturation and social integration; the Mainland Aborigines who settled on the island as waifs, wanderers and spouses, with similar acculturation status to the Lardil, but without enclave and group identity; the third group were the Kaiadilts who were dispossessed, socially fragmented and least acculturated to Western modernity. The latter group, the Kaiadilt, suffered most from mental disorders especially depression, while the more acculturated Lardil suffered the least fragmentation and were the healthiest (Cawte et al., 1968). The study showed, however, that emulation of Western patterns or cultural identity was unrelated with psychiatric symptomatology except for one aspect of cultural identity, namely retention of traditional beliefs. The explanation for this was that mental health may not be linked directly with the individual's various cultural activities, interests and aspirations, but with his or her social and interpersonal conflicts.

Expectations of, and claims upon, indigenous adolescents, from the dominant group through the school and from their group of origin through parents, relatives, etc., can generate feelings of insuffiency, loyalty conflict and stress, particularly if the cultures of these groups are in contrast. In an early study of Aboriginal youth in the Northern territory of Australia their handling of projective cultural conflicts was closely related to their acceptance or rejection of Aboriginal traditional values and behaviors and not to modern value-orientation or psychopathology (Davidson, Nurcombe, Kearney & Davis, 1978). The lack of association between the conflict handling and psychopathology was interpreted as a successful resolving of conflicts. This study also revealed important sex differences. Males were more likely to adhere to traditional social constraints than females. The latter group was more willing to participate in both modern religious and traditional cultural activities.

The impact of acculturation stress experienced through boarding schools has by several sources been found to affect health status and adjustment negatively. In their study of Navajo students Boyce and Boyce (1983) studied the relationship between illness experiences and cultural background in a boarding-school setting. The findings indicated that the number of clinic visits for illnesses that required medical attention was positively associated with cultural incongruity and not with level of acculturation, either in the families or in the communities. Boarding-school students from families and communities that conflicted in cultural orientation experienced higher rates of clinic visits.

One of the main features in Berry's model is that individuals use *accultura-tion strategies* to deal with the acculturative process (Berry & Kim, 1988). Positive relationships to both cultures (integration) seem to provide the strongest sociocultural foundation for good mental health, while marginalization is associated with mental health problems. In a study of Arctic Sami adolescents in Norway, the influence of acculturation factors on different types of behavior problems varied clearly with gender and context. In Sami males, a protective effect of integration attitudes occurred, while marginalization attitudes were a risk factor for mental health problems. Losing ties with the Sami culture may represent a greater risk for psychological maladjustment for Sami males when it is not replaced by an attachment to the Norwegian culture. For Sami females, separation and withdrawal from Norwegian culture represented a risk factor for mental health problems. The association between mental health and acculturation attitudes varied with the context of living for the Sami adolescents. In Sami males living in clear minority positions in majority dominated areas, marginalization attitudes were relatively strongly related to anxiety and depression. In other Norwegian-oriented contexts, which in cultural terms are colored by a "melting pot" ideology, positive attitudes to ethnic interaction (integration) seemed important for healthy development. This may also explain why separation occurred as a risk factor for internalizing problems such as depression and anxiety, particularly in females in these areas. It is likely that adolescents who prefer separation may acquire less bicultural competence and have fewer coping strategies, which can contribute to psychological maladjustment. The effect of acculturation had its weakest influence in indigenous-oriented contexts (Kvernmo & Heyerdahl, 2003).

15.4.3   Substance use

Colonization and its consequences, such as acculturative stress due to culture change, are often used as explanatory factors for increased risk of substance use among indigenous people. Prior to the introduction of alcohol by European colonizers, indigenous cultures in general had no or little experience with psychoactive substance use (Beauvais, 1998; Mancall, Robertson & Huriwai, 2000; Bjerregaard, 2001). Several reasons for the initiation of alcohol use in indigenous people have been suggested, such as parroting and acquirement of habits and practice of the colonizers as a necessary tool in the cultural adaptation process; pressure by Europeans to drink to seal trade agreements or acknowledge special occasions (May, 1982); the desire to induce dream seeking by altering the state of consciousness; and the need for relief from boredom and despair due to relocation into reservations and alienation from traditional work and culture (Mail & Johnson, 1993; Beauvais, 1998). Although the rates of substance use in many indigenous groups and tribes exceed those of the non-indigenous populations and represent a threat of destruction to communities and families and to individuals' health, some tribes and indigenous groups have a lower prevalence than the dominant population (Larsen, 2001; Spein, Sexton & Kvernmo, submitted).

Both personal and societal factors can moderate the effects of acculturation on substance use (Berry, 1990b; Terrell, 1993; De La Rosa, Vega & Radisch, 2000). While traditionalism in cultural orientation has been regarded as protective towards substance use in several studies (Herman-Stahl & Chong, 2002), it has in American Indians been found insignificant when controlling for family history of drinking, psychological stress and gender (Weisner, Weibel-Orlando & Long, 1984). In a longitudinal study of American Indian alcoholics, cultural affiliation was associated to both depression and substance use at baseline, but not at follow-up (Westermeyer & Neider, 1984). Also among indigenous adolescents, contradicting results are found regarding the relationship between substance use and cultural identification. While Oetting and Beauvais (1990) found in one study that bicultural adolescents were less likely to use drugs, results from other studies including other indigenous groups suggested no significant relationship (Oetting, Swaim, Edwards & Beauvais, 1989; Spein et al., submitted). In Arctic Sami adolescents, assimilation attitudes occurred as a risk factor for substance use both at baseline and after three-year follow-up, as did separation attitudes at baseline (Spein et al., submitted). The findings of Herman-Stahl and Chang (2002) among adult American Indians living on reserves showed a bad effect from low orientation to the indigenous culture, and from biculturalism, on multiple types of substance misuse.

Generally, linguistically acculturated ethnic-minority adolescents who only speak the majority language are more likely to drink than bilingual peers (Epstein, Doyle & Botvin, 2003). This is also claimed for indigenous people like the Sami (Spein et al., submitted). Lack of ethnic language can indicate a lost possibility of inclusion in full participation in the indigenous culture, or an orientation away from the culture of origin, including adaptation to majority customs such as alcohol use.

15.4.4 Suicide

High and increasing rates of suicides among adolescents and young people are a major issue in several indigenous groups, such as the Maori people in New Zealand, Native Americans and Alaskan Natives in the USA, First Nations in Canada and Aborigines in Australia (Beautrais, 2001; Cantor, 2000; Clarke, 1997; Grossman, 1991; Lester, 1999). In some indigenous adolescent and young adult groups, the levels of suicides are some two to six times higher than for the nation as a whole, with males constituting approximately two-thirds of all suicides (Borowsky, 1999; Clarke, 1997; Malchy, 1997). However, within the indigenous groups, great variety is found. The highest rates are seen among indigenous people, and particularly among young men, in the Arctic, like the Inuit in Greenland (Thorslund, 1991), in the Arctic parts of Canada (Sigurdson, 1994) and among Alaskan Natives in the USA (Borowsky, 1999). In spite of the recent decrease in the overall suicide rates, the number of suicides among young indigenous individuals is still high and increasing (Hunter, 2002).

The number and types of factors associated with suicidal behavior among indigenous adolescents suggest a multicomponent etiology. Several studies on suicide in indigenous people indicate that minority status, loss of cultural or ethnic identity and a rapid modernization process are contributing to this phenomenon (Bjerregaard, 2001; Lee, Chang & Cheng, 2002). Ethnic communities in Arctic areas where the cultural distance to the mainstream society is prominent, and where a rapid modernization process contributes to extended cultural and societal changes, are perceived as being more vulnerable to suicidal behavior than those which have adapted to this process and made efforts to promote and preserve their original culture (Chandler, 2001; Leineweber & Arensman, 2003).

15.4.5 Physical health

For most indigenous peoples, the acculturation process represented by assimilation has resulted in changes of physical health due to altered living conditions, nutrition and feeding, and limited access to health services. Historically, reservation life and boarding schools contributed to overcrowded living conditions with sanitation and hygiene problems and inferior housing, increasing the death rate and incidences of illnesses such as smallpox, tuberculosis, pneumonia and influenza (Hunter, 1990; Hyer, 2001; Waldram, Herring & Young, 1995). The governments' efforts to reduce the spread of pathogens, which their own ancestors had brought with them and against which many natives had no immunological defenses, failed to a large extent. The use of traditional medicine, healers and shamans who hold impressive knowledge of roots and herbs proven to cure many forms of illnesses, was eroded and replaced by Western medicine. The revitalization of indigenous cultures in the last decades has included the resumption of traditional medicine. In several countries, the use of traditional healers is now acting side-by-side with Western medicine.

In spite of an improved health status for most indigenous groups, today's mortality rate and the prevalence of diseases in many indigenous groups are dismal (Hunter, 1995; Young et al., 2002), particularly regarding life-style diseases which are probably a by-product of rapid acculturation. Indigenous groups who have adopted a Westernized diet and a sedentary life style have rates of overweight, obesity, cardiovascular disease and diabetes equal to or higher than the majority groups (Bjerregaard, Young & Hegele, 2003; Gracey, 1998). The rates of these diseases are also increasing alarmingly among indigenous children and adults (Young et al., 2002).

In some indigenous groups, the health situation can be considered somewhat better such as among the Maori where the mortality rate is falling faster than that for Pakeha (the dominant population) (Hunter, 2002). Among more traditionally oriented tribes or groups, the prevalence of Western life-style diseases is still found to be lower than among more urbanized people, as is seen in the Inuk peoples' high blood pressures. The role of the traditional diet, a rural life style with a low level of psychosocial stress, and genetics are assumed to be of importance for this variation (Bjerregaard *et al.*, 2003; Grace, 2003).

15.4.6 Resilience

Although the effect of acculturation has not inevitably been negative for indigenous peoples, research focusing on the relationship between stress, coping and health has been virtually ignored. Acculturative stressors on health and wellbeing are moderated by cultural, individual and environmental factors or by their interactions. Research has shown that strengthening the tie to the traditional culture by positive identity attitudes is important in enhancing self-esteem, coping with psychological distress and avoiding depression (Walters, 1992). In addition, enculturation or the process by which individuals learn about and identify with their ethnic culture acts protectively either by mitigating the negative effects of stressors or by enhancing the impact of buffers, and thereby increasing the probability of positive outcomes (Zimmerman, Ramirez-Valles, Washienko, Walter & Dyer, 1996). Chandler and Lalonde (1998) also showed that First Nations bands which were engaged in community practices which represented markers of a collective effort to rehabilitate and preserve the cultural continuity of the bands, and thereby the self-continuity in their adolescents, had significantly lower suicide rates than other bands not managing this task. In several indigenous groups, there has been a revitalization of traditional spirituality and healing practices. The relationship between spiritual methods of coping and psychological, social and physical adjustment to stressful life events, as well as physical and mental health status, is suggested in empirical studies (Zimmerman *et al.*, 1996). It is also claimed that traditional health and healing practices may have intrinsic benefits directly tied to positive health outcomes among Native Americans (Buchwald, Beals & Manson, 2000; Marbella, Harris, Diehr, Ignace & Ignace, 1998).

In studies of the effect of acculturation strategies on coping and stress, integration strategy is found to foster academic resiliency among Innu secondary-school female students, while separation was negatively associated with stress (Bourque, 2004). Among Sami young males in Norway, integration has a protective effect on both internalizing and externalizing behavior problems in the Norwegian-dominated context (Kvernmo & Heyerdahl, 2003).

15.5 Conclusions

Across indigenous groups, the acculturation process seems to have common features of colonization and harsh assimilation, using much the same methods in trying to emolliate the native cultures. The results have for too many indigenous individuals been loss of identity, language, sense of group membership and cultural practices, but also loss of dignity, land and traditional ways of living. The outcome of this was low living standards, and increased physical and emotional heath problems. History also shows the strengths of the indigenous cultures worldwide, with increasing cultural revitalization and recapturing of the traditional cultures. Future acculturation research needs to focus once more on indigenous groups and the processes taking place in a modern and globalized world. Studies of common topics across indigenous groups can make important contributions to several indigenous groups and highlight common phenomena. There is also a greater need for focusing on resilience and coping strategies as important aspects of the acculturation process.

In summary, there is growing evidence that a revival of the indigenous culture through identity issues and practice can foster good coping strategies and resilience associated with the acculturative process, but more and extended research among more indigenous groups is needed to make more generalized conclusions.

15.6 References

Beautrais, A. L. (2001). Child and young adolescent suicide in New Zealand. *Australian and New Zealand Journal of Psychiatry, 35*, 647–653.

Beauvais, F. (1998). Cultural identification and substance use in North America – an annotated bibliography. *Substance Use and Misuse, 33*, 1315–1336.

Berry, J. W. (1966). Temne and Eskimo perceptual skills. *International Journal of Psychology, 1*, 207–229.

(1968). Ecology, perceptual development and the Muller Lyer illusion. *British Journal of Psychology, 59*, 205–210.

(1970). Marginality, stress and ethnic identification in an acculturated aboriginal community. *Journal of Cross-Cultural Psychology, 1*, 239–252.

(1971). Psychological research in the north. *Anthropologica, 13*, 143–157.

(1990a). Acculturation and adaptation: a general framework. In W. H. Holtzman & T. H. Hogg (eds.), *Mental health of immigrants and refugees* (pp. 90–102). Austin: Hogg Foundation for Mental Health.

(1990b). Psychology of acculturation. In J. Berman (ed.), *Cross-cultural perspectives. Nebraska symposium on motivation* (pp. 201–234). Lincoln: University of Nebraska Press.

Berry, J. W. & Hart Hansen, J. P. (1985). Problems of family health in circumpolar regions. *Arctic Medical Research, 40*, 7–16.

Berry J. W. & Kim U. (1988). Acculturation and mental health. In P. R. Dasen & J. W. Berry (eds.), *Health and cross-cultural psychology: toward applications* (pp 207–236). London: Sage Publications.

Berry J. W. & Sam D. L. (1997). Acculturation and adaptation. In J. W. Berry, M. H. Segall & C. Kağitçibaşi (eds.), *Handbook of cross-cultural psychology: social behavior applications* (Vol. III, pp. 314–317). Boston: Allyn & Bacon.

Berry J. W., Wintrob Y. H., Sindell P. & Mawhinney T. (1982). Psychological adaptation to culture change among the James Bay Cree. *Le Naturaliste Canadien, 109*, 965–975.

Bjerregaard, P. (2001). Rapid socio-cultural change and health in the Arctic. *International Journal of Circumpolar Health, 60*, 102–111.

Bjerregaard, P., Dewailly, E., Young, T. K., *et al.* (2003). Blood pressure among the Inuk (Eskimo) populations in the Arctic. *Scandinavian Journal of Public Health, 31*, 92–99.

Bjerregaard, P., Young, T. K. & Hegele, R. A. (2003). Low incidence of cardiovascular disease among the Inuk – what is the evidence? *Atherosclerosis, 166*, 351–357.

Blum, R. W. (1992). American Indian – Alaska Native youth health. *Journal of the American Medical Association, 267*, 1637–1644.

Borowsky, I. W. (1999). Suicide attempts among American Indian and Alaska Native youth: risk and protective factors. *Archives of Pediatric and Adolescent Medicine, 153*, 573–580.

Bourque, J. (2004). Education et culture: l'impact des stratégies d'acculturation psychologique sur la résilience scolaire de jeunes Innus [Education and culture: impacts of psychological acculturation strategies on the academic resiliency of Innu youth]. Unpublished Ph.D. thesis: University of Sherbrooke, Faculty of Education.

Boyce, W. T. & Boyce, J. C. (1983). Acculturation and changes in health among Navajo boarding school students. *Social Science and Medicine, 17*, 219–226.

Buchwald, D., Beals, J. & Manson, S. M. (2000). Use of traditional health practices among Native Americans in a primary care setting. *Medical Care, 38*, 1191–1199.

Bull, L. (1991). Indian residential schooling: the Native perspective. *Canadian Journal of Native Education, 18*, 3–63.

Cantor, C. (2000). The epidemiology of suicide and attempted suicide among young Australians. *Australian and New Zealand Journal of Psychiatry, 34*, 370–387.

Cattarinich, X., Gibson, N. & Cave, A. J. (2001). Assessing mental capacity in Canadian Aboriginal seniors. *Social Science & Medicine, 53*, 1469–1479.

Cawte, J. E., Bianchi, G. N. & Kiloh, L. G. (1968). Personal discomfort in Australian Aborigines. *Australian and New Zealand Journal of Psychiatry, 2*, 69–79.

Chance, N. A. (1965). Acculturation, self-identification, and personality adjustment. *American Anthropology, 67*, 372–393.
    (1968). Implications of environmental stress. Strategies of developmental change in the North. *Archives of Environmental Health, 17*, 571–577.

Chandler, M. J. (2001). The time of our lives: self-continuity in native and non-native youth. In R. Kail & H. Reese (eds.), *Advances in child development and behavior* (pp. 175–221). San Diego: Academic Press.

Chandler, M. J. & Lalonde, C. (1998). Cultural continuity as a hedge against suicide in Canada's First Nations. *Transcultural Psychiatry, 35*, 191–219.

Choney, S. K., Berryhill-Paapke, E. & Robbins, R. R. (1995). The acculturation of American Indians: developing frameworks for research and practice. In J. G. Ponterotto & J. M. Casas (eds.), *Handbook of multicultural counseling* (pp. 73–92). Thousand Oaks: Sage Publications.

Clarke, V. A. (1997). Understanding suicide among indigenous adolescents: a review using the PRECEDE model. *Injury Prevention, 3*, 126–134.

Davidson, G. K., Nurcombe, B., Kearney, G. E. & Davis, K. (1978). Culture conflict and coping in a group of aboriginal adolescents. *Culture, Medicine and Psychiatry, 2*, 359–372.

Dawson, J. L. (1967). Cultural and physiological influence upon spatial-perceptual processes in West Africa. *International Journal of Psychology, 2*, 115–128.

De La Rosa, M., Vega, R. & Radisch, M. A. (2000). The role of acculturation in the substance abuse behavior of African-American and Latino adolescents: advances, issues, and recommendations. *Journal of Psychoactive Drugs, 32*, 33–42.

Dick, R. W., Manson, S. M. & Beals, J. (1993). Alcohol use among male and female Native American adolescents: patterns and correlates of student drinking in a boarding school. *Journal of Studies on Alcohol, 54*, 172–177.

Dinges, N. G. & Duong-Tran, Q. (1994). Suicide ideation and suicide attempt among American Indian and Alaska Native boarding school adolescents. *American Indian and Alaska Native Mental Health Research Monograph Series, 4*, 167–182.

Dlugokinski, E. & Kramer, L. (1974). A system of neglect: Indian boarding schools. *American Journal of Psychiatry, 131*, 670–673.

Durie, M. (2000). Maori health: key determinants for the next twenty-five years. *Pacific Health Dialog, 7*, 6–11.

Epstein, J. A., Doyle, M. & Botvin, G. J. (2003). A mediational model of the relationship between linguistic acculturation and polydrug use among Hispanic adolescents. *Psychological Reports, 93*, 859–866.

Freeman, M. M. (1988). Environment, society and health. Quality of life issues in the contemporary north. *Arctic Medical Research, 47(Suppl. 1)*, 53–59.

Grace, S. L. (2003). A review of Aboriginal women's physical and mental health status in Ontario. *Revue Canadienne de Santé Publique, 94*, 173–175.

Gracey, M. (1998). Australian Aboriginal child health. *Annals of Tropical Paediatrics, 18(Suppl.)*, 53–59.

  (2000). Historical, cultural, political, and social influences on dietary patterns and nutrition in Australian Aboriginal children. *American Journal of Clinical Nutrition, 72*, 1361–1367.

Grose, P. R. (1995). An indigenous imperative: the rationale for the recognition of Aboriginal dispute resolution mechanisms. *Mediation Quarterly, 12*, 327–338.

Grossman, D. C. (1991). Risk factors for suicide attempts among Navajo adolescents. *American Journal of Public Health, 81*, 870–874.

Hassle, S., Sjölander, P., Barnekow-Bergkvist, M. & Kadesjö, A. (2001). Cancer risk in the reindeer breeding Saami population of Sweden, 1961–1997. *European Journal of Epidemiology, 17*, 969–976.

Havighurst, R. J., Gunther, M. K. & Pratt, I. E. (1946). Environment and the Draw-A-Man Test: the performance of Indian children. *Journal of Abnormal and Social Psychology, 41*, 50–63.

Havighurst, R. J. & Hilkevitch, R. R. (1944). The intelligence of Indian children measured by a performance scale. *Journal of Abnormal and Social Psychology, 39*, 419–433.

Herman-Stahl, M. & Chong, J. (2002). Substance abuse prevalence and treatment utilization among American Indians residing on-reservation. *American Indian and Alaska Native Mental Health Research, 10*, 1–23.

Honigmann, J. J. & Honigmann, I. (1965). *Eskimo townsmen*. Ottawa: Canadian Research Centre for Anthropology.

Hunter, E. (1990). Using a socio-historical frame to analyse aboriginal self-destructive behaviour. *Australian and New Zealand Journal of Psychiatry, 24*, 191–198.

   (1995). "Freedom is just another word": aboriginal youth and mental health. *Australian and New Zealand Journal of Psychiatry, 29*, 374–384.

   (2002). "Best intentions" lives on: untoward health outcomes of some contemporary initiatives in Indigenous affairs. *Australian and New Zealand Journal of Psychiatry, 36*, 575–584.

Hunter, E. & Harvey, D. (2002). Indigenous suicide in Australia, New Zealand, Canada, and the United States. *Emergency Medicine, 14*, 14–23.

Huriwai, T. (2002). Re-enculturation: culturally congruent interventions for Maori with alcohol- and drug-use-associated problems in New Zealand. *Substance Use and Misuse, 37*, 1259–1268.

Hyer, J. R. (2001). Health issues and the Pala Indian Reservation, 1903–20. *Bulletin Canadien d'Histoire de la Médecine, 18*, 67–84.

Kim, Y. K., Lujan, P. & Dixon, L. D. (1998). "I can walk both ways." Identity integration of American Indians in Oklahoma. *Human Communication Research, 25*, 252–274.

Kleinfeld, J. & Bloom, J. (1977). Boarding schools: effects on the mental health of Eskimo adolescents. *American Journal of Psychiatry, 134*, 411–417.

Krush, T. P & Bjork, J. (1965). Mental health factors in an Indian boarding school. *Mental Hygiene, 49*, 94–103.

Krush, T. P., Bjork, J. W., Sindell, P. S. & Nelle, J. (1966). Some thought on the formation of personality disorder: study of an Indian boarding school population. *American Journal of Psychiatry, 122*, 868–876.

Kvernmo, S. (2004). Mental health of Sami adolescents. *International Journal of Circumpolar Health, 63*, 221–234.

Kvernmo, S. & Heyerdahl, S. (2003). Acculturation strategies and ethnic identity as predictors of behavior problems in arctic minority adolescents. *Journal of the American Academy of Child and Adolescent Psychiatry, 42*, 57–65.

Larsen, S. (2001). The origin of alcohol-related social norms in the Saami minority. *European Journal of Human Genetics, 9*, 724–727.

Lee, C. S., Chang, J. C. & Cheng, A. T. A. (2002). Acculturation and suicide: a case-control psychological autopsy study. *Psychological Medicine, 32*, 133–141.

Leineweber, M. & Arensman, E. (2003). Culture change and mental health: the epidemiology of suicide in Greenland. *Archives of Suicide Research, 7*, 41–50.

Lester, D. (1999). Native American suicide rates, acculturation stress and traditional integration. *Psychological Report, 84*, 398.

MacArthur, R. S. (1968). Some cognitive abilities of Eskimo, White and Indian-Metis pupils aged 9–12 years. *Canadian Journal of Behavioural Science, 1*, 50–59.

   (1969). Some differential abilities of Northern Canadian Native youth. *International Journal of Psychology, 3*, 43–51.

Mail, P. D. & Johnson, S. (1993). Boozing, sniffing, and toking: an overview of the past, present, and future of substance use by American Indians. *American Indian and Alaskan Native Mental Health Research, 5,* 1–33.

Malchy, B. (1997). Suicide among Manitoba's aboriginal people, 1988 to 1994. *Canadian Medical Association Journal, 156,* 1133–1138.

Mancall, P. C., Robertson, P. & Huriwai, T. (2000). Maori and alcohol: a reconsidered history. *Australian and New Zealand Journal of Psychiatry, 34,* 129–134.

Marbella, A. M., Harris, M. C., Diehr, S., Ignace, G. & Ignace, G. (1998). Use of American healers among Native American patients in an urban Native American health center. *Archives of Family Medicine, 7,* 182–185.

May, P. A. (1982). Substance abuse and American Indians: prevalence and susceptibility. *International Journal of the Addictions, 17,* 1185–1209.

Morrissette, P. (1991). The therapeutic dilemma with Canadian Native youth in residential care. *Child and Adolescent Social Work Journal, 8,* 89–99.

O'Neil, J. (1986). Colonial stress in the Canadian Arctic: an ethnnography of young adults changing. In C.R. Janes, R. Stall & S.M. Gifford (eds.), *Anthropology and epidemiology: interdisciplinary approaches to the study of health and disease* (pp. 249–274). Dordrecht: Reidel Publishing Company.

Oetting, E. R. & Beauvais, F. (1990). Orthogonal cultural identification theory: the cultural identification of minority adolescents. *International Journal of the Addictions, 25,* 655–685.

Oetting, E. R., Swaim, R. C., Edwards, R. W. & Beauvais, F. (1989). Indian and Anglo adolescent alcohol use and emotional distress: path models. *American Journal of Drug and Alcohol Abuse, 15,* 153–172.

Shannon, C. (2002). Acculturation: Aboriginal and Torres Strait Islander nutrition. *Asia and Pacific Journal of Clinical Nutrition, 11(Suppl. 3),* 576–578.

Sigurdson, E. (1994). A five year review of youth suicide in Manitoba. *Canadian Journal of Psychiatry, 39,* 397–403.

Sinha, D., Mishra, R. C. & Berry, J. W. (1992). Acculturative stress in nomadic and sedentary tribes of Bihar, India. In S. Iwawaki, Y. Kashima & K. Leung (eds.), *Innovations in cross-cultural psychology* (pp. 396–407). Amsterdam: Swets & Zeitlinger.

Spein, A. R., Sexton, H. & Kvernmo, S. (submitted). Drinking and smoking in indigenous Sami adolescents: an ethnocultural and longitudinal perspective.

Stevenson, M. R. (1998). At risk in two worlds: injury mortality among indigenous people in the US and Australia, 1990–92. *Australian and New Zealand Journal of Public Health, 22,* 641–644.

Terrell, M. D. (1993). Ethnocultural factors and substance abuse: toward culturally sensitive treatment models. *Psychology of Addictive Behavior, 7,* 162–167.

Thorslund, J. (1991). Suicide among Inuk youth in Greenland 1977–86. *Arctic Medical Research, Suppl.,* 299–302.

UNDP (2000). *About indigenous peoples. Definition.* New York: United Nations Development Program.

Vernon, P. E. (1966). Educational and intellectual development among Canadian Indians and Eskimos. *Education Review, 18,* 79–91, 186–195.

Waldram, J. B., Herring, D. A. & Young, T. K. (1995). *Aboriginal health in Canada: historical, cultural, and epidemiological perspectives.* Toronto: University of Toronto Press.

Walters, K. L. (1992). Urban American Indian identity attitudes and acculturative styles. *Journal of Human Behavior and Social Environment, 2*, 163–178.

Weisner, T. S., Weibel-Orlando, J. C. & Long, J. (1984). "Serious drinking," "white man's drinking" and "teetotaling": drinking levels and styles in an urban American Indian population. *Journal of Studies on Alcohol, 45*, 237–250.

Young, T. K., Martens, P. J., Taback, S. P., *et al.* (2002). Type 2 diabetes mellitus in children: prenatal and early infancy risk factors among Native Canadians. *Archives of Pediatrics and Adolescent Medicine, 156*, 651–655.

Zimmerman, M. A., Ramirez-Valles, J., Washienko, K. M., Walter, B. & Dyer, S. (1996). The development of a measure of enculturation for Native American youth. *American Journal of Community Psychology, 24(2)*, 295–310.

PART III

Acculturating contexts: societies of settlement

As we noted above, the range of societies in which acculturation is taking place is much broader than we have been able to accommodate in this *Handbook*. This section presents a highly selective account of acculturation research, mainly focused on immigrants, that has been carried out in some of these societies. It begins with portrayals of issues and findings in the traditional settler societies of Australia and New Zealand (Chapter 16), Canada (Chapter 17), Israel (Chapter 18) and the USA (Chapter 19). This is followed by four overview chapters concerned with issues and research in the more recent acculturation contexts of Northern and Western Europe, including the European Union, Francophone countries, Nordic countries and the United Kingdom. Missing, of course, are chapters that attempt to present work done in other parts of the world. While this is a serious limitation to this *Handbook*, it also presents an opportunity for the development of a companion volume dealing with acculturation in the "Majority World."

16 Acculturation in Australia and New Zealand

David L. Sang & Colleen Ward

Australia has an area of about 7.7 million square kilometers, making it the sixth largest country in the world. Its climate ranges from tropical rainforests, through deserts and cool temperate forests, to snow-covered mountains. New Zealand has three main islands: South Island (150,437 km^2), North Island (113,729 km^2) and Stewart Island (1,680 km^2). The climate ranges from sub-tropical in the north, to sub-arctic in the mountains of South Island.

This chapter consists of two major sections, one for each country. Each section starts with a brief country profile to provide the political and sociocultural backgrounds within which acculturation takes place. Following this is a selective survey of the research on acculturation among the various groups in each country.

16.1 Australia

16.1.1 A diverse population

Until the arrival of the "First Fleet" with around 1,350 people (half of them convicts) in 1788, the population of Australia comprised indigenous peoples, both Aboriginal and Torres Strait Islanders. Today, indigenous people make up 2.4% (about 460,000) of the total Australian population. From the very beginning, immigration to Australia has had, and continues to have, a significant impact on the country, politically, economically and socially.

In 2001, Australia's population was an estimated 19.4 million people, of whom approximately 23% were born overseas. A further 20% of the Australian population has at least one parent who was born overseas. The proportion of the population born overseas is higher in Australia than in any other traditional immigration country (e.g. 20% of the New Zealand population, 18% of the Canadian population and 11% of the population of the United States).

In long-established overseas-born populations (e.g., from the United Kingdom and Ireland, and from northern and southern Europe), second-generation Australians account for more than half of the total population. In more recently arrived groups (mainly from Asia), second-generation Australians form a smaller part of the group.

In the 2001 census, over 200 different ancestries were reported, the most common ancestry being Australian (35.9%), followed by English (33.9%), Irish (10.2%), Italian (4.3%), German (4.0%), Chinese (3.0%), Scottish (2.9%) and Greek (2.0%) (Australian Bureau of Statistics, 2002).

16.1.2   Brief history of immigration policy

In 1901, the six Australian colonies joined together to become the country of Australia, and immigration became an issue controlled by the Federal Government. One of the first Acts of the new Federal Parliament was the Immigration Restriction Act (1901), allowing the Federal Government to restrict non-European immigration. This is the formal beginning of the "White Australia Policy" which especially restricted Chinese immigration (Department of Immigration and Multicultural Affairs, DIMA, 2001). The Commonwealth Naturalization Act (1903) further restricted non-European immigration by preventing people from Asia, Africa and the Pacific Islands (except for New Zealand) from immigrating. Between 1905 and 1914, 390,000 immigrants had entered Australia, mostly from the United Kingdom (DIMA, 2001). Immigration virtually ceased during the First World War, but, as economic prosperity rose in the 1920s, so did immigration. Between 1920 and 1929, 300,000 immigrants entered Australia, mostly under assistance schemes, including the 1921 (British) Empire Scheme, where the costs of an immigrant's passage were shared between the UK and Australian governments. The majority of immigrants were from the UK, with smaller numbers from Italy and Greece (DIMA, 2001).

Immigration fell markedly as a consequence of the Great Depression of the 1930s and remained low during the Second World War. The perceived danger to Australia from foreign invaders, heightened as a result of the Japanese advance through South-East Asia during the Second World War, culminated in the "populate or perish" approach to immigration and population growth (DIMA, 2001). The post-Second World War period saw a rapid increase in the Australian population (from 7.6 million in 1947 to 12.7 million by 1971); 2.2 million (43%) of this growth being attributed to immigration (Borrie, 1988; DIMA, 2001).

A tangible government response to the importance of immigration was the creation in 1945 of the Federal Department of Immigration. The aim was that immigration should lead to a 1% rise in population per annum, with a further 1% rise due to births within the Australian population.

In 1950, immigration numbers reached 153,685, the highest to that time. The year 1951 also heralded in the commencement of the Colombo plan, whereby Chinese students were granted temporary residence in order to study at Australian universities. In 1952, the first elements of a non-European immigration policy commenced. In 1959, Australian citizens were allowed to sponsor non-European spouses and unmarried minor children for immigration. In 1966, eligibility criteria for immigration were further relaxed, allowing selection of non-European immigrants on the basis of their qualifications, ability to integrate and suitability as settlers (DIMA, 2001).

The "White Australia Policy" was officially ended in 1972, at least in terms of Federal Government policy, with race being removed as a criterion for immigration. Priority was given to the reuniting of close dependants and to selected skilled occupations for which there was an un-met demand in Australia. Since 1973, all immigrants were eligible to apply for citizenship after having been resident for three years. In 1976, the first boat with five refugees from Vietnam arrived, and Australia began to accept Indo-Chinese refugees from refugee camps in Thailand. In 1982, an agreement was signed between the Vietnamese and Australian governments, agreeing to an "Orderly Departure Program" (ODP) for immigrants from Vietnam. From 1985 onwards, government policy increasingly concentrated upon economic issues to guide immigration policy, while maintaining a commitment to refugees. In 1989, Chinese citizens, many of them students, were allowed to stay in Australia after their visas expired, as a response to the events in Tiananmen Square. Chinese-born people resident in Australia at this time were granted four-year residence visas, leading to a doubling of the Australian population born in China between 1986 and 1991 (DIMA, 2001).

Throughout the 1990s the shift towards short-term, skilled immigration continued. In 1999 a new points system was brought into being, which was more tightly focused on the potential migrant's employability, based on qualifications, work experience, English proficiency and age. The new system also made it easier for overseas students to apply for permanent residence after completing studies in Australian tertiary education institutions, with points awarded for their Australian qualifications. A further significant event occurred in 1995, when New Zealand became the major source country for immigrants, overtaking the UK for the first time (DIMA, 2001).

In 2000, amendments were made to the Employer Nomination Scheme (ENS), with the view to increasing Australia's competitiveness in attracting skilled immigrants in an increasingly globalized economy. In 2001, New Zealand-born people had to apply for permanent residence in order to access social security payments in Australia (DIMA, 2001).

The Humanitarian Program continues to give priority to *bona fide* refugees, but the government has adopted very tough measures against "illegal" asylum seekers by putting them in detention centers where they are screened for refugee status. Since the introduction of mandatory detention in 1992, many asylum seekers and their children have been held in detention for considerable periods of time. In 2005, the Migration Amendment (Detention Arrangements) Bill was introduced, which allows, *inter alia*, all family units to be removed from detention and placed in the community and the asylum-seeker determination process to be fast-tracked.

In summary, several trends are apparent in the immigration policy of the government of Australia, particularly since 1945. First, there has been a fluctuation in the planned immigrant intake and the actual intake over the post-Second

Table 16.1 *Top ten source countries of immigrants to Australia*

Source country, ranked by population size at 1996 census	1996 census	Estimated population (June, 1999)	Median age (June 1999)	2001 census
1. UK/ Ireland	1,072,562	1,227,193 (1)	50.3 (5)	1,036,245 (1)
2. New Zealand	291,388	361,572 (2)	36.6 (8)	355,765 (2)
3. Italy	238,246	244,614 (3)	60.4 (1)	218,718 (3)
4. Vietnam	151,053	175,249 (4)	35.7 (10)	154,831 (4)
5. Greece	126,520	140,196 (6)	57.3 (2)	116,431 (6)
6. People's Republic of China	111,009	123,466 (7)	53.4 (4)	108,220 (7)
7. Germany	110,331	156,767 (5)	41.2 (6)	142,780 (5)
8. Philippines	92,949	116,887 (8)	37.2 (9)	103,942 (8)
9. Netherlands	87,898	92,741 (10)	55.3 (3)	83,324 9 (10)
10. India	77,551	100,711 (9)	40.2 (7)	95,452 (9)

(Adapted from Australian Bureau of Statistics, 2002)

World War period, largely in response to economic conditions in Australia. Second, there has been a shift away from a strong emphasis on immigrants from the UK towards those of Non-English-Speaking-Background (NESB) countries, initially those of Europe and latterly those of Asia. Third, there has been a shift away from manual and trades occupations towards more skilled occupations. Fourth, there has been a reduction in family reunion immigrants. Fifth, there has been an increase in refugee intake as part of the immigration program since the 1970s. However, screening is more rigorous, and new legislations have been introduced to deal with unauthorized arrivals and stop people-smugglers. The latest changes to immigration laws, whilst "belated" and "inadequate," have provided "a softer edge" on detention.

16.1.3 Profile of immigrants

Table 16.1 presents data on the number of the overseas-born population from the top ten countries of birth at the 1996 census. Data also included are the Estimated Population and median age as calculated for June 1999, and the number and revised rank order of immigrants from each country at the 2001 census. Several issues are noteworthy from these and other data. First, there has been a decrease in the proportion of the immigrant population born in the United Kingdom, and an increase in the proportion from NESB countries, in particular from Asia. Second, there have been changes in the sex ratio and age within different immigrant groups.

16.1.4 Acculturation research: theoretical perspectives and empirical findings

Research on the acculturation of immigrants in Australia is too extensive to be reviewed in detail. Acculturation research with Aborigines is less extensive, but again only a few highlights will be mentioned. This section will focus on key approaches and discuss a sample of studies adopting those approaches.

16.1.4.1 Immigration and acculturation

Australian research began in the early 1950s, at a time of a large influx of immigrants into Australia; it has employed four perspectives for studying the immigrants' acculturation: the multifacet socialization–resocialization perspective of Taft (1977, 1985), the dynamic sequential model of A. Richardson (1974), the acculturative stress model of Berry and associates (Berry, Kim, Minde & Mok, 1987; Berry, 1997), and the functional model of friendship networks and cultural mediation of Bochner and associates (Bochner, McLeod & Lin, 1977; Bochner, 1982, 1986; Furnham & Bochner, 1982).

According to Taft (1977), the adaptation of immigrants can be treated as a case of re-socialization, involving such psychological factors as changes in attitudes, values and identification; the acquisition of new social skills and behavior norms; changes in reference and membership-group affiliations; and emotional adjustment to a changed environment. Following this orientation, and on the basis of factor-analytic studies of various immigrant groups' adaptation (e.g. British, Dutch, Hungarian, Italian, Latvians and Lithuanians, Poles and a mixed group of adolescent boys), Taft developed a multifacet model of immigrants' adaptation. This model consists of one aspect of socio-emotional adjustment and four aspects of integration (National and Ethnic Identity, Cultural Competence, Social Absorption and Role Acculturation). Each of the five aspects is examined from the Internal (subjective) and External (objective) viewpoints. The internal side is reflected in self-judgment and consists of attitudes and perceptions. The external measures are derived from observable behavior or ratings of the immigrant by outsiders. According to this model, the process of adaptation is multidimensional. For example, it is possible to be acculturated with respect to one aspect of life (e.g., language), and not with respect to another, such as commitment to the new country (Taft, 1985). The multifacet model has provided a framework for data ordering based on aspects common to all immigrants, thus enabling comparisons between groups such as British (A. Richardson, 1974) and Soviet (Taft, 1987) immigrants, and over time within groups.

Richardson (1974) describes the process of migration and adaptation as a function of motivation, opportunity, disposition to migrate, energizing experiences and influences before migrating, and corresponding factors after migration. Adaptation proceeds through a series of stages, each of which entailed the migrant reaching a threshold of progress in one before passing on to the next. Richardson observed that new immigrants to Australia began their stay with initially high levels of satisfaction, attributable to a combination of novelty, freedom from normative restrictions, and justification of their decision to migrate. This initial euphoria was said to be followed by a period of depression, resulting from culture shock, nostalgia, and reaction to prejudice from locals. If the immigrant survived this trough, without returning to the "old country," the typical next phase was said to be a resumed high level of satisfaction, which often led finally to acculturation, or adoption of the ways of the society, including use of slang. This has been referred to as the U-curve hypothesis (the honeymoon, crisis, recovery, adjustment of Oberg, 1960). Richardson's model was found unsatisfactory (Scott & Scott, 1989) as it implies a single, monolithic native culture, towards which immigrants move in sequential stages, rather than a variety of partially overlapping, partially coherent cultures that are differentially contacted and experienced by different newcomers, resulting in different acculturation patterns.

The model of acculturation developed by Berry (discussed in detail in Chapter 3) adopts a two-dimensional view of acculturation. One dimension is based upon a person's preference for identification with their ethnic culture, the other dimension based upon a desire to participate in the larger society. Four acculturation strategies may be identified: *assimilation, integration, separation* and *marginalization*. How the different acculturation strategies relate to the individual's sociocultural and psychological adaptation has been reported by Berry *et al.* (1987): integration may be the most adaptive strategy and marginalization the least adaptive for immigrants and other acculturating peoples. In a later review, Berry (1997) presented an explicit and elaborate stress and coping framework of immigration and acculturation. This framework considers the acculturative experience as a major life event that is characterized by stress, and that requires cognitive appraisal of the situation and coping strategies (see Chapter 4).

A number of investigations in Australia have employed Berry's framework. These studies used a variety of acculturation indicators and a diverse set of samples. Gupta (1993) and Green (1994), for example, investigated student sojourners of Chinese origin in Australia and found that separation and marginalization attitudes were related to high levels of stress. Green also found that female international students reported higher levels of stress than males and a lower year of study predicted higher stress.

Levels of acculturative stress have also been found to be affected by the correspondence between expectations and reality following migration (Berry, 1997). Watkins *et al.* (2003) surveyed 1,352 prospective Vietnamese migrants to Australia aged 16 years or more. In general, prospective migrants believed that future educational, socio-economic and employment opportunities in Australia were better than in Vietnam. However, their expectations were modified by individual socio-demographic characteristics (e.g., age, English proficiency, education, vocational experiences) and perceived health status.

Bochner and associates' functional model specifies that international students use three distinct social networks in different ways. The primary network consists of bonds with conationals, its function being to provide companionship and emotional support and to enhance self-esteem and cultural identity. The second network consists of friendships with other non-compatriot foreign students, its function being largely recreational, as well as providing mutual social support based on a shared foreignness. The third network consists of links with host nationals, its function being largely instrumental, to help with academic and professional difficulties. Furnham and Bochner (1982), in their work on "culture shock," argue that the most fundamental difficulties experienced by cross-cultural travelers occur in social situations, episodes and transactions. They emphasize the significance of social skills and social interactions and focus on culturally relevant behavioral skills required for sojourners, immigrants and refugees to survive and thrive in their new societies.

16.1.4.2 Ethnic identification

The concept of ethnic identification involves the kind of identification individuals have with their ethnic roots, both as a cognitive self-categorization and as a sense of attachment (see Chapter 6). Few studies have a multi-focus approach, measuring a range of components of ethnic identity. Exceptions are studies by Rosenthal and colleagues. One study (Rosenthal & Feldman, 1992) of the ethnic identity of first- and second-generation Chinese Australian and Chinese American adolescents found that, in both samples, there was erosion over time of ethnic identification and behavior/knowledge, but not of the importance and evaluative components of ethnic identity. These findings highlight the multifaceted rather than unitary nature of the construct. More research is required to determine the interrelationships among the different components of ethnic identity and, in particular, to consider whether some aspects of ethnic identity are more open to change than others. Rosenthal and Hrynevich (1985) explored the nature of ethnic identity in a sample of Greek-, Italian- and Anglo-Australian adolescents. They found that similar dimensions (i.e., language, religion, social activities, maintenance of cultural traditions, family life and physical characteristics) emerged as important for all the ethnic minority groups. Perceptions of ethnicity, however, differed. For Greek Australians, associated with recognition of their cultural separateness was a positive sense of valuing their ethnic origins. For Italian Australians, cultural separateness was associated with a positive attitude to integration. Rosenthal and Cichello (1986) explored further the perceptions of ethnicity among Italian-Australian adolescents and investigated the relationship between ethnic identity and psychosocial adjustment. Interestingly, they found that parents' maintenance of cultural ties was associated with a strong sense of ethnic identity. However, ethnic identity per se was relatively unimportant in predicting psycho-social adjustment. Of greater significance were cultural variables such as parents' embeddedness in the Italian community, the desire to assimilate into the

Australian culture and the perception of problems arising from minority-group memberships. These findings underline the importance of intergenerational factors and the need for further research into causative models of psycho-social adjustment of immigrant adolescents.

In order to examine the possible relationship between a migrant's ethnic identification and the level of psychological distress experienced in Australia, Nesdale, Rooney and Smith (1997) developed a model in which ethnic identity was predicted to influence personal coping resources (i.e., self-esteem, self-mastery, interpersonal trust) and external coping resources (i.e., appraisal, esteem, sense of belonging, social support) that, in turn, were predicted to influence migrants' psychological wellbeing. The model was tested on a sample of Vietnamese immigrants. The results revealed that ethnic identity was a significant, but not a strong, predictor of distress, mediated by self-esteem.

16.1.4.3   The Longitudinal Survey of Immigrants to Australia (LSIA)

S. Richardson (2002) reported on a survey that compares the experiences of migrants who arrived in Australia between 1993 and 1995 (Cohort 1) with the experiences of those who arrived between 1999 and 2000 (Cohort 2). Immigrants were interviewed about six months after arrival. Further waves of interviews were conducted twelve months and twenty-four months after the first wave.

The two cohorts differed: relative to Cohort 1, Cohort 2 had a higher proportion who immigrated under the visa category of Independent or Business Skills / Employer Nomination Scheme, and a lower proportion who migrated as Preferential Family / Family stream or Humanitarian. Cohort 2 also had a higher proportion of immigrants who had higher levels of formal education, were fluent speakers of English, and fewer who did not speak English well at all. Overall, the labor-market outcomes six months after arrival in Australia were substantially better for Cohort 2 than they were for Cohort 1 (e.g., higher employment, lower unemployment and lower non-participation in the labor force). Both cohorts gave positive reasons for migration to Australia, which were related mainly to family reunion, greater opportunities, a better future for family in Australia, and an attractive climate.

Overall, immigrants in both cohorts believed they had very good health on arrival in Australia: 91% of Cohort 1 and 92% of Cohort 2, in comparison with 83% of the general Australian population. The majority of people with stress or nervous problems in both cohorts were from the Humanitarian visa category. Pre-existing health conditions were more prevalent among older migrants, female migrants, and migrants on a Humanitarian visa. It was found that 26% of the immigrants in both cohorts indicated symptoms of significant psychological distress (compared with 7.5% in the general Australian population). S. Richardson (2002) attributed this higher level of psychological distress to the major life changes occurring in the immigrants' lives.

16.1.4.4 Immigration and mental health

The Australian literature relating to immigration and mental illness is characterized by two distinct features: (a) the dominance of epidemiological research led by Krupinski and his group from the 1960s through to the early 1980s; and (b) the emerging impact of transcultural psychiatry and medical anthropology from the late 1980s. For a comprehensive and critical review of these studies, see Jayasuriya, Sang and Fielding (1992). The following general trends emerged from Krupinski and colleagues' early studies:

1. there is a higher incidence of depression among all immigrants compared to the Australian-born;
2. there is a higher incidence of schizophrenia among NESB immigrants from Eastern and Southern Europe than among other groups;
3. the incidence of mental disorders among males is partly due to the adverse effect of immigration on single men facing economic problems and professional and skilled men whose qualifications are not recognized;
4. the incidence of mental disorders among NESB women is due partly to social isolation caused by a lack of English skills and partly to differential rates of assimilation within the family.

Krupinski (1967) also discussed the social aspects relating to immigrant mental illness, such as difficulties at home and at work, wartime experiences, loss of status, and assimilation problems. The latter was further emphasized by Stoller (1967): the effect of too rapid assimilation may be stressful and detrimental for both the immigrant and Australian populations. Krupinski (1984), in a subsequent review of research extending over twenty years, stated that the changing patterns of immigration to Australia influenced psychiatric morbidity of immigrants, as different groups at risk were identified in specific periods under scrutiny.

The most comprehensive study of refugee youth in Australia is a longitudinal study of young Indochinese refugees over a two-year period (Krupinski & Burrows, 1986), which examined the level of psychiatric disorders in three Indochinese groups: pre-adolescent (5–14 years), adolescent (15–19 years) and young adult refugees (20–24 years) in Melbourne. Whilst the authors describe the physical health of their sample as "good," of particular concern were the psychiatric disorders and emotional distress of refugee children and adolescents. For children, distress was specifically associated with premigration trauma and separation from family members; moreover, compared with other groups, more children who are assessed as disturbed throughout the study were without both parents. Refugees who initially presented with anxiety and depression were found to be free of any symptoms after one or two years in Australia.

Sang (1986) examined the adaptation of Vietnamese refugees who had been in Australia for twelve to twenty-four months. The results showed that the frequency and intensity of the respondents feeling down did not seem to abate significantly after the initial period in the immigrant hostel. Among the factors that distinguish those at risk (above vs. below the General Health Questionnaire cut-off point) are: past traumatic experiences, current problems, and length of residence in Australia. It appears that both past-life events and resettlement problems have an adverse impact on the refugees' health. Sang's results were supported by studies reviewed by Boman and Edwards (1984), who found a common theme underlying the factors that put Indochinese refugees at risk for mental ill-health: the noxious effect of status dislocation between their employment status in Indochina and in the United States.

Whilst no definite conclusions can be drawn on the question of the differential rates for mental illness among immigrant and ethnic groups, a number of sub-groups can be identified as being at greater risk. From the early Australian literature, Krupinski (1984) identified the following high-risk groups: single men, mainly from the UK; non-assimilated housewives; adolescents caught between the two cultures of their parents and their peers; elderly immigrants; and Asian immigrants, especially Indochinese refugees. The international literature on studies of groups with special mental health needs (Canadian Task Force, 1988) provides some confirmatory evidence and suggests four main "at risk" groups: immigrant and refugee children and youth; female immigrants and refugees; elderly immigrants and refugees; and victims of torture and trauma.

The long-term effect of psychological trauma was assessed in a community sample of 1,413 adult Vietnamese refugees resettled in Australia (mean residence of 11.2 years) by Steel et al. (2002). It was found that the risk of mental illness fell consistently across time. However, people who had been exposed to more than three trauma events had heightened risk of mental illness after ten years, compared with people with no trauma exposure. These results are consistent with those of McKelvey et al. (2002): the prevalence of psychiatric disorders for those Vietnamese children and adolescents with limited exposure to the traumas of war and migration was no different from that for the general child and adolescent population in Australia or in other Western countries.

16.1.4.5   More "at risk" groups

Australia has in recent times developed and implemented policies to deter asylum seekers. As already discussed, key components of these policies include the mandatory detention of unauthorized arrivals, the issuing of three-year Temporary Protection Visas for asylum seekers found to be refugees, and, more recently, the transfer of asylum seekers intercepted en route to Australia to a third state for processing and/or removal. Concern about the impact of prolonged detention and the use of Temporary Protection Visas on the psychosocial status of asylum seekers has been raised by a number of organizations, e.g., The United Nations High Commissioner for Refugees, the Australian Human Rights and Equal Opportunity Commission, Amnesty International, and Human Rights Watch, etc.

16.1.4.6 Indigenous peoples

Research with Aboriginal peoples has a long history in Australia, but accul-turation studies by psychologists began in the 1960s. In a series of studies, Dawson (1969) examined attitudinal conflict between being Aboriginal and being Australian and concluded that such conflict gave rise to personal dif-ficulties that required a resolution in order for successful adaptation to take place. Berry and colleagues (e.g., Berry, 1970; Sommerlad & Berry, 1970) took the first steps towards the development of the notion of *acculturation attitudes* presented in Chapter 3 of this volume. This framework was devised as a response to the Government's proposal to begin a process of assimila-tion of Aborigines and the perceived need to examine the views of Aborigines about how they wished to go about their acculturation. The 1970 study was an attempt to distinguish further these various ways of acculturating and their relation to acculturative stress. Since these early studies, little psychological research with Aborigines has been carried out. Recently, more research focus has been placed on the health status of Aboriginal and Torres Strait Islander peoples. For example, their life expectancies have been found to be fifteen to twenty years below those of other Australians. The high levels of mental health problems, high rates of substance misuse, self-injury and suicide rates were further attributed to social and cultural factors such as removal from land, dislocation of communities and separation of families (Australian Institute of Health and Welfare, 1999).

16.2 New Zealand

16.2.1 Immigration policy and practices

New Zealand is a nation of migrants built upon the base of its indigenous Maori population. Indeed, many interpret the Treaty of Waitangi / Te Tiriti o Waitangi (1840), the agreement between Maori and the British Crown, as the country's first immigration policy.

New Zealand's immigration practices have traditionally favored European settlers, particularly those of British, Protestant Anglo-Celtic origins. Migra-tion from Europe grew steadily in the late nineteenth century, due to widespread labor shortages in the country, and increased through the twentieth century. An unofficial "white New Zealand policy" was practiced by all governments until 1945, and at the end of the Second World War New Zealand had one of the most ethnically homogenous societies of European settlement (Brooking & Rabel, 1995).

Prominent Maori scholar Ranginui Walker (1995) has argued that the Treaty of Waitangi / Te Tiriti o Waitangi permits entry to New Zealand for settlers from the regions named in the Treaty's preamble, specifically, Europe, Aus-tralia and the United Kingdom, but that admission from other sources is a matter for consultation with the descendants of the Crown's treaty partners. Despite these contentions, New Zealand had been home to non-European migrants, notably Chinese, Indians and Polynesians, even before the 1986 and 1991 policy changes that permitted and encouraged immigration from non-traditional sources. Historically, the treatment of non-European immigrants, however, has differed considerably from the reception of the European settlers.

The Chinese migration prompted by the 1860s gold rush was restricted by legislation and subjected to poll taxes. South Asians, particularly Punjabis and Gujuratis, who began to enter New Zealand around the turn of the twentieth century, were also subjected to exclusionary immigration legislation. Severe labor shortages of the 1960s and 1970s prompted a dramatic increase in Pacific migration; however, as the labor market cooled, so did the enthusiasm for Pacific settlers. The late 1970s were known for the infamous "dawn raids" to identify and deport Pacific Island over-stayers. The 1970s also saw a stream of refugees from Cambodia, Laos and South Vietnam reach New Zealand.

It was not until the 1986 and 1991 changes in policy that New Zealand entered a new era of immigration and the country saw a large influx of settlers from non-traditional sources. Asian migration experienced an enormous burst of activity, increasing 240% since the mid-1990s, and China and India have been the largest contributors to New Zealand's growing population this century.

Presently, New Zealand grants on average between 40,000 and 50,000 residence approvals per annum, most admitted under the General Skills category, followed by Family, Business and Humanitarian entrants, and smaller numbers for Special Quota categories such as that for Samoans. Up to 750 United Nations mandated refugees and between 200 and 500 asylum seekers are admitted on a yearly basis, with the largest proportions now arriving from Somalia, Ethiopia and Iraq. There are also up to 110,000 international students who enroll in educational institutions in New Zealand each year. The inward migration is countered by a moderately large outward migration, particularly to Australia, and it is not uncommon for New Zealand to lose, rather than to gain, residents due to the emigration–immigration imbalance.

The population of New Zealand reached 4 million in 2003. On the basis of the 2001 census the ethnic origin of the population was: 80% European, 14.6% Maori, 6.5% Pacific (3.2% Samoan), 6.6% Asian (2.8% Chinese) and 6.9% other. Projections indicate that non-European groups will grow significantly between now and 2021, with increases ranging from 28% (Pasifika) to 120% (Asians). Cultural diversity is a reality in New Zealand now and will only increase in the future.

16.2.2   Acculturation research in New Zealand

This section summarizes acculturation research in New Zealand and is organized by type of acculturating group: indigenous peoples, sojourners, immigrants and refugees. A comprehensive review of psychological research on acculturation in this country is well beyond the scope of this chapter, but for current research the reader is advised to consult various university and government web-sites, including those of Waikato University's Migration Research Group (www.waikato.ac.nz/wfass/migration) and Maori and Psychology Research Unit (www.waikato.ac.nz/mpru), Massey University's New Settlers' Programme (http://newsettlers.massey.ac.nz), Victoria University of Wellington's Centre for Applied Cross-cultural Research (www.vuw.ac.nz/cacr), New Zealand Immigration Service (www.immigration.govt.nz), Office of Ethnic Affairs (www.ethnicaffairs.govt.nz) and the Ministry of Education (www.minedu.govt.nz).

16.2.2.1 Indigenous peoples

The nature of the relationship between Maori, as the indigenous peoples of Aotearoa, and the first and later settlers differs in form and content from other types of intercultural contact in New Zealand. In the simplest terms, psychological and social changes arising from the acculturation process are a direct result of colonization and are frequently associated with negative outcomes for Maori. Indeed, in a controversial address to the New Zealand Psychological Society in 2000, the then Associate Minister of Maori Affairs, Tariana Turia, referred to a Post-colonization Traumatic Stress Disorder as being rife in the Maori community and linked this to poor self-image, family violence and victimization through personal, institutional and cultural racism.

Although Maori have enjoyed a revival of language and culture over the last two decades, including the birth and evolution of an indigenous psychology movement, the earlier era of assimilationist policies in New Zealand has taken its toll. Objective indicators of socio-economic status (e.g., education and income) and general wellbeing (e.g., hospital admissions, incarceration rates, mortality figures, adolescent suicide) confirm inequalities between Maori and non-Maori (Durie, 2001). There is also evidence that longstanding negative attitudes towards Maori still exist and that Maori are the victims of discrimination more frequently than other minority groups (Ritchie, 1992). These disadvantages, however, do not consistently manifest themselves in studies of subjective psychological and social adaptation. Indeed, despite relative deprivation, Maori appear remarkably resilient. A number of studies have failed to find differences in adaptation outcomes such as anxiety, depression, self-esteem, academic attitudes and scholastic performance between New Zealanders of Maori and European descent (e.g., Evans, Wilson, Hansson & Hungerford, 1997), and others have demonstrated more positive psychological outcomes for Maori, including higher levels of self-esteem in university students (Harrington & Liu, 2002) and greater life satisfaction in the elderly (Gee, 2002).

A key issue for Maori has revolved around the definition and retention of cultural identity, and this is viewed as a core component of Maori development by indigenous scholars (Durie, 2001). Survey research with Maori students reported that language, culture and customs are seen as the defining features of identity, more so than color, tribal affiliation or descent (Thomas & Nikora,

1992). Overall, Maori retain both stronger ethnic and stronger national identity than New Zealanders of European descent, and they engage in more ethnic exploration. In addition, stronger ethnic identity is associated with positive outcomes, such as greater life satisfaction (Ward, 2006).

The identity politics of dual ethnic persons, those who acknowledge both Maori and European heritage, have been discussed by Gibson (1999), including the tendency for others to identify and label dual ethnics in ways that are incongruent with the way they perceive themselves. Emergent issues relate to the ability to pass as European, being perceived as "not really Maori," and others' expectations that dual ethnics would be expert in all things Maori. Ward's (2006) study of dual heritage youth, however, found that, contrary to discussion in the international literature, "mixed race" persons did not suffer psychological disadvantages. In fact, they adopted values, attitudes and behaviors from both cultures and generally occupied an intermediate position when compared to their Maori and European peers.

16.2.2.2 Sojourners

Studies of sojourners in New Zealand have been concentrated on the experiences of international students and led largely by work by Ward with her students and colleagues. The research has primarily concentrated on the distinction and prediction of psychological and sociocultural adaptation. While the two adaptation outcomes are significantly interrelated, the former is reliably predicted by personality (e.g., emotional resilience, extraversion, internal locus of control), life changes, social support (including related measures such as loneliness, satisfaction of contact with hosts) and perceived discrimination. The latter is associated with underlying factors such as length of residence, cultural knowledge, cultural distance, expected difficulty, cultural identity, and interactions with host nationals (for early studies see Ward, Bochner & Furnham, 2001).

Research by Ward and colleagues with international students has also challenged the U-curve model of adaptation. Their study of Japanese students at entry, and at four, six and twelve months after arrival in New Zealand found that psychological distress was greatest upon arrival, declined markedly at four months and did not vary significantly over the remaining time periods. The pattern of sociocultural adaptation resembled a learning curve, improving significantly in the first four months, continuing to climb and levelling off at the twelve-month period.

Comparisons across a range of student groups converge to suggest that sociocultural adaptation is lower for students who travel overseas, compared to peers who remain at home and for students who make large, as opposed to small, cross-cultural transitions. These differences are not generally apparent in terms of psychological adaptation – at least when the same national group of students (e.g., Malaysian, New Zealand) are examined in different locations. However, a recent study in New Zealand suggested that international students from Asia experience more psychological distress than their peers from Europe and North America (Ward, Masgoret, Berno & Ong, 2004).

16.2.2.3 Immigrants

Identity has been an important theme in migrant research, and studies have strongly supported the preference for integration as an acculturation strategy and its association with positive psychological and social outcomes (Eyou, Adair & Dixon, 2000; Ho, 1995). A separate line of innovative research has compared migrant groups to non-migrant groups in both their country of origin and their country of settlement. Altrocchi and Altrocchi (1995) examined identity, attitudes and behaviors in four groups of Cook Islanders, comparing them with a group of non-Cook Island New Zealanders. Research revealed that identification as a Cook Islander was strongest in an outer island, followed by a more populated and frequently visited island, the first-generation migrant group and a New Zealand-born group, respectively. In addition, the New Zealand-born Cook Islanders more closely resembled other New Zealanders in terms of their attitudes and behaviors than they did Cook Islanders.

Social integration of immigrants has also received attention. Today's migrants are, on the whole, better educated than native-born New Zealanders. Yet they are more likely to be unemployed and earn lower incomes. Discrimination has been one of the varied reasons suggested for these trends, and a recent survey by the New Zealand Immigration Service (2004a) indicated that one in five immigrants reported the experience of discrimination and that this occurred most frequently in work-related areas. Not only do income and employment define the socio-economic status of migrants, but unemployment has also been linked to depression, anxiety and poorer psychological adaptation (Abbott, Wong, Williams, Au & Young, 1999).

Economic and employment constraints have prompted a number of Asian migrants to become "astronaut" families with wives and children residing in New Zealand and husbands living and working abroad. Evidence suggests that these arrangements put considerable strain on family relationships and lead to marital discord and parent–child conflict (Aye & Guerin, 2001). On the positive side, many migrants retain strong links with family and friends in their home countries and use these networks as sources of social support. Connections with friends, family and members of their ethnic communities in New Zealand have been demonstrated to promote effective coping, stress reduction and diminished risk of emotional disorder in migrants (Abbott *et al.*, 1999; Trlin, Henderson, North & Skinner, 2001).

New Zealanders, on the whole, have moderately positive attitudes towards new settlers. They strongly support the principles of multiculturalism, they endorse integration as the preferred acculturation strategy, and they do not view new migrants as a significant source of threat. However, Maori have more negative attitudes towards new migrants than New Zealanders of European descent, and migrants from Australia, Britain and South Africa are viewed more favorably than those from China, India and Samoa (Ward & Masgoret, 2005). Furthermore, a recent poll conducted by the Human Rights Commission indicated that 72% of those surveyed believed that immigrants in New Zealand are subjected to some or a great deal of discrimination.

16.2.2.4 Refugees

As in the international literature on refugees, a significant proportion of New Zealand research has adopted a clinical perspective on refugee mental health. Along these lines, Cheng (1994) reported that 12% of 223 Cambodian refugees living in Dunedin met the diagnostic criteria for Posttraumatic Stress Disorder. Pernice's (1989) earlier study examined depression and anxiety in 129 Indo-Chinese refugees and concluded that 33% were symptomatic with only a gradual decrease occurring over time. She also noted that post-migratory factors such as discrimination, lack of financial support from family members and absence of close friends contributed to negative outcomes.

Post-migration problems for refugees and obstacles to their integration into New Zealand society include language proficiency, access to employment, financial constraints, and discrimination (New Zealand Immigration Service, 2004b; Guerin, Guerin, Diiriye & Abdi, 2004). Refugees face downward job mobility, and a national survey found that after six months only 16% are gainfully employed. The same research reported that 7–8% of both recently arrived and established refugees saw themselves as victims of discrimination over the last month. Despite these difficulties, most studies show that refugees in New Zealand report good health which improves over time, is associated with language fluency and is attributed by the refugees themselves to feeling safe and secure, reduced stress and access to better health care facilities (Guerin, Abdi & Guerin, 2003; New Zealand Immigration Service, 2004b).

Relatively less is known about the social and psychological integration of refugees although Cheng's (1995) study reported that integration was the preferred acculturation strategy for members of the Cambodian community. A national survey of refugees indicated that ethnic communities provided a good source of social support and that 85–91% said it was important to learn about New Zealand culture. Only a small number suggested it was difficult to retain their heritage culture, due primarily to a small community and lack of activity within it.

There has been some suggestion that adaptation is more problematic for refugee children and adolescents than adults. Refugee parents noted difficulties for girls, particularly in terms of cultural and religious factors, including expected dress and standards for socializing with members of the opposite sex. Parents also reported that for sons it was very difficult to balance their own culture and New Zealand culture (New Zealand Immigration Service, 2004b). This is echoed by Guerin et al.'s (2004) work in the Somali community, which cited gender roles, issues pertaining to autonomy, materialism, prohibited activities such as drug and alcohol consumption, differences in time orientation and language deficits as sources of stress in parent–child relations and as having implications for the adaptation of refugee youth.

16.3 Conclusions

In this chapter, a brief portrayal of the historic and contemporary cultural diversity in Australia and New Zealand was presented to set the stage for a subsequent survey of the major theoretical and empirical work on acculturation in each country. This overview attempted to highlight a number of points:

1. Australia and New Zealand both enjoy ethnic diversity in population and immigration policies. The similarity starts with changes in the official policy objectives (the abolition of the "traditional source country" preference, which has resulted in ethnic diversification) and the general structure of the immigration program (division into economic, family and humanitarian migration, implemented as a point system), where points are allocated for employability, age and various settlement factors.
2. More recently, both countries refined their selection process with regard to economic immigrants. The New Zealand approach is human capital-based and emphasizes general skills in its selection. The Australian approach has similar elements, although it appears somewhat more pragmatic by maintaining elements of occupational selection. Finally, in response to the increasing number of asylum seekers since the late 1990s, both governments have introduced regulations designed to hasten the determination of refugee status and to allow for the faster removal of people who enter the countries unlawfully, and for the detention of asylum seekers while their cases are assessed.
3. Research on acculturation in both countries is very extensive and complementary. It examines all the major acculturating groups and the various factors affecting and moderating acculturation on the macro level (characteristics of the society of origin and society of settlement) and micro level (characteristics of the acculturating individual and situational aspects of the acculturative experience), as discussed in previous chapters.

There is a need, however, to follow up on these general findings with longitudinal research over settlement time and into later generations. There is also a need to develop outcome- and solution-focused research with respect to immigrants and refugees, and for studies of reverse culture shock in sojourners returning to home countries.

16.4   References

Abbott, M., Wong, S., Williams, M., Au, M. & Young, W. (1999). Chinese migrants' mental health and adjustment to life in New Zealand. *Australian and New Zealand Journal of Psychiatry, 33,* 12–21.

Altrocchi, J. & Altrocchi, L. (1995). Poly-faceted psychological acculturation in Cook Islanders. *Journal of Cross-Cultural Psychology, 26,* 426–440.

Australian Bureau of Statistics. (2002). *2001 census of population and housing.* Canberra: Australian Government Publishing Service.

Australian Institute of Health and Welfare (1999). *The health and welfare of Australia's Aboriginal and Torres Strait Islander peoples.* Cat. No. 4704.0. Canberra: Australian Institute of Health and Welfare.

Aye, A. & Guerin, B. (2001). Astronaut families: a review of their characteristics, impact on families and implications for practice in New Zealand. *New Zealand Journal of Psychology, 30,* 9–15.

Berry, J. W. (1970). Marginality, stress and ethnic identification in an acculturated Aboriginal community. *Journal of Cross-Cultural Psychology, 1,* 239–252.

   (1997). Immigration, acculturation and adaptation. *Applied Psychology: An International Review, 46,* 5–34.

Berry, J.W., Kim. U., Minde, T. & Mok, D. (1987). Comparative studies of acculturative stress. *International Migration Review, 21,* 491–511.

Bochner, S. (1982). The social psychology of cross-cultural relations. In S. Bochner (ed.). *Cultures in contact: studies in cross-cultural interaction* (pp. 5–44). Oxford: Pergamon.

   (1986). Coping with unfamiliar cultures: adjustment or cultural learning? *Australian Journal of Psychology, 38,* 347–358.

Bochner, S., McLeod, B. M. & Lin, A. (1977). Friendship patterns of overseas students: a functional model. *International Journal of Psychology, 12,* 277–297.

Boman, B. & Edwards, M. (1984). The Indochinese refugee: an overview. *Australian and New Zealand Journal of Psychiatry, 18,* 40–52.

Borrie, W. D. (1988). Changes in migration patterns since 1972. In J. Jupp (ed.), *The Australian people* (pp. 111–118). Sydney: Angus and Robertson.

Brooking, T. & Rabel, R. (1995). Neither British nor Polynesia: a brief history of New Zealand's other immigrants. In S. Greif (ed.), *Immigration and national identity in New Zealand* (pp. 23–49). Palmerston North, New Zealand: Dunmore Press.

Canadian Task Force (1988). *Review of the literature on migrant mental health.* Ottawa: Ministry of Supply and Services.

Cheng, P. (1994). Posttraumatic stress disorder among Cambodian refugees in New Zealand. *International Journal of Social Psychiatry, 40,* 17–26.

   (1995). Acculturation and psychiatric morbidity among Cambodian refugees in New Zealand. *International Journal of Social Psychiatry, 41,* 108–119.

Dawson, J. (1969). Attitude change and conflict among Australian Aborigines. *Australian Journal of Psychology, 21,* 101–116.

DIMA (2001). *Immigration: federation to century's end. 1901–2001.* Canberra, ACT: DIMA. Retrieved from www.immi.gov.au/amep/reports/reports/age_table.pdf.

Durie, M. (2001). *Mauri ora: the dynamics of Maori health*. Oxford: Oxford University Press.

Evans, I. M., Wilson, N. J., Hansson, G. & Hungerford, R. (1997). Positive and negative behaviors of independent adolescent youth participating in a community support programme. *New Zealand Journal of Psychology, 26*, 29–35.

Eyou, M. L., Adair, V. & Dixon, R. (2000). Cultural identity and psychological adjustment of adolescent Chinese immigrants in New Zealand. *Journal of Adolescence, 23*, 531–543.

Furnham, A. & Bochner, S. (1982). Social difficulty in a foreign culture: an empirical analysis of culture shock. In S. Bochner (ed.), *Cultures in contact: studies in cross-cultural interaction* (pp. 161–198). Oxford: Pergamon.

Gee, S. (2002). Happily ever after? Positive aging in three New Zealand cultural groups. Paper presented at the New Zealand Association of Gerontology Conference, Auckland, New Zealand.

Gibson, K. (1999). Maori women and dual ethnicity: non-congruence, "passing" and "real Maori." In N. Roberston (ed.), *Maori and psychology : research and practice* (pp. 1–4). Hamilton: Waikato University Maori and Psychology Research Unit.

Green, S. (1994). The acculturation experience of overseas students of Chinese origin: a study of acculturation attitudes and acculturative stress. Unpublished Honours thesis: Department of Psychology, University of Western Australia.

Guerin, B., Abdi, A. & Guerin, P. (2003). Experiences with the medical and health systems for Somali refugees living in Hamilton. *New Zealand Journal of Psychology, 32*, 27–32.

Guerin, B., Guerin, P., Diiriye, R. O. & Abdi, A. (2004). Living in a close community: the everyday life of Somali refugees. *Network: Australian College of Community Psychologists, 16*, 7–17.

Gupta, D. (1993). The acculturation experience of overseas students of Chinese origin: a study of acculturation attitudes, cognitive appraisal and acculturative stress. Unpublished Masters' thesis: Department of Psychology: University of Western Australia.

Harrington, L. & Liu, J. (2002). Self-enhancement and attitudes toward high achievers: a bi-cultural view of independent and interdependent self. *Journal of Cross-Cultural Psychology, 33*, 37–55.

Ho, E. (1995). Chinese or New Zealander? Differential paths of adaptation of Hong Kong Chinese adolescent immigration in New Zealand. *New Zealand Population Review, 21*, 27–49.

Jayasuriya, L., Sang, D. & Fielding, A. (1992). *Ethnicity, immigration and mental illness: a critical review of Australian research*. Canberra: Bureau of Immigration Research.

Krupinski, J. (1967). Sociological aspects of mental ill health in migrants. *Social Science and Medicine, 1*, 267–281.

(1984). Changing patterns of migration to Australia and their influence on the health of migrants. *Social Science and Medicine, 18*, 927–937.

Krupinski, J. & Burrows, G. D. (1986). *The price of freedom: young Indochinese refugees in Australia*. Sydney: Pergamon Press.

Nesdale, D., Rooney, R. & Smith, L. (1997). Migrant ethnic identity and psychological distress. *Journal of Cross-Cultural Psychology, 28*, 569–588.

New Zealand Immigration Service (2004a). *Migrants' experiences of New Zealand: pilot survey report.* Wellington: New Zealand Immigration Service.

(2004b). *Refugee voices: a journey towards resettlement.* Wellington: New Zealand Immigration Service.

Oberg, K. (1960). Cultural shock: adjustment to new cultural environments. *Practical Anthropology, 7,* 177–182.

Pernice, R. (1989). Refugees and mental health. In M. Abbott (ed.), *Refugee resettlement and well-being* (pp. 155–160). Auckland: Mental Health Foundation of New Zealand.

Richardson, A. (1974). *British immigrants and Australia: a psychosocial inquiry.* Canberra: Australian National University Press.

Richardson, S. (2002). The migrant perspective. In *Migration: benefiting Australia – conference proceeding* (pp. 165–200). DIMA, Canberra: Commonwealth of Australia.

Ritchie, J. (1992). *Becoming bicultural.* Wellington: Huia Publishers.

Rosenthal, D. & Cichello, A. (1986). The meeting of two cultures: ethnic identity and psychological adjustment of Italian-Australian adolescents. *International Journal of Psychology, 21*, 487–501.

Rosenthal, D. & Feldman, S.S. (1992). The nature and stability of ethnic identity in Chinese youth. *Journal of Cross-Cultural Psychology, 23*, 214–227.

Rosenthal, D. & Hrynevich, C. (1985). Ethnicity and ethnic identity: A comparative study of Greek-, Italian-, and Anglo-Australian adolescents. *International Journal of Psychology, 20*, 723–742.

Sang, D. (1986). *Wanted: further research on resettlement of Indochinese refugees.* Melbourne: Ecumenical Rejuvenation Centre.

Scott, W. A. & Scott, R. (1989). *Adaptation of immigrants: individual differences and determinants.* Sydney: Pergamon Press.

Sommerlad, E. & Berry, J. W. (1970). The role of ethnic identification in distinguishing between attitudes towards assimilation and integration. *Human Relations, 23,* 23–39.

Steel, Z., Silove, D., Phan, T. & Bauman, A. (2002). Long-term effect of psychological trauma on the mental health of Vietnamese refugees resettled in Australia: a population-based study. *Lancet, 360,* 1056–1062.

Stoller, A. (1967). Migration and mental health in Australia. *British Journal of Social Psychiatry, 1,* 70–77.

Taft, R. (1977). Coping with unfamiliar cultures. In N. Warren (ed.), *Studies in cross-cultural psychology* (pp. 121–153). London: Academic Press.

(1985). The psychological study of the adjustment and adaptation of immigrants in Australia. In N. Feather (ed.), *Australian psychology: review of research* (pp. 364–386). Sydney: Allen & Unwin.

(1987). The psychological adaptation of Soviet immigrants in Australia. In Y. Y. Kim & W. B. Gudykunst (eds.), *Cross-cultural adaptation: current approaches* (pp. 150–167). Newbury Park: Sage Publications.

Thomas, D. & Nikora, L. W. (1992). From assimilation to biculturalism: changing patterns in Maori–Pakeha relationships. In D. Thomas & A. Veno (eds.),

Psychology and social change (pp. 278–298). Palmerston North: Dunmore Press.

Trlin, A., Henderson, A., North, N. & Skinner, M. (2001). Personal connections and international migration in New Zealand: the importance of relatives and friends. *New Zealand Population Review, 27,* 1–25.

Ward, C. (2006). Acculturation, identity and adaptation in dual heritage adolescents. *International Journal of Intercultural Relations, 30,* 243–259.

Ward, C., Bochner, S. & Furnham, A. (2001). *The psychology of culture shock.* London: Routledge.

Ward, C. & Masgoret, A.-M. (2005). New Zealanders' attitudes toward immigrants and immigration. Paper presented at New Directions, New Settlers, New Challenges: Foundation for Science, Research and Technology End-users Seminar on Migration, Wellington, New Zealand, April.

Ward, C., Masgoret, A.-M., Berno, T. & Ong, A. (2004). The psychological well-being of Asian students in New Zealand. In S. Tse, A. Thapliyal, S. Garg, G. Lim & M. Chatterji (eds.), *Proceedings of the Inaugural International Asian Health Conference* (pp. 115–125). Auckland: School of Population Health, University of Auckland.

Watkins, R., Plant, A. J., Sang, D., *et al.* (2003). Individual characteristics and expectations about opportunities in Australia among prospective Vietnamese migrants. *Journal of Ethnic and Migration Studies, 29,* 157–166.

17 Acculturation in Canada

Kimberly A. Noels & John W. Berry

Canada has been a culturally plural society since before its formal establishment as a nation state in 1867. Indigenous Peoples settled over 10,000
years ago in diverse ecological zones, giving rise to distinct cultural zones
that still persist. Around 500 years ago, Europeans arrived and settled, followed by Africans, Asians and South Americans. As a result of contact
among these groups, many acculturation phenomena have a long history in
Canada. Similarly, acculturation research has been carried out for over 50 years
(e.g. Hallowell, 1945; Honigmann & Honigmann, 1968), and continues as a
focus of psychological research, including a continuing interest in Aboriginal
Peoples, immigrants and refugees. Peoples of British, French and other origins have maintained their cultural heritages to a large extent; as a result,
acculturation studies have also been prominent among these ethnocultural
groups.

In this chapter, we first examine aspects of Canada's socio-historical context, and the policy response to it by various governments. We then present a
selective overview of acculturation research in Canada.

17.1 The Canadian context

17.1.1 History of settlement

In its short history, Canada has become a diverse and pluralistic modern society. When European explorers arrived on the east coast of Canada in the 1500s
they found a land populated by around half a million Indigenous Peoples living
throughout the territory that is now Canada. As the population of French and
British colonialists grew, settlers expanded westward and northward. Following the American Revolution of 1776, colonists loyal to Britain came from the
United States of America and settled in eastern and southern Canada. The eigh-
teenth and nineteenth centuries saw a continuing flow of British immigrants,
as well as Ukrainian, Chinese, Italian and Irish settlers.

In the early twentieth century, many settlers from eastern and southern
Europe came to the Canadian prairies to farm. After the 1930s, with the growth
of cities, immigrants flowed to urban centers, where the majority of Canadians

The authors would like to thank Kristie Saumure for her research and clerical assistance.

resided and worked. Between 1946 and 1954, 96% of the immigrants admitted to Canada came from Europe. Following changes in immigration policy (see section below), since the 1980s, the majority of immigrants have come from Asia, Africa and the Caribbean. Most choose to live in large cosmopolitan cities like Toronto, Montreal and Vancouver. Due to this shift, visible minorities accounted for 13.4% of the population in 2001, making Canada even more multicultural. Even with this influx of immigrants of diverse origins, and with lingering questions surrounding Québec's place in Canada, Canadian national identity has remained strong (Kalin & Berry, 1996).

17.1.2 Demography

Canada is the second-largest country in the world after Russia, with a total area of almost 10 million square kilometers, spanning a distance of over 5,000 kilometers from east to west and over 4,000 kilometers from north to south. For reasons of agriculture, climate, economics and geography, over 90% of the Canadian population of just over 30 million live within 200 km of the Canada–US border. Over three-quarters of all Canadians live in urban areas (77% in 1996; Statistics Canada, 1996); about one half of all Canadians currently live in Canada's ten largest cities. Roman Catholicism remains the single largest denomination (48%), professed mainly by those of French, Irish and Italian origin, followed by various groups of Protestantism (37%) and Asian religions (4%). The economy is characterized by relatively high affluence (GDP = US$26,474 per capita), and immigrants have slightly higher incomes than the average.

Canada is a federal state consisting of ten provinces and three territories. The ethnic mix varies by region and province. For example, in Newfoundland 95% of the population are of British origin, while, in Québec, French origins predominate (85%). In Manitoba and Saskatchewan, the majority of the population is neither British nor French. Ontario and British Columbia are the two provinces where most ethnocultural groups other than British and French have chosen to reside. The Province of Québec and the Territory of Nunavut have social institutions and policies (including language, education, civil law) that reflect their respective French and Inuit cultural origins.

Canada has a high level of immigration, with 18.9% of its population of 31 million not born in the country. In recent years, around two-thirds of the annual flow of 250,000 to 300,000 immigrants have been from Asia. The percentage of immigrants varies widely by region and city. For example, in Toronto, 44.0% of the population are immigrants, the highest of all cities in Canada. Immigration has massively transformed the city over the past fifty years: between 1951 and 2001, the percentage with origins in the UK declined from 73% to 27%, and the most frequent names in the Toronto phone book went from Smith and Brown in 1951 to Smith, Lee, Wong, Brown, Singh, Kim, Mohammed, and Patel at present.

For the country as a whole, the net migration rate is 5.96 migrants/1,000 population, including economic immigrants. The population growth rate is 1.06%, and the fertility rate is 1.65. However, for the Indigenous population, the fertility rate is more than double the overall rate. Since the 1980s, the number of Asian immigrants and Indigenous Peoples in the country has increased, and the relative proportion of British and French origin decreased, such that the current ethnic origins for the country as a whole are: British Isles 40%; French 27%; other European 20%; Indigenous Peoples 1.5%; and other (mostly Asian) 11.5%. As a result of these patterns of growth, Canada is the most diverse country on many international indicators.

17.1.3 Policy

There are several federal policies that are relevant to the study of acculturation in Canada; we will focus this discussion on two: immigration and multiculturalism.

Immigration In the 1950s, the federal government's immigration policy had been to fill the country's needs in the natural resource and industrial sectors; the policy later shifted towards acceptance of professionally educated workers. In the 1960s, Canada halted its previous preferential treatment of British, French and American citizens (Canada Immigration Act, 1952, see Citizenship and Immigration Canada, 2000) and finally implemented immigration policies that did not officially discriminate on the basis of race, color or religion. Some legislative landmarks have also contributed to the shape of Canadian society, particularly the statutes of official bilingualism in 1969 and 1988 (Canadian Heritage, 2004b), multiculturalism in 1971 and 1988 (Canadian Heritage, 2004a), and the Canadian Charter of Rights and Freedoms in 1982 (Department of Justice Canada, 1982).

Under its current immigration policy (Immigration and Refugee Protection Act, 2002), Canada takes in 1% of the population each year (around 300,000 people). These include applicants in the economic class (professionals and skilled workers and their immediate families, comprising 54.7% of those who received permanent residency in 2003; Citizenship and Immigration Canada, 2005), refugees (for those who meet Geneva Convention or other, mainly humanitarian, criteria; 11.7%), and those who come under the family reunification program (family members of permanent residents; 31.2%).

Multiculturalism The fundamental purpose of Canada's Multiculturalism Act (1971/1988; see Berry & Kalin, 2000, for an overview) is to increase inter-group harmony and the mutual acceptance of all groups in the country; this goal is termed the "group acceptance and tolerance" element of the policy (Berry, 1984). Second, the policy seeks to avoid assimilation by encouraging all cultural groups to maintain and develop themselves as distinctive groups within Canadian society; this element has been referred to as the "cultural" focus of the policy. Third, the policy argues that group development by itself is not sufficient to lead to group acceptance; "intergroup contact and sharing" is also required, and has been referred to as the "social" focus of the policy. Fourth, full participation in Canadian society cannot be achieved if some common languages are not learned; thus the "learning of official languages" (English and French) is also encouraged by the policy, and elaborated in the Official Languages Act (1969/1988).

17.2   Acculturation research

Given Canada's demographic characteristics and historical context, it is not surprising that issues related to ethnic diversity and acculturation have been long investigated by Canadian researchers and practitioners (Adair, 1999; Berry, 1993; Dobson, 1997). For instance, Rule and Adair (1984) cite Lambert's work on French immersion education (e.g., Lambert & Tucker, 1972), Berry's work on Aboriginal Peoples' adaptation to ecological and cultural changes (e.g., Berry & Annis, 1974; Berry, Wintrob, Sindell, & Mawhinney, 1982), and the research on inter-group attitudes by Berry, Kalin and Taylor (1977; see also Kalin and Berry, 1982) as early examples of research on distinctly Canadian matters. In this section, we consider three theoretical approaches (outlined in more detail in Chapters 4, 5 and 6) to recent Canadian scholarship on the psychology of acculturation. These include the study of acculturation within (i) a stress, coping and adaptation framework, (ii) an inter-group relations paradigm, and (iii) a communication processes perspective. We then highlight research conducted by Canadian scholars concerning immigrants, sojourning students, refugees and Aboriginal Peoples.

17.3   Theoretical orientations

17.3.1   Stress, coping and adaptation

One prominent theoretical approach focuses on understanding how individuals cope with *acculturative stress*, and, through processes of adaptation, achieve various outcomes, including psychological and physical health and behavioral adjustments (e.g., social, occupational, educational; see Berry & Annis, 1974; Dyal & Dyal, 1981; and Chapter 4, this volume). Two themes are central to Canadian research: the adoption of a multidimensional approach to the study of acculturation; and the effort to model the relations between stressors and outcome variables, taking into account a variety of mediators and moderators of those relations.

Multidimensionality. Consistent with the Canadian multicultural policy's pluralistic ideology, many scholars emphasize that understanding cultural adaptation requires a consideration of two independent aspects: the extent of affiliation with the larger Canadian society; and the degree of involvement with the ethnic group of origin (Berry, 1980, 2001, see also Chapter 3; Dompierre & Lavallée, 1990; Ryder, Alden & Paulhus, 2001; see Vallee, Schwartz & Darknell, 1957, for an early discussion). Although this bidimensional, or "fourfold," model has received criticism on methodological and ideological grounds (Rudmin & Ahmadzadeh, 2001; see Berry & Sam, 2003, for a response), the point remains that a comprehensive understanding of acculturation processes requires an orthogonal consideration of all relevant ethnic referent groups. This has typically meant the group of origin and the dominant ethnic group, although in certain settings additional groups may be relevant (e.g., in some parts of Québec, particularly in and around Montréal and the western border with Ontario, there are two dominant language groups, French and English).

Other researchers have incorporated the orthogonal acculturation model into their examinations of more specific acculturation-related constructs, particularly ethnic identity (e.g., Sayegh & Lasry, 1993; Lasry & Sayegh, 1992). In their *situated ethnic identity model*, Clément and Noels (1992; Noels, Clément & Gaudet, 2004) take the issue of multidimensionality a step further, by arguing that ethnic allegiance with each group may shift depending upon the social situation. This situational variation may have important implications for acculturation, such that cultural change is more likely to occur in less intimate domains (e.g., at work), where there is greater opportunity for inter-ethnic interaction, than in more personal domains (e.g., at home) which may be relatively sheltered from the effects of acculturative contact.

Modeling the acculturation process. Acculturation is not only a multidimensional phenomenon, but also a multivariate phenomenon. Hence, different acculturation patterns may be evident depending upon the variable considered (e.g., attitudes, identity, behaviors; see Clément, Gauthier, & Noels, 1993; Laroche, Kim, Hui & Joy, 1996; Laroche, Kim & Hui, 1997). To capture the relations between variables (including stressors and adaptation outcomes), several scholars have proposed models of the acculturation process (e.g., Young & Gardner, 1990; Masgoret & Gardner, 1999; Noels, Pon & Clément, 1996; Gaudet & Clément, 2005). For example, Safdar, Lay and Struthers' (2003; see also Safdar & Lay, 2003) multidimensional individual differences acculturation model posits that psycho-social adjustment, connectedness to family and culture, and the experience of acculturation-specific and non-specific daily hassles (Lay & Nguyen, 1998) predict ingroup and outgroup behavior and psychological distress, which are mediated by the acculturation attitudes of separation and assimilation. Although empirical tests of such models generally support the proposed relationships, most lack a longitudinal component that would allow a legitimate assessment of causal claims (but see Kealey, 1989). Nonetheless, they provide a much-needed theoretical framework for organizing acculturation-relevant variables.

17.3.2 Inter-group relations and social identity

A second perspective on acculturation is taken by researchers of social identity (see Chapter 6). As Liebkind (2001:399) points out, "acculturation does not take place in a social vacuum, rather it unfolds itself within the context of intra- and intergroup relations." Inter-group theory, particularly social identity theory (Tajfel, 1978; Tajfel & Turner, 1986), arrived in Canada in the 1970s, and was used to examine relations between French and English groups in Québec. Aspects of this theory have now been extended to study relations between immigrant groups and the English and/or French groups.

Although not restricted to ethnic groups, social identity theory and related frameworks (e.g., Moghaddam, 1988; Taylor & McKirnan, 1984) have implications for understanding acculturation patterns because of their predictions regarding the reactions of minority-group members to their relative status in society (Lalonde & Cameron, 1993). An important premise of the inter-group approach, which is outlined in the framework proposed by Berry (1980), is that the dominant group has the power to constrain the attitudes of non-dominant-group members towards cultural maintenance and participation in the larger society. In this vein, Bourhis and his colleagues developed the *interactive acculturation model* (Bourhis, Moïse, Perreault, & Sénécal, 1997). This model is designed to predict the quality of inter-group relations likely to derive from the adoption of different acculturation orientations. They argue that relational outcomes are the product of the acculturation orientations of both the dominant majority and immigrant groups, and that these orientations are influenced by state integration policies. Conflict between groups is most likely to occur with a mismatch in acculturation orientations, or when the two groups have "agreed to disagree" (i.e., both adopt separation/segregation or cultural exclusion as a mode of adaptation).

17.3.3 Intercultural communication

Consistent with the policy of official bilingualism, language and communication have been key variables of interest for several Canadian researchers. Although developed to understand the phenomenon of bilingualism, many of these models are de-facto acculturation models in which communication plays an important role (see Chapter 5, for an extended discussion of language and cultural learning). Lambert's early work on bilingualism was directed not only at understanding the positive and negative cognitive effects of bilingualism, but also at the conditions that contribute to positive and negative social psychological outcomes. Lambert (1967, 1978; see also Lambert & Taylor, 1990; Taylor, Meynard & Rheault, 1977) argued that language acquisition was associated with the acquisition of other cultural characteristics (e.g., identity). These patterns could be "additive" or "subtractive" depending upon the sociostructural status of the group. For members of majority groups, learning another language involved the addition of another language and cultural repertoire, as well as the maintenance of the original language and cultural identity. For minority-group members, proficiency in the language of the dominant group was likely to be associated with the loss of the original language and identity.

More recent work includes Gardner's (1985) socio-educational model which posits that inter-group attitudes (termed "integrativeness") can influence motivation to learn a second language and achievement in that language, and are associated with a variety of social psychological outcomes, including acculturative consequences (Young & Gardner, 1990; Lanca, Alksnis, Roese & Gardner, 1994). Another example is Clément's (1980) socio-contextual model, which claims that the relation between inter-ethnic contact and a variety of acculturative outcomes, including identity and psychological health, is mediated by linguistic and communicative self-confidence (Clément, 1986; Clément, Noels & Denault, 2001; Noels & Clément, 1996; Noels et al., 1996; see also Pak, Dion & Dion, 1985; Lee & Chen, 2000).

17.3.4   Section conclusion

Although each represents a rich scholarly tradition, the three theoretical orientations reviewed here are not mutually exclusive, nor are they exhaustive of all the conceptual perspectives evident in Canadian research. For example, a relatively recent perspective on acculturation that is informed by self-determination theory (Deci & Ryan, 1985) focuses on the motivational processes that underpin the adoption of particular cultural orientations (Chirkov, Ryan, Kim & Kaplan, 2003; Downie, Koestner, ElGeledi & Cree, 2004). As well, although they do not address acculturation processes directly, studies of basic processes (e.g., self-concept, emotions, etc.) in bicultural individuals lend some insight into the experience of biculturality and cultural change (e.g., Heine & Lehman, 2004).

17.4   Acculturating groups

17.4.1   Immigrants

Much of the research using the conceptual perspectives discussed earlier was carried out with immigrant samples. Although this work has contributed to the development of general models to describe the acculturation experience of individuals, several Canadian scholars argue that more attention must be directed to understanding how the immigration experience is instantiated depending upon factors such as gender and age/generation, and to considering interpersonal and family dynamics.

With regards to gender, Dion and Dion (2001; see also Boyd, 1986; Lee & Cochran, 1988; Wittebrood & Robertson, 1991) note that men and women from more gender-segregated societies than Canada may face challenges to their assumptions regarding gender roles and relations. Not infrequently, the desire to improve the life circumstances of the family can necessitate that women seek paid employment outside the family, a role often not previously enacted in the country of origin. According to Noh, Wu, Speechley and Kaspar (1992) women thus face a "double burden" of paid and unpaid occupations, often combined with renegotiation of the power dynamics in the family as Canadian values regarding gendered expectations and responsibilities penetrate the spousal relationship (Ataca & Berry, 2002). A consideration of gender also offers insights into some quandaries that may be experienced by the second generation. Daughters are often expected to embody traditional ideals, and to be responsible for passing them on to the next generation (Dion & Dion, 2004; Tang & Dion, 1999). Such expectations may contrast with the simultaneous desire of immigrant parents for their children, including their daughters, to take advantage of educational, professional and economic opportunities that were the grounds for moving to Canada (Naidoo, 1985).

These gender issues may be especially salient for the families who undergo stage or serial migration, whereby one family member migrates to seek work without the spouse and children, who later join him/her once employment and living arrangements have been established (Hondagneu-Sotelo, 1992; Dion & Dion, 2001). Although the husband is often the initiating member, because of governmental programs such as the Live-In Caregiver Program (www.cic.gc.ca/english/pub/caregiver/), many women too leave their families for several years to initiate the familial migration process. During separation, both spouses may acquire new skills and responsibilities traditionally assumed by the other spouse. Upon reunification, gender expectations for behavior may have changed, such that men may be more involved in domestic duties and women more in family decision-making. Although some changed expectations and behaviors might be perceived positively, these personal changes and lengthy separations have much potential to cause family disruptions (Pratt, in collaboration with the Philippine Women Centre, 1999; Smith, Lalonde & Johnson, 2004).

Astronaut families provide another contemporary illustration of the transnational family involved in contemporary migration to Canada. Astronaut families are those in which some family members, often the father but sometimes both parents (in the case of "parachute" or "satellite kids"), return to the country of origin to work while the remaining family members reside in the new country (Aye & Guerin, 2001). Motivated to immigrate by the security offered by citizenship in a politically and economically stable nation, educational opportunities for their children, and the promise of improved quality of life (Tsang, Irving, Alaggia, Chau & Benjamin, 2003), these families maintain ties with the culture of origin because they desire to return to the country of origin once these goals have been achieved (Waters, 2003). While there are advantages to this strategy, the issues surrounding disruption of familial and spousal relationships, loss of career and support networks, increased domestic responsibilities, loneliness, and the cultural transformation of astronaut wives and satellite children warrant research attention (Waters, 2002, 2003; Tsang *et al.*, 2003). Moreover, the return of these transnational families to the country of origin (should it occur) may also have important psychological implications (cf. Kanno's [2000] study of children of returning Japanese expatriates).

This focus on transnational families is not meant to suggest that immigrant families in other circumstances merit less research attention. A growing body of research on children and adolescents and their families is contributing to a better understanding of immigration and integration into Canadian society. In their review, Hicks, Lalonde and Pepler (1993) concluded that the stresses of migration and resettlement do not invariably lead to higher rates of emotional problems and maladaptive behaviors, but that risk and protective factors can moderate such outcomes (see also Westhues & Cohen, 1998). Their conclusions are consistent with those of Kwak and Berry (2001), whose study of Vietnamese, Korean and East Indian families showed that understanding generational differences and conflicts must be particularized by each group's selective emphasis on different cultural issues (see also Costigan & Su, 2004; Kester & Marshall, 2003; Leung, 2001; Wong, 1997).

17.4.2 Sojourners: international students

Because it is one of the world's top providers of education to international students, Canada's post-secondary student body contains a sizeable proportion of international students at the undergraduate and graduate levels (4.6% and 12.3% respectively; Canadian Bureau for International Education, 2002). Popadiuk and Arthur (in press) note that more than 100,000 international students are currently enrolled in Canadian universities, coming predominantly from countries in Asia, followed by Europe, North America, Africa, South America and Oceania. There is much to be gained from this international contact for both parties: the students acquire an international education, experience and contacts, while Canada benefits in terms of financial gains, enhanced international reputation, and increased commercial, trade and diplomatic linkages (Cunningham, 1991). It is, hence, crucial that a concerted effort be made to ensure a satisfactory experience.

In their review of international student counseling, Popadiuk and Arthur (2004); see also Arthur, 2001 (2004); Heikinheimo & Shute, 1986) point out that, although international students face many of the same challenges as other students (e.g., learning new administrative procedures), they also encounter additional hurdles that render their experience unique. In particular, they must deal not only with the vicissitudes of cultural transition common to most sojourners (e.g., limited communication skills), but also with the problems often associated with being from a non-dominant ethnic background (e.g., prejudice and discrimination). There is some evidence that international students experience more problems than resident students (Chataway & Berry,

1989; Zheng & Berry, 1991); this tendency may be particularly evident for older, graduate and/or female students (Dyal & Chan, 1985; Leung & Berry, 2001; Adrian-Taylor, Noels & Tischler, in press).

Rather than emphasizing the problems that can arise during an educational sojourn abroad, and hence marginalizing international students, Popadiuk and Arthur (2004) suggest that a focus on health promotion, improving the accessibility and legitimacy of counseling services, customizing group interventions, and improving multicultural counseling competencies could go a long way to enhancing these students' international experience. In a parallel effort to promote a more positive perspective on the international students, research attention directed towards identifying the predictors of successful sojourns may prove beneficial, including studies of the benefits of intercultural experiences; how students elicit social support from home, the host nationals, and other international students; and how to improve coping and problem-prevention strategies employed by international students and their hosts.

17.4.3 Refugees

In Canada 118,282 residents currently have refugee status, and in 2002, 31,500 individuals entered the country on humanitarian grounds (Citizenship and Immigration Canada, 2002). There are at least two sources of stress for refugees that are not experienced by other immigrants (Beiser, 1999). These are the atrocities that individuals experience while living in conflict-ridden countries (e.g., imprisonment, assault, seeing family members suffer and/or die) and the challenges of escaping from their country, which often are accompanied by a period of residence in a crowded, and often dangerous, refugee camp. Like other immigrants, refugees selected for resettlement must adapt to their new country, which may or may not be a place they would have chosen to live. As a result, refugees are usually considered to be at risk for psychological distress (Berry & Blondel, 1982; Williams & Berry, 1991; see also Young, 2000; Winter & Young, 1998; and Chapters 13 and 14).

Despite these circumstances, Beiser (1999) argues that most refugees succeed in Canada, although some people do suffer from depression, substance abuse, and posttraumatic stress disorder. Based on the results of his ten-year longitudinal study of Southeast Asian refugees, Beiser (1999) argues that post-migration stresses may affect mental health more profoundly than the traumas of uprooting, flight and incarceration, in part because refugees may disconnect from the past in order to avoid thinking of traumatic events or longing for a lost past before the conflict arose, when things were much better than their current circumstances (see also Beiser, Turner & Ganesan, 1989). The longitudinal nature of this study provides a perspective on cultural change and its link to wellbeing in ways that few other studies can. An important finding is that factors that may facilitate adjustment in the early stages of resettlement, such as having a like-ethnic community, being married or female, may become detrimental to adaptation in later stages. Central to successful adaptation was the acquisition of English language, which was the key to obtaining good employment.

Other factors which would seem to be important for the adaptation of refugees include satisfaction with the new country (Husni, Cernovsky, Koye & Haggarty, 2002), while retaining aspects of the original culture (Donà & Berry, 1994). Young and Evans (1997) report that Salvadorean refugees were no different from native Canadians in psychological distress, and attributed their wellbeing to the type of refugee movement they experienced (anticipatory rather than acute; see Kunz, 1973), the relative similarity between Salvadorean and Canadian cultures (compared to East Asian cultures), youth, the presence of family members, employment, and/or engagement in English language training. Nonetheless, these individuals reported lower life satisfaction and quality of life, particularly with regards to marital relations, parent–child relations, material wellbeing and job satisfaction. To this list of problems, Durst and Lange (1999) add discrimination and a fractured community. Merali (2002) maintains that some of the distress experienced in refugee families may stem from incongruities in estimating intergenerational differences in acculturation, which may result from low levels of verbal sharing and companionship, with a focus on integrating the family unit into the new society (Fantino & Colak, 2001; Hyman, Vu & Beiser, 2000). Moreover, the trauma experienced by refugees may be transmitted intergenerationally to offspring not alive when these events took place (Baranowsky, Young, Johnson-Douglas, Williams-Keeler & McCarrey, 1998).

In sum, although they may be considered an "at risk" group, research suggests that refugees in Canada generally adapt well to their new home. Nonetheless, their psychological health concerns have often been often overlooked because the primary focus has been on providing physical sanctuary (cf. Berry & Sam, 1997), a situation that clearly merits redressing.

17.4.4   Aboriginal peoples

Empirical research with Aboriginal peoples, including First Nations, Métis and Inuit communities, is relatively less well represented in Canadian acculturation scholarship, but generally suggests that the acculturation situation for many individuals from Aboriginal communities is a difficult one (Berry *et al.*, 1982). In his cross-Canada study of Aboriginal cultural identity, Berry (1999) reported that the lives of many research participants had been extensively affected by the nature of contact with non-Aboriginals, particularly through residential schools and the justice system. This colonizing contact resulted in disruptions to cultural identity, expressed as identity loss and confusion, as well as an associated decline in social and psychological wellbeing. The experience of prejudice and discrimination, and attendant cultural dissolution, has been linked to several destructive consequences, including poorer academic achievement, a higher rate of incarceration, more drug, alcohol and gambling addictions, and a higher suicide rate than the Canadian general population.

In his examination of suicide, Kral (1998; Kral & Dyck, 1995) recognizes the importance of distress as a motivating factor, but maintains that the idea of suicide, and how such ideas are spread throughout a cultural community, underlie the higher incidence of suicide attempts in particular communities (for a discussion of an Aboriginal community, see Kral *et al.*, 2000). Chandler (1994) explores the possibility that the distress associated with suicide arises when persons come to view themselves as disconnected from their past and especially their future. In their examination of Aboriginal youths, Chandler and Lalonde (1998; Chandler, Lalonde, Sokol & Hallett, 2003) argue that, by undermining cultural continuity, the assaults directed at Aboriginal societies have added to the array of developmental and social challenges that can undermine a sense of personal continuity, such that individuals come to lack concern for and commitment to a possible future self, and hence may be at greater risk for suicide. An important point made by Chandler and Lalonde (1998; Chandler *et al.*, 2003) is that suicide rates across Aboriginal communities are not uniform; some show low rates of youth suicide, and these communities tend to be those who actively strive for cultural continuity (e.g., regaining legal title to traditional lands and re-establishing forms of self-regulation in various institutions [e.g., government, education, health care, etc.]).

Taylor (1997; Taylor & Wright, 2003) maintains that difficulties experienced by Aboriginal groups stem from a situation of unclear, undefined identity and anomie, although he differs in the presumed origin of this identity vacuum. According to Taylor (1997), Aboriginal groups and others faced with "value-less colonization" exist in a situation in which the original cultural systems have been destroyed by colonizers, and inadequate or inappropriate effort has been made to teach the values, ways of being, and norms of the colonizing culture. Lacking a sense of collective (cultural) identity, individuals struggle to make sense of their own personal identity. Taylor claims that language is an important cultural resource because it is one of the few visible manifestations of collective identity. Consistent with this premise, the results of an examination of Inuit children living in the Québec Arctic demonstrated that early schooling in the heritage language is associated not only with better performance on standardized intelligence tests, but also significant gains in self-esteem (Taylor & Wright, 2003; Wright & Taylor, 1995; Wright, Taylor & MacArthur, 2000).

In sum, this research suggests that some Aboriginal individuals exemplify the marginalized situation that can arise as a result of forced contact with a powerful other (Berry & Sam, 1997). The toll of colonization cannot be underestimated; at the same time, a second current in these and other studies speaks to the resilience, both personal and collective, of many Aboriginal persons and communities (Cheah & Nelson, 2004; Chapter 15, this volume). Future research might well address the manner by which oppression is successfully overcome.

17.5   Conclusions

This chapter has highlighted the context of acculturation in Canada, not only in terms of the socio-historical milieu in which many ethnocultural groups interact, but also in terms of the scholarly perspectives through which the experience of different acculturating groups is studied. Many of the themes and issues identified in this chapter are likely to be important not only in Canada but also in other multicultural societies. Canada's relatively unique emphasis on cultural and linguistic pluralism and tolerance, however, provides a distinctive environment for understanding the processes of acculturation.

17.6   References

Adair, J. G. (1999). Indigenisation of psychology: the concept and its practical implementation. *Applied Psychology: An International Review, 48*, 403–418.

Adrian-Taylor, S. R., Noels, K. A. & Tischler, K. (in press). Conflict between international graduate students and faculty supervisors: towards effective conflict prevention and management strategies. *Journal of Studies in International Education.*

Arthur, N. (2001). Using critical incidents to investigate cross-cultural transitions. *International Journal of Intercultural Relations, 25*, 41–53.

   (2004). *Counseling international students: clients from around the world.* New York: Kluwer Academic/Plenum.

Ataca, B. & Berry, J. W. (2002). Psychological, sociocultural and marital adaptation of Turkish immigrant couples in Canada. *International Journal of Psychology, 37*, 13–26.

Aye, A. & Guerin, B. (2001). Astronaut families: a review of their characteristics, impact on families and implications for practice in New Zealand. *New Zealand Journal of Psychology, 30*, 9–15.

Baranowsky, A. B., Young, M., Johnson-Douglas, S., Williams-Keeler, L. & McCarrey, M. (1998). PTSD transmission: a review of secondary traumatization in Holocaust survivor families. *Canadian Psychology, 39*, 247–256.

Beiser, M. (1999). *Strangers at the gate: The "boat people's" first ten years in Canada.* Toronto: University of Toronto Press.

Beiser, M., Turner, R. J. & Ganesan, S. (1989). Catastrophic stress and factors affecting its consequences among Southeast Asian refugees. *Social Science and Medicine, 28*, 183–195.

Berry, J. W. (1980). Social and cultural change. In H. Triandis & R. Brislin (eds.), *Handbook of cross-cultural psychology* (pp. 211–279). Boston, MA: Allyn & Bacon.

   (1984). Multicultural policy in Canada: a social psychological analysis. *Canadian Journal of Behavioural Science, 16*, 353–370.

   (1993). Ethnic identity in plural societies. In M. E. Bernal & G. P. Knight (eds.), *Ethnic identity: formation and transmission among Hispanics and other minorities* (pp. 271–296). Albany, NY: State University of New York Press.

(1999). Aboriginal cultural identity. *Canadian Journal of Native Studies*, *19*, 1–36.

(2001). A psychology of immigration. *Journal of Social Issues*, *57*, 615–631.

Berry, J.W. & Annis, R.C. (1974). Acculturative stress: the role of ecology, culture and differentiation. *Journal of Cross-Cultural Psychology*, *5*, 382–406.

Berry, J. W. & Blondel, T. (1982). Psychological adaptation of Vietnamese refugees in Canada. *Canadian Journal of Community Mental Health*, *1*, 81–88.

Berry, J. W. & Kalin, R. (2000). Multicultural policy and social psychology: the Canadian experience. In S. Renshon & J. Duckitt (eds.), *Political psychology: cultural and cross-cultural foundations* (pp. 263–284). London: Macmillan.

Berry, J. W., Kalin, R. & Taylor, D. M. (1977). *Multiculturalism and ethnic attitudes in Canada*. Ottawa: Minister of Supply and Services.

Berry, J. W. & Sam, D. L. (1997). Acculturation and adaptation. In J. W. Berry, M. H. Segall & C. Kağitçibaşi (eds.), *Handbook of cross-cultural psychology*, Vol. III: *Social behavior and applications* (pp. 291–326). Needham Heights, MA: Allyn & Bacon.

(2003). Accuracy in scientific discourse. *Scandinavian Journal of Psychology*, *44*, 65–68.

Berry, J. W., Wintrob, R. M., Sindell, P. S. & Mawhinney, T. A. (1982). Culture change and psychological adaptation. In R. Rath, H. Asthana, D. Sinha & J. B. P. Sinha (eds.), *Diversity and unity in cross-cultural psychology* (pp. 157–170). Lisse: Swets & Zeitlinger.

Bourhis, R. Y., Moïse, L. C., Perreault, S. & Sénécal, S. (1997). Towards an interactive acculturation model: a social psychological approach. *International Journal of Psychology*, *32*, 369–386.

Boyd, M. (1986). Immigrant women in Canada. In R. J. Simon & C. B.Bretnell (eds.), *International migration: the female experience*. Totowa, NJ: Rowman & Allanheld.

Canadian Bureau for International Education (2002). *National report on international students in Canada 2000/01*. Retrieved May 27, 2002, from www.cbie.ca.

Canadian Heritage (2004a). *Multiculturalism*. Retrieved February 25, 2005, from www.pch.gc.ca/progs/multi/reports/ann2002-2003/01_e.cfm.

(2004b). *History of bilingualism in Canada*. Retrieved February 25, 2005, from http://www.pch.gc.ca/progs/lo-ol/biling/hist_e.cfm.

Chandler, M. J. (1994) Adolescent suicide and the loss of personal continuity. In D. Cicchetti & S. Toth (eds.), *Disorders and dysfunctions of the self* (pp. 371–390). Rochester Symposium on Developmental Psychopathology, 5. Rochester, NY: University of Rochester Press.

Chandler, M. J. & Lalonde, C. E. (1998). Cultural continuity as a hedge against suicide in Canada's First Nations. *Transcultural Psychiatry*, *35*, 193–211.

Chandler, M. J., Lalonde, C. E., Sokol, B. & Hallett, D. (2003). *Personal persistence, identity development, and suicide: a study of native and non-native North American adolescents*. Monographs of the Society for Research in Child Development, Vol. 68, no. 2, serial no. 273. Boston, MA: Blackwell.

Chataway, C. J. & Berry, J. W. (1989). Acculturation experiences, appraisal, coping and adaptation: a comparison of Hong Kong Chinese, French, and English students in Canada. *Canadian Journal of Behavioural Science*, *21*, 295–309.

Cheah, C. S. L. & Nelson, L. J. (2004). The role of acculturation in the emerging adulthood of aboriginal college students. *International Journal of Behavioral Development, 28*, 495–507.

Chirkov, V., Ryan, R. M., Kim, Y. & Kaplan, U. (2003). Differentiating autonomy from individualism and independence: a self-determination theory perspective on internalization of cultural orientations and well-being. *Journal of Personality & Social Psychology, 84*, 97–109.

Citizenship and Immigration Canada. (2000). *Forging our legacy: Canadian citizenship and immigration, 1900–1977.* Retrieved February 25, 2005, from www.cic.gc.ca/english/department/legacy/.

(2002). *Statistical overview of the temporary refugee and resident claimant population.* Retrieved February 25, 2005, from www.cic.gc.ca.english/pub/facts2002-temp/facts-temp-3.html.

(2005). *Permanent residents by category, 1980 to 2003.* Retrieved May 25, 2005, from www.cic.gc.ca/english/pub/facts2003/permanent/1.html.

Clément, R. (1980). Ethnicity, contact and communicative competence in a second language. In H. Giles, W. P. Robinson & P. M. Smith (eds.), *Language: social psychological perspectives* (pp. 147–154). Oxford: Pergamon Press.

(1986). Second language proficiency and acculturation: an investigation of the effects of language status and individual characteristics. *Journal of Language and Social Psychology, 5*, 271–290.

Clément, R., Gauthier, R. & Noels, K.A. (1993). Choix langagiers en milieu minoritaire: attitudes et identité concomitantes [Language choices in minority settings: correlated attitudes and identity]. *Revue canadienne des sciences du comportement, 25*, 149–164.

Clément, R. & Noels, K. A. (1992). Towards a situated approach to ethnolinguistic identity: the effects of status on individuals and groups. *Journal of Language & Social Psychology, 11*, 203–232.

Clément, R., Noels, K. A. & Denault, B. (2001). Inter-ethnic contact, identity, and psychological adjustment: the mediating and moderating roles of communication: *Journal of Social Issues, 57*, 559–577.

Costigan, C. L. & Su, T. F. (2004). Orthogonal versus linear models of acculturation among immigrant Chinese Canadians: a comparison of mothers, fathers, and children. *International Journal of Behavioral Development, 28*, 518–527.

Cunningham, C. G. (1991). *The integration of international students on Canadian post-secondary campuses.* CBIE Research, 1. Ottawa, ON: Canadian Bureau for International Education.

Deci, E. L. & Ryan, R. M. (1985). *Intrinsic motivation and self-determination in human behavior.* New York: Plenum Press.

Department of Justice Canada. (1982). *Canadian charter of rights and freedom.* Retrieved February 25, 2005, from http://laws.justice.gc.ca/en/charter.

Dion, K. K. & Dion, K. L. (2001). Gender and cultural adaptation in immigrant families. *Journal of Social Issues, 57*, 511–521.

(2004). Gender, immigrant generation, and ethnocultural identity. *Sex Roles, 50*, 347–355.

Dobson, K. S. (1997). Psychology in Canada: the future is not the past. *Canadian Psychology, 36*, 1–11.

Dompierre, S. & Lavallée, M. (1990). Degré de contact et stress acculturatif dans le processus d'adaptation des réfugiés africains [Degree of contact and acculturative stress in the adaptation process of African refugees]. *International Journal of Psychology, 25*, 417–437.

Donà, G. & Berry, J. W. (1994). Acculturation attitudes and acculturative stress of Central American refugees. *International Journal of Psychology, 29*, 57–70.

Downie, M., Koestner, R., ElGeledi, S. & Cree, K. (2004). The impact of cultural internalization and integration on well-being among tricultural individuals. *Personality and Social Psychology Bulletin, 30*, 305–314.

Durst, D. & Lange, A. (1999). Ups and downs: the social integration of Salvador refugees in Regina. Paper presented at the Immigrants and Immigration SPSSI-Sponsored International Conference, Toronto, ON, August.

Dyal, J. A. & Chan, C. (1985). Stress and distress: a study of Hong Kong Chinese and Euro-Canadian students. *Journal of Cross-Cultural Psychology, 16*, 447–466.

Dyal, J. A. & Dyal, R. Y. (1981). Acculturation, stress and coping: some implications for research and education. *International Journal of Intercultural Relations, 5*, 301–327.

Fantino, A. M. & Colak, A. (2001). Refugee children in Canada: searching for identity. *Child Welfare, 80*, 587–596.

Gardner, R. C. (1985). *Social psychology and second language learning: the role of attitudes and motivation.* London: Edward Arnold.

Gaudet, S. & Clément, R. (2005). Ethnic identity and psychological adjustment among the Fransaskois. *Canadian Journal of Behavioural Science, 37*, 110–122.

Hallowell, A. I. (1945). Sociopsychological aspects of acculturation. In R. Linton (ed.), *The science of man in the world crisis* (pp. 310–332). New York: Columbia University Press.

Heikinheimo, P. S. & Shute, J. C. M. (1986). The adaptation of foreign students: student views and institutional implications. *Journal of College Student Personnel, 27*, 399–406.

Heine, S. J. & Lehman, D. R. (2004). Move the body, change the self: acculturative effects on the self-concept. In M. Schaller & C. Crandall (eds.), *Psychological foundations of culture* (pp. 305–331). Mahwah, NJ: Lawrence Erlbaum Associates.

Hicks, R., Lalonde, R. N. & Pepler, D. (1993). Psychosocial considerations in the mental health of immigrant and refugee children. *Canadian Journal of Community Mental Health, 12*, 71–87.

Hondagneu-Sotelo, P. (1992). Overcoming patriarchal constraints: the reconstruction of gender relations among Mexican immigrant women and men. *Gender & Society, 6*, 393–415.

Honigmann, J. & Honigmann, I. (1968). Peoples under tutelage. In V. Valentine & F. Vallee (eds.), *Eskimo of the Canadian Arctic* (pp. 173–185). Toronto: McClelland and Stewart.

Husni, M., Cernovsky, Z. Z., Koye, N. & Haggarty, J. (2002). Sociodemographic correlates of assimilation of refugees from Kurdistan. *Psychological Reports, 90*, 67–70.

Hyman, I., Vu, N. & Beiser, M. (2000), Post-migration stresses among Southeast Asian refugee youth in Canada: a research note. *Journal of Comparative Family Studies, 31*, 281–293.

Kalin, R. & Berry, J. W. (1982). The social ecology of ethnic attitudes in Canada. *Canadian Journal of Behavioural Science, 14*, 97–109.

(1996). Ethnic and civic self-identity in Canada. *Canadian Ethnic Studies, 27*, 1–15.

Kanno, Y. (2000). Kikokushijo as bi-cultural. *International Journal of Intercultural Relations, 24*, 361–382.

Kealey, D. J. (1989). A study of cross-cultural effectiveness: theoretical issues, practical applications. *International Journal of Intercultural Relations, 13*, 387–428.

Kester, K. & Marshall, S. K. (2003). Intergenerational similitude of ethnic identification and ethnic identity: a brief report on immigrant Chinese mother–adolescent dyads in Canada. *Identity: An International Journal of Theory and Research, 3*, 367–373.

Kral, M. J. (1998). Suicide and the internalization of culture: three questions. *Transcultural Psychiatry, 35*, 221–233.

Kral, M. J., Arnakaq, M., Ekho, N., *et al.* (2000). Suicide in Nunavut: stories from Inuit elders. In J. Oakes, R. Riewe, S. Koolage, L. Simpson & N. Schuster (eds.), *Aboriginal health, identity and resources* (pp. 34–44). Winnipeg, MB: Native Studies Press.

Kral, M. J. & Dyck, R. J. (1995). Public option, private choice: impact of culture on suicide. In B. L. Mishara (ed.), *The impact of suicide*. New York: Springer.

Kunz, E. F. (1973). The refugee in flight: kinetic models and forms of displacement. *International Migration Review, 7*, 125–146.

Kwak, K. & Berry, J. W. (2001). Generational differences in acculturation among Asian families in Canada: a comparison of Vietnamese, Korean, and East-Indian groups. *International Journal of Psychology, 36*, 152–162.

Lalonde, R. N. & Cameron, J. E. (1993). An intergroup perspective on immigrant acculturation with a focus on collective strategies. *International Journal of Psychology, 28*, 57–74.

Lambert, W. E. (1967). A social psychology of bilingualism. *Journal of Social Issues, 23(2)*, 91–110.

(1978). Some cognitive and sociocultural consequences of being bilingual. In J. E. Alatis (ed.), *International dimensions of bilingual education* (pp. 214–229). Washington, DC: Georgetown University Press.

Lambert, W. E. & Taylor, D. M. (1990). *Coping with cultural and racial diversity in urban America*. New York: Praeger Publishers.

Lambert, W. E. & Tucker, R. G. (1972). *Bilingual education of children: the St. Lambert experiment*. Rowley, MA: Newbury House.

Lanca, M., Alksnis, C., Roese, N. J. & Gardner, R. C. (1994). Effects of language choice on acculturation: a study of Portuguese immigrants in a multicultural setting. *Journal of Language & Social Psychology, 13*, 315–330.

Laroche, M., Kim, C. & Hui, M. K. (1997). A comparative investigation of dimensional structures of acculturation for Italian Canadians and Greek Canadians. *Journal of Social Psychology, 137*, 317–331.

Laroche, M., Kim, C., Hui, M. K. & Joy, A. (1996). An empirical study of multidimensional ethnic change: the case of the French Canadians in Québec. *Journal of Cross-Cultural Psychology*, 27, 114–131.

Lasry, J. C. & Sayegh, L. (1992). Developing an acculturation scale: a bidimensional model. In L. Sayegh & P. Migneault (eds.), *Transcultural issues in child psychiatry* (pp. 67–86). Montreal, QC: Editions Douglas.

Lay, C. & Nguyen, T. (1998). The role of acculturation-related and acculturation non-specific daily hassles: Vietnamese-Canadian students and psychological distress. *Canadian Journal of Behavioural Science*, 30, 172–181.

Lee, B. K. & Chen, L. (2000). Cultural communication competence and psychological adjustment: a study of Chinese immigrant children's cross-cultural adaptation in Canada. *Communication Research*, 27, 764–792.

Lee, C. C. & Cochran, L. R. (1988). Migration problems of Chinese women. *Canadian Journal of Counseling*, 22, 202–211.

Leung, C. (2001). The sociocultural and psychological adaptation of Chinese migrant adolescents in Australia and Canada. *International Journal of Psychology*, 36, 8–19.

Leung, C. M. & Berry, J. W. (2001). *Psychological adaptation of international and migrant students in Canada*. Victoria, Australia: authors.

Liebkind, K. (2001). Acculturation. In R. Brown & S. Gaertner (eds.), *Blackwell handbook of social psychology: intergroup processes* (pp. 386–406). Oxford: Blackwell.

Masgoret, A.-M. & Gardner, R.C. (1999). A causal model of Spanish immigrant adaptation in Canada. *Journal of Multilingual and Multicultural Development*, 20, 216–235.

Merali, N. (2002). Perceived versus actual parent–adolescent assimilation disparity among Hispanic refugee families. *International Journal for the Advancement of Counselling*, 24, 57–68.

Moghaddam, F. M. (1988). Individualistic and collective integration strategies among immigrants: toward a mobility model of cultural integration. In J. W. Berry & R. C. Annis (eds.), *Ethnic psychology: research and practice with immigrants, refugees, ethnic groups, and sojourners* (pp. 69–79). Lisse, The Netherlands: Swets & Zeitlinger.

Naidoo, J. (1985). Contemporary South Asian women in the Canadian mosaic. *International Journal of Women's Studies*, 8, 338–350.

Noels, K. A. & Clément, R. (1996). Communicating across cultures: social determinants and acculturative consequences. *Canadian Journal of Behavioural Science*, 28, 214–228.

Noels, K. A., Clément, R. & Gaudet, S. (2004). Language and the situated nature of ethnic identity. In S. H. Ng, C. N. Candlin & C. Y. Chiu (eds.), *Language matters: culture, identity and communication* (pp. 245–266). Hong Kong: City University Press.

Noels, K. A., Pon, G. & Clément, R. (1996). Language, identity, and adjustment: the role of linguistic self-confidence in the acculturation process. *Journal of Language & Social Psychology*, 15, 246–264.

Noh, S., Wu, Z., Speechley, M. & Kaspar, V. (1992). Depression in Korean immigrants in Canada: correlates of gender, work, and marriage. *Journal of Nervous and Mental Disease*, 180, 578–582.

Pak, A. W., Dion, K. K. & Dion, K. L. (1985). Correlates of self-confidence with English among Chinese students in Toronto. *Canadian Journal of Behavioural Science*, *17*, 369–378.

Popadiuk, N. & Arthur, N. (2004). Counselling international students in Canadian schools. *International Journal for the Advancement of Counseling*, *26*, 125–145.

Pratt, G., in collaboration with the Philippine Women Centre (1999). Is this really Canada? Domestic workers' experiences in Vancouver, BC. In J. Momsen (ed.), *Gender, migration and domestic service* (pp. 23–42). New York: Routledge.

Rudmin, F. W. & Ahmadzadeh, V. (2001). Psychometric critique of acculturation psychology: the case of Iranian migrants in Norway. *Scandinavian Journal of Psychology*, *42*, 41–56.

Rule, B. G. & Adair, J. G. (1984). Contributions of psychology as a social science to Canadian society. *Canadian Psychology*, *25*, 52–58.

Ryder, A., Alden, L. & Paulhus, D. (2001). Is acculturation unidimensional or bidimensional? A head-to-head comparison in the prediction of personality, self-identity, and adjustment. *Journal of Personality and Social Psychology*, *79*, 49–65.

Safdar, S. & Lay, C. H. (2003). The relations of immigrant-specific and immigrant-nonspecific daily hassles to distress controlling for psychological adjustment and cultural competence. *Journal of Applied Social Psychology*, *33*, 299–320.

Safdar, S., Lay, C. & Struthers, W. (2003). The process of acculturation and basic goals: testing a multidimensional individual difference acculturation model with Iranian immigrants in Canada. *Applied Psychology: An International Review*, *52*, 555–579.

Sayegh, L. & Lasry, J. C. (1993). Immigrants' adaptation in Canada: assimilation, acculturation, and orthogonal cultural identification. *Canadian Psychology*, *34*, 98–109.

Smith, A., Lalonde, R. N. & Johnson, S. (2004). Serial migration and its implications for the parent–child relationship: a retrospective analysis of the experiences of the children of Caribbean immigrants. *Cultural Diversity and Ethnic Minority Psychology*, *10*, 107–122.

Statistics Canada. (1996). *Census of Canada*. Retrieved July 30, 2002, from http://www12.statcan.ca/english.census01/info/census96.cfm.

Tajfel, H. (1978). Interindividual behaviour and intergroup behaviour. In H. Tajfel (ed.), *Differentiation between social groups: studies in the social psychology of intergroup relations* (pp. 27–60). London: Academic Press.

Tajfel, H. & Turner, J. C. (1986). The social identity theory of intergroup behaviour. In S. Worchel & W. S. Austin (eds.), *Psychology of intergroup relations* (pp. 7–24). Chicago, IL: Nelson.

Tang, T. N. & Dion, K. L. (1999). Gender and acculturation in relation to traditionalism: perceptions of self and parents among Chinese students. *Sex Roles*, *41*, 17–29.

Taylor, D. M. (1997) The quest for collective identity: the plight of disadvantaged ethnic minorities. *Canadian Psychology*, 38, 174–190.

Taylor, D. M. & McKirnan, D. J. (1984). Theoretical contributions: a five-stage model of intergroup relations. *British Journal of Social Psychology*, *23*, 291–300.

Taylor, D. M., Meynard, R. & Rheault, E. (1977). Threat to ethnic identity and second-language learning. In H. Giles (ed.), *Language, ethnicity and intergroup relations* (pp. 99–118). New York: Academic Press.

Taylor, D. M. & Wright, S. C. (2003). Do aboriginal students benefit from education in their heritage language? Results from a ten-year program of research in Nunavik. *Canadian Journal of Native Studies, 23*, 1–24.

Tsang, A. K. T., Irving, H., Alaggia, R., Chau, S. B. Y. & Benjamin, M. (2003). Negotiating ethnic identity in Canada: the case of the "Satellite Children." *Youth & Society, 34*, 359–384.

Vallee, F. G., Schwartz, M. & Darknell, F. (1957). Ethnic-assimilation and differentiation in Canada. *Canadian Journal of Economics & Political Science, 23*, 540–549.

Waters, J. L. (2002). Flexible families? "Astronaut" households and the experiences of lone mothers in Vancouver, British Columbia. *Social & Cultural Geography, 3*, 117–134.

   (2003). Flexible citizens? Transnationalism and citizenship amongst economic immigrants in Vancouver. *Canadian Geographer, 47*, 219–234.

Westhues, A. & Cohen, J. S. (1998). The adjustment of intercountry adoptees in Canada. *Children and Youth Services Review, 20*, 115–134.

Williams, C. L. & Berry, J. W. (1991). Primary prevention of acculturative stress among refugees: application of psychological theory and practice. *American Psychologist, 46*, 632–641.

Winter, K. A. & Young, M. Y. (1998). Biopsychosocial considerations in refugee mental health. In S. Kazarian & D. R. Evans (eds.), *Cultural clinical psychology* (pp. 348–376). New York: Oxford University Press.

Wittebrood, G. & Robertson, S. (1991). Canadian immigrant women in transition. *Canadian Journal of Counselling, 25*, 170–182.

Wong, S. K. (1997). Delinquency of Chinese-Canadian youth: a test of opportunity, control and intergeneration conflict theories. *Youth and Society, 29*, 112–133.

Wright, S. C. & Taylor, D. M. (1995). Identity and the language of the classroom: investigating the impact of heritage versus second language instruction on personal and collective self-esteem. *Journal of Educational Psychology, 87*, 241–252.

Wright, S. C., Taylor, D. M. & MacArthur, J. (2000). Subtractive bilingualism and the survival of the Inuit language: heritage versus second language education. *Journal of Educational Psychology, 92*, 63–84.

Young, M. Y. (2000). Psychological consequences of torture: clinical needs of refugee women In S. Okpaku (ed.), *Clinical methods in transcultural psychiatry* (pp. 391–411). Washington, DC: American Psychiatric Press.

Young, M. Y. & Evans, D. R. (1997). The well-being of Salvadoran refugees. *International Journal of Psychology, 32*, 289–300.

Young, M. Y. & Gardner, R. C. (1990). Modes of acculturation and second language proficiency. *Canadian Journal of Behavioural Science, 22*, 59–71.

Zheng, X. & Berry, J. W. (1991). Psychological adaptation of Chinese sojourners in Canada. *International Journal of Psychology, 26*, 451–470.

18 Acculturation in Israel

Gabriel Horenczyk & Uzi Ben-Shalom

18.1 Introduction

Acculturation psychology is becoming increasingly contextual. Dealing specifically with the acculturation of immigrants, Phinney, Horenczyk, Liebkind & Vedder (2001) suggest that "ethnic and national identities and their role in adaptation can best be understood in terms of an interaction between the attitudes and characteristics of immigrants and the responses of the receiving societies, moderated by the particular circumstances of the immigrant group within the new society" (p. 494). The acculturation process is seen as not taking place in a social vacuum; rather, as consisting of intricate communicational transactions in which acculturating groups and individuals try to make sense of what they expect and is expected of them within the context(s) of the larger society (Horenczyk, 1996).

Israel seems to offer a unique laboratory for the examination and application of such a contextual approach, including as it does national non-Jewish minorities striving to find their place in a country which defines itself as "Jewish and democratic," immigrants undergoing acculturation processes within a society with a strong assimilationist history gradually adopting more multicultural policies, and "foreign workers" deprived of legal and social status. In short, Israel is a complex context for numerous groups of newcomers and members of minority groups who are continuously engaged in processes of identity definition and re-definition within the framework of a fragmented and conflicted society heavily laden with ideological and political forces.

This chapter will portray the complex and often conflictual nature of acculturation in Israel. After a brief delineation of the social, political and ideological context of acculturation, we will summarize the research literature dealing with patterns of acculturation and adaptation of various minority and immigrant groups.[1] Following our interactional and contextual approach, we will then review studies that examine the attitudes of the dominant/ host population

---

[1] The choice of acculturating groups to be presented, from among the large number of minority groups, will inevitably be selective. The information on aspects of acculturation and adaptation provided on each of the groups will also be limited due to space constraints and the availability of relevant data.

towards the various acculturating groups. Our last section will bring us back to the "uniqueness" of the Israeli context, focusing on the role of Jewishness and Jewish identity in the acculturation process.

18.2 The acculturative context

The acculturation game requires at least two players – a dominant or majority group and an acculturating or minority group (Berry, 1990). In contemporary Israel, it is sometimes hard to identify the dominant majority society, and it often seems that a group can play the dominant role in one context and the minority role in another. The conflictive social–cultural structure of Israeli society has been described by Tatar (2004) in terms of four – partially overlapping – divisions: (1) a national division between Jewish and non-Jewish citizens; (2) ethnic divisions within the Jewish and non-Jewish populations; (3) socio-political-cultural divisions based on the degree of religiosity; and (4) political divisions within the Jewish and non-Jewish populations, primarily with regards to the resolution of the Israeli–Palestinian conflict.

The resulting map is not one of concentric circles with a central core; rather, it looks more like a complex tapestry with vague demarcation lines. Kimmerling (2004) announced the slow end of "hegemony" in Israel, the gradual collapse of the united, uniform and powerful social "center." He sees Israeli society today as an aggregate of cultures and counter-cultures with varying degrees of autonomy and separate institutional development within a common framework.

There are, nevertheless, still a number of ideological forces that strongly shape the Israeli acculturative context. These are clearly reflected in the widely accepted, albeit problematic, self-definition of the Israeli state as "Jewish and democratic." This formula specifies, to a large extent, the acculturative constraints in respect to non-Jewish minority groups, primarily Arabs. It has been widely interpreted as granting the Jews collective rights as a national group, whereas non-Jews enjoy individual rights as citizens. At the legal and political levels, the Israeli ideological context is best epitomized by the Law of Return, adopted in 1950 after the establishment of the State, according to which "every Jew has the right to come to this country as an *oleh* [immigrant, literally one that ascends]." An amendment specified that "for the purposes of this Law, 'Jew' means a person who was born of a Jewish mother or has been converted to Judaism and who is not a member of another religion." This delicate combination of *jus sanguinis* (ethnic) together with religious criteria delineates a division between those acculturating groups and individuals who are considered members of the larger "imagined community" (Anderson, 1991) and those who are not.

18.3   Acculturating groups – Arab minorities

Arabs living in Israel see themselves as its inhabitants through the ages: they trace their roots in this area to the seventh century (Kimmerling, 2004). But the establishment of the Israeli State, and the subsequent large waves of Jewish immigration, transformed the Arab population from a majority into a numerical and political minority. Approximately 1 million Palestinian Arabs constitute 19 percent of the Israeli population. Their changing acculturation patterns vis-à-vis the Jewish Israeli majority have been influenced by developments in the Israeli–Palestinian conflict; by cultural, political and religious changes in the Arab and Muslim world; and by economic, demographic and cultural processes within both the Jewish and Arab societies in Israel (Amara & Schnell, 2004).

Suleiman (2002a & b) outlined several models for analyzing the identity of Palestinian Arab citizens of Israel. The *bipolar* model (Tessler, 1977) sees the national (Palestinian) and civic (Israeli) identities as contradictory because of the Palestinian–Israeli conflict. Identification with one side of the conflict necessarily negates and precludes identification with the other. Consistent with this model, Suleiman (2002b) showed – using Multidimensional Scaling techniques – that Palestinians perceive the national and civic categories as diametrically opposed in their identity space.

The *integration* model rests on an assumption of orthogonality (Zak, 1976): the Israeli and Palestinian components are perceived as independent, allowing for synthesis between the two identities. Smooha (1992) claims that the Palestinian Arabs in Israel are experiencing two parallel processes: "Palestinization" and "Israelization." The result is a "new Arab," largely bilingual and bicultural: one who successfully integrates the Palestinian and Israeli components of collective identity. He or she feels solidarity with the Palestinian people and at the same time loyalty to the state of Israel. A similar conclusion was reached by Amara and Schnell (2004) who suggest that Arabs in Israel feel strongly attached to various collective identities, in such a way that none of them dominates the others. Each identity relates to a different context of meaning, and plays a different role in their identity repertoire.

An alternative model was put forward by Rouhana (1997). His *accentuated identity* model suggests that the only internalized identity is the national Palestinian one, whereas the civic Israeli identity is secondary and exists only in the formal and legal sense.

The *double marginality* model (Suleiman, 2002b) attempts to reconcile the previous conceptualizations. It posits that Palestinian Arabs in Israel are undergoing a process of "marginalization," as a result of being a group peripheral to both the Jewish-Israeli society and Palestinians residing outside the state of Israel (Al-Haj, 1993). This double marginality (for a similar notion – "trapped minority" – see Rabinowitz, 2001) "enables them to define their identity in national (Palestinian) terms – and to some extent in civic 'Israeli' terms – without the need to commit themselves to either one of the two referent groups. It also enables them to tolerate the friction between the two identities and even to integrate them, despite the fact that they perceive them as contradictory and conflictual" (Suleiman, 2002a, p. 41).

18.3.1   A minority within a minority: Christian Arabs

Palestinian Christians in Israel have been described as "a double minority: Arabs in the midst of the majority Jewish population of Israel, Christians within Israel's dominant Muslim Arab society" (Rossing, 1999:28). According to recent figures (*Statistical Abstract of Israel*, 2003), the Palestinian Christians constitute approximately 1.72 percent of the total population in Israel, and 7.45 percent of the non-Jewish population.

A recent study (Horenczyk & Munayer, submitted) examined acculturation orientations of Palestinian Christian Arabs within this complex Israeli context. Acculturation attitudes and perceived acculturation expectations were measured vis-à-vis the two majority groups: Israeli Jews and Israeli Muslim Arabs. The findings suggest that Palestinian Arab Christians in Israel wish to maintain their ingroup identity; however, they expressed more willingness to adopt elements of the Jewish society, as compared to those of Muslim Arab society. They also feel stronger assimilation pressures coming from Israeli Jews. These results were explained primarily in terms of differences between the two majority groups in their control over valuable resources. The intricate patterns of Israeli Palestinian Christians' cultural allegiances emerged also from Identity Structure Analysis (Weinreich, 1989): the various components of their identity – ethnicity, nationality and religion – seem to play different roles in the complex acculturative processes (Horenczyk & Munayer, 2003).

The problematic nature of this acculturative context seems also to impinge on the Palestinian identity of Christian Arabs in Israel. In Amara and Schnell's (2004) study, Christian Arabs were largely split between those who consider their Palestinian identity as highly relevant and those who see it as unimportant. It would seem that the former tend to view the Palestinian category as one that can unite Muslims and Christians, whereas the latter tend to differentiate themselves from the Palestinian Muslim majority.

18.3.2   A minority outside a minority: Israeli Druze

Another ethno-religious group exposed to various – mostly conflicting – acculturative forces is the Druze minority in Israel. The Druze are a religious group that split from mainstream Islam during the tenth and eleventh centuries. They live mainly in the Middle East and are concentrated in four countries: Syria, Lebanon, Israel and Jordan. Although in all other countries considered by others and themselves to be Arabs, in Israel – due to political and historical circumstances (Firro, 1999) – the approximately 100,000 Druze are generally seen as a separate national group. They speak Arabic and live in villages in the north of the country, constituting an almost independent social, cultural and religious community.

In Halabi's (2003) study, Druze university students report that they live within three main spheres of identity: Druze identity, which for most is a religious identity, and is the most important and stable one; Arab identity, which is a national identity, although most see it primarily as a cultural one; and Israeli identity, which is mainly a civic identity. Palestinian identity emerged in the background and on the margins, as a relatively empty sphere of affiliation (for similar findings reporting a widespread rejection of Palestinian identity by Israeli Druze, see Amara & Schnell, 2004).

The Druze established alliances with the Jews prior to the foundation of the State of Israel; nowadays, the vast majority of Druze men serve in the Israeli army, unlike most other Arab citizens. This has led to a generally hostile attitude among other Arabs towards the Israeli Druze. But, according to Halabi's (2003) interviewees, Israel has made little effort to integrate the Druze fully as equal partners in its society. The result is a conflictual and frustrating acculturative situation marked by feelings of "double rejection," by both Arabs and Jews.

18.4   Acculturating groups – immigrants

Between the establishment of the State (in 1948) and 2002, approximately 3 million immigrants arrived in Israel, multiplying its Jewish population almost eight times. This is clear evidence that practically the whole Israeli population is "acculturating." Two massive waves of immigration drastically affected the makeup of Israeli society. Almost 700,000 newcomers from Europe, Asia and Africa arrived during the 1950s and settled with tremendous economic and social difficulties (Lissak, 1999). The second wave took place after the collapse of the Soviet Union: over a million immigrants have arrived in Israel since 1989. During this same period, almost the entire Ethiopian Jewish community also moved to Israel. Our analysis below will focus on these two main groups of recent immigrants.

18.4.1   Immigrants from the former Soviet Union

Immigrants who arrived from the Former Soviet Union (FSU) since 1989 constitute approximately 15 percent of the Israeli population. The acculturative orientation of this group is a hotly debated issue, in both the academic and public spheres. As noted by Al-Haj (2002), some researchers emphasize the immigrants' efforts to preserve their "cultural uniqueness" within a "Russian bubble" (Kimmerling, 1998). According to this view, they strive to create a "cultural enclave" (Lissak, 1995), one that includes "Russian" cultural organizations, Russian-language media, and community organizations.

But this pattern of cultural affiliation does not necessarily imply separation from the majority society. Horowitz and Leshem (1998), summarizing numerous studies conducted during the first decade of the migration wave from the FSU, suggest that this group is neither assimilating into the host society nor distancing itself from it. Rather, these newcomers seem to fit an "integration" model: they are engaged in the creation of a new community within a changing Israeli society, strengthening its pluralization processes.

Recent data support these claims about the bicultural orientation of FSU immigrants. In a survey (Adler, 2004), adult newcomers were asked about the extent to which they feel Israeli or "members of their group of origin." More than 65 percent chose a bicultural option, whereas the monocultural responses (Israeli or "member of my group of origin") were selected by only 31 percent of the respondents. A study that followed FSU immigrants during the first five years after their arrival reports that the newcomers tend to socialize primarily within their fellow immigrants, but the frequency of interactions with Israeli nationals increases with time. They consider it important to preserve their culture of origin, but they also attach great importance to their involvement in Israeli society (Rosenbaum-Tamari & Damian, 2004))

Two studies have examined acculturation orientations among adolescent immigrants from the FSU in Israel. In their study of students residing in boarding schools for immigrant youngsters, Ben-Shalom and Horenczyk (2000) found a clear preference for the bicultural orientation; *integration* scores were significantly higher than those on the *separation* scale. A similar pattern emerges from the responses of the FSU immigrants within the Israeli sample of the ICSEY study (Horenczyk, 2003): Integration was the most strongly endorsed attitude, followed by Separation and Assimilation; while Marginalization was largely rejected by the newcomers. Length of stay in Israel was uncorrelated with the various acculturation strategies. As to the Separation orientation, this finding is rather surprising, since we would expect such an attitude to weaken over time. It would seem that not only the larger society, but also minority groups, are capable of providing the resources for the maintenance of mono-cultural approaches among immigrants.

In sum, most research evidence conveys a largely bicultural (integrationist) image of Israeli immigrants from the FSU. How can this image be reconciled with the public perception of this immigrant group as markedly separatist? We would like to suggest that the discrepancies are largely based on conceptual grounds with strong ideological roots. Although Israeli society is gradually relinquishing its assimilationist rhetoric in favor of more pluralistic views (Horenczyk & Ben-Shalom, 2001), the unidimensional approach to acculturation (Sayegh & Lasry, 1993) still prevails in much of Israeli public and academic discourse (Horenczyk & Tatar, 2002). When every sign of "cultural retention" is interpreted as rejection of the host culture, FSU immigration is inevitably perceived as "separatist." However, adopting a bidimensional approach to immigration allows for a different discourse and for different research findings: when biculturalism is rhetorically and methodologically available, it becomes clear that this option is strongly endorsed by these immigrants.

The discrepancy can also be attributed to the inherent vagueness of the "integration" attitude. Horenczyk (1996) suggested that the rhetoric of integration might not have the same meaning for the majority and minority groups participating in the acculturation process. Integration involves the maintenance of original culture and the adoption of the host culture, both to a certain degree. It might be the case that the extent of adoption of host culture deemed sufficient by immigrants in order to perceive themselves as "biculturals" is not considered satisfactory by members of the host society.

Many studies have examined the psychological adjustment among immigrants from the FSU. Mirsky (1998) reviewed a decade of psychiatric research which compared psychological distress of newcomers and long-term Israeli nationals. She indicates that the evidence consistently shows relatively high levels of psychological distress among FSU immigrants. More recent studies seem to support her conclusion: newcomers from the FSU report more somatic distress (Ritsner, Ponizovsky, Kurs & Modai, 2000), show more suicide ideation (Ponizovsky & Ritsner, 1999), report higher levels of experienced loneliness (Ponizovsky & Ritsner, 2004), and score higher on general measures of psychological distress (Mirsky, Baron-Draiman & Kedem, 2002), as compared to the general Israeli population. Along similar lines, Ullman and Tatar (2001) reported that – as compared to their Israeli-born classmates – immigrant adolescents express less satisfaction with their lives and show less congruence between their self-concept and the ways in which, in their opinion, they are perceived by others.

Current mental health research is paying increasing attention to risk and resilience factors that moderate the effects of stressors (like those involved in the immigration and acculturation processes) on psychological adjustment. Israeli studies on immigrants from the FSU have examined some of these factors (Mirsky, 1998): higher educational levels were found to be correlated with better adaptation; unemployment emerges as a serious risk factor among the working-age group; physical health seems to contribute to positive adjustment; stressful life events during the transition process add to the acculturation pressures; unmarried immigrants report higher levels of distress; and social support – from both outgroup and ingroup members – promotes improved coping with the hardships of immigration.

Are acculturation orientations related to adaptation among Israeli immigrants from the FSU? Research evidence provides a positive answer to the question, although the exact patterns of relationships vary among studies. In line with the general findings of the acculturation literature (Berry, 1998), many studies found the integrationist/ bicultural orientation to be positively related to adaptation. Among Jewish sojourner youth from the FSU, lower degrees of separation and higher levels of integration were positively linked with measures of sociocultural adaptation, such as a wish to remain in Israel, acceptance by Israelis, and counselors' ratings of student adjustment (Eshel & Rosenthal-Sokolov, 2000). In a study conducted among a representative sample of the adult population of FSU immigrants, both the Israeli and the "immigrant from the FSU" identities were positively related to aspects of social adaptation (Al-Haj & Leshem, 2000).

Other studies show a different pattern of relationship between acculturation orientations and adjustment. Israeli findings from the ICSEY cross-national study (Horenczyk, 2003), for example, showed only the national (Israeli) identity to be related to psychological and sociocultural adaptation, whereas the ethnic (minority) identity was not correlated with adjustment measures. A similar pattern was found among FSU immigrants in the Israeli army – a highly assimilative context (Ben-Shalom & Horenczyk, 2004): bicultural individuals did not report higher levels of adaptation, as compared to assimilative immigrants, whereas newcomers holding to the Separation and Marginalization orientations exhibited relatively low levels of adaptation. These findings emphasize the need for careful contextual analyses, in each of the studies, of the specific intra-group and inter-group conditions within which the acculturation processes take place. Such an "interactional" (Phinney et al., 2001) or "ecological" (Birman, Trickett & Vinokurov, 2002) approach suggests that different contexts call for different orientations among newcomers, and also moderate the relationships between acculturation orientations and adjustment.

18.4.2 Ethiopian immigrants

Almost the entire Jewish Ethiopian population emigrated to Israel in two waves: "Operation Moses" (1984–5) and "Operation Solomon" (1991). Relative to the total Israeli population, the Ethiopian newcomers and their offspring constitute a small immigrant group: less than 75,000 people, they make up 5 percent of the total number of immigrants who settled in the country during the 1980s and 1990s. Ethiopian immigrants, however, exhibit unique patterns of acculturation due to their traumatic geographical and cultural transition as well as to their distinctive characteristics.

The painful journeys that were part of their transition to Israel constitute a central component of the group's narrative and identity. First, they became refugees and were forced to escape their native homeland via hostile desert paths, often by foot, where children and elders died of starvation and fatigue, and robbery and rape were common. After their arrival in Israel, the authenticity of their Jewishness was questioned by Israeli authorities, despite their strong commitment to the Jewish faith, and most of the immigrants had to undergo certain procedures of ritual conversion. Culture shock was almost inevitable due to the sharp contrast between the immigrants' largely religious, patriarchal and rural tradition and life style, and the Israeli primarily secular, modern and urban culture. One result of this cultural clash is the unique pattern of mental illness and psychopathology exhibited by many Ethiopian immigrants (Grisaru, Irwin & Kaplan, 2003).

In addition to their distinctive language and culture, what differentiated this group from other immigrants and from the rest of Israeli population is their black African ancestry. As reported by Shabtay (2001), whereas the first generation of Ethiopian youth in Israel did not experience an identity crisis, in the second generation identity appears to be constructed more strongly on the basis of color than of the Jewish religion.

Israeli findings from the ICSEY study (Horenczyk, 2003) show a similar pattern of acculturation orientations among immigrant youth from Ethiopia and from the FSU: Integration was most strongly endorsed by both groups, followed by Separation, Assimilation and Marginalization. Using a different methodology, Orr, Mana and Mana (2002) compared the structure and strength of adaptation strategies (similar to Berry's, 1990, acculturation orientations) in Israeli immigrants from Ethiopia and from the FSU. Among both groups, the Extended Identity pattern (akin to Berry's Integration) was the most strongly endorsed. However, Secluded Identity (which resembles the Separation orientation) was lower among the Ethiopian respondents, as compared to FSU immigrants.

The vagueness of the Integration rhetoric mentioned above calls for an in-depth examination of cultural identity among the Ethiopian immigrants, a group acculturating within a unique and highly problematic context. Based on qualitative interviews with young Ethiopian Israelis, Ben-Eliezer (2004) suggests that the second generation of Ethiopian immigrants in Israel is engaged in a new construction of their group identity, to a type previously unknown – a hybrid identity that meshes Israeliness, Jewishness and Blackness.

In spite of their wish to become an integral part of Israeli society, the acculturation of Ethiopian Jews is still in its first, and highly problematic, phase. Employment rates, as well as percentages of students passing matriculation exams and of students attending universities, are significantly lower among this group in comparison to the Israeli population at large. As a group, their acculturative state can be described as largely separated, with the immigrants socially and culturally isolated within their own communities. The experience of many of these immigrants is essentially one of painful disillusion, resulting from an inability to become part of the majority group coupled with alienation and bewilderment (Shabtay, 1999).

18.5   An invisible minority group – foreign workers

Since the late 1980s, a steady flow of "foreign workers" (the Israeli term for "labor migrants") has gradually taken the place of Palestinian workers in the Israeli economy. Estimates of the number of foreign workers in Israel range between 200,000 and 300,000; they constitute almost 5 percent of the entire population and about 10 percent of the Israeli labor force. Approximately 65 percent of them are believed to have an illegal resident status (Ellman & Laccher, 2003).

Although foreign workers have become an integral part of the economy, they are placed at the bottom of the labor market and the social order (Raijman, Schammah-Gesser & Kemp, 2003). Foreign workers are employed in low-paid sectors, such as construction, agriculture and nursing. Although they take on jobs that few Israelis want, foreign workers are largely perceived by Israelis as posing a threat to their economic interests (Semyonov, Raijman & Yom-Tov, 2002). Many foreign workers are de facto permanent residents in Israel; however, they are generally excluded from the welfare and benefit system accorded to Israeli citizens. Most of their ethnic communities occupy distinct, often neglected, neighborhoods in the large cities (Amir, 2002).

It is important to note that academic interest in issues of identity and acculturation of foreign workers in Israel is very limited, almost non-existent. An interesting exception is the study by Roer-Strier and Olshtain-Mann (1999) on Latin American workers. When asked about their sense of well-being, 90 percent of the interviewees gave positive responses, and 85 percent provided positive reports concerning their friends and family members. However, the study portrays a non-acculturating minority group – remaining at the borders of Israeli society, not trying to get in, and only wishing not to be thrown out. The study, which compares foreign workers in Jerusalem and Tel Aviv, reveals "unique ecological conditions," such as the interplay among Jewish, Arab Muslim and Christian ecological niches which strongly influence community formation.

The paucity of studies on this minority group is somewhat surprising, considering its unique features and their challenging adaptation struggles. The minimal research interest in foreign workers may reflect the indifference of authorities and funding agencies towards Israeli (supposedly) temporary labor migrants. In fact, they can be described as "invisible" (Roer-Strier & Olshtain-Mann, 1999), not only as residents but as individuals with legitimate social, cultural and psychological needs.

18.6   Back to the uniqueness argument

The uniqueness of Israel as an acculturation context has been attributed to various factors: the cultural pluralism of Israeli society, with its numerous immigrant and minority groups; conflicts between cultural, national and ethnic groups which sharpen divisions and foster occasional alliances between groups against a "common enemy"; and the ideological basis of the State of Israel, with its central – albeit problematic – Jewish self-identification.

18.6.1 Attitudes towards acculturating groups

A central premise of a contextual approach to acculturation is that the attitudes of the host/majority society towards the members of acculturating groups have a powerful effect on the latter's acculturation orientations and on their levels of adaptation. An understanding of such influences has to take into account variations within the majority society in the content, direction and intensity of these attitudes. Moreover, it is important to distinguish between different levels at which the attitudes are expressed: the rhetorical/ideological and the level of behavioral intentions (Horenczyk, 1997). Such a detailed analysis of majority attitudes towards the numerous acculturating groups in Israel is beyond the scope of this chapter. We will limit ourselves only to a brief summary of the research on the attitudes held by the wider Israeli society towards the Arab minority and Jewish immigrants.

Research has documented negative stereotypes of, and prejudice against, Arabs in general and Israeli Arabs in particular, among Israeli Jewish adolescents (Tatar, 2004). Members of the Israeli majority group show very little tolerance for the legitimization of the democratic rights of the Arab minority (Ichilov, Bar-Tal & Mazawi, 1989). Abu-Nimer (1999), in a comprehensive review, reported that over half of Israeli Jewish adolescents believe that Arabs do not deserve full and equal civic rights and that most of the Arabs are not loyal to the state. Suleiman (2002b) showed that Israeli Jewish university students perceive the national (Arab) and civic (Israeli) identities of the Palestinian minority as conflictual.

The attitudes of the Israeli host society towards immigration and immigrants are markedly different from those held towards the Palestinian Arab minority. Many studies reported an overall favorable approach among veteran Israelis towards new immigrants, but they also point to marked sub-group differences in these host attitudes (Horowitz & Leshem, 1998; Isralowitz & Abu-Saad, 1992). As to the ways in which the immigrants perceive the attitudes of majority members, the evidence is inconclusive: some studies (e.g., Al-Haj & Leshem, 2000) report that FSU immigrants attribute negative attitudes to the host society, whereas according to other studies, the immigrants express relatively high levels of satisfaction with the attitudes of members of the host society (Adler, 2004).

According to Bourhis and Dayan (2004), the State of Israel can be characterized as having an assimilationist policy towards "valued" Jewish immigrants and a somewhat ethnist one towards its "devalued" national minority. The Israeli assimilationist policies towards its Jewish immigrants have been widely documented (Horowitz & Leshem, 1998; Kimmerling, 2004). This is explicit in the very name given to the ministry in charge of immigration ("Ministry of Immigration Absorption"). As indicated earlier, assimilationist pressures and rhetoric are gradually weakening and giving way to more multiculturalist norms and policies. Horenczyk (1996) reported that the Integration mode is generally regarded by members of the host community as the preferred acculturation attitude for immigrants. Similarly, the Israeli Jewish university students in Bourhis and Dayan's (2004) study mainly endorsed the Integrationism and Individualism acculturation orientations towards Jewish immigrants, but they were more segregationist and exclusionist towards Israeli Arabs.

This process of "pluralization" seems to be much slower within the educational system. Horenczyk and Tatar (2002) found that Israeli teachers endorsed pluralistic attitudes when referring to the integration of FSU immigrants into the general society, but assimilationist attitudes were more predominant when related to the approach towards immigrants in educational contexts. The teachers seem to view education as the primary means for transforming the immigrant into an "Israeli," and they see the school as the most appropriate setting for attaining this goal. In a study conducted among Israeli educational counselors, Tatar (1998) classified three-quarters of his respondents as "assimilationist" and the remaining one-quarter as "cultural pluralist."

Our brief analysis points to some disparities between the acculturation attitudes held by members of the majority society and those of the various acculturating groups. It would seem, for example, that Palestinian Arabs tend to adopt a bicultural (integrationist) attitude vis-à-vis the Jewish majority, whereas the majority holds a rather segregative attitude towards them. According to the Interactive Acculturation Model (IAM) (Bourhis, Moïse, Perreault & Sénécal, 1997), the relational outcomes of such divergences are likely to be "conflictual" or "problematic." The model further suggests that conflictual outcomes need not be the result of majority–minority disparities in acculturation orientations: when the host community holds policies and attitudes of Exclusion (as seems to be the case with the foreign workers in Israel), all relational outcomes will tend to be conflictual, irrespective of the attitudes held by the minority group. A study by Roccas, Horenczyk and Schwartz (2000) showed the negative effects of acculturation disparities. Their immigrant respondents believed that Israelis want them to relinquish their distinctive identity and to assimilate more than they themselves wish to do. Perceived pressure to assimilate correlated negatively with life satisfaction, but only among those who scored high on the conformity value.

18.6.2 Jewishness and Jewish identity

As noted above, the self-definition of Israel as a "Jewish and democratic" state seems to define a very unique and problematic context for many acculturating groups. Although very little research has explored this aspect of the acculturation context, some studies provide evidence on the role played by Jewish identity in the patterns of immigrants' attitudes and adjustment. Within this context, Jewish identity refers to (i) the self-definition of the person as a member of the Jewish people, and (ii) the extent of the individual's attachment to his or her Jewishness (Jewish religion, culture, nationality or peoplehood).

A few studies compared the acculturation of Jewish and non-Jewish immigrants. Non-Jewish immigrants from the FSU tend to report stronger minority identities, and to express more willingness to leave Israel in the future, as compared to Jewish immigrants (Chaskin, 1999).

Within the Jewish group, the strength of Jewish identity seems to contribute to better adjustment among the immigrants. Epstein and Levin (1996) report that FSU immigrants with low Jewish identity express more distress and less satisfaction with life than newcomers with strong Jewish identity. Horenczyk and Ben-Shalom (2001) measured the strength of three cultural identities among FSU immigrants in Israel – the minority identity, the Israeli identity and the Jewish identity. In line with their "identity accumulation hypothesis," the findings showed that the higher the number of positive cultural identities the better the psychological and sociocultural adaptation. It would seem that Jewishness and Jewish identity can contribute valuable resources (social, normative, spiritual, etc.) to the acculturating individual, thus promoting his or her adaptation to the new society.

18.6.3 Uniqueness – a divergent voice

In this chapter we have attempted to describe the complex and rapidly changing nature of the Israeli acculturative context. For years, not only policy makers but also social scientists in Israel have emphasized the uniqueness of this context. But some diverging voices have recently started to challenge this view. Shuval (1998) critically reviewed aspects of Israeli immigration and concluded that:

> It appears that Israel is becoming more like other societies to which there is large-scale immigration ... Every society has its unique cultural qualities but also shares many characteristics with other societies in which parallel social processes are taking place. The mythology of Israel's "uniqueness" in the field of migration no longer seems appropriate ... It is clear that many elements of the mythology were socially constructed.   (p. 18)

18.7 References

Abu-Nimer, M. (1999). *Dialogue, conflict resolution, and change: Arab–Jewish encounters in Israel*. New York: SUNY Press.

Adler, S. (2004). *Comparative attitude survey – immigrants from the FSU and nationals*. Jerusalem: Ministry of Immigration Absorption.

Al-Haj, M. (1993). The impact of the Intifada on Arabs in Israel: the case of the double periphery. In A. Cohen & G. Wolfsfeld (eds.), *Framing the Intifada, media and people* (pp. 64–75). Norwood, NJ: Ablex.

(2002). Identity patterns among immigrants from the Former Soviet Union in Israel: assimilation vs. ethnic formation. *International Migration, 40*, 49–70.

Al-Haj, M. & Leshem, E. (2000). *Immigrants from the former Soviet Union in Israel: ten years later*. Haifa: The Center for Multiculturalism and Educational Research, University of Haifa.

Amara, M. & Schnell, I. (2004). Identity repertoires among Arabs in Israel. *Journal of Ethnic and Migration Studies, 30*, 175–193.

Amir, S. (2002). Overseas foreign workers in Israel: policy, aims and labor market. *International Migration Review, 36*, 41–57.

Anderson, B. (1991). *Imagined communities*. London: Verso.

Ben-Eliezer, U. (2004). Becoming a Black Jew: cultural racism and anti-racism in contemporary Israel. *Social Identities, 10*, 245–266.

Ben-Shalom, U. & Horenczyk, G. (2000). Cultural identity and adaptation among immigrant adolescents participating in the "Na'aleh 16" project. *Megamot, 40*, 199–217. (In Hebrew.)

(2004). Identity and adaptation in an assimilative setting: immigrant soldiers from the former Soviet Union in Israel. *International Journal of Intercultural Relations, 28*, 461–479.

Berry, J. W. (1990). Psychology of acculturation: understanding individuals moving between cultures. In R. W. Brislin (ed.), *Applied cross-cultural psychology* (pp. 232–253). Newbury Park, CA: Sage Publications.

(1998). Acculturation and health: theory and research. In S. S. Kazarian & D. R. Evans (eds.), *Cultural clinical psychology: theory, research and practice* (pp. 39–57). New York: Oxford University Press.

Birman, D., Trickett, E. J. & Vinokurov, A. (2002). Acculturation and adaptation of Soviet Jewish refugee adolescents: predictors of adjustment across life domains. *American Journal of Community Psychology, 30*, 585–607.

Bourhis, R. Y. & Dayan, J. (2004). Acculturation orientations toward Israeli Arabs and Jewish immigrants in Israel. *International Journal of Psychology, 39*, 118–131.

Bourhis, R. Y., Moïse, L. C., Perreault, S. & Sénécal, S. (1997). Towards an interactive acculturation model: a social psychological approach. *International Journal of Psychology, 32*, 369–386.

Chaskin, A. (1999). Adaptation and identity of immigrants from the CIS, registered as non-Jewish, as compared to immigrants registered as Jewish. Unpublished MA thesis, The Hebrew University of Jerusalem.

Ellman, M. & Laccher, S. (2003). *Migrant worker in Israel: a contemporary work of slavery*. Copenhagen: Euro-Mediterranean Human Rights Network.

Epstein, A. & Levin, R. (1996). The impact of Jewish identity on the psychological adjustment of Soviet Jewish immigrants to Israel. *Israel Journal of Psychiatry and Related Sciences, 33*, 21–31.

Eshel, Y. & Rosenthal-Sokolov, M. (2000). Acculturation attitudes and sociocultural adjustment of sojourner youth in Israel. *Journal of Social Psychology, 140*, 677–691.

Firro, K. (1999). *The Druzes in the Jewish state*. Leiden: Brill.

Grisaru, N., Irwin, M. & Kaplan, Z. (2003). Acute psychotic episodes as a reaction to severe trauma in a population of Ethiopian immigrants to Israel. *Stress and Health, 19*, 241–247.

Halabi, R. (2003). Socio-psychological aspects of Druze identity in Israel. Unpublished doctoral dissertation, The Hebrew University of Jerusalem.

Horenczyk, G. (1996). Migrating selves in conflict. In G. Breakwell & E. Lyons (eds.), *Changing European identities* (pp. 241–250). Oxford: Butterworth Heinemann.

(1997). Immigrants' perceptions of host attitudes and their reconstruction of cultural groups: comments on "Immigration, acculturation, and adaptation" (by John W. Berry). *Applied Psychology: An International Review*, 46, 34–38.

(2003). The benefits of multiple identities: implications from studies on cultural identity and adaptation. In E. Leshem & D. Roer-Strier (eds.), *Cultural diversity: a challenge to human services* (pp. 127–138). Jerusalem: Magnes Press. (In Hebrew.)

Horenczyk, G. & Ben-Shalom, U. (2001). Multicultural identities and adaptation of young immigrants in Israel. In N. K. Shimahara, I. Holowinsky & S. Tomlinson-Clarke (eds.), *Ethnicity, race, and nationality in education: a global perspective* (pp. 57–80). Mahwah, NJ: Lawrence Erlbaum Associates.

Horenczyk, G. & Munayer, S. (2003). Complex patterns of cultural allegiances: the ethnic identity of Palestinian Christian Arab adolescents in Israel. In P. Weinreich & W. Saunderson (eds.), *Analysing identity: clinical, societal, and cross-cultural perspectives* (pp. 171–189). London: Routledge.

(submitted). Acculturation orientations toward two majority groups: the case of Palestinian Arab Christians in Israel. Manuscript submitted for publication.

Horenczyk, G. & Tatar, M. (2002). Teachers' attitudes toward multiculturalism and their perceptions of the school organizational culture. *Teaching and Teacher Education*, 18, 435–445.

Horowitz, T. & Leshem, E. (1998). The immigrants from the FSU in the Israeli cultural sphere. In M. Sicron & E. Leshem (eds.), *Profile of an immigration wave* (pp. 291–333). Jerusalem: The Magnes Press. (In Hebrew.)

Ichilov, O., Bar-Tal, D. & Mazawi, A. (1989). Israeli adolescents' comprehension and evaluation of democracy. *Youth and Society*, 21, 153–169.

Isralowitz, R. E. & Abu-Saad, I. (1992). Soviet immigration: ethnic conflicts and social cohesion in Israel. *International Journal of Group Tensions*, 22.

Kimmerling, B. (1998). The new Israelis: multiple cultures with no multiculturalism. *Alpayim*, 16, 264–308. (In Hebrew.)

(2004). *Immigrants, settlers, natives: the Israeli state and society between cultural pluralism and cultural wars*. Tel Aviv: Am Oved. (In Hebrew.)

Lissak, M. (1995). *The immigrants from the FSU: between segregation and integration.* Jerusalem: Center for Social Policy Research in Israel. (In Hebrew.)

(1999). *The mass immigration in the fifties: the failure of the melting pot policy.* Jerusalem: Bialik Institute. (In Hebrew.)

Mirsky, J. (1998). Psychological aspects of immigration and absorption of immigrants from the Soviet Union. In M. Sicron & E. Leshem (eds.), *Profile of an immigration wave* (pp. 334–367). Jerusalem: The Magnes Press. (In Hebrew.)

Mirsky, J., Baron-Draiman, Y. & Kedem, P. (2002). Social support and psychological distress among young immigrants from the former Soviet Union in Israel. *International Social Work*, 45, 83–97.

Orr, E., Mana, A. & Mana, Y. (2002). Immigrant identity of Israeli adolescents from Ethiopia and the former USSR: culture-specific principles of organization. *European Journal of Social Psychology*, 33, 71–92.

Phinney, J. S., Horenczyk, G., Liebkind, K. & Vedder, P. (2001). Ethnic identity, immigration, and well-being: an interactional perspective. *Journal of Social Issues*, 57, 493–510.

Ponizovsky, A. M. & Ritsner, M. S. (1999). Suicide ideation among recent immigrants to Israel from the former Soviet Union: an epidemiological survey
of prevalence and risk factors. *Suicide and Life Threatening Behavior*, *29*,
376–392.

(2004). Patterns of loneliness in an immigrant population. *Comprehensive Psychiatry*, *45*, 408–414.

Rabinowitz, D. (2001). The Palestinian citizens of Israel, the concept of trapped minority and the discourse of transnationalism in anthropology. *Ethnic and Racial
Studies*, *24*, 64–85.

Raijman, R., Schammah-Gesser, S. & Kemp, A. (2003). International migration,
domestic work, and care work: undocumented Latina migrants in Israel.
Gender and Society, *17*, 727–749.

Ritsner, M., Ponizovsky, A., Kurs, R. & Modai, I. (2000). Somatization in an immigrant
population in Israel: a community survey of prevalence, risk factors, and help-
seeking behavior. *American Journal of Psychiatry*, *157*, 385–392.

Roccas, S., Horenczyk, G. & Schwartz, S. H. (2000). Acculturation discrepancies and
well-being: the moderating role of conformity. *European Journal of Social
Psychology*, *30*, 323–334.

Roer-Strier, D. & Olshtain-Mann, O. (1999). To see and not be seen: Latin American
illegal foreign workers in Jerusalem. *International Migration*, *37*, 413–436.

Rosenbaum-Tamari, Y. & Damian, N. (2004). *FSU Immigrants 2001: first two years
in Israel*. Jerusalem: Ministry of Immigration Absorption. (In Hebrew.)

Rossing, D. (1999). Microcosm and multiple minorities: the Christian communities
in Israel. In N. Greenwood (ed.), *Israel yearbook and almanac* (pp. 28–42).
Jerusalem: IBRT Translation/Documentation.

Rouhana, N. (1997). Accentuated identities in protracted conflicts: the collective identity of the Palestinian citizens in Israel. *Asian and African Studies*, *27*, 97–127.

Sayegh, L. & Lasry, J.-C. (1993). Immigrants' adaptation in Canada: assimilation,
acculturation, and orthogonal cultural identification. *Canadian Psychology*,
34, 98–109.

Semyonov, M., Raijman, R. & Yom-Tov, A. (2002). Labor market competition, perceived threat, and endorsement of economic discrimination against foreign
workers in Israel. *Social Problems*, *49*, 416–431.

Shabtay, M. (1999). *Best brother: the identity journey of Ethiopian immigrant soldiers.*
Tel Aviv: Cherikover. (In Hebrew.)

(2001). Living with threatened identities: the experiences of Ethiopian youth in
Israel living with a color difference in an ethnocentric climate. *Megamot*, *41*,
97–112. (In Hebrew.)

Shuval, J. T. (1998). Migration to Israel: the mythology of "uniqueness." *International
Migration*, *36*, 3–26.

Smooha, S. (1992). *Arabs and Jews in Israel: change and continuity in mutual tolerance*. Boulder, CO: Westview Press.

Statistical Abstract of Israel (2003). No. 54. Jersualem: Central Bureau of Statistics.

Suleiman, R. (2002a). Minority self-categorization: the case of the Palestinians in
Israel. *Peace and Conflict: Journal of Peace Psychology*, *8*, 31–46.

(2002b). Perception of the minority's collective identity and voting behavior: the
case of Palestinians in Israel. *Journal of Social Psychology*, *142*, 753–766.

Tatar, M. (1998). Counselling immigrants: school contexts and emerging strategies. *British Journal of Guidance and Counselling*, 26, 337–352.

— (2004). Diversity and citizenship education in Israel. In J. A. Banks (ed.), *Diversity and citizenship education: global perspectives* (pp. 377–405). San Francisco, CA: Jossey-Bass.

Tessler, M. (1977). Israel's Arabs and the Palestinian problem. *Middle East Journal*, 31, 313–329.

Ullman, C. & Tatar, M. (2001). Psychological adjustment among Israeli adolescent immigrants: a report on life satisfaction, self-concept, and self-esteem. *Journal of Youth and Adolescence*, 30, 449–463.

Weinreich, P. (1989). Variations in ethnic identity: Identity Structure Analysis. In K. Liebkind (ed.), *New identities in Europe* (pp. 41–76). London: Grover.

Zak, I. (1976). Structure of ethnic identity of Arab-Israeli students. *Psychological Reports*, 38, 239–246.

19 Acculturation in the United States

Huong H. Nguyen

This chapter examines acculturation studies in the USA, focusing on how certain contexts and findings are neglected, and yet critical to its understanding. It suggests that to advance acculturation research, we need to: (1) incorporate more contextual, structural and macro-level perspectives; (2) develop more theories about the processes of acculturation; and (3) integrate findings from other disciplines, such as those regarding the Immigrant Paradox. Drawing from disciplines such as sociology, epidemiology and public health, the Immigrant Paradox is the counterintuitive finding that immigrants – despite their numerous risk factors – often do better than US-born peers on an array of adaptation indices, ranging from health to education to criminal behaviors. (See also Sam *et al.*, in press.)

The sections in this chapter are somewhat disparate, mainly because the literatures are disparate. However, they are relevant to each other and should be connected to advance our understanding. This chapter suggests some possible connections. The three sections go from macro- to micro-perspectives, covering historical–structural contexts, epidemiological patterns and psychological processes. The first section discusses the historical and structural contexts of the USA. It explores how immigration policies and demographic changes can impact acculturation studies, how changes in the context of reception can help to explain the Immigrant Paradox, and how racial structures in the USA can shape a person's acculturation. The second section focuses on psychological studies of acculturation; it articulates the need for more theory building, especially theories that examine the contexts and processes of acculturation. Finally, the third section discusses the Immigrant Paradox, a pattern of findings seen by some as a "paradox."[1] It examines how findings from other disciplines can be integrated with psychological studies of acculturation to further our understanding.

19.1 Historical and structural contexts

19.1.1 Immigration policies and demographic changes

The ethnic minority population in the USA today is increasing and increasingly diverse, in large part because of a change in immigration flow. In

---

[1] Whether the patterns are paradoxical or not is debatable. However, it is not the inconsistencies but the findings behind them that are of special interest here.

contrast to immigrants arriving in the 1800s–1900s (mainly from Europe), today's immigrants (post-1965) hail mainly from Asia and Latin America. These new immigrants are more diverse than ever before, with regard to color, class, and country of origin.

This diversity is a result of changing immigration policies that alternatively opened and closed doors to different populations. Historically, these policies have undergone three major phases, beginning with the *laissez-faire* phase (1780–1875), a time of frontier expansion, when the USA welcomed immigrants to help settle a vast country. Then, in the phase of qualitative restrictions (1875–1920), the USA barred certain types of foreigners such as the Chinese and low-skilled workers. Finally, in the phase of quantitative restrictions (1921 to the present), the USA set quotas for those wishing to immigrate, focusing initially on those with certain national origins, and more recently (from 1965 to the present) on family reunification and employer preference (Martin & Midgley, 2003).

For most of the 1800s and 1900s, these policies favored Europeans. Under the Immigration Act of 1924, for example, Congress established the "national-origins quota system" to ensure the dominance of Europeans. Admission to the USA was based on the immigrant's country of birth, and the majority (70–80%) of immigrant slots were given to those coming from Northern and Western Europe (Center for Immigration Studies, 1995). In effect, the Act of 1924, among others, reinforced patterns of European immigration and staved off immigration from Asia, Africa and Latin America.

However, the Act of 1965 changed all that. As an extension of the Civil Rights movement, it sought to end discrimination by removing racial and ethnic restrictions on immigrants. Instead of giving priority to immigrants with certain origins, this new system gave priority to those with US relatives or with special skills and accomplishments. The cornerstone of the Act was family reunification (which facilitated immigration from Latin America) and to a lesser extent, employment preference (which facilitated immigration from Asia). The net effect was striking: immigration from Asia and Latin America skyrocketed. And, even with numerous reforms since 1965 (and since the events of September 11), today's admission policies still rest largely on the Act of 1965 (Martin & Midgley, 2003).

This Act changed US demographics dramatically. In 2000, 76% of the foreign-born were from Asia or Latin America, compared to only 6% in the early 1900s. Of the total population, 20% were of foreign origin, with 11% being foreign-born and 10% having one or two foreign-born parents. Whites made up 72% of the US population, followed by Blacks at 12%, Hispanics at 11%, Asians 4%, and Native Americans 1%. Sixty-two percent of Asians and 36% of Hispanics in the USA were foreign-born, compared to only 6% of Blacks, 5% of Native Americans, and 2% of Whites. In 2000, ethnic minorities[2] (African, Asian, Hispanic and Native Americans) made up 28% of the population, and in 2050 they will make up 47%, mainly because of the increase in Asians and Hispanics (Schmidley, 2001; US Census Bureau, 2000).

Immigrant children These demographic changes have implications for acculturation research. First, they underscore the growing presence of immigrant and minority children, who, in many parts of the country, now constitute 50% or more of the population under 18. In 2000, 39% of all US children were ethnic minorities, and in 2050 this share will jump to 57%. This growth is largely due to immigrant children, who are the fastest-growing segment in the population under eighteen. Currently, one out of five children is an immigrant or a child of an immigrant. The majority of these children are Asian or Hispanic and, as such, are contributing to the increasing diversity in the child population (Hernandez & Charney, 1998).

Such changes have consequences on American society – especially when in 2040, it is projected that 75% of the elderly population will be White (Pollard & O'Hare, 1999). The result is that: "As the predominantly White baby-boom generation reaches retirement age, it will depend increasingly for its economic support on the productivity, health, and civic participation of adults who grew up in minority immigrant families. Indeed, the *long-term* consequences of contemporary immigration for the American economy and society will hinge ... on the future prospects of children in immigrant families" (Hernandez & Charney, 1998:1–2). Thus, the successful acculturation of immigrant children is consequential, not just for the children themselves, to ensure their health and wellbeing, but also for economic, political and social reasons, to ensure the vitality of US institutions.

Furthermore, the debates on immigration today will be decided by immigrant children and their children. As Waters explains, while most of the political and scholarly debates focus on the first generation, "it is only in the second and later-generations that ... these debates (over things like language acquisition, political participation and socioeconomic integration)" will be decided. After all, only so much change can be expected of one generation, "it is over time and generations that these changes happen" (2004:5).

Racial diversity The second implication deals with the racial diversity of new immigrants. Today's diversity challenges the assimilation theories and policies initially erected for early, European immigrants. Such theories assert that assimilation leads to better adaptation. They suggest that there is a process where different ethnic groups "come to share a common culture" and "gain equal access to the opportunity structure of society" (Zhou, 1999:196). To

---

[2] Like "groups of color" and "nonwhites," the term "minorities" or "ethnic minorities" refers collectively to African, Asian, Hispanic and Native Americans. It is used here to signify groups with limited political power and social resources, those with unequal access to opportunities, social rewards and social status. It is not used to denote inferiority or to indicate small demographic size (DHHS, 2001).

do so, one must abandon old cultural behaviors and incorporate new ones. Anything distinctively ethnic (such as native languages, ethnic enclaves) are seen as disadvantages that negatively affect assimilation. Thus, "immigrants must free themselves from their old cultures" so that they can rise up from their marginal position and assimilate into the new society (Zhou, 1999:197).

However, given the racial stratification that persists, this assimilation theory may not be as applicable to today's immigrants (who are mainly nonwhite) as it was for their European predecessors. Put simply, racial discrimination may make it harder for new immigrants to adapt (Waters, 2004). Even if they were to relinquish their "old culture," their "color" or ascribed physical features may be a handicap to their adaptation (Zhou, 1999).

19.1.2   Context of reception: then versus now

Moreover, the contexts of reception that led to the eventual incorporation of early immigrants were not the same as those that greet today's newcomers. While studies of immigration today may be implicitly comparative with immigration in the early 1900s, there are concerns about comparing today's newcomers with this earlier wave. The context of reception, then vs. now, has changed – in the economy, in the concentration of poverty, and in the replenishment of immigrants (Waters, 2004). Such changes can affect one's acculturation.

Economy In today's economy, there is a widening gap between rich and poor and a shrinking middle class. Currently, the income of the top 1% is more than the bottom 90% combined, and the ownership of wealth is "more concentrated in fewer hands" today than it has been since the late 1800s (Reich, 2005:1). Also, the blue-collar jobs today – jobs generally available to newly arrived immigrants – not only pay less, but are less available than before (Zhou, 1999).

Thus, contemporary immigrants are entering an economy where there are *increasing* inequalities in income and wealth. Because of this bifurcated, hourglass structure in the economy, many are climbing a ladder where the "middle rungs are missing" (Waters, 2004:5). They will need a college degree or face limited mobility. Those without a college education may be trapped in a permanent underclass, a hyperghetto human warehouse.

Consequently, the path to achieving the American dream (or to successful acculturation and adaptation) is not the same for today's newcomers as it was for earlier immigrants who flourished on plenty of factory jobs that paid a decent wage. If immigrants then did not have a college education, they could still achieve a middle-class lifestyle through work. In contrast, they entered an economy where there were *decreasing* inequalities – a time (e.g., 1940–1973) where the "rising tide lifted all boats," and in fact, lifted boats at the bottom the fastest (Waters, 2004: 5). While these trends (increasing inequalities, limited mobility) are sociological in nature, they have *psychological* consequences, as evidenced by the oppositional culture (discussed below).

Concentration of poverty In addition to changes in the economy, there are also changes in the concentration of poverty, especially of immigrants and minorities in low-income communities. With institutional discrimination and segregation, and with the suburbanization of middle-class populations and jobs, poverty has become more concentrated in the inner cities where most immigrants settle. It is not just that immigrants and minorities predominate in the inner cities, but also that they are the poorest of their ethnic groups, left behind by more affluent co-ethnics (Zhou, 1999).

Such concentration negatively affects the children growing up in these settings, as they form expectations from the world they see around them (Zhou, 1999). As Zhou explains: "Without middle-class role models, without roles in economic production, and without roles in families, young men in low-income communities tend to become marginalized and alienated . . . [Such] social isolation and deprivation have given rise to an 'oppositional culture' among young people who feel excluded from mainstream American society"(p. 202).

This oppositional culture is felt especially in inner-city minority schools. In a context with "rising hopes and shrinking opportunities," where minorities do not get the same return for their education, minority children reject the notion that school achievement leads to upward mobility (Zhou, 1999:202). Seeing little hope for mobility, they respond with rejection of academic pursuits and resentment towards middle-class adults. They identify teachers as oppressive authority and those who achieve as "sell-outs," "acting white." Thus, in a context where children are learning not to learn, such a culture can negatively affect their educational outcomes. While it is easy to blame these children for perpetuating harmful stereotypes, Zhou (1999) cautions that it is a normal response to blocked mobility. This oppositional culture can be understood as a response to a gap between socially approved goals and an available means for achieving them (Portes & Rumbaut, 2001).

Replenishment of immigrants Finally, a third change in the context of reception is that the USA is experiencing a continual replenishment of immigrants. In contrast to the "great bursts" of European immigrants in the early 1900s, today's immigration flow is more continuous. In the 1920s, European immigration was cut off by the Depression and by restrictive laws. Children of immigrants then did not have new immigrants from their parents' countries to replenish their communities and reinforce their ethnic values. In contrast, today's immigrant children "will come of age while new immigrants are constantly arriving" (Waters, 2004:5). Barring any great changes in the economy or in immigration laws, the USA will continue to greet 1 million legal and 350,000–500,000 non-legal immigrants annually (Martin & Midgley, 2003).

This replenishment, coupled with the ease of communication and travel today, may help new immigrants to sustain their ethnic practices more than before. As such, it may have a large impact on their acculturation (Waters, 2004). Moreover, such replenishment may act to sustain the protective, cultural factors that can help to explain the Immigrant Paradox.

19.1.3   Racial structure: race and ethnic disparities

In addition to these historical and structural changes, the concept of race is also important. In the USA, race is considered the "master status." While people may have many aspects to their identity, one aspect – their race – will be used by society to define them. As Waters explains, "the fact that a person may be male or female, educated or uneducated, immigrant or native, is not noticed. Race serves as a master status defining the person to others" (Waters, 1999:5).

There are costs to this "master status," as suggested by the many inequalities along racial and ethnic lines. The Surgeon General's Report, for example, documents disparities affecting the mental health of minorities (African, Asian, Hispanic and Native Americans). Compared to Whites, ethnic minorities: (i) have less access to mental health services; (ii) are less likely to receive needed services; (iii) receive poorer quality of care when they do receive services; and (iv) are underrepresented in mental health research (DHHS, 2001).

These inequalities occur not just in mental health, but also in other domains including: physical health, crime statistics, housing quality and economic status (Smelser, Wilson & Mitchell, 2001). There are large disparities, for example, in death rates and infant mortality. Blacks are far more likely to die from homicide and HIV, and Native Americans from suicide and unintentional injuries, than other groups. Moreover, Black and Native American babies are more likely to die in infancy than White babies (Blank, 2001).

There are striking disparities, too, in poverty rates. Blacks, Hispanics and Native Americans are three times more likely than Whites to live in poverty, and Asians, two times more likely. In 2002–2003, 24% of Blacks and Native Americans, 22% of Hispanics and 11% of Asians lived in poverty, compared to 8% of Whites (US Census Bureau, 2004). These rates are compelling given that the threshold for poverty is as low as "three times what it would cost . . . to afford a basic diet" (Lalasz, 2004:1).

Furthermore, the "model-minority" appearances of Asians are misleading. As a broad category, "Asian" lumps together very different sub-groups. It thereby masks important variations. For example: although the Japanese, Filipinos and Asian Indians are very affluent, the Southeast Asians – the Hmong, Cambodians, Laotians and Vietnamese – are very poor. In fact, in 1990, 64% of the Hmong population were living in poverty, as were 43% of the Cambodian population (DHHS, 2001). These poverty rates were higher than that of any other group, including Blacks, Hispanics and Native Americans.

What do these disparities mean? And why are they relevant to acculturation research? These disparities suggest that, on an array of social and economic indicators, Blacks, Hispanics, Native Americans and some Asians fare worse than Whites. They suggest that the USA is a racially stratified context, where the main feature or master status used to define a person is race. Moreover, they suggest that race is an important predictor of one's life chances. As Blank (2001) asserts:

> Racial categories [are] defining characteristics for many Americans. They
> are correlated with educational and economic opportunities, with health sta-
> tus, and with where people live and who they live next to. The magnitude
> of these differences ... is extremely significant ... suggesting that these dis-
> parities are widely experienced ... Whatever the cause, these are substantial
> differentials; they shape our life opportunities, and they shape our opinions
> about and behaviors toward each other ... Race continues to be a salient
> predictor of wellbeing in American society.   (p. 38)

Thus, when immigrants acculturate to the USA, they become not just "Americans," but also "minorities."[3] Consequently, they may take on the minority
status and health profiles of their co-race peers. Hence, to understand how
acculturation shapes the adaptation of newcomers, it is essential to understand
the racially stratified context in which this acculturation occurs. As Waters suggests, the adaptation of immigrants "revolves around the interaction between
specific culture and identities of the immigrants ... and how that culture and
those identities are shaped and changed by conditions in America – especially
the American racial structure" (1999:6). It is not just the cultural changes, but
also the racial structure – the differentials in power, the subordination of certain
groups, the racially stratified contexts – that are key to one's acculturation and
adaptation in the USA.

Still, this is not to imply that race is the *cause* of all the disparities. There
may be numerous factors involved. Yet these patterns are compelling; they
urge researchers to test mechanisms that could explain such differences. For
acculturation researchers, they suggest that we should incorporate the psychological aspects of race-stratification into our research, for example, to examine
how social hierarchies, social stigma, racialization and race relations work in
conjunction with cultural changes (acculturation) to affect adaptation (Berry,
2001; Padilla & Perez, 2003). Such efforts may help to illuminate the Immigrant Paradox.

In sum, it is important to consider the structural and historical contexts of the
USA. First, immigration policies and their consequent population changes can
have implications for acculturation studies, by underscoring the growing presence and importance of immigrant children and by challenging the assimilation
theories and policies dominant in the USA. Second, the context of reception
has changed, especially in the economy, in the concentration of poverty, and in
the diversity and replenishment of immigrants. Such changes can profoundly
affect one's acculturation. Finally, given the racial disparities that persist today,
it is not just the cultural changes, but also the racial structures, that are key to
a person's acculturation in the USA.

Taken together, these contexts set the stage for the Immigrant Paradox. The
continual replenishment of immigrants may help newcomers to sustain their

---

[3] Technically, not *all* immigrants become minorities, as some are non-Hispanic Whites. However,
the *majority* (77%) of the foreign-born are ethnic minorities – in this case, Asian, Hispanic and
Black (Martin & Midgley, 2003).

ethnic practices more than ever before. It may reinforce the protective, cultural factors that can help to explain their unexpected, positive outcomes. Moreover, the economic inequalities, the concentration of poverty, and the racial-stratification (especially for minority immigrants today) can help to explain why these positive outcomes deteriorate with time in the USA.

19.2   Acculturation and adaptation: psychological studies

Acculturation has been linked to an array of indices, from clinical symptomatology, to educational achievement, to family harmony. Despite the numerous associations, however, there is no discernible pattern among the body of findings. As a whole, it seems that our understanding of the links between acculturation and adaptation is a contradictory one.

One set of findings indicates that "high acculturation" (or assimilation as measured by many studies)[4] is positively related to adaptation, whereas another set indicates that it is negatively related. Similarly, findings show that "low acculturation" (or separation) is positively related to adaptation, *and* negatively related. To complicate matters further, additional research reveals a "curvilinear relationship" (where biculturalism is linked with adaptation) while other studies reveal no relationships at all.

Such contradictions impede our understanding. Why do they occur, and how can we disentangle them to build a more coherent understanding? There are various reasons for the conflicting findings, ranging from the different conceptualizations of acculturation, to the different adaptation indices used, to the different contexts in which groups reside, both nationally and internationally. Failure to account for any of these differences could lead to conflicting findings.

It is my contention that one of the limitations in acculturation–adaptation research is that it focuses solely on outcomes, rather than mechanisms leading to such outcomes. Hence, it is possible that past research has reported conflicting results because it has failed to acknowledge important mediating and moderating variables that shape acculturation–adaptation links. As suggested earlier, one such variable is "context." The other factors – the conceptualization of acculturation and operationalization of adaptation – have been addressed in our previous work (Nguyen, Messé & Stollak, 1999).

Context: ethnic density, cultural fit, and discrimination Although contextual factors can have a profound impact on adaptation, they have often been overlooked in past research. Few studies have described, let alone measured, the potential influence of context. Most research seems to study

---

[4] Although the author is not an advocate of unidimensional models of acculturation, terms such as "high/low acculturation" are used here to more accurately report findings based on these models. Such conceptualizations are problematic and, in my view, one of the main reasons for the conflicting findings. Bidimensional models such as Berry's framework are preferable (see Chapter 3).

acculturation–adaptation links in isolation, devoid of their historical and sociocultural settings. Until recently, the few that have incorporated a sense of context have only done so descriptively – rather than descriptively *and* empirically.

Yet these studies suggest that contextual factors are vital to one's adaptation. Gil and Vega (1996), for example, studied Cuban and Nicaraguan families in Miami, and found that the Nicaraguans experienced more cultural stress (more experiences of discrimination and language and acculturation conflicts) than their Cuban peers. They attributed these findings to different conditions in the groups' contexts, explaining that the Cubans fared better because they had more established enclaves and resources than their Nicaraguan peers – who, in contrast, encountered greater barriers in their resettlement to Miami (more exploitation by police, more restrictions in obtaining job permits and legal residence, etc.).

Similarly, Murphy (1965) found that contextual factors such as ethnic density were inversely linked to problems among acculturating groups. He demonstrated that individuals who lived in areas with a substantial population of minorities had lower hospitalization rates. His findings underscored the importance of "context" and, furthermore, the concept of "cultural fit" in facilitating one's adaptation (as measured by clinical disorders and hospitalization rates). Murphy further illustrated the importance of context, as he noted that:

> [In] ... districts of Chicago where the foreign-born were in majority, their hospitalisation rates were quite low, lower, for some disorders, than the city-wide rates for the native-born-of-native-parentage ... [F]or rural Michigan, there was a negative correlation between the percentage strength of an ethnic minority and the level of its hospitalisation rate. For Canada, the same thing is illustrated by Chinese hospitalisation rates ... In British Columbia, the only province that has a real Chinatown, the Chinese have the lowest hospitalisation rate of all ethnic minorities. In Ontario, where the Chinese are scattered throughout the province in "penny" numbers and have no real focus, they have the highest rate of all ethnic minorities. In addition, a similar picture was found in Britain, where Polish refugees showed an inverse association between local group size and relative incidence of mental hospitalization.   (p. 25)

While Murphy's research does not focus on acculturation per se, his work, and Gil and Vega's, have important implications in studying acculturation–adaptation links. They suggest that contextual factors (such as ethnic density and cultural fit) are vital in shaping such links.

In addition to these factors, one's experience of poverty and discrimination is also important. Portes and Rumbaut (2001) found that youth's perceptions and experiences of discrimination increased with time and that such experiences were positively linked to their identity. Furthermore, Nguyen (2004a) found that discrimination mediated acculturation–adaptation links and predicted more negative adaptation on an array of psychological, social and academic indices (distress, depression, self-esteem, life-satisfaction, delin-quency; family, peer and teacher relations; school grades, reading scores, academic aspirations). Taken together, these findings demonstrate that it is important to examine contextual factors (cultural fit, discrimination, poverty) when studying acculturation–adaptation links.

Cultural competence and belongingness Similarly, it is important to examine themes of competence and belongingness. Like the contextual fac-tors, these themes have emerged as descriptive explanations for acculturation–adaptation links. They have not been measured empirically, however. Such themes are best exemplified in the following relationships (see Chapter 3 for definitions of assimilation and separation).

Assimilation and distress Research documenting a positive relationship between "acculturation" and distress has linked assimilation with various disorders, including depression, phobia, dysthymia, suicide, and substance abuse/dependence (Burnam, Hough, Karno, Escobar & Telles, 1987; Caetano, 1987). Assimilation has also been linked with higher rates of delinquency and deviant behavior (Szapocznik, Kurtines & Fernandez, 1980) and higher anorexia scores (Pumariega, 1997). Similarly, it has been linked with family conflicts and difficulty in school (e.g., Chun & Akutsu, 2003). Portes and Rum-baut (2001), for example, found that youth who were becoming too "American" were less successful academically.

A review of these findings suggests that assimilation into the mainstream, US culture alienates the individual from his/her supportive ethnic group and gives rise to ethnic- and self-hatred. Assimilation can facilitate internaliza-tions of damaging behaviors and beliefs that are a part of the dominant culture. These beliefs may include prejudices and discrimination towards the person's ethnicity. Consequently, such internalizations may result in self-deprecation, ethnic- and self-hatred, and a weakened ego-structure (Rogler, Cortes & Malgady, 1991). In sum, the rationale here seems to be that belongingness with those in one's culture promotes a sense of support, identity and mental health.

Separation and distress In the second group of findings, separation has also been linked to psychological distress. Whether measured by length of residency, by loyalty to the culture, or by lack of English proficiency, separa-tion has been associated with various problems, including depression, with-drawal and obsession–compulsion (Torres-Matrullo, 1976) as well as somatic symptoms, combat stress, PTSD (posttraumatic stress disorder) and alcohol abuse/dependence (Escobar *et al.*, 1983). Separation has also been linked to negative life events (divorce, death, hospitalizations) and dissatisfaction with life (boredom, dreariness, sadness) (Salgado de Snyder, 1987).

Researchers in this group suggest that when acculturating individuals have been uprooted from traditional relationships, they are likely to experience lone-liness and isolation in their new environment. Such challenges, coupled with an absence of instrumental skills (knowledge of the main language, access to dif-ferent resources), may keep the separated individual from becoming familiar, comfortable and competent in his/her new world. Consequently, these predicaments may lower self-esteem and give rise to dysfunctional behavior (Rogler *et al.*, 1991). In this set of findings, there seem to be themes of competence and belongingness.

It is interesting that while the many findings seem conflicting, their explanations are not. It is possible that *both* themes of competence *and* belongingness play a role in shaping one's adaptation. It does not have to be "either-or." Thus, the seemingly fragmented findings may be better integrated by examining the mechanisms or explanations underlying these findings.

In sum, it is my contention that the conflicting findings are due, in part, to the fact that we have focused only on the outcomes of acculturation, rather than on the mechanisms leading to such outcomes. Moreover, we have failed to acknowledge the importance of context, as most have studied acculturation in isolation, devoid of its sociocultural settings. To counter these limitations, Nguyen (in preparation) developed and tested an ecological theory of acculturation. This theory asserts that if we examine factors such as competence and belongingness, as well as perceptions of context and cultural fit, and poverty and discrimination, we can unravel the contradictions and organize the fragmented parts into a more coherent whole. (Due to space limitations, however, this theory is not detailed here, except to say that findings demonstrated substantial support for it. The interested reader should refer to Nguyen, in preparation.) Using a similar, ecological perspective, Birman, Trickett and Buchanan (2005) also demonstrated the impact of community context, showing too that "acculturation is best understood as a contextual phenomenon" (p. 84).

In short, acculturation research in the USA has grown massively, often without a semblance of a coherent body (of research) or a conceptual guide to understanding its findings. It is therefore critical to develop theories, especially theories that examine the processes and contexts of acculturation. We need to move beyond broad generalizations (e.g., acculturation is related to mental health) and focus instead on theories that examine conditions and principles that govern the relationships (Sue, 2003). Theory building is essential to advance acculturation studies and to help explain the Immigrant Paradox, which current acculturation theories do not seem to do.

19.3 Acculturation and adaptation: the Immigrant Paradox

Drawing from research in sociology, epidemiology and public health, findings show that despite their numerous risk factors (e.g. poverty, low socio-economic status [SES], race / ethnic minority status), immigrants (the foreign-born) do better than US-born peers on an array of indices, ranging from health to education to criminal behaviors. Moreover, research has also shown that despite their low SES, many US-born Latinos have better health and wellbeing than their White peers (Hayes-Bautista, 2004). This pattern – that immigrants (and/or US-born Latinos) have unexpected, positive outcomes and that these positive outcomes deteriorate over time and generation – has sometimes been termed the *Immigrant Paradox*, or the *Hispanic/Latino paradox*, or, in studies of infant mortality, the *epidemiological paradox*.

While it is not surprising that immigrants assimilate to the norms of the USA, what is surprising – i.e., the Paradox – is that they do well initially and oftentimes better than native-born peers and better than White counterparts. Conventional wisdom suggests that immigrants would show more negative outcomes, given their many disadvantages (high poverty, low SES, minority status, barriers to health care and education, exposure to troubled neighborhoods, etc.). Yet, the opposite turns out to be true (Rumbaut, 1999).

Although not the initial intent of the term, what is also paradoxical is that this pattern counters the classical assimilation theory – the idea that assimilation leads to better adaptation. Based on a deficit model, this theory (and many US policies and practices) suggest that: "to get ahead, immigrants need to learn how to become American, to overcome their deficits with respect to the new language and culture, the new health care and educational system, the new economy and society. As they shed the old and acquire the new over time, they surmount those obstacles to make their way more successfully" (Rumbaut 1999:174). Yet, research suggests the opposite: that it is something about the ethnic culture – "the old" – that protects against deteriorating health and wellbeing (e.g., Landale, Oropesa & Gorman, 1999).

The idea of the Paradox is a slippery concept, and some researchers argue that it should not be interpreted as "an unassailable phenomenon," as what is paradoxical is debatable (Palloni & Morenoff, 2001). Moreover, findings regarding the Paradox are not limited to just immigrants, as such protection has also been demonstrated in Latinos who have lived in the USA for six or seven generations (hence "the Hispanic/Latino paradox") (Hayes-Bautista, 2004). The study of the Paradox, however, dates back to the 1960s–1970s, starting with findings regarding the birth outcomes of Mexican immigrants (Palloni & Morenoff, 2001). Today, these patterns extend across outcomes, ages and ethnic groups, and, to some extent, across national boundaries. Here are some examples.

Mental health With regard to mental health, two large-scale, epidemiological studies have shown that Mexican immigrants have lower rates of mental disorders than their US-born peers. Both the Epidemiologic Catchment Area (ECA) Study and the National Comorbidity Study (NCS) examined rates of psychiatric disorders in the USA. The ECA Study found that while the Mexican and White Americans had similar rates of disorders overall, when the Mexican group was further divided, those who were foreign-born had lower rates of depression and phobias than their US-born peers (Robins & Reiger, 1991; Burnam *et al.*, 1987). Similarly, the NCS showed that Mexican immigrants (the foreign-born) had lower prevalence rates of any lifetime disorders (affective disorders, anxiety disorders, substance abuse, any psychiatric disorders) (Ortega, Rosenheck, Alegria & Desai, 2000).

Still a third study confirmed this pattern and demonstrated that, compared to their US-born peers, foreign-born Mexicans had lower rates of mental disorders and substance abuse. Furthermore, it demonstrated that years in the USA made a difference, as immigrants who lived in the USA less than thirteen years had lower rates of mental disorders and substance abuse than did those who had lived in the USA more than thirteen years (Vega, Kolody, Aguilar-Gaxiola, Alderete, Catalano & Caraveo-Anduaga, 1998).

While these findings involved adults, similar patterns have also been demonstrated in adolescents. Swanson, Linskey, Quintero-Salinas, Pumariega and Holzer (1992) did a large-scale survey of Mexican youth on both sides of the Texas–Mexico border and found that youth on the Texas side had more problems (depressive symptoms, suicidal ideation, illicit drug use) than did youth in Mexico. All these studies, including those with other ethnic groups (Canino *et al.*, 1987; Moscicki, Rae, Regier & Locke, 1987), suggested that factors associated with living in the USA may lead to an increased risk of mental disorders (DHHS, 2001).

Physical health and health risk behaviors Turning to physical health, Harris (1999) studied the perceived health and health risk behaviors of adolescents. Using the ADD Health Data (from the National Longitudinal Study of Adolescent Health), she examined a large (20,000+), nationally representative sample of adolescents in grades 7–12. This sample consisted of first-, second- and third- or later-generation youth, from diverse racial/ethnic backgrounds (from Mexico, Asia, Africa, Europe, and Central and South America).

Harris found that, like the mental disorders, health problems and risk behaviors increased with generation status and years in the USA. Compared to their immigrant peers (first-generation), second-generation youth were more likely to have obesity, asthma, learning disabilities, and poor or fair health. They were also more likely to have missed school because of a health or emotional problem and to have engaged in early sexual activity and deviant behaviors (delinquency, violence, drugs). The outcomes of third- or later-generation youth varied with racial and ethnic groups, but in general, US-born minorities had the highest rates of health problems and risk behaviors. The overall pattern then, is that first-generation youth had the lowest rate of health problems and risk behaviors, followed by second-generation youth (whose rates were equal to that of Whites), then third- or later-generation youth, especially ethnic minorities who had the highest rates of all. This effect held across ethnic background and country of origin. In addition to these generational differences, Harris also found that years in the USA made a difference: the more time and exposure youth had to the USA, the greater their health problems and risk behaviors.

In addition, immigrant status (being foreign-born) was also protective with respect to infant health (low birthweight, infant mortality), education (grades, drop-out rates, school attitudes and motivation), criminal propensities, chronic diseases and intestinal cancer (e.g., Landale *et al.*, 1999; Rumbaut, 1999).

Limitations and next steps In sum, the general pattern is that health and wellbeing deteriorate with generational status, years in the USA, and, sometimes, English fluency. In addition to explanations such as migration selectivity ("the hardy immigrant hypothesis") or faulty data (Palloni & Morenoff, 2001), researchers also assert that "acculturation" (assimilation as measured by these proxies) leads to worse outcomes. Many scholars suggest that there is something about the ethnic culture that is protective and that it is the "Americanization [that] is hazardous to your health" (Escobar, Hoyos-Nervi & Gara, 2000; Rumbaut, 1998).

However, the limitation in such research is that there is no direct test of acculturation, as years in the USA and generation status are rough proxies at best. This is because there are many ways in which acculturation can take place, other than by assimilation (see Chapter 3). Furthermore, acculturation is a complicated process, and it is not clear what it is about acculturation that leads to deteriorating health (DHHS, 2001). Is it the changes in cultural values and practices (diet, life style, cultural sanctions), the stressors associated with such changes, the negative encounters with US institutions (Bentacourt & Lopez, 1993), or the socialization into inner-city subcultures (Portes & Rumbaut, 2001)? Still another limitation is that such findings are based on cross-sectional research and, thus, are limited in their ability to examine change over time.

To understand these findings better, we need to test acculturation more directly (DHHS, 2001). For one, we need to examine how proxies vs. direct measures of acculturation reflect different patterns. How do these epidemiological–sociological findings compare with those in psychological studies, where acculturation is more often measured via behavioral and attitudinal scales, rather than single indices? Are the patterns the same?

As a preliminary test, Nguyen (2004b) examined how different measures and proxies (English fluency, US residence, generational status and US involvement) varied in their predictions of adaptation. Findings suggested that, even though these indices were all aspects of "becoming American," they reflected different aspects of Americanization, and, in turn, had different outcomes. While generational status and years in the USA predicted worse psychological, social and academic outcomes (like the Paradox findings), youth's fluency in English and involvement in US behaviors and values (more specific aspects) predicted more positive outcomes. Thus, different measures and proxies of acculturation may suggest not just a measurement issue, but also a conceptual one. They may reflect different segments of assimilation, which, in turn, can lead to different trajectories. Hence, we need to examine how and why various measures of acculturation (including open-ended questions) predict different pathways and outcomes.

Moreover, we need to test specific causes and pathways. We need to examine how contextual and risk and protective factors are associated with acculturation, as such factors are largely unknown and unexplored. For instance, we know very little about the causes and pathways that explain why children of immigrants do better overall, despite their many risk factors, and why their positive outcomes fade over time. We also know very little about the risk or protective factors that account for these changes. Yet such factors are critical. One line of thinking, for example, suggests that even though protective factors, such as strong family bonds (and other, unknown sociocultural and demographic factors), may sustain cultural orientations that lead to healthy behaviors, such factors fade with assimilation, allowing for the deleterious effects of poverty and racism (Hernandez & Charney, 1998). As Berry suggests, "the very process of acculturation may involve risk factors that can reduce one's health status" (1998:49). Hence, we should examine how such factors, in conjunction with acculturation, do or do not lead to negative outcomes.

Finally, we need to examine whether these patterns hold up longitudinally, as the findings are based only on cross-sectional research. Such designs limit our ability to examine developmental and causal processes. Do the same patterns emerge over the life-span? What are the key predictors? Longitudinal studies are essential here. As Hernandez and Charney (1998) suggest,

> Trajectories of healthy development, assimilation, and adaptation occur across periods of years or decades for individuals, and the nature of individual outcomes depends on the timing and sequencing of specific personal, family, neighborhood, and historical events in the child's life. These are best measured and analyzed through longitudinal data collection and research that follows the same individuals over extended periods ... Moreover, several of the most intriguing findings ... on immigrant children – notably those pertaining to unexpected positive outcomes and deteriorating outcomes over time – require longitudinal data and substantial contextual information if their causes and pathways are to be clarified.   (p. 12)

Thus, we need to examine how youth's acculturation and adaptation change over time. Moreover, we need to evaluate the assertions behind the Paradox (e.g., that cultural assimilation leads to deteriorating outcomes) by:

➤   examining how different measures and proxies of acculturation predict outcomes. Do they show the same patterns as the Paradox suggests?
➤   examining whether these patterns emerge longitudinally, as most findings are based only on cross-sectional research.
➤   examining how various contextual and risk and protective factors are associated with acculturation, and how such factors can help to account for the unexpected, positive outcomes and the deterioration over time, if any. What are the causes and pathways involved? To what extent, are these pathways captured in the ecological processes described in the previous section? Furthermore, how do other acculturation theories help to explain the Paradox?

As Harris' research (1999) suggests, when immigrant youth assimilate to the USA, they don't just become "Americans," they become "minorities" – and, as such, may take on the negative health profiles of their native minority peers. As Hayes-Bautista (2004) further suggests, even the US-born Latinos who remain "ethnic" remain healthier. Hence, it could be that immigrant and ethnic youth have a protective quality related to their culture, but as they become "Americanized" or "minorities" in a racially stratified context, this protection is eroded. By studying the processes of acculturation, we may better explain the deterioration in outcomes over time (if any) and the racial disparities that may or may not ensue. The more we can discern the causes and pathways involved, the better we can inform policies aimed at decreasing these disparities.

19.4   Conclusions

To better understand and advance acculturation research in the USA, it is essential to: (i) incorporate more contextual, structural and macro-level perspectives; (ii) develop more theories about the processes of acculturation; and (iii) integrate relevant findings from the Paradox.

First, it is important to consider the structural and historical contexts of the USA. Given the racial disparities that persist today, it is not just the cultural changes, but also the racial structures that are critical to understanding acculturation in the USA. Thus, it is essential to consider the psychological aspects of stratification – for example, to examine how social hierarchies and racialization work in conjunction with cultural changes (acculturation) to affect adaptation.

Furthermore, changes in the context of reception – in the economy, in the concentration of poverty, and in the diversity and replenishment of immigrants – can profoundly affect one's acculturation. Taken together, these contexts set the stage for the Immigrant Paradox. The continual replenishment of immigrants may help new immigrants to sustain their ethnic practices more than ever before. It may reinforce the protective, cultural factors that can help to explain their unexpected, positive outcomes. Moreover, the economic inequalities, the concentration of poverty, and the racial stratification can help to explain why these positive outcomes deteriorate over time and with generation in the USA.

Second, it is important to focus more on theory building. In the USA, acculturation research has grown massively, often without a semblance of a coherent body (of research) or a conceptual guide to understanding its findings. However, more is not necessarily better, as the avalanche of data can make theory building more difficult. The danger is that data will pile up without any guide to what the information means (Portes, 1999). As Portes warns: "A . . . misconception is that the accumulation of evidence leads to theoretical innovation . . . Data may accumulate endlessly without producing any significant conceptual breakthroughs . . . Ideas, especially those of a broader reach, are few and far between and certainly do not emerge out of masses of data" (p. 22).

Further, it is rare to find systematic efforts that determine what factors account for, mediate or moderate findings. Such treatment has led to a literature replete with reports of outcomes that are limited in their scientific contribution. It is not surprising then that acculturation manuscripts have been criticized for their atheoretical nature and over-emphasis on fact-finding (Smith, Harb, Lonner & van de Vijver, 2001). Consequently, theory building is in serious need of attention. We need theories that consider the contexts and processes of acculturation and theories that can help to explain the Paradox.

Finally, it is important to consider findings from the Immigrant Paradox. Since "acculturation" is often used to explain these findings, it is interesting that these patterns do not emerge or are not discussed in psychological studies of acculturation. Why the discrepancy? And how can we bridge the different literatures to further our understanding?

One step is to examine proxies vs. actual measures, risk and protective factors, and longitudinal data, as suggested earlier. Another is to test whether the speculations above (about the context of reception and/or about the ecological theory) can help to explain these findings. Still a third step is to test empirically the interpretations behind the Paradox. To what extent are these findings due to acculturation, social stress, migration selectivity or faulty data? To what extent are these findings aptly named: *are* they really paradoxical? Or are they colored by our choice of risk factors and assumptions that such factors are relevant to all groups? Are they colored by our ethnocentrism, since we can just as well ask: "Given their many advantages, why are Whites doing so poorly?" Furthermore, how do the patterns vary with immigrant groups? And what exactly is the comparison group (Whites, Blacks, US-born co-ethnics)?

As these questions imply, more research is needed. The intent here is not to provide an exhaustive report, but an overview to suggest avenues for further research. As such, the Paradox is a promising frontier, wide-open for acculturation researchers.

19.5   References

Bentacourt, H. & Lopez, S. (1993). The study of culture, ethnicity, and race in American psychology. *American Psychologist, 48*, 629–637.

Berry, J. (1998). Acculturation and health. In S. Kazarian & D. Evans (eds.), *Cultural clinical psychology. theory, research, and practice* (pp. 39 57). New York: Oxford University Press.

Birman, D., Trickett, E. & Buchanan, R. (2005). A tale of two cities. *American Journal of Community Psychology, 35(1)*, 83–101.

Blank, R. (2001). An overview of trends in social and economic well-being, by race. In N. Smelser, W. Wilson & F. Mitchell (2001), *America becoming* (pp. 21–39). Washington, DC: National Academy Press.

Burnam, M., Hough, R., Karno, M., Escobar, J. & Telles, C. (1987). Acculturation and lifetime prevalence of psychiatric disorders among Mexican Americans in L.A. *Journal of Health and Social Behavior, 9*, 105–130.

Caetano, R. (1987). Acculturation and drinking patterns among U.S. Hispanics. *British Journal of Addiction, 82*, 789–799.

Canino, G., Bird, H., Shrout, P., *et al.* (1987). The prevalence of specific psychiatric disorders in Puerto Rico. *Archives of General Psychiatry, 44*, 727–735.

Center for Immigration Studies (1995). *Three decades of mass immigration.* www.cis.org/articles/1995/back395.html.

Chun, K. & Akutsu, P. (2003). Acculturation among ethnic minority families. In K. Chun, P. Organista & G. Marin (eds.), *Acculturation: advances in theory, measurement and applied research* (pp. 95–120). Washington, DC: American Psychological Association.

DHHS (2001). *Mental health: culture, race, and ethnicity. A supplement to mental health: a report to the Surgeon General.* Rockville, MD: US Department of Health and Human Services – DHHS, Public Health Service, Office of the Surgeon General.

Escobar, J., Hoyos-Nervi, C. & Gara, M. (2000). Immigration and mental health. *Harvard Review of Psychiatry, 8*, 64–72.

Escobar, J., Randolph, E., Puente, G., *et al.* (1983). PTSD in Hispanic Vietnam veterans. *Journal of Nervous and Psychological Functioning, 171*, 586–596.

Gil, A. & Vega, W. (1996). Two different worlds. *Journal of Social and Personal Relationships, 13(3)*, 435–456.

Harris, K. (1999). The health status and risk behaviors of adolescents in immigrant families. In D. Hernandez & E. Charney (eds.), *Children of immigrants* (pp. 286–315). Washington, DC: National Academy of Science Press.

Hayes-Bautista, D. (2004). *La nueva California: Latinos in the Golden State.* Berkeley and Los Angeles, CA: University of California Press.

Hernandez, D. & Charney, E. (1998). *From generation to generation: the health and well-being of children in immigrant families.* Washington, DC: National Academy Press.

Lalasz, R. (2004). *Poverty up, number of insured down in the U.S.* Population Reference Bureau. www.prb.org/Template.cfm?Section=PRB&template.

Landale, N., Oropesa, R. & Gorman, B. (1999). Immigrant and infant health. In D. Hernandez & E. Charney (eds.), *Children of immigrants* (pp. 244–285). Washington, DC: National Academy of Science Press.

Martin, P. & Midgley, E. (2003). Immigration: shaping and reshaping America. *Population Bulletin, 58(2)*, 1–43.

Moscicki, E., Rae, D., Regier, D. & Locke, B. (1987). The Hispanic Health and Nutrition Examination Survey: depression among Mexican Americans, Cuban Americans, and Puerto Ricans. In M. Gaviria & J. Arana (eds.), *Health and behavior: research agenda for Hispanics* (pp.145–159). Chicago: Hispanic American Family Center.

Murphy, H. (1965). Migration and the major mental health disorders: a reappraisal. In M. Kantor (ed.), *Mobility and mental health* (pp. 5–47). Springfield: Charles Thomas.

Nguyen, H. (2004a). Discrimination, acculturation, and adjustment. Paper presented at the American Psychological Association (APA) Convention, Honolulu, HI.

(2004b). Paradoxes in acculturation. Paper presented at the Society for Research on Adolescence (SRA) Biennial Meeting, Baltimore, MD.

(in preparation). *Acculturation in context*. The New Americans: Immigration and American Society. Series eds. S. Gold and R. Rumbaut. New York: LFB Scholarly Publishing.

Nguyen, H., Messé, L. & Stollak, G. (1999). Towards a more complex understanding of acculturation and adjustment. *Journal of Cross-Cultural Psychology, 30(1)*, 5–26.

Ortega, A., Rosenheck, R., Alegria, M. & Desai, R. (2000). Acculturation and lifetime risk of psychiatric and substance abuse disorders among Hispanics. *Journal of Nervous and Mental Disease, 188*, 728–735.

Padilla, A. & Perez, W. (2003). Acculturation, social identity, and social cognition. *Hispanic Journal of Behavioral Sciences, 25(1)*, 35–55.

Palloni, A. & Morenoff, J. (2001). Interpreting the paradoxical in the Hispanic Paradox. *Annals New York Academy of Sciences, 954*, 140–174.

Pollard, K. & O'Hare, W. (1999). America's racial and ethnic minorities. *Population Bulletin, 54(3)*, 1–48.

Portes, A. (1999). Immigration theory for a new century. In C. Hirschman, P. Kasinitz & J. DeWind (eds.), *The handbook of international migration* (pp.159–183). New York: Russell Sage Foundation.

Portes, A. & Rumbaut, R. (2001). *Legacies*. New York: Russell Sage Foundation.

Pumariega, A. (1997). Body dissatisfaction among Hispanic and Asian-American girls. *Journal of Adolescent Health, 21(1)*, 1.

Reich, R. (2005). *Cheers for the President's Ownership Society*. http://my.brandeis.edu/news/item?news_item_id=103467.

Robins, L. & Regier, D. (1991). *Psychiatric disorders in America: the Epidemiologic Catchment Area Study*. New York: The Free Press.

Rogler, L., Cortes, D. & Malgady, R. (1991). Acculturation and psychological functioning status among Hispanics. *American Psychologist, 46(6)*, 585–597.

Rumbaut, R. (1998). Children of immigrants: is "Americanization" hazardous to infant health? In H. Fitzgerald, B. Lester & B. Zuckerman (eds.), *Children of color* (pp.159–183). New York: Garland.

(1999). Assimilation and its discontents. In C. Hirschman, P. Kasinitz & J. DeWind (eds.), *The handbook of international migration* (pp. 172–195). New York: Russell Sage Foundation.

Salgado de Snyder, V. (1987). Factors associated with acculturative stress and depressive symptomatology among married Mexican immigrant women. *Psychology of Women Quarterly, 11*, 475–488.

Sam, D., Vedder, P., Ward, C. & Horenczyk, G. (in press). Psychological and sociocultural adaptation of immigrant youth. In J. Berry, J. Phinney, D. Sam & P. Vedder (eds.), *Immigrant youth in cultural transition: acculturation, identity and adaptation across national contexts*. Mahwah, NJ: Lawrence Erlbaum Associates.

Schmidley, A. (2001). *Profile of the foreign-born population in the U.S.: 2000*. Washington, DC: US Government Printing Office.

Smelser, N., Wilson, W. & Mitchell, F. (2001). *America becoming*. Washington, DC: National Academy Press.

Smith, P., Harb, C., Lonner, W. & van de Vijver, F. (2001). The Journal of Cross-Cultural Psychology between 1993 and 2000. *Journal of Cross-Cultural Psychology, 32(1)*, 9–17.

Sue, S. (2003). Foreword. In K. Chun, P. Organista & G. Marin (eds.), *Acculturation: advances in theory, measurement and applied research* (pp. xvii–xxi). Washington, DC: American Psychological Association.

Swanson, J., Linskey, A., Quintero-Salinas, R., Pumariega, A. & Holzer, C. (1992). A binational school survey of depressive symptoms, drug use, and suicidal ideation. *Journal of the American Academy of Child and Adolescent Psychiatry, 31*, 669–678.

Szapocznik, J., Kurtines, W. & Fernandez, T. (1980). Bicultural involvement in Hispanic American youths. *International Journal of Intercultural Relations, 4*, 353–365.

Torres-Matrullo, C. (1976). Acculturation and psychopathology among Puerto Rican women in mainland U.S. *American Journal of Orthopsychiatry, 46,* 710–719.

US Census Bureau (2000). *Census of the U.S.A.* Washington, DC: US Government.
    (2004). *Census of the U.S.A.* Washington, DC: US Government.

Vega, W., Kolody, B., Aguilar-Gaxiola, S., Alderete, E., Catalano, R. & Caraveo-Anduaga, J. (1998). Lifetime prevalence of DSM-III-R psychiatric disorders among urban and rural Mexican Americans in California. *Archives of General Psychiatry, 55,* 771–778.

Waters, M. (2004). Children of immigrants in American Society. Paper presented at the New Young Americans Conference, Suffolk University, Boston, MA.

Zhou, M. (1999). Segmented assimilation. In C. Hirschman, P. Kasinitz & J. DeWind (eds.), *The handbook of international migration* (pp. 196–211). New York: Russell Sage Foundation.

20 Acculturation in European societies

Karen Phalet & Ankica Kosic

Immigration and ethnic minority issues pose major social, political and intellectual challenges to contemporary Europe. European states and societies are coping with very unevenly spread, rapidly diversifying and most often increasing incoming migration streams. New arrivals include asylum seekers, refugees, sojourners and documented or undocumented immigrants from all parts of the world. In addition, growing numbers of European transmigrants, students and highly qualified professionals, the so-called "free movers," are living and working outside their countries of origin within the European Union (Favell, 2003). At the same time, national destinations of South–North and East–West migration streams have spread from the economically most developed North-West to the South and Center of the European continent (European Commission, 2003). Meanwhile, the children of post-1965 immigrant workers in the north-west of Europe are coming of age (Haug, 2002). The ways in which they are able to negotiate multiple identities and cultures are crucial for the success of immigrant incorporation in European societies (Crul & Vermeulen, 2003).

20.1 European acculturation studies: an emerging research field

This chapter aims to contribute to a more accurate understanding of acculturation processes in (actual and prospective) EU countries. To this end, we discuss theoretical and empirical implications of the distinctive contextual characteristics of minority groups, receiving societies and ethnic relations in different parts of Europe. Key contextual and relational features of the acculturation process are documented by examples of acculturation studies in European cities and societies. The first part reviews distinct configurations and meanings of cultural diversity in East-Central and Western Europe, highlighting the varying historical and institutional contexts in which acculturation processes take place. The main part of the chapter discusses conceptual problems and challenges of comparability in cross-cultural acculturation studies. Drawing on examples of acculturation studies in the North-West, South and Center of Europe, we develop a common "derived etics" approach to situated and interactive acculturation strategies (see Bourhis, Moïse, Perrault &

Sénécal, 1997; Kalin & Berry, 1996; Montreuil & Bourhis, 2001; Phalet & Swyngedouw, 2003; Zagefka & Brown, 2002). The last part gives key facts about patterns of migration, ethnic inequalities and prejudice across European receiving societies. To conclude, we discuss new challenges and future directions for comparative acculturation studies in the enlarged European Union.

With its great variety of national and ethnic cultures and institutional arrangements, Europe constitutes an interesting natural laboratory for studying contextual variation and dynamic change in acculturation processes. Definitions of minority and dominant identities, communities and cultures differ widely between national contexts, depending on distinct national histories of migration and nation building. Moreover, public acceptance, let alone full recognition, of cultural diversity within "old" nation states is still the exception rather than the rule. Therefore, the meanings of key terms like *immigrant integration* and *multiculturalism* differ between Canada, Australia or the USA and most European countries.

European cross-cultural and social psychologists are only beginning to address key theoretical and applied issues in the area of ethnic and migration studies. In recent years we have seen steady progress and an emerging coordination of research efforts, not only in the north-west of Europe but increasingly also including South and Central European projects and researchers. Examples of coordinated European studies and perspectives on immigration, acculturation and identity issues are the 2001 special issue of the *Journal of Social Issues* (e.g. Zick, Wagner, van Dick & Petzel 2001), the 2000 special issue of the *Journal of Community and Applied Psychology* (Deaux, 2000) and a few edited volumes – for instance, Breakwell and Lyons (1996) on European identity, and Phalet and Örkeny (2001) on ethnic relations in Western and Central Europe. A major comparative research which includes several countries is the ongoing ICSEY (International Comparative Study of Ethnic Youth) project, applying and extending Berry's (2002) bidimensional acculturation model to the USA, Israel and Europe (Phinney, Horenczyk, Liebkind & Vedder, 2001). Other recent examples of coordinated research efforts are mainly replicating and extending Bourhis *et al.*'s (1997) Interactive Acculturation Model (IAM) in European receiving contexts (Montreuil & Bourhis, 2001; Phalet & Swyngedouw, 2003).

Both the ICSEY project and approaches using the IAM have in common their emphasis on the contextual and interactive nature of psychological acculturation, taking into account cross-national variation in the patterning of ethnic diversity and inter-ethnic relations. Along similar lines, European social psychologists have studied situated and shifting ethnic identity strategies, stressing multiplicity and hybridity in the self-understandings of immigrants and minorities (Liebkind, 2000; Verkuyten, 2004). Taken together, European studies of acculturation and ethnic identity show that the designation of minority and dominant groups and cultures is more complicated than early bicultural models suggest. Still, we are far from a coherent comparative and applied psychological research agenda that fully incorporates the complexities of rapidly changing European societies and cities.

20.2 Acculturation in context: ethnic relations in the two Europes

Post-Second World War migration, along with European integration and enlargement, has given rise to new patterns of geographic mobility, ethnic diversity and (post)national citizenship across Europe. In Western Europe (with notable exceptions like Belgium or Spain) issues and policies of ethnic diversity are almost exclusively concerned with the incorporation of postwar immigrant populations. As distinct from similar debates in multinational settler societies such as Canada, the European multiculturalism debate has rarely been about group rights, such as the legal protection of minority languages or cultures or the right to self-government of minority communities (Bauböck, 1994). In contrast, cultural, linguistic and political minority rights are at the heart of ethnopolitical contention in the (formerly) multinational states of Central and Eastern Europe. There is a debate on what the terms *citizen*, *foreigner*, *national*, *ethnic*, *minority* and *immigrant* stand for in the context of Eastern Europe (Kymlicka, 1995). This issue is related to *jus soli* and *jus sanguinis* citizenship policies. For example, all Baltic states experienced, after the Second World War, significant immigration flows from Russia and from other parts of the former Soviet Union. Since regaining independence, Baltic countries do not recognize their Russian population as citizens. All of them have to pass a naturalization procedure, and naturalization rates are slowly increasing (Brands Kehre & Stalidzane, 2003). For conceptual clarity, the use of national, ethnic and civic categories should be clarified and situated within a particular national context.

20.2.1 Central Europe: the challenge of minority nationalism

Since the fall of the Berlin Wall, East and Central European states are responding to the renewed challenge of minority nationalisms within their borders (e.g., ethnic Hungarians in Rumania) in conjunction with trans-border nationalisms from external "homelands" in neighboring states (e.g., Hungary). Extending Kymlicka's (2000) normative distinction between immigrant and non-immigrant minorities to the European context, national minorities are generally defined as non-immigrant populations whose historic homeland has been incorporated into multinational states. Not only are national minorities typically claiming institutional recognition of their distinct languages, cultures and identities, they are also seeking legal protection against forced assimilation by nationalizing states; and they are commonly aspiring to some degree of self-governance, either through territorial autonomy or through some form of power sharing. In addition, most national minorities in East and Central Europe wish to preserve cross-border cultural ties with external homelands, which are most often neighboring states. Typically, the built-in antagonism between minority and state nationalisms is held in check by symmetric concerns of neighboring states with the treatment of trans-border minorities (Brubaker, 1996). For instance, Hungary's national concern with the preservation of Hungarian culture, language and identity among ethnic Hungarian minorities outside state borders has motivated the development of an exemplary minority rights legislation. This 1993 Act formally protects Hungary's "nations within" from forced linguistic assimilation and grants the group rights necessary to maintain a distinct culture and identity and to preserve close cultural ties with external homelands (Phalet & Örkeny, 2001). Combining multiple criteria such as one's mother-tongue, ethnic descent, ethnic self-definition or externally imposed ethnic labeling, the Act includes such diverse ethnic groups as Roma, Germans, Rumanians and Serbs. At the same time, minority rights are restricted to ethnic groups who have been living on Hungarian territory for at least one century, thus excluding immigrants, refugees and all foreigners who are not Hungarian citizens (e.g., ethnic Hungarian refugees from Transylvania). In general, normative conceptions of cultural diversity and intercultural relations in the post-communist states of the "old New Europe" are less concerned with new immigration than with the historical legacy of multinational empires and federations. Obviously, one reason is that immigration in these countries is a relatively new phenomenon, which became a political issue mostly as a consequence of recent restrictive conditions specified by the EU.

20.2.2   Western Europe: the challenge of immigrant multiculturalism

In the immigrant receiving societies in Western Europe, however, notions of cultural diversity are typically referring to the presence of immigrant minorities. As distinct from ethnic minorities in East-Central Europe, who often have a long history of relative regional autonomy, most immigrant communities have recently settled (post-1965 or later) and are territorially dispersed across major industrial or metropolitan areas. In spite of persistent national differences, most states in the North-West of Europe have gradually and selectively extended to immigrants civil and social rights that used to be the exclusive entitlements of the dominant national group. With a view to incorporating post-war immigrants and their descendants, Western European states are reproducing, and to some extent reinventing, their particular histories of nation building and (post)colonial legacies (Favell, 2001). For example, Dutch minorities policies selectively extend to immigrant communities a typical "pillarization" or segmented pluralism approach, which was originally developed to integrate separate and sovereign communities (e.g., Catholics and Protestants) into one nation state. Therefore, national incorporation regimes differ notably in degrees of cultural closure and in their emphasis on common history or political project ("ethnos" or "demos"). Varying national responses to cultural diversity as a consequence of immigration are commonly conceived as reflecting ideal typical paradigms of incorporation. For instance, British-style "immigrant multiculturalism," or the inclusion of immigrant minorities as ethnic communities, has been opposed to French-style "assimilationism," including immigrants and their descendants as individual citizens only, and German-style "segregationism," or the exclusion of immigrant minorities from the nation (Koopmans & Statham, 2000). The unreflective use of imported vocabularies is common in more recent or reluctant immigration countries, which have not yet defined their own way of understanding and recognizing differences (Kosic & Triandafyllidou, forthcoming). In some cases, e.g. in Italy, "multiculturalism" is the most widely employed and preferred term in institutional and political discourse, but it is used interchangeably with "integration" and "cultural diversity." In practice, however, national policies usually fall short of full recognition, nor do they impose complete exclusion, of immigrant minorities. Recently, comparativists have noted the cross-national convergence of West European states around common vocabularies and policies under the heading of "immigrant integration" (Favell, 2001). For instance, national integration policies have now been officially adopted in France, Belgium and the Netherlands – in search of a politically acceptable middle ground between the equally divisive extremes of cultural differentialism and ethnic exclusionism at both ends of the political spectrum (Phalet & Swyngedouw, 2001). In the case of the Netherlands, the adoption of integration policies meant a dramatic move away from its former exemplary policies, which were – along with similar British and Swedish policies – pioneering a European variant of immigrant multiculturalism. Specifically, Dutch ethnic minorities policies have moved away from the public recognition of ethnic cultures and identities towards a more restrictive and individualized approach to the integration of newcomers.

More generally, proponents of integration – in the European sense of the term – usually require the subordination, though not necessarily the abandonment, of ethnic loyalties to the dominant national culture and identity in order to achieve full citizenship in the receiving society. For instance, integration policies in Belgium specify that immigrant minorities are required to learn the national language(s) and to adhere to national "core values" such as the principles of liberal democracy and women's rights. In contrast, advocates of multiculturalism tend to support some degree of public accommodation and recognition of distinct ethnic cultures and identities. For instance, many state schools in the UK and the Netherlands provide special *halal* food or special prayer places for the benefit of Muslim minorities.

Looking beyond diverse visions of national identity and citizenship, both integration and multiculturalism policies seek to create some sense of belonging across ethnic boundaries by formally redefining national institutions and cultures (Faist, 2000). In so doing, de facto multi-ethnic states are assigning more or less incomplete membership status to different ethnic categories.

In so doing, they are blurring and redrawing the lines between insiders and outsiders. Historically speaking, citizenship regimes have always served as exclusionary devices distinguishing between those who belong and those who don't (Brubaker, 1992). Consequently, changing notions of citizenship do not only include settled or long-established minorities to varying degrees, they also entail new forms of exclusion. Thus, the partial dissociation of citizenship in European states from national cultures and identities has new inclusionary as well as exclusionary implications. For instance, the creation of a superordinate category of "EU citizens" has extended certain prerogatives that were hitherto attached to national membership – such as local voting rights – to non-nationals from other EU countries while at the same time subjecting "third-country nationals" to a double exclusion as non-national and non-EU residents.

20.3   Towards a more integrated approach

One reason why European acculturation research has not (yet) realized its full comparative potential is the persistence of distinct national vocabularies and understandings of migration and multiculturalism (Phalet & Örkeny, 2001). The field of ethnic and migration studies is a terminological quagmire, where ill-defined concepts are typically applied to very different categories and cases (Connor, 1994). Conceptual problems are complicated by the fact that key terms in social science research, such as *nationalism, integration, assimilation, multiculturalism, discrimination, racism* . . . are also used as appraisive and operative tools in policy making. Inevitably, core concepts in acculturation research are associated with normative precepts or idealized projections of society. Since policy models and practices vary considerably between – or even within – national contexts, the same concept is therefore weighted with very different affective or evaluative valences in different contexts. A related problem is the sometimes unreflective use of international concepts and measures that have been developed to examine very different multicultural realities in Canada, Australia or the USA. In our view, the field of cross-cultural acculturation studies in Europe is still in search of a balanced "derived etics" approach, which starts from the "emics" of local ethnopolitical configurations in order to delineate common research units and concepts (Van de Vijver & Leung, 1997).

In what follows, theoretical and empirical implications of the European research context for the study of acculturation are discussed and illustrated with recent examples of studies and findings. Building on Berry's (2002) bicultural acculturation model, an interactive and contextual approach of acculturation processes is developed and applied across national contexts in Europe (Phalet & Swyngedouw, 2003). This approach implies that acculturation is only partly a matter of personal choice, as it is co-determined by the quality of inter-group relations and by the socio-political context in which cross-cultural interactions take place. Most importantly, acculturation contexts not only refer to the immediate situational context of intercultural encounters, but should include the wider political, institutional and historical context of inter-group relations. More often than not, national and ethnic cultures and identities are being politically challenged and mobilized, for instance by competing minority and dominant nationalisms in multinational states or by the new Radical Right campaigning against immigrants or Islam. This has psychological implications for the acculturation strategies that are open to immigrants or minorities. But public cultures and identities have hitherto been under-researched in acculturation studies, which are primarily concerned with the private lives, individual attitudes, and personal adaptation of immigrants. As a consequence, relatively little is known about the psychological consequences of ethno-political tension for immigrant or minority experiences of acculturation. From a contextual and interactive perspective on acculturation in European settings, however, divergence between dominant and minority acculturation orientations (e.g., in the case of Turks in the Netherlands, between dominant Dutch assimilationism and minority Turkish segregationism), and hence inter-group conflict, is most likely in the public domain. These national and ethnic cultures and identities are openly played out against each other in the political arena, in public debates and in the media. Thus, we argue the need to incorporate the public domain into European acculturation studies, with a view to complementing a predominant research emphasis on acculturative transitions in private cultures and encounters.

20.3.1   Ethnic and national categories: what do they mean?

A basic requirement of comparative research is the definition of common categories as units of analysis. By definition then, the acculturation process implies enduring relationships of asymmetrical interdependence between various minority groups and a dominant cultural group within the same state. But inter-group relations in European cities and societies are generally more complex than the deceptively simple divide between "Us" (nationals) and "Them" (immigrants). Commonly used distinctions between "ethnic" and "national" groups take on different meanings in different European countries (Ruiz Jiménez, Kosic & Kiss, forthcoming). Not only do these categories have a different legal status in different countries, but their sociocultural meanings and political implications depend crucially on specific histories of nation formation and institutional reform. While the historical past may carry considerable weight in national and ethnic self-definitions, ethnic categories are not simply given, nor are they invented overnight. Rather, they are socially constructed and politically mobilized in response to changing socio-economic opportunities, institutional arrangements and cultural meaning systems.

Thus, in Central and Eastern Europe, ethnic categories and cultures mostly refer to non-immigrant minorities who have formed distinct cultural or linguistic communities over generations. Most often they are territorially con-centrated in certain regions and historically included in the process of nation formation – in the sense that they have a historical claim on linguistic rights or on other forms of cultural or regional autonomy (e.g., Jews in Russia or Turks in Bulgaria). "National" categories are used to refer to national minorities as well as dominant national groups within multinational states (Brubaker, 1996). National minorities typically have national political status or aspirations and most often also an external national homeland (e.g., Hungarians in Rumania or Russians in Ukraine).

In multi-nation states as historically multicultural settings, acculturation processes between minority and dominant cultural groups are embedded in complex inter-group relations. An interesting example of how ethnic minori-ties negotiate multiple, overlapping and conflicting ethnic identities and cul-tures are the Polish Tatars. In their qualitative study of Polish Tatar self-understandings and public discourse, Cieslik and Verkuyten (in press) show how they try to reconcile being a Tatar, a Muslim and a Pole by interweaving different narratives: a first historical narrative recounts Tatar cultural, military and political involvement in Poland as proof of their true Polishness and patri-otism; a second mythological narrative refers to Tatar ancestors as warriors conquering the steppe, testifying to a uniquely Tatar heritage and a glorious past; and last but not least, a religious narrative casts Polish Tatars as historical mediators between East and West, connecting Christian Poland and Europe to the Muslim world. The case of Polish Tatars shows nicely how political discourse and historical past are being appropriated and reinvented in order to reconcile multiple intersecting identities and cultures.

Conversely, in Western Europe, the attribute "ethnic" applies mostly to var-ious categories of immigrants and their descendants. For example, the term "ethnic minority" in the Netherlands refers to specific groups of immigrant workers and their children, including Turkish and Moroccan labor migrants and Surinamese and Antillian post-colonial migration (Hagendoorn, Vollebergh & Veenman, 2003). Membership of an ethnic minority in the Dutch case is defined by the nativity of at least one parent, which overlaps only in part with foreign nationality or with ethnic self-categorization. Moreover, not all post-migration communities in the Netherlands have obtained the status of ethnic minority, but only those that were officially recognized as culturally distinct and socially dis-advantaged and hence entitled to special minorities policies. Although formal minority policies have been discontinued, similar ethnic criteria and categories are still being used for the purpose of ethnic monitoring of specific groups of immigrants and their children.

Surveying random samples of Turkish and Moroccan minorities and a native-born Dutch comparison sample in the multicultural city of Rotterdam, Phalet, van Lotringen and Entzinger (2000) found that (mostly second-generation) minority youth predominantly self-categorize as Turkish, Moroccan or Muslim. Moreover, they self-identify almost exclusively with the Turkish or Moroccan identity while clearly dissociating themselves from the Dutch national identity. From a contextual approach to acculturation, they prefer separation in private life, while preferring a combination of ethnic and national cultural elements or integration in the public domain. From an interactive perspective, the greatest divergence between minority-group and dominant-group acculturation orientations is found for ethnic culture maintenance in the public domain, with native-born Dutch youth expecting minorities to abandon the Turkish or Moroccan culture, as opposed to most Turkish and Moroccan youth who claim public recognition of their heritage cultures. In so doing, ethnic minorities adhere to official multicultural policies, whereas the endorsement of such policies by the receiving society is mostly limited to the private sphere. More precisely, ethnic minority youth navigate both ethnic and national cultures in the public domain, while simultaneously distancing themselves from the dominant national identity. This pattern of findings illustrates the complexity of diverging and shifting acculturation patterns, depending on distinct perspectives (from minorities, dominant groups or formal policies), contexts (public or private) and aspects of acculturation (cultural preference or identification).

Another study dealing with definitions of social and ethnic–national identities in public vs. private contexts is situated in a Southern European country. Through the analysis of interviews with Albanian immigrants in Italy, Kosic and Triandafyllidou (2003) revealed that most relationships between Albanians and the host society are characterized by some degree of social distance, due to their distinct social status as foreigners or *extracomunitari* (literally, non-EU people) vs. natives, which is especially salient in the public domain. The Albanian immigrants stress their strong sense of civil belonging to the host country and consider acquiring Italian citizenship without hesitation, but they also feel discriminated against and they are aware of being labelled "foreigners" or "Albanians," particularly when dealing with Italian institutions. For those Albanians who are ready to mobilize around the issue of recognition, their participation in ethnic associations does not imply ethnic closure or separation. Rather, ethnic associations are seen as a strategic vantage point to promote their culture and to overcome the ignorance and prejudice of natives towards them.

20.3.2 Insiders and outsiders: competing host communities, remigrants and "remooring"

Multinational states across Europe are increasingly also immigrant receiving states. New immigrants to Belgium, Switzerland or Spain, for instance, are confronted with distinct and competing national host cultures within one host society (e.g., in multilingual cities or regions) instead of one dominant host culture (Jacobs, 2000). Similarly, some receiving states are characterized by deep regional divides, for instance between East and West in Germany or between North and South in Italy, with competing claims to the superordinate level of civil society, public culture and the state. Combined multinational, multi-ethnic and regional configurations in contemporary Europe give rise to complex multi-group systems, which defy a simple bicultural approach to acculturation processes and attitudes towards immigrants.

In her study of shifting social comparison processes in intercultural relations between immigrant and national populations in Greece, Italy and Spain, Triandafyllidou (2000) problematizes the issue of defining who "We" are in receiving societies marked by deep inter-group divides. In Italy, for example, the dominant Northern region maintains a greater inter-group distance from the South than the non-dominant South from the North. Moreover, both regions relate to the Italian state itself as to a distinct outgroup, posed against the Italian people in much the same way that immigrants are posed against the ingroup. The study convincingly argues the need to consider both the political discourses of immigration and the historical and institutional developments which give rise to this discursive space.

In a similar vein, Montreuil and Bourhis (in press) compare the acculturation orientations of dominant and non-dominant national groups towards valued and devalued immigrant groups in Canada, Belgium and Germany. Across national contexts, non-dominant national groups (e.g. French-speaking Canadians, Flemish Belgians or East Germans) were feeling more threatened by cultural diversity and hence were consistently less welcoming of immigrant groups. Moreover, greater perceived inter-group distances between competing national groups were found to predict more exclusionist acculturation orientations towards devalued immigrant groups. The latter findings demonstrate how inter-group relations between competing host communities affect the inclusion or exclusion of immigrants in complex multicultural settings.

Another complication of bicultural approaches to acculturation regards the special case of immigrant groups that are viewed as rightfully returning to their historical homeland. Thus, receiving societies with a predominantly "ethnic" conception of national identity and citizenship may recognize a special category of immigrants as belonging to the same ethnic culture as the dominant national group (e.g., ethnic Hungarian refugees from Transylvania, ethnic German "Aussiedler" from Central Europe, Italians from Latin America, etc.). Depending on varying and often diverging minority-group and dominant-group perceptions in specific situations, these immigrant groups are simultaneously defined as cultural insiders and outsiders.

For example, Jasinskaja-Lahti (2000) finds that distinct categories of ethnic Finnish "remigrants" negotiate multiple partial identities, stressing either their linguistic identity as Russian-speaking, or their common Finnish descent as ethnic Finns in Finland. From their side, Finnish hosts are prone to appropriating the Finnish identity and culture while excluding Russian-speaking re-migrants as Russians, thus questioning the validity of their claim to a common Finnish identity and heritage culture. Marked discrepancies between self- and other-categorizations (e.g., by Finnish hosts or by the Russian and Finnish authorities) raise troubling questions of identity and belonging, especially among the youngest generation who are more often monolingual in Russian or of mixed Finnish–Russian parentage. Similarly, in their study of social perceptions and representations of minorities among Hungarian school children, Örkeny and Szabo (2001) found that ethnic Hungarian refugees from Transylvania occupy an ambivalent middle position in the ethnic hierarchy of their hosts. Typically, ethnic Hungarians are devalued relative to the dominant ingroup of "real Hungarians" but much less so than other immigrants. Overall, the simultaneous insider and outsider status of remigrants calls for an interactive and contextual approach to acculturation, allowing for situational shifts and diverging perspectives from immigrants, hosts and formal policies.

Finally, new immigrants may bring along their ethnic minority status from the country of origin (e.g., Moroccan Berbers in the Netherlands, Kurdish refugees from Turkey in Germany, or Frisian Dutch émigrés in Australia); and most immigrants are received by established ethnic minority communities as their proximal hosts in the destination country. Inevitably, migration implies leaving one environment in which one's ethnic identity and culture have been enacted and supported, and coming to a new environment in which one's culture and identity must be resituated and redefined. Ethier and Deaux (1994) have called "remooring" the processes by which immigrants link their cultures and identities to a system of supports in the new environment.

One example of so-called "remooring" concerns the changing meaning of cross-border citizenship among immigrant minorities in Europe with formal or informal dual citizenship (Icduygu, 1996). Thus, Phalet and Swyngedouw (2001) compared social representations of dual citizenship in the national contexts of origin and residence among Turkish and Moroccan minorities in Brussels. Factor analysis of the valences attached to national institutions, symbols and values in both contexts shows that dual national attachments carry distinct meanings. Typically, long-distance Turkish or Moroccan citizenship is centered around an imaginary ethno-religious community, connecting religious symbols and moral values with national icons, as distinct from a predominant orientation towards equal rights, education and employment as Belgian citizens.

Another example of remooring refers to the changing and multiple meanings of religion among Muslim minorities in Europe, especially among the second generation. A comparative survey of Turkish and Moroccan minorities in Rotterdam documents predominant processes of "boundary blurring" (cf. Lamont & Molnar, 2002) between ethnic and national cultures and between private and public domains (Phalet & Hagendoorn, 2002; Phalet & Güngör, 2004). Boundary blurring refers to the redefinition by Muslim youth of what it means to be a Muslim in Europe, redrawing the lines between (Muslim) insiders and (non-Muslim) outsiders. Factor analysis of religious attitudes and behaviors reveals distinct dimensions of religious identification, religious participation within the ethnic community, and religious mobilization or public claim-making in the wider society. While religious identification is remarkably strong, widely shared and stable across generations, the younger generations typically dissociate their Muslim identity from active participation in religious associations and practices. At the same time, a minority of Muslim youth, who perceive severe ethnic discrimination or political exclusion from the receiving society, support religious mobilization in the public domain. The patterning of distinct religious dimensions shows how Turkish and Moroccan youth are negotiating the symbolic boundaries of Muslim communities in Europe against the backdrop of intergenerational, inter-ethnic and geopolitical tensions.

20.4   Socio-political context and ethnic exclusion

Immigrant as well as non-immigrant ethnic minorities are facing vary-ing degrees and forms of exclusion by European states and societies. To sketch the wider social and political context of European ethnic relations, some basic facts about migration policies, ethnic inequalities and ethnic prejudice in Europe are briefly reviewed below.

Policies regarding the immigration, naturalization and integration of immi-grants have largely remained a prerogative of the member states and are decided at the national level of government. Nevertheless, a series of communications and agreements at the EU level have enabled (limited) free movement of EU cit-izens across national borders (i.e., the 1985 Schengen Agreement) and issued influential directives concerning (among other things) the reception of asylum seekers, the monitoring and combating of ethnic prejudice and discrimination, and the extension of local voting rights to non-nationals. Despite continu-ing efforts to harmonize national policies across EU member states, the main immigrant receiving countries in Europe have developed different regimes of immigrant incorporation. Some migration scholars have heralded the end of the nation state, questioning the feasibility of state control or state regulation and presenting immigrants as pioneers of emerging transnational social spaces (Faist, 2000). Others, in contrast, have convincingly argued the relative stabil-ity and the significant impact of national immigration and citizenship regimes, as well as national social and welfare policies, emphasizing the continued power of nation states to institutionalize the selective inclusion and exclusion of different categories of immigrants (Joppke, 1999).

20.4.1   Ethnic inequalities

Regardless of the ways in which immigrants are incorporated into society, most of them suffer from political and social exclusion. Migrants experi-ence many barriers and disincentives, often in the form of exclusion from the labor market, or from key social, legal and political institutions, as well as exclusion from local communities and neighborhoods (Cremer-Schafer, Pelican, Pilgram, Steinert, Taylor & Vorbuba, 2001).

Employment discrimination poses the most serious problem. Across Western Europe, immigrants have far higher rates of unemployment and economic inactivity than the native-born population. These rising unemployment rates among immigrant workers have caused increasing concern for the prospects of the next generation (European Commission, 2001; OECD, 2003). In many countries net ethnic disparities between the occupational attainment of the second-generation immigrant and the native-born population persist after taking into account educational qualifications and relevant socio-demographic variables (Bonifazi & Strozza, 2003; Heath & Cheung, forthcoming). This concern is deepened by the rise of a significant anti-immigrant vote and widespread anti-immigrant attitudes in a number of EU countries, presenting immigrants as a threat to national culture, unity and prosperity (Lubbers, 2001). Most recently, geopolitical repercussions of September 11 have fueled hostile reactions against Muslim immigrants and minorities across Europe (EUMC, 2003; Phalet & Hagendoorn, 2002). Against the background of economic insecurity and ethno-political tension, national media and – to some extent – public opinion are now overtly framing immigrants and their children as a socio-economic burden, as cultural outsiders and as a security threat (Fetzer, 2000; Sniderman, Hagendoorn & Prior, 2003; ter Wal, 2001). In addition, the fall of the Berlin Wall and European enlargement have brought to the fore the fear of new streams of massive and uncontrolled east–west migration.

20.4.2 Ethnocentrism and prejudice

Going beyond classic prejudice, recent survey data across EU member states document the dynamics of conflicting acculturation orientations and inter-group attitudes in immigrant–host relations, leading to varying degrees of public support for legal immigration, anti-discrimination measures and multicultural policies (ESS, 2002). Thus, the latest wave of the European Social Survey in the UK, the Netherlands, Germany and Belgium reveals interesting cross-national commonalities in host acculturation orientations. Asked what are important criteria in admitting new immigrants, the perceived willingness of newcomers to adopt the culture of the receiving society appears to be the most important requisite, followed closely by their mastery of the national language, with educational qualifications a distant third. In spite of a predominant assimilationist orientation, however, an overwhelming majority does not accept overtly racist selection criteria. Similarly, when asked about the desirability at the societal level of various forms of cultural diversity, a majority across all four countries rejects linguistic diversity and close to half thinks that diverse cultural habits are bad for their country. Finally, the data show a common pattern of conditional support for legal immigration and qualified support for multicultural policies, in line with an emerging cross-national consensus around "national integration" models of immigrant incorporation. Specifically, a majority is in favor of equal rights for minorities and legal protection from discrimination in the workplace, but not the public accommodation or recognition of minority cultures (e.g., special schools for linguistic or religious minorities), nor the granting of full political rights including the right to vote. Interestingly, opposition to new immigration and minority rights in a recent Dutch survey was not restricted to an openly prejudiced segment of the national population, but it was related to widespread perceptions of culture conflict and political threat associated with Islam in Europe (Sniderman et al., 2003). Clearly, ethno-political tension between Muslim communities and receiving societies in Western Europe is at the heart of opposed immigrant and host acculturation orientations and inter-group conflict (Phalet et al., 2000).

20.5   New challenges and directions for future research

Migration and ethnic minority issues will continue to challenge European societies in the near future. Not only can acculturation studies improve our understanding of these key issues, but new forms of cross-border migration and cultural diversity in Europe are rich in possibilities for conceptual and empirical development. While the European research context offers unique comparative opportunities, it is not without its challenges. It has been argued that the meaning of ethnic or national categories and inter-ethnic relations depends crucially on distinct historical, legal and political frameworks and on varying social constructions of identity and otherness from one country to another. In the Center and East of Europe ethnic minority issues are closely related to the challenge of minority nationalism, whereas the West of Europe has been mainly concerned with very different challenges of immigrant multiculturalism. Across Europe, however, established national models of measuring and managing cultural diversity are confronted with new transnational challenges. One major challenge consists of new forms of cross-border migration: examples are so-called "free movers" pursuing European professional careers in Brussels, London or Amsterdam, or "transmigrants" commuting back and forth across the German–Polish border. A related challenge is the increase in cultural diversity in European cities and societies, with established immigrant communities being quickly outnumbered by an increasingly diverse inflow of asylum seekers, refugees and documented or undocumented workers. Last but not least, many European countries now have to reckon with the rise of "islamophobia" in the wake of September 11, and with the electoral sway of a new Radical Right with a populist anti-immigrant discourse.

Complex patterns of ethnic relations in an enlarged European context call for a careful "derived etics" approach to comparative research. Such an approach starts from an "emic" understanding of the acculturation process within its social, cultural and institutional context. This is a necessary first step in search of the common psychological dimensions and dynamics of acculturation across national configurations of ethnic groups and relations. Extending a basic bicultural model of acculturation, the emphasis throughout this chapter has been on an interactive and contextual approach to acculturation. Context does not only refer to the immediate situational setting of intercultural encounters, but takes into account the wider historical, political and discursive embeddedness of the acculturation process. Similarly, a truly interactive approach goes beyond a simple ingroup–outgroup divide between hosts and immigrants, and allows for shifting perspectives across multiple and intersecting ethnic and national groups and cultures. The quest for common patterns as well as areas of difference invites us to fine-tune our conceptual tools and empirical measures, learning and contributing our insights across national as well as disciplinary borders.

20.6 References

Bauböck, R. (1994). *The integration of immigrants*. Strasbourg: The Council of Europe.

Berry, J. W. (2002). Conceptual approaches to acculturation. In K. Chun, P. Balls-Organista & G. Marin (eds.), *Acculturation* (pp. 17–37). Washington: American Psychiatric Association.

Bonifazi, C. & Strozza, S. (2003). Integration of migrants in Europe: data sources and measurement in old and new receiving countries. *Studi Emigrazione, 40(152)*, 870–927.

Bourhis, R. Y., Moïse, L. C., Perrault, S. & Sénécal, S. (1997). Towards an interactive acculturation model: a social-psychological approach. *International Journal of Psychology, 32*, 369–386.

Brands Kehre, I. & Stalidzane, I. (2003). *The role of regional aspects in dealing with citizenship issues*. Riga: The Naturalization Board of the Republic Latvia.

Breakwell, G. M. & Lyons, E. (1996). *Changing European identities: social-psychological analyses of social change*. Oxford: Butterworth-Heinemann.

Brubaker, R. (1992). *Citizenship and nationhood in France and Germany*. Cambridge: Cambridge University Press.

  (1996). *Nationalism reframed: nationhood and the national question in the New Europe*. Cambridge: Cambridge University Press.

Cieslik, A. & Verkuyten, M. (in press). National, ethnic and religious identities: hybridity and the case of Polish Tatars. *National Identities*.

Connor, W. (1994). *Ethnonationalism: the quest for understanding*. Boston: Princeton University Press.

Cremer-Schafer, H., Pelican, C., Pilgram, A., Steinert, H., Taylor, I. & Vorbuba, G. (2001). *Social exclusion as a multidimensional process: subcultural and formally assisted strategies of coping with and avoiding social exclusion*. TSER (Targeted Socio-Economic Research) SOE1-CT98–2048. Brussels: European Commission.

Crul, M. & Vermeulen, H. (eds.) (2003). The future of the second generation: the integration of migrant youth in six European countries. *International Migration Review, 37(4)*.

Deaux, K. (2000). Surveying the landscape of immigration: social-psychological perspectives. *Journal of Community and Applied Psychology, 10*, 421–431.

ESS (European Social Survey) (2002). www.europeansocialsurvey.org/.

Ethier, K. A. & Deaux, K. (1994). Negotiating social identity when contexts change. *Journal of Personality and Social Psychology, 67*, 243–251.

EUMC (European Monitoring Centre) (2003). *Situation of Islamic communities in five European cities.* Vienna: European Monitoring Centre on Racism and Xenophobia.

European Commission (2001). *European social statistics: labour force survey results 2000.* Luxembourg: Office for Official Publications of the European Community.

——— (2003). *Migration and the social integration of migrants: valorisation of research on migration and immigration funded under 4th and 5th European Framework Programmes of Research.* Brussels: European Commission, DG Research, Citizen and Governance. EUR 20641.

Faist, T. (2000). Transnationalism in international migration: implications for the study of citizenship and culture. *Ethnic and Racial Studies, 23(2)*, 189–222.

Favell, A. (2001). Integration policy and integration research in Europe. In T. A. Aleinikoff & D. Klusmeyer (eds.), *Citizenship today* (pp. 349–399). Washington, DC: Brookings Institute / Carnegie Foundation.

——— (2003). Games without frontiers: questioning transnational social power of migrants in Europe. *Archives Européennes de Sociologie, 44(3)*, 397–427.

Fetzer, J. S. (2000). *Public attitudes toward immigration in the US, France and Germany.* Cambridge: Cambridge University Press.

Hagendoorn, L., Linssen, H. & Tumanov, S. (2001). *Intergroup relations in states of the former Soviet Union: the perception of Russians.* European Monographs in Social Psychology Series. Hove: Psychology Press.

Hagendoorn, L., Vollebergh, W. & Veenman, J. (eds.) (2003). *Integrating immigrants in the Netherlands.* Aldershot: Ashgate.

Haug, W. (2002). *The demography of immigrant populations in Europe.* European Population Papers Series, 8. Strasbourg: Council of Europe, DG III, Social Cohesion F-67075.

Heath, A. & Cheung, S.-Y. (forthcoming). *Ethnic minority disadvantage in cross-national perspective.* Oxford: Oxford University Press.

Icduygu, A. (1996). Becoming a new citizen in an immigration country: Turks in Australia and Sweden. *International Migration, 34(2)*, 257–272.

Jacobs, D. (2000). Multinational and poly-ethnic politics entwined: minority representation in the region of Brussels-Capital. *Journal of Ethnic and Migration Studies, 26(2)*, 289–304.

Jasinskaja-Lahti, I. (2000). *Psychological acculturation and adaptation among Russian-speaking immigrant adolescents in Finland.* http://ethesis.helsinki. fi/julkaisut/val/vk/jasinskaja-lahti/psycholo.html. University of Helsinki: Department of Social Psychology.

Joppke, C. (1999). *Immigration and the nation state: the US, Germany and Great Britain.* Oxford: Oxford University Press.

Kalin, R. & Berry, J. W. (1996). Interethnic attitudes in Canada: ethnocentrism, consensual hierarchy and reciprocity. *Canadian Journal of Behavioural Sciences, 28*, 253–261.

Koopmans, R. & Statham, P. (2000). *Challenging immigration and ethnic relations politics*. Oxford: Oxford University Press.

Kosic, A. & Triandafyllidou, A. (2003). Albanian immigrants in Italy: migration plans, coping strategies and identity issues. *Journal of Ethnic and Migration Studies*, *29*, 997–1014.

 (forthcoming). Urban cultural policy and immigrants: multiculturalism or simply "paternalism"? In U. H. Meinhof and A. Triandafyllidou (eds.), *Transcultural Europe: cultural policy in the changing European space*. Basingstoke: Palgrave/MacMillan.

Kymlicka, W. (1995). *Multicultural citizenship*. Oxford: Oxford University Press.

 (2000). *Politics in the vernacular*. Oxford: Oxford University Press.

Lamont, M. & Molnar, V. (2002). The study of boundaries in the social sciences. *Annual Review of Sociology*, *28*, 107–195.

Liebkind, K. (2000). Acculturation. In R. Brown & S. Gaertner (eds.), *Blackwell handbook of social psychology*, Vol. III: *Intergroup processes* (pp. 386–404). Oxford: Blackwell.

Lubbers, M. (2001). *Exclusionistic electorates: extreme right-wing voting in Western Europe*. Nijmegen: Radboud University.

Montreuil, A. & Bourhis, R. Y. (2001). Majority acculturation orientations toward "valued" and "devalued" immigrants. *Journal of Cross-Cultural Psychology*, *32*, 698–719.

 (in press). Acculturation orientations of competing host communities towards valued and devalued immigrants. *International Journal of Intercultural Relations*.

OECD (Organisation for Economic and Cultural Development) (2003). *Employment outlook: toward more and better jobs*. Paris: OECD.

Örkeny, A. & Szabo, I. (2001). Representations of minorities among Hungarian children. In K. Phalet & A. Örkeny (eds.), *Ethnic minorities and inter-ethnic relations in context* (pp. 139–160). Aldershot: Ashgate.

Phalet, K. & Güngör, D. (2004). Religie, etnische relaties en burgerschap. In K. Phalet & J. ter Wal (eds.), *Moslim in Nederland III* (Being Muslim in the Netherlands III). The Hague: Social and Cultural Planning Office.

Phalet, K. & Hagendoorn, L. (2002). *Constructing and mobilising ethno-religious identity and otherness*. Utrecht: ERCOMER Working Paper.

Phalet, K. & Örkeny, A. (eds.) (2001). *Ethnic minorities and inter-ethnic relations in context: a Dutch–Hungarian comparison*. Research in Migration and Ethnic Relations Series. Aldershot: Ashgate.

Phalet, K. & Swyngedouw, M. (2001). National identities and representations of citizenship: a comparison of Turks, Moroccans and working-class Belgians in Brussels. *Ethnicities*, *2(1)*, 5–30.

 (2003). A cross-cultural analysis of immigrant and host values and acculturation orientations. In H. Vinken & P. Ester (eds.), *Comparing cultures* (pp. 185–212). Leiden: Brill.

Phalet, K., van Lotringen, C. & Entzinger, H. (2000). *Islam in de multiculturele samenleving* [Islam in a multi-cultural society]. ERCOMER Report, 2000(1). Utrecht: ERCOMER (European Research Centre on Migration and Ethnic Relations).

Phinney, J. S., Horenczyk, G., Liebkind, K. & Vedder, P. (2001). Ethnic identity, immigration and well-being: an international perspective. *Journal of Social Issues*, *57(3)*, 493–510.

Ruiz Jiménez, A. M., Kosic, A. & Kiss, P. (forthcoming). A public view on European and national identification. In B. Stråth and A. Triandafyllidou (eds.), *Media, elites and citizens: European and national allegiances*.

Sniderman, P., Hagendoorn, L. & Prior, M. (2003). Predisposing factors and situational triggers: exclusionary reactions towards immigrant minorities. *American Political Science Review*, *98*, 35–49.

ter Wal, J. (2001). Minacce territoriali, socio-economiche e di sicurezza. L'immagine degli immigrati nella stampa quotidiana [Territorial, socio-economic and security threats. Images of immigrants in the daily press]. *Incontri*, *16*, 69.

Triandafyllidou, A. (2000). The political discourse on immigration in Southern Europe: a critical analysis. *Journal of Community and Applied Social Psychology*, *10*, 373–389.

Van de Vijver, F. & Leung, K. (1997). *Methods and data analysis for cross-cultural research*. Newbury Park, CA: Sage Publications.

Verkuyten, M. (2004). *The social psychology of ethnic identity*. New York: Psychology Press.

Zagefka, H. & Brown, R. (2002). The relationship between acculturation strategies and relative fit and intergroup relations: immigrant–majority relations in Germany. *European Journal of Social Psychology*, *32*, 171–188.

Zick, A., Wagner, U., van Dick, R. & Petzel, T. (2001). Acculturation and prejudices in Germany: majority and minority perspectives. *Journal of Social Issues*, *57*, 541–557.

21 Acculturation in Francophone European societies

Colette Sabatier & Virginie Boutry

This chapter presents three dimensions of the European Francophone perspective on acculturation research: the context of acculturation in each of the French-speaking countries in Europe, with an emphasis on the similarities and differences; the conceptions that European Francophone people have of the process of acculturation, given their traditional philosophical and political views; and finally some recent empirical studies.

The three neighboring Francophone European countries, France, Belgium and Switzerland, share common histories and a number of points of view on social life, values and intellectual references. Like all neighbors, however, they have pursued some distinctiveness from each other. These shared histories and references allow us to treat them as a group, especially because Francophone researchers within the intercultural field share some theoretical perspectives, refer to the same authors, and share many of the same views on acculturation.

21.1 Political and socio-economic context for acculturation

Dealing with acculturation means taking into account several dimensions of social and political life (Sabatier & Berry, 1994). These include: the hosting traditions of the receiving countries; their demographic needs; immigrant populations (number, diversity of origin, and socio-economic level); and policies concerning social rights of foreigners, civil freedoms, authorization for residence, work and acquisition of nationality. Attitudes of the receiving society members towards immigrants and cultural diversity in daily interactions (school, workplace, living areas, and social and health institutions) are also to be taken into consideration (Bourhis, Moïse, Perreault & Sénécal, 1997). For all of these features, experiences of each of the three countries differ.

21.2 Political histories and founding myths in regard to cultural diversity

National policies regarding inter-group relations and their attitudes towards linguistic and cultural diversity differ across the three countries. France, with 60 million inhabitants, is a centralizing country. Since the French

Revolution, France has emphasized equality for all, whatever their social, cultural and religious origins. This position entails the non-recognition of specific rights for any sub-group. Specific regional and cultural features are scarcely recognized for fear of communitarianism, which is perceived either as the negotiation of specific rights and preferential treatment, or as the domination of one sub-group over others. Cultural and religious specificities are relegated to the private domain, but guaranteed as individual freedom rights. Officially monolingual and secular, France is, nonetheless, in reality multilingual, multicultural and multireligious. Six regional languages have a large number of speakers. Mainly Catholic, France also has the largest Jewish and Islamic populations in the European Union. As a colonizing country since the sixteenth century, France maintains specific bonds with each of her former colonies, through their integration as a territorial part of France, or the establishment of strong economic and cultural bonds. Many formerly colonized individuals and their descendants live in France and have French nationality, which is another source of the country's cultural diversity.

In Belgium and Switzerland, both federal states, several linguistic and cultural communities coexist. These countries have built their national unity on union and compromise between different social groups or territorial communities (Swiss cantons, for example), in order to face a common enemy. In consequence, multilingualism and multiculturalism are part of their respective constitutions. Belgium has 10 million inhabitants among whom are 3.5 million (35%) French speakers. The country's existence as an autonomous and independent country dates from 1831 when it separated from the Netherlands. Belgium became a unitary state, with a constitutional monarchy, and three cultural and linguistic groups (Walloon, Flemish and Germanophones) sharing Catholicism as a religious culture. At the end of the nineteenth century, Belgium engaged in the colonization of the Congo. Switzerland has 7.2 million inhabitants among whom are 1.3 million (18%) French speakers. This nation was born out of its people's need to unite in order to face the expansionism of the House of Habsburg. The Swiss constitution of 1848 established a compromise between centralization and federalism. The Swiss adopted a principle of equal status for the four languages, but recently set up a policy of protection and promotion of the two minority languages (Italian and Romansh). Deeply attached to its neutrality and independence, Switzerland is not a member of the UN, and, while completely encircled by countries of the European Union, it is not a member. Being a pacifist and non-expansionist country, it never had colonies. Altogether, the country seems to be inward-looking.

21.3 Demography and policies towards immigration

These three flourishing countries are proud of their long tradition of welcoming refugees. In the sixteenth century, the canton of Geneva welcomed the Huguenots, who were expelled from France. Since the Revolution, France has also been a land of asylum for political refugees. The three countries have benefited from the supply of immigrant populations for both their demographic and economic development. Without immigration over the past century, the French population would have been reduced to 12 million inhabitants. The need for a supply of labor has been felt since the beginning of the twentieth century, but particularly immediately after the Second World War. This need decreased radically in the 1970s, but, due to demographic problems, the question of immigration is again under discussion. However, in the three countries, policies towards immigrants, and the rights to entrance, residence and work, as well as the rules for acquisition of nationality, are considerably different (Wihtol de Wenden, 1999).

The immigrant populations (the number of foreigners and among them the proportion of non-Europeans) coming to each country are related to their national histories (including bonds with their former colonies), their geographical position and the economic needs of the country. France with 6.1% of foreigners has a lower overall rate but a higher proportion of people not belonging to any of the fifteen countries of the European Union (60%). They come mainly from Africa (Maghreb and Sub-Saharan countries), which has intensified the cultural diversity of the French population. The main immigrant groups are Portuguese (14.4%), Algerians (13.3%), Italians (11.6%) and Moroccans (11.0%). Belgium has a foreign population of 8.4%, which is a little more homogeneous than immigrants in France, being mainly citizens of European Union countries. The main groups are Italians (23.9%), Moroccans (15%), French (10%) and Turks (9%); the formerly colonized Congolese are very few (1%). The presence of foreigners varies according to the different Belgian communities. Within the Flemish community, the proportion is 4.8% foreigners, of whom 2.2% are non-European. Within the Walloon community, it is 10.4%; of these 2.4% are non-European. In the Brussels area, the proportion is 29.7%, of whom 15.5% are non-Europeans. Switzerland has a higher proportion of foreigners (19.6%). These include persons of European origin (89%), mainly from Italy (25%), the former Yugoslavia (23%) and Portugal (10%). However, these statistical data, which simply count the number of people who do not hold citizenship, do not reflect the real degree of openness in the different countries. For example, Leanza, Ogay, Perregaux and Dasen (2001) underline, the harshness of the Swiss laws concerning the acquisition of nationality, and point out that, if Switzerland had adopted the same laws as her neighbors, the percentage of foreigners would be reduced to around 7.2%.

Laws concerning the rights of sojourn and residence for immigrants and for people seeking refugee status, as well as the acquisition of citizenship, have changed several times in recent years. These changes have been due to such factors as economic pressures, the growing migratory flow, and the necessity of coordinated immigration policies among European countries. However, the changes in each country have evolved in opposite directions (Wihtol de Wenden, 1999). In France, the law concerning the acquisition of nationality, which had been more liberal (a combination of *jus soli* and *jus sanguini*, based upon place of birth and parentage, respectively), became tougher in 1993 with restriction of the *jus soli* and an increase in the length of marriage required in the case of acquisition by marriage. One can apply for citizenship after five years of residence. In Belgium, where the right to citizenship from parentage prevailed till 1985, the law has been changed to allow for double citizenship. For second-generation immigrants, it is possible to keep both the citizenship of their parents and that of Belgium. One can apply for citizenship after five years of residence. In Switzerland, laws have been seriously toughened on two occasions, due to concerns about the ability of immigrants to be integrated into Swiss society. In 1991, the Federal Council pronounced on the differential capacities of immigrants to integrate, according to their country of origin. Some are considered to be fully able to integrate here, and some as clearly unable. The Federal Council has adopted a "three circles" policy that distinguishes between Europe; Canada / USA / Eastern Europe; and the rest of the world, with differential quotas. Access to nationality is very difficult: the right from parentage prevails, and application for nationality is possible only after a residence of twelve years.

In France and Belgium, around 36% of foreigners acquire citizenship, but this number varies according to country of origin. In France, Vietnamese acquire it in large numbers, but Portuguese acquire it less often. The variation according to countries of origin is explained by several factors: among them are the possibility of having dual nationality (which is possible in all three countries), as well as the laws in each country of origin. For example, for Portuguese who maintain strong economic and affective links with their home country, it is very important to keep their Portuguese nationality. For Moroccans in France and in Belgium, there is a similar rate of acquiring citizenship and a similar percentage of mixed marriages (15% in Belgium, 20% in France). These indicate an identical quality of welcome, in spite of different integration policies and different laws for the acquisition of citizenship.

21.4   Religious issues

The religious issue is often seen as a sign of cultural distance and as an impediment to the integration of immigrant populations. It is a recurrent question put forward with the increase of xenophobia. This is the case even when immigrants have the same faith but have different practices, customs and rites. For example, at the beginning of the twentieth century, Polish and Italian Roman Catholics in France were rejected by the French population (Dewitte, 2003). Today, the question of religious differences is increasingly being revived in all the European Union countries, especially with Muslim immigrants arriving from the Maghreb and Turkey.

The three Francophone countries are officially secular, but have different conceptions of the notion of secularism (Haarscher, 1996). The Swiss way of life has been founded on the principle of tolerance for different religions since the sixteenth century, when there was tension among the different Christian communities (today, the main religion is still Christianity, mainly Protestant or Catholic). Belgium and France are predominantly Roman Catholic. In Belgium, Catholicism has been a major unifier. Following numerous debates, during the nineteenth and early twentieth centuries the supporters of Catholicism and those of secularism reached a compromise. The Belgian State recognizes and subsidizes the advocates both of secularism and of five cults (Catholic, Protestant, Anglican, Jewish, Islamic). Two large educational networks coexist, one official (community, provinces and municipality), the other private (religious congregations, lay associations and individuals) but subsidized by the state. The organization of Islam began in 1974, but Belgium privileged the influence of Saudi Arabia while the majority of Muslims in Belgium have Moroccan origins. In France, the relationships between the Catholic Church and French state have been tense since the Revolution. The separation of church and state has been strict since 1905, even if some legal exceptions exist in Alsace, as well as in some overseas territories. Any incursion of any church in state life and public institutions (schools, for example) is perceived negatively. The secular character of public life is conceived as a basic guarantee of religious freedom in the private domain. In 2004, the French government changed the relations between Islam and the Republic. These changes included the concretization of the legal and secular organization of Islam and the passing of the "secular law" which prohibits the wearing of all distinctive religious symbols in public institutions. The aim of this law is to guarantee the same treatment for all, and to protect the private right to religious freedom.

21.5 Inter-group attitudes of the host society and models of integration

Attitudes towards foreign populations and religious and racial diversity, as assessed by several European Union surveys of French and Belgian samples, are relatively similar, but with substantial differences in line with the demographic and sociological differences of the two countries (see Tables 21.1 and 21.2). France and Belgium are around the European mean, but in general consider it more necessary to establish conditions for entrance into their country than do the other fourteen European countries. They are racist more often than the European mean, but they are more convinced that immigrants

Table 21.1 *Results of "continuous tracking" surveys of European opinion*

	Europe	France	Belgium
People from other European Union (15) who want to live in your country			
accepted without restriction	38	32	45
accepted with restriction	49	53	42
not accepted	10	14	6
Political asylum			
accepted without restriction	34	36	24
accepted with restriction	49	50	53
not accepted	11	11	13
Rights of people who come from countries not EU members			
extended	47	17	16
as they are	24	33	28
restricted	25	45	44
Number of people in your country not EU members			
too many	57	54	54
just right	18	22	22
not too many	17	13	12
Degree of expressed racism			
very racist	9	16	22
quite racist	24	32	33
a little racist	33	27	27
not at all	34	25	19
Option for integration or assimilation			
immigrants are so different, they can never be fully accepted	39	24	25
agrees with assimilation	25	32	44
agrees with integration	36	44	31

Source: European Commission (1997: Table 1: January 1997, no. 10)

Table 21.2 *Feeling of disturbance*

Are you personally disturbed by the presence of a person of		%			
		Europe	France	Belgium	Switzerland
another nationality?	no	81	79	78	90
	yes	15	17	20	
another race?	no	80	75	70	
	yes	15	19	27	
another religion?	no	81	78	71	90
	yes	14	17	26	
Foreigners are a source of cultural enrichment					73

Sources: Belgium, France and Europe – Eurobarometer (2000); Switzerland – Schäbi and Joye (2000).

can adapt themselves to the receiving country. Differences between Belgium and France are in line with their experience of immigrant groups. Belgium is much more welcoming of European Union members than France, while France is more open to political refugees and less bothered by people of a different religion or race than Belgium. In Switzerland, such surveys are rather rare; they indicate, however, that the Swiss are less bothered by foreigners or people with another religion, a fact which seems to contradict the results of different referendums on immigration and policies towards foreigners.

On the whole, considering all aspects of the legal, economic and social framework, the policies towards immigration and integration in the three countries are embedded in distinct philosophical models. Bolzman (2001) identifies four types of rights: cultural, political, socio-economic and civil. According to the degree to which countries respect each of these sets of rights, he describes eight models of integration. These include the model of "assimilationist citizenship" (the model of the great universalist ideologies), which sees the maintenance of cultural rights as an obstacle to the equality of rights in other domains. France is a typical example of "assimilationist citizenship". Switzerland, which has an ethnic conception of the nation, an immigration policy mainly based on the importation of labor and no tradition of colonization, follows the model of "assimilationist non-participative insertion." In Belgium, where immigration is a federal responsibility while the policies of integration (social programs, school, work, housing) are the responsibility of communities, the model of integration is more complicated. The Flemish have adopted the Dutch philosophy of acknowledgment of cultural diversity (which is opposed by the extreme-right nationalist movements), while the Walloon have adopted the "Republican" French model (Bousetta, 2000). According to Bolzman's terminology (2001), the Belgian Flemish model is the "pluricultural non-participative insertion" one, which considers communities as real entities and grants to immigrants social rights but limits their political participation and does not facilitate the acquisition of citizenship. The Belgian Walloon model is the "participative citizenship" model. In fact, because the Belgian social and school policies allow numerous local initiatives, many researchers agree that the differences between the two communities are more philosophical than true differences in the daily life of immigrants (Bousetta, 2000; Medhoune & Lavallée, 2000). In sum, although Switzerland and Belgium have included multiculturalism in their constitutions, analysis of their policies towards cultural groups who were not involved in their historic compromises reveals an important difference from other countries who have adopted multiculturalism, particularly those that have depended on immigration (such as Canada and Australia). Such analysis underlines the difficulties these two Francophone countries have experienced in their attempts to integrate immigrants, difficulties which are greater in Switzerland.

21.6 Major intellectual and theoretical debates about the concept of acculturation

A search of databases and a review of the literature in the social sciences taking the term *acculturation* as a keyword, reveals the small quantity of studies on acculturation in Francophone European countries. This could give the erroneous impression of a lack of interest in cultural contact issues. However, there is another conceptualization of the contact and change process in these countries. Many authors are critical of the concept of acculturation and impute to it a lack of explanatory value and point out the limitations of its culturalist theoretical framework. Some even consider that the concept is impregnated with ethnocentrism. In their view, making a distinction between two cultural groups in order to analyze their relationships has the effect of establishing closed boundaries between cultural groups and unfairly categorizes persons. Numerous researchers in the Francophone European countries thus prefer the concepts of *interpenetration* or *intertwining* (Bastide, 1968), *interculturation* (Clanet, 1990), *transculturation* (Vasquez, 1984) or more simply *socialization*. However, Francophone authors do not ignore the concept of acculturation. When they do refer to it, they all quote the earlier work of Powell, the first author to use this concept, in 1880, and of Herskovits (Redfield, Linton & Herskovits, 1936). The main ideas of the European and Francophone critics of the concept of acculturation, as well as their alternative views are presented in the following section.

21.7 Contributions and critics of the first authors

Among the intellectual circle of Francophone social science researchers who were contemporaries of Herskovits, the theoretical positions of Durkheim were predominant. This sociologist proposed that social and cultural changes are essentially produced by the internal evolution of society. The interest of researchers was therefore centered on the internal cultural dynamics, rather than on change due to external contact. It was not until the 1950s that Francophone researchers began to have an interest in acculturation. This was due to the publications of two contemporaries of Herskovits, Bastide (a sociologist) and Devereux (an anthropologist and psychoanalyst). Bastide, who like Herskovits had worked with Black Americans, presented the work of the school of cultural anthropology on acculturation to Francophone researchers. However, while he acknowledged the theoretical and empirical contribution of these works, he went beyond their limits and tried to improve the approach.

Bastide's criticisms (1968), which influenced a generation of Francophone researchers, are centered on two issues: the primacy of cultural aspects over social ones, and the non-distinction of primary and secondary effects. Firstly,

Bastide acknowledges that social situations of contact are taken into account by American anthropologists, but according to him these researchers have reduced them to a state of a simple variable and have not considered them as true explanatory factors. Cultural relationships are also inter-group relationships; as such they are linked to social facts which constitute frameworks where they occur and which determine the kind of relationship, whether integration, conflict or competition. The second criticism relates to the researchers ignoring the distinction between infrastructure and superstructure, as well as the impact of changes in infrastructure on superstructure, which explains the chain of reactions observed during the process of acculturation. The modification of one dimension of the society leads to unexpected and unavoidable transformations in other dimensions that are not directly involved in the contact itself. This is why it is crucial to differentiate the primary and secondary effects.

Features of acculturation should be studied as whole social phenomena, observable at all levels of social and cultural life. Thus, the analysis of the situation of acculturation should take into account both groups together, whatever their status. Claiming that acculturation is a two-way process, Bastide suggests the terms of *interpenetration* or *intertwining* of cultures, which he believed reflect more accurately the reciprocity of influences. Moreover, considering that culture is a dynamic process of construction, deconstruction and reconstruction, he suggests examining the process of acculturation as a series of disorganizations and re-organizations, along two main principles: continuities and divisions. When continuities prevail over discontinuities, one observes a "material acculturation" process which concerns only visible and conscious aspects of culture. But, in some cases, factors of deculturation prevail and block any restructuring effort. In these circumstances, one observes manifestations of individual disorientation, with an increase of mental diseases and delinquent conducts in these populations. The deconstruction can also coincide with a first phase of a more or less important cultural reconstitution. Acculturation affects the unconscious psychic structures themselves. This process, called by Bastide "formal acculturation," proceeds from the principle of dividing ("principe de coupure").

Bastide (1968) presents a typology of acculturation that includes three fundamental criteria which produce a number of cultural contacts. The three criteria are the presence or absence of manipulation of cultural and social aspects of life, the degree of heterogeneity or homogeneity, and the degree of openness or closedness of the societies in contact. This typology is completed by an analysis of the phenomena of acculturation with special attention to the demographic (majority and numerical minority), ecological (place of contact) and ethnic or racial (structures of domination/subordination) factors that are all involved in the process of acculturation.

Another contemporary of Herskovits' was Devereux (1970), who was a specialist in the study of American Indians living on reservations. He carried out his analysis from an anthropological, psychiatric and psychoanalytic perspective.

His work has had a profound influence on psychotherapists working with immigrants. He proposed the concept of *antagonistic acculturation* which can take three main forms: defensive isolation which consists of avoiding contact and/or pushing away all the cultural influences; the adoption of a new mean which can, in some cases, lead to the modification of the culture of origins; and the negative dissociative acculturation, which expresses itself by a systematic opposition to cultural traits of the threatening culture. This opposition uses three technical means: regression to cultural models prevailing prior to the contact; differentiation, which ends at the construction of original cultural traits; and negation, which consists of elaborate customs strictly opposed to the other group.

In sum, the earlier works of Bastide and Devereux, mainly with colonized or transplanted populations, have integrated the psychological and social science points of view. Their contributions show that the meeting of cultures is not always a peaceful process: it can be the source of conflicts and dysfunctions at the collective level, which have differential consequences on individuals.

21.8   Studies in the 1980s and 1990s

The next generation of Francophone researchers took up these ideas of acculturation as problematic and conflictual. But, due to changes in society with the end of the colonizing era and with the beginning of a huge familial immigration for settlement, they studied essentially the immigrant population. Researchers of this period continued with the macroscopic observations inherited from the earlier works. They devoted their time to the empirical and theoretical identification of the psychological handling of cultural codes of immigrant groups which allows individuals, as well as groups, to handle their identity and mental equilibrium. According to Camilleri and Vinsonneau (1996), this specific focus on psychic aspects is one of the main distinctive characteristics of French research compared to American and Canadian studies on different immigrant communities. The preference for qualitative and clinical methods of research, combined with repeated investigations, rather than quantitative studies with huge samples, is another distinctive feature of the Francophone research on acculturating populations. However, at the present time several researchers are seriously considering the need for a comparative approach (Dasen & Ogay, 2000; Vatz Laaroussi, 2001). As social psychologists demonstrate very little interest in immigrant populations, studies concerning these populations come predominantly from other fields such as educational sciences, social work and clinical psychology.

Camilleri (1990, 1999), the main representative of this second wave of researchers, exerted a strong influence in Francophone Europe. When he refers to the notion of acculturation, he quotes the 1936 definition of Redfield and colleagues, but insists on some differences: the mutual influence through

indirect contacts between the two cultures; the asymmetrical inter-group relations due to domination or subordination; and the changes in both cultures.
The consequences, at the individual level, of conflict and problems generated
by cultural contact affect particularly a person's cultural identity (Camilleri &
Vinsonneau, 1996). Camilleri and his collaborators (Camilleri & Malewska-
Peyre, 1997) concentrate their interest and research efforts on the identity
mechanisms which are activated when individuals and groups are in a situation
of acculturation. They attribute a specific importance to identity construction
with the notion of *identity strategy*. At the individual level, these strategies pursue a double goal: the protection of the sense of self-worth and the maintenance
of the sense of identity unity (balance between the ontological function and
the pragmatic one). These two requirements are particularly endangered in a
situation of acculturation. On one hand, individuals in a situation of acculturation are subjected to a belittlement through stereotypes and prejudices induced
by the asymmetrical relation between the host society and the immigrant's
group of origin. On the other hand, the unity of sense is deconstructed by
the disparity between the different cultural codes which coexist. On the basis
of numerous observations, Camilleri (1990) elaborated a typology of different identity strategies which shows the multiplicity of the paths followed by
immigrants in their effort to adapt to their new environment.

Moreau (1999) considers, however, that Camilleri's views are too optimistic.
Individuals are not always authors of their own life, conscious of what they are
and what determines them. Camilleri's views minimize the tragedy of loss of
one's cultural framework of origin and the difficulties that individuals can meet
in their effort to maintain their own identity in a cultural environment which
is unfamiliar. He insists on the bipolar dimension of the migration process
and proposes the notion of "emigration–immigration." Without the reference
points which sustain their identity in daily life, immigrants try, on a conscious
or unconscious basis, to rebuild a similar cultural framework to the one in
their country of origin, but at the same time they are faced with the objective
conditions of the actual situation. A paradoxical culture results, neither the one
of origin nor that of the host society but an original cultural product, called
"culture of emigration–immigration" which integrates elements taken from the
culture of origin, elements from the culture of the host society, and original
cultural facts. This construction represents a transitional space which alleviates
the experience of migration.

Vasquez (1984), in a critical literature review, noticed the large range of
studies on cultural change which used the notion of acculturation. Following
arguments presented by Bastide, she stressed that social, economic and political constraints endured by individuals and groups in contact are not taken
into account in the classical studies. She also pointed out the implicit ethnocentrism of these studies. Among the studies published after 1970, she
distinguished two types of approach. The first, "descriptive," provides copious
data and general models of acculturation. The second, "dynamic," underlines

the conflictual characteristic of the processes and the contact situations. All of these studies examine the determining factors of acculturation, such as socio-economic level and power relationships, and try to identify the different social supports for acculturation, such as churches, school institutions and language codes. They suggest a psychological explanation for the underlying process, such as expectancies and desires of persons in a situation of acculturation, internalization of belittlement and loss of identity. They also describe the reaction of individuals and groups in a situation of acculturation, such as identity change and withdrawal versus rejection of traditional values. From these studies, Vasquez developed the notion of *transculturation*. In her perspective, the prefix *trans-* means transition, and transformation without bias towards the direction of the process and its goal. Four main principles are described: the first states that conflicts are a dynamic factor in the process; the second claims a need for a diachronic historical analysis; the third emphasizes power relationships as one explanatory factor of the process; and the fourth takes into account the contradictory demands and ambiguity due to the double system of reference and the distance between representations and expectancies of individuals and groups in contact.

Clanet (1990) replaced the term *acculturation* with the term *interculturation*. In line with Vasquez' arguments, he pointed out that indices of acculturation are usually measures of assimilation of minorities. He argued that "acculturation" is appropriate for a diachronic situation which is not the case of persons embedded in a double cultural reference system, for example minorities within a broader context. The new approach developed by Clanet is based on the paradoxical nature of the cultural dynamic. When in contact, a double movement occurs: the transformation of the system due to their interactions, and the maintenance of the system due to the desire of each person to maintain his own identity. The process of interculturation covers these paradoxical dynamics of transformation and coexistence. As a result, three processes are articulated: assimilation by the group of some values of the others; differentiation through the claim of some unique specificities; and an original synthesis, with the creation of new encompassing realities. Interculturation thus refers to the integration of a plurality of cultural references which will combine and interact with each other, and which cannot be reduced to the different cultural poles in contact.

21.9   Current perspectives

The recent publications of Francophone researchers have come close to the concept of acculturation. They concern three types of concepts: the notions of *otherness* (Krewer, 1999; Sabatier, Malewska-Peyre & Tanon, 2002) of *intercultural* (de Villanova, Hily & Varro, 2001) and of *socialization* or *intercultural competences* (Hily, 2001; Manço, 2002).

Otherness (or the construction of the cultural other) lies within the German and French philosophical tradition of studying the relationship between the self and others. It is conceptually close to the social representation of other cultures and individuals. It is also close to the psychology of attributions and of stereotypes, with two main differences: it takes into account intersubjectivity, and always tries to connect the representation of others with the construction of the self (Sabatier *et al.*, 2002). The analysis of the construction of otherness appears to be essential in order to understand the process of adaptation to another culture, including the attitudes of the society towards the new immigrants. The notion of *intercultural* is closer than *otherness* to the concept of acculturation as described by Herskovits. Researchers have used it to study numerous phenomena which occur at the time of cultural meetings, such as artefacts, architecture, and the dynamics of inter-group relationships in daily life (de Villanova *et al.*, 2001). Other authors consider the process of acculturation to be essentially a question of socialization and of cultural competence in such domains as learning the language, social codes, values, modes of politeness and communication behaviors. Adjustment to complex situations which occur when two cultural groups are in contact is a matter of social learning and social competencies which are learned through various networks, such as family, work and school (see also Chapter 5). This is considered to be part of the normal development of any adolescent, young adult or even middle-aged adult (Manço, 2002; Santelli, 2002).

In sum, Francophone researchers who address the question of changes following culture contact focus on the dynamics of interpersonal relationships, with an emphasis on intersubjectivity. They would like to combine these two approaches – the intersubjectivity and the cultural perspectives – for the analysis of social relationships. They definitely prefer emic methodologies over comparison of cultural groups (Krewer, 1994).

21.10 Recent studies on acculturation

In this section, the objective is not to review once again the numerous empirical studies, nor to offer a new synthesis of studies on acculturation. Such work has already been published in several works, at least with respect to the acculturation of children and adolescents (Sabatier, 1999a & b; Sabatier & Berry, 1994). Nor do we aim to present the different studies on identity changes in immigrants who are settled in the three Francophone countries. Our goal is rather to review several recent studies in the field of acculturation which take into account recent changes in the demography of immigration.

The Interactive Model of Acculturation of Bourhis (Bourhis *et al.*, 1997) has been applied in two studies, one in France, the other in Switzerland. One focused on students in a Parisian suburban university characterized by broad cultural and socio-economical diversity, in terms of percentage and diversity of origins. In this study, they add to Berry's model a fifth attitude (individualism) which is the French political point of view; it puts emphasis on the freedom individuals have to choose their own cultural system of references (Barrette, Bourhis, Personnaz & Personnaz, 2004). Results indicate a good similarity between the two groups of students (French and Maghrebians): they both favor individualism first and then integration. Two main aspects of acculturation of French students emerge: first, students of both groups resist the French political view of assimilation. They very seldom choose this option, and they are not ready to sacrifice their cultural origin and their loyalty to their family. A second finding is that students who suffer from discrimination choose the attitude of separation.

Piontkowski, Florack, Hoelker and Obdrzalek (2000) measured acculturation attitudes and mutual perceptions of members of Swiss society and immigrants from the former Yugoslavia. Results indicate a preference for the integration attitude. There is a convergence in the views of these two populations which facilitates the integration of the immigrants. This confirms that, in spite of the harsh governmental policy towards immigrants which assigns them to a precarious social position, Swiss acculturation attitudes towards immigrants are more open.

Bredendiek and Krewer (1999) try to integrate three different models into their framework: Camilleri's model of identity strategies (1999); Berry's model of acculturation strategies (1980); and Boesch's (1991) model of action theory. They studied international students, and considered both positive and negative aspects of acculturation, despite the Francophone theoretical and empirical approach where research efforts are mainly concentrated on individuals' negative experiences. They believe that the process of acculturation can occur at different levels of human functioning, the *pragmatic* level (that is the overt part of the intercultural field which is in line with the sociocultural dimensions described by Ward & Kennedy,1993), and the *ontological* level of subjective and intersubjective identity change.

Current immigration in the three Francophone European countries is essentially a family reunification (rather than as "guest workers"), and as such it is an immigration of settlement. The question of acculturation of children, adolescents and families as a system is thus a particular subject of research among Francophone European researchers. These studies must take into account the process of family dynamics and familial socialization. It also demands serious consideration of the cognitive capacities of children required to handle social information, as well as the attitudes of the host society towards cultural and ethnic diversity and acculturation. Although distinct from the process for adults, numerous studies indicate the relevance of Berry's model of acculturation for adolescents and even for children as young as eight years old (Kanouté, 2002; Sabatier, 1999b; Van de Vijver, Helms-Lornz & Feltzer, 1999).

Regarding family dynamics we have suggested (Sabatier, 1991) the importance of paying attention to the acculturation attitudes and identities of parents, with a clear distinction between their own attitudes and the attitudes they hold for their children. Research indicates a discrepancy between what parents want for themselves and what they desire for their children in terms of acculturation (in both style and degree). Research also indicates that, for most groups, adolescents feel themselves more bicultural and more oriented towards the host society than their parents. However, the data indicate that the acculturation attitudes of parents, more than their cultural identity, influence the acculturation attitudes and wellbeing of their adolescent children. Moreover, acculturation attitudes are transmitted from parents to adolescents (Sabatier, Schmelck & Glevarec, 1998). Vatz Laaroussi (2001) and Perregaux (2003) carefully examine this familial dynamic. A high value is placed on the family by many immigrant groups, more than in the receiving societies. According to Vatz Laaroussi (2001), for immigrants facing the stress of acculturation, the family unit gains in importance and the links between members are strengthened. Family is not only a context, it is also a core part of immigration. Children who have immigrated with their parents show more solidarity with them and endorse more familial values than children born in the host society. These families try to find a balance between their various needs and demands and the goal that the family as a whole will succeed, and not only some individual members. Perregaux (2003) examined language usage within the family circle and their leisure organization. She underlines the crucial role of the eldest child who acts as a mediator between the familial culture and the host society and opens the route to the host society for the youngest children. She puts forward the hypothesis that the acculturation strategy of eldest children is integration, while the youngest children endorse the values of the host society more than those of the family, even if they are attached to the latter.

Finally, several authors, especially in Switzerland, advocate the necessity of taking into account the acculturation attitudes of adults who are responsible for the education of immigrant children. A few studies emphasize the importance of the sensitivity of actors in the social life of children (pediatricians, teachers) during the process of adaptation of these families. Lanfranchi, Gruber and Gay (2002) describe the diversity of acculturation attitudes of Swiss school teachers and their importance for the child's adaptation during the first year of school. Some teachers are sensitive to the cultural specificities of these children while emphasizing their integration into the social group; others consider that cultural specificities are not welcome at school and what counts is academic performance; yet others hesitate between universalism and specificities. The interaction between practices and attitudes of families on one hand, and attitudes of school teachers on the other, is important for adaptation to school and needs further research. Leanza and Klein (2000) describe how pediatricians use cultural mediators, and adapt their advice in their daily practice to manage the parent's anxiety according to their acculturation attitudes.

21.11 Conclusions

The three Francophone European countries present different contexts for the study of acculturation processes, in terms of percentage of foreigners settled in their country, the origin of the immigrant people, and their political model of integration. France has a huge diversity of immigrants who are more distant culturally than those in the two other countries. France is a strong supporter of universalism and considers that most cultural diversity should belong to the private domain, and as such should be guaranteed as private rights and freedom of thinking and faith. Belgium and Switzerland, although their Francophone populations are influenced by the French ideas, adopt different political views. They have long practiced harsher policies towards immigrants with strict criteria for the acquisition of nationality. These divergent views do not seem to be reflected in the attitudes of the host society towards immigrants, since European surveys do not show any important differences.

At the conceptual level, the notion of acculturation is not directly addressed by Francophone researchers who prefer the concepts of interculturation, socialization or otherness. Francophone researchers definitely prefer the theoretical perspective of sociology (socialization) and phenomenology (intersubjectivity and interculturation) over cultural anthropology (acculturation). Francophone researchers prefer to study transformation of identity rather than the behavioral shifts and attitudes which are the topics of acculturation studies in other societies. This divergent conceptual point of view is not a disinterest in the question of integration of immigrant populations. On the contrary, the number of recent studies, especially with families, attests to their concerns. It is rather a question of a different and original epistemological tradition, as distinct from international (mainly English-speaking) research.

21.12 References

Barrette, G., Bourhis, R. Y., Personnaz, B. & Personnaz, B. (2004). Acculturation orientations of French and North African undergraduates in Paris. *International Journal of Intercultural Relations, 28,* 415–438.

Bastide, R. (1968). Acculturation. In *Encyclopaedia Universalis* (Vol. I, pp. 102–107). Paris: Encyclopaedia Universalis.

Berry, J. W. (1980). Acculturation as varieties of adaptation. In A. Padilla (ed.), *Acculturation: theory, models and some new findings* (pp. 9–25). Boulder: Westview.

Boesch, E. E. (1991). *Symbolic action theory for cultural psychology.* Berlin: Springer.

Bolzman, C. (2001). Quels droits citoyens? Une typologie des modèles d'intégration des migrants aux sociétés de résidence. In C. Perregaux, T. Ogay, Y. Leanza & P. Dasen (eds.), *Intégrations et migrations. Regards pluridisciplinaires* (pp. 159–186). Paris: L'Harmattan.

Bourhis, R. Y., Moïse, L. C., Perreault, S. & Sénécal, S. (1997). Towards an interactive acculturation model: a social psychological approach. *International Journal of Psychology, 32(6)*, 369–386.

Bousetta, H. (2000). Intégration des immigrés et divisions communautaires: l'exemple de la Belgique. In M. McAndrew & F. Gagnon (eds.), *Relations ethniques et éducation dans les sociétés divisées (Québec, Irlande du Nord, Catalogne et Belgique)* (pp. 59–81). Paris: L'Harmattan.

Bredendiek, M. & Krewer, B. (1999). Le processus d'acculturation comme choc et chance pour la construction de l'identité: l'exemple des étudiants étrangers à l'Université de la Sarre. In M.-A. Hily & M. L. Lefebvre (eds.), *Identité collective et altérité. Diversité des espaces / spécificités des pratiques* (pp. 213–228). Montreal: L'Harmattan.

Camilleri, C. (1990). Identité et gestion de la disparité culturelle: essai d'une typologie. In C. Camilleri, J. Kastersztein, E. M. Lipiansky, H. Malewska-Peyre, I. Taboada-Leonetti & A. Vasquez (eds.), *Les stratégies identitaires* (pp. 85–110). Paris: Presses Universitaires de France.

——— (1999). Stratégies identitaires, les voies de la complexification. In M.-A. Hily & M.-L. Lefebvre (eds.), *Identité collective et altérité. Diversité des espaces / spécificités des pratiques* (pp. 197–212). Paris: L'Harmattan.

Camilleri, C. & Malewska-Peyre, H. (1997). Socialization and identity strategies. In J. W. Berry, P. R. Dasen & T. S. Saraswathi (eds.), *Handbook of cross-cultural psychology, second edition*, Vol. II: *Basic processes and human development* (pp. 41–68). Boston: Allyn & Bacon.

Camilleri, C. & Vinsonneau, G. (1996). *Psychologie et culture: concepts et méthodes*. Paris: Armand Colin.

Clanet, C. (1990). *L'interculturel. Introduction aux approches interculturelles en éducation et en sciences humaines*. Toulouse: Presses Universitaires du Mirail.

Dasen, P. & Ogay, T. (2000). Pertinence d'une approche comparative pour la théorie des stratégies identitaires. In J. Costa-Lascoux, M.-A. Hily & G. Vermès (eds.), *Pluralité des cultures et dynamiques identitaires. Hommage à Carmel Camilleri* (pp. 55–80). Paris: L'Harmattan.

Devereux, G. (1970). *Essais d'ethnopsychiatrie générale*. Paris: Gallimard.

de Villanova, R., Hily, M.-A. & Varro, G. (eds.). (2001). *Construire l'interculturel? De la notion aux pratiques*. Paris: L'Harmattan.

Dewitte, P. (2003). *Deux siècles d'immigration en France*. Paris: La documentation française.

Eurobarometer (2000). Report no. 53. May 2000. European Commission. http://europa.ed.int/comm/public_opinion/archives/eb/eb53/eb53_en.pdf.

European Commission (1997). Results of "continuous tracking" surveys of European opinion (January 1997). Monitoring / Suivi EUROPINION, 10. http://eropa.eu.int/comm/public_opinion/archives/europinion_cts/eo10/e10_txten.pdf.

Haarscher, G. (1996). *La laïcité*. Paris: Presses Universitaires de France.

Hily, M.-A. (2001). Rencontres interculturelles. Echanges et sociabilités. In R. de Villanova, M.-A. Hily & G. Varro (eds.), *Construire l'interculturel? De la notion aux pratiques* (pp. 7–14). Paris: L'Harmattan.

Kanouté, F. (2002). Profils d'acculturation des élèves issus de l'immigration récente à Montréal. *Revue des sciences de l'éducation, 28(1)*, 171–190.

Krewer, B. (1994). La première rencontre des associations pour la recherche interculturelle: le congrès conjoint de l'ARIC et de l'IACCP et les perspectives de la recherche interculturelle. In J. Blomard & B. Krewer (eds.), *Perspectives de l'interculturel* (pp. 13–22). Paris: L'Harmattan.

(1999). La construction de l'autre culturel du point de vue de la psychologie. In M.-A. Hily & M.-L. Lefebvre (eds.), *Identité collective et altérité. Diversité des espaces / spécificités des pratiques* (pp. 93–112). Paris: L'Harmattan.

Lanfranchi, A., Gruber, J. & Gay, D. (2002). Succès scolaire des enfants d'immigrés: effets des espaces transitoires destinés à la petite enfance. In H.-R. Wicker, R. Fibbi & W. Haug (eds.), *Les migrations et la Suisse. Résultats du programme national de recherche "Migrations et relations interculturelles."* Zurich: Seismo.

Leanza, Y. & Klein, P. (2000). Professionnels de la santé et de la relation d'aide en situation interculturelle: quelle formation? In P. Dasen & C. Perregaux (eds.), *Pourquoi des approches interculturelles en sciences de l'éducation?* (pp. 281–298). Brussels: De Boeck.

Mançó, A. A. (2002). *Compétences interculturelles des jeunes issus de l'immigration. Perspectives théoriques et pratiques.* Paris: L'Harmattan.

Medhoune, A. & Lavallée, M. (2000). Le système scolaire en Belgique: clivages et pratiques éducatives. In M. McAndrew & F. Gagnon (eds.), *Relations ethniques et éducation dans les sociétés divisées (Québec, Irlande du Nord, Catalogne et Belgique)* (pp. 147–165). Paris: L'Harmattan.

Moreau, A. (1999). Culture de l'entre-deux et adaptation psychique des migrants. In P. Dewitte (ed.), *Immigration et intégration: l'état des savoirs* (pp. 246–251). Paris: La Découverte.

Perregaux, C. (2003). Le rôle de la scolarisation des enfants aînés dans les familles migrantes. Projet financé par le Fonds national suisse.

Redfield, R., Linton, R. & Herskovits, M. J. (1936). Memorandum on the study of acculturation. *American Anthropologist, 38*, 149–152.

Sabatier, C. (1991). Les relations parents–enfants dans un contexte d'immigration: ce que nous savons et ce que nous devrions savoir. *Santé Mentale au Québec, 16(1)*, 165–190.

(1999a). La culture, l'immigration et la santé mentale des enfants. In E. Habimana, L. S. Ethier, D. Petot & M. Tousignant (eds.), *Psychopathologie de l'enfant et de l'adolescent. Approche intégrative* (pp. 533–544). Montreal: Gaetan Morin.

(1999b). Les adolescents issus de l'immigration. Les clichés à l'épreuve des faits. In B. Bril, P. Dasen, C. Sabatier & B. Krewer (eds.), *Propos sur l'enfant et l'adolescent – Quels enfants pour quelles cultures?* (pp. 357–382). Paris: L'Harmattan.

Sabatier, C. & Berry, J. W. (1994). Immigration et acculturation. In R.Y. Bourhis & J.-P. Leyens (eds.), *Stéréotypes, discrimination et relations intergroupes* (pp. 261–291). Brussels: Mardaga.

Sabatier, C., Malewska-Peyre, H. & Tanon, F. (eds.) (2002). *Identités, acculturation et altérité.* Paris: L'Harmattan.

Sabatier, C., Schmelck, M.-A. & Glevarec, F. (1998). Adolescent–parent relationships with second generation adolescents living in France. Impact of conversation about ethnicity, culture and racism on ethnic identity and self-esteem of adolescent. A study with Algerian, Antillais, Moroccan, Portuguese and Vietnamese living in France. Paper presented at the 15th biennial meetings of the International Society for the Study of Behavioral Development, Bern, July.

Santelli, E. (2002). Les formes de sociabilité de cadres et d'entrepreneurs d'origine algérienne. Des résultats empiriques aux enjeux épistémologiques posés par l'étude de cette population. In H. Malewska, F. Tanon & C. Sabatier (eds.), *Identités, acculturation, altérité* (pp. 91–105). Paris: L'Harmattan.

Schäbi, N. & Joye, D. (2000). *Eurobaromètre en suisse 1999*. Neuchâtel: Service suisse d'information et d'archivage des données pour les sciences sociales.

Van de Vijver, F., Helms-Lornz, M. & Feltzer, M. J. (1999). Acculturation and cognitive performance of migrant children in the Netherlands. *International Journal of Psychology*, *34(3)*, 149–162.

Vasquez, A. (1984). Les implications idéologiques du concept d'acculturation. *Cahiers de sociologie économique et culturelle*, *1*, 83–121.

Vatz Laaroussi, M. (2001). *Le familial au cœur de l'immigration. Les stratégies de citoyenneté des familles immigrantes au Québec et en France*. Paris: L'Harmattan.

Ward, C. & Kennedy, A. (1993). Psychological and sociocultural adjustment during cross-cultural transitions: a comparison of secondary students overseas and at home. *International Journal of Psychology*, *28*, 129–147.

Wihtol de Wenden, C. (1999). *L'immigration en Europe*. Paris: La documentation française.

22 Acculturation in the Nordic countries

Charles Westin

The Nordic family of countries consists of Denmark, Finland, Iceland,[1] Norway and Sweden, with a total population of 25 million. The socio-political conditions of acculturation differ considerably as a consequence of different immigration histories and minority, language and integration policies. These policy differences reflect diverse historical experiences of state formation, specific economic and sociocultural traditions and also, quite importantly, geographical location in relation to major European powers. The domination of the Lutheran church for almost five centuries is a factor common to the Nordic countries.

22.1 Historical legacies

The Nordic states share histories that include intermittent periods of conflict and war between Germany and Denmark, Denmark and Sweden, and Sweden/Finland and Russia. However, the Nordic countries also share long periods of common rule. Finland was an integral part of the Swedish kingdom for more than 600 years before it was ceded to Russia in 1809. From 1809 to 1917, Finland was a grand duchy under the Russian Tsar. The Russians supported the development of institutions. Helsinki was established as the capital, replacing Turku, which had served as the center of Swedish rule. Language categorizations, and hence also language identities, are of central importance in the ethnocultural context of Finland.

Norway was subject to Danish rule for more than 400 years up until 1814. This gave rise to two closely related but still different Norwegian languages, one corresponding to written Danish, and the other developed during the era of national romanticism with the aim of establishing a written language corresponding to the spoken tongue. Thus language identity is also important in Norway. From 1816 to 1905, Norway and Sweden constituted a united kingdom. For both Finland and Norway these experiences of "foreign" domination were of profound importance to national identities.

During the seventeenth century, Sweden incorporated by conquest some Danish and Norwegian territories in the south and west of present-day Sweden. Even today, natives of these provinces show a sense of regional distinctiveness.

---

[1] Iceland will not be dealt with in this chapter.

Mostly these identity assertions are acted out jokingly in a relaxed manner. However, a militant xenophobic party is active in the province of Scania, demanding regional autonomy from Stockholm and measures to reduce the non-European migrant population of the province (Peterson, Stigendal & Fryklund, 1988).

Sweden and, in modern times, Finland even more so have had to stand up to the mighty power of Russia / the Soviet Union. Denmark on the other hand has had to contend with its powerful neighbor to the south, Germany. Just as Sweden's, and later Finland's, border with Russia has changed over the centuries, the border between Denmark and Germany has been shifted a number of times.

These shifting national borders are one causal factor behind the presence of ethnocultural and ethnolinguistic minorities in the Nordic countries. Immigration is a second factor. All four countries have small communities of Jews, Roma and traveling people. The societal effects of migration during the latter part of the twentieth century are discussed in the following section. A third historical source of ethnocultural diversity in the Nordic states is expansion, colonization and incorporation of the sub-Arctic interior and, in Denmark's case, of Greenland. The territory of northern Norway, Sweden and Finland is the homeland of the indigenous Saami people whose traditional source of livelihood is reindeer husbandry, hunting and fishing. During the twentieth century, substantial parts of the Saami territories were expropriated for purposes of mining, hydroelectric schemes and forestry.

Before industrialization Denmark was the most prosperous country due to its superior agricultural conditions, but all the Nordic countries were poor by European standards. Denmark has been an independent state since its formation in the tenth century. Sweden unified about half a century later and has also been a sovereign kingdom since then. Norway gained its independence from Denmark in 1814 and discontinued its union with Sweden in 1905. Finland became a sovereign state in 1917. All four countries experienced a heavy loss of population, through emigration to North America, from 1850 to 1950.

During the nineteenth and early twentieth centuries Sweden industrialized to a higher degree than the other countries. Although developing a shipbuilding industry, Denmark remained primarily an agricultural country. Norway also developed a maritime industry around shipping and fishing, but it was not until the discovery of North Sea oil that Norway developed its full industrial potential with the oil money. Finland industrialized at a later stage than Denmark and Sweden.

Denmark and Norway were occupied by Germany in April 1940. By then Finland had already fought its first war against the Soviet Union from November 1939 to March 1940. Soon after the outbreak of this war Helsinki was bombed. The Red Cross and other organizations arranged the evacuation of children from the exposed cities of southern Finland to safety in neutral Sweden. More than 70,000 children were evacuated during the course of the

war. This is known as the largest international evacuation of children ever to
have taken place (Räsänen, 1990). Some children remained with their Swedish
foster parents after the war, but a majority returned home with memories of
Sweden and knowledge of Swedish. In quite a few cases, these children emigrated as adults to Sweden in the post-war labor recruitment. In 1941, Finland
joined forces with Nazi Germany in a second war against the Soviet Union,
aiming to reclaim territory that had been lost in 1940. When the defeat of Nazi
Germany became inevitable, retreating German forces brought about massive
destruction of towns and villages in northern Finland and Norway.

The occupation of Norway and Denmark lasted until the end of the Second
World War. It triggered a wave of refugees seeking protection in Sweden.
In a daring operation across the sound that separates Denmark from Sweden
practically the entire Danish Jewry was rescued, transported in small fishing
vessels in the darkness of night.

Finland was forced to cede territory along its eastern border to the Soviet
Union. In addition to substantial war damages that had to be paid to the
Soviet Union, the resettlement of displaced Karelians was a heavy burden on
the country's economy. Industrial developments were delayed, and the standard of living was maintained at a level considerably below that enjoyed by
the other Nordic countries. Although Finland was the hardest hit by wartime
destruction, Finnish- and Swedish-speakers united for the first time in defence
of their country, with important identity consequences for the post-war period.
Though Denmark and Norway did not suffer material destruction to the same
degree, revenge was taken against those who had collaborated with the German
occupying power, thus creating psychological wounds in society that took a
long time to heal.

22.2   Countries, migration and minorities

Sweden is the largest of the Nordic states by territory and population
(9 million). When Europe was to be rebuilt after World War II with "Marshall
money," Sweden had an intact industrial infrastructure and heavy industry
geared towards the very products in demand. By the end of the 1940s, labor
demands could not be met domestically. Industry then recruited labor in other
Nordic countries, and soon in continental Europe. Well before the other Nordic
countries Sweden had a large immigration of manpower that started in the early
1950s. In 1954 a free Nordic labor market was established (Hammar, 1985).
Sweden, in need of manpower, and Finland, with a surplus of unemployed,
stood to gain. Over half a million people emigrated from Finland to Sweden
during this period (Institute of Migration, 2003). The numbers peaked in 1969
and 1970, approaching a net 70,000 persons per year. By the 1960s companies
also turned to Yugoslavia and Greece for manpower, initiating a substantial
migration from these countries. Later on, Turks from Anatolia found their way
to Sweden

Table 22.1 *Sweden: foreign citizens, foreign-born and first and second generation immigrants in 2003*

Countries of origin	Foreign citizens	Foreign born	1st and 2nd generation
Finland	93,500	189,300	271,500
Yugoslavia	18,600	75,100	108,000
Iraq	41,500	67,600	86,600
Iran	12,500	53,200	67,200
Bosnia-Hercegovina	15,500	53,900	64,500
Turkey	12,400	34,100	60,000
Poland	13,400	41,600	54,100
Norway	35,500	45,000	53,300
Denmark	29,700	40,900	52,200
Germany	19,100	39,500	52,200
Chile	9,100	27,500	37,400
Lebanon	2,200	20,800	37,300
Somalia	8,800	14,800	22,500
Hungary	2,300	13,800	19,700
Ethiopia	1,900	11,300	17,800
USA	9,400	15,100	16,600
Others	150,700	334,600	372,300
Grand total	476,100	1 078,100	1.393,200

Source: Statistics Sweden (2004).

In the early 1970s thoughts about banning labor migration began to appear simultaneously in the countries of Western Europe. Thus labor migration to Sweden from non-Nordic countries ceased in 1972. The following period of immigration was one of asylum seekers and subsequent family reunification from Third World countries (Westin, 1993). A considerable number of refugees from Chile were accepted after the 1973 coup, initiating a process of chain migration from Latin America. During the 1970s and 1980s refugees also came from the Middle East. The Syriani, a Christian minority from Eastern Turkey, Lebanon and Syria, sought asylum on the grounds of religious persecution. Another salient group are the Kurds, emigrating from Eastern Turkey. Iranians represent another large group as do the Iraqis. Significant numbers of refugees have also come from Ethiopia, Eritrea and Somalia. After the fall of Communism, asylum seekers from Bosnia and other former Yugoslav republics exceeded the previous waves of refugees, at the height of the Bosnian war amounting to well over 70,000 annually.

Table 22.1 gives the number of people of foreign background residing in Sweden for important countries of origin. The category "foreign citizens" includes people who have not naturalized to Swedish citizenship, and it also

Table 22.2 *Main sending countries, first- and second-generation migrants in Denmark*

Sending country	1st generation	Children, 2nd generation	Total
Turkey	30,800	22,600	53,400
Germany	22,500	2,700	25,200
Iraq	19,700	4,300	24,000
Lebanon	12,100	9,100	21,200
Bosnia	18,100	2,600	20,600
Pakistan	10,600	8,400	19,000
Somalia	12,300	5,500	17,900
Yugoslavia	12,400	5,300	17,700
Norway	13,600	1,600	15,200
Others	179,400	36,900	216,300
Grand total	331,500	97,000	430,700

Source: Statistikbanken Folketal (2004).

includes children born in Sweden to parents who are not Swedish citizens. The term "second generation" applies to children born and/or raised in the country to which both parents immigrated. Ethnocultural diversity is more pronounced in younger age brackets and it is above all an urban phenomenon. In some suburbs of major cities 75 to 90 percent of the young population are of non-Swedish origin.

Parliament adopted a minority policy in 1975, according to which Sweden was viewed as developing into an ethnically plural society. The program was condensed into three principal objectives: equality, freedom of choice, and partnership. Immigrants were to enjoy the same rights as Swedes. They could decide whether they wished to assimilate to Swedish ways of life or to maintain their native culture in the private domain (Hammar, 1985; Westin, 1996). In 1989 the government decided that applications for political asylum would henceforth be treated strictly in accordance with the Geneva Convention. Humanitarian grounds would no longer suffice. Additional measures have been taken to reduce immigration from Third World countries. A problem of the Swedish multicultural policies is that they were introduced in a societal context where, for the past 150 years, important institutions have been aligned to promote nation-state formation and instill national values (Hagos, 2004; Westin, 2004). Sweden will have to reconsider its restrictive immigration policy, which is in total contradiction to its integration and diversity policies.

Denmark is the smallest of the four states in terms of territory, but the second most populous country (5.4 million). Labor immigration to Denmark started somewhat later than to Sweden and on a smaller scale. Unlike the Swedish experience, there is no large component of immigration from neighboring Nordic countries (see Table 22.2). The influx of manpower came from Germany, the Balkans and Turkey. There is a division in Danish politics between groups expressing very liberal acceptance of cultural diversity on the one hand, and groups airing ethnocentric and populist values on the other. The right-wing Progress Party, voted into parliament in 1972, was highly critical of the immigration policies. One of its demands was that foreign workers should be repatriated. Labor immigration was banned in 1973.

The influx of asylum seekers did not really start until ten years later when Denmark introduced Europe's most liberal refugee act. In a few years the number of asylum seekers increased from a few hundred to well over 8,000. The political community reacted by recommending a more restrictive inter- pretation of the Act. Since the early 1980s, Turkey, Iraq, Pakistan and Soma- lia have been important countries of origin. In the 1990s the republics of the former Yugoslavia also contributed substantially to the intake of foreign citizens.

Unemployment rates are much higher for first-generation migrants than within the Danish population as a whole. In 2002 almost half of the foreign-born population of 16–64 years of age was not part of the workforce (Willadsen, 2004). The situation is somewhat better for the second generation. High rates of social welfare dependency for people of immigrant origin have led to discontent within the Danish electorate. The Danish People's Party is the most recent right-wing party to achieve electoral success by exploiting populist opinion. This party was so successful that the coalition of conservative parties forming the present government was forced to introduce drastic restrictions in Danish refugee policy, by retarding asylum seeking and naturalization. The government has taken exceptional measures to combat arranged or, as the gov- ernment sees it, forced marriages, by requiring a minimum age of 24. Since these rules were introduced, the number of marriages to foreigners has dropped by 90 percent and this measure led to an exodus to southern Sweden of Danish citizens married to a foreigner.

Danish integration policies have focused on equal treatment of people with diverse ethnic backgrounds. However, these policies have not been successful. In a modernized version of the Act on integration in 2001, one novel require- ment was to establish an advisory board to guide municipal and city councils on social, cultural and religious issues. A recent evaluation found, however, that less than 20 percent of the Danish municipalities and cities had established integration committees (Ejrnaes, 2004).

Norway is the smallest of the major Nordic states with a total population of 4.5 million, but with regard to territory it comes second to Sweden. Immigration of labor started later than to Sweden and Denmark (Berg, 2004). Norway was in fact a country of emigration until the early 1960s. The country's economy improved through the exploitation of the offshore oil fields, leading to a scarcity of labor. Norway nevertheless imposed a ban on labor immigration in 1975. Labor migrants were primarily from Sweden and Denmark. However, small settlements of Pakistanis and Turks in the early 1970s gave rise to processes of chain migration that continued well after the immigration ban.

Table 22.3 *Main sending countries, first and second generation, Norway*

Country of origin	1st generation	Country of origin	2nd generation
Sweden	22,000	Pakistan	11,400
Denmark	18,000	Vietnam	5,500
Pakistan	15,000	Turkey	4,200
Iraq	15,000	Sri Lanka	4,000
Bosnia	13,000	Somalia	3 400
Somalia	12,000	Iraq	2,400
Vietnam	12,000	Morocco	2,300
Iran	11,600	India	2,300
Germany	10,500	Serbia	2,200
Others	159,900		22,300
Grand total	289,000		60,000

Source: Statistiska sentralbyrån (2004).

Norway has resettled refugees from Chile, Vietnam, Iran, Somalia, Iraq, Bosnia and Serbia-Montenegro. Today the total number of resettled refugees is 100,000, half of whom have nationalized to Norwegian citizenship. In total, the first-generation immigrants to Norway number 289,000. The total for the second generation, defined as children born in the country to two foreign-born parents, is 60,000. The total of first- and second-generation immigrants (350,000) represents 7.6 percent of the total population. See Table 22.3.

A dispersal policy for refugees was adopted to ease the pressure on the Oslo region where almost 40 percent of the refugees and immigrants have settled. Dispersal is also seen as a means to promote assimilation to Norwegian society, which fits the preferred strategy of incorporation rather than integration. Mastering Norwegian is seen as essential in order to establish a position in the labor market. The anthropologist Karin Harsløf Hjelde (2004) gives a number of examples of how organized hikes in the forests and mountains are employed as a means of resettling young unaccompanied refugees.

Norway has introduced an increasing number of restrictions on refugee acceptance, among them the change from permanent to temporary protection. Once the political situation in the sending country is regarded as stable, refugees are to be repatriated. Despite its strong economy, unemployment rates have risen in Norway hitting the foreign-born residents harder than the ethnic Norwegian population, first-generation migrants harder than second-generation, and migrants of Asian origin harder than those of European origin (Berg, 2004).

Discrimination and prejudice are important explanatory factors of the higher unemployment rates among the migrants, but so also are lack of proficiency in Norwegian, low educational levels, problems in evaluating foreign degrees and exams, and lack of experience of Norwegian working life and social networks.

Norway has the largest Saami population of the Nordic states. It totals more than 40,000 persons. In 1980 conflict about a dam on the Alta River ultimately led to official recognition of Saami heritage and public appreciation of the Saami people as an ethnic minority in its own right. While Norwegian policies today are supportive of the Saami minority and its strivings, the incorporation policy vis-à-vis immigrants, on the other hand, does not actively support the formation of ethnic minorities of immigrant origin. An interesting observation is that the position taken by the Swedish authorities is the opposite. Swedish society supports ethnic-language maintenance and the formation of ethnic minorities among the people of migrant origin but does not recognize Saami claims to various traditional rights (Beach, 2000).

Finland's population (5.2 million) is slightly smaller than Denmark's, and its territory is slightly smaller than Norway's. Finland's geopolitical position with a long land border with the Soviet Union/Russia was decisive for its political maneuvering during the post-war years. A friendship, cooperation and assistance treaty with the Soviet Union was signed in 1948. During the Cold War, the border between Finland and the Soviet Union was sealed. War damages and resettlement of half a million displaced persons from ceded territories were a heavy burden to the post-war economy. Finland remained a country of emigration up until the late 1980s (Institute of Migration, 2003). Sweden was the main country of destination, receiving over half a million labor migrants during the 1950s to 1970s. In the 1970s, Finland established a policy of welcoming return migrants from Sweden and other destinations of earlier Finnish emigration.

With the collapse of the Soviet Union in 1991, Finland's political position altered dramatically. In 1995 Finland joined the European Union and is the only Nordic state to have joined the Euro-zone. However, within the Nordic community Finland was long criticized for its restrictive immigration policy. While the other Nordic states had a large influx of asylum seekers and refugees accepted on a permanent basis, Finland continued to turn people back. It was not until the end of the Cold War that Finland gradually liberalized its refugee policies. The number of foreign citizens currently residing in Finland is approximately 107,000 (2.1 percent of the total population). The number of naturalized citizens is still quite small. The foreign-born population is mainly concentrated in the Helsinki metropolitan area.

In 1990 President Mauno Koivisto extended the return policy to include people of Finnish descent living in the Soviet Union. This declaration triggered a wave of Russian immigration to Finland (Laakonen, 2004). Numbers are increasing every year through family reunification. There were several reasons for the 1990 policy reorientation. First, Finland was facing a labor shortage, which justified a policy of temporary immigration. Secondly, there was a need to give Finnish foreign policy moral credibility in the eyes of the world. Thirdly,

Table 22.4 *Foreign citizens in Finland in 2003*

Citizen of	2003
Russia	25,000
Estonia	13,500
Sweden	8,000
Somalia	4,500
Yugoslavia	4,000
Iraq	3,500
United Kingdom	2,500
Germany	2,500
Iran	2,500
China	2,500
Turkey	2,500
USA	2,000
Thailand	2,000
Bosnia-Hercegovina	1,500
Ukraine	1,500
Afghanistan	1,500
Others	26,500
Grand total	106,000

Source: Statistikcentralen (2004).

there was a genuine interest in the situation of the Ingrians, regarded as a people of Finnish descent. Besides Russians, refugees have been accepted from Vietnam, Somalia, Iran and Iraq. A majority of the Swedish citizens residing in Finland are persons of Finnish origin who migrated to Sweden during the period of labor emigration, naturalized to Swedish citizenship and then, often in conjunction with retirement, returned to Finland.

Unemployment rates are considerably higher among the foreign-born than among native inhabitants (33.5 percent). The highest percentages are found for migrants from Iran, Iraq, Somalia and Vietnam. The Finnish authorities have adopted an integration policy, which includes measures to combat discrimination (Valtonen, 1999).

The constitution of Finland recognizes two founding language groups (or nations): the Finnish-speakers (Finns) and the Swedish-speakers (Finland Swedes). The Finnish-speakers are 94 percent of the total population, the Swedish-speakers 6 percent. The Finland Swedes are not constitutionally a minority but enjoy far-reaching rights to their language in education, culture, political life and the media. Cities and municipalities can be classified as bilingual if both languages are represented within the population to a certain minimum. Bilingual municipalities are mainly found on the south and west coast, while most of the interior is monolingual Finnish (Sandlund, 1991).

The island province of Åland on the other hand is entirely Swedish-speaking. The Helsinki metropolitan area has attracted a large domestic immigration of Finnish-speakers, thus significantly changing the balance between Finnish- and Swedish-speakers. Urbanization has also led to an increasing number of marriages between Finnish- and Swedish-speakers, the outcome normally being a dominance of Finnish over Swedish in the following generation.

22.3   Studies of the Nordic ethnocultural landscapes

Although the Nordic states have a lot in common, there are, as we have seen, important differences in history, experiences of immigration and interethnic relations, popular attitudes and policies that affect the general ethnocultural context. Popular opposition to immigration policies has become increasingly resentful since the mid-1990s in all countries, but most markedly in Denmark. All countries have experienced increasing problems with integrating migrant populations in the labor market, with exceptionally high unemployment levels and social welfare dependency for non-European migrants.

Today, Sweden, Denmark and Norway have significantly large populations of children born in the country to migrants (the second generation) who have reached majority. Studies report that the second generation is not as hard hit by unemployment as their parents are. Yet the second generation shows significantly higher unemployment levels than the native populations (Berg, 2004; Hagos, 2004; Willadsen, 2004). How do these prospects affect young people's lives, identities, ambitions and acculturation strategies?

These questions have been researched by the ICSEY (International Comparative Studies of Ethnocultural Youth) project in Finland, Norway and Sweden. The theory behind the study is John Berry's work on acculturative stress and Jean Phinney's work on ethnic identity, developed on the basis of empirical experiences in Canada and California (Berry, 1990, 1997; Phinney, 1990). A central issue in intercultural encounters is how the individual relates to the ethnic minority group/culture and the majority group/culture respectively. Berry identified four acculturation strategies: assimilation (rejecting ethnic minority culture in favor of the majority culture), integration (combining both cultures), separation (relying on ethnic minority culture only and rejecting majority culture) and marginalization (rejecting both cultures). Psychosocial adjustment of first-generation migrants was found to be related to these strategies. Previous studies suggest that an integrative attitude is the most adaptive of the four options with marginalization as the least adaptive. Results relating to the role of assimilation and separation have varied with regard to different contexts, countries and ethnic groups (Berry, 1997). A number of variables were operationalized by an international team of researchers[2] and data were

---

[2] John W. Berry and Kyunghwa Kwak (Canada), Karmela Liebkind (Finland), Jean Phinney (USA), Colette Sabatier (France), David L. Sam (Norway), Erkki Virta and Charles Westin (Sweden).

collected by means of a questionnaire distributed to second-generation pupils aged 13–18 years, their parents and a control group of pupils from the majority population in each country.

Erkki Virta and Charles Westin (1999) collected data for the Swedish study in Stockholm schools on youth of Chilean, Finnish, Kurdish, Turkish and Vietnamese origin. The Norwegian study conducted by David L. Sam (1998) surveyed second-generation Pakistanis, Turks and Vietnamese. Karmela Liebkind (1998) was responsible for the study in Finland that collected data on young "Russians," Turks and Vietnamese. On the whole the results coming out of these national studies supported the Berry and Phinney theoretical model of acculturative stress. However, in quite a few respects the results were unexpected and contradict popular stereotypes of youth of non-European origin as losers. Space does not suffice to elaborate on the results of all participating groups in this study.

The Finnish study is of interest because, among other things, immigration is a fairly recent phenomenon in Finland. Another reason why the identities reported by the "Russian" respondents are particularly interesting is because, unlike the Turks and the Vietnamese, the "Russians" were invited to settle in Finland as "returnees." That is, they were regarded as having Finnish ancestors. The returnees have mainly come from Ingria, a province that before Stalin's Russianization purportedly had a Finnish-speaking population. This makes the "Russian" migrants different from the Turks and Vietnamese in Finland, and from the other surveyed groups in Norway and Sweden. The "Russians" did in fact mainly originate from the province of Ingria, and were initially regarded as Ingrian Finns by the Finnish authorities and population. It soon turned out, however, that a majority of the returnees were monolingual in Russian with little knowledge of Finnish society and culture. These young respondents in the ICSEY study identified themselves in most cases as Russians (43%), Finns (16%) or Ingrian Finns (30%), and a smaller number in terms of some other nationality from the former Soviet Union (11%) (Liebkind, 1998).

In various analyses reported by Jasinskaja-Lahti (2000) it was found that the ethnic identity of the Russian-speaking youth reflected both Russian and Finnish identity dimensions. Young people who identified themselves as Russians, but also those who thought of themselves as Ingrian Finns, had more of a Russian identity than those who identified themselves as Finns. Identifying as a Finn or a Russian was consistent with the acculturation strategies (assimilation for Finnish identities and separation for Russian identities).

Support was found in the Finnish study for the hypothesis that perceived discrimination is a major psychological stressor that decreases the psychological adjustment of immigrant groups. In Finland, Somalis and Russians had higher reported levels of perceived discrimination than Turks and Vietnamese. The most reasonable explanation is that the Turks and Vietnamese as ethnic groups have longer experience of residence in Finland than the latter groups. But it is worth noting that the Somalis are a group with high visibility in the public spaces of a city, whereas the "Russians" are a low-visibility group that in public spaces can easily pass as members of the majority population. The results of the Finnish study thus supported the idea that high-visibility groups are subjected to, and consequently also experience and perceive, more discriminatory treatment in everyday life.

Surprisingly, however, this result was not supported by the Swedish and Norwegian studies. In the Swedish study, the Vietnamese (high-visibility), the Latin Americans, Turks and Kurds (medium-visibility) and Finns (low-visibility) all reported low values on perceived discrimination (Virta & Westin, 1999). The results of the Norwegian study are closer to the Swedish than to the Finnish results (Sam, 2000). In all three countries the authorities have been made aware of discrimination in public arenas, and measures have been taken to combat it. I am not suggesting that the Swedish authorities have been more successful than the Finnish authorities. Due to their much smaller size the groups in Finland are more likely to be exposed and vulnerable than the fairly large groups residing in Sweden and sampled in schools where a large number of the pupils are non-Swedes.

Second-generation Turkish pupils in Sweden reported better life satisfaction and school adjustment, and fewer psychological symptoms and behavioral problems than Swedish adolescents. These differences were statistically significant and contradict popular stereotypes of the second generation (Virta & Westin, 1999).

Another interesting finding was that second-generation males in general reported better life satisfaction but a poorer social adjustment than females. However, second-generation Turks deviated from this trend, with females reporting better life satisfaction but more problematic social adjustment than males. A possible interpretation is that young members of the second generation in general do not question adult authority at as early an age as Swedish and Finnish adolescents. Educational ideology in Sweden aims at fostering independence and self-reliance at an early age. Young people in Sweden are encouraged to question authorities and elders. In schools, this approach results in discipline problems, particularly in the seventh to ninth years of school. Youth of Turkish origin will undoubtedly also achieve independence, but follow another course. Age was negatively related to school adjustment for second-generation Turks. Turkish self-identification on the other hand predicted a benign adjustment. A Swedish self-identification does not predict good adjustment for the second generation of Turkish and Kurdish origin.

In the Norwegian study, it was found that Turkish adolescents reported poorer psychological adaptation than their peers in Sweden (Sam, 2000). Predictors of good adaptation were a sense of Turkish identity (high in Sweden) and integration (high in Sweden), whereas poor adaptation was related to marginalization (higher in Norway) and perceived discrimination (higher in Norway). Turkish youth in Norway had significantly lower self-esteem and more mental health problems than the Turkish youth in Sweden. They also reported significantly less Turkish identity and more marginalization than their counterparts in Sweden. These results indicate that the poorer adaptation of Turks in Norway compared to that of the Turks in Sweden could be due to a lower degree of Turkish identity and higher degree of perceived discrimination (Virta, Sam & Westin, 2004).

The Turkish community in Norway is smaller than that in Sweden, and it is also a younger community in the sense that it was established later than the Turkish community in Sweden. A larger share of the Turkish youth in Norway than of Turkish youth in Sweden were born in Turkey. These conditions could partly account for the outcome. In a larger community it is obviously easier to maintain and defend one's ethnic identity than in a smaller community. The Turkish youth in Sweden have, as a collective, had more time to work out an integrative acculturation strategy. However, the outcome also clearly lends support to the Swedish policy of integration, which entails measures to support ethnic minority identity, and represents a critical comment upon the Norwegian policy of incorporation, which in actual fact aims at assimilation.

In another analysis of the Norwegian and Swedish ICSEY data, focusing on the variations in self-esteem among the Chileans, Turks and Vietnamese groups between countries and groups, Sam and Virta (2003) report that country differences that were found between Norwegian and Swedish adolescents are reflected in differences between groups with the same origins in each country. Self-esteem is consistently lower for the minority groups in Norway than for the same groups in Sweden. Sam and Virta explored various possible reasons for this difference, and conclude that positive self-esteem for these adolescents of immigrant background appears to be closely linked to an integrative acculturation strategy.

The ICSEY project has not been pursued in Denmark, so comparable information on the second generation in Denmark is not available. However, in a recent book, social psychologist Rashmi Singla (2004) has collected information on ethnic minority youth, mainly of Asian origin, in Denmark and the acculturation problems they face in a society that at an increasing rate is dismantling its multicultural policies. Singla collected her data through a small number of open-ended interviews with young people of migrant origin. Informants report experiences of discriminatory societal treatment. The interviewees have adopted different strategies to counteract the effects of racism and discrimination. Danish youth, on the other hand, tend to be unaware of indirect discrimination in the classroom. Singla also shows the importance of family and, in particular, supportive sibling relationships to second-generation youth. There is very little social mixing with Danish youth, and, especially, young people who are classified as psychologically poorly functioning give expression to feelings of loneliness.

All the young people in Singla's study had some experience of being with people of different origins. Her informants employ different strategies from acceptance to denial of minority ethnicity in self-categorization. On a theoretical level, Singla's analysis comes close to the acculturative strategies proposed by Berry.

While young people belonging to the northern Saami and Finnish-speaking minorities in Sweden are involved in reproducing cultural identities and revitalizing institutions that support these minority identities, the issues of ethnocultural diversity are more complex in migrant communities. Studies indicate that youth of Arabic, Bosnian, Chilean, Iranian, Kurdish, Somali and Turkish origin are not reproducing the Arabic, Bosnian, Chilean, etc., cultures of their parents, but are developing syncretic or hybrid youth cultures. A qualitative study carried out by Ålund (1997) illustrates how new cultural forms are created and given expression in popular music where young teenage musicians and lyricists voice their experiences. Linguists, corroborating Ålund's interpretation, have shown that a new dialect of Swedish is developing in housing estates where the second generation and their parents live. This dialect incorporates not only words from Turkish, Spanish, Persian, Kurdish, Arabic, Finnish etc., but also figures of speech and prosody (Kotsinas, 1994). There is an obvious risk that a new, "ethnically" determined class structure may hinder the second generation from realizing its potential.

In a third study focused on second-generation identities, Catarina Nyberg has concentrated her data collection on youth of Ugandan Asian origin in Sweden (Westin and Nyberg, in press). Many of Nyberg's respondents report that, as children, they thought of themselves as belonging to the country and being no different from native Swedish children. As teenagers, however, their sense of belonging was called into question by some people in their surroundings, and even abandoned by some. They just felt that they did not conform to the stereotype of the blond, blue-eyed Scandinavian. Although practically everyone denies that they were victims of (overt) discrimination, when pressed for information and details respondents describe the incidents as unfair treatment, and some even report that "insults," within a general joking, non-aggressive atmosphere, were returned. It seems that these youngsters were unwilling to assume the role of victims and that they would not let confrontations of this kind get them down.

Feeling that a Swedish identity was largely denied them, many of Nyberg's informants seemed to explore what an Indian identity would imply. However, after visits to India it was all too obvious that they had very little in common with Indian identity as expressed in India and that their outlook on many vital existential, social and political issues (such as gender roles) was colored by values underpinning Swedish society. They really did have a specifically Swedish outlook on many important issues concerned with cultural identities, gender roles, social welfare, justice and equality. Nyberg's qualitative data seem to lend support to an integrative strategy in accordance with Berry's hypothesis.

22.4   Conclusions

Of the four acculturative attitudes in Berry's model it appears that integration was by far the most functional and adaptive in the Nordic ICSEY data. In the Swedish data, separation was a second functional option. Assimilation and marginalization, on the other hand, received very low mean values for all categories and thus do not appear as viable alternatives. Clearly these results should be of great interest to policy makers. The tendency in Norway to stress an assimilative acculturation and incorporation of second-generation migrant youth, an approach that also has its advocates in Sweden and the other Nordic countries, needs to be reconsidered. These results also support the Swedish approach to multiculturalism. Although we have no ICSEY data from Denmark to back up any conclusions, my understanding is that the tough Danish immigration policy is not sending the right kind of positive signals to the people of migrant origin who are settled in Denmark.

Several indications point to the fact that many second-generation youngsters are doing quite well academically and establishing themselves in certain niches of the developing multicultural society.

22.5   References

Ålund, A. (1997). *Multikultiungdom. Kön, ethnictet, identitet*. Lund: Studentlitteratur.

Beach, H. (2000). The Saami. In M. R. Freeman (ed.). *Endangered peoples of the Arctic* (pp. 223–246). Westwood, CT: Greenwood Press.

Berg, B. (2004). *Landsrapport fran Norge*. www.akatemia.org/projektit/invandr/norge.htm. Accessed September 30.

Berry, J. W. (1990). Psychology of acculturation. In J. J. Berman (ed.), *Nebraska symposium on motivation 1989: Cross-cultural perspectives* (pp. 201–234). Lincoln: University of Nebraska Press.

   (1997). Immigration, acculturation and adaptation. *Applied Psychology: An International Review*, 46(1), 5–68.

Ejrnaes, M. (2004). *Flere kommunale integrationsråd!* http://ekspertpanelet.ms.dk/artikler/morten1.htm. Accessed November 11.

Hagos, M. (2004). *Landsrapport från Sverige*. www.akatemia.org/projektit/invandr/sverige.htm. Accessed September 30.

Hammar, T. (ed.) (1985). *European immigration policy. A comparative study*. Cambridge: Cambridge University Press.

Harsløf Hjelde, K. (2004). *Diversity, liminality and silence. Integrating young unaccompanied refugees*. Oslo: University of Oslo, Department of Group Psychiatry.

Institute of Migration, University of Turku (2003). www.utu.fi/erill/instmigr/eng/e02.htm. Accessed August 3.

Jasinskaja-Lahti, I. (2000). *Psychological acculturation and adaptation among Russian-speaking immigrant adolescents in Finland*. Helsinki: University of Helsinki, Department of Social Psychology.

Kotsinas, U.-B. (1994). *Ungdomsspråk*. Uppsala: Hallgren & Fallgren.

Laakonen, R. (2004). *Landsrapport från Finland*. www.akatemia.org/projektit/invandr/finland.htm. Accessed September 30.

Liebkind, K. (1998). Preliminary findings from the Finnish ICSEY Study. Working paper presented to the ICSEY meeting in Los Angeles, February 21–24.

Peterson, T., Stigendal, M. & Fryklund, B. (1988). *Skånepartiet*. Lund: Arkiv.

Räsänen, E. (1990). Finska krigsbarn. In *Separationsupplevelser i barndomen och konsekvenser i vuxenålder*. Stockholm: CEIFO.

Sam, D. L. (1994). *Acculturation of young immigrants in Norway. A psychological and socio-cultural adaptation*. Bergen: University of Bergen, Faculty of Psychology.

(1998). Ethnic identity and acculturation preferences among four ethnic groups in Norway: relationships and their predictors. Presented at the symposium "Acculturation and cultural identities: aspects of intergroup relationships" during the 14th International Congress of the IACCP, Bellingham, Washington, August 3–8.

(2000). The psychological adaptation of adolescents with immigrant backgrounds. *Journal of Social Psychology*, *140*, 5–25.

Sam, D. L. & Virta, E. (2003). Social group identity and its effect on the self-esteem of adolescents with immigrant background. In H. W. Marsh, R. G. Craven & D. M. McInerney (eds.), *International advances in self research* (pp. 347–373). Greenwich, CT: Information Age Publishing.

Sandlund, T. (1991). *Bilingualism in Finland*. Helsinki: Universitetsförlaget.

Singla, R. (2004). *Youth relationships, ethnicity and psychosocial intervention*. New Delhi: Books Plus.

Statistics Sweden (2004). *Population statistics 2003*. Örebro: Statistiska Centralbyran.

Statistikbanken Folketal (2004). 1. januar efter statsborgerskap, herkomst, oprindelses-land og tid www.statistikbanken.dk/statbank5a/selectVarVal/saveselection.asp Accessed September 28.

Statistikcentralen (2004). *Utländska medborgare i Finland*. www.sc.fi/befolkning-statistik Accessed September 28.

Statistiska sentralbyrån (2004). *Befolkningsstatistikk*. www.ssb.no/emner/02/01/10/flyktninger/main.html Accessed September 28.

Valtonen, K. (1999). *The integration of refugees in Finland in the 1990s*. Helsinki: Ministry of Labor.

Virta, E., Sam, D. L. & Westin, C. (2004). Adolescents with Turkish background in Norway and Sweden: a comparative study of their psychological adaptation. *Scandinavian Journal of Psychology*, *45(1)*, 15–25.

Virta, E. & Westin, C. (1999). *Psychosocial adjustment of adolescents with immigrant background in Sweden*. Occasional Papers, 2. Stockholm: Stockholm University, Centre for Research in International Migration and Ethnic Relations.

Westin, C. (1993). Immigration to Sweden 1940–1990 and the response of public opinion. *Migration. A European Journal of International Migration and Ethnic Relations*, *1993:2*, 143–170.

(1996). Equality, freedom of choice and partnership: multicultural policy in Sweden. In R. Bauböck, A. Heller & A. R. Zolberg. (eds.), *The challenge of diversity. Integration and pluralism in societies of immigration* (pp. 207–225). Aldershot: Avebury.

(2004). Diversity, national identity and social cohesion. Keynote address, 13th Nordic Migration Conference, Aalborg, Denmark, November 18–20.

Westin, C. & Nyberg, C. (in press). Three generations of the Ugandan Asian diaspora in Sweden. In V. Colic-Peisker & P. Waxman (eds.), *Refugee resettlement in the West: economic, social and cultural aspects* (pp. 147–164). Hauppauge, NY: Nova Science Publishers, Inc.

Willadsen, P. S. (2004). *Landsrapport från Danmark*. www.akatemia.org/projektit/ invandr/danmark.htm. Accessed September 30.

23 Acculturation in the United Kingdom

Lena Robinson

23.1 Introduction

This chapter will discuss research findings in the field of acculturation, identity and intercultural relations among first-generation immigrants and second- and third-generation minorities living in the UK. It will highlight intergenerational differences in acculturation between the migrant and British-born generations. The chapter will also provide a brief overview of immigration to the UK, the main ethnic groups and their geographical distribution. Some attention will also be given to UK immigration policies and their potential consequences for migrant acculturation.

The chapter will focus on three of the major ethnic minority groups living in Britain: Indian (Punjabi Sikh and Gujarati Hindu), Pakistani and African Caribbean. It will examine aspects of psychological acculturation that are most important for immigrant parents, children and young people. These include: acculturation attitudes; language usage and proficiency; family and social contacts; and religion. It will also examine the ethnic identity of first-, second- and third-generation African Caribbeans and Asians. It will discuss the differences between first- and second-generation minorities, and will examine their perception of the racism and discrimination that they experience.

There is considerable evidence that there is discrimination against Asians and African Caribbeans in education, employment, the health care system, and law, including the criminal justice system. Indeed, racial violence and racial abuse appear to be on the increase in the UK. This chapter will examine these influences on the integration of minority groups into the host society.

Finally, this chapter will briefly outline some of the issues facing Irish immigrants in the UK. According to the 2001 census, the Irish are the largest ethnic group in Britain. However, very few research projects include the Irish as a distinct ethnic group. This means that this chapter will focus mainly on the three major ethnic minority groups mentioned above.

23.2 Background

The size of the ethnic minority population in the UK was 4.6 million in 2001 or 7.9% of the total population of the United Kingdom. Indians were the largest minority group (1.8%), followed by Pakistanis (1.3%), those of mixed ethnic backgrounds, Black Caribbeans, Black Africans and Bangladeshis (0.5%) (National Statistics, 2003). The remaining ethnic minority groups each accounted for less than 0.5% but together accounted for a 1.4% of the UK population. In Great Britain, the ethnic minority population grew by 53% between 1991 and 2001, from 3.0 million in 1991.

Half of the total ethnic minority population were Asians of Indian, Pakistani, Bangladeshi or other Asian origin. The Indians from South Asia are roughly equally divided in numbers between Hindus and Sikhs, with only a small number of Muslims, while the African Asians include a much larger share of Hindus. A quarter of ethnic minority people described themselves as Black, that is Black Caribbean, Black African or Other Black. Another 15% of the ethnic minority population described their ethnic groups as Mixed. About a third of this group were from White and Black Caribbean backgrounds.

Migration from India started after the Second World War and reached its peak in the early 1960s. The majority of people from Pakistan arrived in Britain in the late 1950s and early 1960s. The post-war migration to Britain was a direct response to the demand for labor in certain sectors of the economy. Migrants were employed mainly in the manufacturing industries in the West Midlands, Lancashire and Yorkshire. They accepted jobs which were considered undesirable by the White population. African Asians (mainly Indians) have a different pattern of migration. They were not labor migrants but refugees and settled in London and Leicester in the early 1970s. The majority of this group were educated, had a good command of the English language and had commercial, professional or business experience before entering Britain. A substantial portion of this population came to Britain from East Africa, in particular from Uganda and Kenya. This immigration to the UK got under way as the colonies of East Africa were about to gain independence in the early 1960s.

Large-scale migration from the Caribbean to Britain began in 1948. What prompted the migration to Britain was in part the response to labor shortages in Britain – in particular in British Rail, London Transport and the National Health Service (Peach, 1968) – and under- or un-employment in the Caribbean (Tidrick, 1966). By 1951, there were 17,218 West Indians in Britain (Peach, 1991), the majority of whom were of Jamaican origin. By 1961, the figure had risen to 173,659 (Peach, 1991). Although the Jamaicans remained the largest migrant group, migration from Barbados had begun in the mid-1950s. Migration from both the Leeward and Windward islands and Trinidad appeared to have been equally well established by the mid-1950s, although migration from Guyana did not get underway until the 1960s. In Britain, the 1962 and 1966 Immigration Acts effectively halted migration from the West Indies, although prior to both Acts there was a marked increase in the numbers arriving (Peach, 1991).

The Commonwealth Immigrants Act 1962 introduced the first legislation to limit the right of Indians and other British-protected persons to settle in the United Kingdom. However, quite a substantial immigration of Indians and African Indians took place during the period 1961–1970 through marriage and family reunifications. The Commonwealth Immigrants Act 1962 was further tightened by another Commonwealth Immigrants Act in 1968, which was rushed through parliament to restrict the flow into Britain of East African Asians holding UK passports. The Immigration Act 1971 added further restrictions: to gain the right of abode in Britain, people generally needed to be Commonwealth citizens (or citizens of the UK and colonies), and also to have some substantial connection with the UK (like having a parent born there). The expulsion of the Ugandan Asians in 1972 led to a temporary suspension of the Act and the UK accepted some 40,000 people of Indian and Pakistani descent with an increased proportion of African Indians. The 1981 British Nationality Act means that a person born in the UK is not automatically a UK citizen, as would have been the case before the Act. To qualify for citizenship, the person must have a UK-born parent as well. The 1988 Immigration Act restricted the right to appeal in certain deportation cases, prevented "second wives" of polygamous marriages entering the country to settle, and made overstaying leave in the UK a criminal offence.

The area of the UK government's immigration policy that has attracted most criticism is deportation, and in particular the removal of rights of appeal for those who have been in the UK for lengthy periods. Appeal rights for those who had overstayed their leave to remain there, but had been there for less than seven years, were restricted by the Conservative government in 1988. This is widely held to have led to an increase in asylum applications, since it was the only way to gain an effective right of appeal before removal. In 1997, the incoming Labour government was urged to restore full appeal rights, so that compassionate circumstances could always be argued at appeal. Instead, the new Immigration and Asylum Act (1999) has taken away all pre-removal appeal rights for overstayers, unless they have an asylum claim or a claim under the Human Rights Act. The most recent Act is the Nationality, Immigration and Asylum Act 2002. It is the latest in the long line of increasingly restrictive immigration controls.

The immigration debate in the UK has always been conducted on the assumption that immigration is a problem, not an opportunity. Asylum seekers have for some time been in the eye of the immigration storm, stimulating three major Acts of Parliament over six years. Deterrent measures were put in place to prevent or discourage arrivals. Visa regimes were the first deterrent. They were imposed on countries producing asylum seekers, backed by penalties on airlines that carried people without visas. The second deterrent measure was detention. A third measure was to reduce the support available for asylum seekers, in the belief that such support acts as an incentive for those who have no valid asylum claim.

It is important to note that, since the 1960s, British governments of both main political parties have adopted a two-pronged approach towards race relations. On the one hand, governments have introduced policies to promote equality of opportunity and attack overt racial discrimination (for example, the Race Relations Act 1976, and its principal amendment in 2000). On the other hand, governments have taken a number of steps to limit the population belonging to ethnic minorities through immigration controls.

Calls for immigration controls have always been posed in racist terms, from the 1905 Aliens Act and its preoccupation with Jewish refugees, through the attacks on Black Commonwealth immigration in the period following the Second World War to present-day constructions of asylum seekers:

> What was to become one of the most important expressions of racialised nationalism in the developed capitalist countries in the twentieth century was the entrenchment of immigration controls. Racism was everywhere integral to the development of immigration controls. Particular groups of immigrants were racialised and presented as a threat to the supposedly finite material resources of the receiving nation, as well as its "culture."   (Mynott, 2002:18)

The strength of the anti-immigration position in Britain can be evidenced by the ease with which the far right has grasped the issue: "The asylum seeker issue has been great for us. This issue legitimates us" (Nick Griffin, leader of the far right British National Party, quoted in the *Observer*, October 13, 2002).

Since the middle of the twentieth century, the Nationalist and Liberal models have vied for supremacy. The Liberal view (there is a single political culture in the public sphere but substantial diversity in the private lives of individuals and communities) became the official UK policy (Poulter, 1998). It has been strongly contested, however, by leading politicians and political theorists to the right of the political spectrum, who have upheld the Nationalist model (assimilation policy), and by their supporters in the media.

The ethnic minority population as a whole is heavily concentrated in the south-east region and the West Midlands. London has the highest proportion of people from ethnic minority groups apart from those of Pakistani origin. Nearly half of the Indian population live in the south-east region with 36% in Greater London. There is a higher proportion of Pakistanis in Yorkshire and Humberside (2.9%) and the West Midlands (2.9%). Leicester has the highest proportion of Indians (25.7%) (National Statistics, 2003). African Caribbeans live predominantly in south-east England, 58% in Greater London with another 16% in the West Midlands (Haskey, 1997).

In 1998, the average employment rate for all Black and Asian people was 57%, which is lower than that for Whites (75%) in general. For Indian women the employment rates were even lower. Unemployment rates for the Indians were around 15% in the late 1990s. A larger proportion of the Indians are self-employed than for other ethnic groups, including the White population in general. Yet Indians have increasingly gained top socio-economic status (SES) positions – managerial, professional and as employers. The pattern is similar for both males and females in employment. Retail distribution accounts for a large part of the self-employment. The African Asians tend also to be found in the banking and finance sectors. For women employees there is a high concentration in the distribution and service sectors. Although a high proportion of the males of Indian origin may be found in the top category, there are also high proportions in semi-skilled and unskilled manual jobs (Modood *et al.*, 1997).

There are differences in the educational attainment levels and employment patterns within the Asian group in Britain (Modood *et al.*, 1997). Among people of working age, the Indian and African Asians are better qualified than the Pakistanis and Bangladeshis. However, Indians do not benefit proportionately from their qualifications. They have greater difficulty than White people with the same qualifications in gaining the most sought-after jobs (Modood *et al.*, 1997). Bangladeshi men are half as likely as White men to be working as professionals. The unemployment rate in the non-white population is significantly higher (21%) than that of the White population (9%). However, within that, these figures are lowest for people of Indian origin (14%) and highest for people from Pakistan/Bangladesh (28%) (Office for National Statistics, 1994). The figures for Bangladeshis and Pakistanis were 35% and 41%, respectively. White people are more likely to work for private sector employers (62%) than those from the ethnic minorities (57%). The number of self-employed people in Britain rose by 49% between 1971 and 1992, with the bulk of the growth being in the 1980s. African and African Caribbean people are substantially under-represented in the self-employed category but Bangladeshi, Chinese, Indian and Pakistani people are comparatively prominent (Wrench & Modood, 2000).

African Caribbean household heads were more likely to be employees than those from other ethnic groups but less likely to be self-employed. African Caribbean household heads were much less likely than those from other ethnic groups to be from higher-status social classes, with the largest deficits being in Social Classes I and II. Though African Caribbean household heads were more likely than those from other ethnic groups to be skilled workers, they were also more likely to be semi-skilled or unskilled.

African Caribbean men are half as likely as White men to be working as professionals (Parekh, 2000). The proportion of African Caribbean youngsters achieving five higher-grade GCSE passes (grades A–C) is considerably less than half the national average. Indian pupils achieve results above the national average, while Pakistani and Bangladeshi pupils achieve below the national average. Data from the Higher Education Statistics Agency (1997–1998) show that 18- to 24-year-old people from all Asian and Black communities are over-represented in higher education, in the sense that their proportions in higher education are greater than their proportions in the general population. Students of Indian origin are three times as likely to be in higher education as might be expected from their numbers in the general population. However, about 70% of African Caribbean and 60% of Indian, Pakistani and Bangladeshi students pursue their degree studies at universities that were formerly polytechnics.

Only 35% of White students do so. Surveys of employers have shown that they much prefer to recruit from the older, more prestigious universities.

African Caribbean pupils are more than six times more likely to be excluded from school than their White counterparts (Majors, 2001). Most of those excluded are male. The number of Black exclusions has become so problematic that, in certain areas of London, Black children are up to fifteen times more likely to be excluded from school than their White classmates (Majors, 2001). Some of the pupils are excluded for conduct and behavioral problems, although far too many pupils in this category are excluded for trivial and relatively minor offences. However, many are also excluded simply for exhibiting culture-specific behaviors (wearing dreadlocks, braids, demonstrating "inappropriate" walking styles or gaze behavior). Many of these exclusions occur because of a lack of cultural awareness, miscommunication, racism and negative stereotyping (Majors, 2001).

23.3   Racial/ethnic identity

Two theoretical approaches to the study of ethnic minority adolescents' racial and ethnic identity development are prominent: racial and ethnic identity formation theory and acculturation theory. The first approach has a more developmental focus, in that it looks at individual change and was originally based on ego identity formation theories. The second perspective is concerned with the extent to which ethnic identity is maintained when an ethnic minority group is in continuous contact with the dominant group. Ethnic identity is an aspect of acculturation that is concerned with how individuals feel about or relate to their own ethnic group as part of the larger majority or dominant society. This section focuses on racial/ethnic identity.

Ethnic or racial or cultural identity models have been proposed for Asians, Hispanics (Berry, 1980), African Americans (Cross, 1978) and minorities in general (Atkinson, Morten & Sue, 1989; Phinney, 1990).

Several models of Black racial identity development and transformation were introduced in the United States in the early 1970s. Each hypothesized that identity development was characterized by movement across a series of sequential stages and that it was influenced by an individual's reaction to social and environmental pressures and circumstances (Cross, 1978; Thomas, 1971). Perhaps the best-known and most widely researched model of Black identity development is Cross' (1978, 1980) model of psychological nigrescence – which refers to the process of developing a Black identity – where "Black" is defined as a psychological connection with one's racial group rather than mere identification of the color of one's skin. The nigrescence approach studies Black identity in adolescents and adults.

Robinson (2000) used Cross' model of racial identity development to compare the racial identity attitudes and self-esteem of African Caribbean adolescents in residential care in a city in the West Midlands (UK) and a group of African Caribbean adolescents living with their own families and attending a multi-racial school in the city. Respondents in residential care and the comparison group primarily endorsed positive racial attitudes. Self-esteem and racial identity attitudes were related.

This section will examine some ethnic identity studies of Asians and African Caribbeans in the UK. In a study of Indian, African Caribbean and English adolescents, Hutnik (1991) found that "ethnic consciousness is significantly more salient in each minority group than in the English group, although on different dimensions" (p. 91). Hutnik (1991) also found that "South Asian adolescents in Britain are more aware of their ethnicity than are English or Indian adolescents [in India] and this is probably because they constitute an ethnic minority group within the British society" (p. 95). In a qualitative study of ethnic identities of first- and second-generation Asians and African Caribbeans in the UK, Modood, Beishon and Virdee (1994) found that several young Asians used hyphenated labels (for example, "Pakistani-British") to describe their identity. The authors conclude that "most of the Asian second generation wanted to retain some core heritage, some amalgam of family cohesion, religion and language, probably in an adapted form, but did not expect this to mean segregated social lives, for they lived and wanted to live in an ethnically mixed way" (p.110). Thus, "Those [Asians] who saw themselves in terms of a bi-cultural or hyphenated identity . . . did not think that there was an inevitable conflict between the two sides of their identity" (p. 119). However, a minority of second-generation Asians "felt alienated from British culture which they perceived as hostile to their family-centred and religious values" (p. 119).

Modood *et al.* (1994) reported that both first- and second-generation African Caribbean respondents in their study used the term Black as an identifying label. Indeed, "for some second generation respondents 'Black' referred to all who suffered racism and thus included South Asians" (p. 117). Second-generation respondents were more likely than first- to express the notion of a shared "Black" identity between themselves and South Asians living in Britain, since, for example, "we are all 'of colour'" (p. 85). These respondents "were more likely to recognize the basis for solidarity with South Asians out of a common colonial history, the experience of racism and youth culture" (Modood *et al.*, 1994:87) The authors conclude that most of the African Caribbean respondents found it difficult to use the term "British" as an identifying label, despite "a strong sense of social and cultural commonality with the White British" (Modood *et al.*, 1994:117). For this group "racism rather than any sense of distinctive ethnic heritage was seen as an obstacle to feelings of unity with the white British majority" (p. 118).

In a study of second-generation African Caribbean youth in London, Alexander (1996) found that none of her respondents felt that the label "British" was sufficient; they additionally defined themselves in terms of family history and origins (the Caribbean). It was also clear that strong affiliations with Africa or the Caribbean did not mean that affiliations with Britain were weakened or that this was not an important part of their identity.

In a recent study undertaken as part of the International Comparative Study of Ethnocultural Youth, Robinson (2003) found that ethnic identity scores were high for Indian, Pakistani and African Caribbean adolescents. Ethnic identity was measured with eight items assessing ethnic affirmation (e.g., sense of belonging, positive feelings about being a group member). This scale is based on the Multigroup Ethnic Identity Measure (MEIM; Phinney, 1992). National identity was important for all groups but ethnic identity was more important than majority identity for all groups. There was a significant relationship between high ethnic identity scores and psychological adaptation as measured by mastery and life satisfaction (Robinson, 2003).

23.4 Acculturation strategies

There is little empirical evidence on how individuals from ethnic minority groups in Britain think about and handle their relationship with the two cultures in which they live. Very little empirical work using Berry's acculturation model has been conducted in Britain. Studies of young Asian people have shown that most young people prefer the integration mode of adaptation (Ghuman 1991, 1999; Hutnik, 1991; Robinson, 2003; Stopes-Roe & Cochrane, 1990). Ghuman (1975) devised the Aberystwyth Bi-culturalism scale to measure biculturalism among South Asians in Britain. In his study of Asian adolescents, Ghuman (1999) found that the majority of young Asian people prefer integration and reject assimilation, marginalization and separation strategies. Thus, Ghuman (1999) reports that "a large majority of young [Asian] people are bi-cultural and bi-lingual: they have retained some aspects of their own culture and at the same time adopted some of the British norms ... the majority define their personal identity in a 'hyphenated way' (for example, Indo-English)" (p. 69). However, "this has not changed the fact that they continue to suffer racial abuse both in and out of school and have mixed feelings about whether they belong [in Britain]" (Ghuman, 2003:130). Significant differences were found within the Asian group. Hindus and Sikhs scored higher than the Muslim sample.

Several studies of first- and second-generation Asians in the UK (Ghuman, 1991, 1994; Drury, 1991; Stopes-Roe & Cochrane, 1990; A. Wilson, 1978) report intergenerational tensions and anxieties. Studies of Asians in Britain (e.g., Anwar, 1998; Robinson, 2003; Shaw, 1988) indicate that first-generation Asians employed "separation" as a mode of working and living in Britain. The main reason for this situation was that they had different languages, religions, family values and general life styles. Issues related to dating and arranged marriages are areas of serious intergenerational conflict (Anwar, 1998; Drury, 1991). Almost all the parents in Dosanjh and Ghuman's (1996) study were aware of this. The concept of *izzat* (honor and respect) plays an important part in the lives and thinking of South Asian parents (Shaw, 2000).

In another study, Stopes-Roe and Cochrane (1990) concluded their discussion of the personal identity of first- and second-generation Indians and Pakistanis by noting that the first generation "felt primarily 'Indian' or 'Pakistani' as the case might be, rather than British, whereas 43% of young [second-generation] people identified as British" (p. 198). However, the authors also found that three-quarters of this group felt that there were differences between themselves and the White British. This could be attributed to the "cultural customs which the young Asians valued" (p. 199). The respondents in Stopes-Roe and Cochrane's study were, however, only given two choices – British or Indian/Pakistani. They were not given the option of indicating a bicultural or hyphenated identity.

The authors also found that "on three measures of assimilation, social, cultural and identification, Hindus were most and Muslims were least assimilated. This was so in both generations although somewhat more clearly for younger people than for their parents" (Stopes-Roe & Cochrane, 1990:207).

More recently, Robinson (2003) found that the acculturation attitude most favored by Indian and African Caribbean adolescents was Berry's integration strategy, and marginalization was least favored by all groups. However, the separation strategy was most favored by first-generation respondents.

The British policies towards immigrants and ethnic minorities can impact on the acculturation strategies and ethnic identity of ethnic minority groups in Britain. For instance, Modood *et al.* (1994) note that "in the second generation of every group [Indians, Pakistanis, African Caribbeans] studied here there is a strong sense of ethnic pride, of wanting to know about or at least to affirm one's roots in the face of a history and a contemporary society in which one's ethnicity has been suppressed or tainted with inferiority" (p. 59). Religion was also an important part of their identity. It is important to note that post 9/11, Muslims in Britain "have emerged as the principal focus of racist antagonisms ('Islamophobia') based on cultural difference" (Parekh, 2000:31). This could influence the acculturation strategies of Pakistanis in Britain. The Indians and Pakistanis in Modood's study "felt themselves to a large extent to be culturally British . . . [but] they felt strongly that they were still not accepted by white British" (Ghuman, 1975:72).

23.5 Language proficiency and use

Ethnic and national language proficiency and use are usually regarded as important indicators of acculturation. The main South Asian languages spoken by Indians in the UK are Punjabi, Hindi and Gujarati, while the African Indians mainly speak Gujarati and fewer speak Hindi and Punjabi. Most British-born second-generation Indians are bilingual or multilingual with greater facility in English. Several studies have shown that the British-born generation is highly proficient in English, which often may be the only language that they can read and write (Robinson, 2003). English tends to be used in communication with peers and younger persons, while the native South Asian language tends to be used when speaking with elders (Robinson, 2003). Although often versed in English the first generation has actively maintained the first language.

Modood *et al.* (1994) found that both the first- and second-generation South Asians considered that it was important to maintain the learning and use of their ethnic-group languages. In an ethnographic study of Muslim families in Oxford, Shaw (2000) found that the use of South Asian languages was in decline, with increasing numbers of second-generation respondents not only unable to read or write in their language of origin but also restricting the spoken language to home and family. Ghuman (2003) noted that the vast majority of young people in his sample used both English and their community languages at home. However, only a very small proportion of these were able to read and write their language of origin. Robinson (2003) found that Indian and Pakistani adolescents reported being highly proficient in the English language but less proficient in their language of origin. While many young Asians are able to speak their language of origin, they are not as capable in reading and writing these languages. In Britain, the teaching of community languages is not widespread (Smith & Tomlinson, 1989; Verma, 1986). The present UK government does not have policies which concentrate on promoting bilingualism. However, many supplementary schools or classes are being set up in Asian communities to teach Asians their religion and community languages (Modood *et al.*, 1994).

Generally speaking there is a pecking order among languages that is usually buttressed and supported by the prevailing political order. People make a positive or negative evaluation about the language that others use. In Britain, "there is a temptation to disparage others' language forms as deficient" (Lago & Thompson, 1996:56). Ahmed and Watt (1986:99) quote a Sikh woman who speaks three Indian languages but cannot speak English: "You know, in this country [UK] if you don't know English they make you feel you are nothing, and that attitude makes you feel so small and insignificant." Ghuman (2003) also reports that "such an attitude has also affected the perceptions and attitudes of some South Asian young people" (p. 200).

African Caribbean teenagers use Creole (sometimes referred to as Black English) to establish ingroup identity (Hewitt, 1986; Modood *et al.*, 1994; Wong, 1986). Modood *et al.* (1994) explored the attitudes of first- and second-generation African Caribbeans towards the use of Creole. The first generation felt that the use of Creole was limited as a mode of communication to other Caribbean peoples only, and would not therefore offer employment opportunities to their children. However, the other half of the African Caribbean group sampled felt that it was important for their language to be transmitted to their children as part of a cultural identity. Most of the second generation respondents in Modood *et al.*'s (1994) study felt that it was essential for African Caribbeans to be able to communicate in Creole. Those African Caribbeans who were unwilling or unable to use Creole were viewed negatively by some of the respondents. They were considered to be out of touch with "where they were coming from." These respondents also felt that Caribbean languages should be offered in schools.

23.6 Family and social contacts

Family relationships and social contacts "with members of one's own ethnic group and with members of the host society are another important aspect of acculturation." Modood *et al.* (1994) found that, for first-generation South Asians, "the extended family was an important institution of mutual support and transmission of values, and the main sphere of social life" (p. 112). However, the second-generation Asians in Modood *et al.*'s (1994) study placed more importance on the immediate family. They also had friends from outside their communities. However, their closest friends were Asian. Stopes-Roe and Cochrane (1990, 1992) found that second-generation Asian adolescents had a greater degree of social contact with Whites than the first generation.

Most African Caribbean respondents in Modood *et al.*'s (1994) study "had friends from other ethnic groups, though half of the first generation and a third of the second generation had only other Caribbeans as close friends . . . [however] the experience of racism was often extremely important to the second generation in choosing friends" (p. 112). Robinson (2003) found that Indian, Pakistani and African Caribbean adolescents had more frequent contact with peers from their own ethnic group than with peers from the national group. Family relationship values were assessed with two scales, family obligations and adolescents' rights. For the Indian and Pakistani groups, the obligations score was higher than the rights score.

23.7 Religion

In a survey of ethnic groups in Britain, Modood *et al.* (1997) found that Muslims (74%) were more likely than Hindus (43%) and Sikhs (46%) to say that religion was very important in the way they lived their life. Anwar (1998) reports that for a majority of Asians, religion was the main basis for their ethnic identity . However, there were differences between Asian groups. For example, almost three-quarters of Muslims thought religion was very important for the way they lived their life, compared with less than half of Hindus and Sikhs saying this. Stopes-Roe and Cochrane (1990) observed that over two-thirds of young Asian people in their study thought the teaching of religion to be very important. There were differences between the first and second generation: all of the first generation thought that the teaching of religion was important as opposed to 85% of the second generation. Modood *et al.* (1994) observed that for nearly all the first-generation South Asians and the majority of African Caribbeans religion was important to the way they led their lives. The second-generation Asians and African Caribbeans did not consider religion as important as the first generation. However, among the second-generation Asians, the Muslims "spoke most positively about the value and centrality of their religion. Most said that Islam was 'very important' to how they lived their lives" (p. 115). Similar results were reported in Robinson's (2003) study of Indian and Pakistani adolescents in Britain.

23.8   Racism and discrimination

Ghuman (2003) states that "the state of race relations in the wider society and the political climate (with its impact on discrimination, exclusion, rate of unemployment) affect young people's perceptions and attitudes and consequently how far they are willing to [adapt]."

Modood *et al.* (1997) report that Asians and African Caribbeans are "substantially under-represented in the most elite jobs, . . . as employers and managers in large establishments . . . use a 'glass ceiling' that affects all non-white men equally" (p. 143). We need to understand how racism affects the everyday lives of African Caribbean people in Britain even when they do not experience overt racial abuse or physical harassment. This includes a knowledge of the way in which racism is structured in British society in key areas such as education, employment and housing. M. Wilson (2003:9) reports that: "In general, Asian [and African Caribbean] communities [in Britain] have been vulnerable to poor housing, unemployment or low-paid work, and to racism and abuse (Reid-Galloway, 2003)." Muslim communities in the UK are the most disadvantaged groups (as measured by income, housing, occupation and education) of South Asians (Modood *et al.*, 1997).

Modood *et al.* (1997) found that "there is now a consensus across all groups that prejudice against Asians is much the highest of any ethnic, racial or religious groups; and it is believed by the Asians themselves that the prejudice against Asians is primarily a prejudice against Muslims" (p. 133). However, most of the Indian adolescents in Robinson's (2003) study, reported that they were not at all or only rarely discriminated against. But Pakistani and African Caribbeans perceived more discrimination than Indian adolescents.

The present government has declared that it is committed "to creating One Nation, a country where racism is unacceptable and counteracted . . . racial diversity is celebrated." However, public attitudes vary and studies have shown that some people favor assimilation as opposed to multiculturalism and are intolerant of immigrants' religion (shown, for example, by Islamophobia) and customs. A Policy Studies Institute investigation in the mid-1990s found that overall about one in eight of the people it surveyed – Bangladeshi, Caribbean, Chinese, Indian, Pakistani – had experienced racist insults or abuse during the previous 12 months. It estimated that about 20,000 people suffer a racist physical assault each year, 40,000 have items of property damaged and 230,000 experience abuse or insults (Modood *et al.*, 1997).

British governments of both main political parties have introduced policies to promote equality of opportunity and attack overt racial discrimination. Major anti-discrimination legislation was passed in 1968 and 1976. The Race Relations Act 1976, and its principal amendment in 2000, continue to make it unlawful to discriminate on "racial grounds," defined as "colour, race, nationality or national and ethnic origins." The Act refers to both direct and indirect racial discrimination. This has now been extended in the Amendment Bill to include institutional discrimination.

23.9 Irish immigrants

The Irish are often "neglected in considerations of race and cultural diversity ... owing to the myth of the homogeneity of white Britain" (Parekh, 2000:32). Irish people are often classified with the indigenous population or with other White minorities, and as a result Irish issues often remain invisible (Reid-Galloway, 2000). According to the 2001 census, Irish people make up 1.2% of the population of England and Wales. The Irish live mainly in South-West Scotland, Liverpool and London. The highest proportion of Irish people live in London. Migration from Ireland to the UK took place in three phases: mid nineteenth century; 1948–1968; and 1980s. The Irish remain Britain's "insider-outsiders" (Parekh, 2000). The Irish were considered as insiders because they were White. During the nineteenth century, the Irish were increasingly seen "as a race apart." However, immigration legislation of the 1960s defined the Irish as insiders, and the New Commonwealth immigrants were the aliens.

The Irish people in Britain are an under-researched group. There is little psychological research into Irish immigrants in the UK (Curran, 2003). In a survey carried out by O'Connell (1994) it was found that "only 14% of the children or grandchildren of Irish immigrants felt they had a 'strong' Irish dimension to their identity; 45% felt there was no Irish dimension" (p. 5). In addition, "only 6% of the British consider those who come to Britain from Ireland to be 'foreigners.' " Parekh (2000:33) notes that "Irishness as an identity is sometimes combined with other strong loyalties ... [for instance] in Liverpool there is a strong regional identity."

Studies have shown that Irish people have the highest rates of admission to psychiatric hospitals in the UK (Bracken, 1998; Cochrane and Bal, 1989). Balarajan (1995) found high rates of suicide and physical health problems among the Irish in Britain. In a recent study, Curran (2003) explored the acculturation strategies and mental health problems of Irish immigrants in the UK. He found that participants who adopted an integration strategy "have fewer mental health problems as measured by the General Health Questionnaire" (p. 19). He also found that individuals who adopted a marginalized strategy "seem to have increased mental health problems" (p. 27). He points out that "the direct influence of Integration and Marginalization on GHQ [General Health Questionnaire] gives support to these two acculturation strategies within the Berry framework" (p. 27). Integration and marginalization did show significant correlation with mental health as measured by the GHQ12.

To conclude, Curran (2003) argues that more research is needed on the Irish in Britain – in particular the second-generation Irish in Britain.

23.10 Conclusions

There is a dearth of psychological research into how individuals from ethnic minority groups in the UK think about and handle their relationship with the two cultures in which they live. There is a need for more empirical studies on acculturation, identity and intercultural relations among ethnic minority groups living in the UK.

23.11 References

Ahmed, G. & Watt, S. (1986). Understanding Asian women in pregnancy and confinement. *Midwives' Chronicle and Nursing Notes, 99*, 98–101.

Alexander, C. (1996). *The art of being Black: the creation of Black British identities.* Oxford: Clarendon Press.

Anwar, M. (1998). *Between cultures: continuity and change in the lives of young Asians.* London: Routledge.

Atkinson, D. R., Morten, G. & Sue, D. W. (eds.) (1989). *Counseling American minorities: a cross-cultural perspective.* Dubuque, IA: William C. Brown.

Balarajan, R. (1995). Ethnicity and variations in the nation's health. *Health Trends, 27*, 114–119.

Berry, J. (1980). Acculturation as adaptation. In A. M. Padilla (ed.), *Acculturation: theory, models and some new findings.* Boulder, CO: Westview.

Bracken, P. (1998). Mental health and ethnicity: the Irish dimension. *British Journal of Psychiatry, 172*, 103–105.

Brown, C. (1990). *Racial inequality in the British labour market.* Employment Institute, Economic Report, 5.4 (June). London: Employment Institute.

Cochrane, R. & Bal, S. (1989). Mental hospital admission rates of immigrants to England: a comparison of 1971 and 1981. *Social Psychiatry & Psychiatric Epidemiology, 22*, 2–11.

Cross, W. E. (1978). The Thomas and Cross models of psychological nigrescence: a literature review. *Black World, 20*, 13–27.

(1980). Models of psychological nigrescence: a literature review. In R. L. Jones (ed.), *Black Psychology* (pp. 319–339). New York: Harper and Row.

Curran, M. J. (2003). *Across the water: the acculturation and health of Irish people in London*. Dublin: Allen Library.

Dosanjh, J. S. & Ghuman, P. A. S. (1996). *Child-rearing in ethnic minorities*. Clevedon: Multilingual Matters.

Drury, B. (1991). Sikh girls and the maintenance of an ethnic culture. *New Community*, *17*, 387–400.

Ghuman, P. A. S. (1975). *The cultural context of thinking: a comparison study of Punjabi and English boys*. Slough: National Foundation for Educational Research.

   (1991). Best or worst of two worlds: a study of Asian adolescents. *Educational Research, 33*, 121–132.

   (1994). *Coping with two cultures: a study of British Asian and Indo-Canadian adolescents*. Clevedon: Multilingual Matters.

   (1999). *Asian adolescents in the West*. Leicester: British Psychological Society.

   (2003). *Double loyalties: South Asian adolescents in the West*. Cardiff: University of Wales Press.

Haskey, J. (1997). Population review: the ethnic minority and overseas-born populations of Great Britain. *Population Trends, 88*, 13–30.

Hewitt, R. (1986). *White talk Black talk: inter-racial friendship and communication among adolescents*. Cambridge: Cambridge University Press.

Hutnik, N. (1991). *Ethnic minority identity: a social psychological perspective*. Oxford: Clarendon Press.

Jones, T. (1993). *Britain's ethnic minorities: an analysis of the Labour Force Survey*. London: Policy Studies Institute.

Lago, C. & Thompson, J. (1996). *Race, culture and counselling*. Buckingham: Open University Press.

Majors, R. (2001). *Educating our Black children: new directions and radical approaches*. London: Routledge.

Modood, T., Beishon, S. & Virdee, S. (1994). *Changing ethnic identities*. London: Policy Studies Institute.

Modood, T., Berthoud, R., Lakey, J., *et al.* (1997). *Fourth National Survey of Ethnic Minorities in Britain: diversity and disadvantage*. London: Policy Studies Institute.

Mynott, E. (2002). Nationalism, racism and immigration control. In S. Cohen, B. Humphries & E. Mynott (eds.), *From immigration controls to welfare controls* (pp. 203–219). London: Routledge.

National Statistics (2003). *Census, April 2001*. London: The Stationery Office.

O'Connell, J. P. (1994). *British attitudes to Ireland and the Irish: a special relationship*. Bradford: Department of Peace Studies, Bradford University.

Office for National Statistics (1994). *Labour force surveys*. London: HMSO.

Parekh, B. (ed.) (2000). *The future of multiethnic Britain*. London: Profile Books.

Peach, C. (1968). *West Indian migration to Britain: a social geography*. London: Oxford University Press.

   (1991). *The Caribbean in Europe: contrasting patterns of migration and settlement in Britain, France and the Netherlands*. Coventry: Centre for Research in Ethnic Relations, University of Warwick.

Phinney, J. S. (1990). Ethnic identity in adolescents and adults: review of research. *Psychological Bulletin, 108*, 499–514.

(1992). The multigroup ethnic identity measure: a new scale for use with diverse groups. *Journal of Adolescence*, *7(2)*, 156–176.

Poulter, S. (1998). *Ethnicity, law and human rights*. Oxford: Clarendon Press.

Reid-Galloway, C. (2000). *Mental health of Irish-born people in Britain*. London: Mind Publications.

Robinson, L. (2000). Racial identity attitudes and self-esteem of Black adolescents in residential care: an exploratory study. *British Journal of Social Work*, *30*, 3–24.

(2003). The adaptation of Asian and African Caribbean second generation youth in Britain. Paper presented to the International Conference on Diversity in Organisations, Communities and Nations, Hawaii, February 13–16.

Shaw, A. (1988). *A Pakistani community in Britain*. London: Blackwell.

(2000). *Kinship and continuity: Pakistani families in Britain*. Amsteldijk: Harwood Academic Publishers.

Smith, J. D. & Tomlinson, S. (1989). *The school effect: a study of multi-racial comprehensiveness*. London: Policy Studies Institute.

Stopes-Roe, M. & Cochrane, R. (1990). *Citizens of this country: the Asian British*. Clevedon: Multilingual Matters.

(1992). The child-rearing values of Asians in Britain: a study of Hindu, Muslim and Sikh immigrants and their young children. *British Journal of Social Psychology*, *29*, 149–160.

Thomas, C. (1971). *Boys no more*. Beverly Hills, CA: Glencoe Press.

Tidrick, G. (1966). Some aspects of Jamaican emigration to the United Kingdom 1953–1962. *Social and Economic Studies*, *15*, 11–20.

Verma, G. K. (1986). *Ethnicity and educational achievements in British schools*. London: Macmillan.

Wilson, A. (1978). *Mixed race children: a study of identity*. London: Allen & Unwin.

Wilson, M. (2003). The mental health of black and minority ethnic people. *Mental Health Review*, *8*, 7–15.

Wong, A. (1986). Creole as a language of power and solidarity. In D. Sutcliffe & A. Wong (eds), *The language of the Black experience*. Oxford: Basil Blackwell.

Wrench, J. & Modood, T. (2000). *The effectiveness of integration policies towards immigrants and ethnic minorities in the UK*. London: International Labour Office.

PART IV

Applications

This section deals with acculturation within the school, labor settings, the health sector and the larger society. The section, however, begins by looking at two groups of acculturating individuals – women and children – who have received less research attention, but may be vulnerable to acculturation problems. This chapter discusses how the psycho-social situation of immigrant children and women combines with immigration and acculturation to make them more vulnerable to adaptation problems. The next chapter (Chapter 25) discusses both successful and unsuccessful schooling trajectories for immigrant children, as well as educational strategies that may benefit them. In the labor setting (Chapter 26), the salaries of immigrants are discussed as well as the applicability of classical assimilation theories to economic behavior. Chapter 29 focuses on both the problematic aspects and advantages of cultural diversity, and the need to manage the inevitable diversity that many societies face. This section on applications also looks at two topics that are closely related, but which are the opposite of each other. Chapter 27 focuses on the health of immigrants, and discusses the complexity of the relationship between migration and health in research and theory formulation. Chapter 28 discusses and documents how people manage to adapt very well in spite of adverse conditions during their cross-cultural transitions, employing the concept of resilience. In Chapter 29, the focus is on the relationships that exist between the larger society and ethnocultural groups, drawing out some principles for how to improve these relationships and thereby increase the chance of positive acculturation. The last chapter (30) discusses from both theoretical and practical points of views, how immigrants and sojourners can learn to deal successfully with cross-cultural transitions using intercultural training.

24 Acculturation of immigrant children and women

David L. Sam

Even under the most favorable conditions, people's coping skills are challenged when they leave behind a familiar environment for unknown locations with different cultural values and traditions (Ward, Bochner & Furnham, 2001). It is therefore not surprising that early studies on migration and acculturation tended to paint a grim and negative picture of the consequences of the phenomenon (Eitinger, 1965; Ødegaard, 1932). This picture has, however, changed in recent years, where a number of studies and reviews (see, e.g., Beiser *et al.*, 1988; Berry & Sam, 1997) came to the conclusion that while immigration and acculturation may inherently be risky and make people vulnerable to a number of problems, risks are in themselves not destiny. It is further contended that people's long-term adaptation may not necessarily be poor.

In contemporary times, migration is very often triggered by several unfavorable circumstances, including wars, famine, economic hardships, natural disasters and human rights violations (see Chapters 13 and 14). These factors most likely put extra demands on people's coping abilities and make them more susceptible to maladaptation. The extent to which migration poses adaptation problems for individuals depends on a number of factors such as migration motives, the prevailing socio-demographic, psychological and political conditions in the society of settlement, as well as the cultural similarities and differences between the two societies in question and the person's predisposition to problems (Berry, 2003; see also Chapters 3, 4, 5 and 8, this volume). It follows therefore that, under normal circumstances some individuals may be more vulnerable than others to the risks involved in migration and acculturation, and one's vulnerability may be exacerbated under unfavorable circumstances.

The focus of this chapter is on individuals and groups who, as a result of their socio-demographic and psycho-social situations, may be more vulnerable to adaptation problems during acculturation. Specifically, the chapter focuses on children and women, and their acculturation may be considered as a double jeopardy. The "double jeopardy" children and women face during acculturation refers to the fact that, in addition to the risks all individuals undergoing acculturation are exposed to, women and children may face added risks due to the interaction between their psycho-social situation and gender in the case of women, and age and developmental phase in the case of children (Bashir, 1993; Beiser *et al.*, 1988). This chapter examines some of these psycho-social circumstances and how they combine with gender (i.e., the social meaning assigned to being a female) on the one hand, and age and developmental phase on the other, to make women and children particularly vulnerable to problems during acculturation.

24.1 Immigrant children

From demographic and economic points of view, the future of many societies lies in the hands of their children, since the children of today will be the leaders, workers and parents of tomorrow. The welfare of children is therefore regarded as having important ramifications for societies. However, welfare services directed towards children may be so general that the needs of some particular children may be overlooked; this has been the case with immigrant children (Gelinek, 1974). In many Western societies, not only do immigrant children constitute a sizeable proportion of the national population, they also form one of the fastest expanding sectors of the population (Aronowitz, 1984). In the United States for instance, it was estimated in 1997 that nearly 1 out of every 5 children (14 million) was the child of an immigrant (Hernandez & Charney, 1998), and that, during the period between 1990 and 1997, the number of children in immigrant families grew by 47%. The corresponding increase in children of native-born parents was only 7% during the same period (Hernandez, 1999).

24.1.1 The psycho-social situation of immigrant children

Adolescence falls within the developmental transition between childhood and adulthood and key developmental processes of this period include changes in biological, cognitive and psycho-social domains. These changes are affected, both directly and indirectly, by important contexts, including family, school and peers (Petersen & Leffert, 1995). For immigrant children, these processes are influenced by the varied cultural frameworks in which they grow up (Garcia Coll & Magnusson, 1997).

During the transition from childhood to adulthood, young people make important decisions about who they are and who they hope to be in the future, that is, they form an identity. In addition to developing identity like all adolescents, immigrant adolescents also develop an identity as a member of their own group (Phinney, 1990) and, to varying degrees, as a member of the larger society (Phinney & Devich-Navarro, 1997). The extent to which they develop a preference for either the ethnic or national group or combine them into a bicultural identity has implications for their psychological adjustment (LaFromboise, Coleman & Gerton 1993; Phinney, Horenczyk, Liebkind & Vedder, 2001).

By means of socialization within the family and the community, adolescents learn the values, traditions and practices of their culture. In many immigrant families, these values typically emphasize interdependence among family members (Fuligni, 1998a & b; Phinney, Ong & Madden, 2000; Kwak, 2003; Kağitçibaşi, 2003), including the expectation of mutual support within the family. With increased age, there are countervailing pressures for greater autonomy; peers from other groups provide models of alternative ways of interacting with parents and others. A strong sense of obligation to the family may benefit immigrant youth by providing clear roles and a sense of direction (Fuligni, 1998a & b), but it may also create conflicts, as adolescents strive for more autonomy in their own lives. Concomitantly, immigrant parents may be less willing to grant their children the autonomy they are striving for, resulting in intergenerational discrepancies in value orientations (Szapocznik & Kurtines, 1993; Santisteban & Mitrani, 2002). As they get older, adolescents are more oriented towards peers generally and particularly towards members of the opposite sex. Immigrant parents are often stricter than other parents in Western societies in regulating social behaviors like dating. In some cases, they try to limit social contacts to peers from the same ethnic group (Berry, Phinney, Sam & Vedder, in press). As immigrant youth make friends across ethnic group lines, conflicting pressures from parents and peers regarding social contacts can pose a challenge for these adolescents.

At school, immigrant children may be faced with the disadvantages of language barriers as well as their parents' lack of familiarity with the school system of the society of settlement. Yet, immigrant parents may have very high expectations for their children's academic achievements right from the start as part of their desire to see their children succeed in the new country (Eldering & Kloprogge, 1989).

In each of these situations, adolescents are faced with decisions as to the extent to which they retain the expectations, values and behaviors of their family and community or adopt those of the larger society. Because of the varying influences and opportunities they face in making choices on these issues, immigrant adolescents' development may take many different pathways towards adulthood in a new society (see Chapter 7; Sam & Oppedal, 2002; Sam, in press). These choices may also be conflicting and make the immigrant child vulnerable to maladaptation (Bromley, 1988).

24.1.2 The adaptation outcome

Because of the different developmental pathways down which these influences and choices may lead (Sam, in press), it is not surprising that research findings on immigrant children's adaptation are contradictory and inconsistent. Indeed, reviews point to vulnerabilities and maladaptation (Bashir, 1993; Beiser *et al.*, 1988) as well as resilience and very good adaptation (Fulgini, 1997; Harris, 1999). Generally, while early research studies on immigrant children concluded that they were poorly adapted (see, e.g., Bagley, 1972; Minde & Minde, 1976; Roderguez, 1968; Schaller, 1972, 1974), newer studies (e.g. Berry *et al.*, in press; Fuligni, 1997; Harris, 1999; Kao, 2000; Zhou, 1997) have concluded otherwise.

The discrepancies between the earlier studies confirming poor adaptation and newer studies suggesting better adaptation have been attributed to the use of less rigorous research methodologies in the earlier studies (Aronowitz, 1984). For instance, many of the earlier studies were carried out using theories that were developed for adult immigrants rather than theories that are relevant to the situation of children (see Oppedal, Røysamb & Sam, 2004).

In his literature review on the emotional and social adjustment of young children, Aronowitz (1984) concluded that psychological problems are not exclusive to immigrant children, and immigrant children did not necessarily manifest greater incidence of disorders than their native peers. The review also pointed out that, when immigrant children have adaptation difficulties, they tend to follow a broad pattern: children tend to report more behavioral problems and, in adolescence, identity conflicts. The experience of migration and culture change, nevertheless, it was suggested, could exacerbate the normal developmental crises for immigrant children and result in adaptation problems.

Intergenerational conflicts in family values suggested to be the basis of maladaptation among immigrant children (Rosenthal, Ranieri & Klimidis, 1996; Szapocznik & Kurtines, 1993) have been questioned in recent years, as a psycho-social situation not exclusive to immigrant families (Kwak, 2003). Findings from the ICSEY study (Berry et al., 2006) suggest that some form of discrepancies in intergenerational family values exist in both immigrant and national groups. These discrepancies are not uniquely an immigrant family phenomenon, nor do they inevitably lead to adaptation problems. While some groups of immigrant children may have increased intergenerational conflicts, and these may affect their adaptation, others, in spite of serious intergenerational conflicts, may not experience adaptation problems.

Studies examining how immigrant youth define and relate to their own ethnicity and that of the national group abound (see Chapter 6; Phinney, 1990; Phinney & Chavira, 1992; Phinney & Devich-Navarro, 1997; Rosenthal & Feldman, 1992; Verkuyten, 1994). How an immigrant defines his or her ethnicity, and how this relates to his or her adaptation, has often been examined against the status assigned to the immigrant in the society of residence (Liebkind, in press; Sam & Virta, 2003). It has often been suggested that if the group to which the immigrant belongs is a disparaged one, adaptation problems such as low self-esteem may abound. However, various reviews have found conflicting results (see Sam & Virta, 2003; Verkutyen, 1994, 2001). In their study across thirteen nations, Berry et al. (in press) found that immigrant children generally had high ethnic identity, and this was consistently higher than their national identity (i.e., identity with the society of settlement). In addition, the study found positive relationships between both ethnic and national identities and self-esteem across ethnic groups and across countries. This was irrespective of country of residence. However, the overall adaptation was moderated by the degree of perceived discrimination.

Good academic achievement is seen as a prerequisite for entry into the labor force, and immigrant parents, because they often begin at the low end of the occupation ladder (see Chapter 26, this volume), desire above all things that their children will succeed in school (see Eldering & Kloprogge, 1989). Because children spend the larger part of their life in school, immigrant children's school adjustment has attracted much research (see Chapter 25, this volume). In spite of their concern about their children's school adjustment, immigrant parents often appear to be less involved in the actual school activities of their children (Kiselica *et al.*, 1995). This is in part due to their handicap in not understanding the school system of the new society and partly because of their own belief system regarding the family's role in education (Atkinson, 1986). As Yao (1988) points out with respect to Asian parents, these parents tend to hold school teachers and their authority in such high esteem that they rarely question their work. They believe that parents' responsibility is towards the child at home, and that school officials should be responsible for what happens at school, with which parents should not interfere.

At home, however, immigrant parents regard putting pressure on their children to study as their major contributing role. Even after controlling for initial language disadvantages immigrant children may have, it is not uncommon to find that immigrant children spend much more time studying and do more homework than their national peers (see Rumbaut, 2000). It is also common for immigrant children to feel alienated from their school peers (Kao, 2000). Nevertheless, this alienation does not seem to affect their academic achievement. Indeed, Kao found out, in her study among Hispanic and Black children in the USA, that they not only perform very well in schools, they also outperform their national peers, and Rumbaut (2000) succinctly adds, it is because "they work for it" (p. 499). Notwithstanding the overall positive school adjustment immigrant children have, their ethnic and parental socio-economic backgrounds have been found to affect immigrant children's school adjustment (Kao & Tienda, 1995; Portes, 1995; Suarez-Orozco, 1989; Suarez-Orozco & Suarez-Orozco, 2001).

24.2 Immigrant women

Although women have always constituted a sizeable proportion of worldwide migration, their numbers and presence have until recently been overshadowed by men. For decades, international migration studies, and in particular those dealing with labor issues, either explicitly focused only on men or implicitly assumed that most migrants were males (Houstoun, Kramer & Barrett, 1984; Pedraza, 1991; Zlotnik, 2003). Women's participation in international migration was regarded as negligible (Kofman, 2000), even at a time when several Western countries were seeing large numbers of female migrants (Pedraza, 1991). Prior to the 1970s, international migration was rarely classified by gender, and because many women remained in the private sphere of domestic life, they were largely excluded from public discourse, such as policy formation and research agendas.

The Population Division of the United Nations estimates that, as of the year 2000, females accounted for 48.8% of global migration (United Nations, 2002). Since the mid-1960s, the proportion of female migrants has been rising steadily, such that the annual inflow of female immigrants in developed countries has now surpassed that of men. In 2000, females accounted for 52.4% and 51.1%, respectively, of all immigrants to Europe and North America. In absolute numbers, of the over 700,000 immigrants who were admitted into the USA in 2003, for instance, over 55% were females (USCIS, 2004). While the proportion of female immigrants in developing countries still lags behind that of men, in some countries, such as Argentina, female immigrants now outnumber males (Tyree & Donato, 1986).

Female migration normally takes one of two forms: family reunification or labor migration, with an overwhelming majority as family reunification. In recent years, a new form of migration, albeit an illegal one – human trafficking – has come to the fore. The dynamics of these forms of migration place women in a vulnerable position during acculturation. In the next sections we will present the research context of female migration and then look at how the different forms of female migration may put women in a double jeopardy.

24.2.1 The research context

Although early studies in international migration were gender biased in favor of men, research on female migrants is now a burgeoning field. With few exceptions such as the special issue of the *International Migration Review* in 1984, it was not until the 1990s that the inclusion of women in international studies of migration started to mushroom, and this has continued unabated. There are now over 3,000 references on female immigrants from all fields of study including anthropology, economics, law, medicine, psychology and sociology. Consequently, this review is very selective and touches only the tip of the iceberg. Readers are therefore directed to Hofstetter (2005) for a comprehensive, but by no means exhaustive, bibliography of studies on female immigrants from 1945 to the present.

A characteristic feature of studies on immigrant women is that other than the ones using census data, sample sizes tend to be small compared with studies on male immigrants. This is because many women are seen as remaining within the private sphere and therefore not readily available for large-survey studies. The notion of women staying within the private sphere itself has arisen because much of the work women do, including that of female immigrants, goes unpaid and is therefore not classified as work (Pedraza, 1991; Morokvasic, 1984).

In addition, many of the studies on female immigrants are qualitative and descriptive rather than quantitative and analytic. In spite of their relevance, the generalizations of the findings may be limited. Thus, each study cited here needs to be understood within the context of the society of settlement, the ethnic group in question and country of origin.

24.2.2 Women and family reunification

Immigration laws regarding women have generally been based on coverture law, i.e., the status a woman acquires upon marriage under common law. This means that a wife normally has no legal identity of her own other than that of her husband. In terms of international migration, women's immigration status is often a derivative of her husband's status (Clifford & Pearce, 2004). One form of coverture law in international migration is the family reunification program which allows the spouse and children to join migrants who are already in a country legally. In these programs, women form the largest group.

Women who migrate as part of family reunification programs tend to have an insecure status. As immigrants, they can only stay in a country either as a wage earner, or as dependent on a wage earner. Nevertheless, in the mid-1970s when several European countries placed a moratorium on labor immigration but were opened to family reunification, women who joined their husband were either banned from entering into the labor force or had to wait for a period before they could enter into it (Morokvasic, 1984). In the absence of legal employment opportunities, these women risk being exploited if they decide not to be dependent on their wage-earning husband and enter into the labor force. As illegal workers, they are often placed in low-status jobs, required to put in long working hours and cheated economically. As dependents, their stay is linked to the legal status of the immigrant husband. If the dependency link ceases to exist, for example through divorce or separation, the woman risks being deported (Brouwer & Priester, 1983; Morokvasic, 1984).

Acculturation constitutes a double transition for married immigrants in that both the individual and the marriage adapt to the new culture. The couple has to learn to accommodate each other in a new cultural context (Ataca & Berry, 2002). For women joining their husband as part of family reunification, there is the danger of the couple having grown apart during the transition between the time the husband migrates and when the wife joins him. This may hamper the adaptation process when effort has to be directed towards salvaging the marriage.

Family reunification adds new tasks to the traditional unpaid tasks a woman has. These new tasks include ensuring the survival of the culture of the family and that of the heritage culture (see Hollander & Bukowitz, 1990; Killian, 2002) in a possibly non-supportive social environment; socializing a child in multiple cultures (Maiter & George, 2003); maintaining cordial social networks of kin and networks of obligations, including economic remittances (Curran & Saguy, 2001; Salaff, 2002).

In addition to their own efforts to adjust to two cultural systems (as part of their acculturation), immigrant women, and in particular mothers, have the added responsibility of helping children deal with adjusting to two or more cultures, including the values of their own ethnic group, and those of the society of settlement. For instance, mothers try to support their children in the learning of their heritage language, as well as training them in the national language. Furthermore, as culture bearers, women bear the responsibility of ensuring the survival of their traditional culture in the society of settlement. Using Hong Kong Chinese women in Canada as examples, Salaff (2002) describes how these women struggle to sustain cordial kinship relationships when they are abroad. It is the responsibility of the Chinese woman to build social support networks of a wide variety be they at home in China or overseas. While trying to maintain a good social network support system, the woman may nevertheless be isolated at home (Ataca & Berry, 2002; Mirdal, 1984).

During economic recession, if her husband is laid off from work, immigrant women are expected to take over as the breadwinners of the family, because they are more flexible and more willing to accept menial and low-paying jobs than are men (Morokvasic, 1984; Pedraza, 1991). Changes in gender roles that may arise because the woman is the breadwinner may put her at risk of being abused by the husband. This is because a husband may feel unsure of his masculinity and resort to violence as a means of reaffirming it (Gutmann, 1997).

To conclude this section on family reunification, it is important to indicate that a number of men also join their wife through family reunification programs, but in their case they do so in connection with refugee status granted to their wife. In times of political, ethnic and religious conflicts, women and children tend to be the first to seek refuge outside their habitual abode, and men follow their wives (Pedraza, 1991).

24.2.3   Female migrants in the labor market

Even if the majority of women migrated under family reunification objectives, many of them, once they arrive, are also exposed to a variety of factors (such as high cost of living, failing marriage) which force them to become active in the labor market. A woman's participation in the labor force depends on a number of factors, including her educational and social background, marital status, and whether she has a child or not. Well-educated women and women with middle- or upper-class backgrounds may choose to enter into the labor force as soon as possible, in order to maintain a certain standard of living (Prieto, 1987), even if they were not working outside the house prior to their migration. Being educated increases an immigrant woman's chances of securing a job, and each additional year of education beyond mandatory schooling may increase her chances by 3% (Evans, 1984). However, just like her male counterparts, she may end up in a job well beneath her qualifications (Dustmann & Schmidt, 2001; Meadows, Thurston & Melton, 2001).

Married immigrant women also have lower chances of securing a salary-paying job, compared with unmarried immigrant women of the same age (Chiu, 1998; Evans, 1984; Lee, 1998; Salaff, 2002). Evans (1984) found in her study among immigrant women in Australia that with some exceptions, each child the woman has decreases her labor market participation by about 3%. When a married immigrant woman with a young child enters into the labor market, she very often has to make do with a low-status job and work twice as much as she would otherwise in order to make up for the expenses of having someone else take care of her child.

Migrant women's participation in the labor force is highly gendered and they tend to be concentrated in domestic service and in factory work, particularly in the garment industry (Pedraza, 1991). The incorporation of migrant women into domestic service and care work is not only the result of migratory circumstances (such as a lack of language proficiency, inadequate cultural orientation, and incompatible occupational skills – see Chapter 26, this volume), but rather it reflects the fact that domesticity is one of the few occupations open to migrant women due to gender segregation in the labor market of developed countries (Glenn 1986; Raijman, Schammah-Gesser & Kemp, 2003; Salazar, 2001). The availability of domestic and household service for migrant women has in itself arisen because of increasing numbers of native women entering into the labor force in developed countries, which has created labor for immigrant women in the "newly vacated" homes of the native women. Much as domestic and household work may be a low-status job, for some immigrant women this kind of employment may introduce them to a middle- and upper-class life style, as well as provide them with a healthier work environment (Pedraza, 1991).

The gender-segregated nature of labor and the precarious position that women find themselves in (such as inability to join labor unions) easily make them victims of exploitation: long working hours and low salary (Dustmann & Schmidt, 2001). For instance Morokvasic (1984) points to the fact that the number of daily working hours in the French garment industry was regulated to ten hours a day as far back as 1892, yet almost a century later immigrant women in Parisian sweatshops worked fourteen to sixteen hours a day.

24.2.4 Human trafficking and female immigrants

Some characteristic features of human trafficking are illegal activities such as coercion, deception, fraud, forced labor and sexual exploitation. Accordingly human trafficking is often regarded as a form of illegal immigration.

And as with other illegal immigration, it is difficult to come up with accurate statistics on the scope of the phenomenon. With regards to human trafficking, estimates suggest that, globally, between 500,000 and 1 million people are victims annually (IOM, 2001), of whom the overwhelming majority are women and children.

The desire to migrate and difficulties in fulfilling these dreams make people particularly vulnerable to trafficking and exploitation. Restrictive norms (e.g. gender discrimination) and structures unfavorable to women in the labor market are not in line with demands placed on women to fulfill financial and economic responsibilities such as looking after a child alone. Because of the illegal nature of human trafficking, research findings are scanty, except for police reports. But there is no doubt that the process of placing people into slavery-like conditions entails some form of threat, intimidation, or physical and emotional abuse which together can result in Battered Woman Syndrome (Rubenstein, 2004; Walker, 2000). Battered Women Syndrome is a label given to a pattern of psychological and behavioral symptoms found in women living in abusive relationships. These symptoms may include fear, anger, sadness, self-blame, distrust, generalized belief that the world is unsafe, depression, flashbacks, anxiety, sleep problems and substance abuse. Because human trafficking often results in sexual exploitation such as prostitution, the dangers of sexually transmitted diseases and HIV/AIDS cannot be overemphasized in this context.

24.3 Limitations and conclusions

The focus on children and women in this chapter has been approached as though women and children, and indeed men, are discrete individuals in the acculturation setting. In fact, women, children and men constitute family units, and how families weather the acculturation process is different from how the individual members deal with the process (Santisteban & Mitrani, 2002). More often than not, immigrant women and children are dependent on the male immigrant who has been the basis for much of the theory on immigration and acculturation. There is a need to focus on women and children, and, more importantly, a focus on the family as a functional unit is very much needed.

Immigrant research, just like research with disadvantaged groups in general, very often suffers from the methodological error of focusing almost exclusively on problems, thereby ignoring the strengths and resources of the group under scrutiny. This chapter is no exception as the emphasis has been on the problematic aspects of immigration for women and children. This undoubtedly gives the impression that all immigrant children and, in particular, immigrant women are suffering and are crushed by the weight of these difficulties. This is, indeed, not the case. There are several studies of female labor immigrants who are recruited into leadership and professional positions, which we have not focused on. Similarly the chapter has not focused on refugee children and unaccompanied minors, who may be even more vulnerable (see Sourander, 1998). Focusing on these groups may help offset the skewed picture painted here. This, however, has not been done because of lack of space.

The current state of the art suggests that immigrant children do adapt well, and in some cases better than their national peers. With respect to immigrant women, in particular married ones, their overall wellbeing appears to be mediated by their family-centeredness and their roles as resources for the family more than the difficulties associated with the immigration per se (Anderson, 1987; Meadows *et al.*, 2001).

24.4 References

Anderson, J. M. (1987). Migration and health: perspectives on immigrant women. *Society of Health and Illness*, 9, 410–438.

Aronowitz, M. (1984). The social and emotional adjustment of immigrant children. A review of literature. *International Migration Review*, 18, 237–257.

Ataca, B. & Berry, J. W. (2002). Psychological, sociocultural and marital adaptation of Turkish immigrant couples in Canada. *International Journal of Psychology*, 37, 13–27.

Atkinson, D. R. (1986). Cultural issues in school and family. In L. B. Golden & D. Capuzzi (eds.), *Helping families help children* (pp. 237–244). Springfield. IL: Charles C. Thomas.

Bagley, C. (1972). Deviant behaviour in English and West Indian school children. *Research in Education*, 8, 47–55.

Bashir, M. R. (1993). Issues of immigration for the health and adjustment of young people. *Journal of Paediatrics and Child Health*, 9(Supplement 1), s42–s45.

Beiser, M., Wood, M., Barwick, C., *et al.* (1988). *After the door has been opened: mental health issues affecting immigrants and refugees in Canada*. Ottawa: Ministries of Multiculturalism and Citizenship, and Health and Welfare.

Berry, J. W. (2003). Conceptual approaches to acculturation. In K. Chun, P. Balls-Organista & G. Marin (eds.). *Acculturation. Advances in theory, measurement and applied research* (pp. 17–37). Washington: APA Press.

Berry, J. W., Phinney, J. S., Sam, D. L. & Vedder, P. (eds.) (2006). *Immigrant youth in cultural transition: acculturation, identity and adaptation across national contexts*. Mahwah, NJ: Lawrence Erlbaum Associates

Berry, J. W. & Sam, D. L. (1997). Acculturation and adaptation. In J. W. Berry, M. H. Segall & C. Kağitçibaşi (eds.), *Handbook of cross-cultural psychology*, Vol. III: *Social behaviour and applications*. 2nd edn. (pp. 291–326). Boston: Allyn & Bacon.

Bromley, M. A. (1988). Identity as a central adjustment issue for Southeast Asian unaccompanied refugee minors. *Child and Youth Care Quarterly*, 17, 104–114.

Brouwer, I. & Priester, M. (1983). Living in between: Turkish women in their homeland and in the Netherlands. In A. Phizaclea (ed.), *One way ticket: migration and female labour* (pp. 113–129). London: Routledge and Kegan Paul.

Chiu, C. (1998). *Small family business in Hong Kong: accumulation and accommodation*. Hong Kong: Chinese University of Hong Kong Press.

Clifford, E. J. & Pearce, S. C. (2004). *Women and current US immigration practices*. http://newmedia.colorado.edu/~socwomen/socactivism/womenimm.pdf.

Curran, S. R. & Saguy, A. C. (2001). Migration and cultural change: a role for gender and social networks? *Journal of International Women's Studies, 2*, 54–77.

Dustmann, C. & Schmidt, C. M. (2001). *The wage performance of immigrant women: full-time jobs, part-time jobs and the role of selection*. CEPR Discussion Papers, 2702. London: Centre for Economic and Policy Research.

Eitinger, L. (1965). *Concentration camp survivors in Norway and Israel*. Jerusalem: Weizmann Science Press.

Eldering, I. & Kloprogge, J. (eds.) (1989). *Different cultures, same school: ethnic minority children in Europe*. Amsterdam: Swets & Zeitlinger.

Evans, M. D. R. (1984). Immigrant women in Australia: resources, family and work. *International Migration Review, 28*, 1063–1090.

Fuligni, A. J. (1997). The academic achievement of adolescents from immigrant families. The role of family background, attitudes and behavior. *Child Development, 68*, 261–273.

   (1998a). The adjustment of children from immigrant families. *Current Directions in Psychological Science, 7*, 99–103.

   (1998b). Authority, autonomy, and parent–adolescent relationships: a study of adolescents from Mexican, Chinese, Filipino, and European backgrounds. *Developmental Psychology, 34*, 782–792.

Garcia Coll, C. & Magnusson, K. (1997). The psychological experience of immigration: a developmental perspective. In A. Booth, A. Crouter & N. Landale (eds.), *Immigration and the family: research and policy on U.S. immigrants* (pp. 91–131). Mahwah, NJ: Lawrence Erlbaum Associates.

Gelinek, I. (1974). Migrant children. *International Children's Welfare Review, 21*, 45–71.

Glenn, E. N. (1986). *Issei, Nisei, warbride*. Philadelphia: Temple University.

Gutmann, M. (1997). Trafficking in men: the anthropology of masculinity. *Annual Review of Anthropology, 26*, 385–409.

Harris, K. M. (1999). The health status and risk behavior of adolescents in immigrant families. In D. J. Hernandez (ed.), *Children of immigrants: health, adjustment and public assistance* (pp. 286–315). Washington, DC: National Academy Press.

Hernandez, D. J. (1999). Children of immigrants: health, adjustment and public assistance. In D. J. Hernandez (ed.), *Children of immigrants: health, adjustment and public assistance* (pp. 1–18). Washington, DC: National Academy Press.

Hernandez, D. J. & Charney, E. (eds.) (1998). *From generation to generation: the health and well-being of children in immigrant families*. Washington, DC: National Academy Press.

Hofstetter, E. O. (2005). *Women immigrants: 1945 to the present. A bibliography*. www.towson.edu/users/hofstet/.

Hollander, B. S. &. Bukowitz, W. R. (1990). Women, family culture and family business. *Family Business Review, 3*, 139.

Houstoun, M. F., Kramer, R. G. & Barrett, J. M. (1984). Female predominance of immigration to the United States since the 1930s: a first look. *International Migration Review*, *18*, 908–963.

IOM (2001). Trafficking in immigrants. In *IOM Quarterly Bulletin 23*. Geneva: International Organization for Migration.

Kağitçibaşi, C. (2003). Autonomy, embeddedness and adaptability in immigration contexts. *Human Development*, *46*, 145–150.

Kao, G. (2000). Psychological well-being and educational achievement among immigrant youth. In D. J. Hernandez (ed.), *Children of immigrants. Health, adjustment and public assistance* (pp. 410–477). Washington, DC: National Academy Press.

Kao, G. & Tienda, M. (1995). Optimism and achievement. The educational performance of immigrant youth. *Social Science Quarterly*, *76*, 1–19.

Killian, C. (2002). Culture on the weekend: Maghrebin women's adaptation in France. *International Journal of Sociology and Social Policy*, *22(1–3)*, 75–105.

Kiselica, M. S., Changizi, J. C., Cureton, V. L. L. & Gridley, B. E. (1995). Counselling children and adolescents in schools. Salient multicultural issues. In J. G. Ponteroto, J. M. Casas, L. A. Suzuki & C. M. Alexander (eds.), *Handbook of multicultural counselling* (pp. 516–532). Thousand Oaks, CA: Sage Publications.

Kofman, E. (2000). The invisibility of skilled female migrants and gender relations in studies of skilled migration in Europe. *International Journal of Population Studies*, *6*, 45–59.

Kwak, K. (2003). Adolescents and their parents: a review of intergenerational family relations for immigrant and non-immigrant families. *Human Development*, *46*, 115–136.

LaFromboise, T., Coleman, H., & Gerton, J. (1993). Psychological impact of biculturalism: evidence and theory. *Psychological Bulletin*, *114*, 395–412.

Lee, C. (1998). Counselling the Black adolescent. Critical roles and functions for counselling professionals. In R. J. Jones (ed.), *Black adolescents* (pp. 293–308). Berkeley, CA: Cobb & Henry.

Liebkind, K., Jasinskaja-Lahti, I. & Solheim, E. (2004). Cultural identity, perceived discrimination, and parental support as determinants of immigrants' school adjustments: Vietnamese youth in Finland. *Journal of Adolescent Research*, *19*, 635–656.

Maiter, S. & George, U. (2003). Understanding context and culture in the parenting approaches of immigrant South Asian mothers. *Affilia*, *18(4)*, 411–428.

Meadows, L. M., Thurston, W. E. & Melton, C. (2001). Immigrant women's health. *Social Science and Medicine*, *52*, 1451–1458.

Minde, K. & Minde R. (1976). Children of immigrants: the adjustment of Ugandan Asian primary school children. *Canadian Psychiatric Association Journal*, *21*, 371–381.

Mirdal, G. M. (1984). Stress and distress in migration: problems and resources of Turkish women in Denmark. *International Migration Review*, *18*, 984–1003.

Morokvasic, M. (1984). Birds of passage are also women . . . *International Migration Review*, *24*, 886–907.

Ødegaard, O. (1932). Emigration and insanity. *Acta Psychiatrica et Neurological, Supplement 4.*

Oppedal, B., Røysamb, E. & Sam, D. L. (2004). The effect of acculturation and social support on change in mental health among young immigrants. *International Journal of Behavioural Development, 28,* 481–494.

Pedraza, S. (1991). Women and migration. The social consequences of migration. *Annual Review of Sociology, 17,* 303–325.

Petersen, A. C. & Leffert, N. (1995). What is special about adolescence? In M. Rutter (ed.), *Psychosocial disturbances in young people* (pp. 3–36). Cambridge: Cambridge University Press.

Phinney, J. S. (1990). Ethnic identity in adolescents and adults: a review of research. *Psychological Bulletin, 108,* 499–514.

Phinney, J. S. & Chavira, V. (1992). Ethnic identity and self-esteem: an exploratory longitudinal study. *Journal of Adolescence, 15,* 271–281.

Phinney, J. S. & Devich-Navarro, M. (1997). Variations in bicultural identification among African American and Mexican American adolescents. *Journal of Research on Adolescence, 7,* 3–32.

Phinney, J. S., Horenczyk, G., Liebkind, K. & Vedder, P. (2001). Ethnic identity, immigration, and well-being: an interactional perspective. *Journal of Social Issues, 57,* 493–510.

Phinney, J. S., Ong, A. & Madden, T. (2000). Cultural values and intergenerational value discrepancies in immigrant and non-immigrant families. *Child Development, 71,* 528–539.

Portes, A. (ed.) (1995). *The economic sociology of immigration.* New York: Russell Sage Foundation.

Prieto, Y. (1987). Cuban women in the U.S. labor force: perspectives on the nature of change. *Cuban Studies, 17,* 73–91.

Raijman, R., Schammah-Geser, S. & Kemp, A. (2003). International migration, domestic work, and care work: undocumented Latina migrants in Israel. *Gender and Society, 17,* 727–749.

Roderguez, R. (1968). Difficulties of adjustment in immigrant children in Geneva. *Médecine et Hygiène, 845,* 1–6.

Rosenthal, D. A. & Feldman, S. S. (1992). The nature and stability of ethnic identity in Chinese youth. *Journal of Cross-Cultural Psychology, 23,* 214–227.

Rosenthal, D., Ranieri, N. & Klimidis, S. (1996). Vietnamese adolescents in Australia: relationships between perceptions of self and parental values, intergenerational conflict, and gender dissatisfaction. *International Journal of Psychology, 31,* 81–91.

Rubenstein, L. S. (2004). *What is battered woman's syndrome?* www.divorcenet.com/states/oregon/or_art02.

Rumbaut, R. G. (2000). Passages to adulthood: the adaptation of children of immigrants in Southern California. In D. J. Hernandez (ed.), *Children of immigrants. Health, adjustment and public assistance* (pp. 478–545). Washington, DC: National Academy Press.

Salaff, J. W. (2002). Women's work in international migration. In E. Chow (ed.), *Transforming gender and development in East Asia* (pp. 217–238). London: Routledge.

Salazar, P. (2001). *Servants of globalization: women, migration, and domestic work.* Stanford, CA: Stanford University Press.

Sam, D. L. (in press). Adaptation of children and adolescents with immigrant background: acculturation or development. In M. H. Bornstein & L. R. Cote (eds.), *Acculturation and parent–child relationships: measurement and development.* Mahwah, NJ: Lawrence Erlbaum Associates.

Sam, D. L. & Oppedal, B. (2002). Acculturation as a developmental pathway. In W. J. Lonner, D. L. Dinnel, S. A. Hayes & D. N. Sattler (eds.), *Online readings in psychology and culture* (Unit 8, Chapter 6) (www.edu/~culture), Center for Cross-Cultural Research, Western Washington University, Bellingham, Washington, USA.

Sam, D. L. & Virta, E. (2003). Social group identity and its effect on the self-esteem of adolescents with immigrant background. In R. G. Craven, H. W. Marsh & D. M. McInerney (eds.), *International advances in self research* (Vol. I, pp. 347–373). Sydney: Information Age Publishers

Santisteban, D. A. & Mitrani, V. B. (2002). Influence of the acculturation processes on the family. In K. Chun, P. Balls-Organista & G. Marin (eds.), *Acculturation. Advances in theory, measurement and applied research* (pp. 121–136). Washington, DC: APA Press.

Schaller, J. (1972). Residential change and emotional maladjustment in children and adolescents. A review of research. *Gotenberg Psychological Reports, 2,* 1–11.
   (1974). The relations between geographic mobility and school behaviour. *Gotenberg Psychological Reports, 4,* 1–17.

Sourander, A. (1998). Behavior problems and traumatic events of unaccompanied refugee minors. *Child Abuse and Neglect, 22,* 719–727.

Suarez-Orozco, C. & Suarez-Orozco, M. (2001). *Children of immigrants.* Cambridge, MA: Harvard University Press.

Suarez-Orozco, M. (1989). *Central American refugees and US high schools: a psychosocial study of motivation and achievement.* Stanford: Stanford University Press.

Szapocznik, J. & Kurtines, W. (1993). Family psychology and cultural diversity. *American Psychologist, 48,* 400–407.

Tyree, A. & Donato, K. (1986). A demographic overview of international migration of women. In R. J. Simon. & C. B. Brettell (eds.), *International migration: the female experience* (pp. 21–41). Totowa, NJ: Rowman & Allanheld.

United Nations (2002). *International migration report: 2002.* New York: United Nations.

USCIS (2004). *2004 year book of immigration statistics.* http://uscis.gov/graphics/shared/statistics/yearbook/YrBk04Im.htm.

Verkuyten, M. (1994). Self-esteem among ethnic minority youth in western countries. *Social Indicators Research, 32,* 21–47.
   (2001). Global self-esteem, ethnic self-esteem, and family integrity: Turkish and Dutch early adolescents in the Netherlands. *International Journal of Behavioral Development, 25,* 357–366.

Walker, L. E. A. (2000). *The battered woman's syndrome.* 2nd edn. New York: Springer.

Ward, C., Bochner, S. & Furnham, A. (2001). *The psychology of culture shock.* London: Routledge.

Yao, E. L. (1988). Working effectively with Asian immigrant parents. *Phi, Delta, Kappan, 70*, 223–225.

Zhou, M. (1997). Growing up American: the challenge confronting immigrant children and children of immigrants. *Annual Review of Sociology, 23*, 63–95.

Zlotnik, H. (2003). The global dimensions of female migration. www.migrationinformation.org/Feature/display.cfm?ID=109.

25 Acculturation and the school

Paul H. Vedder & Gabriel Horenczyk

25.1 Introduction

For most immigrant children and adolescents, school and other educational settings are the major arenas for inter-group contact and acculturation. School adjustment can be seen as a primary task, and as a highly important outcome, of the cultural transition process. Schools represent and introduce the new culture to immigrant children. Within many immigrant communities, therefore, the importance attributed to school adjustment is particularly high (Horenczyk & Ben-Shalom, 2001): newcomers tend to see schools as welcome avenues to participation and mobility (Gibson, 1991). And indeed, many succeed in establishing a better life in their new societies than they had in their societies of origin. Nevertheless, for many of them, the process of acculturation is a painful one due to the loss of personal relationships and of the culturally known. Although they succeed in acquiring new competencies, many immigrants do not reach levels of social participation that they – and members of the national society – consider satisfactory. An abundance of studies show that immigrant youth in the Western world benefit insufficiently from schools (Glenn & De Jong, 1996). Too many of these students leave schools without the necessary certificates and qualifications (see Eldering & Kloprogge, 1989).

This chapter aims to explore possible explanations for both successful and unsuccessful schooling trajectories and, in doing so, it describes educational strategies that may benefit immigrant youth. The last three decades of scientific enquiry into school adjustment in multicultural societies have resulted in a proliferation of theoretical models (e.g., Cushner, 1998; Korn & Bursztyn, 2002; May, 1999; Troyna & Carrington, 1990; Hagendoorn & Nekuee, 1999). We will not present a review of these models, but instead opt for describing two broad theoretical approaches. After the presentation of these approaches we will focus on school adjustment in the multicultural society from two perspectives: the school system, and the broader acculturation context.

25.2 Two broad theoretical approaches

The first approach describes immigrant youth's socialization in terms of a combination of enculturation and acculturation. From this perspective, school is seen as a setting aimed at socializing students towards the national culture. The second perspective views school as a setting that functions as a representative of a predominantly global culture, not a national culture. The contrast is then between global and local cultures.

25.2.1 Enculturation and acculturation

Enculturation is the process of becoming skillful in using tools, learning behaviors, knowledge and values that are part of the culture of one's own group. It is a learning process that takes place in the context of a partly school-bound process of intergenerational transmission of culture. Schools, however, are likely to support the enculturation process of majority-group children more than that of minority-group children (see Boekaerts, 1998). Curricula, assessment instruments and instructional methods tend to reflect and focus on the cultural and educational requirements of the majority society (Banks, 1994; Vedder, 1994). These instruments of schooling are rarely adapted to the variety of students' cultural backgrounds. The distance between the school standards and children's socialization experiences is likely to be larger for immigrant children than for national children. Hence, for students with a cultural minority background, schools take less responsibility in terms of enculturation and tend to serve more acculturation functions. Acculturation refers to changes in the course of the development of a cultural group due to contact with other cultural groups. Acculturation at the individual level requires adaptation to behaviors, customs, values and tasks that are typical of another cultural group – for the immigrant, these are those of the majority society. Both enculturation and acculturation are considered to be learning processes that are likely to facilitate future professional and social adaptation. But the challenge of simultaneous enculturation and acculturation which immigrant children face is very demanding. Both the enculturation and the acculturation trajectories can lead to disappointing outcomes. In the enculturation process they may fail to become sufficiently proficient in their own language and to acquire culture-specific skills, knowledge and attitudes which are deemed very important by their parents or by other group members. A failed acculturation in school will result in relatively poor academic achievements, in low levels of wellbeing and, eventually, in dropping-out.

Enculturation and acculturation are not absolutely separate routes. The ease and success of the immigrant's learning process depends on a variety of factors like motivation; cognitive competencies; support from parents, kin and other relatives; actual learning time; but also the distance between the ethnic culture and the national culture. This distance is determined by a myriad of cultural elements (Extra & Vallen, 1989; Mumford & Babiker, 1998), e.g., linguistic, educational, religious, economic and legal differences. Structural linguistic differences, for example, have to do with questions like: "Does English have the same sounds and sound combinations as, for instance, Turkish, and is the relationship between morphemes and graphemes comparable between these two languages?" Cultural differences also impinge on the actual opportunities for oral and written contacts between members of two ethnic groups. Such opportunities are important for second language acquisition (Bialystok, 2001). Many studies that examined differences in value orientations and interaction patterns between home and school or between immigrant and national families tend to attribute differences between children as regards school adjustment to the distance between immigrant and national cultures (Heath, 1983; Snow, Barnes, Chandler, Goodman & Hemphill, 1991; Zentella, 1997). Acculturation is assumed to proceed more smoothly when the difference between two cultures is smaller. If the differences are small, earlier-acquired skills and knowledge related to one's first culture may be useful in contexts typical of the other culture as well. Moreover, when the cultural distance is relatively short, opportunities for learning about the other culture or in settings representing the other culture will be more readily available or accessible to the immigrants and their families.

The first approach, thus, will usually predict that immigrant students will exhibit more school adjustment problems than national students. Support is found in many studies (Glenn & De Jong, 1996; Portes & Rumbaut, 2001; Suarez-Orozco & Suarez-Orozco, 2001; Vedder & Virta, 2005). At the same time, it is not difficult to show that the rule does not hold for all countries and groups. In the case where immigrant students have successful school careers and even outperform national students, such students are likely to be referred to as "model minorities" (Lee, 2001; Ying, Lee, Tsai, Hung, Lin & Wan, 2001). Motivation, support from home and actual learning time are used to explain their school adjustment. But still the primary contrast or comparison remains between nationals and immigrants or ethnic minorities.

25.2.2   The school as a global stage

The second approach is also concerned with cultural distance or cultural differences, but the primary focus is not on groups, but rather on settings. Within this broad framework, studies typically explore how students deal with task demands, norms and communication styles characteristic of the school and the home situation. An exemplary and frequently cited work is Phelan, Davidson and Cao's (1991) study entitled "Students' multiple worlds: negotiating the boundaries of family, peer, and school cultures." Findings show that students with a minority cultural background differ widely in the extent to which they are able to adapt to culture-specific requirements for social participation within the family, in school and with peers. Each setting requires different patterns of adaptation. Most students have no problems at all, but some show severe problems of adaptation and become isolated or marginalized at school.

This second approach draws together studies that show that many students are incapable of experiencing learning in school as learning for life outside school, as learning that is useful for knowing how to accomplish tasks that make sense (Resnick, 1987) and studies that show that schools all over the world are involved in a process of an increasing globalization of education (Plomp & Loxley, 1992; Suarez-Orozco, 2001; Vedder, 1994). Suarez-Orozco describes globalization as a process of change that transcends or supersedes national borders and is characterized by powers that detach important economic, social and cultural practices from the region or location in which they originated and were originally conducted. Financial capital, human resources and information are no longer bound to particular countries – they can, and actually do, move around. He also describes schools as an important power in this process and suggests that, in adapting to this global institution, immigrant children actually do have a head start. After all, they already experienced and learned about the importance of crossing borders in order to improve the availability and accessibility of resources that warrant a better future. This notion of immigrant children's head start has clearly found a support in the repeatedly reported finding in studies in the USA, as well as in Western Europe, that immigrant students outperform national children even when their parents have a lower educational background (Portes & Rumbaut, 2001; Tesser & Iedema, 2001). This is seen as an indication that schools basically have an alienating effect on all students. Schools require acculturation from all students. Purves (1990) even suggested that, all over the world, education leads students away from their past and family. The strength of this second approach also lies in the possibility of using it to compare a much broader range of groups than just immigrants versus nationals. For instance, it may be used as well to explain why some sub-groups of national youth have a more positive school adjustment than others.

Most studies dealing with multicultural education can be categorized as representing one of these two approaches. Of course, there are also studies drawing on both approaches. Although these studies contrast national and immigrant students, they clarify that students have to cope with setting-specific task requirements. Portes' (1995) study of segmented assimilation is an example, as well as studies exemplifying a contextual approach to acculturation. The process of adaptation to a new society involves intricate communication transactions, in which immigrants try to make sense of what they expect and what is expected from them in new settings (Horenczyk, 1996; Phinney, Horenczyk, Liebkind & Vedder, 2001). For example, students respond differently to particular school environments. Birman, Trickett and Vinokurov (2002) examined the adaptation of Soviet Jewish refugee adolescents to a school in the USA characterized by strong assimilationist pressures. In this setting national identity predicted better grades, whereas in other settings adolescents' bicultural orientation and language competencies were more important.

25.3   The school system

Greenfield, Keller, Fuligni and Maynard (2003) contend that children – irrespective of their cultural background – face three major developmental tasks: to establish, maintain and end social relationships; to acquire new knowledge and skills; and to achieve autonomy while maintaining social relationships (Greenfield *et al.*, 2003). Along similar lines, it has been suggested that schools should strengthen three basic qualities or values: relatedness, competence and autonomy (Connell & Wellborn, 1991). These qualities will allow students to experience a strong feeling of the availability of social support, which allows them to feel good and cope with both task demands and emotional stress (Boekaerts, 1992, 1998). In this section, we will have a closer look at each of these tasks.

25.3.1   Relatedness

Youngsters grow up in a mosaic of social settings, and their cognitions, feelings and behaviors are shaped to a great extent by their perceptions and interpretations of these settings. They have had many favorable, and some also many unfavorable, experiences with regard to the role of family members, teachers and peers in their learning and development, which have created diverse mindsets that continue to influence their learning and development. They may feel either secure or insecure with regard to the availability of support from others, they may feel surrounded either by persons who provide for a cognitively and linguistically stimulating environment or by persons who do not care about their cognitive and linguistic competencies. Helgeson (1993), Van der Zee, Buunk and Sanderman (1997) and Wethington and Kessler (1986) showed that perceived availability of social support is a better predictor of wellbeing than actual support given. Generally, young adolescents see parents as more important providers of social support than either peers or teachers (DuBois, Felner, Brand, Adan & Evans, 1992). In the contexts of school and wellbeing in school, however, the teachers' role is important, both with respect to achieving academic goals (instructional support) and with regard to the regulation of emotional and social processes (emotional support) (Berndt, 1999; Furman & Buhrmester, 1992; Tatar & Horenczyk, 1996; Wentzel, 1998).

Little is known about the role of ethnicity or culture in experiencing or perceiving the availability of social support. A recent study by Vedder, Boekaerts and Seegers (2005) showed that Turkish and Moroccan youngsters perceive lower levels of availability of parental instructional support than their Dutch peers do, whereas no such difference was found with respect to the availability of parental emotional support. The Dutch students view instructional support from teacher and parents as being about equal, whereas there is a marked contrast in levels for the Turkish and Moroccan students. They perceive more support from teachers. Interestingly, Dutch students more frequently link school problems with instructional support from parents than immigrant students do. No differences were found between immigrant and national students with respect to support from peers. In their study conducted among Israeli adolescents, however, Horenczyk and Tatar (1998) reported that immigrants assign greater importance to their friendship expectations than their national peers. They seem to perceive of friends as helpers in their struggle to find their position in the new social and cultural environment. To immigrant youth, there is clearly more at stake than just sharing a fun time.

The interest in students' relationships, their sense of belongingness and their feelings of security has increased considerably in recent years due to an increase in the number of serious incidences of violence in schools, both in the USA and in Western European countries. In reaction to these developments, more security measures were implemented, but at the same time many schools have intensified their efforts to strengthen relationships between school staff and students, and amongst students themselves. The improvement of these relationships should serve two purposes. A strong sense of bonding should prevent potential perpetrators from reaching an emotional state in which they become violent. The second purpose is to create a sense of common responsibility for a positive school climate in which both staff and students are willing to discuss problems and report information or incidents that might help in preventing outbursts of violence (Haselton, 1999).

Wentzel and Asher (1995) concluded that students' lack of a sense of relatedness or bonding is likely to lead to aggressive behavior, which in turn negatively affects peer relationships and wellbeing in school. Hofman and Vonkeman's study in the Netherlands (1995) shows that a strong bond with school and with classmates is more important for the immigrants' wellbeing and for preventing them from dropping out, in comparison with national students.

25.3.1.1   Peer relationships

Peer relationships serve as a source of social and emotional support, and as a context for learning and practicing social, cognitive and language skills (Berndt & Ladd, 1989; Hartup, 1992; Newcomb & Bagwell, 1995). Ample evidence (e.g. Newcomb, Bukowski & Pattee, 1993; Inderbitzen, Walters & Bukowski, 1997) showed that children's social status (as popular, rejected, neglected, controversial or average) has predictive value for their psychological adaptation and behavior. The rejected and neglected children are emotionally and cognitively at risk, whereas the popular children are generally resourceful and well adapted (Newcomb et al., 1993). More specifically, several studies show that children's sociometric status is related to their school adjustment and academic achievement (Tuma & Hallinan, 1979; Wentzel, 1994; Wentzel & Asher, 1995).

Kistner, Metzler, Gatlin and Risi (1993) summarized findings from studies that focused on the relationship between children's sociometric status and ethnicity, and concluded that ethnicity has a minor impact on children's sociometric status. Coie, Dodge and Coppotelli (1982) showed that African American children, as compared to Caucasian children, were classified less often as popular and more often as controversial. No difference was found for the category "rejected." Studies using other measures of social competence showed more convincingly that ethnicity is a group-defining characteristic leading to ethnicity-based ingroup preferences (see Hamm, 2000; Schofield & Whitley, 1983; Vedder & O'Dowd, 1999). A few studies since 1990 that used a peer nomination procedure in ethnically mixed classes confirm this ingroup preference, whereas at the same time these studies showed a stronger influence of gender than of ethnicity (Graham & Cohen, 1997; Kupersmidt, DeRosier & Patterson, 1995; Rican, 1996).

25.3.2 Competence

Pursuit of social goals, such as helping classmates with their tasks, and helping each other to learn, contributes significantly to the quality of learning, mainly because these goals promote group cohesion and positive inter-personal inter-actions (Wentzel, 1994; Wentzel & Wigfield, 1998). Pro-social and academic learning goals are closely linked (Covington, 2000). For example, explaining a problem to another student facilitates deeper understanding and consequently promotes competence. The experience of competence is important to students' self-esteem and their willingness to explore new knowledge and skill domains (Hollins & Oliver, 1999). This is especially true for students who experience in schools a denial of their competence, or who have to cope with low grades and decreased support for learning (Black & Wiliam, 1998), which is the case for many immigrant and ethnic-minority students, both in North America and in Western Europe (Glenn & De Jong, 1996; Ogbu, 1992; Portes & Rumbaut, 2001; Suarez-Orozco & Suarez-Orozco, 2001; Vedder & Virta, 2005). Some scholars (Jordan, 1985; Ogbu, 1992; Greenfield & Cocking, 1994) suggest that this can only be overcome when schools' curricula are changed drastically; when knowledge and skills that are important within students' culture-specific arenas of social participation are included in the curriculum; and when attention shifts from self-directed learning, individual initiative and autonomy to positive interdependence amongst students and between students and staff (Campbell, 1997). This is in line with the notion presented earlier that immigrant students have a heavier load in school – as compared to national students – due to the fact that they have to combine enculturation and acculturation tasks. Making schools more culture-sensitive and culture-responsive would mean that schools would invest more in immigrant students' enculturation.

25.3.2.1 Language

In the remainder of this section, we will deal with one particular content or competency domain, namely, language. Language competence is essential for

social participation in all kinds of social settings. It may be a marker of difference that determines the quality of inter-ethnic relationships in a community
(Vedder & O'Dowd, 1999). Language carries information and is an instrument
for structuring thinking processes. As such, its role for learning and development is evident and indisputable. Furthermore, language is instrumental to
satisfying basic needs for bonding and security and, as such, also impacts a
person's identity development. The relationship between language and cultural identity is a highly debated topic. A clear but extreme position in this
discussion is that a person's ethnic identity is largely defined by culture, which
includes language, and, even more specifically, the language in which it is
transmitted between generations. This position corresponds to strong pleas for
language maintenance or language revitalization (Chiang & Schmida, 1999;
Henze & Davis, 1999; Fishman, 1996).

Other scholars (Genesee, 1987; Glenn & De Jong, 1996) are more hesitant
in assigning language such a prominent role in ethnic identity. They suggest
that culture-specific knowledge, skills and feelings can be transmitted through
a newly acquired language as well. They base their argument on evidence
showing that language loss is not synonymous to a loss of group membership,
solidarity and a sense of belonging. Ethnic-language loss may occur without
ethnic identity being weakened (Bentahila & Davies, 1992). On the other hand,
a number of studies show that ethnic language is strongly associated with identity (Gudykunst & Ting-Toomey, 1990; Hurtado & Gurin, 1995). Other studies
(see Cameron & Lalonde, 1994) suggest that ethnic-language maintenance is
important for second- and later-generation immigrants, but not for the first
generation. Phinney, Romero, Nava and Huang (2001) conclude that research
has yielded conflicting findings about the relationship between language maintenance and ethnic identity. However, they found that adolescents from three
American ethnic groups who have higher ethnic-language proficiency and
usage report stronger levels of cultural identity (Phinney et al., 2001). The
same positive relationship was reported in a large survey comparing more than
thirty different immigrant groups from thirteen different immigrant-receiving
countries (Australia, Canada, England, Finland, France, Germany, Israel, the
Netherlands, New Zealand, Norway, Portugal, Sweden and the USA; Berry,
Phinney, Sam & Vedder, 2006).

Language competence also plays an important role in explaining immigrant
students' educational performance. Several models guide research and interpretations. An influential one is the ethnic identity model (Alkan, 1998). It
assumes that immigrant youth grow up between cultures, which leads to identity confusion and adaptation problems if the children experience a lack of
appreciation for the skills, knowledge and feelings that are typical of their cultural background. The model proposes that a strong ethnic identity is important
for immigrants' healthy integration and wellbeing in the new society.

The model, albeit not necessarily under this name, has had a clear impact on
the school curriculum for ethnocultural minority students in countries like the

Netherlands and Sweden (Alkan, 1998; Viberg, 1994). Lessons in students' first language and classes on students' cultural heritage are seen as important for preventing or overcoming adaptation problems. Such lessons are deemed to allow immigrant youth to experience appreciation for their parents' language and culture. The assumptions are that language maintenance and a good knowledge of one's own culture should contribute to adolescents' ethnic identity, and a strong ethnic identity should function as a support for a healthy psychological adaptation.

Some studies confirmed the expectation that a strong ethnic identity is related to a positive adaptation in minority youth (Horenczyk & Ben-Shalom, 2001; Liebkind, 1996; Phinney, Cantu & Kurtz, 1997; Virta & Westin, 1999; Virta, Sam & Westin, 2004). The relationship with ethnic language proficiency was confirmed in a study of Turkish adolescents in Sweden (Vedder & Virta, 2005).

In the ethnic identity model the ethnic language is seen as a symbol of tradition, heritage and ethnicity (see Fishman, 1989, 1996). This function of language is especially important in relation to ethnic identity, since it mostly serves as a criterion for distinguishing between ingroup and outgroup. When a language is given high significance, it is likely to be a defining aspect of a person's or a group's ethnic identity. In the ethnic identity model, ethnic language proficiency is assumed to have an indirect effect on adolescents' learning and development.

Language proficiency in either the first or second language may also have a direct impact on adolescents' learning and development due to its instrumental value for the transmission of information and for regulating cognitive processes (see Baker, 2001). When focusing on this direct relationship between language proficiency and adolescents' learning and development, we emphasize the communicative function of language. This communicative function is central to the second model, the language assimilation model. This model suggests that immigrant youth's proficiency in the national language (L2) is a better predictor of academic performance and social participation than either proficiency in the ethnic language (L1) or measures of ethnic identity (see Driessen, 2000).

The third model to be mentioned here is the language integration model. It is inspired by research on bilingualism showing that children who acquired high levels of proficiency in more than one language developed extra cognitive resources in comparison with children who grew up with one language (for an overview of research, see Baker, 2001). In line with this notion we would expect immigrant students who are proficient in both their ethnic and the national language to report higher wellbeing and more positive social adjustment scores than students who are less balanced in their bilingualism or who lack proficiency in either language. In a sample of Turkish adolescents living in Sweden, we found support for the language integration model (Vedder & Virta, 2005).

25.3.3 Autonomy

Autonomy is considered an important personal drive towards exploring new areas of learning and development and new social relationships. Autonomy is central to students' motivation and their willingness to invest in learning (Deci & Ryan, 1985; Guthrie, 2001). Moreover, autonomy is important for preventing or avoiding negative consequences of being part of a social network that is too tight, such as: not being critical, not knowing how to be critical and not daring to be critical, being susceptible to authoritarian behaviors of leaders, and being indifferent towards injustice incurred by group members. This is a phenomenon that was discussed by Portes (1998) who showed that, in the context of immigrants' acculturation, a strong ingroup preference based on a common ethnic background or religious affiliation may lead to the exclusion or rejection of persons who do not share the ethnic background or religious affiliation, and it may even lead to withholding from group members, e.g. all women, opportunities to express their own opinion and to denying them access to learning opportunities.

Benson (1997) made the distinction between technical, psychological and political versions of students' autonomy. The technical version refers to the aim of equipping students with skills for unsupervised learning. The psychological version refers to fostering attitudes and skills that allow students to take responsibility for their own learning. The political version aims at the learning context and the possibilities for students to control the contents and interactions in this context. All three meanings of autonomy are included in social constructivist notions of learning which stress that learning is a social activity that draws its meaning and significance from the learners' experiences, the directly present social and cultural context in which it takes place, and the anticipated functionality for future social participation (Hickey & McCaslin, 2001). Within this framework, neither learning, nor skills, knowledge or motivation, are seen as individualistic and culture free, but as cooperative, culture-loaded processes and products (Boekaerts, 1998; May, 1994).

The definition of autonomy, however, is problematic, particularly in the context of multicultural education. In a review of studies about learner autonomy, Palfreyman (2001) clarifies that autonomy was defined in opposition to other concepts such as tradition, authority and non-Western culture. It was suggested that autonomy is something that students need for doing well in school. Non-Western students do not sufficiently avail themselves of this quality and therefore have problems in school and society. Parallel to these conceptual conflicts, there are very real conflicts about learning and teaching practices in which the autonomy concept plays a role. For instance, Tesser (Tesser & Iedema, 2001), addressing the primary school situation in the Netherlands and inspired by Chall (2000) who refers to the situation in the USA, warns of a possible conflict between teacher-initiated and teacher-guided attempts to strengthen students' learning and attempts to give students more autonomy by leaving it up to them how they solve problems and complete tasks. He points out that particularly ethnic-minority students perform better in schools that grant them less autonomy in this respect. However, the concept of autonomy used in this argument is somewhat akin to teacher negligence. Another study in the Netherlands (Eldering & Vedder, 1999) showed that the notion of children's autonomy held by immigrant parents conflicts with the significance they attach to children's respect for and obedience to adults. Immigrant parents, more than national parents, express worries about the way schools deal with the notions of autonomy, respect and obedience.

25.4   The broader acculturation context

Societal factors affecting the experience of immigrants and members of minority groups, such as discrimination and group-based inequalities, are undeniable realities that multicultural education has to seriously confront and address. We will briefly discuss the three factors which, according to Portes (1995), determine immigrants' vulnerability for negative adaptation processes and outcomes in the new society: color, location, and the absence of mobility ladders.

Individuals' physical characteristics – like skin color and hair type – serve as important markers of ethnicity. Both in the USA and in West European countries, ethnicity has and continues to be an important reason for (when a quest for belongingness and security is involved; Massey & Espinoza, 1997; Portes, 1998) or cause of (when having to deal with prejudice and discrimination; Kromhout & Vedder, 1996; Sellers & Shelton, 2003) separation and segregation. In many societies, immigrant and minority youth experience discrimination, often linked with – or attributed to – physical characteristics. Results of the international study exploring the acculturation experiences of immigrant youth in thirteen different Western countries cited above suggest that adolescents' subjective experience of discrimination has a strong impact on their wellbeing and social adjustment (Jasinskaja-Lahti, Liebkind, Horenczyk & Schmitz, 2003; Phinney *et al.*, 2001).

Providing children with opportunities for positive inter-group and intercultural contact, and exposing them to instances and examples of good inter-ethnic relationships in schools and other contexts, are two important means for reducing prejudice and discrimination. These notions are based on the well-known contact hypothesis. Elaborated versions of this hypothesis have received ample empirical support (see Liebkind & McAlister, 1999; McClenahan, Cairns, Dunn & Morgan, 1996; Pettigrew & Tropp, 2000). It is thus tempting to rely on the contact hypothesis in order to promote the improvement of inter-ethnic relationships. A major obstacle, however, is that, both in the USA and in Western European countries, a large proportion of schools have ethnically segregated populations. Parental choice, together with particular contextual and demographic factors, have led to an increasing number of schools with a student body consisting of only or predominantly immigrant or ethnic-minority children. One of the additional factors is a housing policy in cities that is incapable of avoiding a high concentration of migrants in particular neighborhoods. A second is a comparatively higher birth rate in immigrant families than in national families. A third is a common-sense notion of many White parents that immigrant children jeopardize the quality of their children's school career. They therefore prefer to find schools for their children with no or low levels of ethnic mixing (White flight) (see Massey & Espinoza, 1997; Reardon & Yun, 2002; Suarez, 1999; Vermeulen, 2001). The resulting schools generally have an ethnically mixed immigrant population, although some may have students of one particular ethnic or cultural background, e.g. Turkish students. Attempts to promote dispersal of students in order to avoid ethnic segregation in schools were largely unsuccessful, not only in the USA (Kahlenberg, 2001; Orfield, 2001) but also in, for instance, the Netherlands (Rutten, 2004; Vermeulen, 2001).

School adjustment depends on schools, but also on the broader context in which schools function and students grow up. Some parents choose to leave a neighborhood because they think that available schools, but also the broader living area, do not meet with the standards which they think are desirable for their children's development. This has negative consequences for the development of the neighborhood and for the quality of life in inner cities (suburban migration), due to an accumulation of problems (Larsen *et al.*, 2004): the average income of the people in such neighborhoods is generally low, as is the general level of schooling; a lack of constancy or continuity of people living in the neighborhood and a related experience of an increasing sense of insecurity; and a deterioration of the quality of housing due to a lack of maintenance and a lack of new investments in the neighborhood. The lack of constancy and continuity of inhabitants is caused, as stated before, by families leaving the neighborhood, but also by newcomers. In immigrant neighborhoods, these are likely to be other immigrants having strong ties with those already living in the neighborhood (Massey & Espinoza, 1997). Such neighborhoods lack activities and relationships with economic and political institutions that benefit both individual inhabitants and the neighborhood as a whole (Hero, 2003; Larsen *et al.*, 2004). In such neighborhoods, where children experience hunger, violence, neglect and a lack of impetus for social participation, even good schools will have a hard time functioning as a mobility ladder for their students.

25.5 Conclusions

This chapter is about conceptual models and empirical studies explaining school adjustment in the context of acculturation. Two of the notions presented in the preceding sections will be highlighted here with a focus on the challenges they entail for further studies and the improvement of educational practices.

We discussed two broad conceptual approaches to school adjustment in a multicultural context. The second one, in which schools are seen as global cultural arenas, lacks a clear empirical basis. Suarez-Orozco (2001) suggests that immigrant students are in a beneficial position if the school is indeed a global arena, since they have already experienced processes of loosening strong bonds with their primary local and group-bound culture. Although, in fact, there is increasing evidence that immigrant students outperform their national classmates who have a comparable socio-economic background, we need studies analyzing the processes involved in the acculturation processes of immigrant as well as national students. Only further studies can clarify whether students' school adjustment is based on the processes described by Suarez-Orozco. Such studies should also clarify the conditions under which the advantageous outcomes will occur. After all, a strong commitment towards the global school culture may be combined with loosening or even losing social relationships anchored in the immigrant culture. Studies (Nesdale, Rooney & Smith, 1997; Phinney & Vedder, 2006) show that this may correspond to lower levels of wellbeing and more social adjustment problems.

More generally, we may contend that theory and research are needed in order to understand better the delicate balance between enculturation and acculturation – the expectations of students, school staff, minority communities and the larger society with regards to the school's enculturating and acculturating roles, and the strategies and techniques for maximizing the benefits of each and both of these processes. Horenczyk and Tatar (2002), for example, showed that Israeli teachers hold highly assimilationist attitudes towards the integration of immigrants in schools; in other words, they emphasize their acculturating roles and almost neglect any enculturating function of the schools.

Peer relationships are important for the school adjustment of immigrant and minority students. As pointed out earlier, extensive literature has shown social support to be positively correlated with psychological wellbeing. Searle and Ward (1990) and Ward and Searle (1991) qualified this by showing that this is particularly the case for immigrants during cultural transitions. The formation of strong relationships may function as an entrée to the majority society; friends from the majority group are able to provide the immigrants with information, as well as social and institutional contacts, which may help to alleviate their sense of estrangement and cultural shock and improve their personal, social and academic adjustment. For schools, and for education in general, the important question is how this function can be optimized. What brings immigrant and national youth together in the first place? What can be done to facilitate youth from a variety of cultural backgrounds finding a common ground for common activities, and what makes them stay together while supporting the cultural transition?

25.6   References

Alkan, M. (1998). Ethnicity and underachievement in the Netherlands: a curricular analysis. In C. Wulf (ed.), *Education for the 21st century* (pp. 195–212). Münster: Waxman.

Baker, C. (2001). *Foundations of bilingual education and bilingualism*. Clevedon: Multilingual Matters.

Banks, J. A. (1994). *An introduction to multicultural education*. Boston: Allyn & Bacon.

Benson, P. (1997). The philosophy and politics of learner autonomy. In P. Benson & P. Voller (eds.), *Autonomy and independence in language learning* (pp. 18–34). London: Longman.

Bentahila, A. & Davies, E. (1992). Convergence and divergence: two cases of language shift in Morocco. In W. Fase, K. Jaspaert & S. Kroon (eds.), *Maintenance and loss of minority languages* (pp. 197–210). Amsterdam: John Benjamins.

Berndt, T. (1999). Friends' influence on students' adjustment to school. *Educational Psychologist*, *34*, 15–28.

Berndt, T. J. & Ladd, G. W. (eds.) (1989). *Peer relationships in child development*. New York: Wiley.

Berry, J., Phinney, J., Sam, D. & Vedder, P. (eds.) (2006). *Immigrant youth in cultural transition: acculturation, identity, and adaptation across national contexts*. Mahwah, NJ: Lawrence Erlbaum Associates.

Bialystok, E. (2001). Metalinguistic aspects of bilingual processing. *Annual Review of Applied Linguistics*, *21*, 169–181.

Birman, D., Trickett, E. J. & Vinokurov, A. (2002). Acculturation and adaptation of Soviet Jewish refugee adolescents: predictors of adjustment across life domains. *American Journal of Community Psychology*, *30*, 585–607.

Black, P. & Wiliam, D. (1998). Inside the black box. Raising standards through classroom assessment. *Phi Delta Kappa*, *80*, 139–148.

Boekaerts, M. (1992). The adaptable learning process: initiating and maintaining behavioural change. *Journal of Applied Psychology: An International Review*, *41*, 377–397.

  (1998). Do culturally rooted self-construals affect students' conceptualization of control over learning? *Educational Psychologists*, *33*, 87–108.

Cameron, J. E. & Lalonde, R. N. (1994). Self, ethnicity, and social group memberships in two generations of Italian Canadians. *Personality and Social Psychology Bulletin*, *20*, 514–520.

Campbell, L. (1997). *Antioch's efforts to develop culturally congruent teacher education*. www.newhorizons.org/strategies/multicultural/lindacampbell.htm. Accessed October 25, 2004.

Chall, J. S. (2000). *The academic achievement challenge*. New York: Guilford Press.

Chiang, Y. S. D. & Schmida, M. (1999). *Language identity and language ownership: linguistic conflicts of first-year university writing students*. Mahwah, NJ: Lawrence Erlbaum Associates.

Coie, J., Dodge, K. & Coppotelli, H. (1982). Dimensions and types of social status: a cross age perspective. *Developmental Psychology*, *18*, 557–571.

Connell, J. & Wellborn, J. (1991). Competence, autonomy, and relatedness: a motivational analysis of self-system processes. In M. Gunnar & A. Sroufe (eds.), *Self processes and development. The Minnesota symposia on child psychology* (Vol. XXIII, pp. 43–77). Hillsdale, NJ: Lawrence Erlbaum Associates.

Covington, M. V. (2000). Goal theory, motivation, and school achievement: an integrative review. *Annual Review of Psychology*, *51*, 171–200.

Cushner, K. (ed.) (1998). *International perspectives on intercultural education*. Mahwah, NJ: Lawrence Erlbaum Associates.

Deci, E. L. & Ryan, R. M. (1985). *Intrinsic motivation and self-determination in human behavior*. New York: Plenum.

Driessen, G. (2000). The limits of educational policy and practice? The case of ethnic minorities in the Netherlands. *Comparative Education*, *36*, 55–72.

DuBois, D. L., Felner, R. D., Brand, S., Adan, A. M. & Evans, E. G. (1992). A prospective study of life stress, social support, and adaptation in early adolescence. *Child Development*, *63*, 542–557.

Eldering, L. & Kloprogge, J. (eds.) (1989). *Different cultures, same school: ethnic minority children in Europe*. Amsterdam: Swets & Zeitlinger.

Eldering, L. & Vedder, P. (1999). The Dutch experience with the home intervention program for preschool youngsters (HIPPY). In L. Eldering & P. Leseman (eds.), *Effective early education: crosscultural perspectives* (pp. 259–285). New York: Falmer.

Extra, G. & Vallen, T. (1989). Second language acquisition in elementary school. In L. Eldering & J. Kloprogge (eds.), *Different culture, same school: ethnic minority children in Europe* (pp. 153–188). Amsterdam: Swets & Zeitlinger.

Fishman, J. (1989). *Language and ethnicity in minority sociolinguistic perspective*. Clevedon: Multilingual Matters.

(1996). "What do you lose when you lose your language?" In G. Cantoni (ed.), *Stabilizing indigenous languages* (pp. 80–91). Flagstaff, AZ: Center for Excellence in Education.

Furman, W. & Buhrmester, D. (1992). Age and sex differences in perceptions of networks of personal relationships. *Child Development*, *63*, 103–115.

Genesee, F. (1987). *Learning through two languages*. Cambridge, MA: Newbury House.

Gibson, M. (1991). Minorities and schooling: some implications. In M. A. Gibson & J. U. Ogbu (eds.), *Minority status and schooling: a comparative study of immigrant and involuntary minorities* (pp. 357–381). New York: Garland.

Glenn, C. & De Jong, E. (1996). *Educating immigrant children: schools and language minorities in twelve nations* New York: Garland.

Graham, J. & Cohen, R. (1997). Race and sex as factors in children's sociometric ratings and friendship choices. *Social Development*, *6*, 355–373.

Greenfield, P. & Cocking, R. (eds.) (1994). *Cross-cultural roots of minority child development*. Hillsdale, NJ: Lawrence Erlbaum Associates.

Greenfield, P. M., Keller, H., Fuligni, A. & Maynard, A. (2003). Cultural pathways through universal development. *Annual Review of Psychology*, *54*, 461–490.

Gudykunst, W. B. & Ting-Toomey, S. (1990). Ethnic identity, language and communication breakdowns. In W. P. Robinson & H. Giles (eds.), *Handbook of language and social psychology* (pp. 309–327). Oxford: Wiley.

Guthrie, J. T. (2001). Contexts for engagement and motivation in reading. www. readingonline.org/articles/art_index.asp?HREF=/articles/handbook/guthrie/index.html. Accessed October 26, 2004.

Hagendoorn, L. & Nekuee, S. (eds.) (1999). *Education and racism*. Aldershot: Ashgate.

Hamm, J. (2000). Do birds of a feather flock together? The variable bases for African American, Asian American, and European American adolescents' selection of similar friends. *Developmental Psychology, 36*, 209–219.

Hartup, W. (1992). Friendships and their developmental significance. In H. McGurk (ed.), *Childhood social development: contemporary perspectives* (pp. 175–205). Hillsdale, NJ: Lawrence Erlbaum Associates.

Haselton, B. (1999). Elements of a model alternative school. www.ccsso.org/content/pdfs/ggnov00.pdf . Accessed November 3, 2004.

Heath, S. (1983). *Ways with words*. Cambridge: Cambridge University Press.

Helgeson, V. (1993). Two important distinctions in social support: kind of support and perceived versus received. *Journal of Applied Social Psychology, 23*, 825–845.

Henze, R. & Davis, K. A. (1999). Authenticity and identity: lessons from indigenous language education. *Anthropology and Education Quarterly, 30*, 3–21.

Hero, R. (2003). Social capital and racial inequality in America. *Perspectives on American Politics, 1*, 113–122.

Hickey, D. & McCaslin, M. (2001). A comparative, sociocultural analysis of context and motivation. In S. Volet & S. Järvelä (eds.), *Motivation in learning contexts* (pp. 33–55). Amsterdam: Pergamon.

Hofman, R. & Vonkeman, E. (1995). *School, schaal en probleemgedrag* [School, scale, and behavioral problems]. Groningen: GION.

Hollins, E. R. & Oliver, E. I. (eds.) (1999). *Pathways to success in school: culturally responsive teaching*. Mahwah, NJ: Lawrence Erlbaum Associates.

Horenczyk, G. (1996). Migrant identities in conflict: acculturation attitudes and perceived acculturation ideologies. In E. Lyons & G. M. Breakwell (eds.), *Changing European identities: social psychological analyses of social change* (pp. 241–250). Woburn, MA: Butterworth-Heinemann.

Horenczyk, G. & Ben-Shalom, U. (2001). Multicultural identities and adaptation of young immigrants in Israel. In N. K. Shimahara, I. Holowinsky & S. Tomlinson-Clarke (eds.), *Ethnicity, race, and nationality in education: a global perspective* (pp. 57–80). Mahwa, NJ: Lawrence Erlbaum Associates.

Horenczyk, G. & Tatar, M. (1998). Friendship expectations among immigrant adolescents and their host peers. *Journal of Adolescence, 21*, 69–82.

   (2002). Teachers' attitudes toward multiculturalism and their perceptions of the school organizational culture. *Teaching and Teacher Education, 18*, 435–445.

Hurtado, A. & Gurin, P. (1995). Ethnic identity and bilingualism attitudes. In A. M. Padilla (ed.), *Hispanic psychology: critical issues in theory and research* (pp. 89–103). Thousand Oaks, CA: Sage Publications.

Inderbitzen, H., Walters, L. & Bukowski, H. (1997). The role of social anxiety in adolescent peer relations: differences among sociometric status groups and rejected subgroups. *Journal of Clinical Child Psychology, 26*, 338–348.

Jasinskaja-Lahti, I., Liebkind, K., Horenczyk, G. & Schmitz, P. (2003). The interactive nature of acculturation: perceived discrimination, acculturation attitudes and stress among young ethnic repatriates in Finland, Israel and Germany. *International Journal of Intercultural Relations, 27*, 79–97.

Jordan, C. (1985). Translating culture: from ethnographic information to educational program. *Anthropology and Education Quarterly, 16*, 105–123.

Kahlenberg, R. (2001). Beyond Brown: the new wave of desegregation litigation. *Educational Leadership, 59*, 13–19.

Kistner, J., Metzler, A., Gatlin, D. & Risi, S. (1993). Classroom racial proportions and children's peer relations: race and gender effects. *Journal of Educational Psychology, 85*, 446–452.

Korn, C. & Bursztyn, A. (eds.) (2002). *Rethinking multicultural education*. Westport, CT: Bergin & Garvey.

Kromhout, M. & Vedder, P. (1996). Cultural inversion in children from the Antilles and Aruba in the Netherlands. *Anthropology and Education Quarterly, 27*, 568–586.

Kupersmidt, J., DeRosier, M. & Patterson, C. (1995). Similarity as the basis for children's friendships: the roles of sociometric status, aggressive and withdrawn behavior, academic achievement, and demographic characteristics. *Journal of Social and Personal Relationships, 12*, 439–452.

Larsen, L., Harlan, S., Bolin, B., *et al.* (2004). Bonding and bridging; understanding the relationship between social capital and civic action. *Journal of Planning Education and Research, 24*, 64–77.

Lee, S. J. (2001). More than "model minorities" or "delinquents": a look at Hmong American high school students. *Harvard Educational Review, 71*, 505–528.

Liebkind, K. (1996). Acculturation and stress: Vietnamese refugees in Finland. *Journal of Cross Cultural Psychology, 27*, 161–180.

Liebkind, K. & McAlister, A. (1999). Extended contact through peer modeling to promote tolerance in Finland. *European Journal of Social Psychology, 29*, 765–780.

Massey, D. & Espinoza, K. (1997). What is driving Mexico–US migration? *American Journal of Sociology, 102*, 939–999.

May, S. (1994). *Making multicultural education work*. Clevedon: Multilingual Matters.
(ed.) (1999). *Critical multiculturalism*. London: Falmer Press.

McClenahan, C., Cairns, E., Dunn, S. & Morgan, V. (1996). Intergroup friendships: integrated and desegregated schools in Northern Ireland. *Journal of Social Psychology, 136*, 549–558.

Mumford, D. B. & Babiker, I. E. (1998). Validation of a self-administered version of the Cultural Distance Questionnaire among young British volunteers working overseas. *European Journal of Psychiatry, 12*, 244–253.

Nesdale, D., Rooney, R. & Smith, L. (1997). Migrant ethnic identity and psychological distress. *Journal of Cross-Cultural Psychology, 28*, 569–588.

Newcomb, A. & Bagwell, C. (1995). Children's friendship relations: a meta-analytic review. *Psychological Bulletin, 117*, 306–347.

Newcomb, A., Bukowski, W. & Pattee, L. (1993). Children's peer relations: a meta-analytic review of popular, rejected, neglected, controversial, and average sociometric status. *Psychological Bulletin, 113*, 99–128.

Ogbu, J. (1992). Understanding cultural diversity and learning. *Educational Researcher*, *21*, 5–14.

Orfield, G. (2001). *Schools more separate: consequences of a decade of resegregation*. Cambridge, MA: Harvard University, The Civil Rights Project.

Palfreyman, D. (2001). The socio-cultural construction of learner autonomy and learner independence in a tertiary EFL institution. Unpublished doctoral thesis, Canterbury Christ Church University College / University of Kent at Canterbury, May. www.7385.tripod.com/Thesis/.

Pettigrew, T. & Tropp, L. (2000). Does intergroup contact reduce prejudice? Recent meta-analytic findings. In S. Oskamp (ed.), *Reducing prejudice and discrimination* (pp. 93–114). Mahwah, NJ: Lawrence Erlbaum Associates.

Phelan, P., Davidson, A. L. & Cao, H. T. (1991). Students' multiple worlds: negotiating the boundaries of family, peer, and school cultures. *Anthropology and Education Quarterly*, *22*, 224–250.

Phinney, J., Cantu, C. & Kurtz, D. (1997). Ethnic and American identity as predictors of self-esteem among African American, Latino, and White adolescents. *Journal of Youth and Adolescence*, *26*, 165–185.

Phinney, J., Horenczyk, G., Liebkind, K. & Vedder, P. (2001). Ethnic identity, immigration, and well-being: an interactional perspective. *Journal of Social Issues*, *57*, 493–510.

Phinney, J., Romero, I., Nava, M. & Huang, D. (2001). The role of language, parents and peers in ethnic identity among adolescents in immigrant families. *Journal of Youth and Adolescence*, *30*, 135–153.

Phinney, J. & Vedder, P. (2006). Family relationship values of adolescents and parents: intergenerational discrepancies and adaptation. In J. Berry, J. Phinney, D. Sam & P. Vedder (eds.), *Immigrant youth in cultural transition* (pp. 167–184). Mahwah, NJ: Lawrence Erlbaum Associates.

Plomp, T. & Loxley, W. (1992). IEA and the quality of education in developing countries. In P. Vedder (ed.), *Measuring the quality of education* (pp. 135–147). Amsterdam: Swets & Zeitlinger.

Portes, A. (1995) Children of immigrants: segmented assimilation and its determinants. In A. Portes (ed.), *The economic sociology of immigration: essays on networks, ethnicity and entrepreneurship* (pp. 248–279). New York: Russell Sage Foundation.

(1998). Social capital: its origins and applications in modern sociology. *Annual Reviews of Sociology*, *24*, 1–24.

Portes, A. & Rumbaut, R. (2001). *Legacies: the story of the immigrant second generation*. Berkeley, CA: University of California Press.

Purves, A. (1990). The world as an educational laboratory. In P. Vedder (ed.), *Fundamental studies in educational research* (pp. 209–222). Amsterdam: Swets & Zeitlinger.

Reardon, S. & Yun, J. (2002). *Private school racial enrolments and segregation*. Cambridge, MA: Harvard University, The Civil Rights Project.

Resnick, L. B. (1987). Learning in school and out. *Educational Researcher*, *16*, 13–20.

Rican, P. (1996). Sociometric status of Gypsy children in ethnically mixed classes. *Studia Psychologica*, *38*, 177–184.

Rutten, S. (2004). *Een eindeloze haastklus; een halve eeuw gelijke kansenbeleid in het Amerikaanse onderwijs* [Rushing endlessly; 50 years of equal opportunities policy in US schools]. Utrecht: Sardes.

Schofield, J. & Whitley, B. (1983). Peer nomination vs. rating scale measurement of children's peer preferences. *Social Psychology Quarterly, 46*, 242–251.

Searle, W. & Ward, C. (1990). The prediction of psychological and sociocultural adjustment during cross-cultural transition. *International Journal of Intercultural Relations, 14*, 449–464.

Sellers, R. & Shelton, J. (2003). The role of racial identity in perceived racial discrimination. *Journal of Personality and Social Psychology, 84*, 1079–1092.

Snow, C., Barnes, W., Chandler, J., Goodman, I. & Hemphill, L. (1991). *Unfulfilled expectations. Home and school influences on literacy.* Cambridge, MA: Harvard University Press.

Suarez, R. (1999). *The old neighborhood: what we lost in the great suburban migration.* New York: Free Press.

Suarez-Orozco, C. & Suarez-Orozco, M. M. (2001). *Children of immigration.* Cambridge, MA: Harvard University Press.

Suarez-Orozco, M. (2001). Globalization, immigration, and education: the research agenda. *Harvard Educational Review, 71*, 345–365.

Tatar, M. & Horenczyk, G. (1996). Immigrant and host pupils' expectations of teachers. *British Journal of Educational Psychology, 66*, 289–299.

Tesser, P. & Iedema, J. (2001). *Rapportage minderheden 2001: vorderingen op school* [The minorities report 2001: school progress]. The Hague: Social and Cultural Planning Office.

Troyna, B. & Carrington, B. (1990). *Education, racism and reform.* London / New York: Routledge.

Tuma, N. & Hallinan, M. (1979). The effects of sex, race and achievement on schoolchildren's friendships. *Social Forces, 57*, 1265–1285.

Van der Zee, K., Buunk, B. & Sanderman, R. (1997). Social support, locus of control, and psychological well-being. *Journal of Applied Social Psychology, 27*, 1842–1859.

Vedder, P. (1994) Global measures for the quality of education; a help to developing countries? *International Review of Education, 40*, 5–17.

Vedder, P., Boekaerts, M. & Seegers, G. (2005). Perceived social support and well being in schools; the role of students' ethnicity. *Journal of Youth and Adolescence, 34(3)*, 269–278.

Vedder, P. & O'Dowd, M. (1999) Swedish primary school pupils' interethnic relationships. *Scandinavian Journal of Psychology, 40*, 221–228.

Vedder, P. & Virta, E. (2005). Language, ethnic identity, and the adaptation of Turkish immigrant youth in the Netherlands and Sweden. *International Journal of Intercultural Relations, 29(3)*, 317–337.

Vermeulen, H. (2001). *Etnisch culturele diversiteit als feit en norm* [Ethnocultural diversity as fact and standard]. Amsterdam: Vossiuspers / Universiteit van Amsterdam.

Viberg, A. (1994). Bilingual development of school-age students in Sweden. In G. Extra & L. Verhoeven (eds.), *The cross-linguistic study of bilingual development* (pp. 181–198). Amsterdam: North-Holland.

Virta, E., Sam, D. L. & Westin, C. (2004). Adolescents with Turkish background in Norway and Sweden: a comparative study of their psychological adaptation. *Scandinavian Journal of Psychology*, *45*, 15–25.

Virta, E. & Westin, C. (1999). *Psychosocial adjustment of adolescents with immigrant background in Sweden.* Occasional Papers, 2. Stockholm: CEIFO, Stockholm University.

Ward, C. & Searle, W. (1991). The impact of value discrepancies and cultural identity on psychological and sociocultural adjustment of sojourners. *International Journal of Intercultural Relations*, *15*, 209–225.

Wentzel, K. (1994). Relations of social goal pursuit to social acceptance, classroom behavior, and perceived social support. *Journal of Educational Psychology*, *86*, 173–182.

(1998). Social relationships and motivation in middle school: the role of parents, teachers, and peers. *Journal of Educational Psychology*, *90*, 202–209.

Wentzel, K. & Asher, S. (1995). The academic lives of neglected, rejected, popular, and controversial children. *Child Development*, *66*, 754–763.

Wenztel, K. & Wigfield, A. (1998). Academic and social motivational influences on students' academic performance. *Educational Psychology Review*, *10*, 155–175.

Wethington, E. & Kessler, R. (1986). Perceived support, received support, and adjustment to stressful life events. *Journal of Health and Social Behavior*, *27*, 78–89.

Ying, Y. W., Lee, P. A., Tsai, J. L., Hung, Y., Lin, M. & Wan, C. T. (2001). Asian American college students as model minorities: an examination of their overall competence. *Cultural Diversity & Ethnic Minority Psychology*, *7*, 59–74.

Zentella, A. C. (1997). Latino youth at home, in their communities, and in school: the language link. *Education and Urban Society*, *30*, 122–130.

26 Immigrants in the labor market

John E. Hayfron

26.1 Introduction

The first empirical study on immigrants' earnings assimilation was conducted in the United States (see Chiswick, 1978). According to this study, when immigrants arrive in the USA, they earn less on average than the native-born Americans with comparable human capital: education and work experience. However, after spending some years in the USA, not only do immigrants' earnings "catch-up" to the native-born earnings, but they also surpass them. This phenomenon is referred to as earnings assimilation. This empirical evidence was published at a time when most OECD countries, particularly the non-traditional immigrant-receiving countries, were grappling with the question of how to integrate their growing immigrant population successfully into the mainstream of society. For policy makers in these countries, the need to understand how new immigrant arrivals respond to policy initiative and adapt quickly to the way of life in their new country became crucial.

In the subsequent years, labor economists. as well as other social scientists in several countries, have tested the hypothesis underlying immigrants' earnings assimilation using the individual countries' data, and the results are somewhat mixed. Some of these studies have provided evidence of an entry earnings gap between immigrants and the native-born workers. They concluded that, on average, immigrants' earnings tend to grow at a much faster rate than the earnings of the native-born, and that the initial immigrant–native-born earnings gap disappears over time. Other empirical studies, while corroborating the entry earnings gap notion, reject the hypothesis that immigrants' earnings converge to the native-born earnings. They argue that, depending on the skill and ethnic composition of immigrant arrivals, immigrants' earnings may not necessarily converge to the earnings of the native-born over time. In other words, not every immigrant assimilates. The question is: why do the earnings of some immigrants assimilate but those of others do not? Why should immigrants' earnings rise faster than those of the comparable native-born?

These questions are addressed in two parts. First, the underlying theory of economic assimilation is examined. This should shed some light on the sources of the entry earnings gap, and the factors that determine the rapid growth of immigrants' earnings over time. Next, a review of some empirical research findings on immigrants' earnings assimilation from the United States, Canada and Norway will be carried out. This is followed closely by a discussion of some psychological research findings relevant to the study of economic assimilation. The chapter concludes with a summary.

26.2   The theory of economic assimilation

The theory of economic assimilation basically states that recently arrived immigrants at different stages of their adaptation process in the host country may differ from the native-born, or their immigrant counterparts who migrated several years ago in various aspects. These could include the number of hours immigrants work, their earnings (which is the wage rate multiplied by the number of hours worked) or occupational attainment. But in this chapter, the analysis of economic assimilation is limited to immigrants' relative earnings at the initial stage of the adaptation process, and how that changes over time. This is best seen using an age–earnings profile. An age–earnings profile shows how earnings change as individuals (native-born and immigrants alike) grow older (i.e., acquire more experience) during their working life. Specifically, for immigrants, it also shows how their earnings change over time due to their continuous stay in the host country. A positive relationship between individual immigrants' earnings and length of stay in the host country (measured as the difference between census period and year of immigration) is considered to be a measure of earnings assimilation.

The hypothetical age–earnings profiles of immigrants and native-born in Figure 26.1, are drawn under the simplifying assumption that the age at migration is also the age at which the newly arrived immigrant enters the host country's labor market. Suppose that a native-born individual of the same age, say twenty years old, enters the labor market at the same time as the newly arrived immigrant. The question labor economists seek to address is whether these two labor-market entrants with comparable human capital would be paid the same wage. Although these two individuals may have different unobservable characteristics, such as innate ability, motivation and ambition, the human capital theory suggests that employers would normally base their hiring and compensation decisions solely on the individual observable characteristics, such as educational qualifications, years of work experience, language skills etc. The reason is that employers believe that there is a positive correlation between observed and unobserved characteristics. It is common knowledge that individuals with higher abilities perform better at school on average than those with lesser abilities. The other question is whether an entry earnings gap between recently arrived immigrants and the native-born will disappear over time because of assimilation.

Recently arrived immigrants may initially not enjoy a greater economic success like the native-born for the following reasons. First, the pre-migration human capital that would determine their economic success may not be

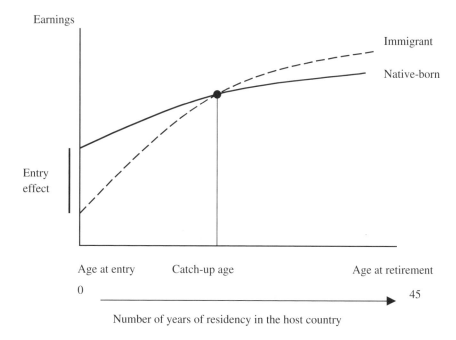

Figure 26.1 *Hypothetical age–earnings profile*

recognized in the host country's labor market. It is commonly argued that, since different countries have different educational systems and labor-market operation, employers in the host country may have less information about the content and quality of the educational qualifications and work experience most immigrants bring with them to the host country's labor market. For this reason, potential employers may devalue immigrants' credentials, particularly those obtained from the developing countries during hiring (see Chiswick 1986a, 1986b; Aycan & Berry, 1996; Friedberg, 2000; Li, 2001; Reitz, 2001; Ferrer & Riddell, 2002; Bratsberg & Terrell, 2002). As a result of non-recognition of pre-migration human capital, recently arrived immigrants may be hired to carry out less well-paid menial jobs, or may experience a period of unemployment. Moreover, recent immigrants may lack the host-country-specific skills that employers seek.

Second, recent immigrants normally exhibit cultural diversity, one such difference being their various native languages. This may have implications for their earnings assimilation process, depending on the linguistic distance between the individual immigrants' native language and the host country's language (see Chiswick & Miller, 1995; Hayfron, 2001). An entry earnings gap may arise because of the language barrier that immigrants face when they arrive in the host country. Given that job vacancies are normally advertised in the local language(s), language deficiency may prolong a recent immigrant's job search. Even if there are job vacancies in the labor market, employability and earnings of recent immigrants would depend on how well individual immigrants speak the host country's language (see Weiermair, 1976; Kossoudji, 1988; Dustmann, 1994, 1997; Chiswick & Miller, 1995; Beenstock, 1996; Chiswick, 1998; Gonzalez, 2000; Hayfron, 2001; Berman, Lang & Siniver, 2003). This is because employers normally prefer job seekers who can communicate in the host country's language(s) to those who cannot. Therefore, a poor knowledge of the language may lead to an exclusion of the recently arrived immigrants from higher-paying jobs in the labor market. Furthermore, since language is one of the norms of the host country's culture, recent immigrants with poor knowledge of the language may be perceived by potential employers as less acculturated. On the other hand, recent immigrants who share a native language with the host country are likely to enjoy a greater economic success (Evans, 1987).

Third, apart from the non-transferability of pre-migration human capital and the language barrier, the economic conditions in the country at the time of the immigrants' arrival may also be a source of an entry earnings gap between immigrants and native-born workers. Economists call this the "period or entry effects." It is generally difficult for an individual to find a job if there is a high rate of unemployment in the country. It is even more difficult, if not impossible, for immigrants who arrive in the host country at the time of economic recession to find a decent job. Empirical studies have shown that, compared to the native-born, immigrants are more likely to face a period of unemployment during economic downturn (McDonald & Worswick, 1998; Barth, Bratsberg & Raaum, 2004). Moreover, in times of economic hardship, scarcity of jobs in the labor market may give rise to hiring discrimination or nepotism, since the native-born job seekers would be given a priority during hiring, even if immigrant job seekers have similar human capital to the native-born. This differential treatment may have an adverse effect on the personal and psychological wellbeing of individual immigrants, who may in turn develop mistrust for the authorities (Liebkind & Jasinskaja-Lahti, 2000). In theory, this type of discrimination should not persist over time because of assimilation.

In reality, some recent immigrants may experience a period effect of unemployment, others will find part-time jobs even if they are willing and capable of working full-time (i.e., underemployment), and some line up a full-time job. These differences in employment status are partly due to differences in the individual unobservable characteristics. To examine the effect of differences in unobserved characteristics (e.g. innate ability, psychological characteristics) on immigrants' earnings assimilation, economists distinguish between positively selected immigrants and negatively selected immigrants. "Positively selected immigrants" refers to individuals who, prior to immigrating, belonged to the upper tail of the skill and income distributions in the individual countries of origin. The negatively selected immigrants are individuals who belonged to the bottom tail of the skill and income distributions in the source country.

The initial assumption in the migration literature was that only the positively selected individuals would have the incentives to emigrate from their countries of origin. However, recent evidence has shown that, because of push factors, such as political upheavals and poor economic conditions in most developing countries, negatively selected immigrants are also immigrating to the resource-rich countries. The influx of refugee immigrants to Western Europe during the 1990s is a case in point. To a group of labor economists, most notably George Borjas (1985a), the fact that individuals from different countries with different unobserved abilities arrive in a particular host country at different points in time may explain why we observe an entry earnings gap between recently arrived immigrants and the native-born. This may also explain why some immigrants do not assimilate economically. They propose an alternative framework for analyzing immigrants' assimilation process. This framework draws on the theory of self-selection.

Before discussing the alternative framework, or the "cohort effects" analysis as it is otherwise known, it is important to note that the idea of using the theory of self-selection to analyze immigrants' earnings assimilation does not resonate well with some economists. Some labor economists argue that immigrants, particularly refugee immigrants, do not self-select, rather they are sorted globally by the differences in immigration policies across countries, and by the dictates of the Geneva Refugee Convention.

26.3 Earnings assimilation and cohort effects

The cohort effects analysis assumes that the entry earnings gap between recent immigrants and native-born arises as a result of skill differentials across successive immigrant waves at different points in time. The thrust of this argument is that, in one period, it might be the case that immigrants arriving in a host country may be more talented and highly motivated individuals (i.e., positively selected), while in another period less talented and less motivated individuals may arrive (i.e., negatively selected). It is also assumed that individuals immigrating to a particular host country may not be randomly selected (in terms of ability) from the population of the source country. For these reasons, if, in a cross-sectional dataset, it is shown that the current earnings of newly arrived immigrants are lower than the current earnings of the native-born, or immigrants who have been in the country for several years, then this may be due to two separate effects: differences in the returns to length of stay in the host country as implied in the "assimilationist" model, and differences in unobserved characteristics (cohort effects). Precisely, this may be due to the fact that the earlier immigrant cohorts may be positively selected while the recently arrived immigrants are negatively selected. This alternative school argues that the earnings of positively selected immigrants are more likely to attain parity with the earnings of the native-born, while the earnings of negatively selected immigrants are less likely to converge to the earnings of the native-born individuals.

26.4   Evidence on cohort effects and immigrant-earnings assimilation

With these theoretical insights behind us, let us now turn to the more practical question of whether immigrants experience a rapid earnings growth (i.e., assimilate), and, if they do, how long does it take for their earnings to "catch up" to the earnings of the comparable native-born? To answer these questions, I conduct a kind of "meta-analysis" based on the findings of empirical studies that were conducted in three immigrant-receiving countries: the United States, Canada and Norway.

26.4.1   The US evidence

The natural starting point in this cross-country comparison is the United States, where the assimilation hypothesis was first tested by Barry Chiswick (1978). Chiswick used a cross-sectional dataset from the 1970 US census to trace the age–earnings profiles of male native-born Americans and comparable male immigrants originating from Western Europe. He constructed age–earnings profiles that look like Figure 26.1. Interpreting the age–earnings profiles of immigrants and the comparable native-born men, Chiswick arrived at an obvious conclusion. Upon arrival in the United States, the average immigrant worker received earnings that were 15 percent lower than the native-born with the same human capital (i.e., the entry earnings gap). However, the immigrant earnings grew at a faster rate (as indicated by the steeper slope of the immigrants' earnings profile) and, after fourteen years of residency in the USA (i.e., the catch-up period), exceeded the earnings of the comparable native-born workers (as indicated by the portion of the immigrants' earnings profile lying above that of the native-born).

It is interesting that the earnings of seemingly positively selected immigrants to the USA rise at a faster rate than those of the native-born Americans. Why should this be the case? One reason, which draws on the human capital theory, is that acquiring US-specific human capital in addition to the pre-migration human capital would lead to a faster growth in immigrants' earnings. There is also the self-selection argument that immigrants are on average more ambitious and hardworking than the native-born. Therefore, with the strong desire for success in their new country, immigrants tend to take multiple jobs and work longer hours on average than the native-born.

Borjas (1985a) argued that Chiswick's cross-sectional approach provides an imperfect measure of immigrants' earnings assimilation. The reason is that Chiswick's age-earnings profile does not reveal the actual life-cycle earnings profile of immigrants. A cross-sectional age pattern inherently cannot separate across-cohort differences from those that represent the pure effects of aging or length of stay (a measure of assimilation). As the number of years of residency is increasing, so is the aging process of the individual. For this reason, the two effects should be separated.

Moreover, a second problem concerns the non-random return migration among the immigrant population. Borjas pointed out that immigrants who do not succeed in the US labor market may decide to return to their country of origin, or move to another country. Evidence of return migration has been found in a study of Israeli-born Jewish in the USA (Cohen & Haberfield, 2001), and of the least economically successful OECD immigrants in Sweden (Edin, LaLond & Åslund, 2000). According to Borjas, since the less economically successful immigrants choose to leave, return migration cannot be considered to be random. To the extent that the unsystematic return migration would filter out the least able individuals from the immigrant population, this suggests that, in any given cross-sectional analysis, there is the likelihood that one would be comparing a randomly drawn sample of a native-born population with a selected group of highly skilled and more motivated immigrants. In this case, the average earnings of immigrants are likely to be higher than those of the native-born workers. These two problems, together with the fact that assimilation is a long-term and not a short-term process, create several forms of bias that tend to make the cross-sectional approach overestimate immigrants' actual earnings assimilation.

In view of the significance of the issues associated with the selection bias, Borjas (1985a, 1994) used a synthetic-panel data set to test the hypothesis underlying immigrants' earnings assimilation. Pooling two cross-sectional data sets together allowed Borjas to track the earnings of arrival cohorts across two censuses. His finding was consistent with the theoretical argument that the cross-sectional approach makes it appear that there is earnings convergence between immigrants and the native-born, when in fact there is none. For example, he found that newly arrived immigrants to the United States do not perform as well as their immigrant counterparts who have spent several years in the US, and their earnings do not catch up to or overtake the earnings of the native-born Americans over time (i.e., zero assimilation). Borjas attributed the absence of immigrants' earnings assimilation to the changing national origin mix of the recent immigrant flows to the USA.

26.4.2 The Canadian evidence

Chiswick's findings spawned a lot of research worldwide, including in Canada, which is one of the traditional immigrant-receiving countries. Most of the earlier Canadian studies used cross-sectional data to examine the earnings assimilation of immigrants (Meng, 1987; Abbot & Beach, 1993). The authors of these studies concluded that the entry wage (or earnings) gap between immigrants to Canada and the native-born Canadians is about 15 percent, and the "catch-up" period is between nine and fourteen years of immigrants' residency in Canada.

In contrast to the cross-sectional studies, a number of recent empirical studies (Baker & Benjamin, 1994; McDonald & Worswick, 1998) have used two or more cross-sections (synthetic-panel data) to test the assimilation hypothesis, and arrived at conclusions similar to Borjas' findings in the USA. According to these studies, the earnings of immigrants grouped by arrival cohorts do not attain parity with the earnings of the native-born Canadians over time. They also found that the average skill level of immigrants arriving in Canada is declining over time. They attributed this decline to changes in both the Canadian immigration policy and the source countries of immigrants arriving in Canada during the 1970s. The only exception is Grant (1999) who also used the synthetic-panel approach but found significant evidence of an immigrant assimilation rate of 17 percent for the 1976-1980 arrival cohorts. This is much in line with Chiswick's finding in the USA.

A psychologically oriented study (Aycan & Berry, 1996) found this pattern of earnings change over time in Canada among Turkish immigrants. These workers reported lower entry-level employment in Canada than their departure-level jobs in Turkey, and a subsequent rise to levels that surpassed their pre-departure job status. They also reported that the degree of their "status loss" and a slower rate of status recovery negatively impacted their overall adaptation and psychological wellbeing.

26.4.3 The Norwegian evidence

Unlike the United States and Canada, Norway is not a traditional immigrant-receiving country, and research on immigrants' earnings assimilation is just of recent years. Hayfron (1998a & b) was the first to verify the earnings assimilation of immigrants in Norway. Using randomly drawn samples from the 1980 and 1990 Norwegian censuses, Hayfron was able to compare the cross-sectional estimates of the rate of earnings growth (i.e., rate of assimilation) with those obtained from the synthetic-panel analysis. He found that immigrants who arrived in Norway during the 1970s earned 5.6 percent less than Norwegians with comparable human capital. However, over a ten-year period, the 1970–1979 immigrant arrival cohorts experienced an earnings growth that exceeded that of Norwegian men by 11 percent. This is considerably lower than the 19 percent earnings growth rate predicted by the cross-sectional approach. This finding supports the claim that the cross-sectional approach overestimates the rate of immigrants' earnings assimilation.

Regarding the 1960–1969 arrival cohort, there was no evidence of earnings parity between them and the comparable Norwegians. Compared to the 1960s arrivals, the immigrants that arrived in the 1970s were positively selected individuals from the other OECD countries, particularly the United Kingdom and North America. These were mainly labor migrants with specialized skills who came to Norway because of the increased demand for skilled workers in the Norwegian oil and gas industry.

Recently, Longva & Raaum (2003) have used a large data set and a better measure of length of stay in Norway to replicate Hayfron's study. They found a much smaller entry earnings gap (2.3 percent) between the 1970–1979 arrival cohort and Norwegians, and a moderate earnings growth of 6 percent relative to the earnings of Norwegians during the first ten years in Norway. Longva and Raaum found that, despite the larger assimilation effect for immigrants from non-OECD countries relative to those from OECD countries, their earnings do not attain parity with the earnings of Norwegians with comparable skills.

The lesson from the cross-country analysis is that both the theoretical analysis and the empirical evidence from the three selected countries examined support the claim that the entry wage (or earning) is lower for recent immigrants than for comparable native-born individuals. However, the answer to the question of whether immigrants manage to overcome the initial earnings penalty and probably do better economically than the native-born depends on the type of data (cross-section versus synthetic panel) used and the methodology employed.

26.5   Applying psychology to economics of immigration

Much as economic success (a faster earnings growth, in our case) has a positive effect on the physical and psychological wellbeing of individual immigrants, economic failure (as measured by periods of unemployment, underemployment, and sluggish earnings growth) would have an opposite effect. Both effects are directly contingent upon the performance of immigrants in the host country's labor market. Yet, economic studies on the labor market outcome of immigrants have not taken into account how the psychological problems immigrants face may impact their assimilation process. This is probably because most economists consider this the domain of psychology.

This section discusses the psychological implications of economic assimilation. It is important to note that the vast majority of the cross-cultural psychology literature focuses on immigrant acculturation, and treats assimilation as one mode of acculturation (see Berry, 1980, 1997, 2001; Sam, 1994). It is not all that clear, for example, how economics of immigration and cross-cultural psychology differ, especially when they address a common topic such as immigrant assimilation. One thing is certain, language proficiency and length of stay in the host country are important indicators of both acculturation and assimilation.

Suppose an immigrant arrives in a particular host country with a university degree or a professional qualification. This immigrant expects to line up a job that not only is relevant to his or her qualification, but also pays a wage higher than the wage the immigrant would earn in his or her home country. If the immigrant gets his or her wish (e.g., a decent job and a higher salary), this immigrant is more likely to have a sound and stable mind and less likely to experience acculturative stress. In their study of immigrant health, selectivity and acculturation, Jasso, Massey, Rosenzweig & Smith (2002) found a positive relationship between income gain from immigration and individual health. However, if the immigrant's degree is not recognized, he or she may end up doing jobs that the native-born do not want, or may experience a period of unemployment. According to Lev-Wiesel and Kaufman (2004), immigration and unemployment create three sources of stressors: uncertainty about the future, financial and emotional distress due to lack of job, and exclusion from mainstream society. They contend that incidence of unemployment would also lead to increased mortality rates, physical and mental ill-health (see also Beiser *et al.*, 1998; Aycan & Berry, 1996).

Unemployment is one factor that can slow down an immigrant's earnings growth (i.e., rate of assimilation) and therefore prevent immigrants' earnings from converging to the native-born earnings over time. An unemployed person earns less on average than an employed person, since the former's current earnings are not directly related to the number of hours worked (one dimension of assimilation). Since immigrants are more likely to be unemployed than the native-born (and this is supported by empirical evidence), assimilation will occur only if the unemployment is short-term – that is, if reemployment makes it possible for immigrants to work longer hours, or take multiple jobs, as alluded to earlier on. However, a longer duration of unemployment may eventually turn some immigrants into discouraged workers – that is, immigrants form a strong belief that there is a remote possibility of lining up a job in the future, and therefore give up looking for work. These immigrants may experience a cognitive dissonance, since their decision not to look for a job would under normal conditions not be the preferred choice of action. Another way to look at this is that immigrants may take such a decision because they have justifiable "reasons" for taking this decision, rather than because of underlying preferences. A longer duration of unemployment may also influence the psychological wellbeing of immigrants (Jacobsen, 1986; Lev-Wiesel & Kaufman, 2004).

26.6 Conclusions

To economists, earnings assimilation is a labor-market phenomenon. It occurs when immigrants suffer an earnings penalty upon arrival in a host country's labor market. However, through acquisition of (or investment in) host-country-specific skills, information, language proficiency, and attitudes needed to function effectively in the labor market, immigrants are able to overcome the initial earnings shortfall. Some economists argue that immigrants may even perform better economically than the native-born having spent some time in the host country. Others argue that, on the contrary, immigrants may not be able to outperform their native-born counterparts. These differing theoretical views on economic assimilation have formed the basis of empirical studies in several countries. In the three selected countries that were considered in this analysis, the empirical findings and conclusions are divided along similar lines. All the studies (whether in the US, Canada or Norway) show the existence of an entry earnings gap between recent immigrants and the native-born workers with the same human capital (or physical culture). However, while the cross-sectional studies provide evidence that immigrants' earnings "overtake" those of the native-born over time, the synthetic panel studies (except for one in Canada) show that most immigrant cohorts do not experience any rapid earnings growth relative to the native-born. In this case, the question of whether immigrants experience a more rapid earnings growth than the native-born depends on how one conducts the research: the type of data used, the methodology used and the period of research.

Finally, this analysis considered the psychological implications of immigrants' economic assimilation – that is, the potential mental health problems that are encountered in some stages of immigrants' adaptation process, an issue that is central to the thinking of cross-cultural psychologists.

26.7 References

Abbott, M. G. & Beach, C. M. (1993). Immigrant earnings differentials and birth-year effects for men in Canada: post-war 1972. *Canadian Journal of Economics, 26 (August)*, 505–524.

Aycan, Z. & Berry, J. W. (1996). Impact of employment-related experiences on immigrants' psychological well-being and adaptation to Canada. *Canadian Journal of Behavioural Science, 28*, 240–251.

Baker, M. & Benjamin, D. (1994). The performance of immigrants in the Canadian labor market. *Journal of Labor Economics, 12 (July)*, 396–405.

Barth, E., Bratsberg, B. & Raaum, O. (2004). Identifying earnings assimilation of immigrants under changing macroeconomic conditions. *Scandinavian Journal of Economics, 106(1)*, 1–22.

Beenstock, M. (1996). The acquisition of language skills by immigrants: the case of Hebrew in Israel. *International Migration, 34(1)*, 3–30.

Beiser, M., Barwick, C., Berry, J. W., *et al.* (1998). *After the door has been opened: mental health issues affecting immigrants and refugees in Canada*. Ottawa: Ministry of Multiculturalism and Citizenship, and Health and Welfare Canada.

Berman, E., Lang, K. & Siniver, E. (2003). Language-skill complementarity: returns to immigrant language acquisition. *Labor Economics, 10(3)*, 265–290.

Berry, J. W. (1980). Social and cultural change. In H. C. Triandis & R. Brislin (eds.), *Handbook of cross-cultural psychology* (Vol. V, pp. 211–279). Boston: Allyn & Bacon.

(1997). Immigration, acculturation and adaptation. *Applied Psychology*, *46*, 5–68.

(2001). A psychology of immigration. *Journal of Social Issues*, *57(3)*, 615–631.

Borjas, G. J. (1985a). Assimilation, changes in cohort quality, and the earnings of immigrants. *Journal of Labor Economics*, *3(October)*, 463–489.

(1985b). Assimilation and changes in cohort quality revisited: what happened to immigrant earnings in the 1980s. *Journal of Labor Economics*, *3(2)*, 201–245.

(1994). The economics of immigration. *Journal of Economic Literature*, *32*, 1667–1717.

Bratsberg, B. & Terrell, D. (2002). School quality and returns to education of U.S. immigrants. *Economic Inquiry*, *40(2)*, 177–198.

Chiswick, B. (1978). The effect of Americanization on the earnings of foreign-born men. *Journal of Political Economy*, *86 (October)*, 897–921.

(1986a). Is the new immigration less skilled than the old? *Journal of Labor Economics*, *4*, 168–192.

(1986b). Human capital and the labor market adjustments: testing alternative hypotheses. *Research in Human Capital and Development*, *4*, 1–26.

Chiswick, B. R. & Miller, P. W. (1995). The endogeneity between language and earnings: international analyses. *Journal of Labor Economics*, *13(2)*, 246–288.

Cohen, Y. & Haberfield, Y. (2001). Self-selection and return migration: Israeli-born Jews returning home from the United States during the 1980s. *Population Studies*, *55(1)*, 79–91.

Dustmann, C. (1994). Speaking fluency, writing fluency and earnings of migrants. *Journal of Population Economics*, *7*, 133–156.

Edin, P. A., LaLond R. J. & Åslund, O. (2000). Emigration of immigrants and measures of immigrant assimilation: evidence from Sweden. *Swedish Economic Policy Review*, *7*, 163–204.

Evans, M. D. R. (1987). Language skill, language usage and opportunity: immigrants in the Australian labour market. *Sociology*, *21(2)*, 253–274.

Ferrer, A. M. & Riddell, W. C. (2002). The role of credentials in the Canadian labour market. *Canadian Journal of Economics*, *35*, 879–905.

Friedberg, R. M. (2000). You can't take it with you? Immigrant assimilation and portability of human capital. *Journal of Labor Economics*, *18*, 221–251.

Gonzalez, A. (2000). The determinants of and labour market returns to understanding, speaking, reading and writing proficiency. *Contemporary Economic Policy*, *18(3)*, 259–269.

Grant, M. (1999). Evidence of new immigrant assimilation in Canada. *Canadian Journal of Economics*, *32 (August)*, 930–955.

Hayfron, J. E. (1998a). The labor market experience of immigrants in Norway. Unpublished Ph.D. thesis, Department of Economics, University of Bergen, Norway.

(1998b). The performance of immigrants in the Norwegian labor market. *Journal of Population Economics*, *11*, 293–303.

(2001). Language training, language proficiency and earnings of immigrants in Norway. *Applied Economics*, *33*, 1971–1979.

Jacobsen, D. (1986). Individual reactions to occupational uncertainty: a theoretical model. *Social Welfare*, *7(2)*, 95–115.

Jasso, G., Massey, D. S., Rosenzweig, M. R & Smith, J. P. (2002). Immigrant health – selectivity and acculturation. A paper prepared for the National Academy of Science Conference on Racial and Ethnic Disparities in Health.

Kossoudji, S. A. (1988). English language ability and the labor market opportunities of Hispanic and East Asian immigrant men. *Journal of Labor Economics*, *6*, 205–228.

Lev-Wiesel, & Kaufman (2004). *International Migration*, *42(3)*, 57–75.

Li, D. (2001). The market worth of immigrants' educational credentials. *Canadian Public Policy*, *27*, 1.

Liebkind, K. & Jasinskaja-Lahti, I. (2000). The influence of experiences of discrimination on psychological stress: a comparison of seven immigrant groups. *Journal of Community and Applied Social Psychology*, *10*, 1–16.

Longva, P. & Raaum, O. (2003). Earnings assimilation of immigrants in Norway – a reappraisal. *Journal of Population Economics*, *16*, 177–193.

McDonald, T. & Worswick, C. (1998). The earnings of immigrant men in Canada: job tenure, cohort and macroeconomic conditions. *Industrial Relations Review*, *51*, 465–482.

Meng, R. (1987). The earnings of Canadian immigrant and native-born males. *Applied Economics*, *19*, 1107–1119.

Reitz, J. G. (2001). Immigrant skill utilization in the Canadian labour market: implications of human capital research. *Journal of International Migration and Integration*, *2(3)*, 347–378.

Sam, D. L. (1994). Acculturation of young immigrants in Norway. A psychological and socio-cultural adaptation. Unpublished thesis, Faculty of Psychology, University of Bergen, Norway.

Schmitter, B. E. (1983). Immigrant minorities in West Germany: some theoretical concerns. *Ethnic and Racial Studies*, *6*, 308–319.

Weiermair, K. (1976). Economic effects of language training to immigrants: a case study. *International Migration Review*, *1–4*, 205–219.

27 Acculturation and health

David L. Sam

27.1 Introduction

Migration is a social process whereby an individual moves from his or her cultural setting (often a nation state) into another one for the purpose of settling down either permanently or for a prolonged period of time (Syed & Vangen, 2003). The reasons for the movement can vary from adventure to economic, educational, political or social causes, but they all boil down to the search for a better life (Evans, 1987; Furnham & Bochner, 1986). However, the sought-for better life may not always be found, due to difficulties associated with the migration process and subsequent acculturation. One area in which difficulties associated with migration and acculturation may be manifested is health. The possible effect migration and acculturation may have on health has been of interest to health professionals for years. These interests are not limited to the health problems immigrants face, but also cover the risks the host society faces should the immigrant be a carrier of diseases previously unknown in that society, and the demands such a disease may make on its public health service. Moreover, changes in health following immigration have the potential of increasing our understanding of the etiology of different health problems from a public health perspective (Evans, 1987).

Concerned about health problems immigrants posed to the host society, countries such as the United States were initially wary of the type of immigrants they received on the grounds that they were of inferior stock and more liable to fall sick (Littlewood & Lipsedge, 1989). Consequently, as early as 1648, immigrants had to show that they would not become a burden on the receiving society as a result of ill health. There are numerous anecdotes of travelers who have been quarantined because of the fear that they carried diseases. The recent outbreak of SARS (Severe Acute Respiratory Syndrome) in South-East Asia, and the consequent quarantining of travelers, is one such example. As Carballo, Divino and Zeric (1998) put it, immigration has become one of the most important determinants of global health and social development.

The link between migration and health raises a number of questions, such as whether immigrants have poorer health; whether they are predisposed to have poor health; and whether there are some factors in the acculturation process (i.e., the meeting between two different cultures) that jeopardize people's (i.e., the newcomer's) health. Closely related to the latter question is whether migrants, as part of their acculturation, acquire some health-compromising behaviors that make them unhealthy.

These questions and attempts to answer them have resulted in various hypotheses regarding the link between migration and health. These have included the *selection hypothesis* (i.e., immigrants who are predisposed to have health problems are those who migrate – see, e.g., Ødegaard, 1932; Grob, 1965); the *stress hypothesis* (i.e., the health problems immigrants have are as a result of inability to cope with the stresses associated with migration and the acculturation thereafter – see, e.g., Beiser, 1990; Clare, 1974; Chapter 4, this volume); and of late the *healthy immigrant effect* or the *Immigrant Health Paradox* (Hyman, 2001; Chapter 19, this volume). The healthy immigrant effect is subsumed in the immigrant Health Paradox. The *healthy immigrant effect* suggests that immigrants who migrate are healthier than those who do not migrate. The *immigrant paradox* contends that immigrants have better health than their socio-economic backgrounds suggest, and that, while they start off (i.e., first-generation immigrants) with better health than their non-immigrant counterparts, this better health deteriorates with time (i.e., with second and later generations).

The main focus of this chapter is a review of some of the health problems that have been found to vary between immigrants and the host nationals. Many of the chapters in Part II of this *Handbook* have touched on some specific health problems migrants have (e.g., posttraumatic stress disorder [PTSD] among refugees), and these will not be dealt with here. This chapter takes a more general approach to the health issues of migrants and limits itself to some major health problems. The chapter is in two parts: the first part reviews some research findings on immigration and health, and the second part discusses the complexity of researching the relationship between migration and health. In the second part, references will be made to some of the different hypotheses mentioned above. Finally, the link between migration and health will be discussed in the light of some central acculturation theories.

Regardless of the fact that immigrants have moved from their habitual place of abode to another, as humans they may not be "immune" to any of the health problems humans face. Thus, there is the need to be highly selective in such a review chapter. In deciding which health problems to focus on, we have limited our attention to: (i) health problems with some known differential rates among immigrants and non-immigrants; and (ii) health problems with relatively high Global Burden of Disease and high Disability Adjusted Life Years[1] (see Lopez, 2005; Murry & Lopez, 1996; WHO, 2004). Against this background the chapter looks at two infectious diseases (tuberculosis and HIV/AIDS), cardiovascular diseases, cancer and mental health (focusing on schizophrenia and depression).

---

[1] Global Burden of Disease (GBD), which is measured in Disability Adjusted Life Years (DALY), is a comprehensive assessment of mortality and disability from diseases. DALY is a measure that expresses one year of life lost to premature death and years lived with a disability of specified severity and duration: one year of life lost to poor health.

Health problems such as posttraumatic stress disorder, often associated with refugees, have not been dealt with in this chapter, not because they carry low DALY, but because they have been dealt with in the chapters on refugees.

27.2   Migration and physical health

27.2.1   Infectious diseases

27.2.1.1   Tuberculosis

In spite of major advances in virology, pharmacology and vaccine development, infectious diseases continue to plague the world. And this is due in part to the fact that many infectious diseases are transmitted from one part of the world to another and, in the process, they mutate and become resistant to normal treatment. One such infectious disease, which has undoubtedly been responsible for one of the largest numbers of deaths through disease worldwide and continues to have a high rate of infection, is tuberculosis (TB). In 1997, it was estimated that there were 6.3 to 11.1 million new cases of TB globally (Dye, Scheele, Dolin, Pathania & Raviglione, 1999), and migration has been implicated in its spread. In Denmark, for instance, there was an increase of 42% in the number of new TB cases among new immigrants (from 18% to 60%) in the period between 1986 and 1996 (Prinsze, 1997). Similarly, Karmi (1997) estimated that 40% of all new TB cases in England and Wales occurred among people arriving from the Indian sub-continent. In Canada, while there has been a decline of 28% in new TB cases among the Canadian-born non-Aboriginal population, there has been an increase of 29% among new immigrants in the period between 1980 and 1995 (Health Canada, 1998). A similar trend of increase has been found among immigrants to the United States (Walker & Jaranson, 1999).

Although TB is a bacterial infection it thrives in poverty-stricken areas and populations. Carballo and his colleagues (1998) point out that many immigrants to Western developed countries not only come from backgrounds where TB is still common, but many of them also move into living conditions that offer little protection from TB. Many immigrants enter into sub-standard housing and areas of overcrowding and poor sanitation, and these are areas where the disease can very easily be spread. Furthermore, immigrants are not the most ardent users of the health care system of their new society, making them less likely to receive proper medical care following infection (see Nejimi, 1983).

27.2.1.2   Human Immunodeficiency Virus/Acquired Immuno-Deficiency Syndrome (HIV/AIDS)

Not only does the scale of the HIV/AIDS epidemic continue to exceed all expectations since its identification in the early 1980s, but its spread to different areas and countries has been greater than predicted (Piot, Bartos, Ghys,

Walker & Schwartländer, 2001). Globally, an estimated 37.8 million people were living with HIV, and some 20 million people had died, by the end of 2003 (NIAID, 2004). The magnitude of this problem has called for global targeting of all possible sources of new outbreaks of the epidemic, among them global traveling.

However, it was only in recent years that the possible role of population movement in the spread of HIV/AIDS began to attract attention (Carballo & Siem, 1996; Carballo, Grocutt & Hadzihasanovic (1996), even though its role could logically have been identified from the outset. Excluding the role of the transport of contaminated blood products, the virus could only enter an HIV/AIDS-free area via a carrier, and that carrier must be either an outsider coming into the area with the disease or an insider returning to the area with the disease (Skeldon, 1999). Against this background, it was not uncommon for countries to look at immigrants/travelers as possible culprits when the disease was first identified (Jürgens, 2001; Morrison, 2002). However, it is important to differentiate between immigration and the behavior of migrants. It is the behavior of migrants that is largely responsible for the spread of HIV/AIDS, rather than immigration per se. Furthermore, it is important to distinguish between the possible role of long-term immigrants and that of short-term travelers such as tourists who, as a result of frequent traveling between places, can easily spread the disease over wider areas. Interestingly enough, the age group that is most mobile is also the most sexually active age group, and one major means of transmission is through sexual intercourse.

There are differences in the rates of HIV/AIDS among immigrants in different countries. While the prevalence rate among immigrants in Italy and Belgium is lower than that of the nationals (Carchedi & Picciolini, 1997; Muynck, 1997) the opposite is the case in Germany (Huismann, 1997). Many of those infected in Germany come from the Americas, Africa and Asia, including Turkey and Eastern Europe.

27.2.2 Cardiovascular diseases (CVD)

Cardiovascular disease is a broad, all-encompassing term for a collection of diseases and conditions. It covers dysfunctional conditions of the heart, veins and arteries that supply oxygen to vital life-sustaining areas of the body such as the brain, the heart itself and other vital organs. If its oxygen supply is curtailed, the tissue or organ deprived will die. These diseases include arteriosclerosis, angina, high blood pressure, high cholesterol, heart attack, stroke and arrhythmia. Heart diseases and stroke are the leading causes of death in both industrialized nations and many economically developing countries. CVD makes up nearly 10% of GBD, killing about 17 million people each year – i.e., about a third of all deaths globally (American Heart, 2004; WHO, 2004). In the United States it is estimated that one person dies of heart disease every thirty seconds.

The interest in the relationship between immigration and CVD is because acculturation following migration may result in observable changes in areas of life style such as physical activities, eating habits, smoking and use of alcohol, and stress, and these have all been implicated in the development of CVD. Monitoring immigrants' life style may help epidemiologists and public health workers gain better understanding of the development of the disease and associated risks (Kliewer, 1992).

Several studies have identified differential rates of CVD among the foreign-born and host nationals and these differential rates may be attributed to genetic factors, changes in life style and some environmental conditions. The classical studies in this field (see Kagan, Harris & Winkelstein 1974; Marmot & Syme, 1976) involved comparing rates of heart disease among Japanese immigrants to California and Hawaii with those among Japanese in Japan. Findings suggest that heart disease prevalence and mortality rates for the subjects in the immigrant cohort approach those of settlement society, suggesting that environmental factors may be involved in heart diseases.

Using WHO data and Canadian census data, Kliewer (1992) examined changes in CVD among immigrants to Canada from twenty-nine countries. One striking finding in this study was that the mortality rate of immigrants from twenty-six countries shifted towards the level of the Canadian native-born, giving further support to the role of environmental factors. However, these findings do not exclude the possible role of the immigrant's early environment in later CVD, as has been suggested to be the reason for the above-average rates of obesity and heart diseases among Finnish immigrants to Sweden (Carballo et al., 1998).

McKeigue and his colleagues (McKeigue, Ferrie & Pierpoint, 1993) found that, in the United Kingdom, people from South Asia (primarily India) appeared to be particularly prone to coronary heart disease. Furthermore, both men and women from South Asia have been found to have 30–40% higher rates of coronary heart disease than the native English, or people of European backgrounds (Balajaran, 1991). Similar findings regarding South Asians have been found in Canada. Using census information and the Canadian Mortality database, Sheth, Nair, Nargundkar, Anand and Yusuf (1999) examined differences in heart disease mortality rates among Canadian-born, South Asian-born and Chinese-born populations. Findings indicated that, for males, mortality from ischemic heart disease was higher in the South-Asian-born and Canadian-born populations and significantly lower in the Chinese-born population. For females, mortality was higher among South Asians than in the Canadian-born and Chinese-born. However, in a self-reported rate of heart disease and hypertension, Pomerleau and Ostbye (1997) found no differences among immigrant groups when other risk factors had been controlled for.

As an explanation for the higher risks of heart disease among South Asians, Jolly, Pais and Rihal (1996) have suggested that this might be genetic, in that there appear to be ethnic differences in insulin resistance. South Asians have been found to have a high prevalence of glucose intolerance, and high insulin levels even in the presence of normal blood sugars.

27.2.3 Cancer

Cancer is another global health problem, and estimates from 2000 suggest that there were 10 million new cases in that year, 6 million deaths, and 22 million people living with the disease (Parkin, 2001). The most common forms of cancers in terms of new cases were lung, breast, colorectal, stomach and liver. The profile varies greatly in different populations, and the evidence suggests that this variation is mainly a consequence of different life style and environmental factors.

Many studies on cancer mortality consider the influence of life style (smoking, drinking and diet), physical environment (solar exposure, air pollution, etc.) and predisposition factors such as hereditary factors. The link between certain environmental or genetic risk factors and mortality from specific diseases is well documented. In the case of immigrants, researchers have been interested in changes in their mortality rates following immigration. One research area has been the testing of the *convergence hypothesis* (see Adelstein, Staszewski & Muir, 1979; Head, Marmot & Swerdlow, 1993; Rosenwaike & Shai, 1986) which, briefly stated, means that the rates of cancer among immigrants tend to converge towards those of the settlement society.

Review of studies seems to support the *convergence hypothesis* (Hyman, 2001; McKay, Mcintyre & Ellaway, 2003). Convergence is most evident when there is a large difference in rates between the society of settlement and the country of origin; otherwise, when the rates in both societies are similar, immigrants' rates tend to diverge from those of host nationals. Studies using different generations of immigrants also show that the risk experienced by immigrants' offspring is somewhere inbetween that of the native-born of the society of settlement, and that in the country of origin of the parents, and also that the risk increases for each later generation.

27.3 Migration and mental health

Since mental health problems in a number of cases are not the direct cause of death (e.g., depression may be the reason for a suicide, but the cause of death will rarely be listed as depression, but as suicide), to appreciate fully the toll mental health has on humanity, it is becoming increasingly common to look at this in terms of GBD and DALY. Mental illness accounts for about 10% of all GBD and it affects about 450 million people (WHO, 2001). In terms of years lived with disability, mental health problems account for 31% of the global total.

Mental health problems constitute an array of different illnesses ranging from anxiety, through depression, to schizophrenia, and it will be impossible to review studies on all these areas. In this section therefore, we will limit ourselves to schizophrenia and depression in immigrant populations. Because both schizophrenia and depression have been linked to suicide (see Baldwin, 2000; Guze & Robins, 1970; Mortensen & Juel, 1993) a brief look will also be taken at suicide as part of the mental health problems faced by immigrants. The reason for focusing on depression and schizophrenia is because these two problems have respectively been described as the most widespread and the most debilitating of all mental illnesses (Desjarlais, Eisenberg, Good & Kleinman, 1995; WHO, 2001).

27.3.1 Schizophrenia

In the 1930s, Ødegaard reported that immigrants were liable to have an excess incidence rate of schizophrenia because this disease interferes with its victim's attachments to his/her native community and predisposed him/her to migrate. Using a group of Norwegian immigrants to the United States and a reference group of Norwegians back at home, Ødegaard (1932) found support for this hypothesis. However, while a number of studies have found evidence of the relatively higher incidence of schizophrenia among immigrants compared to natives (e.g., Cantor-Graaf, Pedersen, McNeil & Mortensen, 2003; Cochrane & Bal, 1987; Harrison et al., 1997; Selten, Slaets & Khan, 1997), the explanation for the findings has been disputed (see, e.g., Bhugra, 2004; Murphy, 1977).

In one population-based cohort study in Denmark, Cantor-Graaf et al. (2003) found that the relative risks of developing schizophrenia were 2.45 and 1.92 among first-and second-generation immigrants (from the Middle East, Africa, Australia, North and South America) respectively, and 1.60 among Danes with a history of foreign residence. Reviewing studies that have compared rates of schizophrenia among immigrants and nationals, Bhugra (2004) found that, in less rigorous studies (with failure to standardize the rates of the illness), the rate of schizophrenia for African and Caribbean immigrants ranged from 2.5 to 8.4 times the rate for Whites. With age standardization and more controlled selection, the rates were still higher among the immigrants: between 1.9 and 14.6 times.

Other than the selection hypothesis put forward by Ødegaard (1932) to account for the differential rates of schizophrenia between immigrants and host nationals, a number of other hypotheses have been put forward. These have included: sending countries having high rates of schizophrenia; migration produces stress and elevates rates of schizophrenia; misdiagnosis; differences in symptoms; ethnic density in society of settlement; differences in self-concepts and discrepancies in aspirations; and achievement disparity (see Bhugra, 2004 for a discussion of these). However, not a single one of the hypotheses has been found to account for the differential rates. It appears that the different factors implicated in the different hypotheses interact with each other to account for the rates.

27.3.2 Depression

Unlike schizophrenia, where immigrants appear to have higher prevalence rates than the host nationals, findings with respect to depression among immigrants, as compared with nationals, are inconsistent and contradictory. The contradictory findings may be due to the mode of assessment, which ranges from the use of un-validated and un-standardized self-reports (see, e.g., Sam, 1994a) and standardized instruments such as the Beck Depression Inventory (see, e.g., Gutkovich, Rosenthal, Galynker, Muran, Batchelder, & Itskhoki, 1999) to the use of clinical interviews such as the WHO's Composite International Diagnostic Interview (see, e.g., Carta, Kovess, Hardoy, Morosini, Murgia, & Carpiniello, 2002). In addition, immigrant samples used in the studies have varied from clinical samples, such as those at outpatient clinics (see, e.g., Gutkovich et al., 1999), to samples drawn from the general population or a local community (see, e.g., Noh, Wu, Speechley & Kaspar, 1992). The fact that the use of health services varies among ethnic groups (e.g., it has been suggested that Asian men in the United Kingdom are more likely to consult a medical officer than their White peers, in spite of having fewer longstanding illnesses than Whites – Murry & Williams, 1986) implies that studies using outpatients to compare rates of depression among immigrants with those among nationals will very likely find higher rates among the immigrants.

Contradictory findings with respect to rates of depression among immigrants and host nationals have been observed when similar research instruments have been used among the same group of immigrants in the same country of residence (Rogler, Cortes & Malgady, 1991). Using the Center for Epidemiological Studies' Depression (CES-D) scale in a community-based study among Korean immigrants in Toronto, the depression rates among the over 800 adults were not different from rates typical of a North American community sample (Noh et al., 1992). In another community-based study using the CES-D scale among older (mean age 70.6 years) Mexican Americans in California, the immigrants were found to have higher rates of depression compared to non-Hispanic Caucasians and African Americans (Gonzalez, Haan & Hinton, 2001). On the other hand, the use of the Hamilton Depression Scale and the Beck Depression Scale among Russian-Jewish immigrants at a primary care clinic in the United States found that over 40% of the 57 consecutive patients had clinically significant depression (Gutkovich et al., 1999). This is in spite of excluding individuals with a known history of mental illness from the study.

Depression among immigrants may be attributed to a number of possible explanations ranging from psychoanalytic models of loss and grief to cognitive models of failure and locus of control (Bhugra, 2003). Given that migration involves leaving family, friends and other aspects of one's former life behind, psychoanalytic models of depression among immigrants focus on mourning and grieving following the symbolic loss of friends and social and physical milieu. In cognitive models, thoughts of being a failure and a pessimistic view of the future because the person has problems coping with the life changes following migration may all contribute towards depression. The acculturative stress model of Berry (see Chapter 4, this volume) is one such cognitive model. Bhugra (2003), in his model of migration and depression, argues that some individuals may be more vulnerable to depression partly because of lack of social skills, coupled with internal locus of control (see Chapter 8, this volume) and this is akin to the cultural learning perspective (see Chapter 5, this volume).

27.3.3 Suicide

While not all suicide is caused by mental health problems, it has been estimated that mental health problems, and in particular depression, may be implicated in between 40% and 70% of all suicides in the USA for instance (Desjarlais *et al.*, 1995). Thus, a look at changes in suicide rates following immigration may shed some light on the relationship between migration and depression.

A number of studies have found both a higher attempted suicide rate and a higher actual suicide rate among immigrants, compared to non-immigrants (Bayard-Burfield, Sundquist, Johansson & Traskman-Bendz, 1999; Johansson, Sundquist, Johansson, Bergman, Qvist & Traskman-Bendz, 1997; Raleigh & Balarajan, 1992; Strachan, Johansen & Nair, 1990). Johansson and his colleagues (Johansson *et al.*, 1997) examined the influence of ethnicity, age, sex, marital status and date of immigration on suicide rates in Sweden. The study was based on all individuals over fifteen years old in Sweden in 1985. Suicides and undetermined deaths, during the follow-up period 1986–1989, were taken from the central Cause of Death Register. Analyses indicated that being foreign-born was a risk factor for suicide for both men and women, with risk ratios of 1.21 and 1.36 respectively, with control for age and marital status. The highest risk ratios for suicide in Sweden, adjusted for age, were found among males born in Russia and Finland. They also showed higher suicide risks than in their countries of birth. Females born in Hungary, Russia, Finland and Poland all had high risks of committing suicide in Sweden, and they also had higher risks than in their countries of birth.

Kliewer and Ward (1988) investigated factors influencing the 1969 to 1973 suicide rates among twenty-five immigrant groups in Canada. Their findings, based on age-standardized suicide rates, suggested that the suicide rates of immigrants converged with those of the destination native-born population. Among immigrants from low-risk countries (i.e., countries with lower suicide rates than Canada), suicide rates increased to those of Canada, and among immigrants from high-risk countries, suicide rates decreased. Length of residence was also positively related to the degree of convergence. These findings were confirmed in a later study which also suggested that migration may be more deleterious for females than males (Kliewer, 1991).

27.4 Acculturation and health: research and conceptual issues

The health of immigrants and the pattern of their mortality and morbidity are influenced not only by the factors within their country of origin, but also by factors within the society of settlement and by the process of immigration. After migration, migrants' mortality/morbidity rates for a particular cause of death or disease may remain relatively close to the norm of their country of origin. On the other hand, these may change for better or for worse depending on the reference group used. With respect to the country of settlement, immigrant health may converge towards the norm (see Kliewer, 1992) but convergence may be either an improvement or a worsening with respect to the norms of the original society. Furthermore, changes in, or the stability of, mortality and morbidity rates an immigrant may experience may be due to predisposing genetic factors the individual has, or due to carrying over of certain life style choices (e.g., diet) from the native country, or to the acquisition of new habits akin to the new society. They could equally be due to environmental factors within the new society or a combination of or interaction among these factors. There is no doubt that the relationship between immigration and health is a complex one with no easy and clear answer. In addition, there is the unresolved critical question of whether immigrants are a select group and their original health plays a role in their decision to move or not and the subsequent health outcome.

The array of factors involved in the health of an immigrant *complicates* any research attempt to isolate the precise link between migration and health.

In an English study, Marmot, Adelstein and Bulusu (1984) compared the mortality rates for different diseases, including heart diseases, among migrants from Ireland, Poland, Italy, the Indian sub-continent and the Caribbean with the rates of the respective sending countries. They found that, with the exception of the Irish, all the immigrant groups' mortality rates were much lower than those of residents in the country of origin. These findings were seen as an indication that the healthiest migrated, albeit the health selection effects may also vary across countries.

A closely related finding to the one above is what has become known in the United States as the "Latino or Hispanic (Health) Paradox." By many measures, Hispanic immigrants to the United States have superior health compared to non-Hispanics, and to what one might expect given their socio-economic situation (see Chapter 19, this volume). The reasons for the Hispanic Health

Paradox have received much research attention, but the two explanations given for it are the healthy migrant effect and the protective effects of the Hispanic culture (see Vega & Amaro, 1994). The healthy migrant effect rests on the assumption that it is the healthy individuals who migrate. The selectivity of immigrants in the context of better health is the exact opposite of what the original selection hypothesis proposed.

Using data from the National Health Interview Survey in the United States,[2] Jasso, Massey, Rosenzweig and Smith (2004) found that, when self-reports of general health status are utilized, the foreign-born population in the United States appear to be slightly worse off than their native-born peers. However, when these same individuals are compared in terms of disease prevalence rates, the foreign-born appear to have much lower rates of chronic disease than the native-born. These differences could be due to methodological artefacts where the foreign-born under-report their health problems because of unfamiliarity with Western diagnostic techniques. In the same study, they found a reversal in ranking among older households; the rates of heart disease were slightly higher among the oldest foreign-born group than the native-born, suggesting the tendency for differences to converge to near equality among the older populations. The older foreign-born also appeared to experience more rapid health deterioration during their stay in the United States than is typical of the native-born population.

27.5   The role of acculturation in the migration–health link

For many people, migration entails changes in their original way of living (e.g., changes in life style), exposure to a new physical environment (e.g., new bacteria and viruses) and a breakdown in their social support network. All these changes can be summed up as "acculturation." Thus picking up new eating habits (such as high consumption of fast-food), turning to alcohol as a means of dealing with difficulties in one's life because one has lost the social support provided by friends and family, or starting to smoke because it is affordable in the new country or facilitates socializing, may all contribute towards the risks of developing poor health.

The focus on the link between immigration and health is perhaps more concerned about a decline in health, but there is no doubt that migration and the acculturation that follows can also result in better health because of exposure to better health facilities and services. The acculturation strategies people choose may also influence their health behavior and subsequently their health. For instance, Sam (1994b) found that immigrant youth who preferred assimilation

---

[2] The National Health Interview Survey (NHIS) is conducted annually by the National Center for Health Statistics' (NCHS') Centers for Disease Control and Prevention (CDC). The NHIS annually administers interviews to a nationally representative sample of about 43,000 households comprising about 106,000 people.

and integration had a higher risk of engaging in health-compromising behavior, such as smoking and drinking alcohol, than their peers who preferred separation. Similarly, Thuen and Sam (1994) found immigrant youth in Norway who scored high on Separation were less likely to use safety devices such as a cycle helmet, compared to their Norwegian peers. In their comparative study involving over 5,000 immigrant youth in 13 different countries, Berry, Phinney, Sam and Vedder (2006) found that immigrant youth with an Integration profile had better psychological adaptation compared with those with an Ethnic or National profile, and much better adaptation than youth who had a Diffuse (Marginal) profile. In this study, the Integration profile included adolescents who highly endorsed the integration acculturation attitude, and also held both strong ethnic and strong national identities. They also had high national language proficiency and had high peer contacts with both the nationals and their own ethnic group members. Individuals with Ethnic profile were those who scored high on ethnic identity, had more contacts with their own ethnic group and were high on ethnic language proficiency and use. The National profile was more or less the opposite of the Ethnic profile, and included those with, among other things, high national identity but low ethnic identity. Those in the Diffuse profile had low integration attitudes, and were low on both identities. The psychological adaptation variable included measures of psychological problems such as anxiety, depression and psychosomatic symptoms.

The relationships between immigration, acculturation and health are highly variable. There are major individual differences in how people deal with the stresses of migration. Some individuals are more resilient to the adverse factors (see Chapter 28, this volume). Some individuals may be better prepared for the migration than others, and a pre-migration preparation may serve as a protective factor against ill health.

27.6 Conclusions

Does migration result in poor health? There is evidence that the prevalence rates of some health problems may be higher among immigrants than non-immigrants, suggesting that immigration may affect one's health, but this is not enough to conclude that migration results in poor health. Indeed, most immigrants do not become seriously ill, and some show improved health (see Kliewer, 1992). The link between migration and health is not a straightforward and linear one. This link is affected by both personal factors (e.g. age, coping skills and resources, and genetic makeup) and factors existing within the country of origin and the country of settlement (e.g., the resettlement policies, and social support), the immigration process itself (e.g., pre-migration preparation, etc.) and the interaction among these. Any one of these can easily tilt the balance between poor health and good health.

27.7 References

Adelstein, A. M., Staszewski, J. & Muir, C. S. (1979). Cancer mortality in 1970–1972 among Polish-born migrants to England and Wales. *British Journal of Cancer*, *40(3)*, 464–475.

American Heart (2004). *Biostatistical factsheet: population.* www.americanheart.org/downloadable/heart/1023898043312CVD_stats.pdf.

Balajaran, R. (1991). Ethnic differences in mortality from ischemic heart disease and cerebrovascular disease in England and Wales. *British Medical Journal*, *302*, 560–564.

Baldwin, R. C. (2000). Prognosis of depression. *Current Opinion in Psychiatry*, *13*, 81–85.

Bayard-Burfield, L., Sundquist, J., Johansson, S.-E. & Träskman-Bendz, L. (1999). Attempted suicide among Swedish-born people and foreign-born migrants. *Archives of Suicide Research*, *5*, 43–55.

Beiser, M. (1990). Migration: opportunity or mental health risk. *Triangle*, *29*, 83–90.

Berry, J. W., Phinney, J. S., Sam, D. L. & Vedder, P. H. (eds.) (2006). *Immigrant youth in cultural transition: acculturation, identity and adaptation across national contexts.* Mahwah, NJ: Lawrence Erlbaum Associates.

Bhugra, D. (2003). Migration and depression. *Acta Psychiatrica Scandinavica*, *108*, 67–72.

(2004). Migration and mental health. *Acta Psychiatrica Scandinavica*, *109*, 243–258.

Cantor-Graaf, E., Pedersen, C., McNeil, T. F. & Mortensen, P. B. (2003). Migration as a risk factor for schizophrenia: a Danish population-based cohort study. *British Journal of Psychiatry*, *182*, 117–122.

Carballo, M., Divino, J. & Zeric, D. (1998). Migration and health in the European Union. *Tropical Medicine and International Health*, *3*, 936–944.

Carballo, M., Grocutt, M. & Hadzihasanovic, A. (1996). Women and immigration: a public health issue. *World Health Statistics Quarterly*, *49*, 158–164.

Carballo, M. & Siem, H. (1996). Migration policy and AIDS. In M. Haour & R. Rector (eds.), *Crossing borders: migration, ethnicity and AIDS* (pp. 31–49). London: Taylor & Francis.

Carchedi, F. & Picciolini, A. (1997). Migration and health in Italy. In A. Huismann, C. Weilandt & A. Greiger (eds.), *Country reports on migration and health in Europe* (pp. 316–378). Bonn: Wissenschaftliches Institut der Ärzte Deutschlands e.V.

Carta, M. G., Kovess, V., Hardoy, M. C., Morosini, P., Murgia, S. & Carpiniello, B. (2002). Psychiatric disorders in Sardinian immigrants to Paris: a comparison with Parisians and Sardinians resident in Sardinia. *Social Psychiatry and Psychiatric Epidemiology*, *37*, 112–117.

Clare, A. W. (1974). Mental illness in the Irish emigrant. *Journal of the Irish Medical Association*, *67(1)*, 20–24.

Cochrane, R. & Bal, S. S. (1987). Migration and schizophrenia: an examination of five hypotheses. *Social Psychiatry*, *22*, 181–191.

Desjarlais, R., Eisenberg, L., Good, B. & Kleinman, A. (1995). *World mental health: problems and priorities in low income countries.* Oxford: Oxford University Press.

Dye, C., Scheele, S., Dolin, P., Pathania. V. & Raviglione, M. C. (1999). Consensus statement. Global burden of tuberculosis: estimated incidence, prevalence, and mortality by country. WHO Global Surveillance and Monitoring Project. *Journal of the American Medical Association, 282,* 677–686.

Evans, J. (1987). Migration and health. *International Migration Review, 21(3),* v–xiv.

Furnham, A. & Bochner, S. (1986). *Culture shock: psychological reactions to unfamiliar environments.* London: Methuen.

Gonzalez, H. M.,Haan, M. N. & Hinton, L. (2001). Acculturation and the prevalence of depression in older Mexican Americans: baseline results of the Sacramento Area Latino Study on Aging. *Journal of the American Geriatrics Society, 49,* 948–953.

Grob, G. N. (1965). *The state of the mentally ill.* Chapel Hill: University of North Carolina.

Gutkovich, Z., Rosenthal, R. N., Galynker, I., Muran, C., Batchelder, S. & Itskhoki, E. (1999). Depression and demoralization among Russian-Jewish immigrants in primary care. *Psychosomatics, 40,* 117–125.

Guze, S. B. & Robins, E. (1970). Suicide and primary affective disorders. *British Journal of Psychiatry, 1117,* 437–438.

Harrison, G., Glazebrook, C., Brewin, J., *et al.* (1997). Increased incidence of psychotic disorders in migrants from the Caribbean to the United Kingdom. *Psychological Medicine, 27,* 799–806.

Head, J., Marmot, M. G. & Swerdlow, A. J. (1993). "Cancer in Italian migrant populations. England and Wales: mortality." *IARC Scientific Publications, 123,* 166–177.

Health Canada (1998). *Tuberculosis in Canada.* Ottawa: Ministry of Health. www.hc-sc-gc.ca/hbp/lcdc.

Huismann, A. (1997). Migration and health in Germany. In A. Huismann, C. Weilandt & A. Greiger (eds.), *Country reports on migration and health in Europe.* Bonn: Wissenschaftliches Institut der Ärzte Deutschlands e.V.

Hyman, I. (2001). *Immigration and health.* Health Policy Working Paper Series. Ottawa: Health Canada. www.hc-sc.gc.ca/iacb-dgiac/arad-draa/english/rmdd/wpapers/immigration01.html.

Jasso, G., Massey, D. S., Rosenzweig, M. R. & Smith, J. P. (2004). Immigrant health-selectivity and acculturation. In N. B. Anderson, R. A. Bulatao & B. Cohen (eds.), *Critical perspectives on racial and ethnic differences in health in late life* (pp. 227–266). Washington, DC: National Academy Press.

Johansson, L. M., Sundquist, J., Johansson, S.-E., Bergman, B., Qvist, J. & Traskman-Bendz, L. (1997). Suicide among foreign-born minorities and native Swedes: an epidemiological follow-up study of a defined population. *Social Science and Medicine, 44,* 181–187.

Jolly, K. S., Pais, P. & Rihal, C. S. (1996). Coronary artery disease among South Asians: identification of a high risk population. *Canadian Journal of Cardiology, 12,* 569–571.

Jürgens, R. (2001). *Immigration and HIV: a new report demands justice, not prejudice.* Montreal: The Canadian HIV/AIDS Legal Network. www.aidslaw.ca/Media/speaking-notes/e-speak-jun1201.htm.

Kagan, A., Harris, B. R. & Winkelstein, W. Jr. (1974). Epidemiologic studies of coronary heart disease and stroke in Japanese men living in Japan, Hawaii and

California: demographic, physical, dietary and biochemical characteristics. *Journal of Chronic Diseases, 27*, 345–364.

Karmi, G. (1997). Migration and health in the United Kingdom. In A. Huismann, C. Weilandt & A. Greiger (eds.), *Country reports on migration and health in Europe*. Bonn: Wissenschaftliches Institut der Ärzte Deutschlands e.V.

Kliewer, E. V. (1991). Immigrant suicide in Australia, Canada, England and Wales, and the United States. *Journal of the Australian Population Association, 8*, 111–128.

(1992). Epidemiology of diseases among migrants. *International Migration Quarterly Review, 30*, 141–165.

Kliewer, E. V. & Ward, R. H. (1988). Convergence of suicide rates to those in the destination country. *American Journal of Epidemiology, 127*, 640–653.

Littlewood, R. & Lipsedge, M. (1989). *Aliens and alienists: ethnic minority and psychiatry*. London: Unwin Heyman.

Lopez, A. D. (2005). The evolution of the Global Burden of Disease framework for disease, injury and risk factor quantification: developing the evidence base for national, regional and global public health action. *Globalization and health, 1(5)*. www.globalizationandhealth.com/content/pdf/1744-8603-1-5.pdf.

Marmot, M. G., Adelstein, A. M. & Bulusu, L. (1984). Lessons from the study of immigrant mortality. *Lancet, 8392*, 1455–1457.

Marmot, M. G. & Syme, S. L. (1976). Acculturation and coronary heart disease in Japanese Americans. *American Journal of Epidemiology, 104*, 225–247.

McKay, L., Mcintyre, S. & Ellaway, A. (2003). *Migration and health. A review of the international literature*. Occasional Paper, 12. Glasgow: Medical Research Council, Social and Public Health Sciences Unit.

McKeigue, P. M., Ferrie, J. E. & Pierpoint, T. (1993). Association of early onset coronary heart disease in South Asian men with glucose intolerance and hyperinsulinemia. *Circulation, 87*, 142–161.

Morrison, J. S. (2002) *HIV testing requirement for immigrants and visitors to the United States: time to reconsider?* Center for Strategic and International Studies Task Force on HIV/AIDS. www.csis.org/africa/0302_hivtesting_immigrants.pdf.

Mortensen, B. P. & Juel, K. (1993). Mortality and causes of death in first admitted schizophrenic patients. *British Journal of Psychiatry, 163*, 183–189.

Murphy, H. B. M. (1977). Migration, culture and mental health. *Psychological Medicine, 7*, 677–684.

Murray, C. J. L. & Lopez, A. D. (1996). *The global burden of disease*. Geneva: World Health Organization, Harvard School of Public Health, World Bank.

Murry, J. & Williams, P. (1986). Self-reported illness and general practice consultations among Asian-born and British-born residents of West London. *Social Psychiatry, 21*, 136–145.

Muynck, A. (1997). Migration and health in Belgium. In A. Huismann, C. Weilandt & A. Greiger (eds.), *Country reports on migration and health in Europe*. Bonn: Wissenschaftliches Institut der Ärzte Deutschlands e.V.

Nejimi, S. (1983). Social and health care of Moroccan workers in Europe. In M. Colledge, H. A. van Guens & P. G. Svensson (eds.), *Towards an understanding of the health care needs of ethnic minorities* (pp. 138–149). Copenhagen: WHO, Regional Office for Europe.

NIAID (2004). *HIV/AIDS statistics.* Bethesda, MD: National Institute of Allergy and Infectious Diseases, National Institute of Health.

Noh, S., Wu, Z., Speechley, M. & Kaspar, V. (1992). Depression in Korean immigrants in Canada. II. Correlates of gender, work, and marriage. *Journal of Nervous and Mental Disease, 180,* 578–582.

Ødegaard, O. (1932). Emigration and insanity. *Acta Psychiatrica et Neurologica, Supplement 4.*

Parkin, D. M. (2001). Global cancer statistics in 2000. *Lancet Oncology, 2,* 533–543.

Piot, P., Bartos, M., Ghys, P. D., Walker, M. & Schwartländer, B. (2001). The global impact of HIV/AIDS. *Nature, 410,* 968–973.

Pomerleau, J. & Ostbye, T. 1997. The relationship between place of birth and some health characteristics in Ontario. *Canadian Journal of Public Health, 88,* 337–345.

Prinsze, F. (1997). Tuberculosis in countries of the European Union. *Infectieziekten-bulletin, 8,* 25–27.

Raleigh, V. S. & Balarajan, R. (1992). Suicide levels and trends among immigrants in England and Wales. *Health Trends, 24,* 91–94.

Rogler, L. H., Cortes, D. E. & Malgady, R. G. (1991). Acculturation and mental health status among Hispanics. Convergence and new directions for research. *American Psychologist, 46,* 585–597.

Rosenwaike, I. & Shai, D. (1986). Trends in cancer mortality among Puerto Rican-born migrants to New York City. *International Journal of Epidemiology, 15(1),* 30–35.

Sam, D. L. (1994a). The psychological adjustment of young immigrants in Norway. *Scandinavian Journal of Psychology, 35,* 240–253.

(1994b). Acculturation of young immigrants in Norway. Unpublished Ph.D. dissertation, University of Bergen, Norway.

Selten, J. P., Slaets, J. P. J. & Khan, R. (1997). Schizophrenia in Surinamese and Dutch Antillean immigrants to the Netherlands: evidence of an increased incidence. *Psychological Medicine, 27,* 807–811.

Sheth, T., Nair, C., Nargundkar, M., Anand, S. & Yusuf, S. (1999). Cardiovascular and cancer mortality among Canadians of European, South Asian and Chinese origin from 1979 to 1993: an analysis of 1.2 million deaths. *Canadian Medical Association Journal, 161,* 131–138.

Skeldon, R. (1999). Population mobility and HIV vulnerability in South East Asia: an assessment and analysis. Paper presented to the UNDP South East Asia HIV and Development Project Workshop on Population Movement and HIV Vulnerability, Chiang Rai, Thailand, November 10–12.

Strachan, J. H., Johansen, C. & Nair, C. 1990. Canadian suicide mortality rates: first-generation immigrants versus Canadian-born. *Health Reports, 2,* 327–341.

Syed, H. R. & Vangen, S. (2003). *Health and migration. A review.* Oslo: Norwegian Center for Minority Health Research.

Thuen, F. & Sam, D. L. (1994). Use of safety equipment among young immigrants in Norway. A comparison with Norwegian children. *Journal of Norwegian Medical Association, 114,* 195–198. (In Norwegian with English abstract.)

Vega, W. & Amaro, H. (1994). Latino outlook: good health, unhealthy prognosis. *Annual Review of Public Health, 15,* 39–67.

Walker, P. F. & Jaranson, J. (1999). Refugee and immigrant health care. *Medical Clinics of North America, 83,* 1103–1120.

WHO (2001). *Mental health: new understanding, new hope.* World Health Report 2001. Geneva: World Health Organization.

(2004). *Changing history.* World Health Report 2004. Geneva: World Health Organization.

28 Immigration and resilience

Esther Ehrensaft & Michel Tousignant

Immigration is a long-term process; its roots begin in one's country of origin long before departure and extend far into the future when a sense of familiarity with the host country has finally been achieved. Much has been said about the hardships of resettlement: mourning, uprooting, alienation, poverty, discrimination and the acquisition of a new identity have all been amply documented in empirical and clinical literature. And yet, at the core of the immigrant's experience is the rekindling of a sense of hope with one's new departure and a vision of opportunities to accomplish goals that were previously seen as beyond one's reach.

While biographies and fiction have provided narratives of the success of immigrants, the social sciences literature has been more reserved about analyzing in detail the arduous road of survival during the immigration process. The scientific snapshot approach, the questionable validity of retrospective procedures, and the pressure to publish have all played against the widespread use of longitudinal approaches. As a result, we have only just begun to construct a coherent picture of the lengthy process of resilience necessary to overcome the chronic hardships of starting life anew, far from one's homeland.

The literature in social sciences on the subject of resilience is largely centered on pre-migratory trauma among refugees who fled their country of origin. Since refugee populations are of particular interest to organizations assisting newcomers, they will constitute the major focus of this chapter. While the refugee experience is highly varied, there are certainly common denominators of challenge and loss. These include living as a survivor and carrying the memory of personal and collective drama, leaving behind deceased parents or ones who have disappeared, and slowly shedding one's identity of being exiled. This said, immigrants also share their load of adversity, such as professional exploitation, semi-clandestine or illegal status, and family disruptions. It is safe to assume that most newcomers hold a personal and collective history of hardship, struggle and a remarkable capacity for survival at the heart of their life experiences.

Ehrensaft (2002) provides an extensive and up-to-date review of the literature on the concept of resilience and its application to refugee populations in trans-cultural psychology. The author highlights Rutter's (1993) theory of resilience as an appropriate framework for refugee groups. Rutter elegantly captured the essence of the concept when he wrote that resilience is a phenomenon observed in subjects who develop positively, even though they have endured experiences of stress which, in the general population, would have likely led to a serious risk of negative outcome. Furthermore, "resilience" is not synonymous with "coping mechanism" or "protective factor." Rather, it is an enduring process that integrates various coping mechanisms. Regarding psychiatric morbidity, resilience is not simply the absence of visible symptoms. For many individuals, there appears to be a dimension of transformation, of taking the opportunity of the trauma to channel one's energy into new directions. It may take many years to conclude that one is in the presence of true resilience. The resilient person may show vulnerability, and may even experience crises and failures, but will ultimately emerge stronger in the long run. Perhaps most importantly, resilience is a process, not a personal quality. It is the result of positive resources within the individual, and also of supporting factors in the immediate network and the community.

With regard to the field of immigration, each culture has its own specific ways of facilitating or impeding resilience. In their exploration of the role of culture in development, adjustment, and psychopathology, Cohler, Stott and Musick (1995) argue that resilience, as defined by Western researchers, is a construct that may not be applicable to other cultures. They stress that the majority of studies on vulnerability and resilience do not consider culture and ethnicity as factors associated with the origins or evolution of personal distress over the developmental life course. These authors suggest that it is critical to recognize the specific trajectory of resilience within particular groups, since every culture has its own unique form of expressing and treating metaphors of distress. Adjustment takes place within a culture that is composed of shared understandings of meaning, including those concerning the passage of time and changes that can be expected over time, as well as the continuity of self and relationships with others both within the family and in society at large (Cohler, Stott & Musick, 1995; Antonovsky, 1986).

Cohler, Stott & Musick (1995) also call attention to the cultural values upon which the Western concept of resilience is founded. Resilience is rooted in the values of autonomy, the capacity to face adversity alone and to resolve one's problems without the support of others. The cultural roots of these values become evident when one considers that different capacities and qualities are valued in other cultures. For example, Asian cultures tend to place a high value on the capacity of the individual to live harmoniously in collective family and social groups. It is thus highly likely that alternative definitions of resilience may exist in cultures in which a high value is placed on interdependence, harmony and collective living (Ehrensaft, 2002). This point is important in discussing the themes of integration and adaptation.

Few studies have specifically targeted the process of resilience. It is tempting in this field to rely only on qualitative reports and occasional autobiographies, which are valuable and important for the formulation of hypotheses but lack the necessary scientific distance to prove a point. As appropriately pointed out by Beiser (1999), the field is littered by this sort of tautology. Therefore, this review will be limited to research using systematic, scientific approaches. We have also decided to provide in-depth description of particular, highly thorough studies of resilience in order for the reader to grasp better what underlies the concept and process. The reader will also hopefully forgive our bias towards Canadian studies, which also reflects the high local interest in resilience.

28.1 Making sense out of chaos

In countries such as Cambodia and Rwanda, the vast majority of the population has been exposed to extreme violence. According to a study published in 1996 by UNICEF (Bellamy, 1996), virtually all Rwandan children were directly exposed to scenes of violence during the genocide of 1994 and remained profoundly marked by these experiences: 80 percent of children witnessed a murder or an attack, one-third witnessed the death of a member of their own family, and two-thirds witnessed an execution; 84 percent of children found themselves in situations in which they thought that they were going to die. A central issue for survivors was the daunting task of making meaning out of life in the wake of senseless atrocity. In this respect, it is necessary to underscore that the concepts of resilience, trauma and wellbeing are the products of a system of signs, meanings and actions developed by a cultural group (Corin & Lauzon, 1992), as well as of the collective meaning ascribed by this group to past, present and future events (Antonovsky, 1986).

Narrative construction plays a critical role for those developing resilience in the wake of trauma. Bruner (1990), a key theorist in narrative psychology, conceptualizes narrative construction as a fundamental, adaptive human process that serves to reconcile normative, ordinary experience with exceptional events that constitute breaches in the normal and canonical. The construction of narratives helps, psychologically, to manage and tolerate the conflicts and contradictions engendered by social life. According to Neimeyer and Levitt (2001:7), the process of resilience involves the development of coping strategies for "narrative repair." They argue that: "By formulating coping as a narrative endeavour, we are advancing a framework in which people are viewed as 'motivated storytellers,' an approach that helps us think in an integrated fashion about adaptation and self-change" (p. 10). The development and restructuring of one's life narrative is in fact conceived as a psychological need which enables individuals and their larger social communities to ascribe meaning to their experience by using a story-telling structure. By structuring a setting for his story, the narrator enables both himself and his audience to relate and re-enter the event and its story in an "experientially vivid way" (p.15). The narrator thereby achieves "verisimilitude" or a detailed story, believable in the mind's eye of the listener (Bruner, 1990), and elicits empathy and a dialogical relationship in the listener (Josselson, 1995). In other words, does the individual relate his story in a detailed, fluid manner, or are there contradictory and unclear elements in the story, either for the teller or for his audience? The *setting* enables resilience in that it may create a space for a new perspective and a shift in one's perspective from a "symptom position" to an active stance of coping (Neimeyer and Levitt, 2001, p. 15). The challenge of narrative emplotment is particularly Herculean for survivors of massive trauma since they are torn between loyalty to the past and the perceived responsibility to remember on the one hand, and, on the other, the desire to forget exceedingly painful memories (Becker, Beyene & Ken, 2000). In a sense, the successful or resilient trauma narrative must negotiate these ambiguous needs by integrating and reframing the past in order to make room for a positive, meaningful present and orientation towards the future.

In her research on resilience among Rwandan refugee adolescents in Quebec, Ehrensaft (2002) analyzed the meaning attributed to war events by sub-samples of most- and least-resilient youth. One of her conclusions was that meaning was not linked to resilience in a linear fashion. Youth did not adhere to a single meaning about war and genocide, but rather constructed complex, polysemic patterns of meaning. The most resilient group tended to employ either a pattern of a core meaning with a related constellation of meaning, or a "counterweight meaning" structure, in which seemingly conflicting meanings of events were integrated into a framework of significance. On the other hand, the least resilient group tended to demonstrate a fragmented polysemic structure of meaning, in which grounding meanings were conspicuously absent.

Indeed, this study revealed a widespread tendency of youth to emulate the political and ethnic discourse heard in the family: a general comparative analysis of the meaning-making of parents' interviews about their children revealed that these adolescents absorbed and repeated parental discourse on the causes of the war and the responsibility for ethnic suffering and divide. The fact that the most resilient group of adolescents evoked ethnic attributions of war also merits reflection (Ehrensaft, 2002). Discourse on ethnic innocence and victimization seems to be relatively widespread among those youth showing a higher level of resilience. Rousseau, Bertot, Mekki-Berrada, Measham & Drapeau (2001) also found that, among Algerians, the possibility of attributing some meaning to the memory of horrendous massacres, perpetrated by organized groups, was the only escape from the vacuum of absurdity. In this respect, ethnic attributions in fact perpetuate rather than repair ethnic divide. This suggests that conflict resolution efforts and interventions aimed at collective forgiveness and rapprochement are in direct opposition to the meaning-making found in resilient youth (Ehrensaft, 2002).

In Ehrensaft's (2002) study of Rwandan youth, virtually no adolescent in the most resilient group rejected family meaning or held the family responsible for his or her war misfortunes while those in the least resilient group tend largely to have differences with family interpretations. While the finding of the pattern of a core meaning with a related constellation of meanings corresponds closely to Antonovsky's (1986) concept of the sense of coherence, the pattern of the counterweight meanings suggests that a resilient narrative may also be achieved by managing contradictions without dissolving them into a single, core meaning. In fact, the existence of this type of pattern implies that some youth may derive their resilience from their ability to live comfortably with conflicting, contradictory explanations of the causes of war. Doubt, ambivalence, absurdity, uncertainty, rage and sadness may coexist with meaning, rather than being fully repressed. A useful metaphor might be that of a juggler, who maintains a sense of balance by alternately keeping a given meaning up in the air and others weighted in his hands (Ehrensaft, 2002).

These observations about Rwandan youth point to the possible risks for non-Western immigrants who integrate too rapidly to a Cartesian epistemological approach, that is less open to the ambiguous, mysterious or contradictory meanings of life.

28.2 Personal and collective memory

As mentioned, personal experience is always embedded within collective stories which form the background of personal narratives (Schiff, Noy & Cohler, 2001). The personal account will take its meaning from the larger historical interpretation. Transporting this principle to the survival of refugees, we could argue that the meaning of the war in the eyes of the listener will greatly contribute to ensuring the resilience of the victim. Refugees coming from Chile and Rwanda were seen as victims of immoral massacres by the Canadian population, and their experience was attributed a meaning of sacrifice within the secular Christian values of the host culture. It took a longer time for the Haitians to be accepted as victims, until images of violence transmitted on the news started to indicate the high insecurity of daily life in Haiti. Most likely, refugees from Guatemala, Argentina or Peru, and many African countries, have come from regions with a less publicized conflict and have consequently not enjoyed the same spontaneous compassion in the land of exile. Thus, the suffering of the immigrant and the refugee has to be legitimized by the host culture in order to facilitate their inclusion.

The collective aspect of memory, especially with regard to war, does not imply universal forms of remembering within a culture. The way memory is voiced may depend on small differences within a cohort of refugees (Rousseau, Morales & Foxen, 2001). For example, when Rios Montt, former president of Guatemala, organized political repression against Mayan villages in the north, there followed a flight of entire villages to the state of Chiapas in Mexico. Fearing the overflow of the revolutionary movement within its own borders, the government of Mexico tried to spread the refugee population in areas more remote from the Mayan population of Chiapas. The sub-group who were displaced to the states of Yucatan and Quintana Roo had, from there on, a different exile experience. When the hour of the return came, this group, who had been more exposed to the discourse of the international help organizations and cut from its traditional ties to home, used its memory to assert its new dream of reconquering its status in the old country. It chose a strategy of confrontation and strength, naming its new homeland community "La Victoria" in direct challenge to the authorities. On the other hand, another group who had stayed near the border and tried to live as close as possible to the traditional ways chose a more silent path when returning two years later. They avoided reference to history and tried to revert to their old ways without drawing local or international attention to themselves. Their new village was named "La Esperanza" (hope). In this instance, we see how differential acculturation in exile has modified the process of facing adversity among members of the same culture.

28.3   Family continuity and disruption

Parental separation is sometimes considered to be more traumatic for young persons than exposure to violence and the dangers of war (Ressler, Boothby & Steinbock, 1988). In clinical practice, suicide attempts appear to be high among young immigrant and refugees with a story of lengthy separation from their families (Rousseau et al., 2001:16). Among Congolese, the dislocation of the family during exile to Canada is a real moral torture and reunification provides a second life. On the level of representations, the intact family appears as an anchor for salvation. A discourse analysis shows the theme of family to be a source of meaning, around which projects are built and the psyche is structured. Reunification becomes the raison de vivre. Yet, problems that were left behind often resurface when the family is back together. However painful, the separation is not without some advantages. Both spouses have learned to become autonomous from one another, and it then becomes easier to adopt new roles abroad. Some children even claim that the distance has brought them closer to their parents. The literature on family separation has also produced other unexpected observations. A spontaneous reaction for parents is to bequeath their cultural traditions to their children to ensure a symbolic intergenerational continuity during periods of stress. In fact, many African intellectuals, raised in religious boarding schools, become conscious of their own uprootedness in the process. The separation is not experienced as a black spot in the history of the family, but as a fundamental reference illustrating its capacity to survive. Rousseau et al. (2001) claim that women are more prepared for the challenge made inevitable by change because they are oriented towards the project of bringing children to life. Adaptation during exile is made easier by being conscious that life is change.

In her research on resilience among Rwandan adolescents living in Quebec, six to seven years after genocide and the retaliatory massacres in its aftermath, Ehrensaft (2002) came upon an unexpected finding. Those who had been separated from their mothers for the longest period of time showed fewer externalizing symptoms than those separated for a shorter period, and those separated the longest from their fathers indicated stronger prosocial abilities. It was interpreted that these adolescents had learned how to self-soothe, or to calm and regulate their feelings of anger and loss autonomously. The situation of these Rwandan youth appears to have been quite different from that of the British children investigated in Freud and Burlingham's (1943) classic study after the bombing of London in the Second World War. The British children who were brought up in a so-called "safe" environment were anguished by a possible loss of their parents, while those who had stayed in the shelters were at least assured that their parents were alive. In Rwanda, parents were forced to mourn their dead and were not necessarily in a position to support their children psychologically in their grieving process. At the same time, it should be kept in mind that these Rwandan refugee adolescents often had guardians who were part of the extended family and they were not left alone with strangers.

Refugee adolescents, particularly those raised by single mothers, also tend to take on more family responsibilities, compared to their North American peers (Tousignant, Habimana, Biron *et al.*, 1999). They take pride in helping their parents financially and guiding them in their dealings with various institutions, or even in securing employment.

Few studies bear on resilience as such among non-refugee immigrant groups. For the poor and less-educated immigrants, ensuring continuity between generations remains a considerable challenge. Mexican families migrating to the United States face a situation where mere reproduction of tradition will not necessarily help their children in achieving success. Faced with poor symbolic resources, these parents engage in a career of hard work, hoping that their self-sacrifice will be an example for their children to follow in order to succeed in the United States (Lopez & Stanton-Salazar, 2001). Immigrant families with greater social standing and resources may face just as much difficulty in imbuing cultural values and motivation for achievement in their children. Immigrant children from wealthier families tend to have a more lax attitude towards academic achievement, since they generally have not witnessed firsthand the struggles and sacrifices required for success and social mobility (Portes & Rumbaut, 2001).

28.4 Inner mechanisms

28.4.1 Religion

In Canada, a government program allows foreign domestic workers to apply for permanent residency after completing an initial three-year work contract. Many other countries such as Singapore, Malaysia, Hong Kong and Middle East nations rely on foreign domestic employees. Bals (1999), who was herself a participant in this program when she entered Canada, investigated the stress factors, the negative outcomes, as well as the resilience strategies in this professional group. She conducted in-depth interviews with forty Filipina women, fifteen of whom had complied with the requirements of residency, as well as eight Moroccan women. The majority were in their early thirties. The Filipina sample was highly educated, one half having some university education, and 40 percent were married and had left their children back home with the intention of bringing them to Canada at the end of their contract. The typical Moroccan worker was divorced and without children.

Working conditions were chronically stressful for these women, including long working hours, isolation in a suburban house, and an average of eighty hours a week on duty. There were numerous reports of psychological, physical and sexual abuse. The employer had the upper hand, knowing that the domestic worker was at risk of being deported if she were to break her contract. The fact that no more than twelve of the forty women interviewed stayed in the same family for the full three years was a good indication of the underlying tensions.

Results uncovered interesting findings on the role of meaning-making in building resilience among domestic workers. Filipina domestic workers fared better psychologicaly than the Moroccans, in spite of a higher level of adversity. While results should be interpreted with caution due to the small sample size of Moroccan women, important differences emerged with regard to meaning-making between the two groups. Most Moroccan women participated in the program to flee their failed marriages and did not have children, while many of the Filipinas were struggling to offer a better future to their children. Moreover, the Filipina government hailed these women as new heroes because of the money brought back to the country of origin. Religion was the main solace in enduring professional difficulties. It was reportedly helpful for the Filipina women to give spiritual meaning to their suffering and to invoke God regularly as their confidant. In fact, spiritual solace was sometimes preferred to the support of friends, for fear that a breach of confidence could endanger their social identity in such a close-knit community. Family-meaning also emerged as a key source of strength for Filipina women. More than two-thirds of the women had a family member living in Canada, and many shared a part-time apartment with another domestic worker when not living in their employers' home. Distance from their husband and children was certainly a challenge, but some confessed that emigrating alone was an attempt to save their faltering union. One supporting factor was hope for improvement in their lives, though this was often frustrated by unexpected delays. Here, the role of culturally sanctioned notions of self and wellbeing seemed to have enabled Filipina women to build resilient migration narratives. But a more extendable notion of time helped them to tolerate the slow process of achieving their dream. Moreover, their "self" was not as central as is expected in Western culture, and the frustration of their original plans was less painful. Moreover, much of their psychological tension was channeled into somatic symptoms, which they were also used to suppressing in view of the lack of health insurance in their country of origin.

Religion has also been reported as highly valued among South Asian Canadian women (Naidoo, 2003). The trauma experienced during migration was met with a religious answer. One's identity was viewed as more sacred after extreme hardship and suffering had been endured.

Religion also proved an important source of support for Congolese of Montreal, Canada, in Rousseau *et al.*'s work (2001). The belief that God was the supreme power sustained the values of respect, generosity and love in the community. The same was true of the Rwandan refugees, many of whom were raised in boarding schools.

Reliance on religion to cope with adversity has certainly proved to be positive in the experience of refugees. Paradoxically, these groups now fill the churches emptied by the host population. They now occupy the sacred sanctuaries considered to be at the heart of ethnic identity for French Canadians a generation ago. The boundaries between the center and the margin have thus been significantly transformed within a generation.

28.4.2 Emotion-focused coping

A long tradition of research shows that North Americans cope more successfully with life stresses by using more problem-focused strategies than emotion-focused strategies. Racial discrimination is a chronic source of stress faced by a significant percentage of immigrants. In a sample of South-East Asian refugees, Beiser (1999) found a quarter of respondents reporting this difficulty. Westerners, with their sense of entitlement and confrontational strategies, are usually highly vulnerable in such situations.

According to Beiser (1999), South-East Asians are more likely to cope with discrimination by means of passive avoidance rather than confrontation. The author claims that more collectively oriented cultures tend to prefer to mitigate tensions rather than to confront their adversaries, so as to preserve relationships. He has also observed that the more strongly an individual identifies with his own culture, the more protective his emotion-focused strategies. Again, we observe that assimilating the coping mechanisms of the Western host culture could prove dangerous and counter-productive for adaptation and resilience among newcomers.

28.4.3 Time orientation

Cottle (1976) conducted a series of psychological studies to demonstrate that people cope with adversity by splitting the spheres of time: in other words, by focusing on the immediate necessities of the present rather than digging up the past or roaming into the future. Similar observations were made by Friedlander

(1979) on the Jews of Europe. South-East Asian refugees in Beiser's (1999) study developed a similar attitude as illustrated by the following testimonies: "When you live as we have for the past few years, never knowing what will happen, you live day by day. We do not think about the past. We cannot let ourselves think about the future" (p. 126, Nong); "I'm not sure I'll still be alive tomorrow. How can you ask me about medical school?" (p. 127, Toura, who was preparing to emigrate to Sacramento).

The atomistic notion of time, shared by 80 percent of Beiser's sample, was associated in 1981 with half the rate of depression than those with an attitude of time-binding or overlapping perceptions of past, present and future (Beiser & Hyman, 1997). Two years later, those who had changed their attitude towards time had shifting rates of depression in the direction predicted by the first association. But ten years later, when a sense of normality had been reached, attitude towards time no longer mattered. There was also evidence that the 10 percent of refugees who reported a nostalgic attitude at the first stage of research, that is according relatively more importance to the past than to present and future, were more at risk for mental health problems. Elderly, unemployed refugees and those with little or no English were over-represented in this group.

These data indirectly bring into question the idea of debriefing victims of trauma, a procedure not tested on people having experienced a genocide (Mitchell & Dyregrov, 1993). The UNICEF program based on this approach has been criticized by some experts as not being the most adequate in the case of civil wars. As verbalized by Larry, a survivor of the Holocaust: "If I did not remember all of the events we had traversed, life would be meaningless. If I did not forget selectively, life would be intolerable." There is an unending battle with traumatic memory, and the process of resilience is probably never completely achieved. Many Polish and Russian refugees who fled to England and had coped well professionally during their adult stage in fact, met serious mental health problems towards the end of their lives (Hitch & Rack, 1980).

28.5   Life projects and new departures

The process of resilience needs to be fed by life projects offering a new direction. Brown, Adler and Bifulco (1988) have termed life events at the closing of an episode of depression as "new departures" in the sense that they offer a goal to structure latent energies. Acquiring employment, even if well below the occupational status in the country of origin, is a significant source of resilience among refugees. Our own research on adolescents from refugee families (Tousignant *et al.*, 1999) found that adolescents whose fathers had been unemployed for an extended period during the first year of resettlement in Quebec were faring significantly worse in terms of mental health, years after arrival, than those with a father who had quickly succeeded in securing employment.

Immigrant parents weathering the hardships of poverty during the first year of integration are sustained by the hope for a better future for their children. In our investigation quoted above (Tousignant *et al.*, 1999), a former university president reported that he was happy to reinvent himself in the field of psycho-social intervention knowing that his sons were living in security and could receive a good education.

Another strong factor contributing to the resilience of immigrants and refugees entering more democratic countries is the feeling that one can trust the justice system and be promoted in the absence of family contacts. While staying in India, the second author noted that people who approached him about the possibilities of immigration were often more frustrated by the unfairness of procedures of promotion in their professional setting than by their income level.

The restoration of peace after exile can have a positive impact on mental health for many refugees and immigrants fleeing a dire situation in their homeland. First, it provides a sense of hope for the future of their nation of origin; and second, it diminishes anguish for friends and relatives who stayed behind. In a symposium in March 2004 commemorating the Rwandan genocide, the sociologist Yvon Lefebre called attention to the fact that the invading army's quick control of the situation after thirteen weeks of atrocities at least helped the Tutsi community in Quebec to slowly come to terms with their future.

28.6 Social support of the community

On the basis of Canadian epidemiological data on mental illness among immigrants, Murphy (1973) proposed a critical mass theory as a protective factor. He hypothesized that it is protective to maintain a basic support network of a certain size composed of peers from one's country of origin. The empirical literature on social support and immigration is surprisingly scant. Research in the United States has yielded results that are mixed and difficult to summarize and interpret. Most of the studies have been conducted among Hispanic groups of Mexican origin (Lafontaine & Tousignant, 2002). They indicate that this latter group has a smaller support network than the group of American origin, relies more on family than friends, and maintains friendships with those who live nearby. Beiser (1999) also found that social support during the early years of residence in Canada prevents the later occurrence or persistence of posttraumatic stress disorder among refugees. Interestingly, in his Indochinese sample, Beiser (1999) concluded that the ethnic Chinese subgroup fared better during the first years than the rest of the sample, noting that they found more historical continuity within the local Chinatown community, but not necessarily more sources of employment. In contrast, being matched with private sponsors prevented adaptation, although it seemed like a rather good idea at first glance. The situation was especially dire when refugees and the sponsoring family did not belong to the same religion, as the former felt intruded upon and a latent pressure to convert. They also resided close to their sponsor family rather than to their own ethnic community.

In the United States, living in a racial or ethnic ghetto has provided a source of cohesiveness, sometimes helping to integrate better into the national institutions of business and higher education. Families progressively moved from ethnic enclaves into the mainstream suburbs by acquiring wealth. With the immigration of more racially diverse groups, discrimination has become more overt and young people have felt the urge to assert their difference aggressively as a means of self-defence (Portes & Rumbaut, 2001). However, this process cannot be called a retreat back to the culture of origin. Parental guidance and authority is often sorely compromised for immigrant youth. For example, in stride with the Black youth movement, the second-generation immigrants in this study have rallied around their Mexican identity and their Haitian identity, often using English with rhetoric closer to their American peers' than to that of their parents. The same has been true among North African female youth elsewhere in Europe and in Quebec, who adopted the Islamic *hijab* as an act of assertiveness. Many have traded their jeans and t-shirts for more traditional clothes, often to the surprise of their own parents who were more comfortable with the advantages of acculturation. These coping strategies raise new questions and call for a revision of the classic model of linear acculturation.

New evidence shows that support provided by family must be linked to community support in order to lead to resilience. For instance, Haitians and Nicaraguans in Florida are confronted with harsh discrimination and lack the protection of an ethnic enclave, and are thus much more likely to face a bleak future (Portes & Rumbaut, 2001). Allegiance to American values does not necessarily pay off, since the closer the newcomers get to mainstream institutions, the more likely they are to face discrimination. The ideology of nativism runs the risk of isolation and entrapment within an inferior status, while assimilation is synonymous with dissonant acculturation. The solution appears to point to selective acculturation under the umbrella of well-structured ethnic communities.

28.7 Conclusions

The early literature on the notion of culture shock tended to portray immigration as a form of trauma and immigrants as survivors. Some immigrants have certainly experienced serious hardships before or after their arrival, or a high level of chronic stress. However, at least in Canada, such indices as mortality by suicide or mental health status show immigrants to be at an advantage compared to the host population. Fortunately, research has begun to focus on resilience and is gradually providing a portrait of the immigrant, not as a victim of life circumstance, but as an actively coping agent engaged in a life-long project of improving his/her life conditions.

From the reviewed studies, it becomes increasingly clear that resilience is not a short-term success story; it develops over many years and can include failures along the way. For children, it is difficult to state a definitive conclusion to resilience until full passage to adult life. Similarly, it has been observed that some adults who lead apparently fulfilling lives sometimes succumb to psychological dysfunction later in life. This raises interesting and as yet unanswered questions about the trajectory of resilience over the life course. It is also possible that, for some individuals, resilience may be a compartmentalized process. Some may be sufficiently resilient to adapt successfully in most domains of life, but maintain a vulnerable area that can lead to dysfunction under stress.

Our final point is that resilience does not develop in a social or cultural vacuum. The immigrant is part of a family, which is in turn part of a community, which also interacts with a host society. All these levels contribute to the success or failure of the process of resilience. Furthermore, resilience is not the mechanical product of interacting protective factors. Rather, it is experienced and achieved in the mind as much as in the body, and meaning-making is central to its process. Ultimately, resilience encompasses morality as much as psychology, by forcing one to grapple with the meaning of life in the face of absurdity, and by engaging one's ability to forge hope and maintain strength of character.

28.8 References

Antonovsky, A. (1986). Intergenerational networks and transmitting the sense of coherence. In N. Datan, A. L. Greene & H. W. Reese (eds.), *Life-span developmental psychology: intergenerational relations* (pp. 211–222). Hillsdale, NJ: Lawrence Erlbaum Associates.

Bals, M. (1999). *Les employées domestiques étrangères au Canada: esclaves de l'espoir* [Female foreign domestic employees in Canada: slaves of hope]. Montreal: l'Harmattan.

Becker, G., Beyene, Y. & Ken, P. (2000). Memory, trauma, and embodied distress: the management of disruption in stories of Cambodians in exile. *Ethos, 28*, 320–345.

Beiser, M. (1999). *Strangers at the gate. The "boat people's" first ten years in Canada.* Toronto: University of Toronto Press.

Beiser, M. & Hyman, I. (1997). Refugees' time perspective and mental health. *American Journal of Psychiatry, 154*, 996–1002.

Bellamy, C. (1996). *The state of the world's children.* Oxford: Oxford University Press.

Brown, G. W., Adler, Z. & Bifulco, A. (1988). Life events, difficulties and recovery from chronic depression. *British Journal of Psychiatry, 152*, 487–498.

Bruner, J. (1990). *Acts of meaning.* Cambridge, MA: Harvard University Press.

Cohler, B. J., Stott, F. M. & Musick, J. S. (1995). Adversity, vulnerability and resilience: cultural and developmental perspectives. In D. Cichetti & D. J. Cohen (eds.), *Manual of developmental psychopathology*, Vol. II: *Risk, disorder, and adaptation* (pp. 753–800). Oxford: John Wiley and Sons.

Corin, E. & Lauzon, G. (1992). Positive withdrawal and the quest for meaning: the reconstruction of experience among schizophrenics. *Psychiatry: Journal for the Study of Interpersonal Processes*, 55, 266–278.

Cottle, T. J. (1976). *Perceiving time: a psychological investigation of men and women.* New York: Wiley.

Ehrensaft, E. (2002). The relationship between resilience, adversity and meaning Construction among Rwandan refugee adolescents exposed to armed conflict. Unpublished doctoral dissertation, University of Quebec in Montreal, Canada.

Freud, A. & Burlingham, D. T. (1943). *War and Children.* London: Medical War Books.

Friedlander, S. (1979). *When memory comes.* Toronto: McGraw Hill.

Hitch, P. & Rack, P. 1980. Mental illness among Polish and Russian refugees in Bradford. *British Journal of Psychiatry*, 137, 206–211.

Josselson, R. (1995). Imagining the real: empathy, narrative and the dialogic self. In R. Josselson & A. Lieblich (eds.), *Interpreting experience: the narrative study of lives* (Vol. III, pp. 27–44). Thousand Oaks, CA: Sage Publications.

Lafontaine, P. & Tousignant, M. (2002). Environnement de soutien [Support environment]. In *Santé et bien-être, immigrants récents au Québec: une adaptation réciproque? Etude auprès des communautés culturelles 1988–1999* [Health and wellbeing, newly arrived immigrants in Quebec: an interactive adaptation? A study among ethnic communities 1988–1999] (pp. 289–302). Quebec: Institut de la statistique du Québec, Gouvernement du Québec.

Lopez, D. E. & Stanton-Salazar, R. D. (2001). Mexican Americans: a second generation at risk. In R. G. Rumbaut & A. Portes (eds.), *Children of immigrants in America* (pp. 57–90). Los Angeles: University of California Press.

Mitchell, J. T. & Dyregrov, A. (1993). Traumatic stress in disaster workers and emergency personnel: prevention and intervention. In J. P. Wilson & R. Beverley (eds.), *International handbook of traumatic stress syndromes* (pp. 905–914). The Plenum Series on Stress and Coping. New York: Plenum Press.

Murphy, H. B. M. (1973). Migration and the major mental disorders: a reappraisal. In C. Zwingmann & M. Pfister-Ammende (eds.), *Uprooting and after* (pp. 204–220). New York: Springer-Verlag.

Naidoo, J. C. (2003). South Asian Canadian women: a contemporary portrait. *Psychology and Developing Societies*, 15, 51–67.

Neimeyer, R. A. & Levitt, H. (2001). Coping and coherence: a narrative perspective on resilience. In C. R. Snyder (ed.), *Coping with stress: effective people and processes* (pp. 7–29). New York: Oxford University Press.

Portes, A. & Rumbaut, R. G. (2001). Conclusion – the forging of a new America: lessons for theory and policy. In R. G. Rumbaut & A. Portes (eds.), *Children of immigrants in America* (pp. 301–318). Los Angeles: University of California Press.

Ressler, E. M., Boothby, N. & Steinbock, D. J. (1988). Separation, trauma, and intervention. In *Unaccompanied children: care and protection in wars, natural disaster, and refugee movements* (pp. 153–180). New York: Oxford University Press.

Rousseau, C., Bertot, J., Mekki-Berrada, A., Measham, T. & Drapeau, A. (2001). *Etude longitudinale du processus de réunification familiale chez les réfugiés* [Longitudinal study of the family reunification process among refugees]. Research report presented to the Quebec Council of Social Research. Montreal: McGill University Health Center.

Rousseau, C., Morales, M. & Foxen, P. (2001). Going home: giving voice to memory strategies of young Mayan refugees who returned to Guatemala as a community. *Culture, Medicine and Psychiatry, 25*, 135–168.

Rutter, M. (1993). Resilience: some conceptual considerations. *Journal of Adolescent Health, 14*, 626–631.

Schiff, B., Noy, C. & Cohler, B. J. (2001). Collected stories in the life narrative of Holocaust survivors. *Narrative Inquiry, 11*, 159–194.

Tousignant, M., Habimana, E., Biron, C., Malo, C., Sidoli-Leblanc, E. & Bendris, N. (1999). The Quebec Adolescent Refugee Project: psychopathology and family variables in a sample from 35 nations. *American Journal of the Academy of Child and Adolescent Psychiatry, 38*, 1426–1432.

29 Intercultural relations in plural societies

Colleen Ward & Chan-Hoong Leong

The review and synthesis of the global literature on intercultural relations in plural societies for an international handbook of acculturation is a daunting task. Not only is there a massive empirical database on this topic, but the underlying theory and research derive from quite separate and distinct traditions in social and cross-cultural psychology. The first strand originates from social psychological studies of inter-group perceptions and relations, particularly research undertaken in North American settings. This work draws on both field- and lab-based investigations and relies primarily on survey and experimental designs. Pertinent to this chapter are studies of established ethnic communities (e.g. Blacks, Whites and Hispanics in the United States) and more recent applications of social psychological theories to the analysis of inter-group relations between newly arrived immigrant groups and members of the receiving society (e.g., Indo- and Anglo-Canadians).

The second research tradition arises from theoretical and empirical work in cross-cultural psychology, most notably from studies of acculturation. This body of work has been more international in scope and relies more heavily on field-based than lab-based studies and on surveys rather than experimental interventions. Attention has conventionally been focused on the experiences and perspectives of acculturating groups such as immigrants, sojourners and refugees, rather than members of the receiving society; nevertheless, acculturation and inter-group relations are intertwined, and contemporary investigations of acculturation processes are now emerging from the perspective of host nationals.

Social and cross-cultural psychological theories converge to offer a comprehensive overview of intercultural relations in plural societies. These theories, which form the core of this chapter, are outlined in Table 29.1. Note that the table is not comprehensive in terms of the theories and models that *could be* applied to the analysis of acculturation and inter-group relations; instead, this chapter has concentrated on those theoretical frameworks that *have been* applied to real-world studies of ethnocultural groups in plural societies in international research.

Plural societies are made up of diverse ethnocultural groups, and the boundaries between them and the terms used to describe them are sometimes blurred. Migrant groups, for example, evolve into established ethnocultural communities, and they eventually become members of the host or receiving society

Table 29.1 *Theoretical approaches to the study of intercultural relations in plural societies*

RESEARCH TRADITIONS	GROUPS	
	Dominant ethnocultural groups	Non-dominant ethnocultural groups
Social psychology: inter-group research	• Integrated Threat Theory • Instrumental Model of Group Conflict	• Social Identity Theory
	• Contact hypothesis • Theory of Common Ingroup Identity	
Cross-cultural psychology: acculturation research	• Interactive Acculturation Model	• Model of acculturation attitudes

with respect to new settlers. Although the social psychological literature commonly refers to majority and minority groups, this nomenclature is not uniformly applicable across nations and cultures (e.g., Ward & Hewstone, 1986). The acculturation literature often discusses migrants and hosts, but these are not the only relevant terms, particularly as indigenous peoples have also been included in acculturation research (Berry, Kim, Minde & Mok, 1987). "Ethnocultural group" is a useful term for the consideration of intercultural relations in plural societies as this term is neutral, inclusive and does not make distinctions on the basis of social, political and economic status or migration history. Various terms will be used throughout this chapter, but "dominant ethnocultural groups" and "non-dominant ethnocultural groups" are used to make basic distinctions within a society as a whole, and "migrants" and "hosts" (or "members of the receiving society") are used more specifically in the context of migration research.

This chapter provides an overview of the international literature on intercultural relations in plural societies and draws on social psychological and cross-cultural theory and research to address the following questions.

1. What are the characteristics of inter-group relations in plural societies?
2. What factors influence the inter-group perceptions held by dominant groups and the relationships between them and members of non-dominant groups?
3. What are the antecedents, correlates and outcomes of perceived discrimination in non-dominant groups?
4. How do members of non-dominant acculturating groups manage issues of identity and relationships with members of the dominant group?
5. What acculturation expectations do members of the receiving society have for immigrant groups?
6. How can intercultural relations be improved in plural societies?

29.1   Inter-group processes in plural societies

29.1.1   Ethnocentrism

Ethnocentrism has been one of the most frequently studied aspects of inter-group relations, with differential evaluations of ingroups and outgroups commonly examined in terms of stereotypes and attributions. Stereotypes are widespread and readily accessible, and although outgroups may be perceived moderately positively, they are generally viewed less favorably than members of the ingroup. DeRoza and Ward (2005), for example, found ingroup favoritism in each of the four major ethnic groups in Singapore: Chinese, Malays, Indians and Eurasians. Research in Thailand has demonstrated ingroup favoritism by Thais in their perceptions of Hmong tribal peoples, Chinese minorities and American sojourners (Wibulswasdi, 1989). International research from Greece, Germany and the United States has also shown that members of the receiving societies hold less positive stereotypes of short- and long-term migrant groups than of their own group (Georgas, 1998; Kosmitzki, 1996; Triandis & Vassiliou, 1967).

Attribution research generally converges with studies of stereotypes and attitudes. Group-serving attributions, those that favor the ingroup and derogate the outgroup, have been commonly observed. More specifically, individuals are inclined to offer internal attributions for desirable behaviors and external attributions for undesirable behaviors of ingroup members, while the reverse is true for the causal attributions of outgroup behaviors. These outcomes have been observed cross-culturally in studies of religious and ethnocultural groups in India (Taylor & Jaggi, 1974), Malaysia, Singapore (Hewstone & Ward, 1985) and New Zealand (Lynskey, Ward & Fletcher, 1991), although there has been some variation across dominant and non-dominant group status and other socio-political conditions.

Inter-group contact has been explored as a means of reducing ethnocentrism, but research has shown that contact per se is insufficient to improve inter-group relations and that perceptual changes resulting from increased contact have been for the better and the worse. Amir and Ben-Ari (1988) reviewed the characteristics of inter-group contact that are most likely to result in enhanced inter-group relations (e.g., voluntary, equal status, pleasant, intimate, cooperative), and Islam and Hewstone (1993) demonstrated that it was the qualitative, rather than the quantitative, aspects of contact that were the strongest predictors of outgroup attitudes in their study of Hindus and Muslims in Bangladesh. Despite the mutually beneficial effects of positive inter-group contact, members of non-dominant groups, including sojourners, recent immigrants and ethnocultural minorities, are more willing to interact across ethnocultural lines than members of the dominant group (Ward, 2001).

The reduction of ethnocentrism has also been examined in connection with techniques designed to induce a common ingroup identity. Gaertner and colleagues have argued that ethocentrism and inter-group conflict can be diminished by interventions that shift cognitive representations of membership in ingroups and outgroups to an inclusive social identity within a single group (Gaertner, Dovidio & Bachman, 1996). Surveys of national identity and attitudes towards ethnic outgroups undertaken in Canada, Belgium and Singapore have lent support to Gaertner's model (Berry, 2000; Billiet, Maddens & Beerten, 2003; DeRoza & Ward, 2005).

29.1.2 Inter-group relations: "A view from the top"

To a large extent research has shown that members of receiving societies have more positive impressions of migrants who are ethnically, culturally and linguistically similar to themselves. New Zealanders, for example, hold significantly more favorable perceptions of immigrants from Australia and Great Britain, compared to those from Asia, the Pacific and Africa; however, indigenous Maori evaluate Samoan migrants more positively than do New Zealanders of European descent (Ward & Masgoret, 2004). Australians, on the whole, are more likely to recommend the restriction of immigration from Asia and the Middle East than from Great Britain and Southern Europe (Ho, Niles, Penney & Thomas, 1994). In Canada, British- and French-Canadians are seen as more acceptable than groups from Northern, Southern or Eastern Europe, who are, in turn, viewed as more acceptable than those from South and East Asia and the West Indies (Berry, 2000). Research from non-Western countries, however, has produced a somewhat different pattern of results, suggesting that there may be a global status hierarchy that also affects perceptions of immigrants. Research in Singapore, for example, has revealed more favorable responses to Americans than to Mainland Chinese, at least in the employment realm (Lim & Ward, 2004), and a similar study conducted in Malawi demonstrated a preference for Westerners compared to Africans from neighboring countries (Carr, Ehiobuche, Rugimbana & Munro, 1996).

The most systematic international investigations of inter-group relations in plural societies undertaken from the perspective of socially dominant groups have been studies by Stephan and colleagues testing the Integrated Threat Theory (ITT; Stephan & Stephan, 2000) and work by Esses and associates on the Instrumental Model of Group Conflict (IMGC; Esses, Jackson & Armstrong, 1998). Both theories highlight the significant role of threat in prejudice and discrimination, although the models differ in the relative emphasis placed on other factors such as stereotypes, inter-group anxiety, social dominance and zero sum beliefs. This is elaborated in the following sections.

29.1.2.1 Integrated Threat Theory

Drawing on a range of theories that emphasize cognition, comparison and conflict, and building on a solid base of empirical research (e.g., Berry, Kalin & Taylor, 1977; Levine & Campbell, 1972), ITT identifies four types of threat that play a significant role in precipitating prejudice: realistic threats, symbolic threats, inter-group anxiety and negative stereotyping. Realistic threats include perceived threats to the welfare of a group or its members. Symbolic threats are associated with values, beliefs and attitudes and are perceived to undermine or jeopardize the world-view of a group. Inter-group anxiety constitutes threat as it arises in response to fears of diminished self-concept and negative evaluations by others. Finally, negative stereotypes contain elements of threat in that they lead to the anticipation of negative events and interactions. Stephan and Stephan (2000) argue that these four threats predict outgroup attitudes, and their contentions have received substantial support in international research on migration.

Realistic threats, particularly the threat of job loss and increased social assistance to newcomers, are strong predictors of negative outgroup attitudes. Findings from American, Canadian and Spanish research converge on this point (Esses *et al.*, 1998; Stephan, Ybarra & Bachman, 1999; Stephan, Ybarra, Martínez, Schwarzwald & Tur-Kaspa, 1998). Unemployment trends are strongly related to opposition to immigration (Palmer, 1996), and Quillian's (1995) analysis of attitudes towards immigrants in twelve countries in the European Union noted that poorer economic conditions and large immigrant numbers predicted anti-immigrant attitudes.

Symbolic threat is also important and was a major predictor of attitudes towards Ethiopian immigrants in Israel (Stephan *et al.*, 1998). Similarly, stereotypes lead to prejudice and discrimination against immigrants as demonstrated by Ybarra and Stephan's (1994) study of attitudes towards Mexican Americans in the United States. Finally, inter-group anxiety has predicted negative attitudes towards Moroccan immigrants in Spain and Hindus in Muslim-dominated Bangladesh (Islam & Hewstone, 1993; Stephan *et al.*, 1998).

29.1.2.2 The Instrumental Model of Group Conflict

A more recent model for the analysis of relations between hosts and immigrants is the Instrumental Model of Group Conflict based on the work of Esses and colleagues (e.g., Esses *et al.*, 1998; Esses, Dovidio, Jackson & Armstrong, 2001). Inspired by realistic group conflict theory (LeVine & Campbell, 1972), the model identifies two conditions leading to inter-group antagonism. The first is resource stress or the "perception that, within a society, [that] access may be limited to certain groups" (Esses *et al.*, 1998:702). Resource stress may arise from limited resources, unequal access, and desire for or acceptance of unequal access based on a social hierarchy. The last of these three factors is regarded as an individual difference variable and is often discussed under the rubric of social dominance orientation. The second determinant of conflict is the presence of a relevant outgroup. The outgroup should be salient, distinctive and a viable competitor for valued resources. Salience and distinctiveness are accentuated by increasing numbers of outgroup members and by relevant outgroup characteristics (e.g., skills) for obtaining limited resources.

The combination of resource stress and a relevant outgroup results in inter-group competition and is accompanied by the cognitive and affective perception of threat. The cognitive component revolves around a zero-sum belief system, where there is a perception that any opportunities and benefits given to one group are regarded as directly reducing the concomitant opportunities and benefits available to the other, in essence, a zero-sum trade off between the two groups. The affective component encompasses the perceptions of fear and anxiety as a result of the challenges posed by outgroup competitors.

To resolve inter-group conflict, dominant groups can adopt a variety of strategies to remove the source of the competition. These include improving the actual or perceived performance or competitiveness of the ingroup, decreasing the performance of the outgroup by limiting their competitiveness or derogating their members, and avoiding or denying social comparisons between groups. The selection of strategy may reflect what is considered more convenient and appropriate in a particular cultural context. For example, to increase the actual competitiveness of a host national ingroup, skills re-training programs can be initiated; to reduce the competitiveness of an immigrant outgroup, discriminatory actions may be introduced. In either approach, the final objective is to reduce or remove the source of competition.

Esses' Canadian research, which examined the effects of experimental manipulations of characteristics of a fictitious immigrant group, found that more negative perceptions arose in response to immigrant competitiveness in a scarce labor market and as a function of participants' social dominance orientation (Esses, Jackson, Nolan & Armstrong, 1999). Later research similarly confirmed that zero-sum beliefs mediated the relationship between social dominance orientation and attitudes towards Asian and Black migration to the United States (Esses *et al.*, 2001). More recently, aspects of the Instrumental Model of Group Conflict, in particular the role of social dominance and zero-sum beliefs, have received support in both lab- and field-based studies in New Zealand, which have examined attitudes towards international students and new immigrants (Gezentsvey, Masgoret & Ward, 2004; Masgoret, 2004; Ward & Masgoret, 2004).

29.1.3 Inter-group relations: "Looking up and looking out"

29.1.3.1 Perceived discrimination

Research with non-dominant ethnocultural groups in plural societies has concentrated less on their attitudes towards members of the dominant group and more on their perceptions of personal and group discrimination. Along these lines investigations have shown that perceptions of discrimination vary considerably across acculturating individuals and groups. Over 80% of Korean migrants in Canada have acknowledged experiencing discrimination (Noh & Kaspar, 2003), and seven out of ten second-generation adolescent migrants in France reported feeling deeply affected by prejudice and discrimination (Malewska-Peyre, 1982). Cultural differences underpin such perceptions: greater cultural distance is associated with increased perceptions of discrimination (Sodowsky & Plake, 1992). In the United States East Asians are more likely to report discrimination than their peers of African, Latino or European descent (Fisher, Wallace & Fenton, 2000). In Finland, Arabs, Somalis and Turks perceived greater discrimination than Russians, Estonians and Vietnamese (Liebkind & Jasinskaja-Lahti, 2000). Nevertheless, even groups who are linguistically, ethnically and culturally similar to majority members of the host culture may feel socially disadvantaged. Ward and Leong (2005), for example, found that sojourners from the People's Republic of China perceived at least a moderate level of prejudice and discrimination in Singapore and that this was heightened with stronger ingroup identification.

Research typically reveals a higher reported incidence of group, as compared to personal, discrimination (Taylor, Wright, Moghaddam & Lalonde, 1990). But are perceptions of personal and group discrimination accurate and valid? It is likely that these perceptions are one view of reality and overlap with actual patterns of inter-group relations. There has been some suggestion, however, that incidences of personal discrimination are likely to be under-reported because of the psychological benefits of reacting this way (Finch, Kolody & Vega, 2000).

Discrimination perceived by new and successive generations of migrants has been associated with stronger ethnic identity, weaker national identity, and a lower commitment to the new culture. It has also been related to a variety of negative outcomes including increased stress, lowered self- and group esteem, impaired health, antisocial behaviors such as drug use and delinquency, identity conflict and poorer work adjustment and job satisfaction (Ward, Bochner & Furnham, 2001).

Perceived discrimination has been examined as a function of inter-group interactions, and findings have provided at least indirect support of the contact hypothesis. In general, increased contact with majority group members is associated with more positive inter-group perceptions, and decrements in perceived individual and group discrimination (Ward & Leong, 2005; Islam & Hewstone, 1993). However, there is also evidence that length of residence in a new country is linked to stronger perceptions of discrimination (Barry & Grilo, 2003; Liebkind & Jasinskaja-Lahti, 2000).

29.1.3.2 Dealing with prejudice and discrimination

How do non-dominant ethnocultural groups, sojourners, refugees, immigrants and native peoples, respond to prejudice and discrimination? Their choice of strategy is influenced by individual, group and societal factors, and Social Identity Theory (SIT) offers a perspective on the inter-group processes.

According to SIT (Tajfel, 1981), human beings tend to strive for positive distinctiveness through their membership in a particular social category. To achieve this objective, individuals engage in a process of *self-categorization*, relying on salient or contextually relevant cues that will define membership in the ingroup and outgroup. They then strive to enhance personal self-esteem through *social identification* with members of their ingroup. These processes are followed by *social comparison,* where ingroup members compare their group's status and performance with a relevant outgroup. If the comparison favors the ingroup, a sense of positive distinctiveness emerges. However, if the comparison places the ingroup in an unfavorable position, individuals may engage in either social mobility or social change strategies to improve their relative status.

Social mobility is likely to occur when the inter-group boundaries are seen as permeable. In this case, individual members of lower-status groups are able to dissociate from their negatively distinctive ingroup and "cross-over" to become a member of a higher-status group. "Switching" group membership takes place at the individual level, but the relative position of lower- and higher-status groups remains unchanged.

Social change is more likely to arise when the boundaries between dominant and non-dominant groups appear to be relatively stable and impermeable. The limitations imposed on lower-status group members by institutional and psychological constraints encourage them to rely on collective strategies to change the status quo, in order to achieve a sense of positive distinctiveness. Changes may result from successfully competing with members of the dominant group or by reframing evaluative aspects of group identity. In either event, collective strategies are used to improve the relative standing of all members of the non-dominant group.

Moghaddam, Taylor and Lalonde (1987) investigated these strategies in their study of Iranian immigrants in Canada. An individualistic approach, concerned primarily with personal social mobility rather than maintenance of cultural heritage, was adopted by one group. Collectivist strategies, including reliance upon the support of Iranian cultural organizations and the larger Iranian community to help with social advancement, were engaged by the others. These groups differed on a number of salient characteristics, including willingness to remain in Canada and perceived necessity of liaisons with the Iranian community. Most importantly, however, those who adopted collectivist strategies had a stronger belief in the justice and fairness of the Canadian system. Later research with Indian, Caribbean, Italian and Greek migrants to Canada suggested that members of visible minorities are more likely to prefer collectivist strategies (Lalonde & Cameron, 1993). The use of collectivist strategies is also associated with greater perceived group, as opposed to personal, discrimination (Moghaddam & Perreault, 1991).

Interestingly, it is not only ingroup perceptions that are important for social identity, but also "meta-perceptions," or how outgroups are believed to perceive the ingroup. Issues about own group, other groups and meta-perceptions are considered in greater detail from the perspective of non-dominant groups in the next section on acculturation models and strategies.

29.2   Acculturation processes in plural societies

29.2.1   Acculturation attitudes: immigrant and indigenous populations

The most popular model for examining acculturation attitudes has arisen from work by John Berry (1974, 1994) and is discussed in depth in Chapter 3. The model identifies four acculturation strategies: integration, separation, assimilation and marginalization. Berry and colleagues have produced persuasive evidence that integration is consistently the most favored acculturation response across sojourners, immigrants, refugees and native peoples (Berry, Kim, Power, Young & Bujaki, 1989; Berry, Wintrob, Sindell & Mawhinney, 1982; Donà & Berry, 1994). Not only is integration preferred by acculturating groups, it is also associated with better psychological and sociocultural adaptation in long- and short-term migrants and native peoples (Berry et al., 1987; Berry & Sam, 1997; Ward & Kennedy, 1994).

Although new settlers may prefer integration, what members of the host society permit necessarily influences the ultimate selection of acculturation strategies. For example, separation and marginalization are more likely to occur and assimilation is less likely to be adopted under conditions of greater perceived discrimination (Barry & Grilo, 2003). Evidence suggests that it is important to look beyond the acculturation attitudes of short- and long-term migrants to the acculturation expectations of members of the receiving society. The Interactive Acculturation Model by Bourhis, Moïse, Perreault and Sénécal (1997) provides an avenue for that line of research.

29.2.2   Acculturation expectations: national groups and members of receiving societies

Bourhis and colleagues have provided a framework to examine public policy and issues relating to immigrant and host community relations in the development of their Interactive Acculturation Model. The investigators begin by distinguishing four state ideologies that can be placed on a continuum: pluralist, civic, assimilationist and ethnist. They then go on to identity five acculturation orientations: integration, segregation, assimilation, exclusion and individualism, the first three being conceptually similar to Berry's (1994, 1997) notions of integration, separation and assimilation and the last two representing variations on marginalization. Although Berry discussed these four responses in terms of acculturation attitudes, linking them to the strategies used by non-dominant ethnocultural groups, he also broadly considered the acculturation expectations of members of the receiving society in his early work (Berry *et al.*, 1977) and more recently described these as multiculturalism, melting pot, segregation and exclusion orientations (Berry, 2001).

According to Bourhis *et al.* (1997), integration represents an accommodative approach in which host nationals believe that immigrants are entitled to preserve their heritage culture while simultaneously adopting aspects of the national culture. Those who endorse this strategy anticipate the gradual evolution of multicultural society. Host nationals who espouse segregation believe it is in the best interest of the larger community to separate immigrant cultures from the mainstream society. Those who support assimilation express a desire to see immigrants relinquish their heritage culture in favor of the one from their adopted homeland. Individualism is preferred by those who believe that there is no one right way to manage identity issues as individuals should be empowered to adopt any strategy that they see fit. Finally, exclusionism reflects the belief that immigration and immigrants are perilous to the national community and that the country would benefit most from a closed, as opposed to an open, immigration policy.

Bourhis and colleagues proposed that the acculturation expectations of host nationals vary as a function of political ideologies. Although this has not been systematically tested in multinational research, there is some empirical evidence that lends support to Bourhis *et al.*'s contention. Zick, Wagner, Van Dick and Petzel (2001) reported a preference for assimilation in German nationals and commented that this reflected the widespread anti-foreigner sentiment and the nation's closed-border immigration policy. Ward and Masgoret (2004), however, found a preference for integration in New Zealand, where there is a relatively high rate of immigration and a national policy of biculturalism. Dutch research has identified strong support for both integration and assimilation (Van Oudenhoven, Prins & Buunk, 1998).

Convergence between host and migrant acculturation preferences do not always occur, and Bourhis *et al.* have argued that dissimilar attitudes result in problematic or conflictual outcomes. Horenczyk's (1996) research revealed that both Russian migrants and Israeli hosts preferred integration, but tensions arose over assimilationist pressures. Members of the receiving community had a stronger preference for assimilation than did migrants; they also believed that migrants were more willing to assimilate than was actually the case. Van Oudenhoven *et al.* (1998) noted that Dutch nationals strongly endorsed both integration and assimilation, that they believed Moroccan and Turkish migrants favored separation, but that integration was actually preferred by both immigrant groups. The outcomes of host and migrant mismatches, however, have not been widely investigated. One exception to this is research with ethnic repatriates in Finland, Germany and Israel, which linked discordant acculturation preferences to greater perceived discrimination and increased psychological distress (Jasinskaja-Lahti, Liebkind, Horenczyk & Schmitz, 2003).

Variations in acculturation expectations have also been examined as a function of both immigrant characteristics and perceptions of threat. Florack, Piontkowski, Rohmann, Balzer and Perzig (2003) found that threat was associated with more ethnocentric acculturation expectations – assimilation, segregation and exclusion – in their examination of German attitudes towards Turkish immigrants. Montreuil and Bourhis (2001) highlighted the significance of social categorization, i.e., the perception of immigrant groups as "valued" or "devalued," in their study of attitudes towards immigration in Quebec. The research targeted migrant groups from France and Haiti in a survey of over 600 students in Canada. As hypothesized, integration and individualism were preferred when the would-be migrants originated from France. In the case of Haiti, however, segregation and exclusionism were most strongly advocated. Echabe and Gonzales (1996) found similar results in Spain when they asked a sample of Spanish nationals for their opinions about immigrants and the open border policy. When immigrants from Third World countries were anticipated, an opened, as compared to a closed, border was viewed more negatively. In contrast, when positive images of immigrants from other European countries were invoked, the open border was seen as more acceptable. These studies, along with some of the Asian and African research on ethnocentrism, suggest that further consideration of a possible global status hierarchy and its influence on immigration attitudes is warranted.

29.2.2.1   Cross-cultural studies of acculturation and inter-group relations

This chapter has provided a broad overview of the international literature on acculturation and inter-group relations and applied these to the understanding of intercultural relations in plural societies. While there has been a great amount of convergence across the empirical investigations, there is also evidence to suggest some culture-specific trends. A glaring gap in the literature concerns the cross-cultural analysis of inter-group and acculturation processes. To date, most studies have been undertaken in single countries, resulting in piecemeal and unsynthesized research, and the cross-cultural generalizability of theoretical formulations has not been adequately tested. For example, recent research has suggested that Social Identity Theory may not account as well for inter-group behaviors in collectivist societies (Yuki, 2003). Two cross-cultural projects that receive special attention in this section are the International Comparative Study of Ethnocultural Youth led by John Berry, Jean Phinney, David Sam and Paul Vedder, and the Cultural Level Analysis of Attitudes towards Immigrants and Multiculturalism by Chan-Hoong Leong.

29.2.3   The International Comparative Study of Ethnocultural Youth

The International Comparative Study of Ethnocultural Youth is a large thirteen-nation project involving host-national and immigrant adolescents and including over fifty ethnocultural groups. The participating countries are: Australia, Canada, Finland, France, Germany, Israel, the Netherlands, New Zealand, Norway, Portugal, Sweden, the United Kingdom and the United States. The project examines identity (ethnic and host-national), acculturation strategies (integration, separation, assimilation and marginalization), various values and attitudes (e.g. family obligations, children's rights), perceived discrimination, and psychological (symptoms, life satisfaction) and sociocultural (behavioral problems, school adjustment) outcomes. The project aims to assess both within- and between-country variation in these and other variables, and to construct a predictive model of psychological and sociocultural adaptation. Grand and comprehensive in its design and analysis, only a portion of the findings related to acculturation and inter-group relations will be described here.

A systematic examination of Berry's model of four acculturation strategies revealed that overall, integration was endorsed most strongly by both host-national and immigrant groups; however, stronger endorsement emerged in immigrants. Separation was the next preferred option for migrants; however, this was not uniform for all ethnocultural groups and in all countries. The Vietnamese in France, Norway, Sweden and the United States, for example, preferred assimilation as did the Turks in Finland and several groups in Portugal. In contrast to immigrant perspectives on acculturation, host-national youth more strongly endorsed assimilation than separation. Acculturation preferences were associated with inter-group relations more broadly; specifically, separation and marginalization were linked to greater perceived discrimination in migrant youth. Acculturation preferences were also related to psychological and sociocultural outcomes, with integrated youth experiencing the most positive outcomes.

Above and beyond the analysis of acculturation attitudes and expectations, the intercultural variables under examination were subjected to cluster analysis, yielding four profiles: integrated, national, ethnic and diffuse. The integrated profile was characterized by high endorsement of integration, low endorsement of marginalization, separation and assimilation, strong ethnic and host-national peer relations, high host-national language proficiency and average ethnic language proficiency. The ethnic profile reflected a strong orientation towards one's heritage culture, including high ethnic identity and language proficiency, endorsement of separation strategies, weak national identity, and few contacts with the host-national group. Ethnic youth were described as "embedded within their own cultural milieu and show[ing] little involvement with the larger society" (Berry, Phinney, Sam & Vedder, in press). This contrasts with the national profile where a strong orientation to the host society is apparent. Strong national identity, weak ethnic identity, and endorsement of assimilation were the primary characteristics of this group. In addition, host-national language proficiency was good and social contacts with members of the national group were common. The diffuse profile was associated with high proficiency and use of native language, but weak ethnic identity. Endorsement of the conflicting acculturation strategies of marginalization and assimilation suggests that these youth would like to be part of larger society but are lacking the skills to do so.

There was ample variation in the profiles across countries and groups. Integrated profiles were common in the United States (53.5%), United Kingdom (53%), Australia (51.1%) and Canada (50.4%). In contrast, Finland (44.1%) and Israel (40.3%) had the highest proportions of diffuse profiles. Furthermore, there was significant variation across groups within countries. Most importantly, the diffuse group demonstrated poor intercultural relations, reporting the most perceived discrimination; the integrated and national groups reported the least. Overall, this large-scale international study provided strong evidence of the preference for integration and the positive consequences arising from it. The project has also moved towards synthesizing and refining theory on acculturation and adaptation, which has been more commonly investigated in single-country studies.

29.2.4   A cultural level analysis of attitudes towards immigrants and multiculturalism

Leong's (2005) doctoral work offers other important cross-cultural insights into inter-group relations in plural societies through a cultural level analysis of attitudes towards immigrants and attitudes towards multiculturalism. This was accomplished by reliance on the archival data from the Eurobarometer Survey (Eurobarometer, 2000) and Hofstede's (1980) dimensions of cultural variability in examining the relations between culture (i.e., cultural level differences) and attitudes towards immigrants. The dimensions of cultural variability included: power distance (respect and deference based on position in a social hierarchy); uncertainty avoidance (the establishment of rules and regulations and the avoidance of change as a means of ensuring stability and dealing with life's uncertainties); individualism (the relative emphasis on personal over collective goals and choices); and masculinity (the relative emphasis on achievement over interpersonal harmony).

The Eurobarometer Survey is a public opinion research engine under the umbrella of the European Union. It has examined a diverse range of social attitudes in the fifteen European nations, and it lays claim to one of the most comprehensive and reliable databases from European polls. Based on a recent survey of racism and xenophobia (Eurobarometer, 2000), the open-source archival data revealed at least five factors pertinent to immigration attitudes: (1) blame – the extent to which respondents attribute their individual and social misfortune to new immigrants; (2) social coexistence – the level of support for policies to enhance social relations between host-national and migrant groups; (3) disturbance – the perception of psychological disturbance on the basis of immigrants' nationality, race and religion; (4) multicultural optimism – the recognition of the benefits of multiculturalism for national wellbeing; and

(5) cultural assimilation – preference for cultural assimilation over heritage retention.

Leong examined the relationship between national culture and attitudes to multiculturalism by correlating the country-level responses in the Eurobarometer study with their respective indices of Hofstede's four dimensions of cultural variability.[1] Results indicated that all measures of cultural variability were correlated with social coexistence, i.e., support for policies that enhance intergroup relations. Countries rated high on masculinity ($r = -.62$, $p < .05$), power distance ($r = -.55$, $p < .05$), and uncertainty avoidance ($r = -.76$, $p < .01$) and low on individualism ($r = .63$, $p < .05$) were less in favor of institutional policies that promote multiculturalism. In addition, masculinity was related to lower multicultural optimism ($r = -.69$, $p < .01$). More specifically, countries where achievement is valued over interpersonal harmony are less likely to show support for multiculturalism.

Analyses across the four cultural dimensions across the fourteen European nations, however, revealed significant multi-collinear relations between power distance and uncertainty avoidance ($r = .78$, $p < .01$) and between individualism and uncertainty avoidance ($r = -.68$, $p < .01$). Masculinity, on the other hand, was unrelated to the other measures of cultural variability; it was also the only domain that correlated with multicultural optimism. On that basis, Leong postulated that masculinity is the single and most parsimonious predictor of anti-immigrant attitudes.

29.3   Applications and concluding comments

"Diversity is a fact of life; whether it is the 'spice of life' or a significant irritant to people is the fundamental psychological, social, cultural and political issue of our times" (Berry, 2000:1).

Increased intercultural understanding and enhanced intercultural relations can be achieved by a number of routes. At the individual level, training has been used effectively to improve intercultural knowledge, attitudes and skills, including decreased stereotyping, increased world-mindedness, better intercultural problem-solving skills and greater enjoyment of intercultural relations (Ward, 2004). These techniques are discussed in detail in the following chapter.

At the institutional level, particularly in schools, the contact hypothesis has provided a framework for the implementation of programs utilizing cooperative learning techniques that have led not only to better academic performance but also to more intercultural friendships (Ward & Rzoska, 1994). The contact hypothesis also underpins research findings that attitudes towards ethnic outgroups improve as a function of their proportional representation in their neighborhoods (Berry, 2000), although it has been noted that this trend has been confined to groups that do not exceed 20% of the population. Of greater

[1] Luxembourg was eliminated from the analysis as it was not included in Hofstede's study.

interest in this chapter, however, are political discourse and national policies, particularly as articulated in the media, and their influences on intercultural perceptions and relations.

An excellent discussion of this is provided by Pratto and Lemieux (2001) in their analysis of the psychological ambiguity of immigration. They note that immigration is associated with two different and contradictory discourses – one of social inclusion and one of group threat. In terms of theorizing, the former may be associated with the Common Ingroup Identity Model where "framing immigration as an opportunity for group inclusion may induce empathy, which is associated with lower prejudice and discrimination" (Pratto & Lemieux, 2001:414). The latter discourse may be linked to Integrated Threat Theory, the Instrumental Model of Group Conflict and aspects of Social Identity Theory. Its converse is reflected in the "multicultural assumption" or the contention that a sense of security and confidence in one's identity lead to greater outgroup acceptance (Berry et al., 1977).

Pratto and Lemieux (2001) have convincingly demonstrated that political rhetoric affects immigration attitudes in a field experiment with Californian voters and their endorsement of immigration policy. Extrapolating from lab-based research, rhetoric that diminishes perceptions of threat and undermines zero-sum beliefs is likely to improve attitudes towards migrants, although, in the latter case, the positive effects may be limited to those low in social dominance orientation (Esses, Hodson & Dovidio, in press). Discourse that appeals to a sense of a common ingroup identity also precipitates more favorable impressions of immigrants (Esses et al., in press), and messages that depict immigrants as neither more nor less successful than host nationals in the labor market lead to more positive perceptions (Masgoret, 2004).

Societies that support maintenance of ethnocultural heritage while at the same time promoting a super-ordinate national identity show high levels of outgroup tolerance. Canada is a familiar example of this. Most residents identify as Canadians as opposed to by ethnic group, support for multiculturalism and outgroup tolerance is moderately high, and both have increased since the early 1990s (Berry, 2000). Research from Belgium has also shown that stronger national identity, couched in terms of a civic ideology respecting cultural diversity and encouraging inter-group harmony, is associated with more positive attitudes towards immigrants (Billiet et al., 2003). Similar trends have been observed in Singapore's multicultural society. There, research has shown that ethnic and national identity are strong and positively correlated in the four major ethnic groups, that Singaporeans typically refer to themselves in terms of a hyphenated identity (e.g., Singaporean-Chinese), and that stronger national identity is associated with more positive outgroup attitudes (De Roza & Ward, 2005). Indeed, the strategies adopted by the Singapore government to promote a multicultural and harmonious society after the racial turbulence of the 1960s have proven very successful.

At the individual level, there is abundant evidence that integration (i.e., maintenance of heritage culture and adoption of aspects of the larger national culture) is conducive to psychological and social wellbeing. When integration as an acculturation strategy is combined with the construction of national culture as an inclusive super-ordinate identity, this leads to benefits not only for individuals and ethnocultural groups, but also for plural societies more broadly. Integration at the individual and group levels, however, cannot be achieved without widespread acceptance of multiculturalism. With that in place, cultural diversity may be celebrated and intercultural relations in plural societies enhanced. Multiculturalism is the key to positive intercultural relations and holds the promise for the future in an era of increasing globalization.

29.4   References

Amir, Y. & Ben-Ari, R. (1988). A contingency approach for promoting intergroup relations. In J. W. Berry & R. C. Annis (eds.), *Ethnic psychology: research and practice with immigrants, refugees, native peoples, ethnic groups and sojourners* (pp. 287–296). Lisse, Netherlands: Swets & Zeitlinger.

Barry, D. T. & Grilo, C. M. (2003). Cultural, self-esteem and demographic correlates of perception of personal and group discrimination among East Asian immigrants. *American Journal of Ortho-psychiatry, 73*, 223–229.

Berry, J. W. (1974). Psychological aspects of cultural pluralism. *Topics in Culture Learning, 2*, 17–22.

 (1994). Acculturation and psychological adaptation. In A.-M. Bouvy, F. J. R. van de Vijver, P. Boski & P. Schmitz (eds.), *Journeys into cross-cultural psychology* (pp. 129–141). Lisse, Netherlands: Swets & Zeitlinger.

 (1997). Immigration, acculturation and adaptation. *Applied Psychology: An International Review, 46*, 5–34.

 (2000). Socio-psychological costs and benefits of multiculturalism: a view from Canada. In J. W. Dacyl & C. Westin (eds.), *Governance and cultural diversity* (pp. 1–89). Stockholm: UNESCO & CIEFO, Stockholm University.

 (2001). A psychology of immigration. *Journal of Social Issues, 57*, 615–631.

Berry, J. W., Kalin, R. & Taylor, D. M. (1977). *Multiculturalism and ethnic attitudes in Canada.* Ottawa: Minister of Supply and Services.

Berry, J. W., Kim, U., Minde, T. & Mok, D. (1987). Comparative studies of acculturative stress. *International Migration Review, 21*, 491–511.

Berry, J. W., Kim, U., Power, S., Young, M. & Bujaki, M. (1989). Acculturation attitudes in plural societies. *Applied Psychology, 38*, 185–206.

Berry, J. W., Phinney, J., Sam, D. L. & Vedder, P. (eds.) (2006). *Immigrant youth in cultural transition: acculturation, identity and adaptation across national contexts.* Mahwah, NJ: Lawrence Erlbaum Associates.

Berry, J. W. & Sam, D. (1997). Acculturation and adaptation. In J. W. Berry, M. H. Segall & C. Kağitçibaşi (eds.), *Handbook of cross-cultural psychology,* Vol. III: *Social behavior and applications* (pp. 291–326). Boston: Allyn & Bacon.

Berry, J. W., Wintrob, R., Sindell, P. S. & Mawhinney, T. A. (1982). Psychological adaptation to culture change among the James Bay Cree. *Naturaliste Canadien, 109*, 965–975.

Billiet, J., Maddens, B. & Beerten, R. (2003). National identity and attitude toward foreigners in a multinational state: a replication. *Political Psychology, 24*, 241–257.

Bourhis, R. Y., Moïse, C., Perreault, S. & Sénécal, S. (1997). Towards an interactive acculturation model: a social psychological approach. *International Journal of Psychology, 32*, 369–386.

Carr, S. C., Ehiobuche, I., Rugimbana, R. & Munro, D. (1996). Expatriates' ethnicity and their effectiveness: "similarity-attraction" or "inverse resonance?" *Psychology and Developing Societies, 8*, 177–197.

DeRoza, C. & Ward, C. (2005). National identity, ethnic identity and intergroup perceptions in Singapore. Manuscript submitted for publication.

Donà, G. & Berry, J. W. (1994). Acculturation attitudes and acculturative stress of Central American refugees. *International Journal of Psychology, 29*, 57–70.

Echabe, A. E. & Gonzales, J. (1996). Images of immigrants: a study on the xenophobia and permeability of intergroup boundaries. *European Journal of Social Psychology, 26*, 341–352.

Esses, V., Dovidio, J., Jackson, L. & Armstrong, T. (2001). The immigration dilemma: the role of perceived group competition, ethnic prejudice, and national identity. *Journal of Social Issues, 57*, 389–412.

Esses, V. M., Hodson, G. & Dovidio, J. F. (in press). Public attitudes toward immigrants and immigration: determinants and policy implications. In C. C. Beach, A. G. Green & J. G. Reitz (eds.), *Canadian immigration policy for the 21st century*. Kingston, Ontario: John Deutsch Institute, Queen's University.

Esses, V. M., Jackson, L. M. & Armstrong, T. L. (1998). Intergroup competition and attitudes toward immigrants and immigration. *Journal of Social Issues, 54*, 699–724.

Esses, V. M., Jackson, L. M., Nolan, J. M. & Armstrong, T. L. (1999). Economic threat and attitudes toward immigrants. In S. Halli & S. Drieger (eds.), *Immigrant Canada: demographic, economic and social challenges* (pp. 212–229). Toronto: University of Toronto Press.

Eurobarometer (2000). *Attitudes toward minority groups in the European Union: a special analysis of the Eurobarometer 2000 opinion poll on behalf of the European Monitoring Center on Racism and Xenophobia*. Eurobarometer Opinion Poll. http://europa.eu.int/comm/public_opinion/index_en.htm. Accessed September 1, 2003.

Finch, B. K., Kolody, B. & Vega, W. A. (2000). Perceived discrimination and depression among Mexican-origin adults in California. *Journal of Health and Social Behavior, 41*, 295–313.

Fisher, C. B., Wallace, S. A. & Fenton, R. E. (2000). Discrimination distress during adolescence. *Journal of Youth and Adolescence, 29*, 679–695.

Florack, A., Piontkowski, U., Rohmann, A., Balzer, T. & Perzig, S. (2003). Perceived intergroup threat and attitudes of host community members toward immigrant acculturation. *Journal of Social Psychology, 143*, 633–648.

Gaertner, S., Dovidio, J. & Bachman, B. A. (1996). Revisiting the contact hypothesis: the induction of a common in-group identity. *International Journal of Intercultural Relations, 20*, 271–290.

Georgas, J. (1998). Intergroup contact and acculturation of immigrants. Paper presented to the Fourteenth International Congress of the International Association for Cross-cultural Psychology, Bellingham, WA, August.

Gezentsvey, M., Masgoret, A.-M. & Ward, C. (2004). Attitudes toward international students and international education: a test of the Instrumental Model of Group Conflict. Paper presented to the Fourth International Conference of the International Academy of Intercultural Research, Taipei, Taiwan, May.

Hewstone, M. & Ward, C. (1985). Ethnocentrism and causal attribution in Southeast Asia. *Journal of Personality and Social Psychology*, *48*, 614–623.

Ho, R., Niles, S., Penney, R. & Thomas, A. (1994). Migrants and multiculturalism: a survey of attitudes in Darwin. *Australian Psychologist*, *29*, 62–70.

Hofstede, G. (1980). *Culture's consequences: international differences in work-related values*. Beverly Hills, CA: Sage Publications.

Horenczyk, G. (1996). Migrant identities in conflict: acculturation attitudes and perceived acculturation ideologies. In G. Breakwell & E. Lyons (eds.), *Changing European identities: social psychological analyses of social change* (pp. 241–250). Oxford: Butterworth-Heinemann.

Islam, R. M. & Hewstone, M. (1993). Dimensions of contact as predictors of intergroup anxiety, perceived out-group variability, and out-group attitude: an integrative model. *Personality and Social Psychology Bulletin*, *19*, 700–710.

Jasinskaja-Lahti, I., Liebkind, K., Horenczyk, G. & Schmitz, P. (2003). The interactive nature of acculturation: perceived discrimination, acculturation attitudes and stress among young ethnic repatriates in Finland, Israel and Germany. *International Journal of Intercultural Relations*, *27*, 79–90.

Kosmitzki, C. (1996). The reaffirmation of cultural identity in cross-cultural encounters. *Personality and Social Psychology Bulletin*, *22*, 238–248.

Lalonde, R. & Cameron, J. (1993). An intergroup perspective on immigrant acculturation with a focus on collective strategies. *International Journal of Psychology*, *28*, 57–74.

Leong, C.-H. (2005). A multi-level research framework for the analysis of attitudes toward immigrants. Unpublished Ph.D. thesis, Victoria University of Wellington, New Zealand.

LeVine, R. A. & Campbell, D. T. (1972). *Ethnocentrism: theories of conflict, ethnic attitudes, and group behavior*. New York: Wiley.

Liebkind, K. & Jasinskaja-Lahti, I. (2000). The influence of experiences of discrimination on psychological stress: a comparison of seven immigrant groups. *Journal of Community and Applied Social Psychology*, *10*, 1–16.

Lim, A. & Ward, C. (2004). The effects of nationality, length of residence and occupational demand on the perception of "foreign talent" in Singapore. In K. S. Yang, K. K. Hwang, P. Pedersen & I. Daibo (eds.), *Progress in Asian social psychology: conceptual and empirical contributions* (pp. 247–259). Westport, CT: Praeger.

Lynskey, M., Ward, C. & Fletcher, G. J. O. (1991). Stereotypes and intergroup attributions in New Zealand. *Psychology and Developing Societies*, *3*, 113–127.

Malewska-Peyre, H. (1982). L'expérience du racisme et de la xénophobie chez jeunes immigrés [The experience of racism and xenophobia in young immigrants]. In H. Malewska-Peyre (ed.), *Crise d'identité et déviance chez jeunes immigrés*

[Identity crisis and deviance in young immigrants] (pp. 53–73). Paris: La Documentation Française.

Masgoret, A.-M. (2004). Examining the bases of intergroup competition and its role in determining immigration attitudes in New Zealand. Paper presented to the Twenty-eighth International Congress of Psychology, Beijing, China, August.

Moghaddam, F. M. & Perreault, S. (1991). Individual and collective mobility strategies among minority group members. *Journal of Social Psychology*, *132*, 343–357.

Moghaddam, F. M., Taylor, D. & Lalonde, R. (1987). Individualistic and collectivistic integration strategies among Iranians in Canada. *International Journal of Psychology*, *22*, 301–313.

Montreuil, A. & Bourhis, R. (2001). Majority acculturation orientations toward "valued" and "devalued" immigrants. *Journal of Cross-Cultural Psychology*, *32*, 698–719.

Noh, S. & Kaspar, V. (2003). Perceived discrimination and depression: moderating effects of coping, acculturation and ethnic support. *American Journal of Public Health*, *93*, 232–238.

Palmer, D. L. (1996). Determinants of Canadian attitudes toward immigration: more than just racism? *Canadian Journal of Behavioral Science*, *28*, 180–192.

Pratto, F. & Lemieux, A. (2001). The psychological ambiguity of immigration and its implications for promoting immigration policy. *Journal of Social Issues*, *57*, 413–427.

Quillian, L. (1995). Prejudice as a group threat: population composition and anti-immigrant and racial prejudice in Europe. *American Sociological Review*, *60*, 586–611.

Sodowsky, G. R. & Plake, B. S. (1992). A study of acculturation differences among international people and suggestions for sensitivity to within-group differences. *Journal of Counseling and Development*, *71*, 53–59.

Stephan, W. G. & Stephan, C. W. (2000). An integrated threat theory of prejudice. In S. Oskamp (ed.), *Reducing prejudice and discrimination* (pp. 23–46). Hillsdale, NJ: Lawrence Erlbaum Associates.

Stephan, W. G., Ybarra, P. & Bachman, G. (1999). Prejudice toward immigrants: an integrated threat theory. *Journal of Applied Social Psychology*, *29*, 2221–2237.

Stephan, W. G., Ybarra, P., Martínez, C. M., Schwarzwald, J. & Tur-Kaspa, M. (1998). Prejudice toward immigrants to Spain and Israel: an integrated threat theory analysis. *Journal of Cross-Cultural Psychology*, *29*, 559–576.

Tajfel, H. (1981). *Human groups and social categories*. Cambridge: Cambridge University Press.

Taylor, D. M. & Jaggi, V. (1974). Ethocentrism in a South Indian context. *Journal of Cross-Cultural Psychology*, *5*, 162–172.

Taylor, D. M. & Moghaddam, F. M. (1987). *Theories of intergroup relations: international and social psychological perspectives*. New York: Praeger.

Taylor, D. M., Wright, S., Moghaddam, F. M. & Lalonde, R. (1990). The personal/group discrimination discrepancy: perceiving my group but not myself to be a target of discrimination. *Personality and Social Psychology Bulletin*, *16*, 254–262.

Triandis, H. C. & Vassiliou, V. (1967). Frequency of contact and stereotyping. *Journal of Personality and Social Psychology*, 7, 316–328.

Van Oudenhoven, J. P., Prins, K. S. & Buunk, B. P. (1998). Attitudes of minority and majority members towards adaptation of immigrants. *European Journal of Social Psychology*, 28, 995–1013.

Ward, C. (2001). The ABCs of acculturation. In D. Matsumoto (ed.), *The handbook of culture and psychology* (pp. 411–445). New York: Oxford University Press.

  (2004). Theories of culture contact and their implications for intercultural training and interventions. In D. Landis, J. M. Bennett & M. J. Bennett (eds.), *Handbook of intercultural training*. 3rd edn. (pp. 185–216). Thousand Oaks, CA: Sage Publications.

Ward, C., Bochner, S. & Furnham, A. (2001). *The psychology of culture shock*. London: Routledge.

Ward, C. & Hewstone, M. (1986). Ethnicity, language and intergroup relations in Malaysia and Singapore: a social psychological analysis. *Journal of Multilingual and Multicultural Development*, 6, 271–296.

Ward, C. & Kennedy, A. (1994). Acculturation strategies, psychological adjustment and socio-cultural competence during cross-cultural transitions. *International Journal of Intercultural Relations*, 18, 329–343.

Ward, C. & Leong, C.-H. (2005). Acculturation, identity and perceived discrimination: a study of Malaysian and P. R. C. Chinese in Singapore. In Y. Kashima, Y. Endo, E. S. Kashima, C. Leung & J. McClure (eds.), *Progress in Asian social psychology* (Vol. IV, pp. 125–138). Seoul: Kyoyook-Kwahak-Sa Publishing.

Ward, C. & Masgoret, A.-M. (2004). New Zealanders' attitudes toward immigrants and immigration. Paper presented to New Directions, New Settlers, New Challenges: Foundation for Science, Research and Technology End-users Seminar on Migration. Wellington, New Zealand, April.

Ward, C. & Rzoska, K. (1994). Cross-cultural perspectives on cooperation and competition: educational applications in plural societies. In E. Thomas (ed.), *International perspectives on culture and schooling* (pp. 455–482). London: University of London.

Wibulswasdi, P. (1989). The perception of group self-image and other ethnic group images among the Thai, Chinese, Thai Hmong hill tribes and Americans in the province of Chiang Mai. In D. M. Keats, D. Munro & L. Mann (eds.), *Heterogeneity in cross-cultural psychology* (pp. 204–209). Lisse, Netherlands: Swets & Zeitlinger.

Ybarra, O. & Stephan, W. (1994). Perceived threat as a predictor of stereotypes and prejudice: Americans' reactions to Mexican immigrants. *Boletin de Psicología*, 42, 39–54.

Yuki, M. (2003). Intergroup comparisons versus intragroup relationships: a crosscultural examination of Social Identity Theory in North American and East Asian cultural contexts. *Social Psychology Quarterly*, 66, 166–183.

Zick, A., Wagner, U., Van Dick, R. & Petzel, T. (2001). Acculturation and prejudice in Germany: majority and minority perspectives. *Journal of Social Issues*, 57, 541–557.

30 Intercultural training

Dharm P. S. Bhawuk, Dan Landis & Kevin D. Lo

A review of intercultural training literature shows that researchers have been preoccupied with identifying the best way to prepare people for international assignments or living abroad. This is natural to a new discipline as researchers search for tools to solve problems they face in their discipline. The lecture method did not serve the sojourners well, and thus other methods were explored. The experiential method was quite effective in sensitizing people to cultural differences, and complemented the lecture method well (Bhawuk, 1990; Harrison & Hopkins, 1967). The culture assimilator emerged as a tool to prepare sojourners better to learn to make isomorphic attribution, and emerged as the winner among intercultural training methods, and has been quite well researched (Albert, 1983; Bhawuk, 2001; Cushner & Landis, 1996). Triandis (1984) codified a theoretical approach to developing culture assimilators, and, following a somewhat similar approach, Brislin and colleagues developed the first culture-general assimilator (Brislin, Cushner, Cherrie & Yong, 1986). These developments, combined with the development of culture theories, led to some applications of the culture theory of individualism and collectivism to intercultural training (Bhawuk, 2001; Bhawuk & Brislin, 1992; Triandis, Brislin & Hui, 1988). There are many other examples of theoretical innovations (Black & Mendenhall, 1990), and the field has embraced theory quite passionately in the last decade or so (Bhawuk, 1998, 2001; Bhawuk & Triandis, 1996; Landis, Bennett & Bennett, 2004; Landis & Bhagat, 1996; Landis & Bhawuk, 2004), though the link between theory and practice has not always been clear.

Reviewing the intercultural training literature over its first fifty years, Bhawuk and Brislin (2000) identified four trends. First, they noted that the construct of culture shock (Oberg, 1960) was still being actively researched, which was reflected in the advances made in the theoretical conceptualization of culture shock (Triandis, 1994; Ward, Bochner & Furnham, 2001) and the interest in the development of an instrument to measure this construct (Mumford, 1998). Further refinement of theory and instruments of culture shock may lead to a better understanding of the process of intercultural adjustment. For example, one reason for culture shock is that sojourners break norms and receive negative reactions from hosts, but do not know exactly why. Future research on this construct may help us better understand the dynamics of such interactions, and how they lead to culture shock. This area of research would have interest for acculturation researchers as well. For example, extreme culture shock may be the cause of acculturation modes like marginalization, separation or assimilation (Berry, 1990), and, if so, training programs can effectively prepare people to adapt to the more productive acculturation path of integration.

Second, the development of the field of cross-cultural training shows that the field is evolving towards more theoretically meaningful training methods and tools, and these researchers expected that more theory-based training methods and material are likely to be developed (Bhawuk & Brislin, 2000). For example, the Individualism and Collectivism Assimilator (Bhawuk, 2001, 1995), theory-based exercises and simulations (Brislin & Yoshida, 1994; Cushner & Brislin, 1997), and behavior modeling types of programs (Harrisson, 1992; Landis, Brislin & Hulgus, 1985) based on social learning theory have emerged, and many such methods and materials are likely to emerge in the future. Culture assimilators are also likely to remain the most popular method as this tool has evolved from culture-specific to culture-general to culture theory-based format (Bhawuk, 2001, 1998), and many computer-based and multimedia assimilators (Bhawuk et al., 1999) are likely to emerge in future. This is another area where acculturation and intercultural training literatures could be gainfully bridged.

Third, it is likely that many more criterion measures will be developed in future to meet the demands of evaluating cross-cultural training programs (Bhawuk & Brislin, 2000). An inventory to measure sensitivity to cultural differences between individualist and collectivist cultures was one such dependent measure. This construct is particularly useful in bridging acculturation and intercultural training literatures, and we discuss it in the next section of the chapter. This would be especially important for intercultural training programs geared towards facilitating acculturation of people.

Finally, Bhawuk and Brislin speculated that we are likely to see the development of more innovative experiential exercises in the future. Practitioners are likely to encounter more sophisticated participants who have some exposure to cross-cultural issues through coursework at universities or through orientation programs conducted by international student offices in student dormitories. People are likely to have participated in popular simulations like *BAFA BAFA*, *Barnga*, *Albatross*, etc., or might have traveled abroad, making such simulations irrelevant, since the purpose of simulations is to sensitize participants to consequences of cultural differences experienced while living abroad. Thus, there would be an increased demand for newer and more sophisticated training tools, challenging both research and practice, and the experiential exercises are likely to become more complex, and would probably use more than one medium (e.g., audio, visual, discourse, models and so forth). Again, the field of acculturation is likely to spur various experiential programs for people choosing different acculturating modes or going through different phases of acculturation.

Landis and Bhawuk (2004) presented a theoretical framework in which they attempted to capture the process of intercultural training. Traversing backward from intercultural behavior, which is where the rubber meets the road, they showed how variables like host support, behavioral intentions, centrality of goals, intercultural sensitivity and many others come to impact intercultural interactions. This framework provides a meaningful meeting point between acculturation and intercultural training in that, ultimately, when people acculturate they are involved in intercultural interactions, and success or failure lies in how well they do in these interactions. The success or failure of intercultural training similarly lies in how well the trained sojourners involve in intercultural interactions. Also, the antecedent variables, and other process variables leading to intercultural behavior identified by Landis and Bhawuk (2004), impact people's decision about how they choose to acculturate.

Since there are many chapters in this volume that review the literature on acculturation, we do not delve into that here. We use Berry's (1990) four-part typology of acculturation as a model to demonstrate how to bridge the acculturation and intercultural training literatures. Starting with Berry's model, we accept that these acculturating strategies depend on whether the person chooses to value his or her own native cultural values more or less than the host cultural values (Separation or Assimilation), or decides to create a balance between the two (Integration), or fails to choose either of the two value systems (Marginalization). However, by synthesizing this model in the Landis & Bhawuk (2004) framework, we provide an integrated framework that shows how we can attempt to bridge these two disciplines. We also discuss how different intercultural training strategies may need to be used to deal with people who choose different acculturation strategies. We hope that this seminal attempt to synthesize these two disciplines will stimulate future research and benefit both the disciplines of intercultural training and of acculturation.

30.1   Intercultural sensitivity, acculturation and intercultural training

In attempting to define links between the intercultural training literature and acculturation literature, one necessary step is assessing a sojourner's or immigrant's potential for adaptation to a new culture. This assessment is necessary in both disciplines. For intercultural training, assessing the motivation levels of the trainees is critical, to ensure that they will experience some heightened level of success in their intercultural interactions following the training program. Any well-meaning trainer would consider how effectively the training program would reach out to the target audience. Traditionally, this assessment takes the form of screening and self-selection processes. However, there are also means by which to assess not only the motivation of trainees entering a training program, but also the degree of intercultural success they might be expected to experience based upon their intercultural sensitivity.

Various researchers have already developed scales by which to measure intercultural sensitivity. Bhawuk and Brislin (1992) developed the 46-item Intercultural Sensitivity Inventory (ICSI). The items in their ICSI arc behavioral and examine the following three dimensions of intercultural sensitivity: (i) differences in behavior as a function of being in an individualistic or collectivist culture, (ii) open-mindedness towards differences found in other cultures, and (iii) flexibility towards behaving in unfamiliar ways that are norms in other cultures. At the time when they were developing their scales, the intercultural training field recognized that intercultural sensitivity was highly important to the success of intercultural endeavors. However, at the time, researchers had also failed to develop a reliable means of measuring intercultural sensitivity. Their instrument took a step towards providing such an implement for the field. Tested on samples from the University of Hawaii College of Business Administration and the East-West Center, this scale also incorporates the cultural theory of individualism and collectivism as a starting point for people to start thinking about intercultural interactions. Overall, the study concluded that people could be motivated to alter their behaviors to be culturally specific and experience a greater level of intercultural success related to their tasks.

There are two generally accepted statements regarding intercultural training and global business. First, in the intercultural training field, trainers acknowledge that sojourners who are inadequately prepared for their work overseas or who lack intercultural sensitivity will experience difficulty completing their tasks (Bhawuk & Brislin, 2000; Dotlich, 1982). Second, global business has progressed to such a state that no country can dismiss the benefits, or necessity, of competing on a worldwide scale. By virtue of the second statement, it is expected that companies will be sending their employees abroad to compete in the global market. An understanding of the first statement suggests that when these people are sent on overseas assignments, their intercultural sensitivity and preparedness will factor heavily into the degree of success that they will experience while abroad.

Using the cultural theory of individualism and collectivism, as well as concepts of flexibility and open-mindedness that are regarded as critical to success in intercultural interactions, Bhawuk and Brislin (1992) developed their instrument, which is designed "to capture behaviors rather than attributes or traits" (p. 420). Based on voluntary participation and a self report questionnaire, testing their two sample populations revealed the following two findings that might be applied in principle to acculturation training.

First, intercultural sensitivity is correlated to number of years of intercultural experience. The findings in this study indicate that three years of intercultural interaction marks a period at which intercultural sensitivity generally increases. However, there was also indication that experience extending beyond this three-year period might be even more valuable.

Second, individualism and collectivism can be a starting point for getting people to start thinking about differences in intercultural interactions. Perhaps the acculturation literature could distinguish between novices, lay people, experts and advanced experts in the same way that Bhawuk (1998) differentiated between those who use cultural theories in an intercultural training context and those who do not.

For acculturation perhaps, the tools are less defined than in intercultural training. However, these findings might indicate that cultural theories should also be at the heart of acculturation training, and that it might take as long as three years of interaction between people of two cultures in the acculturation process before many of the intercultural misunderstandings and difficulties are ironed out.

Acculturation describes the changes that occur between individuals of different cultural origins as a result of continuous firsthand contact (Redfield, Linton & Herskovits, 1936). According to Ward (1996), acculturation can be viewed as either a state or a process. For the purposes of this chapter, it seems that the process view fits better with Berry's framework because it considers changes over time. When this view is adopted, some of the other variables that should be considered include: training and prior experience, intercultural communication and language fluency, expectations, social support, personality and cultural distance (Ward, 1996).

Another approach to intercultural sensitivity training comes from a model and the associated scale developed by Bennett and colleagues (Bennett, 1986; Hammer, Bennett & Wiseman, 2003). Bennett's model is quite close to both the intercultural training literature and the acculturation literature. According to Bennett, there are six different phases in the development of intercultural sensitivity. Moving from the ethnocentric to the ethnorelative these phases are: denial, defense, minimization, acceptance, adaptation and integration. Bennett's model can demonstrate the progression from different states of acculturation for both trainees in an intercultural training program and people acculturating in another culture.

"Denial" or "parochialism" refers to a situation where physical or social isolation precludes contact with another culture. Therefore, people tend not to perceive differences. Cultural activities that simply increase awareness of differences are the best strategy for moving towards defense. It is perhaps preferable at this stage not to discuss any large cross-cultural differences. Simple awareness of their existence is sufficient. "Defense" refers to the phase when individuals defend against the differences that threaten their own worldviews. Because there is acknowledgment of differences, defense represents higher intercultural sensitivity than denial. In the defense mode, individuals might likely create negative stereotypes (also known as "denigration of differences") or assume airs of cultural superiority that may typically manifest as openly hostile statements. These behaviors are difficult to change, but highlighting similarities between cultures, as well as precluding negative statements against other cultures, can help to elevate intercultural sensitivity.

Furthermore, discussing the functionality of differences in training programs might enable participants to understand the underlying causes of differences. If people understand that cultural differences frequently exist for a reason, rather than merely existing, there is an avenue for understanding the difference rather than simply finding a coping mechanism.

"Minimization" refers to negative, rather than overt, acknowledgment of cultural differences. Individuals in the minimization phase acknowledge cultural differences, then footnote their significance in favor of larger cultural similarities. Quite near the center on the ethnocentrism/ethnorelativism continuum, individuals in this phase of intercultural sensitivity development frequently adopt a universalistic world-view along the lines of "we are all children of God." Thus, there is the building of cross-cultural tolerance, but it remains superficial (almost "nicey nicey"). Reaching deeper levels of intercultural sensitivity requires additional attitudinal and behavioral shifts.

As the name suggests, in the acceptance stage individuals acknowledge and accept cross-cultural differences. As such, it represents the first move into the ethnorelativism stage. As an overall strategy for movement towards this phase, emphasizing the recognition of differences and respect without judgment is key. Empathy and cultural pluralism characterize adaptation. The empathetic responses which Bennett refers to seem to be akin to making isomorphic attributions in cross-cultural training. Clearly, this behavior represents a very deep cross-cultural sensitivity: one that allows the individual to think as a member of the other culture. "Adaptation" skills that will lead to the "Integration" stage need to be practiced in real-life situations. Finally, individuals who have attained the "integration" level of cultural sensitivity are able to "evaluate phenomena relative to cultural context" (Bennett, 1986:186). This ability also seems to mirror the ability to make isomorphic attributions in a cross-cultural training context.

One important feature of Bennett's model is that it includes "developmental strategies" that can also be considered as training strategies upon which people can design a training program. Perhaps matching up Bennett's model with Berry's model will further reveal possibilities for bridging the intercultural training and acculturation literatures. Table 30.1 provides such a matching.

Table 30.1 *Comparison of the Bennett and Berry models*

Bennett	Berry
Denial	Marginalization, Separation
Defense	Separation
Minimization	Assimilation
Acceptance, Adaptation	Towards Integration
Integration	Integration

A criticism of both models is that they generally fail to specify the antecedent conditions leading to each stage (Bennett) or acculturation strategy (Berry). It is to such a specification that we now turn.

30.2 An integrated model of acculturation and intercultural behavior process

In this section we synthesize Berry's model in the framework proposed by Landis and Bhawuk (2004) for bridging intercultural research and acculturation, which leads us to present an integrated process model of acculturation and intercultural training. The basic idea of the model is that variables like centrality of goals, past experience, intercultural sensitivity, and perceived differences in roles, norms and values are antecedents to the type of acculturation strategy chosen by people – namely, Integration, Assimilation, Separation and Marginalization (Berry & Kim, 1988) – and these in turn shape the behavioral intention, leading to the ultimate intercultural behavior. We view intercultural behavior as the final variable of interest to both intercultural training and acculturation researchers. Berry's model hardly needs elaboration in this *Handbook*, so we will start by discussing the antecedent variables, and then discuss the consequent variables.

30.2.1 Centrality of goals

We posit that centrality of goals shapes how people acculturate in a new culture. Most interactions have a functional component in them, and intercultural interactions are no exception. For example, a manager needs to run an international organization or a project, a student needs to earn a degree abroad, a volunteer needs to carry out a development project, a doctor or nurse needs to provide health care services, a peacekeeping force needs to maintain peace, and so forth. Therefore, it is reasonable to argue that tasks take the center stage in all intercultural interactions, and centrality of goal is likely to have direct impact on how people choose to acculturate. Also implied in the discussion of goals is the motivation level of those being trained. Thus, it would be prudent for designers of acculturation training programs to consider the motivation levels of those in the program.

In Locke's theory of goal setting (e.g., Locke & Latham, 2004, 1990), highly challenging goals produce better performance than easy or non-specific goals. There is also evidence that people have different orientations to goals (Dweck, 1986; Dweck & Leggett, 1988). People who have a learning orientation see the task as one of gaining mastery. When difficulty occurs, these individuals are likely to increase their effort even at the risk of increasing stress. A recent exploratory study has demonstrated that people with a learning orientation produced positive change in both academic and interaction behaviors, while those with a performance orientation only improved academically (Gong, 2003). Thus, based on centrality of goal, one's predisposition to learning or performance, and so forth, people are going to choose different strategies to acculturate. For example, the salesperson who wants to succeed may choose to change his name, or change the way he dresses or talks and so forth to fit in, or assimilate. However, a person who feels strongly about retaining his or her ethnic identity may choose not to do any of the above, and discard the goal of success as a salesperson or restrict such activity to culture mates. It is plausible that people who often do not have a central goal, or are confused about what their goal in the new culture should be are marginalized, and those who know their goals, but still want to balance the two cultures, follow the Integration strategy.

30.2.2 Past experience

Often the affective side of intercultural interactions is ignored. Past experience shapes affect in two ways: as a predisposition to be emotionally labile, or affective predisposition, and the display of actual emotional states or affective response. Additionally, the Stephans (C. Stephan & Stephan, 1992; W. Stephan & Stephan, 1985) have pointed to the intercultural interaction as being inherently anxiety-producing. Much research is needed to examine how past experience shapes affective predisposition, which in turn influences affective responses, and finally the acculturation strategy. However, it makes intuitive sense that a person who is extremely predisposed to show their emotions, and chooses to express them in intercultural interactions, is likely to experience separation or, in the extreme case, marginalization. On the other hand, a person whose past experience has shaped a less affective attitude, and who can choose to show affect less in intercultural interactions, is likely to follow the Integration or Assimilation strategy.

For the purposes of the trainers, careful efforts should be made to ascertain what past acculturation experiences trainees have had, because these experiences could strongly impact the trainees' perceptions and, thus, demand the use of different strategies. For example, negative past experiences might magnify the anxiety that the trainees are experiencing, and they may adopt marginalization, separation or assimilation as the mode of acculturation. Conversely, if a trainee has had positive past experiences, he or she may opt for the Integration strategy. Thus, past experience would shape the choice of acculturation strategy, which in turn would shape the choice of training methodology. It is also important to note that positive past experiences can mitigate the anxiety of negative past experiences, so trainers might consider highlighting positive past experiences to trainees. Once these determinations are made, they can deal with all the past experiences, both positive and negative, and move on to the next phase of the training program. One logical follow-up step in dealing with past experiences might be goal setting and establishing goal centrality, discussed in the previous section.

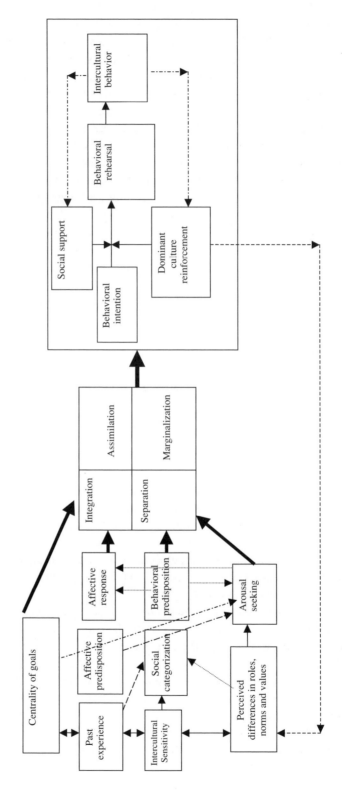

Figure 30.1 A model of acculturation and the intercultural behavior process (adapted from Landis & Bhawuk, 2004)

30.2.3 Intercultural sensitivity

Intercultural sensitivity can be viewed from the perspective of personality or as a set of acquirable skills. From the earliest development of interest in training for international assignments, researchers have searched for individual differences that could predict success in such situations (e.g., Kealey, 1996; Jasinskaja-Lahti & Liebkind, 2000; Mak & Tran, 2001). These efforts have met with mixed success. For example, Mak and Tran (2001) looked at the effect of the so-called "Big Five" personality dimensions on intercultural social self-efficacy and found that only extraversion and openness to experience had significant impacts. The weights, however, were fairly small. Ethnic identity, host language fluency and co-ethnic social self-efficacy had much stronger effects. Similar effects were found by Jasinskaja-Lahti & Liebkind (2000). One possible reason may be that the behaviors being examined tend to be rather specific, whereas the individual difference measures are far more diffuse and can apply to many situations. Another plausible reason is the presence of a number of intervening variables between the personal characteristics that the person brings to the situation and the actual intercultural behavior. Therefore, it should not be surprising to find the direct effect to be rather modest, at best.

Bennett and colleagues (Hammer, Bennett & Wiseman, 2003) view inter-cultural sensitivity as a stage that is malleable. People move from being ethnocentric to being ethnorelative, through denial, defense, minimization, acceptance, adaptation and integration, and a training program can help people make progress from one stage to another, towards ethnorelativism. These researchers use an instrument to recognize the stage that a person is in, and then suggest a suitable training program. In their approach, people who are in denial are given a different training program, compared to people who are in the stage of defense or adaptation. Matsumoto and colleagues (Matsumoto *et al.*, 2001) view intercultural sensitivity as a personality variable, and have developed a measure that correlates with other personality variables. Bhawuk and Brislin (1992) view intercultural sensitivity as the ability to recognize appropriate behaviors in a different culture, and to be able to enact those behaviors. These researchers use their intercultural sensitivity scale to sensitize people to differences between individualist and collectivist cultures, and encourage trainees to acquire the behaviors that they do not have in their repertoire. The tacit assumption in their model is that people need to identify culturally different behaviors, and then learn them through behavior modification.

There is some evidence coming from research on category width that those who are interculturally sensitive use social categorizations more broadly, and are thus able to accept cultural differences in behaviors and attitudes (Detweiler, 1980). Many attempts at reducing prejudice have focused on increasing the permeability of social categories (e.g. Shachar & Amir, 1996; Gaertner & Dovidio, 2000; Brewer & Gaertner, 2002). These studies have mostly assumed that the affect towards the ingroup is quite different from that directed at outgroups (Amir, 1959; Brewer, 1999; Allport, 1954). It is that difference that reinforces the strength of the boundaries. Accordingly, many studies have worked on changing the cognitions and affects associated with the outgroups so that they are seen as similar to the ingroup. These studies have worked generally when the two groups have been in a dominant/submissive relationship (e.g., Caucasian/African-American; Israeli/Arab, etc.). Therefore, we suggest that intercultural sensitivity is an antecedent of social categorization, which in turn shapes the behavioral predisposition of people. The least sensitive people are likely to have rigid social categories and behavioral predisposition, and are likely either to choose Separation or Marginalization as their acculturation strategy. Interculturally sensitive people are, on the other hand, likely to have broader social categories and behavior predisposition, and are likely to choose Assimilation or Integration as their acculturating strategy.

30.2.4 Perceived differences

Triandis (1972) suggested that the greater the perceived differences in subjective culture, the greater will be the affective reaction. In the acculturation paradigm, the more different individuals perceive their culture to be from the dominant culture, the more anxiety they will experience both in simple interactions and in trying to bridge the gap. At the extreme, a large perceived difference might lead to a form of paralysis, in which the individual sees the two cultures as impossibly different. In cases such as these, the individual might be inclined to give up, because the personal change required to bridge the difference is too large to make the effort worthwhile. The possibility of failure might also be a strong deterrent to making these efforts. Individuals facing large perceived differences might, therefore, choose the Separation or Marginalization strategies.

Ward and Searle (1991) empirically demonstrated the phenomenon described above. Their findings support the cultural distance hypothesis that cultural distance and psychological disturbances are interrelated. Such findings are largely intuitive, but the principles should be incorporated into acculturation training programs. Paying special attention to the needs of trainees who perceive large cultural differences, and must therefore work harder and make more changes to acculturate, should be on the checklist of those designing acculturation training programs.

We suggest that at some optimum level of difference the individual will seek greater information, even at the risk of increasing levels of stress. At a point above this level, the arousal seeking will decrease and the person will seek to return to earlier homeostatic levels. The trajectory we propose bears similarity to the Yerkes-Dodson curve relating motivation to performance (Spence, 1951). Thus, depending on the perceived cultural difference between the acculturating person and the dominant culture, the individual is likely to experience separation or marginalization if the cultural difference is immense,

Table 30.2 *Relationship of acculturative strategies and psychological antecedents*

	Marginalization	Separation	Integration	Assimilation
Goal centrality	(−)	(−)	(+)	(+)
Intercultural sensitivity	(−)	(−)	Moderate	Low to moderate
Perceived differences	(+)	High	Moderate	(++)
Past experiences	0 or (−)	(−)	(+)	0

but if the culture difference is not that stunning, he/she is likely to sample Assimilation or Integration strategies.

In order to reduce the perceived differences between cultures, program designers and trainers might elect to focus on differences at the individual level, rather than the cultural level, and also highlight the functionality of differences. Contextualizing differences and providing a reason for their existence makes for better cognitive acquisition and understanding of concepts rather than simply stating that cultural differences exist and leaving the trainees to wrestle with them.

All these four sets of antecedent variables are likely to interact with each other, and the interaction can finally lead one to choose one of the acculturating strategies. For example, if a person is driven by their goals, then despite the negative influence of past experience, lack of intercultural sensitivity and large perceived differences in values, he or she may choose to follow the Integration or Assimilation strategy. Similarly, an immense gap in perceived difference in values may lead one to choose a Separation or Marginalization strategy, despite positive past experience, goal centrality and ability to be interculturally sensitive. Table 30.2 summarizes the antecedents of acculturation and the respective strategies that they might lead to.

Referring to Table 30.2, we hypothesize, for example, that marginalized individuals will have few, if any, relevant goals, poor intercultural sensitivity, perceived clear differences between the home and host cultures, and have neutral to negative past experiences. Separatist individuals are similar to marginalized except that the differences between the two cultures are perceived to be greater and have led to negative past experiences. Similar hypotheses can be drawn for the last two Berry categories. Having discussed the antecedents that may shape the acculturating strategies of an individual, we now turn to the consequences of choosing these strategies on intercultural behaviors.

30.2.5 Behavioral intention, rehearsal and intercultural behavior

As one chooses an acculturating strategy, this will shape one's behavioral intention, which would ultimately shape the intercultural behavior. The relationship between behavioral intention and intercultural behavior is derived from attitude research where it is quite well established that behavioral intention is the best predictor of a behavior (Fishbein & Ajzen, 1975). It is important that intercultural behaviors are measured directly and not through self-report questionnaires, which are necessarily affected by memory and demand characteristics. Such behaviors can be measured using host ratings, or actual observations by research personnel. Another technique can be adapted from personnel psychology, in which employees are rated by themselves, as well as by their peers, subordinates and superiors: the so-called "360 degrees" approach. It is also desirable to assess intercultural behaviors at various periods during the sojourn, much as Ward (1996) has done.

Social support has a number of meanings, and is viewed as a moderator variable in the model. A skein of mechanisms provided by the home culture or organization is one such meaning. Personal support by a trailing spouse and other family members is another. In any case, this is an under-researched variable (Landis & Wasilewski, 1999; De Verthelyi, 1995; Fontaine, 1996). There is some research pointing to the importance of the wellbeing of the trailing spouse for the expatriate sojourner, but it is preliminary and the findings to date are not strong. Also unstudied is the impact of cross-cultural marriages on successful intercultural behaviors. To be sure, there are considerable data on dual-culture marriages (Baldwin, 1995), but these researchers have not linked such arrangements to the intercultural situation.

Dominant culture reinforcement is another significant moderator of intercultural behavior. In the acculturation and diversity literature, the role of public and organizational policies in helping the migrants have been emphasized (Triandis *et al.*, 1988; Bhawuk, Podsiadlowski, Graf & Triandis, 2002). For example, the Canadian multicultural policy has been lauded for facilitating inter-group interaction between Native populations in Canada, as well as migrants from other parts of the world. Similarly, most theories in intercultural adaptation suggest that what the host does, and how often he or she does it, is important to the sojourner, but this aspect has been quite difficult to measure. A recent study by Ward and Rana-Deuba (2000) found that the quality, rather than the quantity, of the host's behavior is a predictor of total mood disturbance in the sojourner.

We propose that behavioral rehearsal is necessary in the intercultural context, because people are acquiring new behaviors from another culture, and acquisition of such behaviors necessarily follows the social learning theory (Bandura, 1977). The acquisition of these new cultural behaviors will be moderated by social support as well as host reinforcement. If spouse and other family members as well as the expatriate or migrant community, as may be the case, support the target person in acquiring these new behaviors, the person is likely to do a better job of learning them. Similarly, if the host nationals or members of the dominant culture support the acquisition of the new behaviors, and encourage the target person, then the learning process is likely to be more effective. These ideas can be tested for a number of intercultural behaviors, from learning foreign languages, to learning gestures and body language, to acquiring work-related behaviors.

30.3 Matching acculturation strategy and intercultural training approaches

Researchers have examined the effectiveness of different training tools (Bhawuk, 1998), and how combining different intercultural training methods could lead to effectiveness in preparing people for international assignments (Landis, Brislin & Hulgus, 1985; Harrisson, 1992). Though the basic idea that different training approaches should be used is well accepted, there is no clear guidance from either researchers or seasoned practitioners about how we should approach people who are going through different phases of acculturation or are employing different acculturating strategies. By using Berry's four-part acculturation typology and three different types of intercultural training approaches – cognitive, affective and behavioral – we explore what sequence may be theoretically most meaningful. Although we talk about cognitive, affective and behavioral modes of training, it is important to recognize that the *content* of the technique will be governed by the lacks in antecedent conditions described above.

People who are marginalized are likely to experience emotional stress, since they are not able to accept the dominant cultural values, and are also not able to stand up for their own cultural values and the associated way of life. People going through such an emotional upheaval need therapy or counseling, depending on the severity of their inability to adjust in the dominant culture. Thus, it seems plausible that we should approach people using marginalization strategy with affective intercultural training first. Only when people are able to gain emotional balance can we start with cognitive training to provide them with an explanation of why they were experiencing the cultural conflict. Once they have become emotionally stable, and have acquired the necessary cognitive framework to deal with cultural differences, then we could provide behavioral training so that they can start changing their behaviors, and learning new behaviors that are culturally appropriate. Thus, for Marginalization strategy, we should use first affective, then cognitive, and finally behavioral training approaches. We should also use smaller differences to increase awareness, which is consistent with Bennett's recommendation.

For people who are using the Separation strategy, we should start with the cognitive approach to be able to provide them a mental framework to deal with cultural differences. Once they have acquired the cognitive framework, we can help them learn behaviors to concretize the learning, and also to provide them positive reinforcement for learning new behaviors, because only if they learn new behaviors are they going to receive support from the members of

Table 30.3 *Order of affective, cognitive and behavioral training approaches as a function of acculturative strategy*

	Affective	Cognitive	Behavioral
Marginalization	X————→	————→	————→
Separation		X———————→	
←			
Assimilation	←———————	←———————	←——————X
Integration		X————→	
←			

the dominant culture. Once they start developing a network by interacting with people of the dominant culture, they could be provided training to deal with the emotional issues. Thus, it seems appropriate to start with a cognitive training for those who are using the Separation strategy, then use behavioral training, and finally provide affective training.

Those who are using the Assimilation strategy are ready to change, and eager to learn new behaviors. Starting with behavioral training in this case may help the learning motive of these people. Thus, it may be best to start with behavioral training so that the participants feel the trainers are responsive to their needs. Once the trainees are making good progress in learning new behaviors, they should be provided with cognitive training so that they can develop a framework to appreciate cultural differences. Finally, they can be provided with affective training to help them deal with the emotional issues of sacrificing one's cultural values to assimilate completely in the dominant culture.

Finally, those who are using the Integration strategy are likely to have thought through the issues of acculturation, and, therefore, it may be best to start the training program with discussion to help them further develop their framework. This should be followed by behavioral training, so that they get to practice what they have thought about and start interacting with the dominant culture, as well as their own ethnic group, to maintain a healthy balance between the two. Finally, affective training should be provided to help them confront the tough emotional issues related to cultural differences. Affective training could address the core of their values as this group of people is likely to be ready to confront themselves with serious questions pertaining to their values and adaptation.

It should be noted that the training strategies for people adopting Separation or Integration modes of acculturation are in the same sequence, whereas the strategies for Marginalization and Assimilation are exactly the opposite of each other. Table 30.3 shows the suggested order in which affective, behavioral and cognitive training should be used for each of the acculturation strategies. Interestingly, in all phases except for Marginalization, the affective strategy is recommended to be the last to be dealt with, especially since it does require

Table 30.4 *Suggested training techniques as a joint function of acculturative strategy and best training approach*

	Affective	Behavioral	Cognitive
Goal Centrality	Fowler and Mumford (1995:Ch. 3, "Role play"); Self-awareness inventories (Fowler & Mumford, 1999:Chs. 3–5), Cold water (Fowler & Mumford, 1999:Ch. 12)	Draw a house (Pedersen, 1999)	Culture theory-I/C Cushner and Brislin (1997:Ch. 3)
Perceived Differences	Talk about differences in a neutral context, Contrast-American technique, Cushner and Brislin (1997:Ch. 4)	Experiential exercises (BAFA BAFA; Shirts, 1973), videotapes (Fowler & Mumford, 1999:Chs. 8–10)	Explain functionality of differences, cultural assimilators, Brislin and Yoshida (1994:Ch. 13)
Intercultural Sensitivity	Piglish (Fowler and Mumford, 1999:Ch. 15), Visual imagery (Fowler & Mumford, 1999:Ch. 20), Cushner and Brislin (1997: Ch. 12)	Experiential exercises	University Model, cultural assimilators, Cushner and Brislin (1997:Ch. 6)
Past Experiences	Talk about them in a neutral context. Therapy in extreme cases, inoculation techniques. Use of film to reduce affectivity of past experiences.	Experiential exercises, role playing, simulations	Journal, documenting past experiences

some preparation to deal with emotional issues. It seems that Integration would be the ideal acculturating strategy since it goes beyond tolerance of other cultures, and people are likely to become bicultural or multicultural in their thinking and being. It may not be ethical to advise people to move towards Integration, but, hopefully, with cognitive, affective and behavioral training given in the right sequence, people would gravitate towards the Integration mode, which would help foster multicultural societies.

We reviewed the literature further to examine what training techniques and tools were available, and how they could be used effectively, given the framework we have proposed above. We provide a summary of suggested training techniques as a joint function of acculturative strategy and best training approach in Table 30.4. This should help practitioners to use the existing training tools in a theoretically rigorous manner, following the ideas discussed in this chapter.

30.4 Conclusions

Intercultural training researchers have been concerned about the development of the best training approach for most of the past fifty years, as much as they have been concerned about the evaluation of the effectiveness of intercultural training programs. This might have been because the field has been in its early phase of development, and needed to create its identity and defend its turf. With the *Handbook of Intercultural Training* in its third edition, the *International Journal of Intercultural Relations* in its twenty-eighth year, and the International Academy for Intercultural Research having held its fourth biannual conference in 2005, the discipline of intercultural training needs to go beyond fear of identity crisis. The discipline needs to boldly start building bridges between associated research disciplines. We take the first step towards this goal, and have attempted to build a bridge between the disciplines of intercultural training and acculturation. Another example of how bridging disciplines using the principles from intercultural training might be possible can be found in Brislin and Kim (2003). They discuss how cultures can differ on ten different dimensions of time including (but not limited to): clock vs. event time, monochronic vs. polychronic time, punctuality, fast vs. slow paces of life, and time orientation (past, present or future). An intercultural training program that uses time as its central construct of focus would follow the same spirit of bridging disciplines that we have advocated in this chapter.

We noted various applications of the theory of individualism and collectivism in intercultural training, and suggested that perhaps acculturation literature should also take advantage of this theory more rigorously, which would further help us bridge the two disciplines through a common theoretical foundation. We also attempted to connect intercultural sensitivity and acculturation literature by showing commonality between Bhawuk and Brislin's approach to intercultural sensitivity, and Bennett's model of intercultural development. We hope in future researchers would further examine these and other constructs more closely to establish a relationship between intercultural training and acculturation.

We attempted to integrate Berry's four-part typology of acculturation strategies into a theoretical framework developed by Landis and Bhawuk (2004), and this seems to open new avenues towards synthesizing these two disciplines. This approach may also serve to bridge intercultural training and other research disciplines like sojourner adaptation, stress management techniques and learning theories.

Finally, we also explored how different training tools could be effectively used to train people who are using different acculturating strategies. It is reasonable to treat those who are using an Integration strategy differently from those who are using Marginalization, Separation, or Assimilation. We hope scholars will examine our ideas and test some of them in future research so that we can advance the field of intercultural training and acculturation together.

30.5 References

Albert, R. D. (1983). The intercultural sensitizer or culture assimilator: a cognitive approach. In D. Landis & R. W. Brislin (eds.), *Handbook of intercultural training: issues in training methodology* (Vol. II, pp. 186–217). New York: Pergamon.

Allport, G. (1954). *The nature of prejudice*. Cambridge, MA: Addison-Wesley.

Amir, Y. (1959). Contact hypothesis in ethnic relations. *Psychology Bulletin, 71,* 319–342.

Baldwin, J. (1995). Dual-culture marriages: an annotated bibliography. Unpublished manuscript.

Bandura, A. (1977). *Social learning theory*. Englewood Cliffs, NJ: Prentice-Hall.

Bennett, M. J. (1986). A developmental approach to training for intercultural sensitivity. *International Journal of Intercultural Relations, 10,* 179–195.

Berry, J. W. (1990). Psychology of acculturation: understanding individuals moving between cultures. In R. W. Brislin (ed.), *Applied cross-cultural psychology* (pp. 232–253). Newbury Park, CA: Sage Publications.

Berry, J. W. & Kim, U. (1988). Acculturation and mental health. In P. Dasen, J. W. Berry & N. Sartorius (eds.), *Health and cross-cultural psychology* (pp. 207–236). London: Sage Publications.

Bhawuk, D. P. S. (1990). Cross-cultural orientation programs. In R. W. Brislin (ed.), *Applied cross-cultural psychology* (pp. 325–346). Newbury Park, CA: Sage Publications.

(1995). The role of culture theory in cross-cultural training: a comparative evaluation of culture-specific, culture-general, and theory-based assimilators. Unpublished doctoral dissertation, University of Illinois at Urbana-Champaign.

(1998). The role of culture theory in cross-cultural training: a multimethod study of culture-specific, culture-general, and culture theory-based assimilators. *Journal of Cross-Cultural Psychology, 29(5),* 630–655.

(2001). Evolution of culture assimilators: toward theory-based assimilators. *International Journal of Intercultural Relations, 25(2),* 141–163.

Bhawuk, D. P. S. & Brislin, R. W. (1992). The measurement of intercultural sensitivity using the concepts of individualism and collectivism. *International Journal of Intercultural Relations, 16,* 413–436.

(2000). Cross-cultural training: a review. *Applied Psychology: An International Review, 49(1),* 162–191.

Bhawuk, D. P. S., Lim, K., Copeland, J., White, B. & Yoshida, W. (1999). *Multimedia individualism and collectivism assimilator*, a one-hour CD-ROM cross-cultural training program.

Bhawuk, D. P. S., Podsiadlowski, A., Graf, J. & Triandis, H. C. (2002). Corporate strategies for managing diversity in the global workplace. In G. R. Ferris, M. R. Buckley & D. B. Fedor (eds.), *Human resource management: perspectives, context, functions, and outcomes.* 4th edn. (pp. 112–145). Englewood Cliffs, NJ: Prentice-Hall.

Bhawuk, D. P. S. & Triandis, H. C. (1996). The role of culture theory in the study of culture and intercultural training. In D. Landis & R. Bhagat (eds.), *Handbook of intercultural training.* 2nd edn. (pp. 17–34). Newbury Park, CA: Sage Publications.

Black, J. S. & Mendenhall, M. (1990). Cross-cultural training effectiveness: a review and theoretical framework for future research. *American Management Review, 15,* 113–136.

Brewer, M. (1999). The psychology of prejudice: ingroup love or outgroup hate? *Journal of Social Issues, 55(3),* 429–444.

Brewer, M. & Gaertner, S. (2002). Toward the reduction of prejudice: intergroup contact and social categorization. In R. J. Brown & S. Gaertner (eds.), *Blackwell handbook of social psychology: intergroup processes.* Oxford: Blackwell.

Brislin, R. W., Cushner, K., Cherrie, C. & Yong, M. (1986). *Intercultural interactions: a practical guide.* Beverly Hills, CA: Sage Publications.

Brislin, R. & Kim, E. (2003). Cultural diversity in people's understanding and use of time. *Applied Psychology: An International Review, 52,* 363–382.

Brislin, R. W. & Yoshida, T. (eds.) (1994). *Improving intercultural interactions: models for cross-cultural training programs.* Thousand Oaks, CA: Sage Publications.

Cushner, K. & Brislin, R. W. (eds.) (1997). *Improving intercultural interactions: models for cross-cultural training programs,* Vol. II. Thousand Oaks, CA: Sage Publications.

Cushner, K. & Landis, D. (1996). The intercultural sensitizer. In D. Landis & R. Bhagat (eds.), *Handbook of intercultural training.* 2nd edn. (pp. 185–202). Thousand Oaks, CA: Sage Publications.

Detweiler, R. (1980). Intercultural interaction and the categorization process: a conceptual analysis and behavioral outcome. *International Journal of Intercultural Relations, 4,* 275–295.

De Verthelyi, R. (1995). International students' spouses: invisible sojourners in the culture shock literature. *International Journal of Intercultural Relations, 19,* 387–412.

Dotlich, D. (1982). International and intercultural management development. *Training and Development Journal, 36(10),* 26–31.

Dweck, C. (1986). Motivational processes affecting learning. *American Psychologist, 41,* 1040–1048.

Dweck, C. & Leggett, E. (1988). A social-cognitive approach to motivation and personality. *Psychological Review, 95,* 256–273.

Fishbein, M. & Ajzen, I. (1975). *Belief, attitude, intention, and behavior: an introduction to theory and research.* Reading, MA: Addison-Wesley.

Fontaine, G. (1996). Social support and the challenges of international assignments. In D. Landis & R. Bhagat (eds.), *Handbook of intercultural training.* 2nd edn. (pp. 264–282). Thousand Oaks, CA: Sage Publications.

Fowler, S. & Mumford, M. (eds.) (1995). *Intercultural sourcebook: cross-cultural training methods,* Vol. I. Yarmouth, ME: Intercultural Press.

(eds.) (1999). *Intercultural sourcebook: cross-cultural training methods,* Vol. II. Yarmouth, ME: Intercultural Press.

Gaertner, S. & Dovidio, J. (2000). *Reducing intergroup bias: the common ingroup identity model.* Philadelphia, PA: Taylor and Francis.

Gong, Y. (2003). Goal orientations and cross-cultural adjustment: an exploratory study. *International Journal of Intercultural Relations, 27,* 297–305.

Hammer, M., Bennett, M. & Wiseman, R. (2003). Measuring intercultural sensitivity: the intercultural development inventory. *International Journal of Intercultural Relations, 27,* 421–444.

Harrison, R. & Hopkins, R. L. (1967). The design of cross-cultural training: an alternative to the university model. *Journal of Applied Behavioral Science, 3,* 431–460.

Harrisson, J. K. (1992). Individual and combined effects of behavior modeling and the culture assimilator in cross-cultural management training. *Journal of Applied Psychology, 77,* 952–962.

Jasinskaja-Lahti, I. & Liebkind, K. (2000). Predictors of the actual degree of acculturation of Russian-speaking immigrant adolescents in Finland. *International Journal of Intercultural Relations, 24,* 503–518.

Kealey, D. (1996). The challenge of international personnel selection. In D. Landis & R. Bhagat (eds.), *Handbook of intercultural training,* 2nd edn. (pp. 81–105). Thousand Oaks,CA: Sage Publications.

Landis, D., Bennett, M. & Bennett, J. (2004). *Handbook of intercultural training,* 3rd edn. Thousand Oaks, CA: Sage Publications.

Landis, D. & Bhagat, R. (1996). *Handbook of intercultural training,* 2nd edn. Thousand Oaks,CA: Sage Publications.

Landis, D. & Bhawuk, D. P. S. (2004). Synthesizing theory building and practice in intercultural training. In Dan Landis, Milton Bennett & Janet Bennett (eds.), *Handbook of intercultural training,* 3rd edn. (pp. 451–466). Thousand Oaks, CA: Sage Publications.

Landis, D. & Brislin, R. (1983). *Handbook of intercultural training.* 3 vols. Elmsford, NY: Pergamon Press.

Landis, D., Brislin, R. W. & Hulgus, J. (1985). Attribution training versus contact in acculturative training: a laboratory study. *Journal of Applied Social Psychology, 15,* 466–482.

Landis, D. & Wasilewski, J. (1999). Reflections on 22 years of the International Journal of Intercultural Relations and 23 years in other areas of practice. *International Journal of Intercultural Relations, 23,* 535–574.

Locke, E. & Latham, G. (1990). *A theory of goal setting and task performance.* Englewood Cliffs, NJ: Prentice-Hall.

(2004). What should we do about motivation theory? Six recommendations for the twenty-first century. *Academy of Management Review, 29(3),* 388–403.

Mak, A. & Tran, C. (2001). Big Five personality and cultural relocation in Vietnamese Australian students' intercultural self-efficacy. *International Journal of Intercultural Relations, 25,* 181–201.

Matsumoto, D., LeRoux, J. A., Ratzlaff, C., *et al.* (2001). Development and validation of a measure of intercultural adjustment potential in Japanese sojourners: the intercultural adjustment potential scale (ICAPS). *International Journal of Intercultural Relations, 25,* 483–510.

Mumford, D. B. (1998). The measurement of culture shock. *Social Psychiatry and Psychiatrical Epidemiology*, *33*, 149–154.

Oberg, K. (1960). Culture shock: adjustment to new cultural environments. *Practical Anthropology*, *7*, 177–182.

Pedersen, P. B. (1999). Identifying culturally learned patterns: two exercises that help. In S. Fowler & M. Mumford (eds.), *Intercultural sourcebook: cross-cultural training methods* (Vol. II, pp. 123–129). Yarmouth, ME: Intercultural Press.

Redfield, R., Linton, R. & Herskovits, M. J. (1936). Memorandum for the study of acculturation. *American Anthropologist*, *38*, 149–152.

Shachar, H. & Amir, Y. (1996). Training teachers and students for intercultural cooperation in Israel. In D. Landis & R. Bhagat (eds.), *Handbook of intercultural training*, 2nd edn. (pp. 400–413). Thousand Oaks, CA: Sage Publications.

Spence, K. (1951). Theoretical interpretations of learning. In S. S. Stevens (ed.), *Handbook of experimental psychology* (pp. 690–729). New York: Wiley.

Stephan, C. & Stephan, W. (1992). Reducing intercultural anxiety through contact. *International Journal of Intercultural Relations*, *16*, 89–106.

Stephan, W. & Stephan, C. (1985). Intergroup anxiety. *Journal of Social Issues*, *41*, 157–176.

Triandis, H. (1972). *The analysis of subjective culture*. New York: Wiley.

(1984). A theoretical framework for the more efficient construction of culture assimilators. *International Journal of Intercultural Relations*, *8*, 301–330.

(1994). *Culture and social behavior*. New York: McGraw-Hill.

Triandis, H., Brislin, H. & Hui, C. (1988). Cross-cultural training across the individualism–collectivism divide. *International Journal of Intercultural Relations*, *12*, 269–289.

Ward, C. (1996). Acculturation. In D. Landis & R. Bhagat (eds.), *Handbook of intercultural training*, 2nd edn. (pp. 124–147). Thousand Oaks, CA: Sage Publications.

Ward, C., Bochner, S. & Furnham, A. (2001). *The psychology of culture shock*. London: Routledge.

Ward, C. & Rana-Deuba, A. (2000). Home and host culture influences on sojourner adjustment. *International Journal of Intercultural Relations*, *24*, 291–306.

Ward, C. & Searle, W. (1991). The impact of value discrepancies and cultural identity on psychological and socio-cultural adjustment of sojourners. *International Journal of Intercultural Relations*, *15*, 209–225.

31 Conclusions

John W. Berry, David L. Sam & Amanda Rogers

31.1 Introduction

Psychology of acculturation is now a thriving and flourishing field of study with numerous publications in both general psychological journals and some specialized journals in the areas of cultural, cross-cultural and intercultural psychology. The chapters in this volume, and the lists of references at the end of each chapter, all testify to the growing interest in this field, and there is no sign that this interest will abate in the near future.

The last hundred years has seen the field develop many theories and research frameworks, although these have not always been well integrated into existing and established bodies of knowledge within psychological science (Liebkind, 2000; Padilla & Perez, 2003). The need for a systematic body of knowledge that is useful for both research and practice therefore cannot be over-emphasized. This volume is one attempt to help integrate and systematize the field, as well as to display its great variety. Indeed, it is a core claim of the field of cross-cultural psychology that only when human behavior in all its variation is available for examination will we be able to discern its common features, and progress towards systematic theory development and the identification of universal features of how individuals go about their acculturation and achieve some measure of successful adaptation (Berry, Poortinga, Segall & Dasen, 2002). We believe that the present volume can serve as a starting point for theory development, and as a basis for the search for universals.

There are numerous changes in the ways acculturation is now taking place. First, many current events are bringing about new forms of intercultural contact, resulting from geopolitical turmoil, globalization, and advances in information technology. These more remote forms of contact are bringing new challenges that the field of acculturation has to incorporate into theory and practice. Second, many societies that are already plural as a result of their earlier colonial experiences are now undergoing rapid urbanization, which is creating metropolitan communities that are not only plural, but increasingly cosmopolitan in nature. Third, the acculturating contexts for individuals and groups in many societies are no longer simply a meeting between two cultures (in the traditional "us-and-them" fashion), but are involving interactions among a number of cultures at the same time. This development can presently be found in large metropolises such as London, Los Angeles or Toronto, where no one ethnocultural group can claim the privileged position of being a "host" or a "majority" society. This means that acculturation theory needs to examine multiple sources of cultural influences, and develop more complex frameworks for their study. Finally, since patterns of co-residence are increasingly common among settled immigrant and ethnocultural populations, it is possible for some individuals to remain within their ethnocultural community within the larger cosmopolitan community and to be oblivious to the acculturative influences that their group is exposed to.

31.2 The challenges

In nearly all the chapters in this *Handbook*, the concluding remarks raised some critical issues for future consideration; these will not all be reiterated here. In this section, however, some of these issues will be given special attention, and these are briefly highlighted below.

Acculturation research has over the years drawn heavily on affective, behavioral and cognitive theories, in what Ward (2001) referred to as the "ABCs of acculturation." Rather than continuing to develop theories in just one of these perspectives, efforts should be aimed at developing integrative models that incorporate all three perspectives, as well as elements from developmental and personality psychology. Cognitions, attitudes and values all change as part of normal human development. Hence, acculturation theories should take cognizance of the fact that these changes will still take place in the absence of acculturative influences.

As human developmental issues gain a stronger position in acculturation theories, there is no doubt that more efforts will be directed towards longitudinal studies. These studies are very much needed for a broader understanding of the *change* that underlines acculturation phenomena. Such research designs will allow us to distinguish between actual change in individuals experiencing acculturation, and cohort effects. They will also help us answer the question of whether change takes place in a uniform or variable fashion across different groups of people and in different cultural settings.

Many acculturation studies, as can be seen in the numerous studies cited in this volume, have examined one ethnocultural group in one specific society. Occasionally the focus is on a heterogeneous category of an acculturating group, such as refugees or immigrants in a given country. Any attempt to develop a universal theory of acculturation will require multi-group, multi-society studies, in order to determine which acculturation factors are specific to a group or a country, and which factors are global or universal. An effort to accomplish this goal has recently appeared (Berry, Phinney, Sam & Vedder, 2006), in which thirty immigrant groups were studied, following their settlement in thirteen societies.

Efforts aimed at multi-group, multi-society studies will be very much limited by the present general lack of standardized instruments. However, the creation of such instruments may offend some basic principles of assessment across cultural groups, since they may overlook some unique aspects of people's acculturation. In other words, much as such instruments are needed to facilitate comparative research across groups, they also carry the danger of overlooking novel features of people's acculturation.

While acculturation research is interested in all the changes that arise following a meeting between two or more cultural groups, its focus boils down to two fundamental goals. The first is the promotion of positive psychological acculturation and the wellbeing of individuals. The second is the attainment of harmonious intercultural relations among all groups in contact, leading to a more congenial larger society for everyone involved in the process of acculturation. Many of the chapters have identified individual, contextual and interactional factors that may be involved in what might be called "successful acculturation." However, an issue that is still far from clear is *who* is responsible for achieving successful acculturation: is it the individual, the group to which the person belongs, or the members of the larger society? These issues have policy implications; as we gain better understanding of the factors involved in providing answers, the findings need to be translated into policies.

Although acculturation affects all individuals and groups in contact, much research effort to date has been directed towards the non-dominant groups such as immigrants, indigenous peoples or ethnocultural groups within a larger society. With few exceptions, acculturation studies rarely look at how the larger society is affected and responds. There is obviously a need for more studies of how the dominant group itself changes and weathers the process of acculturation.

31.3   Limitations and future directions

While most acculturation phenomena are taking place in the "Majority World" of Africa, China, India, and elsewhere in the non-Western world, this volume has been limited mainly to an examination of acculturation that is taking place in the Western world. Initially, however, acculturation was studied by anthropologists during colonial contact with peoples in these majority societies. We believe that it is high time for psychologists to return to the roots of the field, and to expand our focus to include these other populations in our research and practice. Some work has been accomplished, for example with Adivasi in India (Mishra, Sinha & Berry, 1996), but much more is required if we wish to establish broad, even universal, theories of psychological acculturation.

Since acculturation is a complex phenomenon, collaboration between researchers in many disciplines is essential. Obviously such collaboration should include anthropology, but also demography, economics, sociology, education and political science; these disciplines can all add valuable ideas and evidence to designing, conducting and interpreting research. While this volume has been focused mainly on the psychology of acculturation, many chapters did reach out to include relevant ideas and findings from these other disciplines. However, more needs to be done in this direction in a systematic way, rather than selecting literature from these other disciplines, and attempting to fit it to our psychological perspective.

A further aspect for researchers to consider is the feedback loop between research and clinical work on acculturation. While more comprehensive theories and empirical research are essential, it is important to ensure that this research feeds into practice and that practice in turn feeds back into research. Clinicians working with populations such as immigrants, refugees and international students have produced a wealth of raw information and case studies that could aid research in both a formal and informal manner. In turn, this body of scientific knowledge that is growing rapidly should be accessible to those individuals and groups in the helping professions who can directly influence and assist in the acculturation of others. Only with this continuous feedback will we develop comprehensive, practical and relevant theories that are of use to the many acculturating individuals, groups and societies.

31.4 References

Berry, J. W., Phinney, J. S., Sam, D. L. & Vedder, P. H. (2006). *Immigrant youth in cultural transition: acculturation, identity and adaptation across national contexts*. Mahwah, NJ: Lawrence Erlbaum Associates.

Berry, J. W., Poortinga, Y. H., Segall, M. S. & Dasen, P. R. (2002). *Cross-cultural psychology: research and applications*. New York: Cambridge University Press.

Liebkind, K. (2000). Acculturation. In R. Brown. & S. L. Gaertner (eds.), *Blackwell handbook of social psychology: in-group processes* (pp. 386–406). Oxford: Blackwell Publishers.

Mishra, R. C., Sinha, D. & Berry, J. W. (1996). *Ecology, acculturation and psychological adaptation*. New Delhi: Sage Publications.

Padilla, A. & Perez, W. (2003). Acculturation, social identity and social cognition: a new perspective. *Hispanic Journal of Behavioral Sciences*, 25, 110–122.

Ward, C. (2001). The ABCs of acculturation. In D. Matsumoto (ed.), *The handbook of culture and psychology* (pp. 411–445). Oxford: Oxford University Press.

Author index

Subject index